CRITICAL READING, CRITICAL THINKING

A CONTEMPORARY ISSUES APPROACH

Second Edition

RICHARD PIROZZI

PASSAIC COUNTY COMMUNITY COLLEGE

Longman

New York San Francisco Boston
London Toronto Sydney Tokyo Singapore Madrid
Mexico City Munich Paris Cape Town Hong Kong Montreal

T 79926

Vice President and Editor in Chief: Joseph Terry
Senior Acquisitions Editor: Steven Rigolosi
Associate Editor: Barbara Santoro
Senior Marketing Manager: Melanie Craig
Supplements Editor: Donna Campion
Production Manager: Joseph Vella
Project Coordination, Text Design, and Electronic Page Makeup:
    Electronic Publishing Services Inc., NYC
Cover Design Manager: John Callahan
Cover Designer: Kay Petronio
Cover Illustration: © Artville
Photo Research: Photosearch, Inc.
Manufacturing Buyer: Lucy Hebard
Printer and Binder: Courier Corporation—Stoughton
Cover Printer: Coral Graphics Services

For permission to use copyrighted material, grateful acknowledgment is made to the copyright holders on pp. 499–504, which are hereby made part of the copyright page.

Library of Congress Cataloging-in-Publication Data
Pirozzi, Richard C.
    Critical reading, critical thinking: a contemporary issues approach /
Richard Pirozzi.--2nd ed.
      p. cm.
    Includes index.
    ISBN 0-321-08835-2
      1. Reading (Higher education). 2. Critical thinking. I. Title.

LB2395.3 .P56 2003
428.4'071'1--dc21
                                                                          2002025681

Please visit our website at http://www.ablongman.com

ISBN 0-321-08835-2

1 2 3 4 5 6 7 8 9 10—CRS—05 04 03 02

This book is dedicated to:

Richard

Jessica

Jonathan

"The joys and sorrows of parenthood are silent."

BRIEF CONTENTS

DETAILED CONTENTS

CHAPTER 5

Basic Problem Solving 268

Part 3

CRITICAL READING: EVALUATING WHAT YOU READ 321

CHAPTER 6
Using Inference 322

CHAPTER 7
Distinguishing Between Facts and Opinions 366

CHAPTER 8
Recognizing Purpose and Tone 392

- At the end of each chapter is "Looking Back," which in this edition asks students to summarize and/or paraphrase the most important information learned from the chapter and determine how it can be put to use in other classes.

- Also new to this edition is "The Dashing Detective," which can be found at the end of every chapter and provides students with the opportunity to have fun by applying critical thinking skills while solving short mysteries. These complement "Playing Sherlock Holmes and Dr. Watson," a semester-long, mystery-solving feature from the first edition.

- "Eye on Vocabulary"—a new feature attached to the contemporary issue passages—asks students to use context, word parts, or the dictionary to determine the meanings of unfamiliar words and to list them along with their definitions in a notebook or on note cards.

- The contemporary issue passages have been updated and expanded, while others have been replaced in response to the suggestions of those who used the first edition. More short stories and information from the Internet, longer textbook passages, and some poetry, song lyrics, and a movie review also have been included to accommodate a variety of instructional needs. Problem-solving exercises, dealing with hypothetical and real-life situations, continue to be an intricate part of most of the chapters.

- Finally, there are "Mastery Tests" at the end of all chapters, which in many instances are somewhat longer than in the previous edition. After completing them, students can remove them from the textbook and hand them in to the instructor for grading purposes.

BOOK-SPECIFIC ANCILLARIES

An *Instructor's Manual* (ISBN 0-321-08838-7), with suggestions and answers to the exercises, is available and should prove useful to instructors. The suggested answers should serve as guides, because the passages used for many of the activities allow for a variety of possible answers. Thus, they will encourage different points of view, which should make for lively, interesting class discussions.

A Testbank (ISBN 0-321-08839-5) of skill questions is also available for additional testing and reinforcement.

THE LONGMAN DEVELOPMENTAL READING PACKAGE

In addition to the book-specific ancillaries discussed above, Longman offers many other supplements to instructors and students. All of these supplements are available either free or at greatly reduced prices.

Instructor Supplements

Electronic Test Bank for Developmental Reading CD ROM. Offers more than 3,000 questions in all areas of reading, including vocabulary, main idea, supporting details, patterns of organization, critical thinking, analytical reasoning, inference, point of view, visual aids, and textbook reading. Instructors simply choose questions, then print out the completed test for distribution OR offer the test online. FREE TO ADOPTERS. (ISBN 0-321-08179-X)

Printed Test Bank for Developmental Reading. Offers more than 3,000 questions in all areas of reading, including vocabulary, main idea, supporting details, patterns of organization, critical thinking, analytical reasoning, inference, point of view, visual aides, and textbook reading. FREE TO ADOPTERS. (ISBN 0-321-08596-5)

The Longman Instructor's Planner. This planner includes weekly and monthly calendars, student attendance and grading rosters, space for contact information, Web references, an almanac, and blank pages for notes. (ISBN 0-321-09247-3)

The Longman Guide to Classroom Management. This guide is designed as a helpful resource for instructors who have classroom management problems. It includes helpful strategies for dealing with disruptive students in the classroom and the "do's and don'ts" of discipline. (ISBN 0-321-09246-5)

Instructor Access Card for Reading Road Trip on the Web. (ISBN 0-321-10187-1)

Student Supplements

The Longman Textbook Reader (with answers). Offers five complete chapters from our textbooks: computer science, biology, psychology, communications, and business. Each chapter includes additional comprehension quizzes, critical thinking questions, and group activities. Available FREE when packaged with any Longman Reading text. (ISBN 0-321-11895-2)

The Longman Textbook Reader (without answers). Offers five complete chapters from our textbooks: computer science, biology, psychology, communications, and business. Each chapter includes additional comprehension quizzes, critical thinking questions, and group activities. (ISBN 0-321-12223-2)

The Longman Reader's Journal. Written by Kathleen McWhorter and the first journal for readers, *The Longman Reader's Journal* offers a place for students to record their reactions to and questions about any reading. Available FREE valuepacked with any Longman Reading text. (ISBN 0-321-08843-3)

The Longman Planner. Ideal for organizing a busy college life! Included are hour-by-hour schedules, monthly and weekly calendars, an address book, and an almanac of tips and useful information. Available FREE valuepacked with any Longman Reading text. (ISBN 0-321-0453-4)

The Longman Reader's Portfolio. This unique supplement provides students with a space to plan, think about and present their work. The portfolio includes a diagnostic area (including a learning style questionnaire), a working area (including calendars, vocabulary logs, reading response sheets, book club tips, and other valuable materials), and a display area (including a progress chart, a final table of contents, and a final assessment). (ISBN 0-321-10766-7)

10 Practices of Highly Effective Students. This study skills supplement includes topics such as time management, test-taking, reading critically, stress, and motivations. Available FREE valuepacked with any Longman Reading text. (ISBN 0-205-30769-8)

Newsweek Discount Subscription Coupon. *Newsweek* Subscription (12 weeks) gets students reading, writing, and thinking about what's going on in the world around them. The price of the subscription is added to the cost of the book. Instructors receive weekly lesson plans, quizzes, and curriculum guides as well as a complimentary *Newsweek* subscription. Available with any Longman text. The price of the subscription is .57 cents per issue (a total of $6.84 for the subscription). (ISBN 0-321-08895-6)

Interactive Guide to *Newsweek*. (Available with the 12-week subscription to *Newsweek*, this free guide serves as a workbook for students who are using the magazine. FREE when valuepacked with any Longman text. (ISBN 0-321-05528-4)

Penguin Program. For instructors who like to use novels, a series of Penguin Putnam Inc. paperbacks is available at a significant discount when packaged with any Longman text. Some titles available are: Julia Alvarez's *How the Garcia Girls Lost Their Accents*, Mark Twain's *Huckleberry Finn*, John Steinbeck's *The Pearl*, James McBride's *The Color of Water*, and more. For a complete list of titles or more information, visit Clubhouse or the Longman-Penguin website: www.ablongman.com/penguin (http://www.ablongman.com/penguin).

The New American Webster Handy College Dictionary. A paperback reference text with more than 100,000 entries. Available for a nominal fee with any Longman text. Call the Valuepack Group for current pricing. (ISBN 0-451-18166-2)

Merriam-Webster Collegiate Dictionary. A hardcover comprehensive dictionary. Call the Valuepack Group for current pricing. Available for approximately $10 when packaged with any Longman text. (ISBN 0-87779-709-9)

Reading Road Trip 2.0 CD-ROM. Taking students on a tour of 15 cities and landmarks throughout the United States, each of the 15 modules corresponds to a reading or study skill (for example, finding the main idea, understanding patterns of organization, thinking critically). All modules contain a tour of the location, instruction and tutorial, exercises, interactive feedback, and mastery tests. FREE when valuepacked with any Longman Reading text. (CD-ROM ISBN 0-321-07900-0)

Student Access Card for Reading Road Trip On the Web. www.ablongman.com/readingroadtrip. A Web version of this popular reading software program. Available FREE when valuepacked with any Longman Reading text. (ISBN 0-321-09706-8)

The English Pages Web Site. http://www.ablongman.com/englishpages. Both students and instructors can visit this free, content-rich Website for additional reading selections and writing exercises. Visitors can conduct a simulated web search, find additional reading and writing exercises, or browse a wide selection of links to various writing and research resources

The Vocabulary Web Site. Offers activities, exercises and games to help students practice and improve their vocabulary skills. Free and open access (http://www.ablongman.com/vocabulary).

For Florida Adopters: Thinking Through the Test: A Study Guide for the Florida College Basic Skills Exit Tests by D.J. Henry. FOR FLORIDA ADOPTIONS ONLY (ISBN 0-321-08066-1). This workbook helps students strengthen their reading skills in preparation for the Florida College Basic Skills Exit Test. It features both diagnostic tests to help assess areas that may need improvement and exit tests to help tests skill mastery. Detailed explanatory answers have been provided for almost all of the questions. Available FREE valuepacked with any Longman Reading text.

For Florida Adopters: Thinking Through the Test: A Study Guide for the Florida College Basic Skills Exit Tests (Version without answers) by D.J. Henry. FOR FLORIDA ADOPTIONS ONLY (ISBN 0-321-09988-5)

Reading Skills Summary for the Florida State Exit Exam by D. J. Henry. FOR FLORIDA ADOPTIONS ONLY (ISBN 0-321-08478-0). An excellent study tool for students preparing to take Florida College Basic Skills Exit Test for Reading, this reading grid summarizes all the skills tested on the Exit Exam. Available FREE valuepacked with any Longman Reading text.

ACKNOWLEDGMENTS

I am indebted to many people who helped to make this second edition a reality. The administration of Passaic County Community College was flexible with my schedule, which allowed me the time to devote to the project. Once again, my students were very willing to use and evaluate the manuscript. As usual, Arlene Trzcinski of the copy center provided copies efficiently and pleasantly, and Alice Ferrer, our graphic artist, came up with wonderful designs for some of the "Think About It!" and "Think Again!" sections of the book. Rosemarie Weinmann was very conscientious and efficient with the index. Mark Hillringhouse was very generous with his poetry, for which I am most grateful.

The hard-working people at Longman Publishers were both creative and efficient, for which I am very appreciative. Steven Rigolosi, senior editor, came up with his usual good ideas, and associate editor Barbara Santoro worked persistently to make this into a better book. Gail Kehler, who is very pleasant to work with, did an outstanding job of chasing down the permissions for both editions. The high quality of the Testbank was the result of the efficiency and efforts of Tim Florschuetz of Mesa Community College. I am indebted to all those other individuals who put their time and energy into the project, but are too numerous to name.

The following reviewers made valuable suggestions for which I am very appreciative:

Maureen Connolly, *Elmhurst College;* Martha Funderburk, *University of Arkansas Community College at Hope;* Elise Gorun, *Truman College;* Susan B. Kanter, *University of Houston;* Linda Mulready, *Bristol Community College;* Carolyn E. Rubin-Trimble, *University of Houston;* Victoria F. Sarkisian, *Marist College;* Janith Stepheson, *College of the Mainland.*

Robert Bunner, *Northern Virginia Community College;* Elizabeth Cassidy, *Adirondack Community College;* Kathleen Engstrom, *Fullerton College;* Michael Kamil, *Stanford University;* Peter Kyper, *West Chester University;* Dr. Sharona A. Levy, *Borough of Manhattan Community College;* Alice Mackey, *Missouri Western State College;* Jane Melendez, *East Tennessee State University;* Jane Rhoads, *Wichita State University;* Susan Riley, *DeVry Institute of Technology, Columbus;* Victoria Sarkisian, *Marist College;* Bonnie M. Smith, *St. Mary's University of Minnesota;* and Suzanne Weisar, *San Jacinto College South.*

Finally, at home, my wife Susan had to put up with me once again as I spent long hours on the manuscript. She also led me to some very interesting, valuable material that was ultimately incorporated into the text. As usual, Lucas knew enough to leave me alone, for which he received much praise and a few dog biscuits, which unfortunately turned out to be not as many as he anticipated and wanted.

PART ONE
BACK TO BASICS

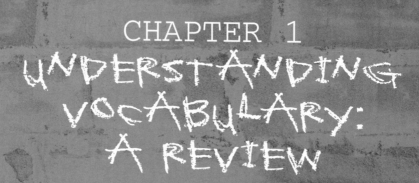

CHAPTER 1
UNDERSTANDING VOCABULARY: A REVIEW

CHAPTER OUTLINE

THINK ABOUT IT!

Every chapter in this textbook begins with "Think About It!" and ends with "Think Again!" sections. They are fun and are designed to get you into the mood and keep you in the mood to think critically. Enjoy them.

Critical thinkers are very careful about observing their surroundings. As a critical thinker, look carefully at the photographs below. There is something strange in each of the scenes. Do you know what it is? In photograph 1, look for something unusual. In photographs 2, 3, and 4, look for something that is not right. Discuss the photographs with your classmates.

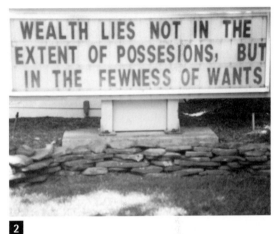

CHAPTER OUTCOMES

After completing Chapter 1, you should be able to:

- Use context clues to uncover word meanings.
- Use word parts to uncover word meanings.
- Use a glossary to find word meanings.
- Use the dictionary effectively.

When you looked at the outcomes and outline for this chapter, you probably said to yourself, "I already had this stuff!" or "I already know this stuff!" In fact, you may react the same way to the next two chapters, which deal with developmental reading skills. At this point in your education, it is understandable that you are not very enthusiastic about covering material that you may consider basic and familiar. Keep in mind, however, that this review will help you make better sense of the kind of reading you are asked to do in college and serve as a foundation on which to build the advanced critical reading and thinking skills presented in the other chapters.

Throughout this book, you will encounter some very interesting topics that should add to and enrich your educational experience as a college student. In addition, you will confront issues and problems that are both controversial and thought-provoking. Therefore, try to be patient as you make your way through the first three chapters even if you feel that they are too elementary. Remember that the skills reviewed in them will help you deal more effectively with the "good stuff" that comes later.

USING CONTEXT CLUES

An inescapable part of your college education is to learn new words. Facing that fact and approaching the task in a systematic way are crucial for several reasons. First, on tests instructors will often ask you to define at least the key terms used in their particular subject areas. Second, the more words you know, the easier you will understand both textbook and lecture material. Third, in a general sense, broadening your vocabulary will enable you to become a more effective reader, listener, writer, and speaker. Not only will you comprehend better, but you will also have more words at your disposal to fulfill your responsibilities as a student. Finally, when you graduate you will be better equipped to understand and deal with the world around you.

This chapter explores four ways of finding the meanings of unfamiliar words: using the context, using word parts, using a glossary, and using the dictionary. The method you employ will depend upon the given situation, and sometimes on your personal preference. However, when you are comfortable with all the methods, you increase your chances of finding word meanings quickly and efficiently.

Which of the following is the correct definition of the word *bar?*

1. The legal profession
2. A room or counter where alcohol is served
3. A piece of solid material longer than it is wide
4. Anything that impedes or prevents
5. All of the above

The answer to the question is "All of the above" because the meaning of *bar* depends on how it is used in a sentence. For example, the following sentences all use the word correctly:

1. Jessica was admitted to the *bar* two years after she graduated from law school.
2. After class, the students went to a *bar* to relax and have a few drinks.
3. Hold on to the *bar* so you don't fall if the subway comes to a sudden stop.
4. The police set up a roadblock to *bar* his escape.

The **context** refers to the surrounding words in a sentence that give a word its specific meaning. Like the word *bar,* many other words have multiple meanings, and you can determine which meaning applies by the way those words are used in a sentence. Thus you can often use the context to help you figure out the meanings of unfamiliar words without consulting a dictionary.

Various aspects of the context can be used to reveal word meanings, including punctuation, synonyms, antonyms, examples, and general sentence clues, individually or in combination.

Punctuation

After mentioning a word, writers sometimes provide its meaning and set it off through the use of punctuation marks, making the definition easy for readers to recognize. For example, a definition can be introduced with a colon:

> Pedro's general condition deteriorated after the physician discovered that he was suffering from **edema**: the accumulation of fluid in various organs of the body.

edema = the accumulation of fluid in various organs of the body

It can be set off between commas (or just one comma if it falls at the end of a sentence):

> Lovelock's theory is intricately tied to **cybernetics,** the study and analysis of how information flows in electronic, mechanical, and biological systems.
>
> F. Kurt Cylke Jr., *The Environment,* p. 78

cybernetics = the study and analysis of how information flows in electronic, mechanical, and biological systems

For greater emphasis, dashes can be used instead of commas:

> Regulation increased substantially during the 1970s. By the end of that decade, numerous proposals for **deregulation**—the removal of old regulations—had been made.
>
> Roger LeRoy Miller, *Economics Today,* p. 648

deregulation = the removal of old regulations

Definitions can also be enclosed in parentheses:

> Music consists of three basic elements: **pitch** (melody); **rhythm** (sounds grouped according to a prescribed system); and **timbre** (the qualities of a tone that make a C-sharp sound different, say, on a tuba than on a guitar). From these building blocks, human beings have created rock and roll, rap, sonatas, blues, folk songs, chants, symphonies, jazz, opera,... the variations are endless. Where there are human beings, there is music.
>
> <div align="right">Carol Tavris and Carole Wade, <i>Psychology in Perspective</i>, p. 575</div>

pitch = melody

rhythm = sounds grouped according to a prescribed system

timbre = the qualities of a tone that make a C-sharp sound different, say, on a tuba than on a guitar

The definition of a term in a foreign language is usually placed in quotation marks:

> The *Ceteris Paribus* Assumption: All Other Things Being Equal. Everything in the world seems to relate in some way to everything else in the world. It would be impossible to isolate the effects of changes in one variable on another variable if we always had to worry about the many other variables that might also enter the analysis. As in other sciences, economics uses the *ceteris paribus* assumption. *Ceteris paribus* means "other things constant" or "other things equal."
>
> <div align="right">Roger LeRoy Miller, <i>Economics Today</i>, p. 10</div>

ceteris paribus = "other things constant" or "other things equal"

The same is true of a definition taken from an outside source:

> **Affirmative action**—"programs instituted by private and public institutions to overcome the effects of and to compensate for past discrimination" (Greenberg and Page, 1997, p. 576)—has recently come under attack in many parts of the United States.

affirmative action = programs instituted by private and public institutions to overcome the effects of and to compensate for past discrimination

Synonyms

Writers sometimes use **synonyms,** or words that mean the same, to provide you with the meanings of unfamiliar words, as in the following sentence.

> First, **psychotropic** or **mood-altering** drugs became increasingly popular among health practitioners, made patients easier to handle and increased their chances of being released.
>
> <div align="right">Richard Sweeney, <i>Out of Place: Homelessness in America</i>, p. 69</div>

Psychotropic and **mood-altering** are synonyms. Therefore, psychotropic drugs are drugs that alter or change our mood.

Antonyms

Writers may use **antonyms,** or words that mean the opposite, to help you figure out the meanings of unfamiliar words, as in the following sentence.

> **Whereas** Princess Diana was rather **tall**, Mother Teresa was **diminutive**.

Whereas indicates that a contrast is being drawn between Princess Diana and Mother Teresa. **Tall** and **diminutive** must be antonyms; therefore, *diminutive* means "short" or "small."

Examples

Sometimes writers use familiar examples that *may* be helpful in determining word meanings, as in the following sentence.

> The United States, Canada, England, and France are all examples of **autonomous** nations, because they are not controlled by any other governments.

> If you have knowledge about some or all of these countries and are aware of what they have in common, perhaps you can figure out that **autonomous** means "independent" or "self-governing."

General Sentence Clues

You may be able to figure out the meaning of an unfamiliar word by studying the general sense of the sentence and focusing on the key words used in it, as in the following example.

> The **driver's eyes** were **bloodshot** and his **speech** was **slurred**; the **police officer** quickly concluded that he was **inebriated**.

> The sense of the sentence—with the use of the key words **driver, bloodshot** with reference to **eyes, slurred** with reference to **speech**, and **police officer**—is that this is a scene involving a drunken driver and hence that **inebriated** must mean "intoxicated" or "drunk."

ACTIVITY 1

DIRECTIONS: Using the context, try to determine the meanings of the words that appear after the sentences. In each case, be prepared to discuss what clues are present to help you. Many of the sentences are taken from college textbooks.

1. She arrived at the party wearing a sari: the garment worn by Hindu women.

   sari: _____

2. Judy does not talk very much at the staff meetings, but James is quite loquacious.

   loquacious: _____

3. Would you like ketchup on your hamburger, or do you prefer some other condiment?

   condiment: _____

4. For years, cigarette manufacturers denied that cigarette smoke was carcinogenic even though millions of smokers were dying from lung cancer.

   carcinogenic:_____

5. Adolf Hitler, Fidel Castro, and Saddam Hussein are good examples of authoritarian leaders.

   authoritarian: _____

6. The rainstorm is expected to mitigate the extremely high temperature.

   mitigate: _____

7. Although the movie character James Bond is always involved in "clandestine" or "secret" activities, some intelligence work today is actually accomplished out in the open.

   clandestine: _____

8. Whereas the center is very slow, the quarterback is extremely nimble.

   nimble: _____

9. Because of his attitude and harsh treatment of women in general, the captain has been called a misogynist by the female officers.

   misogynist: _____

10. There are examples in the Koran, the Muslim Bible, of female saints and intellectuals, and powerful women often held strong informal powers over their husbands and male children.

    Janell L. Carroll and Paul Root Wolpe, *Sexuality and Gender in Society*, p. 19

    Koran: _____

ACTIVITY 2

DIRECTIONS: Using the context, try to determine the meanings of the words that appear after the sentences.

1. We define inflation as an upward movement in the average level of prices. The opposite of inflation is deflation, defined as a downward movement in the average level of prices.

   Roger LeRoy Miller, *Economics Today*, p. 153

   inflation: _____

   deflation:_____

2. From the larynx, inhaled air passes toward the lungs through the trachea, or windpipe.

   Neil A. Campbell, Lawrence G. Mitchell, and Jane B. Reece, *Biology*, 3rd ed., p. 456

   trachea: _____

3. Welfare reform has often been couched in terms of workfare—the requirement that welfare recipients perform public service jobs in exchange for benefits.

   Roger LeRoy Miller, *Economics Today*, p. 689

   workfare:_____

4. Morals, or personal standards of right and wrong, are central to dealing with sexual matters.

   George Zgourides, *Human Sexuality*, p. 382

   morals:_____

5. Then the orgy started. During 1928, the market rose to 331. Many investors and speculators began to buy on margin (borrowing to invest).

   Gary B. Nash and Julie Roy Jeffrey, The American People, 5th ed., p. 764

   buy on margin: _____

6. Having briefly discussed sexual laws, morals, and ethics, let's now turn our attention to a particularly important area of legal concern, that of sexual coercion, or the forcing of sexual remarks, pressure, or behavior on another person.

   George Zgourides, Human Sexuality, p. 384

   sexual coercion:_____

7. For example, studies of twins and adopted children suggest that there may be a genetic component in bipolar disorder ("manic depression"), a mood disorder involving alternating episodes of extreme depression and abnormal states of exhilaration.

   Carol Tavris and Carole Wade, Psychology in Perspective, p. 176

   bipolar disorder: _____

8. The reliance on empirical evidence—evidence gathered by careful observation, experimentation, and measurement—is the hallmark of the psychological method.

   Carol Tavris and Carole Wade, Psychology in Perspective, p. 13

   empirical evidence: _____

9. The distinction between problematic and unproblematic drug use is not just a distinction between legal and illegal substances. In terms of avoidable and thus unnecessary morbidity (illness) and mortality (death), all of the illegally abused drugs *combined* take nowhere near the annual toll that alcohol and nicotine take.

   James D. Wright and Joel A. Devine, Drugs as a Social Problem, pp. 2–3

   morbidity: _____

   mortality: _____

10. During the 1920s and 1930s, they were accused of being part of an international conspiracy to take over U.S. business and government, and anti-Semitism—prejudice or discrimination against Jews—became more widespread and overt.

    Alex Thio, Sociology, 4th brief ed., p. 226

    anti-Semitism:_____

ACTIVITY 3

DIRECTIONS: Using the context, try to determine the meanings of the words that appear after the sentences.

1. We can gain further insight into ourselves and our society by going beyond our national boundaries to study other societies. Today the whole world has become a global village, a closely knit community of all the world's societies. Whatever happens in a faraway land can affect our lives here. Consider the various ways in which economic

globalization—the interrelationships among the world's economies—can influence the U.S. economy and society at large.

Alex Thio, Sociology, 4th brief ed., p. 6

global village: _____

economic globalization: _____

2. Terrorism, which involves "the use of violence to express extreme discontent with a particular government" (Johnson, 1992, p. 5), is all too common today.

terrorism:_____

3. Childbirth, or parturition, begins with labor—contractions of the uterine muscles and opening of the cervix—and concludes with delivery—expelling the child and placenta from the vagina.

George Zgourides, Human Sexuality, p. 249

parturition: _____

labor:_____

delivery:_____

4. Scientists usually start out with a hypothesis, a statement that attempts to describe or explain behavior. Initially, the hypothesis may be stated quite generally, as in "Misery loves company." But before any research can be done, the hypothesis must be put into more specific terms. For example, "Misery loves company" might be rephrased as "People who are anxious about a threatening situation tend to seek out others who face the same threat."

   Some hypotheses are suggested by previous findings or casual observation. Others are derived from a general theory, an organized system of assumptions and principles that purports to explain certain phenomena and how they are related.

Carol Tavris and Carole Wade, Psychology in Perspective, p. 41

hypothesis: _____

theory:_____

5. Antidepressant drugs are used primarily in treating mood disorders such as depression, anxiety, and phobias (irrational fears), and symptoms of obsessive-compulsive disorder, such as endless hand washing and hair pulling.

Carol Tavris and Carole Wade, Psychology in Perspective, p. 191

antidepressant drugs: _____

phobias:_____

obsessive-compulsive disorder: _____

6. The term **scarcity** is used differently in economics from everyday language. Scarcity exists if the amount of the good or resource offered to users is less than they would want if it were given away free of charge. Scarcity has little to do with wealth or poverty. It exists in both rich and poor societies. The only requirement is that there

be an imbalance between what is available and what people would want if the good were free.

Paul R. Gregory, *Essentials of Economics*, 4th ed., p. 5

scarcity:_____

7. Although many diseases today seem to defy our best medical tests and treatments, one that is particularly frustrating is **fibromyalgia,** a chronic, painful, rheumatoid-like disorder that affects as many as 5 to 6 percent of the general population.

Rebecca J. Donatelle, *Access to Health*, 7th ed., p. 512

fibromyalgia:_____

8. Graphs reveal whether two variables are positively or negatively related. A **positive** (or **direct**) **relationship** exists between two variables if an increase in the value of one variable is associated with an increase in the value of the other variable.

A **negative** (or **inverse**) **relationship** exists between two variables if an increase in the value of one variable is associated with a reduction in the value of the other variable.

Paul R. Gregory, *Essentials of Economics*, 4th ed., p. 16

positive relationship:_____

inverse relationship: _____

9. Nicodemus—named for an African prince who became the first slave in this country to buy his freedom—was a mecca for black people during its heyday in the late 1870s. Posters boasting the town's virtues drew men and women who just a few years before had been slaves.

Angela Bates, "New Promise for Nicodemus," *National Parks*, July/August 1992

Nicodemus: _____

10. Interest groups have generally used two methods to pursue their goals through the judicial process. The first is to initiate suits directly on behalf of a group or class of people whose interests they represent (such suits are commonly referred to as "class actions"). The second method is for the interest group to file a brief as a "friend of the court" (*amicus curiae*) in support of a person whose suit seeks to achieve goals that the interest group is also seeking.

Richard F. Cord et al., *Political Science: An Introduction*

class action:_____

amicus curiae: _____

ACTIVITY 4

DIRECTIONS: Using the context, try to determine the meanings of the words that appear after the sentences.

1. Ecology is usually defined as the study of the interactions between organisms and their environment. "Environment" is given a very broad meaning here; it is taken to embrace all those things extrinsic to the organism that in any way impinge on it—not only light,

temperature, rainfall, humidity, and topography, but also parasites, predators, mates, and competitors. Anything not an integral part of a particular organism is considered part of the organism's environment.

William T. Keeton, *Elements of Biological Science*

ecology:_____

environment:_____

extrinsic: _____

2. A loan made to finance the purchase of residential real estate is typically secured by means of a mortgage against such property. The real estate mortgage, in one form or another, has probably been used as long as the right of private property has been recognized. The borrower in such a loan transaction is called the mortgagor; the lender, the mortgagee.

Carl A. Dauten and Merle T. Welshans, *Principles of Finance*

mortgage: _____

mortgager: _____

mortgagee: _____

3. Homeostasis in all organisms is continually disturbed by stress, which is any stimulus that creates an imbalance in the internal environment.

Gerard J. Tortora and Nicholas P. Anagnostakos, *Principles of Anatomy and Physiology*

homeostasis: _____

4. Both Ottoman strength and the weakness of Ottoman adversaries accounted for these rapid conquests. When the expansion began, *ghazis*, warriors for the faith, were attracted in large numbers to Osman's forces, for he was struggling against Islam's chief enemy at the time—Byzantium.

Don Peretz, *The Middle East Today*

adversaries: _____

ghazis:_____

5. Although there is some debate among the experts, another characteristic seems to be machismo—an emphasis on male strength and dominance.

James M. Henslin, *Essentials of Sociology*, 4th ed., p. 314

machismo:_____

6. As Max Weber (1913/1947) pointed out, we perceive **power**—the ability to get your way, even over the resistance of others—as either legitimate or illegitimate. Legitimate power is called **authority**. This is power that people accept as right. In contrast, illegitimate power—called **coercion**—is power that people do not accept as just.

James M. Henslin, *Essentials of Sociology*, 4th ed., p. 274

power:_____

authority: _____

coercion: _____

7. The term *ghetto* originated in Venice, where the section of the city in which Jews were required to live was, in late medieval times, called the "borghetto." This word derived from the Italian word *borgo,* which meant "borough," which is a major section of a city. *Borghetto* was the diminutive form meaning "little borough." Over time the word was shortened to *ghetto,* and its use spread to all European languages. Today the term is often applied to any neighborhood occupied by an ethnic or racial minority.

Rodney Stark, *Sociology*

borgo: _____

borghetto: _____

ghetto: _____

8. Plants counter **herbivores**—plant-eating animals—with both physical defenses, such as thorns, and chemical defenses, such as distasteful or toxic compounds.

Neil A. Campbell et al., *Biology,* 3rd ed., p. 672

herbivores: _____

9. If the crime charged is within the jurisdiction of a municipal court, the arrestee may also be asked to make a **plea,** a statement of innocence or guilt, at the initial appearance. For minor crimes this appearance is sometimes called an **arraignment.** The judge then sets a date for trial in municipal court.

Jay S. Albanese, *Criminal Justice,* p. 160

plea: _____

arraignment: _____

10. In **predation,** an interaction where one species eats another, the consumer is called a **predator** and the food species is known as the **prey.** We will use these terms not only for cases of animals eating other animals, but also for plant-herbivore interactions, where the plant is prey.

Neil A. Campbell et al., *Biology,* 3rd ed., p. 718

predation: _____

predator: _____

prey: _____

ACTIVITY 5

DIRECTIONS: Using the context, try to determine the meanings of the words that appear after the sentences.

1. When unemployment increased and factory orders declined, the Federal Reserve Board boosted the economy by lowering interest rates; when employment and inflation rose,

the Federal Reserve slowed growth by raising interest rates. The result was what economists termed a "Goldilocks economy," neither too cold nor too hot.

John W. Garraty and Mark C. Carnes, *The American Nation,* 10th ed., p. 937

Goldilocks economy: _____

2. At the northernmost limits of plant growth, and at high altitudes just below areas covered permanently with ice and snow, is the **tundra** (from the Russian word for "marshy plain").

Neil A. Campbell et al., *Biology,* 3rd ed., p. 696

tundra: _____

3. Abandoning a lifetime of treating communism as a single worldwide conspiracy that had to be contained at all costs, Nixon decided to deal with China and the Soviet Union as separate powers and, as he put it, to "live together and work together" with both. Nixon and Kissinger called the new policy *détente,* a French term meaning "the relaxation of tensions between governments."

John W. Garraty and Mark C. Carnes, *The American Nation,* 10th ed., p. 850

*détente:*_____

4. The Smoot-Hawley Tariff, like most of the preceding 18 tariff acts stretching back to 1779, was the result of political *logrolling* in the U.S. Congress. Logrolling occurs when some politicians trade their own votes on issues of minor concern to their constituents in return for other politicians' votes on issues of greater concern to their constituents. Tariffs, historically, are the best example of the sacrifice of general interests for special interests.

Paul R. Gregory, *Essentials of Economics,* 4th ed., p. 242

logrolling: _____

5. Many animals exhibit territorial behavior. A **territory** is an area, usually fixed in location, that individuals defend and from which other members of the same species are usually excluded. The size of the territory varies with the species, the function, and the resources available. Territories are typically used for feeding, mating, rearing young, or combinations of these activities.

Neil A. Campbell et al., *Biology,* 3rd ed., p. 754

territory: _____

6. You'll need to know fallacies—errors in argument—as both a reader (to spot them) and a writer (to avoid them). The many common fallacies fall into two groups. Some evade the issue of the argument. Others treat the argument as if it were much simpler than it is.

H. Ramsey Fowler et al., *The Little, Brown Handbook,* 8th ed., p. 155

fallacies: _____

7. All the workers in a honeybee hive are sterile females. They never reproduce, but spend their lives laboring on behalf of the one fertile queen that lays all the eggs in the hive. When a worker stings an intruder in defense of the hive, the worker usually dies. Such behavior, which reduces an individual's fitness while increasing the fitness

of a recipient (in a beehive, the queen), is known as **altruism.** It is an important component of social behavior in many animal species.

Neil A. Campbell et al., *Biology,* 3rd ed., p. 758

sterile: _____

altruism: _____

8. Kin selection does not explain all types of altruism. In some cases, animals behave altruistically toward others who are not relatives. Jane Goodall has discovered that chimpanzees sometimes save the lives of nonrelatives. Similarly, female dolphins without young will often help unrelated mothers care for their young. In these cases, there can be no immediate enhancement of the altruists' fitness. However, in the future, the current beneficiary may reciprocate—that is, "return the favor"—by performing some other helpful act. Thus, we can explain altruism toward nonrelatives as **reciprocal altruism:** an altruistic act repaid at a later time by the beneficiary (or by another member of the social system).

Neil A. Campbell et al., *Biology,* 3rd ed., p. 758

enhancement: _____

reciprocate: _____

reciprocal altruism: _____

9. The scarcity concept arises from the fact that resources are insufficient to satisfy our every desire. Resources are the inputs used in the production of the things that we want. **Production** can be defined as virtually any activity that results in the conversion of resources into products that can be used in consumption. Production includes delivering things from one part of the country to another. It includes taking ice from an ice tray to put it in your soft-drink glass. The resources used in production are called *factors of production,* and some economists use the terms *resources* and *factors of production* interchangeably. The total quantity of all resources that an economy has at any one time determines what that economy can produce.

Roger LeRoy Miller, *Economics Today,* p. 27

resources: _____

production: _____

conversion: _____

factors of production: _____

10. A century ago, belief that a civilization lived on Mars was so widespread that the term "Martian" became essentially synonymous with "alien." Although occasional speculation about life on Mars goes far back into history, the craze began in 1877, when Italian astronomer Giovanni Schiaparelli reported seeing linear features across the surface of Mars through his telescope. He named these features *canali,* the Italian word for "channels." English accounts mistranslated the term as "canals," and coming amidst the excitement surrounding the recent opening of the Suez Canal (in 1869), Schiaparelli's discovery soon inspired visions of artificial waterways built by a Martian civilization.

Jeffrey Bennett, *On the Cosmic Horizon,* p. 9

synonymous: _____

canali: _____

ACTIVITY 6

DIRECTIONS: Bring to class ten examples of context clues taken from your other textbooks, and include the word meanings you were able to figure out using those clues. If you do not have other textbooks at this time, ask your classmates who are using other books to share their examples with you.

USING WORD PARTS: ROOTS, PREFIXES, SUFFIXES

In some instances your knowledge of word parts (roots, prefixes, suffixes) can help you determine the meanings of unfamiliar words. A root is the basic part, or stem, from which words are derived. For example, the root *tang* means "touch," and the word *tangible* is formed from it. A prefix is a word part or group of letters added *before* a root or word to change its meaning or to create a new word. For instance if we add the prefix *in*—which means "not"—to *tangible* we get *intangible*. Thus, we change the meaning from touchable to untouchable. Finally, a suffix is a word part or group of letters added *after* a root or word to create another word or to affect the way a word is used in a sentence. As you saw in the example above, the suffix *ible*, meaning "capable of being," can be added to the root *tang* to form *tangible* or *intangible*. Thus, the word *intangible* is made up of the prefix *in* (not), the root *tang* (touch), and the suffix *ible* (capable of being), which add up to the literal meaning "not capable of being touched." The more roots, prefixes, and suffixes that you know, the greater the likelihood that you will be able to use at least some of them to figure out word meanings.

ACTIVITY 7

DIRECTIONS: Following is a table that lists some of the more common word parts, their meanings, and an example for each. When possible, use the word parts to help you figure out the definitions of the examples that are unfamiliar to you. Write your definitions in the spaces provided. Also try to provide an example of your own for each of the roots, prefixes, and suffixes. If you have difficulty coming up with some of the definitions or examples, your instructor or classmates may help you when this exercise is discussed in class.

ROOTS				
Root	*Meaning*	*Example*	*Definition*	*Your Example*
aqua	water	aquatic		
audi	hear	audible		
auto	self	autobiography		
bene	good, well	benign		
bio	life	biography		

Root	Meaning	Example	Definition	Your Example
chron	time	synchronize		
cred	believe	credible		
culp	blame	culprit		
derm	skin	dermatology		
geo	earth	geology		
graph	to write	polygraph		
log	speech	dialog		
micro	small	microbiology		
mort	death	mortal		
ped	foot	pedicure		
phob	fear	claustrophobia		
phon	sound	phonics		
poly	many	polygamy		
port	to carry	transport		
pseud	false	pseudonym		
psych	mind	psychology		
script	to write	Scripture		
spec	to look	spectacles		
therm	heat	hyperthermia		

PREFIXES

Prefix	Meaning	Example	Definition	Your Example
a–	not, without	atheist		
ante–	before, in front of	anterior		
anti–	against, opposite	antiseptic		
bi–	two	bilingual		
circum–	around	circumference		
con–	together, with	congregate		
contra–	against	contraception		
extra–	more than	extraterrestrial		
hyper–	over	hyperactive		
hypo–	under	hypodermic		
il–	not	illegitimate		

Prefix	Meaning	Example	Definition	Your Example
im-	not	immobile		
in-	not	inoperative		
inter-	between	interstate		
intra-	within	intrastate		
ir-	not	irrational		
mal-	bad	malignant		
mis-	wrong	misadvise		
mono-	one	monologue		
non-	not	nonprofit		
post-	after	posterior		
pre-	before	prejudice		
pro-	for	proponent		
re-	back, again	recede		
retro-	backward	retroactive		
semi-	half	semiconscious		
sub-	under	subservient		
super-	over	supernatural		
trans-	across	transfer		
tri-	three	tripod		
un-	not	uncivil		

SUFFIXES

Suffix	Meaning	Example	Definition	Your Example
-able	capable of	readable		
-ar	relating to	solar		
-en	made of	golden		
-er	person who	adviser		
-ful	full of	plentiful		
-fy	to make	pacify		
-hood	condition	bachelorhood		
-ible	capable of	edible		
-ize	to make	sterilize		
-less	without	penniless		

Suffix	Meaning	Example	Definition	Your Example
-logy	study of	sociology		
-ment	state of being	harassment		
-or	person who	conductor		
-ward	direction	westward		

ACTIVITY 8

DIRECTIONS: You now are aware of the definitions for all of the examples provided in the table above. In your notebook, make up sentences using each of the examples.

ACTIVITY 9

DIRECTIONS: Taking *your* examples from the exercise above, make up sentences in your notebook using each one of them.

USING A GLOSSARY

Glossaries often are found in the back matter—or sometimes within the chapters themselves—of content textbooks dealing with such subjects as business, health, psychology, and sociology. A **glossary** is alphabetized and provides definitions for the most important terms used in the textbook. Unlike a dictionary, which generally lists several meanings and provides additional important information about each word, a glossary only gives the one meaning that is appropriate for the specific subject matter of that textbook. It also provides definitions for specialized combinations of words generally not found in the dictionary. For example in the sample glossary on the following pages, you will find definitions for *crawling peg* and *elastic demand*. Although the dictionary does give separate meanings for each of these words, it does not define them when they are used together, as does this particular glossary. In short, glossaries are useful tools because they provide you with a rapid means of finding the appropriate definitions of the most important terms used in a given subject area.

ACTIVITY 10

DIRECTIONS:

1. Find the meanings of the following words using the pages from the partial glossary beginning on page 21. Write out the definition.

   deregulation:_____

   _____

   _____

barter: _____

_____

_____

collective bargaining: _____

_____

_____

depreciation is also called: _____

_____

_____

economics: _____

_____

_____

balance of trade:_____

_____

_____

certificate of deposit: _____

_____

_____

average total costs is sometimes called:_____

_____

_____

closed shop:_____

_____

_____

another way of saying automatic stabilizers is: _____

_____

_____

black market: _____

_____

_____

another way of saying active policymaking is:_____

_____

_____

DIRECTIONS:

2. Use the partial glossary to answer the following questions.
   a. If a share of stock is bought for $25 and then sold for $150, the capital gain is:

   _____

   b. The pronunciation guide for *ceteris paribus* is:_____

   c. In Canada or England, the discount rate is referred to as the: _____

glossary

Action time lag   The time between recognizing an economic problem and implementing policy to solve it. The action time lag is quite long for fiscal policy, which requires congressional approval.

Active (discretionary) policymaking   All actions on the part of monetary and fiscal policymakers that are undertaken in response to or in anticipation of some change in the overall economy.

Adverse selection   The likelihood that individuals who seek to borrow money may use the funds that they receive for unworthy, high-risk projects.

Age-earnings cycle   The regular earnings profile of an individual throughout his or her lifetime. The age-earnings cycle usually starts with a low income, builds gradually to a peak at around age 50, and then gradually curves down until it approaches zero at retirement.

Aggregate demand   The total of all planned expenditures for the entire economy.

Aggregate demand curve   A curve showing planned purchase rates for all final goods and services in the economy at various price levels, all other things held constant.

Antitrust legislation   Laws that restrict the formation of monopolies and regulate certain anticompetitive business practices.

Automated clearinghouse (ACH)   A computer-based clearing and settlement facility that replaces check transactions by interchanging credits and debits electronically.

Automated teller machine (ATM) network   A system of linked depository institution computer terminals that are activated by magnetically encoded bank cards.

Automatic, or built-in, stabilizers   Special provisions of certain federal programs that cause changes in desired aggregate expenditures without the action of Congress and the president. Examples are the federal tax system and unemployment compensation.

Autonomous consumption   The part of consumption that is independent of (does not depend on) the level of disposable income. Changes in autonomous consumption shift the consumption function.

Average fixed costs   Total fixed costs divided by the number of units produced.

Average physical product   Total product divided by the variable input.

continued on page 22

Average propensity to consume (APC). Consumption divided by disposable income; for any given level of income, the proportion of total disposable income that is consumed.

Average propensity to save (APS) Saving divided by disposable income; for any given level of income, the proportion of total disposable income that is saved.

Average tax rate The total tax payment divided by total income. It is the proportion of total income paid in taxes.

Average total costs Total costs divided by the number of units produced; sometimes called average per-unit total costs.

Average variable costs Total variable costs divided by the number of units produced.

Balance of payments A system of accounts that measures transactions of goods, services, income, and financial assets between domestic households, businesses, and governments and residents of the rest of the world during a specific time period.

Balance of trade The difference between exports and imports of goods.

Balance sheet A statement of the assets and liabilities of any business entity, including financial institutions and the Federal Reserve System. Assets are what is owned; liabilities are what is owed.

Bank runs Attempts by many of a bank's depositors to convert checkable and time deposits into currency out of fear for the bank's solvency.

Barter The direct exchange of goods and services for other goods and services without the use of money.

Base year The year that is chosen as the point of reference for comparison of prices in other years.

Bilateral monopoly A market structure consisting of a monopolist and a monopsonist.

Black market A market in which goods are traded at prices above their legal maximum prices or in which illegal goods are sold.

Bond A legal claim against a firm, usually entitling the owner of the bond to receive a fixed annual coupon payment, plus a lump-sum payment at the bond's maturity date. Bonds are issued in return for funds lent to the firm.

Capital consumption allowance Another name for depreciation, the amount that businesses would have to save in order to take care of the deterioration of machines and other equipment.

Capital controls Legal restrictions on the ability of a nation's residents to hold and trade assets denominated in foreign currencies.

Capital gain The positive difference between the pur-

chase price and the sale price of an asset. If a share of stock is bought for $5 and then sold for $15, the capital gain is $10.

Capital goods Producer durables; nonconsumable goods that firms use to make other goods.

Capital loss The negative difference between the purchase price and the sale price of an asset.

Certificate authority A group charged with supervising the terms governing how buyers and sellers can legitimately make digital cash transfers.

Certificate of deposit (CD) A time deposit with a fixed maturity date offered by banks and other financial institutions.

Ceteris paribus [KAY-ter-us PEAR-uh-bus] **assumption** The assumption that nothing changes except the factor or factors being studied.

Checkable deposits Any deposits in a thrift institution or a commercial bank on which a check may be written.

Clearing House Interbank Payment System (CHIPS) A large-value wire transfer system linking about 100 banks that permits them to transmit large sums of money related primarily to foreign exchange and Eurodollar transactions.

Closed shop A business enterprise in which employees must belong to the union before they can be hired and must remain in the union after they are hired.

Collateral An asset pledged to guarantee the repayment of a loan.

Collective bargaining Bargaining between the management of a company or of a group of companies and the management of a union or a group of unions for the purpose of setting a mutually agreeable contract on wages, fringe benefits, and working conditions for all employees in all the unions involved.

Collective decision making How voters, politicians, and other interested parties act and how these actions influence nonmarket decisions.

Common property Property that is owned by everyone and therefore by no one. Air and water are examples of common property resources.

Comparable-worth doctrine The belief that women should receive the same wages as men if the levels of skill and responsibility in their jobs are equivalent.

Comparative advantage The ability to produce a good or service at a lower opportunity cost compared to other producers.

Complements Two goods are complements if both are used together for consumption or enjoyment—for example, coffee and cream. The more you buy of one, the more you buy of the other. For complements, a change in the price of one causes an opposite shift in the demand for the other.

Constant-cost industry An industry whose total output can be increased without an increase in long-run per-unit costs; an industry whose long-run supply curve is horizontal.

Consumer optimum A choice of a set of goods and services that maximizes the level of satisfaction for each consumer, subject to limited income.

Consumer Price Index (CPI) A statistical measure of a weighted average of prices of a specified set of goods and services purchased by wage earners in urban areas.

Consumption Spending on new goods and services out of a household's current income. Whatever is not consumed is saved. Consumption includes such things as buying food and going to a concert. *Can also be viewed as the use of goods and services for personal satisfaction.*

Consumption function The relationship between amount consumed and disposable income. A consumption function tells us how much people plan to consume at various levels of disposable income.

Consumption goods Goods bought by households to use up, such as food, clothing, and movies.

Contraction A business fluctuation during which the pace of national economic activity is slowing down.

Cooperative game A game in which the players explicitly cooperate to make themselves better off. As applied to firms, it involves companies colluding in order to make higher than competitive rates of return.

Corporation A legal entity that may conduct business in its own name just as an individual does; the owners of a corporation, called shareholders, own shares of the firm's profits and enjoy the protection of limited liability.

Cost-of-living adjustments (COLAs) Clauses in contracts that allow for increases in specified nominal values to take account of changes in the cost of living.

Cost-of-service regulation Regulation based on allowing prices to reflect only the actual cost of production and no monopoly profits.

Cost-push inflation Inflation caused by a continually decreasing short-run aggregate supply curve.

Craft unions Labor unions composed of workers who engage in a particular trade or skill, such as baking, carpentry, or plumbing.

Crawling peg An exchange rate arrangement in which a country pegs the value of its

Continued on page 24

currency to the exchange value of another nation's currency but allows the par value to change at regular intervals.

Crude quantity theory of money and prices The belief that changes in the money supply lead to proportional changes in the price level.

Cyclical unemployment Unemployment resulting from business recessions that occur when aggregate (total) demand is insufficient to create full employment.

Debit card A plastic card that allows the bearer to transfer funds to a merchant's account, provided that the bearer authorizes the transfer by providing personal identification.

Decreasing-cost industry An industry in which an increase in output leads to a reduction in long-run per-unit costs, such that the long-run industry supply curve slopes downward.

Deflation The situation in which the average of all prices of goods and services in an economy is falling.

Demand A schedule of how much of a good or service people will purchase at any price during a specified time period, other things being constant.

Demand curve A graphical representation of the demand schedule; a negatively sloped line showing the inverse relationship between the price and the quantity demanded (other things being equal).

Demand-pull inflation Inflation caused by increases in aggregate demand not matched by increases in aggregate supply.

Demerit good A good that has been deemed socially undesirable through the political process. Heroin is an example.

Dependent variable A variable whose value changes according to changes in the value of one or more independent variables.

Depository institutions Financial institutions that accept deposits from savers and lend those deposits out at interest.

Depreciation Reduction in the value of capital goods over a one-year period due to physical wear and tear and also to obsolescence; also called *capital consumption allowance. Can also be viewed as* a decrease in the exchange value of one nation's currency in terms of the currency of another nation.

Depression An extremely severe recession.

Deregulation The elimination or phasing out of regulations on economic activity.

Derived demand Input factor demand derived from demand for the final product being produced.

Development economics The study of factors that contribute to the economic development of a country.

Direct relationship A relationship between two variables that is positive, meaning that an increase in one variable is associated with an increase in the other and a decrease in one variable is associated with a decrease in the other.

Dirty float Active management of a floating exchange rate on the part of a country's government, often in cooperation with other nations.

Discounting The method by which the present value of a future sum or a future stream of sums is obtained.

Discount rate The interest rate that the Federal Reserve charges for reserves that it lends to depository institutions. It is sometimes referred to as the rediscount rate or, in Canada and England, as the bank rate.

Discouraged workers Individuals who have stopped looking for a job because they are convinced that they will not find a suitable one.

Diseconomies of scale Increases in long-run average costs that occur as output increases.

Disposable personal income (DPI) Personal income after personal income taxes have been paid.

Dissaving Negative saving: a situation in which spending exceeds income. Dissaving can occur when a household is able to borrow or use up existing assets.

Distribution of income The way income is allocated among the population.

Dividends Portion of a corporation's profits paid to its owners (shareholders).

Durable consumer goods Consumer goods that have a life span of more than three years.

Economic goods Goods that are scarce, for which the quantity demanded exceeds the quantity supplied at a zero price.

Economic growth Increases in per capita real GDP measured by its rate of change per year.

Economic profits Total revenues minus total opportunity costs of all inputs used, or the total of all implicit and explicit costs. *Can also be viewed as* the difference between total revenues and the opportunity cost of all factors of production.

Economic rent A payment for the use of any resource over and above its opportunity cost.

Economics The study of how people allocate their limited resources to satisfy their unlimited wants.

Economies of scale Decreases in long-run average costs resulting from increases in output.

Effect time lag The time that elapses between the onset of policy and the results of that policy.

Efficiency wage theory The hypothesis that the productivity of workers depends on the level of the real wage rate.

Efficiency The case in which a given level of inputs is used to produce the maximum output possible. Alternatively, the situation in which a given output is produced at minimum cost.

Efficiency wages Wages set above competitive levels to increase labor productivity and profits by enhancing the efficiency of the firm through lower turnover, ease of attracting higher-quality workers, and better efforts by workers.

Elastic demand A demand relationship in which a given percentage change in price will result in a larger percentage change in quantity demanded. Total expenditure and price changes are inversely related in the elastic region of the demand curve.

Entrepreneurship The factor of production involving human resources that perform the functions of raising capital, organizing, managing, assembling other factors of production, and making basic business policy decisions. The entrepreneur is a risk taker.

Roger LeRoy Miller, *Economics Today*, pp. G1–4

USING THE DICTIONARY

The dictionary is a very valuable tool not only for finding word meanings, but also because it provides additional important information about each word, including correct spelling, pronunciation, part of speech (noun, pronoun, adjective, verb, adverb, conjunction, preposition), various endings, and derivation (origin). The derivation, or etymology, of a word refers to its historical development, including what language it came from.

As you know, the dictionary is alphabetized. At the top of each page, two bold-faced words appear; these are the first and last entries on that page. Thus, if the word you are looking up fits alphabetically between the guide words on a particular page, you can find it there.

Let us look at a typical entry taken from *The Random House Dictionary*.

prim-i-tive (prim' i tiv), *adj* [L. *primitivus*, from *primus*, first] **1** being the first or earliest of the kind **2** characteristic of early ages or of an early state of human development **3** simple or crude—*n* **4** a person or thing that is primitive **5** a naive or unschooled artist—**prim'•i•tive•ly**, *adv*—**prim'•i•tive•ness, prim'•i•tiv'•i•ty,** *n*—**prim'•i•tiv'•ism,** *n*

The word *primitive* is located on the dictionary page between the guide words **primary accent** and **principle.** Right after the correct spelling of the word comes the pronunciation (in parentheses). Most dictionaries provide a pronunciation key for the symbols that they use, which usually is located either at the front of the dictionary or on the bottom of the individual pages. The next entry tells us the part of speech; *primitive* is an adjective. The derivation of the word—located within the brackets—is Latin from *primitivus,* which comes from *primus,* meaning first. Five definitions follow, the last two of which are for when *primitive* is used as a noun. Finally, the various endings are provided. These endings change the part of speech of the word to an adverb or a noun. Most dictionaries furnish a key that explains the abbreviations used for such things as parts of speech and derivation.

As you can see, dictionaries provide much valuable information about words that can be very useful as you make your way through college. If you do not own a dictionary, purchase one immediately, and refer to it often. In fact, you should buy two dictionaries—an unabridged, hardcover one for use at home and a smaller, paperback one to carry with you while you are at school. Also, the school library has very large dictionaries that come in handy when you are studying there.

ACTIVITY 11

DIRECTIONS: Use your dictionary to answer the following questions.

1. Which of the following words would you find on a page with the guide words **narrative–natural?**

narrow	narthex	natural history
nativism	natural gas	nascent
nasalize	narrator	naturalism
narrate	nationwide	natty

2. Find and write down the correct spellings for the following words.

   nationalise:_____   salamandar: _____

   premrose: _____   slouche: _____

   envesion: _____   bressiere: _____

3. Write out the pronunciation guide for each of these words.

   chamois:_____   mullah:_____

kamikaze:_____   hacienda: _____

ubiquitous:_____   decimate: _____

4. Indicate the parts of speech for the words below.

confluence: _____   deposit: _____

insolvable: _____   truly: _____

within: _____   an: _____

5. Provide the derivation for each of the following words.

terrapin:_____   laudable: _____

voodoo: _____   geriatrics:_____

tapioca: _____

6. Give the various endings for these words.

demolish: _____   asphyxiate:_____

vibrate:_____   condense:_____

obfuscate: _____   sage:_____

7. Write out the definitions for the words listed below.

apathy: _____

bourgeois: _____

conservative:_____

entrepreneur: _____

heterogeneous: _____

homogeneous:_____

liberal: _____

metabolism:_____

neurosis: _____

physiological: _____

psychosis: _____

prognosis: _____

verbose:_____

whimsical: _____

zealous: _____

LEARNING AND REVIEWING VOCABULARY WORDS

Whether you use the context, word parts, a glossary, or the dictionary to find the meanings to the most important words that you encounter in college, it is a good idea to keep a written record of them either in a notebook or on note cards. Writing them down helps you learn, remember, and review them for tests without having to look them up again. In addition to writing down the definitions, always include the sentences in which the words appeared so that you are aware of the context and indicate what textbooks or other sources they came from.

ACTIVITY 12

DIRECTIONS: Following the format below, start a vocabulary notebook by recording in your notebook 25 unfamiliar words that you come across while reading your textbooks or various other sources. If you prefer, you may use note cards instead.

Model

NAME OF TEXTBOOK OR OTHER SOURCES

Word	Context	Definition

Example 1

Introduction to Business

Word	Context	Definition
consolidate	It is important for businesses to consolidate (combine) their resources.	combine

Example 2

Western Civilization

Word	Context	Definition
capitulate	Because the army was surrounded and very low on ammunition, the general was forced to capitulate.	give up

――――   ―――――――――――――――――   ――――
――――   ―――――――――――――――――   ――――
――――   ―――――――――――――――――   ――――
――――   ―――――――――――――――――   ――――

LOOKING BACK

With two of your classmates, come up with a list of the most important points you learned from this chapter and determine how they can be put to use in other classes. Be prepared to discuss both the list and the uses.

THINK AGAIN!

How can you prove that 3 is half of 8?

AND AGAIN!

For each of the signs that follow, write a paragraph in your notebook in which you discuss your interpretation of the message.

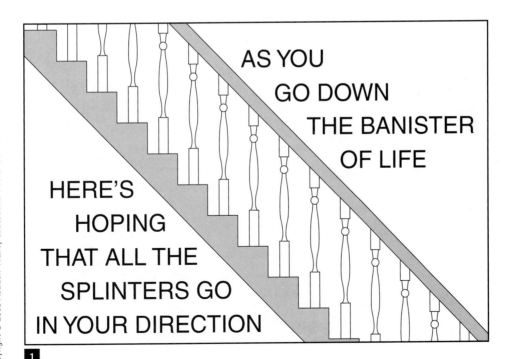

1

The Dashing Detective

At the end of each chapter in this textbook you will have the opportunity to play "the dashing detective" by using your critical thinking skills to solve a picture mystery provided by Lawrence Treat in his book, *Crime and Puzzlement*.

For each mystery:

- first, read the narrative and all the questions
- second, examine the picture carefully
- third, answer the questions in the order they appear and come up with the solution

Have lots of fun!

Boudoir

Amy LaTour's body was found in her bedroom last night, as shown, with her pet canary strangled in its cage. Henry Willy and Joe Wonty, her boyfriends; Louis Spanker, a burglar known to have been in the vicinity; and Celeste, her maid, were questioned by the police.

Wilbur Unisex, who happened to be in the area pursuing the *Heliconius charitonius,* put down his butterfly net and solved the case. Can you?

Questions

1. How was Amy apparently killed?   ☐ Shot   ☐ Stabbed   ☐ Strangled   ☐ Beaten

2. Is there evidence of a violent struggle?   ☐ Yes   ☐ No

3. Was her murderer strong?   ☐ Yes   ☐ No

4. Was Amy fond of jewelry?   ☐ Yes   ☐ No

4. Was she robbed?   ☐ Yes   ☐ No

5. Do you think she had been on friendly terms with her killer?   ☐ Yes   ☐ No

6. Was the canary strangled before Amy's death?   ☐ Yes   ☐ No

7. Was this a crime of passion?   ☐ Yes   ☐ No

8. Did Willy have a motive?   ☐ Yes   ☐ No

9. Who killed Amy?   ☐ Henry   ☐ Willy   ☐ Joe Wonty   ☐ Louis Spanker   ☐ Celeste

Laurence Treat, *Crime and Puzzlement,* pp. 2–3

Name _____ Date _____

MASTERY TEST 1–1

DIRECTIONS: Using the context, write the meanings next to the words that appear after the sentences.

1. Finally, the concept of **social engineering** was born—the belief that *strong governmental leaders, advised by social scientists, could use social science to design a preferred social order.* This notion remains a central ingredient in modern sociological thought.

   Richard P. Appelbaum and William J. Chambliss, *Sociology,* pp. 18–19

   social engineering: _____

   _____

2. Your readers will expect an essay you write to be focused on a central idea, or thesis, to which all the essay's paragraphs, all its general statements and specific information, relate. The thesis is the controlling idea, the main point, the conclusion you have drawn about the evidence you have accumulated. Even if you create a composition on the World Wide Web, you'll have a core idea that governs the links among pages and sites.

   H. Ramsey Fowler et al., *The Little, Brown Handbook,* 8th ed., p. 30

   thesis: _____

3. Communicating via electronic devices, especially facsimile (fax) machines and computerized electronic mail (e-mail), speeds up correspondence but also creates new challenges. For both fax transmissions and e-mail, the standards are the same as for other business correspondence: state your purpose at the outset and write straightforwardly, clearly, concisely, objectively, courteously, and correctly.

   H. Ramsey Fowler and Jane E. Aaron, *The Little, Brown Handbook,* p. 757

   fax: _____

   e-mail:_____

4. When the press secretary announced that the president had "passed away" instead of saying that he had died, he was using a euphemism.

   euphemism:_____

   _____

5. **Antipsychotic drugs,** or *major tranquilizers,* include chlorpromazine (Thorazine), haloperidol (Haldol), clozapine (Clozaril), and risperidone. These drugs have transformed the treatment of schizophrenia and other **psychoses** (extreme mental disorders that involve distorted perceptions and irrational behavior).

   Carol Tavris and Carole Wade, *Psychology in Perspective,* p. 190

   antipsychotic drugs: _____

   _____

psychoses: _____

_____

6. You will often have multiple audiences, some *primary* (the people for whom your document is specifically intended) and some *secondary* (other people who may have reason to read all or part of the document). For example, your engineering report may be read by people who need to analyze the details of what you've written and by those who need to know only the conclusions and recommendations. If you know this in advance, you can make decisions about the document that can accommodate both types of readers. For example, you can decide whether it would be better to "front-load" the document...by putting the recommendations first or to begin with the back-ground discussion.

Kristin R. Woolever, *Writing for the Technical Professions*, pp. 12–13

primary audience: _____

_____

secondary audience: _____

_____

frontload: _____

7. In the autumn, groves of quaking aspen trees turn Colorado mountainsides a rich gold. Up close you can hear the soft rustling of the leaves. It's almost constant, and in a gust of wind, whole trees seem to tremble, or quake. The trembling is an unusual property of the leaves....The stalk of each aspen leaf is flattened and acts like a hinge, letting the small, light leaf blade flutter back and forth in the slightest breeze. The fluttering seems to help the leaves breathe—that is, take up carbon dioxide and give off oxygen gas to the air. Plants use carbon dioxide and solar energy to make food (sugar mole-cules) by photosynthesis. They give off oxygen as a by-product of photosynthesis.

Neil A. Campbell et al., *Biology*, 3rd ed., p. 16

photosynthesis: _____

_____

8. Many people in the United States are still very much opposed to miscegenation, mar-riage between whites and blacks.

miscegenation: _____

9. Abortion will remain a contentious issue for many years to come.

contentious: _____

10. Whereas the professor's lecture last night was very clear, her remarks today were ambiguous.

ambiguous: _____

11. Those who oppose capital punishment offer incarceration for life with no chance for parole as an acceptable alternative.

    incarceration: _____

12. Demography—the study of populations—reviews the ways populations change in size. Births (natality) and deaths (mortality) account for most changes in a population. The difference between the two rates determines its growth or decline.

    Robert Leo Smith and Thomas M. Smith, *Elements of Ecology,* 4th ed., p. 150

    demography: _____

    natality: _____

13. While some people become addicted to prescription drugs and painkillers, we focus our attention here on **illicit drugs**—those drugs that are illegal to possess, produce, or sell.

    Rebecca J. Donatelle, *Health: The Basics,* 4th ed., p. 167

    illicit: _____

14. The canopies, or treetops, of forests are one of nature's great showplaces of different kinds of living organisms.

    Neil A. Campbell et al., *Biology,* 3rd ed., p. 1

    canopies: _____

15. The major constituent of urine is water. The amount of urine excreted daily by an adult may vary from 500 to 2500 ml (milliliters). The exact amount depends on liquid intake and the amount of water lost through perspiration. Heavy perspiration decreases the volume of urine formed. Coffee, tea, or alcoholic beverages have a diuretic (stimulate formation of urine) effect.

    Robert J. Ouellette, *Introductory Chemistry*

    constituent: _____

    excreted: _____

    diuretic: _____

16. Over five million are of Mexican origin or descent. A growing number of this group, especially the younger people in urban areas, prefer the name "Chicano" rather than "Mexican-American" or Hispano.

    Raymond E. Glos, Richard D. Steade, and James R. Lowry, *Business: Its Nature and Environment*

    Chicano: _____

17. An unusual type of capitalism is laissez-faire: a term borrowed from the French that means the noninterference of government in the business sector.

    laissez-faire: _____

18. Slavery established a ground for the seeds of racism. When, during the late eighteenth century, abolitionists (people who opposed slavery) increasingly denounced the slave trade, advocates of slavery were forced to find new arguments to defend their actions.

    Institute for Contemporary Curriculum Development, *Patterns of Civilization: Africa*

    abolitionists: _____

    advocates: _____

19. Much of the violent crime in the United States is committed by recidivists, and it is simply amazing that our society lets these habitual criminals back on the street.

    recidivists: _____

20. The chemist converted the liquid into gas by heating it over a slow flame.

    converted: _____

21. Nomads—Bedouins, or desert Arabs—dwelt with their herds in the neighborhood of Mecca.

    Sydney Nettleton Fisher, *The Middle East: A History*

    Bedouins:_____

22. Urethritis, inflammation of the urethra, is usually an ascending infection. It may be caused by a bacterial or viral infection or by trauma from an indwelling catheter or repeated cystoscopic examinations.

    Lillian S. Brunner and Doris S. Suddarth, *Textbook of Medical-Surgical Nursing*

    urethritis: _____

23. What was needed was a way to identify the sphere of influence of a city: the area whose inhabitants depend on the central city for jobs, recreation, newspapers, television, and a sense of common community.

    Rodney Stark, *Sociology*

    sphere of influence: _____

24. When researchers first glance at a distribution, they probably look for the range—the difference between the lowest and highest values.

    William C. Himstreet, Wayne Murlin Baty, and Carol M. Lehman, *Business Communications*

    range: _____

25. Breathing in is called inspiration or inhalation.

    Gerard J. Tortora and Nicholas P. Anagnostakos, *Principles of Anatomy and Physiology*

    inspiration: _____

26. When negotiations do break down, disagreements between union and management representatives may be settled by mediation—the process of bringing in a third party,

called a mediator, to make recommendations for the settlement of differences. The final step in settling union-management differences is arbitration—the process of bringing in an impartial third party, called an arbitrator, who renders a binding decision in the dispute. The impartial third party must be acceptable to the union and to management, and his or her decision is legally enforceable. In essence, the arbitrator acts as a judge, making a decision after listening to both sides of the argument.

Louis E. Boone and David L. Kurtz, Contemporary Business

mediation: _____

arbitration: _____

27. The physicians decided to treat the cancer with radiation rather than drugs. This change in treatment plans was for the purpose of palliation: to relieve the pain without curing.

palliation: _____

28. Since the time of John Locke, David Hume, David Hartley, and other British philosophers of the 1660s and 1700s, association (the linking of sensations or ideas) has been regarded as central to all thought processes.

James W. Kalat, Introduction to Psychology

association: _____

29. The term "triage" was first described in the *Annals of Military Medicine* as the process of sorting the sick and wounded on the basis of urgency and type of condition presented so that the patient can be properly routed to the appropriate medical area. It is, therefore, right that triage be used in the emergency situations encountered daily in the streets.

J. A. Young and Dean Crocker, Principles and Practice of Respiratory Therapy

triage: _____

30. When the fort was enveloped by the enemy on all sides, it was only a matter of time before it fell.

enveloped: _____

Name _____   Date _____

MASTERY TEST 1–2

DIRECTIONS: Using word parts, try to figure out the meanings of the words listed below.

1. aquanaut: _____

_____

_____

2. inaudible: _____

_____

_____

3. biology: _____

_____

_____

4. creed:_____

_____

_____

5. culpable: _____

_____

_____

6. dermal: _____

_____

_____

7. monosyllable: _____

_____

_____

8. microcomputer:_____

_____

_____

9. immortal:_____

_____

_____

10. phobia: _____

_____

_____

11. polysyllable:_____

_____

_____

12. hypothermia:_____

_____

_____

13. asexual: _____

_____

_____

14. antidote: _____

_____

_____

15. bisect: _____

_____

_____

16. substandard: _____

_____

_____

17. normalize: _____

_____

_____

18. mindless: _____

_____

_____

19. embarrassment:_____

_____

_____

20. lunar:_____

_____

_____

Name _____   Date _____

MASTERY TEST 1–3

A. *DIRECTIONS:* Using the partial glossary on pages 44–47, answer the following questions.

1. A "run-on sentence" can also be referred to as a_____ sentence.

2. An example of an "acronym" is:_____.

3. Another word for "trite expressions" is _____.

4. Provide an example of a "dangling modifier": _____

   _____

   _____

5. What is a "search engine?" _____

   _____

   _____

6. To "upload" is to:_____

   _____

   _____

7. What is the difference between "abstract" and "concrete" words? _____

   _____

   _____

8. A word's "denotation" can be found in the _____.

9. Define "sentence fragment" and provide an example: _____

   _____

   _____

10. A "database" is a collection and organization of_____.

B. *DIRECTIONS:* Answer the following questions by using the dictionary page on page 48.

1. Name the guide words:_____

2. Write out the pronunciation illustration for the word "happenstance." _____

3. What is the part of speech of the word "hapless?" _____

4. Name the various endings of the word "hanker." _____

_____

_____

5. What is the meaning of the word "harangue?" _____

_____

_____

6. "Harakiri" is also called_____.

7. What is the derivation of the word "happy?"_____

_____

_____

8. Another word for Hansen's disease is _____.

_____

_____

9. Name five synonyms for the word "happen." _____

_____

_____

10. Two other ways of spelling "Hanukkah" are: _____

Glossary

This glossary defines terms of grammar, rhetoric, literature, and Internet research.

absolute phrase   A phrase consisting of a noun or pronoun plus the *-ing* or *-ed* form of a verb (a participle): *Our accommodations arranged, we set out on our journey. They will hire a local person, other things being equal.* An absolute phrase modifies a whole clause or sentence (rather than a single word), and it is not joined to the rest of the sentence by a connector.

abstract and concrete   Two kinds of language. Abstract words refer to ideas, qualities, attitudes, and conditions that can't be perceived with the senses: *beauty, guilty, victory.* Concrete words refer to objects, persons, places, or conditions that can be perceived with the senses: *Abilene, scratchy, toolbox.* See also *general and specific.*

acronym   A pronounceable word formed from the initial letter or letters of each word in an organization's title: NATO (North Atlantic Treaty Organization).

active voice   See *voice.*

adjectival   A term sometimes used to describe any word or word group, other than an adjective, that is used to modify a noun. Common adjectivals include nouns (*wagon train, railroad ties*), phrases (*fool on the hill*), and clauses (*the man that I used to be*).

adjective   A word used to modify a noun (*beautiful morning*) or a pronoun (*ordinary one*). Nouns, some verb forms, phrases, and clauses may also serve as adjectives: *book sale; a used book; sale of old books; the sale, which occurs annually.* (See *clauses, prepositional phrases,* and *verbals and verbal phrases.*)

Adjectives come in several classes:

> A descriptive adjective names some quality of the noun: *beautiful morning, dark horse.*

> A limiting adjective narrows the scope of a noun. It may be a possessive (*my, their*); a demonstrative adjective (*this train, these days*); an interrogative adjective (*what time? whose body?*); or a number (*two boys*).

> A proper adjective is derived from a proper noun: *French language, Machiavellian scheme.*

courseware   A program for online communication and collaboration among the teacher and students in a course.

critical thinking, reading, and writing   Looking beneath the surface of words and images to discern meaning and relationships and to build knowledge.

cumulative (loose) sentence   A sentence in which modifiers follow the subject and verb: *Ducks waddled by, their tails swaying and their quacks rising to heaven.* Contrast *periodic sentence.*

dangling modifier   A modifier that does not sensibly describe anything in its sentence.

> **Dangling**   *Having arrived late*, the concert had already begun.

> **Revised**   Having arrived late, *we found that* the concert had already begun.

data   In argument, a term used for *evidence*. See *evidence*.

database   A collection and organization of information (data). A database may be printed, but the term is most often used for electronic sources.

declension   A list of the forms of a noun or pronoun, showing inflections for person (for pronouns), number, and case.

demonstrative adjective   See *adjective*.

demonstrative pronoun   See *pronoun*.

denotation   The main or dictionary definition of a word. Contrast *connotation*.

dependent clause   See *clause*.

derivational suffix   See *suffix*.

description   Detailing the sensory qualities of a thing, person, place, or feeling.

purpose   For a writer, the chief reason for communicating something about a topic to a particular audience. Purposes are both general (usually explanation or persuasion) and specific (taking into account the topic and desired outcome).

quotation   Repetition of what someone has written or spoken. In direct quotation (direct discourse), the person's words are duplicated exactly and enclosed in quotation marks: *Polonius told his son, Laertes, "Neither a borrower nor a lender be."* An indirect quotation (indirect discourse) reports what someone said or wrote but not in the exact words and not in quotation marks: *Polonius advised his son, Laertes, not to borrow or lend.*

rational appeal   See *appeals*.

reciprocal pronoun   See *pronoun*.

reflexive pronoun   See *pronoun*.

rhetoric   The principles for finding and arranging ideas and for using language in speech or writing to achieve the writer's purpose in addressing his or her audience.

rhetorical question   A question asked for effect, with no answer expected. The person asking the question either intends to provide the answer or assumes it is obvious: *If we let one factory pollute the river, what does that say to other factories that want to dump wastes there?*

run-on sentence   See *fused sentence*.

sans serif   See *serifs*.

continued on page 46

search engine   A computer program that conducts Internet searches from keywords or directories.

secondary source   A source reporting or analyzing information in other sources, such as a critic's view of a work of art or a sociologist's summary of others' studies. Contrast *primary source.*

second person   See *person.*

sentence   A complete unit of thought, consisting of at least a subject and a predicate that are not introduced by a subordinating word. Sentences can be classed on the basis of their structure in one of four ways. A simple sentence contains one main clause: *I'm leaving.* A compound sentence contains at least two main clauses: *I'd like to stay, but I'm leaving.* A complex sentence contains one main clause and at least one subordinate clause: *If you let me go now, you'll be sorry.* A compound-complex sentence contains at least two main clauses and at least one subordinate clause: *I'm leaving because you want me to, but I'd rather stay.*

sentence fragment   A sentence error in which a group of words is set off as a sentence even though it begins with a subordinating word or lacks a subject or a predicate or both.

Fragment	She lost the race. *Because she was injured.* [*Because,* a subordinating conjunction, makes the underlined clause subordinate.]
Revised	She lost the race because she was injured.
Fragment	He could not light a fire. *And thus could not warm the room.* [The underlined word group lacks a subject.]
Revised	He could not light a fire. Thus *he* could not warm the room.

sentence modifier   An adverb or a word or word group acting as an adverb that modifies the idea of the whole sentence in which it appears rather than any specific word: *In fact, people will always complain.*

server   A computer that links other computers in a network. Servers transfer data and store files.

setting   The place where the action of a literary work happens.

sexist language   Language expressing narrow ideas about men's and women's roles, positions, capabilities, or value.

signal phrase   Words that indicate who is being quoted: *"In the future,"* said Andy Warhol, *"everyone will be world-famous for fifteen minutes."*

simile   See *figurative language.*

simple predicate   See *predicate.*

simple sentence   See *sentence.*

simple subject See *subject.*

simple tense See *tense.*

thesis The central, controlling idea of an essay, to which all assertions and details relate.

thesis statement A sentence or more that asserts the central, controlling idea of an essay and perhaps previews the essay's organization.

transitional expression A word or phrase, such as *thus* or *for example,* that links sentences and shows the relations between them. The error known as a comma splice occurs when two main clauses related by a transitional expression are separated only by a comma.

transitive verb A verb that requires a direct object to complete its meaning.

trite expressions (clichés) Stale expressions that dull writing and suggest that the writer is careless or lazy.

two-word verb A verb plus a preposition or adverb that affects the meaning of the verb: *jump off, put away, help out.*

uniform resource locator (URL) An address for a source on the World Wide Web, specifying protocol (the standard for transferring data and files), domain (the computer, or server, housing the source), and path (the location and name of the source).

unity The quality of an effective essay or paragraph in which all parts relate to the central idea and to each other.

upload To transfer data or files from your local computer to another computer.

variety Among connected sentences, changes in length, structure, and word order that help readers see the importance and complexity of ideas.

verb A word or group of words indicating the action or state of being of a subject. The inflection of a verb and the use of helping verbs with it indicate its tense, mood, voice, number, and sometimes person. See separate listings for each aspect and *predicate.*

H. Ramsey Fowler et al., *The Little, Brown Handbook,* 8th ed., pp. 943, 950, 963, 964, 967

han·gar (hăng′ər) *n.* A shed or shelter; especially, a structure for housing aircraft. [French, from Old French, probably from Medieval Latin *angarium*†, shed for shoeing horses.]

hang·bird (hăng′bûrd′) *n.* A bird, such as an oriole, that builds a hanging nest. Also called "hangnest."

Hang·chow (hăng′chou′; *Chinese* hăng′jō′). The capital of Chekiang, China, a port located in the northeast on Hangchow Bay. Population, 794,000.

Hang·chow Bay (hăng′chou′; *Chinese* hăng′jō′). An inlet of the East China Sea in northeastern Chekiang, China.

hang·dog (hăng′dôg′, -dŏg′) *adj.* 1. Shamefaced or guilty. 2. Downcast; intimidated. —*n.* A sneak.

hang·er (hăng′ər) *n.* 1. One that hangs. 2. A contrivance to which something hangs or by which something is hung. 3. A device around which a garment is draped for hanging from a hook or rod. 4. A loop or strap by which something is hung. 5. A bracket on an automobile's spring shackle designed to hold it to the chassis. 6. A decorative strip of cloth hung on a garment or wall.

hang·er·on (hăng′ər-ŏn′, -ôn′) *n., pl.* hangers-on (hăng′ərz-). A sycophant; parasite.

hang·ing (hăng′ĭng) *n.* 1. An execution on a gallows. 2. Something hung, as: **a.** Drapery. **b.** Wallpaper. 3. A descending slope or inclination. —*adj.* 1. Situated on a sharp declivity. 2. Projecting downward; overhanging. 3. Suited for holding something that hangs. 4. **a.** Susceptible to or meriting death by hanging: *a hanging crime.* **b.** Disposed to inflict the sentence of death by hanging: *a hanging judge.*

hanging indention. The indention of every line in a paragraph except the first.

hang·man (hăng′mən) *n., pl.* -men (-mĭn). One employed to execute condemned prisoners by hanging.

hang·nail (hăng′nāl′) *n.* A small piece of dead skin at the side or the base of a fingernail that is partly detached from the rest of the skin. [By folk-etymology from AGNAIL.]

hang out. 1. To project downward. 2. *Slang.* To hang around. 3. To suspend for public display: *hang out one's shingle.*

hang·out (hăng′out′) *n.* A frequently visited place.

hang·o·ver (hăng′ō′vər) *n.* 1. Unpleasant physical effects following the heavy use of alcohol. 2. A letdown or deflation, as after a period of excitement or elation. 3. A vestige; holdover: *hangovers from prewar legislation.*

hang up. 1. To suspend on a hook or hanger. 2. To replace (a telephone receiver) on its cradle. 3. To retard, impede, or interrupt: *hang up a project.* 4. To halt the movement or action of. 5. To end a telephone conversation. 6. To become halted or snagged.

hang·up (hăng′ŭp′) *n. Informal.* 1. **a.** A source of irritation or inhibition. **b.** An inhibition or fixation. 2. An obstacle; inconvenience.

Han·hai. The Chinese name for the Gobi Desert.

hank (hăngk) *n.* 1. A coil or loop. 2. A ring on a stay attached to the head of a jib or staysail. 3. A looped bundle, as of yarn. [Middle English, from Scandinavian, akin to Old Norse *hŏnk*†, hank, skein.]

Han·ka. See Lake Khanka.

han·ker (hăng′kər) *intr.v.* -kered, -kering, -kers. To have a longing; crave. See Synonyms at yearn. [From dialectal *hank*, probably from Dutch (dialectal) *hankeren*. See konk- in Appendix.*] —**hank′er·er** *n.*

Han Kiang. A Chinese name for the Han.

Han·kow (hăng′kou′; *Chinese* hăng′jō′). A former city of southeastern Hupei, China; now part of Wuhan (*see*).

han·ky-pan·ky (hăng′kē-păng′kē) *n. Slang.* 1. Devious or mischievous activity. 2. Foolish talk or action. [Coined on analogy with HOCUS-POCUS.]

Han·nah (hăn′ə). A feminine given name. [Hebrew *Hannāh*, "graciousness," from the stem of *hānah*, be gracious.]

Han·ni·bal (hăn′ə-bəl). 247–183 B.C. Carthaginian general.

Ha·noi (hă-noi′, hä-). The capital of North Vietnam; an industrial center on the Red River in the northeast. Population, 415,000.

Han·o·ver¹ (hăn′ō′vər). *German* **Han·no·ver** (hä-nō′vər). The capital of Lower Saxony, West Germany; a commercial and industrial center located on the Leine, 60 miles southeast of Bremen. Population, 571,000.

Han·o·ver² (hăn′ō′vər). 1. An electoral house of Germany (1692–1815). 2. A royal family of England (1714–1901).

Han·o·ve·ri·an (hăn′ō-vîr′ē-ən) *adj.* Of or pertaining to the city of Hanover, the electoral house, or the royal family of Hanover.

Han·sard (hăn′sərd) *n. British & Canadian.* The official report of the proceedings and debates of Parliament. [After its first printer Luke *Hansard* (1752–1828).]

hanse (hăns) *n.* 1. A medieval merchant guild or trade association. 2. *Capital H.* A town belonging to the Hanseatic League. Also called "Hanse town." 3. *Capital H. Rare.* The Hanseatic League. [Middle English *hans*, from Old French *hanse*, from Middle Low German *hanse*, from Old High German *hansa*, troop, company, from Germanic *khansō* (unattested).] —**hans′e·at′ic** (hăn′sē-ăt′ĭk) *adj.*

Hanseatic League. A protective and commercial association of free towns in northern Germany and neighboring areas, formally organized in 1358 and dissolved in the 17th century.

han·sel. Variant of handsel.

Han·sen's disease (hăn′sənz). Leprosy (*see*). [After the Norwegian physician A.G.H. *Hansen* (1841–1912), who discovered the bacillus that causes leprosy.]

Han Shui. The Chinese name for the Han.

han·som (hăn′səm) *n.* A two-wheeled covered carriage with the driver's seat above and behind. [After its designer, English architect Joseph A. *Hansom* (1803–1882).]

Hants. See Hampshire (county).

Ha·nuk·kah, Ha·nu·kah. Variants of Chanukah.

han·u·man (hä′nŏŏ-mən) *n., pl.* -mans. A monkey, *Presbytis entellus*, of southern Asia, having bristly hairs on the crown and the sides of the face. [Sanskrit *hanumant*, "having jaws," from *hanu*, jaw. See genu-² in Appendix.*]

Han·yang (hän′yăng′). A former city of southeastern Hupei, China, now part of Wuhan (*see*).

hap (hăp) *n. Archaic.* 1. Fortune; chance. 2. A happening; an occurrence. —*intr.v.* happed, happing, haps. *Archaic.* To happen. [Middle English, from Old Norse *happ*, good luck, chance. See kob- in Appendix.*]

ha·pax le·go·me·non (hā′păks′ lə-gŏm′ə-nŏn′) *pl.* hapax legomena (-ə-nə). *Greek.* A word or form that occurs only once in the recorded corpus of a given language. Often shortened to "hapax." [Greek, "a thing said only once."]

hap·haz·ard (hăp-hăz′ərd) *adj.* Dependent upon or characterized by mere chance. See Synonyms at chance. —*n.* Mere chance; fortuity. —*adv.* Casually; by chance. [HAP + HAZARD.] —**hap·haz′ard·ly** *adv.* —**hap·haz′ard·ness** *n.*

haph·ta·rah (hăf′tä-rä′, -tôr′ə) *n., pl.* -taroth (-tä-rōt′, -tôr′ōt, -ōth′, -ōs′). Also **haf·ta·rah.** A reading selected from the Prophets, read in the synagogue service on the Sabbath following each lesson from the Torah. [Mishnaic Hebrew *haphtārah*, "conclusion," from *haphtēr*, conclude, discard, dismiss, from Hebrew *pātar*, separated, discharged.]

hap·less (hăp′lĭs) *adj.* Luckless; unfortunate.

hap·lite. Variant of aplite.

hap·loid (hăp′loid′) *adj. Genetics.* Having the number of chromosomes present in the normal germ cell, equal to half the number in the normal somatic cell. Compare diploid. —*n.* A haploid individual. [Greek *haploeidēs*, single : *haplo(u)s*, single, simple : *ha-*, one (see sem-¹ in Appendix*) + *-plo(u)s*, -fold (see pel-³ in Appendix*) + -OID.]

hap·loi·dy (hăp′loi′dē) *n. Genetics.* The state or condition of being haploid.

hap·lol·o·gy (hăp-lŏl′ə-jē) *n.* The shortening of a word by contraction of a sound or syllable in its pronunciation. [Greek *haplos*, single, simple (see haploid) + -LOGY.]

hap·lo·sis (hăp-lō′sĭs) *n. Genetics.* Reduction of the diploid number of chromosomes by one half to the haploid number by meiosis. [New Latin : Greek *haplos*, single, simple (see haploid) + -OSIS.]

hap·ly (hăp′lē) *adv. Archaic.* By chance or accident; perhaps.

hap·pen (hăp′ən) *intr.v.* -pened, -pening, -pens. 1. To come to pass; come into being; take place. 2. To take place or come about by chance. 3. To come upon something by chance. 4. To appear by chance; turn up. [Middle English *happenen*, from *hap*, HAP.]

Synonyms: happen, occur, chance, befall, betide, supervene. These verbs mean to come about. *Happen* and *occur*, the most common, are frequently interchangeable in this sense. *Happen* often implies coming about by accident; *occur* is applicable both to what is accidental and to what comes about through obvious cause. In sentences in which *occur* might be misconstrued in the sense of come to mind, only *happen* is possible: *Nothing of the sort happened to her.* When the desired sense is to be met with or appear, only *occur* is possible: *Violence occurs often in his later plays. An epidemic of this kind seldom occurs now.* *Chance* stresses lack of apparent cause or plan. *Befall* and *betide* generally apply to what comes about from human control, and especially to misfortune. *Supervene* refers to coming about as an additional development, often an unexpected one.

hap·pen·ing (hăp′ə-nĭng) *n.* 1. An event. 2. An improvised spectacle or performance. —See Synonyms at occurrence.

hap·pen·stance (hăp′ən-stăns′) *n.* Also **hap·pen·chance** (-chăns′, -chäns′). A chance circumstance. [HAPPEN + (CIRCUM)STANCE.]

hap·py (hăp′ē) *adj.* -pier, -piest. 1. Characterized by luck or good fortune; prosperous. 2. Having or demonstrating pleasure or satisfaction; gratified. 3. Well-adapted; appropriate; felicitous: *a happy turn of phrase.* 4. Characterized by a spontaneous or obsessive inclination to use something. Used in combination: *trigger-happy.* —See Synonyms at fit, glad. [Middle English, from HAP.] —**hap′pi·ly** *adv.* —**hap′pi·ness** *n.*

hap·py-go-luck·y (hăp′ē-gō-lŭk′ē) *adj.* Taking things easily; trusting to luck; carefree.

Haps·burg (hăps′bûrg′). Also *German* **Habs·burg** (häps′bŏŏrk′). 1. A princely German family furnishing sovereigns to Austria (1278–1918) and to Spain (1516–1700). 2. A member of this family.

hap·ten (hăp′tĕn′) *n.* Also **hap·tene** (-tēn′). An antigen that is incomplete and cannot by itself cause antibody formation but can neutralize specific antibodies in an artificial environment outside the body. [German *Hapten* : Greek *haptein*, to fasten (see synapse) + -ENE.]

HAR Airport code for Harrisburg, Pennsylvania.

ha·ra-ki·ri (här′ə-kîr′ē) *n.* Ritual suicide by disembowelment as formerly practiced by the Japanese upper classes. Also called "seppuku." [Japanese *harakiri*.]

ha·rangue (hə-răng′) *n.* 1. A long, pompous speech; especially, one delivered before a gathering. 2. A speech characterized by strong feeling or vehement expression; tirade. —*v.* haranged, -ranguing, -rangued. —*tr.* To deliver a harangue to. —*intr.* To deliver a harangue. [Middle English *arang*, from Old French *arenge, harangue*, from Medieval Latin *harenga*, perhaps from Germanic. See koro- in Appendix.*] —**ha·rangu′er** *n.*

---

† tight/th thin, path/*th* this, bathe/ū cut/ûr urge/v valve/w with/y yes/z zebra, size/zh vision/ə about, item, edible, gallop, circus/ à *Fr.* ami/œ *Fr.* feu, *Ger.* schön/ü *Fr.* tu, *Ger.* über/KH *Ger.* ich, *Scot.* loch/N *Fr.* bon. *Follows main vocabulary. †Of obscure origin.

CHAPTER 2
UNDERSTANDING WHAT YOU READ: A REVIEW

CHAPTER OUTLINE

THINK ABOUT IT!

Look carefully at the photographs. There is something strange in each of the scenes. Do you know what it is? In photographs 1 and 3, look for something that is not right. In photograph 2, look for something unusual. Discuss the photographs with your classmates.

1

2

3

CHAPTER OUTCOMES

After completing Chapter 2, you should be able to:

- Distinguish main ideas, major details, and minor details
- Recognize patterns of organization (simple listing of facts, time sequence, comparison and contrast, and cause and effect)
- Uncover the central message of a longer selection
- Summarize and paraphrase the most important points

DISTINGUISHING MAIN IDEAS, MAJOR DETAILS, AND MINOR DETAILS

In addition to uncovering word meanings, being able to differentiate among main ideas, major details, and minor details is an extremely important skill because it contributes to a much better understanding of what you are reading. Read the following paragraph; then answer the question "What is this about?"

> One way to recover the past is through music. Popular songs not only provide insight into attitudes and beliefs but also quickly convey the mood and feelings of an era. Through their lyrics, songwriters express the hopes and fears of a people and the emotional tone of an age. Consider, for example, the powerful message conveyed in the Democratic party adoption of "Happy Days Are Here Again" as a campaign theme during the Great Depression. The decline of pop music and the rise of rock and roll in the 1950s tells historians a great deal about the mood of that period. Similarly, the popularity of both folk music and rock in the 1960s provides another way of following social change in that turbulent decade.
>
> Gary B. Nash and Julie Roy Jeffrey, *The American People*, 5th ed., p. 976

If your answer to the question was "music," you are correct: Virtually all of the sentences in the paragraph deal with that particular topic. The **topic** is the subject of a given paragraph, and it can usually be expressed in a word or phrase that can serve as a title.

Now reread the same paragraph, and try to answer the following question: "What is the overall message the writer is communicating about the topic?" The answer to that question can be found in the first sentence, which states: "One way to recover the past is through music." That sentence is the **main idea** of the paragraph because it lets you know in a general sense what the writer wants to say about the topic, and it sums up all or most of the remaining sentences. In fact, the main idea always mentions the topic, which explains why the main idea—when it is stated—is also referred to as the **topic sentence.** The rest of the paragraph then consists of **details** that provide more information in order to make the main idea clearer.

Not all details, however, are of equal importance. Some lend direct support to the main idea and are called **major details.** Others, called **minor details,** lend direct support to the major details but only indirect support to the main idea. In other words, major details explain main ideas more specifically, and minor details explain the major details more specifically. For instance, the second and third sentences in the paragraph on music are the major details because they support the main idea directly by telling you specifically how or why the past can be recovered through music. In short, they supply more information to help make the main idea clearer. The remaining sentences are minor details that explain the major details further by providing very specific examples. Look again at the paragraph, reprinted here, and take note of the main idea, major details, and minor details.

Main idea   One way to recover the past is through music. Popular songs not only provide insight into attitudes and beliefs but also quickly convey the mood and feelings of an era. Through their lyrics, song-writers express the hopes and fears of a people and the emotional tone of an age. — **Major details**

Consider, for example, the powerful message conveyed in the Democratic party adoption of "Happy Days Are Here Again" as a campaign theme during the Great Depression. The decline of pop music and the rise of rock and roll in the 1950s tells historians a great deal about the mood of that period. Similarly, the popularity of both folk music and rock in the 1960s provides another way of following social change in that turbulent decade. — **Minor details**

It is very important for you, as a reader, to be aware of the main idea of every paragraph that you encounter, because it sums up the other sentences and focuses on the overall message that the writer is trying to convey about a given topic. Details give you additional information that make it easier for you to understand the main idea.

When the main idea is stated, as in the example on music, it can be found anywhere in a paragraph—at the beginning, at the end, or somewhere in between. In addition, sometimes a paragraph will have a main idea expressed in more than one sentence. Look at the following examples illustrating each of these, and pay particular attention to the main ideas, major details, and minor details, which have been labeled for you.

Main idea at the beginning   The total number of insect species is greater than the total of all other species combined. — **Main idea**

About a million insect species are known today, and researchers estimate that at least twice this many exist (mostly in tropical forests) but have not yet been dis- — **Major detail**

covered. Insects have been prominent on land for the last 400 million years. They have been much less successful in aquatic environments; there are only about 20,000 species in freshwater habitats and far fewer in the sea. — **Minor details**

Neil A. Campbell, Lawrence G. Mitchell, and Jane B. Reece, *Biology*, 3rd ed., p. 382

Main idea at the end   Throughout U.S. history, various groups that believed the government would not respond to their needs have resorted to — **Minor detail**

some form of violence. — **Major detail**

Analyzing fifty-three U.S. protest movements, William Gamson (1975) found that 75 percent of the groups that used violence got what they wanted, compared with only 53 percent of those that were nonviolent.

Violence, it seems, can pay off. — **Main idea**

Alex Thio, *Sociology: A Brief Introduction*, 4th ed., p. 369

Children usually experience strong short-term reactions to being sexually abused but are often too confused or frightened to tell. They feel upset, helpless, frightened, and guilty; if physically injured, the pain experienced makes them particularly fearful of future contacts. <u>The child's experience of abuse can be minimized or exacerbated by a nonabusing significant adult's management of the event.</u> Parents (nonabusers) who handle the event as an unfortunate but not devastating experience and who can reassure the child that he or she is in no way to blame reduce the impact on the child significantly. On the other hand, the impact of the event may be very much intensified by the parents' negating, angry, and hostile responses. Parents often react so strongly and negatively out of their own feelings of anger, powerlessness, and (too often) denial that they cannot focus constructively on the child, thus isolating the child and providing inadequate help to prevent long-term consequences.

Main idea somewhere in between — Minor details / Main idea / Major details / Minor detail

Kay Johnston Starks and Eleanor S. Morrison, *Growing Up Sexual*, p. 183

Main idea expressed in more than one sentence

Twenty or thirty years ago, high school health and safety courses may have mentioned some of the hazards of sustained alcohol abuse but with that exception, drug education would not have been found in the high school curriculum. <u>Today, one would be hard-pressed to find a single school in America that does not offer anti-drug education as part of its basic curriculum.</u> Usually, anti-drug programming begins in the elementary grades and intensifies in junior high and high school. <u>In addition to school-based programs, the Partnership for a Drug-Free America and other advocacy groups have sponsored national anti-drug media campaigns targeted mainly at youth</u> ("This is your brain. This is your brain on drugs"). Contemporary youth are bombarded with messages about the evils of drugs and exhortations to avoid their use. If American children watch as much television as alleged, the average teenager is exposed to anti-drug messages several times each day.

Minor detail / Main idea / Major detail / Main idea / Major details

James D. Wright and Joel A. Devine, *Drugs as a Social Problem*, p. 51

Occasionally, certain phrases and words, such as "in short," "in brief," "in summary," "in fact," "clearly," "thus," "yes," and "as these examples show," introduce the main idea. Be on the lookout for them. Major and minor details are sometimes preceded by the words "for example" or "for instance," because details generally are examples or instances of something. Look carefully for the main idea directly above those words! Finally, simple lists of sentences that begin with such words as "first," "second," "third," and "finally" are often major details, and you usually can find the main idea just before the first item on those lists. As you know, a simple listing of facts is a common pattern of organization.

Unstated Main Ideas

Sometimes a paragraph will consist of just details with no topic sentence or stated main idea. However, that does not mean that there is no overall message regarding the topic. It is simply unstated and therefore cannot be found in the paragraph. When that occurs, the details should point you in the direction of the message, which you can then put into your own words. Look at this example:

> The average major-league baseball player today earns about $1.2 million a year. The average professional football player earns about $68,000 a year. The average professional basketball player earns about $2 million a year. At the same time, professional sports team owners continue to buy and sell professional franchises for tens and hundreds of millions of dollars.
>
> Roger LeRoy Miller, *Economics Today*, p. 628

The topic of the paragraph has to do with the salaries paid to professional athletes and the money involved when owners buy and sell professional sports franchises. Although no sentence expresses the overall message regarding the topic, three of the four major details provide examples of the high salaries paid to professional athletes, and the last one talks about the large sums of money involved in the buying and selling of professional franchises. Therefore, the **unstated main idea** of the paragraph could be expressed as "Professional athletes get paid very high salaries, and the teams they play for are worth huge amounts of money."

Every paragraph has a topic or subject and an overall message about the topic that is expressed as the main idea. When there is no stated main idea, remember to consider carefully what most or all of the major details in a paragraph have in common, which should then help you figure out the unstated main idea. Remember that major details explain main ideas further while minor details provide more information about major details. Whether the main idea is stated or not, be sure to come away from each paragraph that you read with the overall message clearly in mind.

ACTIVITY 1

DIRECTIONS: For each of the passages that follow, find and label the topic, the main idea, and the major details. If the main idea is unstated, write it out in your own words after the passage. Remember that the topic is the answer to the question "What is this about?" and the main idea answers the question "What is the overall message the writer is communicating about the topic?" Also keep in mind that the major details are *major* because they lend direct support to the main idea.

1

One major difference between arithmetic and algebra is the use of *variables* in algebra. When a letter can represent a variety of different numbers, that letter is called a **variable**. For example, if *n* represents the number of students enrolled in a college's 8 A.M. section of Elementary Algebra, the number *n* will vary, depending on how many students drop or add the class. Thus the number *n* is a variable. If each student pays $600 for the course, the college collects a total of 600 • *n* dollars from the students. Since the cost to each student is consistently $600, the number 600 is called a **constant**.

Marvin L. Bittinger and David J. Ellenbogen, Elementary Algebra, p. 2

2

Have you ever found yourself sitting at the breakfast table reading the label on a box of cereal or loaf of bread? It can be interesting to compare the way a product is advertised on the front of the package with the actual nutritional information on the side or back. For instance, so-called fiber-enriched white bread may have less fiber than an unenriched whole-grain product. Similarly, products like cheese and chips are often labeled "low fat" or "lite." This merely means that they have less fat than the same products without these labels. In fact, their actual fat content may be surprisingly high, and by eating just a few more "lite" chips than regular ones, you may consume just as much fat.

Neil A. Campbell et al., Biology, 3rd ed., p. 447

3

One of the greatest benefits of studying psychology is that you learn not only how the brain works in general but also how to use yours in particular—by thinking critically. **Critical thinking** is the ability and willingness to assess claims and to make objective judgments on the basis of well-supported reasons. It is the ability to look for flaws in arguments and to resist claims that have no supporting evidence. Critical thinking, however, is not merely negative thinking. It also fosters the ability to be *creative and constructive*—to come up with various possible explanations for events, think of implications of research findings, and apply new knowledge to a broad range of social and personal problems. You can't separate critical thinking from creative thinking, for it is only when you question *what is* that you can begin to imagine *what can be*.

Carol Tavris and Carole Wade, Psychology in Perspective, p. 10

4

During the past few years, diversity has become one of the most urgent concerns of business, education, and government. Many of the nation's largest companies have hired executives who are responsible for corporate diversity. There are videos available on the topic, consultants specializing in the subject who have more business than they can handle, and nationally prominent diversity institutes. One educational publisher has begun to market a game called "Diversity Bingo." The management training programs of many of the nation's most successful companies include a module on diversity. Newsletters devoted to the topic have thousands of readers.

B. Eugene Griessman, Diversity, p. 1

5

Sex was taboo at our house, you couldn't say that "dirty" three letter word without somebody blushing, trying to hush it up, or giggling. If you'll pardon the pun, you could say that sex was kept under the blankets at our house. My parents never really told me about the "facts of life"—my mother made a vain attempt by asking my older brother to read a book about sex, but that's as far as it went with us kids. Just recently I got into a bit of an argument with my mom when she expressed her negative feelings about sex education in the public school system. I got angry and told her she was being hypocritical because neither she nor my Dad had educated any of us kids about sex. It is important that kids learn about sex in school because some parents don't do it at all.

Kay Johnston Starks and Eleanor S. Morrison, Growing Up Sexual, p. 83

6

It would be nice if everything we said was understood exactly as intended. Unfortunately, this is not the case. Messages are filtered by listeners' attitudes, values, and beliefs; consequently, changes in their meaning may occur. Someone who distrusts others and is skeptical of what people say, for example, will interpret the words "I like you a lot" differently from someone who is more trusting. A skeptic might think, "He doesn't really mean that, he's only saying it to get on my good side." A more trusting person will accept the message and treat it as a genuine expression of affection. The difference in interpretation between what the "speaker said" and what the "receiver heard" is called the interpersonal gap. Other examples include:

Lisa: "I'm really feeling angry. That's the last time I want to see you do that."

Manuel's interpretation: She is always blaming me for things. I wish she would stop.

Jasmine's interpretation: It was my fault. She is right. I'll try to do things differently in the future.

Courtney's interpretation: She's got to be kidding. What I did could not be that important.

Anthony F. Grasha, Practical Applications of Psychology, p. 259

7

Americans have a history of disapproving of relationships that take place between blacks and whites. After all, we must remember that such relationships were actually illegal in many states until the Supreme Court overturned these laws in 1967. In many other countries, interracial couples are not unusual. Latino-white relationships, as well as Asian-white, Native American–white, Latino-black, and other combinations—while still often looked upon negatively—are more acceptable in the United States than black-white. Unfortunately, these negative feelings can lead to discrimination against such couples and their children.

Janell L. Carroll and Paul Root Wolpe, Sexuality and Gender in Society, p. 287

8

The preferred drug among youth is alcohol and has been for as long as we have gathered data. Alcohol use among the young is a serious social problem. A fairly large minority of the young will also experiment with marijuana. The proportion of young people who have used marijuana in the last year (about a quarter) is in the same range as the proportion of the adult population who have used marijuana (about a third). There are some young people, a few percent at most, who will also experiment with hard drugs, and an even smaller number who will become regular users or even addicts. The usual pattern of drug use is relatively high rates of use in the early adult years and fairly sharp declines as people mature into adulthood.

James D. Wright and Joel A. Devine, *Drugs as a Social Problem*, p. 58

9

Perhaps the most important business trend of the decade was the emergence of a new kind of manager. No longer did family entrepreneurs make decisions relating to prices, wages, or output. Alfred P. Sloan, Jr., an engineer who reorganized General Motors, was a prototype of the new kind of manager. He divided the company into components, freeing the top managers to concentrate on planning new products, controlling inventory, and integrating the whole operation. Marketing and advertising became as important as production, and many businesses began to spend more money on research. The new manager often had a large staff, but owned no part of the company. He was usually an expert at cost accounting and analyzing data. Increasingly, he was a graduate of one of the new business colleges.

Gary B. Nash and Julie Roy Jeffrey, *The American People*, 5th ed., p. 737

10

Over the past two decades, most Americans have become familiar with such terms as environmental disaster, acid rain, ozone depletion, deforestation, and global warming. Many of these environmental issues, like acid rain and ozone depletion, are global in nature and appear remote and only vaguely threatening. Other issues, such as air pollution and pesticide residues on our foods, confront us in our homes on a daily basis. However, both the seemingly remote global issues and the more immediately threatening environmental problems are intricately intertwined. Like a pebble thrown into a pond, changes in a local ecosystem cause ripple effects. They have the potential to initiate or contribute to changes in the global ecosystem.

F. Kurt Cylke Jr., *The Environment*, p. 1

11

Who discovered America? This is not as easy a question to answer as one might think. The first human beings to set foot on the continents of North and South America came from Asia. Perhaps 80,000 years ago they settled an area stretching from northeastern Siberia through the Aleutian islands in Alaska. Scholars refer to the region as "Beringia," named after the explorer Vitus Bering. Most of the area is now submerged beneath the Bering Strait and adjacent waters. During the Ice Age, however, when more precipitation was trapped on land as snow or ice, the ocean was far shallower, exposing much of the ocean bed. During this period, some of the people of "Beringia" moved in search of game and green grass to what is now the North American continent. Almost certainly the settlers of the Americas, the ancestors of the modern Indians, were unaware that they were entering "new" territory. So we must look elsewhere (and much later in time) for the "discoverer" of America as we use that word.

Probably the first European to reach America was a Norseman, Leif Ericson. He ventured before the day of the compass into the void of the North Atlantic and, around the year 1000, reached the shores of Labrador. Yet Ericson's discovery passed practically unnoticed for centuries, and to most modern inhabitants of the New World he lives only in legend.

John A. Garraty and Mark C. Carnes, *The American Nation,* 10th ed., p. 3

12

It is referred to as "underground," "gray," "subterranean," "informal," "off-the-books," or "unofficial." Whatever it is called, the underground economy exists in a big way in the United States and in an even bigger way in Latin America, Europe, and elsewhere. Have you ever bought a cheap umbrella or a pair of earrings from a street vendor? If so, both you and the vendor were partaking in the off-the-books underground economy. If you have ever done odd jobs and been paid in cash or paid someone else in cash to do odd jobs for you, you have participated in the underground economy.

Roger LeRoy Miller, *Economics Today,* p. 163

13

Time is a big problem in the fight against AIDS. Drugs and vaccines must be thoroughly tested for efficacy and for toxic side effects before they can be released for general use. While hearing the outcry of AIDS patients and activists, some experts predict that it may take decades to develop effective vaccines and affordable drugs. At present, education remains our best weapon against AIDS. The World Health Organization concurs with Magic Johnson's campaign for practicing safer sex. Reducing promiscuity and increasing the use of condoms could save millions of lives. To learn more about AIDS and its mode of transmission, anyone may call the National AIDS Hotline, 1–800–342–AIDS.

Neil A. Campbell et al., *Biology: Concepts and Connections,* p. 500

14

Afghanistan suffered through 18 years of war until the mid–1990s, when the Taliban militia took over and proclaimed a Muslim fundamentalist state. As part of the Muslim principles as interpreted by the ruling clerics, women's activities were severely restricted. Women and girls were forbidden to go to offices and schools. The restriction on gainful employment for women was particularly painful to those who were sole supporters of their families. After 18 years of war, there were many fewer men around to support families.

Roger LeRoy Miller, *Economics Today,* p. 265

15

We need relationships with others to know that we are truly alive. While we strive for positive relationships with our friends, family, and significant others, we sometimes find ourselves in relationships that result in an emotional roller coaster. While negative relationships may cause us distress, intimate relationships that have gone bad can send us in a downward spiral emotionally and physically. How can we ensure that the relationship in which we are investing our time, energy, and emotion is a healthy one? What are the characteristics of a healthy relationship? How do our relationships contribute to our overall health and well-being?

Rebecca J. Donatelle, Health: The Basics, 4th ed., p. 96

16

A short 20 years ago, we had few choices when we wanted to communicate with one another: We could send letters through the U.S. Postal Service, make telephone calls on the "fixed" telephone lines of the Bell System, or send telegrams through Western Union. Through the unleashing of competition and vast changes in technology, we now have a much broader range of choices. We can substitute cellular for fixed telephone services, faxes for mail, e-mail for faxes, one long-distance provider for another, and the various overnight mail delivery services for the U.S. Postal Service. We can even use our computers for "free" long-distance telephone calls to foreign countries.

Paul R. Gregory, Essentials of Economics, p. 27

17

Why is the air in cities so polluted from automobile exhaust fumes? When automobile drivers step into their cars, they bear only the private costs of driving. That is, they must pay for the gas, maintenance, depreciation, and insurance on their automobiles. But they cause an additional cost, that of air pollution, which they are not forced to take account of when they make the decision to drive. Air pollution is a cost because it causes harm to individuals—burning eyes, respiratory ailments, and dirtier clothes, cars, and buildings. The air pollution created by automobile exhaust is a cost that individual operators of automobiles do not yet bear directly. The social cost of drivng includes all the private costs plus at least the cost of air pollution, which society bears. Decisions made only on the basis of private costs lead to too much automobile driving or, alternatively, to too little money spent on the reduction of automobile pollution for a given amount of driving. Clean air is a scarce resource used by automobile drivers free of charge. They will use more of it than they would if they had to pay the full social costs.

Roger LeRoy Miller, Economics Today, p. 761

18

Whenever Mary Jane and her husband have an argument, she begins to feel dizzy and to experience tight feelings in her chest. Jim has missed most of his major exams this semester—he always seems to get the flu or a bad cold at the wrong time. Gary sometimes wakes in the middle of the night with asthma attacks and has to be rushed to the hospital—adding another problem to his already stressful life. Ruth's doctors are puzzled by the fainting spells she has from time to time—usually after losing her temper and screaming at her children.

M. Levy et al., *Essentials of Life and Health*, p. 5

19

For years it was believed that our natural resources were free goods which, although wasted and exploited, would be replenished by nature. This nation did not recognize that it was destroying the ability of nature to maintain a balanced ecological system. Today many of our lakes and streams are too polluted to support plant and fish life. In strip-mine areas, the wasted land lies barren. Energy sources that took nature thousands of years to create are consumed within minutes. As indicated by these few examples, a realistic program of environment and energy conservation should be adopted by every business.

Raymond E. Glos et al., *Business: Its Nature and Environment*

20

Analogies can hamper thinking, however. Once you think of things in terms of one relationship, it can be hard to think of them in terms of any other. You can forget that any pair of items has many possible relationships. Suppose someone said that a teacher's use of chalk is like a bookkeeper's use of a quill pen. In this case, the *teacher/chalk* relationship is no longer simply that between a person and a tool the person uses. The analogy with the bookkeeper and the quill pen suggests that there is something old-fashioned and out-of-date about a teacher using chalk.

Or, suppose that someone said that a teacher and chalk were like an artist and paint. Now the chalk is no longer being thought of as a tool at all (whether old-fashioned or not), but as an artistic medium through which something pleasing is created.

In short, an analogy can be a trap if you think it sums up all the relationships between two objects. You can, however, open up your thinking if you use analogies imaginatively to help you find and think about relationships.

Robert Boostrom, *Developing Creative and Critical Thinking*, p. 76

21

What, then, are the realities? There is a distinction which it is important to make in any discussion of Islam. The word "Islam" is used with at least three different meanings, and much misunderstanding can arise from the failure to distinguish between them. In the first place, Islam means the religion taught by the Prophet Muhammad and embodied in the Muslim revelation known as the Qur'ån. In the second place, Islam is the subsequent development of this religion through tradition and through the work of the great Muslim jurists and theologians. In this sense it includes the mighty structure of the Sharï'a, the holy law of Islam, and the great corpus of Islamic dogmatic theology. In the third meaning, Islam is the counterpart not of Christianity but rather of Christendom. In this sense Islam means not what Muslims believed or were expected to believe but what they actually did—in other words, Islamic civilization as known to us in history. In discussing Muslim attitudes on ethnicity, race, and color, I shall try to deal to some extent at least with all three but to make clear the distinction between them.

Bernard Lewis, Race and Slavery in the Middle East

22

The danger of their work makes police officers especially attentive to signs of potential violence and lawbreaking. Throughout the socialization process, the recruit is warned to be suspicious, to be cautious, and is told about fellow officers who were shot and killed while trying to settle a family squabble or write a ticket for speeding. In 1990, seventy-six officers were killed in the line of duty, a figure much lower than the average yearly number. The folklore of the corps emphasizes that officers must always be on their guard. They must look for the unusual, including everything from persons who do not "belong" where they are observed to businesses open at odd hours. They must watch for and interrogate persons, including:

   those known to the officer from previous arrests, field interrogations, and observations;

   emaciated-appearing alcoholics and narcotics users, who may turn to crime to pay for their habit;

   anyone who fits the description of a wanted suspect;

   known troublemakers near large gatherings;

   persons who attempt to avoid or evade the officer, who are visibly "rattled" when near the officer, and who exhibit exaggerated unconcern over contact with the officer;

   "lovers" in an industrial area (make good lookouts);

   persons who loiter about places where children play or around public restrooms;

   persons wearing a coat on a hot day;

   cars with mismatched hubcaps, or dirty cars with clean license plates (or vice versa);

   uniformed "deliverymen" with no merchandise or truck

With these as examples, it is not hard to understand how police officers become suspicious of everyone and all situations.

George F. Cole, The American System of Criminal Justice

23

Picture yourself near a mountain lake as twilight falls on a crisp, clear summer evening. You've arrived here on foot, with only the sounds of nature for company. Sitting near the water's edge, you watch patiently as the sky fills slowly with stars. Soon the band of the Milky Way comes into view, stretching high across the sky and shining with a brilliance city dwellers never see. The depths of the heavens are reflected in shimmering lights on the lake, creating an image of infinity both above and below you. If you set your mind free, you cannot help but ask some of the most fundamental questions imaginable. What is the universe and what is Earth's place in it? How did it all come to be? As you let your thoughts wander through time and space, you could be anyone at any time in history. After all, your questions are the same ones that humans of every culture have asked since history began.

Jeffrey Bennett, *On the Cosmic Horizon*, p. 1

24

As a young child growing up in Brooklyn, New York, during the 1940s, I experienced firsthand the effects of relative poverty and discrimination. In the schools I attended, a common perception was that my culture and language were inferior. I spoke only Spanish when I entered first grade, and I was immediately confronted with the arduous task of learning a second language while my developed native language was all but ignored. Almost 50 years later, I still remember the frustration of groping for English words I did not know to express thoughts I could say very capably in Spanish. Equally vivid are memories of some teachers' expectations that my classmates and I would not do well in school because of our language and cultural differences. This explains my fourth-grade teacher's response when mine was the only hand to go up when she asked whether anybody in the class wanted to go to college. "Well, that's okay," she said, "because we always need people to clean toilets."

Sonia Nieto, *Affirming Diversity*, 3rd ed., p. 1

25

In our culture, excess body fat is considered unattractive. In contrast, some other cultures tend to equate a well-rounded or plump body with beauty and prosperity. Whatever our cultural perspective, fats and related lipids are essential components of the human body. For instance, body fat helps insulate us against cold, and, in moderate amounts, it seems to correlate with a healthy immune system. Extremely thin people tend to have lower levels of vitamin A and beta-carotene in their blood, which may make them more susceptible to certain forms of cancer. Healthy women may have as much as 20–25% of their body weight in fat; for healthy men, the amount is typically 15–19%. When we are too fat, our body fat may be 20% or more above these amounts. Being too fat, or obese, can increase our chances of developing certain diseases (such as heart disease) and decrease our life span.

Neil A. Campbell et al., *Biology*, 3rd ed., p. 443

ACTIVITY 2

DIRECTIONS: Using your other textbooks, find examples of paragraphs with the types of main ideas that we have discussed. Find a variety with topic sentences in the beginning, at the end, and somewhere in between. Also look for examples of paragraphs with a main idea expressed in more than one sentence and ones that have unstated main ideas. If you do not have other textbooks at this time, ask your classmates who are using other books to share their examples with you.

RECOGNIZING PATTERNS OF ORGANIZATION

Look carefully at this sequence of numbers:

16–1–20–20–5–18–14–19   1–18–5   8–5–12–16–6–21–12

Does this mean anything to you? Can you see a message? Probably not. What if you were told that each number corresponds to a letter in the alphabet, numbered in order from 1 to 26? Is that better? After a few minutes, you should be able to figure out that the message is "Patterns are helpful"!

Once you determine the arrangement or pattern of something, it is much easier to understand. Have you ever heard someone say, "I am starting to see a pattern here." That comment usually means that several pieces of similar information are enabling the person to come to a particular conclusion. For example, if Jonathan has consistently arrived late for psychology class during the first three weeks of the semester, his instructor would see a pattern and might conclude that Jonathan is not a very responsible student. Again, patterns can be useful by adding meaning to given situations.

Writers often help readers recognize important details by arranging them in a certain way. These arrangements of details are called **patterns of organization,** and there are four major ones: **simple listing of facts, time sequence, comparison and contrast,** and **cause and effect.** When reading material is organized using one or more of these patterns, it should help you see not only details but also the main idea. Or the main idea may tip you off to the presence of a specific pattern of organization. So it is a two-way process. Let us take a look at each of the patterns.

Simple Listing of Facts

This pattern involves a list of details that could include the causes, characteristics, examples, or types of something. Writers will often use **transition words** such as the following to help you recognize this pattern:

---

also, another, examples, factors, finally, following, in addition, last, list, many, numbers (first, second, etc.), other, part, several, types

---

Determining the main idea can also be of help, because it will let you know exactly what is being listed. Look at the following example.

1   At least three factors contributed to the steady increase in concern about environmental issues during the 1980s. First, there was a great deal of highly publicized political controversy surrounding environmental issues. The Reagan administration's pro-business and anti-environmental regulation position, as well as a series of scandals involving con-

flicts of interest by key officials in the Environmental Protection Agency (EPA), were criticized by many of the nation's leading environmental organizations. Controversy and media coverage increased significantly when the Reagan administration slashed EPA funding dramatically. During President Ronald Reagan's first year in office, the EPA budget was cut by 29 percent, resulting in a 30 percent reduction in staff.

2   A second factor which contributed to the rise of public concern was the increased coverage of specific environmental problems. Global issues such as climate change and ozone depletion received substantial attention. Also, a series of specific environmental disasters captured the nation's attention, not the least of which was a 1989 oil spill which occurred after the Exxon corporation's supertanker *Valdez* ran aground in Prince Edward Sound, Alaska.

3   A third contributing factor was increased media coverage of the activities of environmental activists. This included not only protest marches, but also video images of Greenpeace activists in small inflatable rafts risking their lives by placing themselves between the harpoons of whale hunters and the whales they were trying to save. Environmentalists were aware of the necessity for media coverage, and during the 1980s, many dedicated and hard-working activists capitalized on strategies designed to attract the attention of the mass media.

F. Kurt Cylke Jr., The Environment, pp. 26 and 28

Notice how the main idea—"At least three factors contributed to the steady increase in concern about environmental issues during the 1980s"—covers three paragraphs and lets you know that the list involves three factors. In fact, in most instances, the main idea will be found right before the beginning of a list. The transition words *three factors, first, second,* and *third* also help you recognize the presence of the list, which includes the following major details:

- "First, there was a great deal of highly publicized political controversy surrounding environmental issues."
- "A second factor which contributed to the rise of public concern was the increased coverage of specific environmental problems."
- "A third contributing factor was increased media coverage of the activities of environmental activists."

The rest of the passage includes minor details that provide more specific examples of the major details.

A simple listing of facts does not always involve numbered details, as illustrated by the following example:

America can be fairly called a "drug culture" in the sense that nearly everyone uses drugs of one sort or another. When we are ailing, we expect to be given some drug that will make us feel better. If we have trouble sleeping, we take sleeping medications, whether over-the-counter or prescribed. If we feel anxious, we want anti-anxiety drugs and if we feel depressed we seek antidepressants. If we want sex without the risk of pregnancy, we take "the pill." Millions of us get "up" with caffeine and come "down" with alcohol. It has even been argued that mood-altering drugs satisfy an *innate* human need to suspend ordinary awareness, a need much like sexual tension that "arises spontaneously from within, builds to a peak, finds relief, and dissipates" (Weil, 1972: 22). The use of drugs to make one feel better or to solve one's problems, whatever they might be, is deeply entrenched in our culture and our expectations.

James D. Wright and Joel A. Devine, *Drugs as a Social Problem*, p. 2

In this example, the main idea is stated in both the first and last sentences, which convey just about the same overall message. Writers will sometimes repeat the same—or close to the same—main idea in the first and last sentences of a paragraph, which makes it easier to spot. All the rest of the sentences in the paragraph are major details that list the kinds of drugs people take and their reasons for taking them. Although there is no numbering, you are helped to recognize the presence of the list by the repetition of the words *when we* and *if we*.

Time Sequence

This pattern involves details placed in the order in which they occur in time. Transition words often found in time sequence include these:

after, before, beginning, dates, finally, first, last, later, next, once, prior, repeat, steps, then, thereafter, times of day, when, year

Historical and other material with dated events or times of the day are the most obvious place to find this pattern, as in the following example.

American cities grew rapidly in the last part of the nineteenth and the first part of the twentieth centuries. New York, which had a population of 1.2 million in 1880, grew to 3.4 million by 1900 and 5.6 million in 1920. Chicago expanded even more dramatically, from 500,000 in 1880 to 1.7 million in 1900 and 2.7 million in 1920. Los Angeles was a town of 11,000 in 1880, but multiplied ten times by 1900, and then increased another five times, to more than a half million, by 1920.

Gary B. Nash and Julie Roy Jeffrey, *The American People*, 5th ed., p. 680

Once again, the main idea is stated in the first sentence, which informs you that the time sequence organizes details that illustrate how "American cities grew rapidly in the last part of the nineteenth and the first part of the twentieth centuries." The *dates* throughout the paragraph make it easy to identify the major details that directly support the overall message.

This pattern can also include the steps in a process, directions, or anything else that is accomplished in a definite time order, as in the example below.

In courtship, a male and female loon swim side by side while performing a series of displays. (1) The courting birds frequently turn their heads away from each other. (In sharp contrast, a male loon defending his territory often charges at an intruder with his beak pointed straight ahead.) (2) The birds then dip their beaks in the water, and (3) submerge their heads and necks. Prior to copulation, the male invites the female onto land by (4) turning his head backward with his beak held downward. There, (5) they copulate.

Neil A. Campbell et al., Biology, 3rd ed., pp. 754–755

The main idea is stated in the first sentence, which tells you that "In courtship, a male and female loon swim side by side while performing a series of displays." That sentence, along with the transition words *series*, *then*, and *prior*, lets you know that a behavior process is being traced that must be accomplished in a definite sequence. The rest of the sentences, with the exception of the one in parentheses, are major details that trace the steps in the process. Although the major details are numbered, the pattern of organization here is time sequence rather than a simple listing of facts because the steps in the process must be done in that order. In other words, step 1 must be accomplished before step 2, step 2 must be accomplished before step 3, step 3 must be accomplished before step 4, and step 4 must be accomplished before step 5. With a simple listing, the items on a given list are not in any specific time order. This is the key difference between those two patterns.

Comparison and Contrast

This pattern organizes details that deal with the similarities (comparison) and differences (contrast) between persons, events, ideas, or things. Transition words that are often found with comparison and contrast include these:

> alike, between, common, commonalities, compare, contrast, debate, difference, disagree, distinction, distinguish, like, likeness, on the other hand, same, similarity, unlike, whereas

Also, the main idea usually tells you exactly what is being compared or contrasted. Read the following example.

1   Think of all the ways that human beings are alike. Everywhere, no matter what their backgrounds or where they live, people love, work, argue, dance, sing, complain, and gossip. They rear families, celebrate marriages, and mourn losses. They reminisce about the past and plan for the future. They help their friends and fight with their enemies. They smile with amusement, frown with displeasure, and glare in anger. Where do all these commonalities come from?

2   Think of all the ways that human beings differ. Some of us are extroverts, always ready to throw a party, make a new friend, or speak up in a crowd; others are shy and introverted, preferring the safe and familiar. Some are trailblazers, ambitious and enterprising; others are placid, content with the way things are. Some take to book learning like a cat to catnip; others don't do so well in school but have lots of street smarts and practical know-how. Some are overwhelmed by even the most petty of problems; others, faced with severe difficulties, remain calm and resilient. Where do all these differences come from?

Carol Tavris and Carole Wade, Psychology in Perspective, p. 83

The first paragraph deals with how human beings are similar as stated by the main idea: "Think of all the ways that human beings are alike." The transition words *alike* and *commonalities* help you recognize the pattern. All of the remaining sentences, with the exception of the last one, are major details that directly support the overall message by giving examples of similarities. The main idea of the second paragraph—"Think of all the ways that human beings differ"—tells you that it is concerned with how human beings are different, and the transition words *differ* and *differences* are also revealing. Again, the rest of the sentences in the paragraph, except the last one, are major details that directly support the overall message by providing examples of differences.

Do you notice that there is an additional pattern of organization in both paragraphs? A simple listing of facts. The repetition of the word *they* in the first paragraph and *some* and *others* in the second one gives strong indication that lists are present. As you can see, writers sometimes use a *combination of patterns*, which is very helpful to you, because it gives you more than one opportunity to recognize important details and thus better understand what you are reading.

Cause and Effect

This pattern organizes details that present causes or reasons along with their effects or results. In other words, it explains why something has happened. For example, if one of your classmates asked you how you got an A + on the last history test (*effect*), you might proceed to explain that you attended all classes (*cause*), took down every word the professor said (*cause*), read all the assignments (*cause*), and studied on a daily basis (*cause*). In essence, you would be using the cause-and-effect pattern to give the reasons why you earned such a high grade.

Transition words to look for when this pattern is present include these:

affects, because, brings out, cause, consequences, contributed, create, effect, leads to, reaction, reason, result, therefore, whereas

Sometimes the causes are stated first, as in the following example.

During the late 1980s, news articles, TV shows, and radio commentaries proclaimed that the nation was facing a shortage of scientists. The growth in high-tech industries was going to create demands for scientists and engineers that would not be met. The government even suggested that this shortage would endanger national security. The result was an increase in the number of students seeking postgraduate education, especially doctoral degrees in engineering, the sciences, mathematics, and computer science. For example, in 1981–1982, a total of 2,621 Ph.D.s were granted in engineering; by 1991–1992, the number had more than doubled, to 5,488. Similar, though less dramatic, increases were seen in the number of doctorates awarded in the sciences and mathematics.

Roger LeRoy Miller, *Economics Today*, p. 77

The first three sentences in the paragraph provide causes:

- "During the late 1980s, news articles, TV shows, and radio commentaries proclaimed that the nation was facing a shortage of scientists."
- "The growth in high-tech industries was going to create demands for scientists and engineers that would not be met."

- "The government even suggested that this shortage would endanger national security."

The fourth sentence states the effect:

- "The result was an increase in the number of students seeking postgraduate education, especially doctoral degrees in engineering, the sciences, mathematics, and computer science."

More specific information, which directly supports the effect, is found in the remaining sentences, preceded by the words *for example*. Notice the two transition words *create* and *result*, which help you recognize the pattern. The main idea, which for the most part is unstated, would read something like this: "There was an increase in the number of students seeking postgraduate education in engineering, sciences, mathematics, and computer science as a result of national concern in the late 1980s that there was a serious shortage of scientists and engineers."

This pattern sometimes presents effects first, followed by causes, as in the following example.

> People became homeless for a variety of reasons. Some started life in seriously disturbed families. Others fell prey to alcohol and drugs. Still others had health or learning problems that eroded the possibility of a stable life. For millions of working Americans, homelessness was just a serious and unaffordable illness away. Though many Americans initially regarded the homeless as "bag ladies, winos, and junkies," they gradually came to realize that the underclass category included others as well.
>
> Gary B. Nash and Julie Roy Jeffrey, *The American People,* 5th ed., p. 1013

The first sentence—"People became homeless for a variety of reasons"—has the transition word *reasons* and also lets you know that *homelessness* is the effect. Causes are presented in the second, third, and fourth sentences, which are the major details:

- "Some started life in seriously disturbed families."
- "Others fell prey to alcohol and drugs."
- "Still others had health or learning problems that eroded the possibility of a stable life."

Did you notice a second pattern of organization? Right again! The words *some, others,* and *still others* indicate that the causes are also organized in a simple listing of facts. When you read, recognizing one or more than one pattern of organization enables you to focus on important information and thus helps you comprehend better.

ACTIVITY 3

DIRECTIONS: In the following passages, find the main ideas, patterns of organization, and the most important details organized by the patterns. Write your answers in your notebook. Be prepared to discuss the transition words that help you identify the patterns.

1

1   If you follow tennis, you know that John McEnroe was famous for his on-court antics and spectacular temper tantrums; he was the bad boy of the tennis circuit. Once, when McEnroe noticed a small microphone that could pick up what the players were saying, he walked over and hit it with his racquet, breaking a string. Then he strolled to the sidelines and got a new racquet. There was no penalty for this little episode. In fact, it seemed to work to his advantage: He got all charged up for the game, while his opponent's performance suffered from the interruption. McEnroe also received plenty of attention from fans and the media, who loved him or loved to hate him.

2   In contrast, Bjorn Borg, another tennis champion, was controlled and civilized on the court. "Once I was like John [McEnroe]," he told a reporter. "Worse. Swearing and throwing rackets. Real bad temper. Ask anyone who knew me in Sweden then, 10 or 11 years ago. Then, when I was 13, my club suspended me for six months. My parents locked my racket in a cupboard for six months. Half a year I could not play. It was terrible. But it was a very good lesson. I never opened my mouth on the court again. I still get really mad, but I keep my emotions inside" (quoted in Collins, 1981).

Carol Tavris and Carole Wade, *Psychology in Perspective*, p. 211

2

Victims of rape often suffer battered faces with cut lips and broken noses, bruises, abrasions, broken ribs, bites, and internal damage and bleeding. These immediate effects can bring on emotional symptoms characteristic of a severe anxiety reaction, a condition termed *rape trauma syndrome* (Burgess & Holmstrom, 1988; Rynd, 1988). Some women react with uncontrolled crying, anxiety, restlessness, depression, and feelings of self-blame. In addition to the pain and discomfort from the physical abuse suffered during the rape, they may have other physical complaints, including gastrointestinal upsets, headaches, insomnia, and loss of appetite. Other women encase themselves behind a smiling, cool, and relaxed exterior, masking the trauma and emotional turmoil held inside.

George Zgourides, *Human Sexuality*, pp. 389–390

3

John Rempel (1986) and John Holmes (1989) suggest that answers to three questions can help us make decisions about whether to trust someone. Each is based on an important element of trust.

1. *How predictable is that individual?* A predictable person is someone whose behavior is consistent—consistently good or bad. An unpredictable person keeps us guessing about what might happen next. Such volatile people may make life interesting, but they don't inspire much in the way of confidence.

2. *Can I depend upon him or her?* A dependable person can be relied upon when it counts. One way to tell is to see how a partner behaves in situations where it is possible to care or not to care.

3. *Do I have faith in that person?* Are you able to go beyond the available evidence and feel secure that your friend or partner will continue to be responsible and caring? We have faith in another person when our doubts are put aside and we feel safe in a relationship.

Anthony F. Grasha, Practical Applications of Psychology, p. 295

4

A view from the window of a plane on a transcontinental flight from Boston to California is revealing to an ecology-minded passenger. Below, the pattern of vegetation changes from the mixed coniferous-hardwood forests of the northeast to the oak forests of the central Appalachians with patches of high-elevation spruce forests. Then the forest cover merges with midwestern croplands of corn, soybean, and wheat, land that once was the domain of tallgrass prairie. Wheat fields yield to high-elevation shortgrass plains, and then the plains give way to the coniferous forest of the Rocky Mountains, capped by tundra and snowfields. Beyond the mountains to the southwest lie the tan-colored desert regions.

Robert Leo Smith and Thomas M. Smith, Elements of Ecology, p. 378

5

A lecture hall, for example, provides lots of opportunity to listen but very few opportunities to respond. Research shows that such settings promote a **one-way communication** pattern in which the teacher talks and students, for the most part, listen. For example, 70 percent of the time in a typical college classroom is spent with the teacher talking. Of the remaining time in a class period, students spend about 15 percent of it either responding to questions or asking questions and 15 percent remaining silent (Bonwell and Eison, 1991). When snuggling close to someone you care about, you and your partner have opportunities to talk and to listen. Thus, a **two-way communication** pattern is established.

Anthony F. Grasha, Practical Applications of Psychology, p. 262

6

Virtually every discussion of the history of American environmental concern identifies two major events, both occurring after World War II, as having helped popularize environmental issues. One notable event was the 1962 publication of *Silent Spring*, Rachel Carson's shocking exposé of the harmful environmental effects of pesticides. Carson's book quickly became a best-seller, eventually winning eight literary awards. Perhaps even more influential than Carson's book was the celebration of the first Earth Day on April 22, 1970. Millions of Americans participated in celebrations across the nation.

F. Kurt Cylke Jr., The Environment, p. 17

7

The person most responsible for the growth of the automobile industry was Henry Ford, a self-taught mechanic from Greenfield, Michigan. In 1908 he designed the Model T Ford, a simple, tough box on wheels. In a year he sold 11,000 Model Ts. Thereafter, relentlessly cutting costs and increasing efficiency by installing the assembly-line system, he expanded production at an unbelievable rate. By 1925 he was turning out more than 9,000 cars a day, one approximately every ten seconds, and the price of the Model T had been reduced to below $300.

John A. Garraty, *A Short History of the American Nation*, p. 431

8

American blacks were deeply involved in the Revolution. In fact, the conflict provoked the largest slave rebellion in American history prior to the Civil War. Once the war was under way, blacks found a variety of ways to turn events to their own advantage. For some, this meant applying revolutionary principles to their own lives and calling for their personal freedom. For others, it meant seeking liberty behind English lines or in the continent's interior.

Gary B. Nash and Julie Roy Jeffrey, *The American People*, p. 201

9

1   The extraordinary popularity of sports in the postwar period can be explained in a number of ways. People had more money to spend and more free time to fill. Radio was bringing suspenseful, play-by-play accounts of sports contests into millions of homes, thus encouraging tens of thousands to want to see similar events with their own eyes.

2   There had been great athletes before, such as Jim Thorpe, a Sac and Fox Indian, who won both the pentathlon and the decathlon at the 1912 Olympic Games, made Walter Camp's All-America football team in 1912 and 1913, then played major league baseball for several years before becoming a pioneer founder and player in the National Football League. But what truly made the 1920s a Golden Age was the emergence of a remarkable collection of what today would be called "superstars."

John A. Garraty, *A Short History of the American Nation*, p. 423

10

If the 1920s was the age of the bathroom, the 1930s was the era of the modern kitchen. The sale of electrical appliances increased throughout the decade, with refrigerators leading the way. In 1930, the number of refrigerators produced exceeded the number of iceboxes for the first time. Refrigerator production continued to rise throughout the decade, reaching a peak of 2.3 million in 1937. At first, the refrigerator was boxy and looked very much like an icebox with a motor sitting on top. In 1935, however, the refrigerator, like most other appliances, became streamlined. Sears, Roebuck advertised "The New 1935 Super Six Coldspot... Stunning in Its Streamlined Beauty." The Coldspot, which quickly influenced the look of all other models, was designed by Raymond Loewy, one of a group of industrial designers who emphasized sweeping horizontal lines, rounded corners, and a slick modern look. They hoped modern design would stimulate an optimistic attitude and, of course, increase sales.

Gary B. Nash and Julie Roy Jeffrey, *The American People*, p. 865

ACTIVITY 4

DIRECTIONS: In the following passages, find the main ideas, patterns of organization, and the most important details organized by the patterns. Write your answers in your notebook. Be prepared to discuss the transition words that help you identify the patterns.

1

1   Sexual freedom also contributed to the revival of the women's rights movement. For one thing, freedom involved a more drastic revolution for women than for men. Effective methods of contraception obviously affected women more directly than men, and the new attitudes heightened women's awareness of the way the old sexual standards had restricted their entire existence. In fact, the two movements interacted with each other. Concern for better job opportunities and for equal pay for equal work, for example, fed the demand for day-care centers for children.

2   Still another cause of the new drive for women's rights was concern for improving the treatment of minorities. Participation in the civil rights movement encouraged women to speak out more forcefully for their own rights. Feminists argued that they were being demeaned and dominated by a male-dominated society and must fight back.

John A. Garraty, *A Short History of the American Nation*, p. 540

2

No one disputes the worldwide influence of Sigmund Freud (1856–1939). But there is plenty of dispute about the lasting significance of his work, reflected in three current attitudes toward Freud and his ideas. The first, held by Freud himself and by his most devoted followers to this day, is that Freud was one of the geniuses of history, an intellectual revolutionary like Copernicus, Darwin, and Newton; with minor exceptions, his theory is correct, universal, and timeless. The second view, probably the most common among psychiatrists and clinical psychologists today, is that Freud was a great thinker and that many of his ideas have lasting value, but some are dated, and others are plain wrong. The third view, held by many scientists and by psychologists in other perspectives, is that Freud was a fraud—a poor scientist and even an unethical therapist (Crews,

1995). The British scientist and Nobel laureate Peter Medawar (1982) called psycho-analysis a dinosaur in the history of ideas, doomed to extinction. For good measure, he added that it is "the most stupendous intellectual confidence trick of the twentieth century."

Carol Tavris and Carole Wade, *Psychology in Perspective,* p. 509

3

Collective behavior is relatively spontaneous, unorganized, and unpredictable social behavior. It contrasts with *institutionalized behavior,* which occurs in a well-organized, rather predictable way. Institutionalized behavior is frequent and routine. Every weekday, masses of people hurry to work. On every campus, groups of students walk to classes. These predictable patterns of group action are basically governed by social norms and are the bedrock of social order. Collective behavior, however, operates largely outside the confines of these conventional norms.

Alex Thio, *Sociology: A Brief Introduction,* 4th ed., p. 438

4

The aspect of the physical environment that places the greatest constraint on organisms is climate. Climate is one of those terms we use loosely. In fact, people sometimes confuse climate with weather. **Weather** is the combination of temperature, humidity, precipitation, wind, cloudiness, and other atmospheric conditions at a specific place and time. **Climate** is the long-term average pattern of weather. We can describe the local, regional, or global climate.

Robert Leo Smith and Thomas M. Smith, *Elements of Ecology,* p. 31

5

1   Adam Smith, in his classic *Wealth of Nations,* used the pin factory to illustrate the benefits of specialization. In Adam Smith's day (the late eighteenth century), pins were manufactured through a large number of separate operations. Then and now, pin making consists of seven basic operations: (1) drawing wire, (2) straightening, (3) pointing, (4) twisting, (5) cutting heads and heading the wire, (6) tinning and whitening, and (7) papering and packaging. According to Adam Smith's calculations, each specialized worker produced almost 5000 pins a day (the number of pins produced per day divided by the number of workers in the pin factory). If each person worked alone, only a few pins would be produced per worker. In the late eighteenth century, specialization was achieved by separating pin production into many separate operations: One set of workers would do the straightening, another the pointing, another group the twisting, another group the cutting of heads, and so on.

2   Since the days of Adam Smith, there have been substantial improvements in pin making. According to the 1832 study of English statistician Charles Babbage, daily pin pro-

duction per employee had risen to about 8000 pins. In recent years, English pin factories were producing an astonishing 80,000 pins per day per employee!

Paul R. Gregory, *Essentials of Economics*, p. 6

6
Health in a Diverse World

Contraception around the World

Nearly 50 percent of all the world's couples of reproductive age currently use some form of contraception. Sterilization is the most commonly used method of birth control worldwide, followed by IUDs, oral contraceptives, condoms, and natural family-planning methods. The differences among countries and contraceptive use can be quite dramatic and are influenced by a variety of factors, such as access to services, availability, cost, and political, cultural, and religious factors. Examples of such differences can be seen by examining the following countries:

Brazil
- The most popular methods of contraception are female sterilization (44%), the pill (41%), vasectomy (9%), abstinence and withdrawal (6.2%), condoms (2.5%), IUDs (1.5%), other (3.5%).
- Sterilization, the most common form of birth control, is illegal.
- The government in Brazil provides no public system for delivery of contraceptives or the funding of contraceptives.

Germany
- Oral contraceptive pills, IUDs, barrier methods, and sterilization are available and are covered by insurance.
- The most popular methods of contraception are birth control pills (55%), some sort of barrier method (10%), or IUD (13%), sterilization (5%), and natural methods of contraception (8%).
- In Germany's eastern states, women under 20 years of age can legally obtain contraceptives free of charge.

Kenya
- Cultural and religious beliefs prohibit the use of contraceptives.
- Pills, IUDs, injectables, and "natural planning" are methods currently used, with injectables being the preferred method because they can easily be hidden from the men.
- Only 12 percent of Kenyan men currently use condoms.

China
- In 1979 China developed a one-child family policy.
- Contraceptives are provided free of charge.

- Contraception is still seen only as family planning and not as prevention of sexually transmitted infections.
- IUDs, tubectomies, vasectomies, and induced abortions are considered birth control.

Source: S. L. Caron, *Cross Cultural Perspectives on Human Sexuality* (Boston: Allyn and Bacon, 1998).
Rebecca J. Donatelle, *Health: The Basics,* 4th ed, p. 133

7

1   When it comes to nudity, actresses are just like you and me—self-conscious, vain, insecure, eager to please and sometimes miserable. Except that when they take their clothes off, they have to do it in front of the people they work with, knowing that they have little if any control over how the images of their naked bodies—which will then be projected onto 30-foot screens in front of millions of complete strangers—will ultimately be presented in the context of the finished project. And that their families will probably see them. And their friends. And that owing to the miracle of video rental, the Internet and enormous media interest, these images will be preserved, if not forever, at least for long enough that whatever the actresses' original thoughts about getting naked were, they'll probably have second, third and fourth thoughts about it.

2   On the other hand, being a hot body can be extremely lucrative, and even career-making. It is increasingly a job requisite, with, for example, actresses in their late teens and early 20's, like those in "American Beauty," appearing topless as a matter of course, a circumstance that would have caused at least a mild stir 20 years ago. Nevertheless, other than a *pro forma* disclaimer that the script called for it or a rare, and usually roundly mocked, claim of pride in nudity (think Demi Moore) or exploitation (think about the raised-eyebrow doubts that greeted Sharon Stone's contention that she was tricked into showing more than she knew in "Basic Instinct"), the women themselves rarely get a chance to say how they feel about this state of affairs. No one wants to look like a braggart or a whiner, and anyway, it's embarrassing to talk about. Rosie Perez, whose first film role, in "Do the Right Thing," had such a memorable nude scene that a decade later she's still living it down (or up), convened a round table of some of her friends and colleagues, inviting a reporter to participate, to talk about the pressures, rewards and plain facts about getting naked in public.

Mim Udovitch, "The Pressure to Take It off," *New York Times Magazine,* June 25, 2000, p. 36

8

Did you know that within three months after the Pilgrims landed at Plymouth Rock, half of them had died from malnutrition and illness because of the harsh conditions they encountered? Some of the surviving Pilgrims gave up and returned with the *Mayflower* when it sailed back across the Atlantic. The remaining Pilgrims struggled with famine. After three years of enduring conditions bordering on starvation, and after some Pilgrims became so desperate that they took to stealing from the others, the colonists began to reconsider a key method they had adopted in an effort to promote their new society. This was the practice of "farming in common," which entailed pooling what they produced and then rationing this "common property" in equal allotments. Following much thought and discussion, the colonists decided instead to parcel the *land* equally among families, who could then either consume or trade all fruits of their labors. This change in the Pilgrims' incentive structure worked wonders. Soon they had such bountiful harvests that they decided to have a day of thanksgiving—the forerunner of the modern American Thanksgiving holiday.

Roger LeRoy Miller, Economics Today, p. 760

9

The rate of weathering depends on the type of rock and on environmental conditions. Geologists define three major types of rock: igneous, sedimentary, and metamorphic. **Igneous rocks** are formed by the cooling of volcanic flows, surface or subterranean. The properties of these rocks depend on the rate and temperature at which they form. **Sedimentary rocks** are formed by the deposition of mineral particles (sediments). The properties of sedimentary rocks depend on the type of sediment from which they are formed. Some sediments are of biological origin; for example, shells of ocean invertebrates may fall to the sea floor. **Metamorphic rocks** are either igneous or sedimentary rocks that have been altered by heat and the pressure of overlying rock.

Robert Leo Smith and Thomas M. Smith, Elements of Ecology, 4th ed., p. 97

10

1   One major reason for Clinton's success was his expressed intention to effect changes in health insurance and the welfare system, and to bring the budget deficit under control. His solid knowledge of these and other public issues was impressive. He seemed, as a reporter put it, "a torrent of information" on any subject that came up at his news conferences.

2   Another reason he won the election was his command of English—unlike President Bush, who often responded to questions with rambling, disconnected phrases, Clinton's off-the-cuff remarks were typically clear and concise. This created a general impression of mastery and self-confidence that many voters found reassuring.

3   A third reason for Clinton's success was his apparent reasonableness, his willingness to reconcile differences. "Cooperation is better than conflict," he said on more than one occasion. But however valuable during a campaign, reasonableness was sometimes a disadvantage once the power of the presidency was at Clinton's command. He set out to reverse many of the policies of the Reagan-Bush era, but when opposition developed, circumstances often persuaded him to back down. He lacked Lyndon Johnson's ability to overwhelm opposition with the aura of power surrounding the presidency and the sheer force of his personality. More important, having received only 43 percent of the popular vote in the election, he did not have the kind of mandate Johnson had won in thrashing Barry Goldwater in 1964.

John A. Garraty and Mark C. Carnes, The American Nation, 10th ed., pp. 930–931

ACTIVITY 5

DIRECTIONS: Using your other textbooks, find examples of passages that illustrate the four patterns of organization that we have discussed. If you do not have other textbooks at this time, ask your classmates who are using other books to share their examples with you.

UNCOVERING THE CENTRAL MESSAGE OF A LONGER SELECTION

To this point, we have been discussing using context to find word meanings; distinguishing main ideas, major details, and minor details; and recognizing patterns of organization in paragraphs. All of these skills, of course, can be applied to selections or passages containing several paragraphs. Examples are articles, essays, textbook sections, and chapters.

Just as every paragraph has a main idea, every longer selection also has a main idea that gives the central message of all of the paragraphs within that selection. The **central message** represents the specific aspect of the topic that the writer wishes to discuss, and it is supported by the information in the selection, including the main ideas of the individual paragraphs and most, if not all, of the details. Patterns of organization can help you uncover the central message by directing you to the most important details.

Once again, it is important to determine first what the topic is by answering the question "What is this about?" Most longer selections will have a title or a heading to help you determine the topic. If there is no title or heading, you can usually figure out the topic by reading the selection carefully, concentrating particularly on sentences near the beginning, which will often mention the subject matter. Once you have determined the topic, you identify the central message by answering the question "What is the central message that the writer is communicating about the topic?"

The main idea of a longer selection can be stated or unstated, as is the case with main ideas in paragraphs. When it is stated, it can usually be found somewhere within the first few paragraphs or the last few paragraphs. When it is unstated, a very careful reading of the selection will usually enable you to figure out the overall main idea. Read the following example, determine the topic, and see if you can identify the main idea by answering the question "What is the central message that the writer is communicating about the topic?"

Homeless Advocates

1   Robert Hayes and Mitch Snyder, although differing in many respects, were both catalysts for change during the dreary days of homelessness in the early 1980s. Both helped to awaken Americans to the appalling conditions of homelessness and convinced them that something could be done.

2   Robert Hayes saw firsthand the plight of New York City's homeless and decided to do something about it. In 1979, the recent law school graduate sued the city and the state seeking adequate shelter for his six clients, including one whose residence was a cardboard box on Park Avenue. Even though it was his first court appearance and he was scared to death, he claimed that the state had a constitutional responsibility to provide shelter for anyone who requested it. The judge agreed and New York began to turn armories and other public buildings into shelters with cots, showers, and simple meals. Requests from other states led Hayes to quit his job with a top corporate law firm and to form the National Coalition for the Homeless. Over the years, dozens of cities have learned from Hayes and the Coalition and have persuaded municipal officials and private organizations to pool their resources to help the homeless.

3   Mitch Snyder also left a well-paying job to take up the cause of the homeless. As passionate and zealous as Hayes was studious and methodical, Snyder typified the label of "activist" by being bothersome to many, particularly the Reagan administration. Losing sixty pounds during a fifty-one-day hunger strike, Snyder prodded President Reagan in 1984 to agree to fund an emergency shelter in Washington, D.C. But one accomplishment simply led to another goal in Snyder's ongoing battle to "kick in doors where necessary" to help the homeless. Although a laudatory movie about him starring Martin Sheen made him famous, he continued to live in a shelter, and persistently challenged reluctant authorities to act on his recommendations. He persuaded members of Congress to hold hearings at his Community for Creative Non-Violence shelter, and was instrumental in the creation of the McKinney Homeless Assistance Act of 1988.

Richard Sweeney, *Out of Place: Homelessness in America*, pp. 98–100

The heading of the textbook passage lets you know that the subject matter deals with "homeless advocates," and the first paragraph gives their names. Thus the topic of the selection is "Homeless advocates Robert Hayes and Mitch Snyder." The two sentences in the first paragraph, which express the main idea of the entire selection, provide the central message: "Robert Hayes and Mitch Snyder, although differing in many respects, were both catalysts for change during the dreary days of homelessness in the early 1980s. Both helped to awaken Americans to the appalling conditions of homelessness and convinced them that something could be done." The first sentences of the remaining two paragraphs are main ideas that support the central message:

Paragraph 1:   "Robert Hayes saw firsthand the plight of New York City's homeless and decided to do something about it."

Paragraph 2:   "Mitch Snyder also left a well-paying job to take up the cause of the homeless"

The rest of the selection, which consists of details organized by the comparison-and-contrast pattern of organization, also lends support to the central message.

Let's look at another example, which was also taken from a textbook. As you read the selection, take note of how the information is structured differently than it was in our first example, and think carefully about the topic and central message.

Tragedy at Sea

1   During the height of tensions during the Iran-Iraq war, a number of United States Navy warships were in the Persian Gulf protecting the shipment of oil and other commodities. On July 3, 1988, the *USS Vincennes,* a high-tech warship, was on routine patrol when one of its helicopters was attacked by Iranian gunboats. The *Vincennes* moved into Iranian territorial waters to help and opened fire with superior weapons on the gunboats.

2   To some observers, this was like shooting at rabbits with a radar guided-missile. However, to Captain Will Rogers and the crew of the *USS Vincennes,* this was the combat for which they had trained for years. As the shooting at the gunboats continued, tension aboard the *Vincennes* remained high. They were still positioned inside Iranian waters, and uncertainty about possible attacks by Iranian missiles and F–14 fighter planes lurked in the back of their minds.

3   Besides the threat of Iranian attack, stress was higher than usual under such circumstances. Neither Captain Rogers nor the crew were combat veterans. This was their first hostile encounter outside of wargames and other naval simulations where the ship's captain had developed a reputation as a risky decision maker.

4   At 9:47 A.M. an Iran Air 655 airbus took off from Bandar Abbas, Iran, with 290 civilian passengers aboard on a commercial air route over the Persian Gulf. Almost immediately, the radar on the *Vincennes* picked up the airliner and fed information about the aircraft into a sophisticated computer system designed to identify airplanes as "friendly," "hostile," or "unidentified."

5   The computer initially labeled the aircraft as a commercial flight. Unfortunately, in the tension and semidarkness of the ship's command center, a crew member checking commercial flight schedules for the Persian Gulf missed the listing for the airbus. Direct radio contact with the plane was initiated; but the aircraft's radio channels were busy with air traffic control information and the plane did not receive the initial messages or later warning from the *Vincennes.*

6   By this time, Captain Rogers had taken complete control of the situation. He was directing the fight with the gunboats and was trying to monitor information provided by the computer and his staff about the unidentified airplane. There were simply too many things to think about.

7   Then something happened that psychologists call scenario fulfillment—you see what you expect. In the tension of the moment, anxious crew members tagged the unidentified aircraft as an F–14 fighter and reported that it was descending, picking up speed, and closing in on the *Vincennes.* A later review of the tapes from the warship would reveal that no such thing occurred. In reality the passenger plane was slowing down and climbing to 12,000 feet.

8   Captain Rogers was confronted with incomplete and inaccurate information. He had seconds to make a decision and accepted his crew's conclusion that the aircraft was hostile. He gave the command to fire, and two SM–2 surface-to-air missiles were launched. Within seconds, the airbus, with its crew and 290 passengers, was destroyed.

Anthony F. Grasha, *Practical Applications of Psychology,* pp. 82–83

The heading, "Tragedy at Sea," gives a general idea of the topic, but you have to read the entire passage to find out exactly what happened. Although there is no stated main idea, a careful look at all of the information presented helps you uncover the central message. Notice how many of the sentences in the selection are organized in the time-sequence pattern of organization, which makes it easier to focus on the most important details and thus follow the events described. As a result, you are in a better position to piece together the facts and come up with the central message, which should read something like:

> In 1988, the United States Navy warship *USS Vincennes* shot down an Iran Air 655 airbus in the Persian Gulf, resulting in the deaths of the crew and 290 civilian passengers. Due to the stress involved in a conflict situation and the combat inexperience of Captain Will Rogers and his crew, the airbus was mistaken for an F–14 fighter plane that was about to attack the warship.

As you can see, uncovering the topic and central message of a selection is very useful, because it requires that you focus on the most important information. That should help you derive more meaning from textbook material and other kinds of reading. It will also help you master the approach to contemporary issues discussed in Chapter 4 by enabling you to determine what is at issue, distinguish among opposing viewpoints, and arrive at an informed personal viewpoint.

ACTIVITY 6

DIRECTIONS: Find the topic and central message for each of the selections that follow by answering the questions "What is this about?" and "What is the central message that the writer is communicating about the topic?" Remember to look carefully at main ideas within the paragraphs and any patterns of organization that may be present, because they will help you focus on the most important information.

1
Problem Solving and Decision Making: Two Sides of the Same Coin

1   Each of us needs to solve problems and make decisions under a variety of circumstances. Some of them, like the situation faced by the captain of the *Vincennes*, are tension arousing. Incomplete information exists; there is little room for error; and quick decisions are needed. Other circumstances, while not life threatening, are just as important and demand our best efforts to manage them. Included here are such things as where to invest money, what career path to choose, whether or not to marry, how to resolve a personal problem, choosing what car to purchase, and deciding how to decorate a room or repair a small appliance.

2   Problem solving and decision making are sometimes treated in the literature as if they were separate topics. In reality, they are very much interrelated. To solve **problems** we have to make a number of important **decisions.** We must decide, among other things: how to adequately define our problem; what information is most important; which alternative **solutions** are possible and which one would be the "best" choice; and how to implement a particular solution or course of action. Having to deal with problems forces us to make decisions.

3   Similarly, whenever we say to ourselves, "I have got to make a decision. What should I do?" we are responding to a problem in our lives. That is, we are reacting to something for which we do not have a readily available response. The need to make a decision reflects the fact that we have a problem. *Consequently, suggestions for improving one process ultimately help us to do the other more effectively.*

Anthony F. Grasha, *Practical Applications of Psychology,* p. 83

2

1   It was Michael's first day at the university. Besides feeling a little overwhelmed, he was concerned about obtaining the right signatures from the right advisors, dealing with the financial aid office, locating the right buildings, and finding his classrooms. During orientation week, Michael had also found registering for classes to be a nightmare. Long lines. Short tempers. And he couldn't get into all the classes he wanted, at least not at convenient times. Michael certainly didn't relish the thought of being in class at 8:00 every weekday morning.

2   Michael had signed up for some of the usual courses: Math, History, Art Appreciation, English, and Human Sexuality. These classes sounded interesting, but the idea of also taking Human Sexuality really appealed to him: "Taking a sex class is going to be a breeze! I'm already an expert. I probably won't even have to open the book. I can look for dates. X-rated videos. Sexy stories. Way to go, Mike! At least I'll have one 'easy A' this semester!"

3   If you're like Michael, your initial expectation of a course in human sexuality might be to watch sex education films, listen to people talk about their sex lives, and follow the instructor's discussion of sexual activities you've already experienced. You may see the class as a way of meeting potential sexual partners or maintaining a good grade point average. If you already think of yourself as a sexual expert, you may even consider this course a less than valuable way to spend your time.

4   You'll soon realize, however, that studying human sexuality involves much more than just reading stimulating sexual case studies and watching videos. You'll encounter a great deal of new material. You'll spend time rethinking your values and attitudes about sexuality. The differing viewpoints of your classmates will at times challenge your beliefs about what is acceptable. You'll come to view human sexuality for what it is—a beautiful and integral, but complex, part of life.

George Zgourides, *Human Sexuality,* pp. 2–3

3

Are Car Phones Too Dangerous?

1   On January 13, 1996, Kayla Segerstron was driving in a minivan along a winding country road in Texas when her cellular phone rang. Reaching down to answer it, she missed a sharp turn and plowed into a car carrying the Colvin family.

2   Three-year-old Cole Colvin died; two-year-old Briana broke her neck. Their father suffered brain damage, rendering his left side virtually useless; their mother sustained minor injuries. Segerstron, 17, emerged virtually unhurt.

3   "This accident was directly attributable to the cell phone," says Steven DeWolf, the Colvins' attorney. "They're dangerous as hell." Last May, a jury awarded the Colvins $7 million in damages, to be paid by the insurance company of the Segerstron's family business.

4   Cell phones are becoming almost as common as VCRs in the United States—an estimated 50 million are in use today. Yet society may be paying a high price for this convenience. A widely publicized 1997 study by the University of Toronto indicates that using a cell phone while driving quadruples the risk of having an accident—about the same risk as driving after having had two to three alcoholic drinks.

5   Even hands-free cell phones (which utilize speakers) didn't cut the risk factor in the study. "It's losing your concentration that's dangerous, much more than losing your grip on the steering wheel," says study author Donald A. Redelmeier, M.D. Other research reveals that even the most careful, experienced drivers increase their risk of accident if they talk on the phone and drive.

6   A number of countries, including Great Britain, Sweden, Italy, Brazil and Singapore, have passed or are considering legislation to limit the use of cell phones by drivers. Similar laws are under consideration in several states—yet cell phones also have determined advocates, from police officers to working mothers.

7   Many law enforcement officials defend the use of car phones because they turn drivers into emergency spotters. Approximately 60,000 calls are placed daily to 911 centers by motorists reporting accidents, fires or crimes. And alerts to radio stations about delays have helped improve traffic conditions.

8   Those opposed to banning cell phones also view the proposed legislation as drastic. The increased risk of accident, they point out, appears to be related to intense conversation coupled with driving maneuvers that require caution. But many who dial and drive limit themselves to quick check-ins or fast exchanges of information.

9   "Some argue that cell phones pose no more risk than other distractions, like fiddling with the radio or putting on makeup," notes Michael Goodman, Ph.D., an engineering research psychologist with the National Highway Traffic Safety Administration. "Of course, it's not possible to outlaw all those things. The bottom line is, *all* distractions at inopportune times can cause crashes."

10   Millions of commuters would be loath to give up calls, particularly parents eager to stay in touch with their kids and baby-sitters, and to be reachable in case of an emergency. On-the-go workers also find that talking in transit boosts productivity. Yet for women,

having a cell phone is often an issue of safety—and peace of mind. "I work late and I'd be afraid to leave my car if there was a problem," says Cathy Barker, a nurse living in Birmingham, Alabama. "My cell phone makes me feel secure."

Glamour, September 1997, p. 232

4

Close Your Eyes. Hold Your Nose. It's Dinner Time.

Eric Asimov

1   Got a hankering for some calf testicles?

2   Wait, don't gag just yet. In the Rocky Mountain states, calf testicles—sliced, lightly battered and fried—are considered a delicacy by people who themselves might turn vivid shades of green at the thought of devouring a clam. And if neither calf testicles nor clams repulse you, something in humanity's vast pantry will surely turn your stomach.

3   Humans eat just about anything that can be speared, hooked, shot or reared, from rooster coxcombs (the red things on their heads) to ox tails to grasshoppers to, yes, puppies and kittens. The species' wide-ranging tastes, which so easily arouse disgust among those who do not partake, are reflected in recent reports about two prized regional delicacies: squirrel brains, considered a treat in rural western Kentucky, and geoducks, freakishly large clams that thrive in the saltwater tidelands of the Pacific Nortwest.

4   It seems that consuming squirrel brains can transmit to humans a fatal variant of mad cow disease, which essentially shreds human brain tissue. Scientists last month warned devotees to lay off the gray matter of the gray rodents, though those outside the Squirrel Brain Belt might argue that consuming the delicacy in the first place suggests that the damage has already been done.

5   And then there is the geoduck (oddly enough, pronounced GOO-ee-duck), a clam that can weigh as much as 16 pounds, with a neck like a flexible fire hydrant. Why a geoduck? Organized crime has apparently gotten into the business, smuggling this especially homely bivalve to Asia, where a single clam can sell for $50.

6   The mind may say "Yuck" to such formidable meals, but somewhere, sometime, a mouth first watered at the prospect. Who, after all, would have thought to eat an animal as hideous as a lobster?

7   "What's a lobster other than an insect, but slightly larger?" asked Andrew F. Smith, author of *The Tomato in America* (North Carolina University Press, 1994). Mr. Smith, who teaches culinary history at the New School for Social Research in New York, noted that crickets and grasshoppers were commonly eaten in the United States through the 19th century. "If you're hungry, you tend to eat things," he said, simply enough.

8   That logic might explain the cannibalistic Donner Party, settlers trapped in the Sierra Nevada a century and a half ago—but squirrel brains? "I'm sure that people who lived on the frontier, if they shot a squirrel—what's wrong with eating the brains?" Mr. Smith asked. "What's wrong with eating eyeballs? In Asian societies, eyeballs are considered common foods. If I were hungry, would I eat eyeballs? You bet I would!"

9   You may as well ask who was brave enough to taste a tomato. Mr. Smith said northern Europeans considered tomatoes too revolting to eat when Spanish conquistadors first brought them back from the New World. "Squeamishness depends on cultural background," he said, noting that slime from the surfaces of rivers and lakes was a prized food of the Aztecs.

10   While Mr. Smith's personal diet has occasionally included calf testicles, he does draw the line at the durian, a spiked, football-shaped fruit popular in Southeast Asia that is so famously stinky that Singapore, for one, prohibits slicing them open in public places.

11   It's a shame people can't do a better job of adapting to foods they consider gross, argued Calvin W. Schwabe in his 1979 book *Unmentionable Cuisine* (University Press of Virginia); he asserted that the world, and Americans in particular, may face dire long-term consequences by irrationally rejecting such foods, which can help sustain the food supply and are often cheap, nutritious and tasty. He has collected recipes for foods that are actually eaten, somewhere in the world, including Samoan baked bat, Turkish lamb tongues and Hawaiian broiled puppy.

12   "How strange that we think it natural to eat *some* arthropods—even crabs, which are notorious scavengers of the deep—but just the idea of eating any of our really beautiful bugs and caterpillars, which feed on clean vegetation, makes us shudder," he lamented.

13   Paul Rozin, a professor of psychology at the University of Pennsylvania who studies human choices, says foods that disgust are almost all animal products. Asking why humans find a few scattered animal foods disgusting is the wrong question, he said. "We eat so few animal products that the real question is, why aren't all animal products revolting?" he said.

14   In the United States, which he termed "basically a muscle-eating country," viscosity—that state between solid and liquid that characterizes, say, squirrel brains—generally repulses, as does the odor of decay. But he pointed out that every culture has its exceptions.

15   "We prize cheese, which is rotted milk and smells that way," he said. "Fish sauce, which is rotted fish, is prized in Southeast Asia."

16   Clearly, people's tastes in food depend on what they grew up eating. Those who vow that rodent entrails will never pass between their lips think nothing of eating strips of pig flesh. But maybe if people were more familiar with the smells, squeals and butchery required to turn the pig into bacon, they would be less likely to shrink back from the innards and oddities of other cultures. Or maybe they would give up bacon.

17   Perhaps examining the food on the plate too closely is something we should all avoid. Have you ever looked closely at a Cheez Doodle? Now you can gag.

New York Times, September 14, 1997, p. 2

5

Today's Athletes Owe Everything to Ali

He Took a Stand and Lost Much of His Career. Would Anyone Do That Now?

Max Wallace

1   This weekend, the nation's newspapers are caught up in two separate events. While the news sections focus on the 25th anniversary of the end of the Vietnam War, the sports pages are dissecting last night's heavyweight championship fight between Lennox Lewis and Michael Grant.

2   But 33 years ago this week, Vietnam and the world of boxing loudly converged on both the front page and the sports page when Muhammad Ali refused to be inducted into the United States Army.

3   Ordinarily, such anniversaries offer little more than a chance for reflective nostalgia. But this one may present a long-overdue opportunity to reassess the legacy of Ali and the broader impact of the modern athlete on society.

4   Before Ali came along, the history of American boxing had mirrored the social and political currents of the day. When Jack Johnson became the first African-American heavyweight champion in 1908, his victory was widely considered a blow to white supremacy and declared by The New York Herald "an event more calamitous than the San Francisco earthquake."

5   Subsequent Johnson victories set off race riots in American cities. The novelist Jack London publicly implored the former champion Jim Jeffries to come out of retirement to "restore the title to White America." After Johnson was persecuted by the government and subsequently run out of the country, white boxers simply refused to fight blacks for more than a generation.

6   When Joe Louis came along 30 years later in a new era of condescending tolerance toward blacks, his handlers counseled him to act docile, humble and obedient—a "credit to his race." America accepted Louis, even admired him, and his meek image was to become the expected model for African-Americans for another quarter century. Once Louis outlived his usefulness, his mob handlers discarded him and he died penniless.

7   Ali was also determined to be a credit to his race. But for him, those words had a very different meaning than they did for Joe Louis.

8   The seeds of the revolution Ali led were planted in February 1964 when Cassius Clay defeated the heavily favored Sonny Liston to win his first heavy-weight championship.

9   The following day, Clay, bolstered by his mentor Malcolm X, stepped in front of a room of journalists to declare his conversion to the Nation of Islam. After fielding hostile questions, he voiced the words that would become his lifelong anthem and would forever change the world of sports: "I don't have to be what you want me to be."

10   His affiliation with the Black Muslims, and subsequent name change, made him a national pariah and outraged many of the country's leading sportswriters, who were

stunned by an athlete who dared to voice a political opinion. As a result, most of America's sports pages continued to refer to Ali by what he called his "slave name," Cassius Clay.

11   But if his religious conversion inspired petty revenge, this paled in comparison to what came next.

12   In 1966, J. Edgar Hoover and the American government, paranoid about Ali's influence on young blacks, decided that the easiest way to keep a troublemaker in line would be to keep him under the watchful eye of Uncle Sam for two years. Although Ali had already been declared ineligible for military service, the Army changed its eligibility standards, and suddenly Ali was targeted for induction.

13   When the notice came as he was training for his next bout, Ali uttered the phrase that would earn him a place as the most despised man in America: "I ain't got no quarrel with the Vietcong. No Vietcong ever called me nigger."

14   Ali's words set off a firestorm, earning him vicious condemnation throughout much of the news media and the country.

15   Widespread protests against the Vietnam War had not yet begun, but with that one phrase, Ali articulated the reason to oppose the war for a generation of young Americans, and his words served as a touchstone for the racial and antiwar upheavals that would rock the 60's. Ali's example inspired Martin Luther King Jr.—who had been reluctant to alienate the Johnson administration and its support of the civil-rights agenda—to voice his own opposition to the war for the first time.

16   Ali, claiming conscientious objector status, instinctively understood that America had no business in Vietnam where, in the words of Stokely Carmichael, "Black folks are fighting a war against yellow folks so that white folks can keep a land they stole from red folks."

17   The government offered Ali the same opportunity given to Joe Louis in World War II. He could fight exhibitions for the troops and keep his title without seeing a battlefield. But Ali refused, saying, "I'd be just as guilty as the ones doing the killing."

18   Within minutes of his induction refusal on April 28, 1967, the New York State Athletic Commission stripped him of his title, declaring his actions "detrimental to the best interests of boxing," despite having granted licenses to more than 200 murderers, rapists and other convicted felons over the years. Ali's most serious offense was a traffic violation two years earlier.

19   He was convicted of draft evasion and sentenced to five years in prison, a sentence subsequently overturned by the Supreme Court, after Ali endured four years in internal exile and a legal battle tougher than fighting Liston, Joe Frazier and George Foreman combined. He lost millions of dollars and the peak years of his career. Through it all, he declared, "My principles are more important than the money or my title."

20   When he finally regained his title seven years later and emerged as a worldwide icon, he spent most of his time and money outside the ring fighting for economic justice and human rights. His example was cited by Arthur Ashe, Billie Jean King and others as they fought their own battles to change the face of sports and society.

21   The sports sociologist Harry Edwards argues that Ali's actions paved the way for the unparalleled influence of Michael Jordan and other present-day superstars. "Before Ali," Edwards said, "black athletes were merely 20th-century gladiators in the service of white society."

22   And how have today's superstar athletes carried on Ali's legacy of principles over profit? By shilling running shoes made under sweatshop conditions in Third World countries, including Vietnam. By demonstrating a consistent example of greed and bad behavior. And by pretending the world outside sports does not exist.

23   It is time to measure athletes for more than just their athletic accomplishments and to hold them accountable for their behavior outside the arena, to recognize their significant impact on a large segment of society. Today's generation needs sports heroes whose principles and aspirations extend beyond the next pair of Air Nikes.

24   Today, Ali—despite his Parkinson's syndrome—spends more than 200 days a year on the road as a roving ambassador for human rights and as a spokesman for the Jubilee 2000 campaign to cancel Third World debt. Now a traditional Muslim, he regularly denounces the anti-Semitism of Louis Farrakhan, the leader of the movement he once belonged to.

25   It's time to make Muhammad Ali, not today's two-dimensional corporate pitchmen, the standard by which all athletes are judged.

New York Times, April 30, 2000, p. 11

ACTIVITY 7

DIRECTIONS: Find the topic and central message of the following poem, remembering to answer the questions "What is this about?" and "What is the central message that the writer is communicating about the topic?"

A Quiet House in the Suburbs

Mark Hillringhouse

I'm the only one home
until the mail arrives and the kids return
from school. Sunlight falls on my face
as yet unshaved. The lazy and the industrious
5   live in two separate worlds. Day laborers and
commuters go their separate ways.
I'm blessed to have blue skies and summer
clouds in October. The leaves turn golden
and shimmer in the light breeze.
10   Without a burning desire it is impossible
to write great poems. I should pay bills
and organize bank statements but spend
my time listening to birds and sipping coffee.
A screened porch,
15   a half-finished house,
an old Chevy—a salary
that only gets me through three weeks of the month

20 though I am not starving or unclothed.
  I don't bother keeping up appearances.
20 I pursue my daydreams in quiet
  passing one day after another reading poems.
  I know I should rake and weed but let nature
  take over. Human affairs have little to do
  with this world: from ancient times
25 politics and government have not changed.
  People still suffer poverty and despair.
  But here on this porch mornings and evenings,
  I forget my chores and clear a space for dreaming.
  The squirrels chatter and busy themselves for winter,
30 the crows fight for scraps of leftover food,
  fallen leaves cover my yard and driveway.
  I have not swept, I have not washed or prepared dinner,
  I will do nothing all day.

SUMMARIZING AND PARAPHRASING

If you truly understand reading material, you should be able first to interpret it, then to condense or shorten it, and finally to put it into your own words. When you condense information, you are *summarizing* the main points by using many of the writer's own terms. Putting the information into your own words is called *paraphrasing*—a skill you use when writing out unstated main ideas. In short, paraphrasing involves rewording or substituting your own words—not your opinions—for the author's, except for certain key terminology essential to the meaning of the material. We often use both summarizing and paraphrasing in our everyday lives. For example, when you try to explain to someone what happened in class or what a particular movie or television program was about, you are summarizing and paraphrasing. In those instances, you generally use your own words to provide a short description without relating, word for word, everything that occurred.

  Given the vast amount of information normally presented in a typical college reading assignment, you need to find a way to reduce the information to manageable proportions. Summarizing and paraphrasing, when you do it correctly, should make textbook material easier to learn and remember. To summarize you must be able to pick out the most important information usually found in main ideas, major details, and context definitions. Underlining and highlighting with a marker are techniques that help you focus better by getting you more actively involved in your reading, while enabling you to separate the information you need for your summary.

  Underlining and highlighting are very useful for several reasons. First, the physical act forces you to be more attentive, thereby aiding your concentration; you are less likely to daydream or fall asleep. Second, in determining what you should underline or highlight, you first must evaluate carefully what you are reading, resulting in better comprehension. Third, because underlining and highlighting involve increased concentration, thought, and evaluation, they help you remember. Finally, when done properly, underlining and highlighting help you to locate quickly only the most important information when you review; you need not read the material in its entirety again. In short, make it a habit to underline or highlight with a marker, particularly when you are dealing with textbook material.

The major problem with underlining and highlighting is that students sometimes do too much, finding it difficult to determine what is important. You can avoid this problem by concentrating only on the information you find in main ideas, major details, and context definitions. Use patterns of organization and context clues to help you locate them.

After underlining or highlighting and then summarizing material, you can attempt to paraphrase it. To do this correctly, you must understand fully what the writer is saying, otherwise you may omit important information and lose some of the meaning. For example, look at the passage that follows.

> There are three types of noise that can block communication. The first, external noise, includes those obvious things that make it difficult to hear, as well as many other kinds of distractions. For instance, too much cigarette smoke in a crowded room might make it hard for you to pay attention to another person, and sitting in the rear of an auditorium might make a speaker's remarks unclear. External noise can disrupt communication almost anywhere in our model—in the sender, channel, message, or receiver.
>
> The second type of noise is physiological. A hearing disorder is probably the most obvious type of physiological barrier, although many more exist. Consider, for instance, the difficulty you experience as a listener when you are suffering from a cold or are very tired. In the same way you might speak less when you have a sore throat or a headache.
>
> Psychological noise refers to forces within the sender or receiver that make these people less able to express or understand the message clearly. For instance, an outdoorsman might exaggerate the size and number of fish caught in order to convince himself and others of his talents. In the same way, a student might become so upset upon learning that she failed a test that she would be unable (perhaps unwilling is a better word) to clearly understand where she went wrong.
>
> Ronald B. Adler and Neil Towne, *Looking Out/Looking In: Interpersonal Communication*, pp. 24–25

Notice how the main idea and the details (some of which are organized by the simple listing pattern of organization) have been underlined to make them stand out. A summary of the passage would read something like the following.

> External, physiological, and psychological noise can block communication. External noise, which includes distractions that make it difficult to hear, can disrupt communication in the sender, channel, message, or receiver. There are many physiological barriers, such as a hearing disorder. Psychological noise refers to forces within the sender or receiver that make these people less able to express or understand the message.

Although the information has been condensed, many of the writer's words have been repeated, which by itself does not necessarily mean that true understanding has taken place. Therefore, if we were to go one final step and paraphrase the passage, we might end up with something like the following.

> Outside distractions, physical problems, and mental factors can all interfere with communication. Distractions can disrupt the sender, channel, message, or receiver. Any kind of

a physical disorder, such as a hearing or speaking problem, makes it difficult to communicate. Finally, forces within the mind of the sender or receiver can have a negative effect on a message.

As you can see, very few of the writer's words have been used to paraphrase the passage, but the most important information has been included through the use of other, perhaps more familiar, terms. The ability to paraphrase demonstrates a more complete understanding of whatever you are reading because you are able to translate the material into words that are more meaningful to you, which should make it easier to learn and remember.

Until this point the skills of summarizing and paraphrasing have been separated for purposes of discussion. However, you may want to combine them as they become more familiar to you. For example, look at the following passage, paying particular attention to the sentences that have been underlined.

> One of the first women to make a career in psychology was Mary Calkins. <u>When Henry Durant founded Wellesley College in 1870,</u> he decided to hire only women to teach the all-female student body. But he could find no woman with an advanced degree in psychology. <u>Finally, in 1890, he hired a bright young woman, Mary Calkins, who had a B.A. degree in classics, to teach psychology,</u> promising that he would pay for her graduate education in psychology. <u>Then the problem was to find a graduate program that would accept a female student. After much debate and stiff resistance, nearby Harvard University finally agreed to let her attend graduate classes,</u> although at first it would not allow her to register officially as a student. <u>In 1895, when she passed the final examination for the Ph.D. degree, one of her professors remarked that she had performed better on the examination than had any other student in the history of the department.</u>
>
> <u>The Harvard administration, however, was still unwilling to grant a Ph.D. degree to a woman.</u> It suggested a compromise. <u>It would grant her a Ph.D. degree from Radcliffe College, the recently established women's undergraduate college associated with Harvard. She refused,</u> declaring that to accept the compromise would violate the high ideals of education. She never gave in, and neither did Harvard. <u>Although Mary Calkins never received a Ph.D. degree, she became a pioneer in psychological research, inventing a technique of studying memory, known as the paired-associates method, that is still used today.</u>
>
> James W. Kalat, *Introduction to Psychology*

Remember that the goal here is to first reduce the amount of information by eliminating unimportant material. So concentrating on the topic, main ideas, major details, and context definitions is crucial. Next the information should be translated into the reader's own words—except those words used by the writer that are crucial to the meaning of the passage. A summary that has been paraphrased could possibly look like the following.

> Henry Durant founded Wellesley College in 1870 and hired Mary Calkins to teach psychology. Because she did not have a degree in that field, she tried to get into a graduate program. After much resistance because she was a woman, Harvard agreed to have her attend classes. Although she passed the Ph.D. exam with a performance that was the best ever, Harvard refused to give her the degree because she was a woman. Instead it offered to have Radcliffe College, which was an undergraduate woman's college associated with Harvard, grant her the degree. She refused to accept the offer and never received

her Ph.D. However, she still contributed to the field by inventing a way of studying memory called the paired-associates method that is still used today.

Notice how only certain key words, such as the names of the schools, the names of individuals, and specialized terms like "paired-associates method," are included. Nevertheless, the information is condensed and different words are used without losing the basic meaning of the passage. Thus, the material should be easier to understand, learn, and remember. Make it a practice to underline or highlight and then summarize and paraphrase your reading assignments whenever you can.

In this textbook, you can practice your underlining, highlighting, summarizing, and paraphrasing skills, particularly when distinguishing among opposing viewpoints and rationales as part of the approach to contemporary issues introduced in Chapter 4. Also, at the end of this and all the remaining chapters there is "Looking Back," which asks you to summarize or paraphrase the most important points you learned from the chapter and determine how they can be put to use in other classes. Because of the importance of these skills, take advantage of the opportunities provided to practice them.

ACTIVITY 8

DIRECTIONS: In "Looking Back" at the end of Chapter 1, you were asked only to list the most important points because we had not yet reviewed summarizing and paraphrasing. Now that we have, summarize and paraphrase those points you learned from that chapter.

ACTIVITY 9

DIRECTIONS: Underline or highlight the most important information in the short story that follows and then summarize and/or paraphrase it in your notebook.

The Tell-Tale Heart

Edgar Allan Poe

1   TRUE!—nervous—very, very dreadfully nervous I had been and am; but why *will* you say that I am mad? The disease had sharpened my senses—not destroyed—not dulled them. Above all was the sense of hearing acute. I heard all things in the heaven and in the earth. I heard many things in hell. How, then, am I mad? Hearken! and observe how healthily—how calmly I can tell you the whole story.

2   It is impossible to say how first the idea entered my brain; but once conceived, it haunted me day and night. Object there was none. Passion there was none. I loved the old man. He had never wronged me. He had never given me insult. For his gold I had no desire. I think it was his eye! yes, it was this! He had the eye of a vulture—a pale blue eye, with a film over it. Whenever it fell upon me, my blood ran cold; and so by degrees—

very gradually—I made up my mind to take the life of the old man, and thus rid myself of the eye for ever.

3   Now this is the point. You fancy me mad. Madmen know nothing. But you should have seen *me*. You should have seen how wisely I proceeded—with what caution—with what foresight—with what dissimulation I went to work! I was never kinder to the old man than during the whole week before I killed him. And every night, about midnight, I turned the latch of his door and opened it—oh, so gently! And then, when I had made an opening sufficient for my head, I put in a dark lantern, all closed, closed, so that no light shone out, and then I thrust in my head. Oh, you would have laughed to see how cunningly I thrust it in! I moved it slowly—very, very slowly, so that I might not disturb the old man's sleep. It took me an hour to place my whole head within the opening so far that I could see him as he lay upon his bed. Ha!—would a madman have been so wise as this? And then, when my head was well in the room, I undid the lantern cautiously—oh, so cautiously—cautiously (for the hinges creaked)—I undid it just so much that a single thin ray fell upon the vulture eye. And this I did for seven long nights—every night just at midnight— but I found the eye always closed; and so it was impossible to do the work; for it was not the old man who vexed me, but his Evil Eye. And every morning, when the day broke, I went boldly into the chamber, and spoke courageously to him, calling him by name in a hearty tone, and inquiring how he had passed the night. So you see he would have been a very profound old man, indeed, to suspect that every night, just at twelve, I looked in upon him while he slept.

4   Upon the eighth night I was more than usually cautious in opening the door. A watch's minute hand moves more quickly than did mine. Never before that night, had I *felt* the extent of my own powers—of my sagacity. I could scarcely contain my feelings of triumph. To think that there I was, opening the door, little by little, and he not even to dream of my secret deeds or thoughts. I fairly chuckled at the idea; and perhaps he heard me; for he moved on the bed suddenly, as if startled. Now you may think that I drew back—but no. His room was as black as pitch with the thick darkness (for the shutters were close fastened, through fear of robbers), and so I knew that he could not see the opening of the door, and I kept pushing it on steadily, steadily.

5   I had my head in, and was about to open the lantern, when my thumb slipped upon the tin fastening, and the old man sprang up in bed, crying out—"Who's there?"

6   I kept quite still and said nothing. For a whole hour I did not move a muscle, and in the meantime I did not hear him lie down. He was still sitting up in the bed listening;—just as I have done, night after night, hearkening to the death watches in the wall.

7   Presently I heard a slight groan, and I knew it was the groan of mortal terror. It was not a groan of pain or of grief—oh, no!—it was the low stifled sound that arises from the bottom of the soul when overcharged with awe. I knew the sound well. Many a night, just at midnight, when all the world slept, it has welled up from my own bosom, deepening, with its dreadful echo, the terrors that distracted me. I say I knew it well. I knew what the old man felt, and pitied him, although I chuckled at heart. I knew that he had been lying awake ever since the first slight noise, when he had turned in the bed. His fears had been ever since growing upon him. He had been trying to fancy them causeless, but could not. He had been saying to himself—"It is nothing but the wind in the chimney—it is only a mouse crossing the floor," or "it is merely a cricket which has made a single chirp." Yes, he had been trying to comfort himself with these suppositions: but he had

found all in vain. *All in vain;* because Death, in approaching him had stalked with his black shadow before him, and enveloped the victim. And it was the mournful influence of the unperceived shadow that caused him to feel—although he neither saw nor heard —to *feel* the presence of my head within the room.

8   When I had waited a long time, very patiently, without hearing him lie down, I resolved to open a little—a very, very little crevice in the lantern. So I opened it—you cannot imagine how stealthily, stealthily—until, at length a single dim ray, like the thread of the spider, shot from out the crevice and fell full upon the vulture eye.

9   It was open—wide, wide open—and I grew furious as I gazed upon it. I saw it with per-fect distinctness—all a dull blue, with a hideous veil over it that chilled the very marrow in my bones; but I could see nothing else of the old man's face or person: for I had directed the ray, as if by instinct, precisely upon the damned spot.

10   And have I not told you that what you mistake for madness is but over-acuteness of the senses?—now, I say, there came to my ears a low, dull, quick sound, such as a watch makes when enveloped in cotton. I knew *that* sound well, too. It was the beating of the old man's heart. It increased my fury, as the beating of a drum stimulates the soldier into courage.

11   But even yet I refrained and kept still. I scarcely breathed. I held the lantern motion-less. I tried how steadily I could maintain the ray upon the eye. Meantime the hellish tattoo of the heart increased. It grew quicker and quicker, and louder and louder every instant. The old man's terror *must* have been extreme! It grew louder, I say, louder every moment!—do you mark me well? I have told you that I am nervous: so I am. And now at the dead hour of the night, amid the dreadful silence of that old house, so strange a noise as this excited me to uncontrollable terror. Yet, for some minutes longer I refrained and stood still. But the beating grew louder, louder! I thought the heart must burst. And now a new anxiety seized me—the sound would be heard by a neighbour! The old man's hour had come! With a loud yell, I threw open the lantern and leaped into the room. He shrieked once—once only. In an instant I dragged him to the floor, and pulled the heavy bed over him. I then smiled gaily, to find the deed so far done. But, for many minutes, the heart beat on with a muffled sound. This, however, did not vex me; it would not be heard through the wall. At length it ceased. The old man was dead. I removed the bed and examined the corpse. Yes, he was stone, stone dead. I placed my hand upon the heart and held it there many minutes. There was no pulsation. He was stone dead. His eye would trouble me no more.

12   If still you think me mad, you will think so no longer when I describe the wise pre-cautions I took for the concealment of the body. The night waned, and I worked hastily, but in silence. First of all I dismembered the corpse. I cut off the head and the arms and the legs.

13   I then took up three planks from the flooring of the chamber, and deposited all between the scantlings. I then replaced the boards so cleverly, so cunningly, that no human eye—not even *his*—could have detected anything wrong. There was nothing to wash out—no stain of any kind—no blood-spot whatever. I had been too wary for that. A tub had caught all—ha! ha!

14   When I had made an end of these labours, it was four o'clock—still dark as midnight. As the bell sounded the hour, there came a knocking at the street door. I went down to open it with a light heart,—for what had I *now* to fear? There entered three men, who

introduced themselves, with perfect suavity, as officers of the police. A shriek had been heard by a neighbour during the night; suspicion of foul play had been aroused; information had been lodged at the police office, and they (the officers) had been deputed to search the premises.

15   I smiled,—for *what* had I to fear? I bade the gentlemen welcome. The shriek, I said, was my own in a dream. The old man, I mentioned, was absent in the country. I took my visitors all over the house. I bade them search—search *well*. I led them, at length, to *his* chamber. I showed them his treasures, secure, undisturbed. In the enthusiasm of my confidence, I brought chairs into the room, and desired them *here* to rest from their fatigues, while I myself, in the wild audacity of my perfect triumph, placed my own seat upon the very spot beneath which reposed the corpse of the victim.

16   The officers were satisfied. My *manner* had convinced them. I was singularly at ease. They sat, and while I answered cheerily, they chatted of familiar things. But, ere long, I felt myself getting pale and wished them gone. My head ached, and I fancied a ringing in my ears: but still they sat and still chatted. The ringing became more distinct:—it continued and became more distinct: I talked more freely to get rid of the feeling: but it continued and gained definiteness—until, at length, I found that the noise was *not* within my ears.

17   No doubt I now grew *very* pale;—but I talked more fluently, and with a heightened voice. Yet the sound increased—and what could I do? It was *a low, dull, quick sound—much such a sound as a watch makes when enveloped in cotton.* I gasped for breath—and yet the officers heard it not. I talked more quickly—more vehemently; but the noise steadily increased. I arose and argued about trifles, in a high key and with violent gesticulations; but the noise steadily increased. Why *would* they not be gone? I paced the floor to and fro with heavy strides, as if excited to fury by the observations of the men—but the noise steadily increased. Oh God! what *could* I do? I foamed—I raved—I swore! I swung the chair upon which I had been sitting, and grated it upon the boards, but the noise arose over all and continually increased. It grew louder—louder—*louder!* And still the men chatted pleasantly, and smiled. Was it possible they heard not? Almighty God!—no, no! They heard!—they suspected!—they *knew!*—they were making a mockery of my horror!—this I thought, and this I think. But anything was better than this agony! Anything was more tolerable than this derision! I could bear those hypocritical smiles no longer! I felt that I must scream or die! and now—again!—hark! louder! louder! louder! *louder!*

18   "Villains!" I shrieked, "dissemble no more! I admit the deed!—tear up the planks! here, here!—it is the beating of his hideous heart!"

Tales of Mystery and Imagination, pp. 17–21

LOOKING BACK

Summarize and/or paraphrase the most important points you learned from this chapter and determine how they can be put to use in other classes. Be prepared to discuss with your classmates what you have written.

THINK AGAIN!

Identify the central message of each of the signs in the photographs that follow. In other words, what is the overall point of each of them?

1

2

3

4

The Dashing Detective

Remember to follow these steps:

- first, read the narrative and all the questions
- second, examine the picture carefully
- third, answer the questions in the order they appear, and come up with the solution

Have fun!

Bankward Ho!

The body of Charles Townsend III was found lying on the floor near his desk, which is shown. He had been shot and killed, and a gun was lying on the floor next to his body.

The elevator boy told the police that around the time Mr. Townsend was believed to have been killed a flashily dressed brunette left the Townsend apartment. According to the elevator boy, she had been a frequent visitor. Subsequently, the police identified her as Ruth L. Frye, a masseuse.

From these facts and an examination of Townsend's desk and the objects on it, can you decide how he met his death?

Questions

1. Do you think that Townsend was having an affair with Mrs. Frye?   ☐ Yes   ☐ No

2. Was he in financial straits?   ☐ Yes   ☐ No

3. Did he gamble?   ☐ Yes   ☐ No

4. Was he a proud man?   ☐ Yes   ☐ No

5. Had he formerly been wealthy?   ☐ Yes   ☐ No

6. Do you think he robbed a bank?   ☐ Yes   ☐ No

7. Had he been drinking alone?   ☐ Yes   ☐ No

8. Do you think that he had had a falling out with Mrs. Frye?   ☐ Yes   ☐ No

9. How do you think he met his death?
   ☐ Mrs. Frye killed him
   ☐ The elevator boy killed him
   ☐ He committed suicide

Lawrence Treat, *Crime and Puzzlement*, pp. 32–33

Name _____ Date _____

MASTERY TEST 2–1

DIRECTIONS: Write out the main idea for each of the following passages.

1

Many people report that speaking in front of an audience is their number-one fear. Even many experienced and polished speakers have some anxiety about delivering an oral presentation, but they use this nervous energy to their advantage, letting it propel them into working hard on each presentation, preparing well in advance, and rehearsing until they're satisfied with their delivery. They know that once they begin speaking and concentrate on their ideas, enthusiasm will quell anxiety. They know, too, that the symptoms of anxiety are usually imperceptible to listeners, who cannot see or hear a racing heart, upset stomach, cold hands, and worried thoughts. Even speakers who describe themselves as nervous usually appear confident and calm to their audiences.

H. Ramsey Fowler et al., *The Little, Brown Handbook,* 8th ed., pp. 923–924

Main idea: _____

_____

_____

2

The term "technical profession" applies to a broad spectrum of careers in today's changing workplace where technology is making astonishingly rapid advances and boundaries between companies, countries, and continents are blurring and jobs are being redefined. In the past, the term "technical" conjured up an image of a male engineer with his T-square and slide rule, who made his living by his prowess at mathematical calculations. Today the computer has replaced the slide rule, and the technical professionals include an expanding cast of characters: women as well as men, engineers and scientists of all types, computer programmers, MIS professionals, technicians, laboratory personnel, biotechnical workers—anyone whose job entails working with specialized skills and knowledge in the hands-on fields of science, engineering, and technology.

Kristin R. Woolever, *Writing for the Technical Professions,* p. 1

Main idea: _____

_____

_____

3

For most people, choosing a spouse has never been an inexpensive or easy activity. Not long ago, some people were arguing that the institution of marriage was dying. Yet recent statistics show that the opposite is true: The percentage of Americans getting married has increased. Spouse selection is clearly an activity that most people eventually choose to engage in. A variety of considerations are involved. For example, the ease or difficulty of obtaining a divorce may have an effect on how spouses are chosen; so may the factor called love. Is there a rational, economic reason why individuals prefer a marriage in which there is mutual love? To answer this question, you need to know about the nature of economics.

Roger LeRoy Miller, *Economics Today*, p. 3

Main idea: _____

_____

_____

4

John, age 10, accompanies his mother on a shopping trip to some department stores. He notices the numerous sales and discounts across each of the stores. He asks his mother, "Why do stores offer all these discounts? Wouldn't they be better off keeping the same high price?" Mary, age 10, frequently accompanies her dad on grocery shopping trips. She notices how prices change regularly on hundreds of products. She asks, "Why do retailers change the prices on hundreds of items each week? Wouldn't they be better off finding one price for each item and sticking to it?" Indeed, wouldn't everyday high prices make for higher profit, greater efficiency and easier management?

Gerard J. Tellis, *Advertising and Sales Promotion Strategy*, p. 217

Main idea: _____

_____

_____

5

Currently, 25 nations suffer from chronic water shortages. The number of countries affected by such shortages is expected to increase to at least 90 within ten years. International tension over water availability is increasing rapidly. Currently there are 155 rivers and lakes shared by two or more countries. More than 30 are shared by three countries and 20 are shared by dozens of countries. United Nations estimates suggest that there is a real danger of war erupting in at least 10 areas around the world as a direct result of international competition over water resources. Shortages do not stem from the disappearance of water.

The nature of the planet's hydrologic cycle is such that, for the most part, the total supply of freshwater never increases or diminishes. Shortages stem from population growth, misuse and waste, the latter two frequently making water unfit for human consumption.

F. Kurt Cylke Jr., *The Environment,* p. 58

Main idea: _____

_____

_____

6

For a time after World War II, the nation seemed on the verge of a literary outburst comparable to that which followed World War I. A number of excellent novels based on the military experiences of young writers appeared, the most notable being Norman Mailer's *The Naked and the Dead* (1948) and James Jones's *From Here to Eternity* (1951). Unfortunately, a new renaissance did not develop. The most talented younger writers rejected materialist values but preferred to bewail their fate rather than rebel against it. Jack Kerouac, founder of the "beat" (for beatific) school, reveled in the chaotic description of violence, perversion, and madness. At the other extreme, J. D. Salinger, perhaps the most popular writer of the 1950s and the particular favorite of college students—*The Catcher in the Rye* (1951) sold nearly 2 million copies in hardcover and paperback editions—was an impeccable stylist, witty, contemptuous of all pretense; but he too wrote about people entirely wrapped up in themselves.

John A. Garraty, *A Short History of the American Nation,* p. 530

Main idea: _____

_____

_____

7

The environmental movement is a child of the sixties that has stayed its course. Where other manifestations of that decade of protest—pacifism, the counter-culture and the civil rights struggle—have either lost out or lost their way, the green wave shows no sign of abating. The environmental movement has refused to go away and, some would say, refused to grow up, retaining the vigor and intensity but also the impatience and intolerance of an ever-youthful social movement. Alone among the movements of the sixties, it has gained steadily in power, prestige and, what is perhaps most important, public appeal.

Ramachandra Guha, *Environmentalism: A Gobal History,* p. 1

Main idea: _____

_____

_____

8

All relationships involve a degree of risk. However, without the risk of friendships, intimacy, and shared experiences, most of us would not grow, would not be sufficiently stimulated, and life would hold no excitement. Those of us who choose to take risks—who let ourselves feel, love, and express our deepest emotions—are vulnerable to great love as well as great unhappiness. Taking a look at our intimate and non-intimate relationships, components of our sexual identity, our gender roles, and our sexual orientation may help us better understand who we are in our life and our relationships. Ultimately, this understanding will prepare us to make healthful, responsible, and satisfying decisions about our relationships and sexuality.

Rebecca J. Donatelle, *Health: The Basics,* 4th ed., p. 96

Main idea: _____

_____

_____

9

What is the particular problem you have to resolve? Defining the problem is the critical step. The accurate definition of a problem affects all the steps that follow. If a problem is defined inaccurately, every other step in the decision-making process will be based on that incorrect point. A motorist tells a mechanic that her car is running rough. This is a symptom of a problem or problems. The mechanic begins by diagnosing the possible causes of a rough-running engine, checking each possible cause based on the mechanic's experience. The mechanic may find one problem—a faulty spark plug. If this is the problem, changing the plug will result in a smooth-running engine. If not, then a problem still exists. Only a road test will tell for sure. Finding a solution to the problem will be greatly aided by its proper identification. The consequences of not properly defining the problem are wasted time and energy. There is also the possibility of hearing "What, that again! We just solved that problem last month, or at least we thought we did."

Joseph T. Straub and Raymond F. Attner, *Introduction to Business*

Main idea: _____

_____

_____

10

Fertility is a mixed blessing for some women. The ability to participate in the miracle of birth is an overwhelming experience for many. Yet the responsibility to control one's fertility can also seem overwhelming. Today, we not only understand the intimate details of reproduction but also possess technologies designed to control or enhance our fertility. Along with information and technological advance comes choice, and choice goes hand in hand with responsibility. Choosing if and when to have children is one of our greatest responsibilities. A woman and her partner have much to consider before planning or risking a pregnancy. Children, whether planned or unplanned, change people's lives. They require a lifelong personal commitment of love and nurturing.

Rebecca J. Donatelle, *Access to Health,* 7th ed., p. 178

Main idea: _____

_____

_____

11

The departments of anesthesiology and internal medicine usually assume the medical direction of the respiratory therapy department. Historically, many respiratory therapy departments have been organized under the direction of anesthesiologists. This was due in part to the fact that the pulmonary physiologic abnormalities of patients require a basic understanding that practitioners of both fields have in common. In addition, there is similarity in the equipment used in both fields. Another important factor is the presence of the anesthesiologist in the hospital for extended periods of time. Thus, his availability for such day-to-day tasks is considered somewhat ideal.

J. A. Young and Dean Crocker, *Principles and Practice of Respiratory Therapy*

Main idea: _____

_____

_____

12

Many reasons have been advanced to account for nonreporting of crime. Some victims of rape and assault fear the embarrassment of public disclosure and interrogation by the police. Increasingly, evidence reveals that much violence occurs between persons who know each other—spouses, lovers, relatives—but the passions of the moment take on a different character when the victim is asked to testify against a family member. Another reason for nonreporting is that lower socioeconomic groups fear police involvement. In some neighborhoods, residents believe that the arrival of the law for one purpose may result in the discovery of other illicit activities, such as welfare fraud, housing code violations, or the presence of persons on probation or parole. In many of these same places the level of police protection has been minimal in the past, and residents feel that they will get little assistance. Finally, the value of property lost by larceny, robbery, or burglary may not be worth the effort of a police investigation. Many citizens are deterred from reporting a crime by unwillingness to become "involved," go to the station house to fill out papers, perhaps go to court, or to appear at a police lineup. All these aspects of the criminal process may result in lost workdays and in the expense of travel and child care. Even then, the stolen item may go unrecovered. As these examples suggest, multitudes of people feel that it is rational not to report criminal incidents because the costs outweigh the gains.

George F. Cole, *The American System of Criminal Justice*

Main idea: _____

_____

_____

13

Whereas anatomy and its branches deal with structures of the body, physiology deals with *functions* of the body parts—that is, how the body parts work. As you will see in later chapters, physiology cannot be completely separated from anatomy. Thus you will learn about the human body by studying its structures and functions together. Each structure of the body is custom-modeled to carry out a particular set of functions. For instance, bones function as rigid supports for the body because they are constructed of hard minerals. Thus the structure of a part often determines the functions it will perform. In turn, body functions often influence the size, shape, and health of the structures. Glands perform the function of manufacturing chemicals, for example, some of which stimulate bones to build up minerals so they become hard and strong. Other chemicals cause the bones to give up minerals so they do not become too thick or too heavy.

Gerard J. Tortora and Nicholas P. Anagnostakos, *Principles of Anatomy and Physiology*

Main idea: _____

_____

_____

14

Imagine you are standing before an enormous clock on which the hands tick away the years of the earth's history. The clock is set so that 24 hours represent the nearly 5-billion-year history of our planet. On this cosmic scale, a single second equals nearly 60,000 years; a single minute, 3.5 million years. The first life on earth—the simple one-celled organisms that emerged in the oceans some 2.5 to 3.5 billion years ago—do not make their appearance until at least 7 hours on the clock have passed by. The dinosaurs appear at about the twenty-third hour; they walk the planet for less than 42 minutes, then disappear forever. On this 24-hour clock, the first humanlike creatures appear during the last 2 minutes (4.5 million years ago), and *Homo sapiens* emerges in the last 4 seconds, some 250,000 years ago. What we call human history has barely appeared at all. Written languages, cities, and agriculture, which date back some 12,000 years, emerge only in the last quarter second, representing not even a tick.

On a planetary scale, human beings are very recent arrivals indeed, and what we proudly refer to as human history barely registers. Yet, although we arrived only an instant ago, we have certainly made our presence known. Our population has exploded a thousandfold during the last 17 seconds on the planetary clock, from five million people before written language heralded the dawn of human history to nearly six billion people today. Within 40 years, another five billion people will be added to our crowded planet. Human beings already occupy every corner of the earth, crowding out other forms of plant and animal life. Thanks to modern science, technology, and industry, each of us today is capable of consuming a vastly greater amount of the planet's limited resources than were our prehistoric ancestors. The damage to our planet caused by this explosion in the population is one of the major global issues facing the world today.

P. Appelbaum and William J. Chambliss, Sociology, p. 4

Main idea: _____

_____

_____

15

"Among the nations of the earth today America stands for one idea: *Business,*" a popular writer announced in 1921. "Through business, properly conceived, managed and conducted, the human race is finally to be redeemed." Bruce Barton, the head of the largest advertising firm in the country, was the author of one of the most popular nonfiction books of the decade. In *The Man Nobody Knows* (1925), he depicted Christ as "the founder of modern business." He took 12 men from the bottom ranks of society and forged them into a successful organization. "All work is worship; all useful service prayer," Barton argued. If the businessman would just copy Christ, he could become a supersalesman.

Business, especially big business, prospered in the 1920s, and the image of businessmen, enhanced by their important role in World War I, rose further. The government reduced regulation, lowered taxes, and cooperated to aid business expansion at home and abroad. Business and politics, always intertwined, were especially allied during the decade. Wealthy financiers such as Andrew Mellon and Charles Dawes played important roles in formulating both domestic and foreign policy. Even more significant, a new kind of businessman was elected president in 1928. Herbert Hoover, international engineer and efficiency expert, was the very symbol of the modern techniques and practices that many people confidently expected to transform the United States and the world.

Gary B. Nash and Julie Roy Jeffrey, The American People, 5th ed., p. 758

Main idea: _____

_____

_____

16

    A friend of ours attended a conference in which psychologists were discussing the case of a troubled girl. The girl was disruptive and belligerent, and this behavior made her mother angry. The father, who worked long hours, came home tired most nights and didn't want to deal with the situation.

    The first psychologist thought the problem was that the child was temperamentally difficult from birth—a biological matter that could be treated with drugs. The second psychologist thought the problem was that the child had learned to behave inappropriately and aggressively in order to get the attention of her father; this pattern could be treated with behavior therapy. The third psychologist thought the problem was the mother, who was misinterpreting her daughter's behavior as an intentional effort to provoke her; the mother could be helped with cognitive therapy. The fourth psychologist saw the situation as stemming from traditional gender roles within this family's culture (the "absent" father, the "overprotective" mother) and the role of each individual in a family network; all of them would benefit from family therapy. The fifth psychologist thought that the problem was the child's unresolved Oedipal feelings, the mother's displacement of affectional needs for her husband onto the child, and the father's unconscious anxieties about being a father; the child and the parents could be helped with psychodynamic therapy.

Carol Tavris and Carole Wade, Psychology in Perspective, p. 573

Main idea: _____

_____

_____

Name _____   Date _____

MASTERY TEST 2-2

DIRECTIONS: Identify the pattern of organization for each of the following passages.

1

Managing stress is not unlike training to participate in any sport. Those who are healthy are in good physical condition, get proper amounts of rest, and eat a healthy diet typically perform well. Such individuals have the physical endurance and strength to handle the stresses of the event. In much the same way, we need "to be in shape" to handle the demands and challenges of daily living. People who are physically fit become fatigued less easily; they remain alert to cope with the demands placed upon them; their immune systems are stronger; they possess more energy for handling events in their lives; and they are less susceptible to illnesses.

Anthony F. Grasha, Practical Applications of Psychology, p. 413

Pattern of organization: _____

2

The overhead door installation has caused delays and cost overruns for the HOTCELL chamber operation. The door motor terminal strip was not labeled, and the terminals were not consistent. This required significant time for the electrical contractor to troubleshoot and complete accurate terminations. The overhead door installer was not able to provide assistance, since he had no way of knowing how they were factory wired. In addition, at least one motor was factory wired incorrectly, which was corrected by the electrical contractor. The door limit switch and safety edges have had to be periodically reset on frequent failures of operation. The door seals have also been a problem. In addition, the wall panels have had to be returned because of a lack of fit at the joints.

Kristin R. Woolever, Writing for the Technical Professions, p. 316

Pattern of organization: _____

3

1   Although it was easy to romanticize the West, that region lent itself better to the realistic approach. Almost of necessity, novelists writing about the West described coarse characters from the lower levels of society, and dealt with crime and violence. It would have

been difficult indeed to write a genteel romance about a mining camp. The outstanding figure of western literature, the first great American realist, was Mark Twain.

2   Twain, whose real name was Samuel L. Clemens, was born in 1835. He grew up in Hannibal, Missouri, on the banks of the Mississippi. After having mastered the printer's trade and worked as a riverboat pilot, he went west to Nevada in 1861. Soon he was publishing humorous stories about the local life under the *nom de plume* Mark Twain. In 1865, while working in California, he wrote "The Celebrated Jumping Frog of Calaveras County," a story that brought him national recognition. A tour of Europe and the Holy Land in 1867–1868 led to the writing of *The Innocents Abroad* (1869), which made him famous.

John A. Garraty, *A Short History of the American Nation*, p. 342

Pattern of organization: _____

4

Rebates are a guarantee by firms to reimburse consumers directly for the purchase of a product, subject to certain conditions. Technically, the term has the same meaning as **refund,** except that *rebate* is used for durables and *refund* for nondurables. The typical conditions for a rebate are the mailing in of (1) the refund voucher, (2) a proof of purchase from the product container or package and (3) the sales receipt. The rebate is similar to the coupon. Thus much of our discussion about coupons would apply to rebates. However, rebates differ from coupons in one important way: they require much greater effort to redeem.

Gerard F. Tellis, *Advertising and Sales Promotion Strategy*, p. 282

Pattern of organization: _____

5

Economics is a social science that employs the same kinds of methods used in other sciences, such as biology, physics, and chemistry. Like these other sciences, economics uses models, or theories. Economic **models,** or **theories,** are simplified representations of the real world that we use to help us understand, explain, and predict economic phenomena in the real world. There are, of course, differences between sciences. The social sciences—especially economics—make little use of laboratory methods in which changes in variables can be explained under controlled conditions. Rather, social scientists, and especially economists, usually have to examine what has already happened in the real world in order to test their models, or theories.

Roger LeRoy Miller, *Economics Today,* p. 9

Pattern of organization: _____

6

1   The public's attention was often diverted from the budgetary and political wranglings by a story that seemed scripted for a television melodrama—the murder trail of O. J. Simpson, an African American who had been a football star for the University of Southern California and the Buffalo Bills. On retiring from football, he became an instant celebrity who exploited his good looks and broad, high-wattage simile to make commercials and movies.

2   On June 12, 1994, his estranged wife, Nicole Brown Simpson, who was white, and another man were found stabbed to death near the entry of her condominium in Brentwood, Los Angeles. Five days later, as police were about to arrest Simpson for her murder, he fled south on Freeway Five in a Ford Bronco driven by a former teammate. The police set off in pursuit. A bizarre, low-speed highway chase ensued, with Simpson's driver talking to police on a cell-phone ("Just back off. He's still alive. He's got a gun to his head"). Seven news helicopters swooped in to film the spectacle, crowds gathered on overpasses to witness it ("Go, O. J., Go!"), and millions watched it live on TV. The chase ended quietly and Simpson was charged with murder.

3   Several weeks later Simpson pleaded "absolutely, 100 percent not guilty." His trial lasted nine riveting months. The victims' blood was found in his car and on his clothing. But defense lawyers discovered that Mark Fuhrman, a detective at the crime scene, had previously made inflammatory remarks about blacks; Simpson's lawyers accused Fuhrman of planting the evidence. After deliberating only four hours, the jury acquitted Simpson. A year later, however, he lost the judgment in civil proceedings on the "wrongful deaths" of the victims and was forced to pay substantial sums to their families.

4   The media attention to the case—the networks devoted twice as much air time to the Simpson case as to the 1994 political campaign—reflected both its dramatic character and the cultural divide between white and black Americans. To many whites, Simpson was yet another violent black male, while to many African Americans, he was another innocent black abused by the prejudiced criminal justice system. According to polls, 85 percent of blacks agreed with the not guilty verdict of the first Simpson trial, white only 34 percent of whites did. For the most part, neither race could understand the other's reasoning.

John A. Garraty and Mark C. Carnes, *The American Nation*, pp. 933–934

Pattern of organization: _____

7

1   Economics provides powerful tools to analyze the real world. The large issues, such as inflation, unemployment, the business cycle, economic growth, and balance of international payments, attract the most attention. They influence presidential elections, when we buy new cars and homes, whether we are laid off from jobs, and whether we view the future with optimism or pessimism. The study of the economy in the large is called **macroeconomics.** Macroeconomics treats the economy as a whole. It studies the deter-

minants of total output and its growth, total employment and unemployment, and the general movement in prices.

2   Economists study the small issues as well—how individual businesses behave in different competitive environments; how we choose to use our time; how prices of individual commodities are determined; whether a farmer plants wheat or rye. Although these routine decisions seemingly have a less dramatic effect, they determine the way we live our daily lives. The small issues determine how our television sets and automobiles are built; the prices we pay for cable television; whether soft drinks are sweetened with sugar or corn syrup; whether shoe leather is cut by hand or lasers; and whether the prices of airline tickets rise or fall. This study of the economy in the small is called **microeconomics**. Microeconomics looks at the behavior of the economy's small parts—business firms and households.

Paul R. Gregory, Essentials of Economics, p. 3

Pattern of organization: _____

8

1   Humans are strongly attracted to the seashore. Travel brochures show scenic, empty sandy beaches and pristine shore vegetation. Rarely do they show the real picture: crowded beaches backed by strands of hotels, boardwalks, and shops. Recreational and commercial development of seashores, along with intensive seasonal human use, has had a long-term impact on intertidal ecosystems, the severity of which will increase as human populations grow.

2   This use has had serious effects on intertidal wildlife, especially that of sandy shores. Beach-nesting birds such as the piping plover *(Charadrius melodus)* and the least tern *(Sterna antillarum)* are so disturbed by bathers and dune buggies that both species are in danger of extinction. Other terns and shore birds are subjected to competition for nest sites and to egg predation by rapidly growing populations of large gulls that are highly tolerant of humans and thrive on human garbage. Sea turtles and the horseshoe crab *(Limulus polyphemus)*, dependent on sandy beaches for nesting sites, find themselves evicted and are declining rapidly for that reason.

3   Habitat destruction is only one aspect of human impact on intertidal ecosystems. Another is pollution. Seashore cottages use septic tanks that drain into sandy soil; commercial developments drain all sorts of wastes into the ground; and coastal cities and small towns pour raw sewage into shallow waters off the coast.

4   Each incoming tide brings into the beaches feces-contaminated water that makes beaches unhealthy for humans and wildlife alike. Tides also carry in old fishing lines, plastic debris and other wastes, and blobs of oil, all hazardous to humans and wildlife.

Robert Leo Smith and Thomas M. Smith, Elements of Ecology, p. 506

Pattern of organization: _____

9

In the real world, not everyone gains from international trade, but the law of comparative advantage demonstrates that the average person gains. To say that the average person gains from trade is to say that the people who gain from international trade benefit by a greater dollar amount than the dollar costs imposed on those who lose. For example, prohibiting international trade in automobiles would impose costs on many Americans. First, consumers would pay higher prices for American cars because they could not purchase German and Japanese substitutes. Second, as we shall see, the reduced volume of imports would lead to fewer exports, so American farmers and other export-oriented businesses would lose. The costs imposed on these invisible Americans would be greater than the benefits to the American automobile industry since, according to the law of comparative advantage, restricting international trade reduces the overall efficiency of the economy.

Paul R. Gregory, *Essentials of Economics,* p. 237

Pattern of organization: _____

10

1   **Sexually transmitted infections (STIs)** have been with us since our earliest recorded days on earth. In spite of our best efforts to eradicate them, prevent them, and control their spread, they continue to increase, affecting millions more Americans than previously thought, according to the first new STI estimate in a decade. Today, there are more than 20 known types of STIs. Once referred to as "venereal diseases" and then "sexually transmitted diseases," the most current terminology is believed to be broader in scope and more reflective of the number and types of these communicable diseases. More virulent strains and more antibiotic-resistant forms spell trouble for at-risk populartions in the days ahead.

2   Several reasons have been proposed to explain the present high rates of STIs. The first relates to the moral and social stigma associated with these infections. Shame and embarrassment often keep infected people from seeking treatment. Unfortunately, these people usually continue to be sexually active, thereby infecting unsuspecting partners. People who are uncomfortable discussing sexual issues may also be less likely to use and/or ask their partners to use condoms as a means of protection against STIs and/or pregnancy.

3   Another reason proposed for the STI epidemic is our casual attitude about sex. Bombarded by media hype that glamorizes easy sex, many people take sexual partners without considering the consequences. Others are pressured into sexual relationships they don't really want. Generally, the more sexual partners a person has, the greater the risk for contracting an STI.

4   Ignorance about the infections themselves and an inability to recognize actual symptoms or to acknowledge that a person may be asymptomatic yet still have the infection are also factors behind the STI epidemic.

Rebecca, J. Donatelle, *Health: The Basics,* 4th ed., pp. 328–329

Pattern of organization: _____

Name _____   Date _____

MASTERY TEST 2-3

DIRECTIONS: Write out the central message for each of the following selections.

1
Life in a Nursing Home

1   *Life in a nursing home is almost never the idyll pictured in brochures. Inside, residents are sometimes neglected by the staff, often abandoned by family, and almost always diminished physically and mentally by advancing age. Men and women in wheelchairs are lined up in day rooms and hallways, dozing in and out of reality; others are curled up in their beds, tubes dangling from their bodies. Diminished though they may be, residents still cling to their dignity.*

2   "Don't tie me in, please," a lady named Anna cries out. She sees an aide approach with a tan waist belt that will bind her to the wheelchair. "I don't care if I fall out. Don't tie me up. That's terrible." Her bony fingers reach out to push away the hated restraint. "I'm not going to be tied." Her hands tremble as she grasps the hand rail along the corridor. "No, that's cruel. Don't tie me, don't tie me. Thoughtless. That's what they are," she shouts, her voice firm and determined. Anna is lucky that day. A visitor questions a nurse at the Beverly Hills Nursing Center, in Royal Oak, Mich. Is there a doctor's order for the restraint, as there must be? The nurse backs off. For a while, Anna is free.

3   Helga, dressed in pink with a bandage on her leg, sobs uncontrollably. She misses Roy, her special friend. She doesn't remember Roy has just come to see her. The admissions director, whose name is Nancy, stops a tour to reassure her. Roy has been here and will come again. "I know you miss him," Nancy says gently. Down the hall, Theresa, another resident, misses Archie, her husband of many years. Archie and Theresa both lived at the Moroun Nursing Home, on the east side of Detroit—Theresa on one floor for residents with dementia and Archie on another. Archie died a week ago, and Theresa, 87, is working through her initial grief. She is better dressed than most nursing-home residents and her hair is carefully set. Theresa cries and caresses Archie's picture. She says she had five sons—or was it four? The admissions director again stops, looks at the picture, and listens. "He was a good husband," Theresa says. "Part of loving is letting go," Nancy tells her.

4   Boris, in a purple jogging suit with no place to run, struggles to stand up. Catheter tubes tangle around his legs. He tries to walk, but a waist belt traps him in his wheelchair. His fingers tug at the belt. He tries to loosen it. Unable to free himself, he calls out to the nurse working at the station a few feet in front of him. "What is it, Boris?" she snaps. "Don't get excited. Your daughter's coming." Boris yanks at the belt again, but it is stubborn. He remains tethered to his chair. "You can't take it off," the nurse tells him. "It's to keep you safe." She makes no effort to release Boris even for a moment, or

hold his hand, or give him a hug, or otherwise comfort him in his isolated world at the Hillhaven nursing facility, in San Francisco, Calif.

Consumer Reports, August 1995, p. 521

Central message: _____

_____

_____

2
The Cost of Being Different:
Effects of Lesbian and Gay Prejudices

JODY:

1   Jody is a junior in the honors program, majoring in women's studies. She is energetic, outgoing, affectionate, and an animated speaker. She has very short hair and wears no make up. She says that people attribute her appearance to her feminism and do not recognize her lesbian identity until told.

2   In class, she feels very comfortable talking about lesbian issues as well as the issues facing other oppressed groups. She is aware that there is some negative reaction to her. Sometimes she sees other students rolling their eyes and hissing while she talks; other times, she feels that instructors are trying to placate her and move on to safer topics very hastily. She must also bear hearing teachers say things that are false such as, "There were no gay or lesbian people in colonial times. We can't dwell on irrelevant issues."

3   Her activism sometimes brings her close to burnout. She gets tired of answering questions such as, "In lesbian couples, who is the man and who is the woman?" The burden of educating others at times seems unreasonable to her. Jody also chooses her courses carefully, based on advice she hears within her community on which instructors are receptive.

GREGG:

4   Gregg is a sophomore with a major in mechanical engineering. He comes across as a serious, intelligent, and likeable college student. Although his friends and family now know of his identity, he is still reluctant to come out publicly, fearing violence or verbal attacks that he does not feel strong enough to handle. Gregg views his mental agony as "hellish," and he has difficulty concentrating on his coursework. He once told a friend, "I'm one step short of a nervous breakdown." The worst part was that he felt so alone.

5   He hadn't anticipated the overt and subtle ways fellow students and teachers show their disapproval of gay men. When he hears students snickering about "faggots" and "fruitcakes," he cringes. When teachers tolerate homophobic remarks by ignoring them, he feels furious but not empowered to take the initiative. He is hoping that one day he will feel strong enough to confront such negative stereotypes and hatreds. For now, he is silent. He is reluctant to write about gay topics, fearing there will be grade retaliation or that his papers will be considered too "personal" rather than scholarly. Gregg also recognizes

he is majoring in a field where there is discrimination against gay men, so he has to be very cautious about his identity—something he will have to do for the rest of his life.

Anthony F. Grasha, *Practical Applications of Psychology*, p. 307

Central message: _____

_____

_____

3

Kipling and I

Jesús Colón

1   Sometimes I pass Debevoise Place at the corner of Willoughby Street...I look at the old wooden house, gray and ancient, the house where I used to live some forty years ago...

2   My room was on the second floor at the corner. On hot summer nights I would sit at the window reading by the electric light from the street lamp which was almost at a level with the windowsill.

3   It was nice to come home late during the winter, look for some scrap of old newspaper, some bits of wood and a few chunks of coal, and start a sparkling fire in the chunky fourlegged coal stove. I would be rewarded with an intimate warmth as little by little the pigmy stove became alive puffing out its sides, hot and red, like the crimson cheeks of a Santa Claus.

4   My few books were in a soap box nailed to the wall. But my most prized possession in those days was a poem I had bought in a five-and-ten-cent store on Fulton Street. (I wonder what has become of these poems, maxims and sayings of wise men that they used to sell at the five-and-ten-cent stores?) The poem was printed on gold paper and mounted in a gilded frame ready to be hung in a conspicuous place in the house. I bought one of those fancy silken picture cords finishing in a rosette to match the color of the frame.

5   I was seventeen. This poem to me then seemed to summarize, in one poetical nutshell, the wisdom of all the sages that ever lived. It was what I was looking for, something to guide myself by, a way of life, a compendium of the wise, the true and the beautiful. All I had to do was to live according to the counsel of the poem and follow its instructions and I would be a perfect man—the useful, the good, the true human being. I was very happy that day, forty years ago.

6   The poem had to have the most prominent place in the room. Where could I hang it? I decided that the best place for the poem was on the wall right by the entrance to the room. No one coming in and out would miss it. Perhaps someone would be interested enough to read it and drink the profound waters of its message...

7   Every morning as I prepared to leave, I stood in front of the poem and read it over and over again, sometimes half a dozen times. I let the sonorous music of the verse carry me away. I brought with me a handwritten copy as I stepped out every morning looking for work, repeating verses and stanzas from memory until the whole poem came to be part

of me. Other days my lips kept repeating a single verse of the poem at intervals through-out the day.

8   In the subways I loved to compete with the shrill noises of the many wheels below by chanting the lines of the poem. People stared at me moving my lips as though I were in a trance. I looked back with pity. They were not so fortunate as I who had as a guide to direct my life a great poem to make me wise, useful and happy.

9   And I chanted:
If you can keep your head when all about you
Are losing theirs and blaming it on you...
If you can wait and not be tired by waiting,
Or being lied about, don't deal in lies,
Or being hated don't give way to hating...
If you can make one heap of all your winnings;
And risk it on one turn of pitch-and-toss,
And lose, and start again at your beginnings...

10   "If—," by Kipling, was the poem. At seventeen, my evening prayer and my first morn-ing thought. I repeated it every day with the resolution to live up to the very last line of that poem.

11   I would visit the government employment office on Jay Street. The conversations among the Puerto Ricans on the large wooden benches in the employment office were always on the same subject. How to find a decent place to live. How they would not rent to Negroes or Puerto Ricans. How Negroes and Puerto Ricans were given the pink slips first at work.

12   From the employment office I would call door to door at the piers, factories and storage houses in the streets under the Brooklyn and Manhattan bridges. "Sorry, noth-ing today." It seemed to me that that "today" was a continuation and combination of all the yesterdays, todays and tomorrows.

13   From the factories I would go to the restaurants, looking for a job as a porter or dishwasher. At least I would eat and be warm in a kitchen.

14   "Sorry"..."Sorry"...

15   Sometimes I was hired at ten dollars a week, ten hours a day including Sundays and holidays. One day off during the week. My work was that of three men: dishwasher, porter, busboy. And to clear the sidewalk of snow and slush "when you have nothing else to do." I was to be appropriately humble and grateful not only to the owner but to every-body else in the place.

16   If I rebelled at insults or at a pointed innuendo or just the inhuman amount of work, I was unceremoniously thrown out and told to come "next week for your pay." "Next week" meant weeks of calling for the paltry dollars owed me. The owners relished this "next week."

17   I clung to my poem as to a faith. Like a potent amulet, my precious poem was clenched in the fist of my right hand inside my secondhand overcoat. Again and again I declaimed aloud a few precious lines when discouragement and disillusionment threatened to over-whelm me.

If you can force your heart and nerve and sinew
To serve your turn long after they are gone...

18   The weeks of unemployment and hard knocks turned into months. I continued to find two or three days of work here and there. And I continued to be thrown out when I rebelled at the ill treatment, overwork and insults. I kept pounding the streets looking for a place where they would treat me half decently, where my devotion to work and faith in Kipling's poem would be appreciated. I remember the worn-out shoes I bought in a secondhand store on Myrtle Avenue at the corner of Adams Street. The round holes in the soles that I tried to cover with pieces of carton were no match for the frigid knives of the unrelenting snow.

19   One night I returned late after a long day of looking for work. I was hungry. My room was dark and cold. I wanted to warm my numb body. I lit a match and began looking for some scraps of wood and a piece of paper to start a fire. I searched all over the floor. No wood, no paper. As I stood up, the glimmering flicker of the dying match was reflected in the glass surface of the framed poem. I unhooked the poem from the wall. I reflected for a minute, a minute that felt like an eternity. I took the frame apart, placing the square glass upon the small table. I tore the gold paper on which the poem was printed, threw its pieces inside the stove and, placing the small bits of wood from the frame on top of the paper, I lit it, adding soft and hard coal as the fire began to gain strength and brightness.

20   I watched how the lines of the poem withered into ashes inside the small stove.

A Puerto Rican In New York and Other Sketches, 1982 International Publishers Co., Inc.

Central message: _____

_____

_____

4
Letter to Olivia

Mel Allen

1   Dear Olivia,

2   I am writing this letter to you on November 27, 1999, your father's 31st birthday. I want to tell you about your father, Wil Smith, and about your time together at Bowdoin College. One day you will probably ask him about these years, when he was a single dad with a young daughter, struggling to stay in school, compete in a tough Division III basketball program, and provide a home for you. Everyone knows how modest your father is, so I suspect he'll leave out the details.

3   You are a bouncy, pretty little four-year-old girl with braided pigtails and happy brown eyes. During the games you roam through the stands as the free-spirited, trusting child you are. The students are drawn to you as if by magnet, and it must seem as if the whole world knows your name. Wil says he plays with his head on a swivel, always looking for you during breaks in the action.

4   You live together in a two-bedroom apartment a few blocks from campus. Both of you eat in the student cafeteria. Most nights you are in bed by nine; Wil turns in soon after so he can get up to study, often as early as 5 a.m.

5   You have always come first, but he is also co-captain of the men's basketball team, a four-year starter on a nationally ranked team at 31—an age when other men are playing weekly pickup games at the YMCA. He led Bowdoin in assists and steals, and he made the conference All-Defensive team.

6   Nearly half the Bowdoin students arrive from private schools. Your father came from the Navy, a decade after graduating from a public high school. His first year at college he had to work twice as hard to keep up with the others.

7   He is a black student at a college and in a state with few people of color, and he has made it his business to make life better for others who come after him. "I try to educate people about the people I come from," he says.

8   Wil's story begins in Jacksonville, Fla., with a woman you never knew, your grandmother Mildred. "My mother was the most incredible person I ever met," Wil says. "I was the last of ten children she raised, pretty much on her own, and she always put us first. She worked every day and still found time to coach boys' and girls' baseball and basketball."

9   Everyone knew the Smith boys because they were athletes. At five-foot-ten, Wil was the smallest of all the boys, but he was fast and tough, and nobody worked harder. He wanted to play on his mother's teams, but she sent her sons to play for coaches who knew the sport better than she did. Wil was an all-star in football, basketball and baseball. Mildred learned to drive at age 49 just so she could get to the games; she never missed one.

10   When she died of cancer on November 27, 1983, Wil's 15th birthday, she took much of Wil's passion for sports with her. "My mother was my biggest fan," he says. "When she passed away, I asked myself, 'Why am I still playing?' A lot of my joy in sports came from my mother's look."

11   Wil struggled to cope. He still played, but he was drifting. "I never reached the heights everyone thought I would," Wil says. When colleges sent recruiting letters, he didn't bother to respond.

12   Reluctantly Wil attended Florida A&M in Tallahassee for a year and a half. He played a season of baseball, but his heart wasn't in it. Wil left school in 1988, and started spending time with a crowd that was dealing drugs and fighting.

13   "I was hanging out at a store with my friends," Wil says, "and ESPN came on. It was a baseball highlight. One guy said, 'Wil, man, you don't belong here. You're different. I expected to see you up there, playing ball on TV.' I always remember that. I witnessed heavy stuff, but there's no way to get away from good roots."

14   Three years after graduating from high school, Wil enlisted in the Navy. He was trained to be an aviation electronics technician. In June 1991 his orders sent him to the Naval Air Station in Brunswick, Maine. In his spare time he volunteered as a football coach for middle-school students.

15   "I had sixty white kids on my team," Wil says. "Most had never been in contact with a black man. I had no problem with the kids, but the parents said I was too intense. I told them that every day I'd ask the kids, 'Anybody hurt? Anybody not having fun?' The

kids always said they were fine. I told the parents, 'As long as your kids are with me, they're mine for three hours a day.'"

16   By the season's end, some of those same parents told Wil their kids were slipping in their work. As someone they looked up to, would he talk with them? Soon he became a community fixture, coaching basketball and football.

17   His teams played hard, and they won. In the summer of 1995, while coaching at a basketball camp, Wil's ability and character caught the eye of Tim Gilbride, the men's basketball coach at Bowdoin. Gilbride asked Wil if he'd considered applying to Bowdoin College.

18   Wil was at a crossroads. He'd served seven years in the Navy and was due to re-enlist. But the Navy meant six months overseas every year, and you, Olivia, had been born a couple of months before. He'd met your mother in Portland after returning from overseas duty. Their relationship ended and you lived with your mom, but Wil came for you every Thursday and kept you until Monday.

19   Wil applied to Bowdoin while on a six-month assignment in Sicily. He decided he would not leave you again for that length of time. His last day of active duty, April 25, 1996, was also the day your mother gave him full custody of you, then 11 months old.

20   Though Wil had been accepted to Bowdoin, he didn't know the questions to ask—questions that so many parents of college students take for granted. He didn't know how to apply for student aid or room and board. Wil started school in September 1996. You were 16 months old, and he had no choice but to bring you to class. When you were sick, he wouldn't go. The money he'd saved from the Navy went faster than he could have imagined. At times he didn't eat for three days so he'd have enough food to feed you.

21   "I lost seventeen pounds," Wil said. "I couldn't sleep. I got an F in a course that required you to read about twenty books. I didn't have money for books; I didn't know about books being on reserve in the library."

22   What he told the dean was simply, "Things are hard for me right now." The dean called Betty Trout-Kelly, who oversees Bowdoin's multicultural programs and affirmative action.

23   "I know you feel you shouldn't need this support," Trout-Kelly told Wil, "but if you don't take our help, you won't make it."

24   For the first time, Wil told her about his struggles. Later, after meeting with school officials, Trout-Kelly notified Wil that an anonymous donor would give nearly $25,000 for Olivia's day care and after-school care. Wil would be able to move to campus housing and eat regularly with his daughter. "Thank you," Wil told her. "I'll prove myself worthy."

25   In four years, Olivia, your father has become as well known off-campus as on. A sociology major, he puts what he learns in the classroom to work. He is the community adviser for civil rights teams at Brunswick and Mount Ararat high schools. He travels around the state of Maine giving talks to educators about the problems and challenges of diversity. "I feel like I have an obligation to every young person I come in contact with," Wil says. During the summer he is a counselor at Seeds of Peace International Camp in Otisfield, Maine, where teenagers from regions of conflict around the world live together.

26   None of this has come easily, Olivia. You have asthma, and when you're sick, he has trouble trusting anybody else with your care. Last season you had a fever when the team had a weekend road trip. It took all of Coach Gilbride's skills of persuasion, and his saying his wife had raised three kids and would care for you, before Wil agreed to go.

27   During spring semester of his junior year, Wil was called to active duty—he's still in the Navy reserves—during the Balkan conflict. Before leaving, he scrambled to get you to your aunt in Florida, finished work for two courses, and took incompletes in the rest. He came back before summer, picked you up, finished some papers, and got ready for his final year as a student-athlete.

28   Wil is torn about what to do in the future. Whatever he decides will be in large part because of you, Olivia, because you are more important to him than anything in the world. "I know people look at it as a disadvantage having Olivia," Wil says. "I see it as an advantage. If it was just me, I'd never have made it. There've been nights I've been so tired, I've been ready to quit on papers. But then I look in on Olivia sleeping, and I go back to my paper."

29   Once when you were two, he was walking you to school, holding your hand. "My mind was in turmoil," he says. "I had midterms, my car had broken down and we had no money. Olivia was talking about leaves and trees. I didn't even realize she had let go of my hand. I had taken ten steps without her, then suddenly turned. 'Dad,' she said, 'talk to me!' She was saying, in her own way, 'None of this other stuff matters.'

30   "All she cared about is that we were there. She was glad the car had broken down; that meant we could walk to school together. She put life in perspective for me."

31   Olivia, I hope when you're older you'll read this and understand what an extraordinary man your father is.

32   *Mel Allen*

33   On May 27, 2000, more than 400 students graduated from Bowdoin College. At the ceremony on the campus quadrangle, when Bowdoin president Robert H. Edwards read off the names "Wil and Olivia Smith," the crowd cheered and gave a standing ovation.

34   Wil, now 33, works as Bowdoin's coordinator of Multicultural Student Programs.

35   Olivia, five years old, is in kindergarten. She accompanies Wil when he does volunteer work. "She is right there along for the ride," Wil says. "I can't imagine a life without her."

Bowdoin Magazine, Winter 2000

Central message: _____

_____

_____

Name _____   Date _____

DIRECTIONS: Underline or highlight the most important information in each of the passages that follow and then summarize and/or paraphrase them in your notebook.

1
Conflict Interaction

1   As do most things in life, conflict offers a mixture of the good, the bad, and the uncertain. On the positive side, conflicts allow us to air important issues, they produce new and creative ideas, they release built-up tension. Handled properly, conflicts can strengthen relationships; they may lead groups and organizations to re-evaluate and clarify goals and missions; and they can also initiate social change to eliminate inequities and injustice. These advantages suggest that conflict is normal and healthy, and they underscore the importance of understanding and handling conflict properly.

2   But, perhaps more familiar is the negative side of conflict. Heated exchanges spiral out of control, resulting in frustration, tension, hard feelings, and, ultimately, more conflict. Low-grade family conflicts, prosecuted through criticism, arguments, nagging, and verbal abuse, not only distance parents from children and husbands from wives, but also lower self-esteem and create problems that may follow people through their entire lives. Additionally, conflicts are sometimes violent, not only between strangers, but also in the workplace and within the family. Sometimes **not** being able to start a conflict is the source of frustration. If one friend persistently denies that a problem exists or changes the subject when it comes up, the other cannot discuss the things that are bothering her, and the friendship suffers. The various negative experiences we all have with conflict are reinforced in the media, where it often seems that the only effective way to solve problems is to shoot somebody.

3   Conflicts also bring uncertainty. As we will see, the great "unpredictables" in life often center around how interactions will go. Conversations, meetings, conflicts all have in common the fact that they may suddenly turn in unexpected directions. Indeed, the uncertainties that arise in conflicts often cause them to turn in negative directions.

Joseph P. Folger et al., *Working Through Conflict*, p. 1

2
The Mystery of the Semi-Detached

Edith Nesbit

1   He was waiting for her; he had been waiting an hour and a half in a dusty suburban lane, with a row of big elms on one side and some eligible building sites on the other— and far away to the south-west the twinkling yellow lights of the Crystal Palace. It was not quite like a country lane, for it had a pavement and lamp-posts, but it was not a

bad place for a meeting all the same; and farther up, towards the cemetery, it was really quite rural, and almost pretty, especially in twilight. But twilight had long deepened into night, and still he waited. He loved her, and he was engaged to be married to her, with the complete disapproval of every reasonable person who had been consulted. And this half-clandestine meeting was tonight to take the place of the grudgingly sanctioned weekly interview—because a certain rich uncle was visiting at her house, and her mother was not the woman to acknowledge to a moneyed uncle, who might "go off" any day, a match so deeply ineligible as hers with him.

2   So he waited for her, and the chill of an unusually severe May evening entered into his bones.

3   The policeman passed him with but a surly response to his "Good night." The bicyclists went by him like grey ghosts with fog-horns; and it was nearly ten o'clock, and she had not come.

4   He shrugged his shoulders and turned towards his lodgings. His road led him by her house—desirable, commodious, semi-detached—and he walked slowly as he neared it. She might, even now, be coming out. But she was not. There was no sign of movement about the house, no sign of life, no lights even in the windows. And her people were not early people.

5   He paused by the gate, wondering.

6   Then he noticed that the front door was open—wide open—and the street lamp shone a little way into the dark hall. There was something about all this that did not please him—that scared him a little, indeed. The house had a gloomy and deserted air. It was obviously impossible that it harboured a rich uncle. The old man must have left early. In which case—

7   He walked up the path of patent-glazed tiles, and listened. No sign of life. He passed into the hall. There was no light anywhere. Where was everybody, and why was the front door open? There was no one in the drawing-room, the dining-room and the study (nine feet by seven) were equally blank. Every one was out, evidently. But the unpleasant sense that he was, perhaps, not the first casual visitor to walk through that open door impelled him to look through the house before he went away and closed it after him. So he went upstairs, and at the door of the first bedroom he came to he struck a wax match, as he had done in the sitting-rooms. Even as he did so he felt that he was not alone. And he was prepared to see *something;* but for what he saw he was not prepared. For what he saw lay on the bed, in a white loose gown—and it was his sweetheart, and its throat was cut from ear to ear. He doesn't know what happened then, nor how he got downstairs and into the street; but he got out somehow, and the policeman found him in a fit, under the lamp-post at the corner of the street. He couldn't speak when they picked him up, and he passed the night in the police-cells, because the policeman had seen plenty of drunken men before, but never one in a fit.

8   The next morning he was better, though still very white and shaky. But the tale he told the magistrate was convincing, and they sent a couple of constables with him to her house.

9   There was no crowd about it as he had fancied there would be, and the blinds were not down.

10   As he stood, dazed, in front of the door, it opened, and she came out.

11   He held on to the door-post for support.

12   "*She's* all right, you see," said the constable, who had found him under the lamp. "I told you you was drunk, but you *would* know best—"

13   When he was alone with her he told her—not all—for that would not bear telling—but how he had come into the commodious semi-detached, and how he had found the door open and the lights out, and that he had been into that long back room facing the stairs, and had seen something—in even trying to hint at which he turned sick and broke down and had to have brandy given him.

14   "But, my dearest," she said, "I dare say the house was dark, for we were all at the Crystal Palace with my uncle, and no doubt the door was open, for the maids *will* run out if they're left. But you could not have been in that room, because I locked it when I came away, and the key was in my pocket. I dressed in a hurry and I left all my odds and ends lying about."

15   "I know," he said; "I saw a green scarf on a chair, and some long brown gloves, and a lot of hairpins and ribbons, and a prayer-book, and a lace handkerchief on the dressing-table. Why, I even noticed the almanac on the mantelpiece—October 21. At least it couldn't be that, because this is May. And yet it was. Your almanac is at October 21, isn't it?"

16   "No, of course it isn't," she said, smiling rather anxiously; "but all the other things were just as you say. You must have had a dream, or a vision, or something."

17   He was a very ordinary, commonplace, City young man, and he didn't believe in visions, but he never rested day or night till he got his sweetheart and her mother away from that commodious semi-detached, and settled them in a quite distant suburb. In the course of the removal he incidentally married her, and the mother went on living with them.

18   His nerves must have been a good bit shaken, because he was very queer for a long time, and was always inquiring if any one had taken the desirable semi-detached; and when an old stockbroker with a family took it, he went the length of calling on the old gentleman and imploring him by all that he held dear, not to live in that fatal house.

19   "Why?" said the stockbroker, not unnaturally.

20   And then he got so vague and confused, between trying to tell why and trying not to tell why, that the stockbroker showed him out, and thanked his God he was not such a fool as to allow a lunatic to stand in the way of his taking that really remarkably cheap and desirable semi-detached residence.

21   Now the curious and quite inexplicable part of this story is that when she came down to breakfast on the morning of the 22nd of October she found him looking like death, with the morning paper in his hand. He caught hers—he couldn't speak, and pointed to the paper. And there she read that on the night of the 21st a young lady, the stockbroker's daughter, had been found, with her throat cut from ear to ear, on the bed in the long back bedroom facing the stairs of that desirable semi-detached.

A Treasury of Victorian Ghost Stories, pp. 266–268

CHAPTER 3
GETTING THE MOST OUT OF YOUR TEXTBOOKS: A REVIEW

CHAPTER OUTLINE

Overviewing Your Textbooks

Previewing Textbook Chapters

Reading a Textbook Chapter Critically:
    Questions and Answers

THINK ABOUT IT!

Look carefully at the signs in the photographs. Why are they examples of clever advertising strategies? Discuss your answers with your classmates.

1

2

3

CHAPTER OUTCOMES

After completing Chapter 3, you should be able to:

- ■ Overview a textbook
- ■ Preview a textbook chapter
- ■ Read a textbook chapter critically by developing questions from all chapter headings and then answering them

OVERVIEWING YOUR TEXTBOOKS

If you were to move to a new town, one of your chief concerns would be getting to know your way around as quickly and efficiently as possible. You would want to become familiar with your neighborhood in order to locate the nearest bank, the best store for food shopping, the movie theaters, the hospital, the post office, and any other establishments that are important or helpful to you. By accomplishing this task at the very beginning, you would feel more secure and comfortable with your new surroundings, and it would save you time by enabling you to get places faster.

As a college student, at the beginning of every semester, you should get to know your way around your new textbooks as quickly and efficiently as possible. Other than instructors, textbooks are the most important sources of information that you use in most of your courses. Thus you want to become very familiar with them in order to save time and feel secure and comfortable when reading them. You accomplish this through the use of **overviewing,** which is a quick method of getting acquainted with textbooks.

Overviewing involves **skimming,** or quickly glancing over, the front and back parts of a textbook in order to find out what it is about, how it is organized, and what aids to understanding are offered to help you comprehend it better. **Aids to understanding,** or **learning aids**—which make it easier to use your textbooks—could include appendixes, bibliographies, glossaries, graphic aids, indexes, objectives, outlines, prefaces, previews, questions, reference sources, summaries, tables of contents, and vocabulary lists.

At the very least, the front pages of a textbook usually include a title page, table of contents, and preface. As you know, the **title page** tells you what the book is about in addition to providing the name of the author, the publishing company, and the edition. The back of the title page gives the copyright date or the date of publication of that particular edition of the book so you know if you are dealing with material that is current. After the title page, you will most often find the **table of contents,** which is a blueprint of the entire book's organization. It lists not only the section and chapter titles but also all the main headings in each chapter. In short, it tells you more specifically what the textbook is about and helps you understand how the chapter headings are related to one another. For example, if headings such as "Anxiety Disorders," "Schizophrenia," "Anger," and "Depression" are listed under a larger heading like "Understanding Emotional Disorders," you would recognize immediately that the four subheadings are all examples of emotional disorders. Recognizing these kinds of connections or relationships would help make it easier to understand the chapter when you read it later on.

The **preface,** which generally comes after the table of contents, is also referred to as an introduction. Sometimes it is divided into "To the Instructor" and "To the Student" sections, or it may be a combination of both. Regardless of how it is structured or for whom it is written, the preface is valuable because it usually gives the author's purpose for writing the textbook, lists the features that make the book noteworthy, tells how the book is organized to help the reader, and lists and explains the aids to understanding. All of this information lets you know what you should accomplish as a result of reading the book and what is provided by the writer to help you to use it more efficiently. Although the table of contents shows what is included in the back part of a textbook, you should take a quick look for yourself.

The back pages of a textbook almost always include an alphabetically arranged **index,** which gives page locations for very specific information. Sometimes the index is divided into name and subject sections, which makes it faster to use. As you know from the discussion in Chapter 1, an alphabetically arranged **glossary** is also often found in the back, and it provides definitions of either individual words or combinations of words that fit the context of a given text. Many of those combinations of words will not even be found in a dictionary. For example, the glossary in a biology textbook defines *neutral variation* as "genetic variation that provides no apparent selective advantage for some individuals over others." Although the dictionary provides separate definitions for *neutral* and *variation,* it does not define them in combination. Thus glossaries give the meanings for specialized terms. They are also quicker to use than a dictionary because you do not have to search through a long list of definitions to find the specific one that fits the subject matter.

A **bibliography** containing sources used by the author to write the book, often supplemented by a list of **reference sources** or **suggested readings,** may be located at the back of a textbook or at the end of each chapter. **Credits** and **notes** are sometimes listed as well. They are all useful if research is necessary in order to read further on a given topic or perhaps to write a paper. On occasion, you can also find an **appendix** that includes supplementary or additional information such as definitions, experiments, maps, or diagrams that can prove helpful in understanding the subject matter of the textbook.

Overviewing takes only a short time, but it is well worth the effort. The sooner you become familiar with a textbook, the better your chances of reading it faster and with much more understanding. Furthermore, your awareness of all the aids to understanding included in the book by the writer should make the whole experience easier and more rewarding—and these elements come in very handy when studying for exams.

ACTIVITY 1

DIRECTIONS: Overview the following pages (pp. 129–153) taken from the front and back of a college textbook. Then, in your notebook, answer the overview questions. Be prepared to discuss where you found your answers to the questions.

Photo Researcher: Julie Tesser
Project Manager: Dora Rizzuto
Design Manager: Wendy Ann Fredericks
Text Designer: Nancy Sabato
Electronic Page Makeup: Allentown Digital Services Division of RR Donnelley & Sons Company

Detailed Contents

Detailed Contents   **v**

Preface

With our entry into the new millennium, the need to understand the swift social changes around us is greater than ever. We will explore many of the ongoing changes in this new edition of *Sociology: A Brief Introduction*. It is a major revision packed with up-to-date and useful information and new ideas from the latest sociological research.

This book is designed to help students have fun learning sociology. Thus the fast-paced and lively writing style, the frequent use of examples, and abundant illustrations should stimulate student interest in sociology. I have, however, continued to present the essentials of sociology without a loss of substance or concreteness. By studying this book, students will learn to think analytically and critically about the society in which they live. Armed with new information and better tools for thinking, they will look at the world, their society, and their own lives with enhanced clarity and insight and will be able to live their own lives more effectively and fruitfully.

FEATURES

A unique combination of style and substance makes this text stand out from the rest. In addition to the trusted, hallmark features of the book, I have added a number of new features to this edition in order to make it easier for students to learn sociology.

Myths and Realities

This text is unique for opening each chapter with a list of "Myths and Realities" about social behavior, which are then addressed in the chapter. Many students tend to assume that sociology is only common sense—that what sociology has to teach, they have known all along. In this text, students will find some of their firmest assumptions challenged, and they will start to look at the familiar world around them with a fresh, critical eye. A myth and reality in Chapter 10 (Families), for example, questions the popular belief that the high U.S. divorce rate discourages Americans from getting married, which is later discussed in the chapter. In addition, a photo box featuring one "Myth and Reality" appears in each

chapter, along with icons in the margin indicating where the myths are dispelled in the text.

Thinking Critically—New!

To further strengthen critical thinking skills, a number of "Thinking Critically" questions are provided throughout every chapter. The questions challenge students to critically analyze and examine the world around them. In Chapter 9 (Gender and Age), for example, the reader is asked: "What experiences have you had with gender inequality throughout your educational career? Have you ever felt mistreated or stereotyped because of your gender? Explain." Questions like this will not only sharpen students' critical-thinking skills, but will also show how sociology can be applied to their own lives.

Virtual World—New!

In this increasingly high-tech, information-rich society, we are now exposed more and more to new technology in our daily lives. The advertising on television, in magazines, and in other media now routinely invites us to go to the World Wide Web for more information. Many of us have already acquired the habit of surfing the Net for whatever information we need, and e-mail seems to be getting more popular than snail mail. In this ever-changing virtual world, a new frontier of social behavior is emerging, and it is important for us to understand it. In this text we will learn about, for example, the spreading of online chat, the global computer network, the proliferation of cyberporn, and the development of e-mail etiquette. These Internet-related subjects are discussed in boxes to elaborate on what is presented in the text.

Internet Exercises—New!

Each chapter contains two detailed activities that are designed to teach students how to use the Internet effectively as a tool for sociological research and how to learn more about the major topics introduced in the text. These exercises guide students to useful and relevant Web sites and then encourage them to think critically about the information they have gathered from the Internet.

xi

Applied Sociology—New!

To show how sociological knowledge can help us to understand the world around us, most chapters include a boxed article that illustrates how sociology can be applied to everyday life. These "Applied Sociology" boxes deal with such issues as what humor can do for us, how to become a millionaire, how to have affirmative action without racial preference, and how to use a new, effective way to solve marital problems. These boxes also elaborate on what is discussed in the text.

Global Analysis

Unique to this book, *all* chapters contain a section that analyzes how people around the world live. These analyses enhance and deepen our understanding of other cultures. They also help us gain special insight into our own society by looking at it more objectively—from the outsider's point of view. The global analysis section in Chapter 7 (U.S. and Global Stratification), for example, explores the link between women's participation in the labor force and a society's prosperity, which suggests one reason for the relatively high level of economic success in the United States.

Social Diversity

The diversity of U.S. society, which comprises various racial and ethnic groups, as well as women and men of different social classes and sexual orientations, is high-lighted in "Social Diversity" sections that appear in virtually all chapters. The text does not focus only on the problems of women and minorities; instead, their strengths and achievements are also revealed. Chapter 10 (Families), for example, discusses differences among Native American, African American, Hispanic American, and Asian American families. Social diversity in Chapter 3 (Socialization) deals with differences in child rearing among various U.S. groups.

Feminist Perspective

Consistently provided throughout the text are explanations of feminist views on various social issues. Feminist theorists have made important contributions to sociology by shedding light on many previously ignored subjects and offering a new way of looking at familiar social issues. In this book students will learn from the feminist perspective about numerous important matters, such as how feminists conduct social research, why women run organizations differently than men, and how the oppression of women is related to environmental problems.

NEW TO THIS EDITION

The text has been extensively revised and updated to reflect the changes and trends affecting society in the United States and throughout the world. I have also responded to suggestions and questions from faculty and students who have used previous editions.

The presentation of the three major perspectives has been significantly improved: summary-like subtitles have been added to the titles of sections about these perspectives. These new subtitles make it easier for students to learn and remember how the same perspective is used in different chapters to give its unique insight into different concrete subjects. Students will see, for example, in the conflict perspective how in Chapter 2 "culture supports social inequality" and how in Chapter 7 stratification "creates problems."

More items have been added to the chapter-opening "Myths and Realities," along with a new photo box featuring one "Myth and Reality" in each chapter, and new marginal icons showing where the myths are refuted in the text. Also, all chapters now have a greatly increased number of maps, figures, and tables. Moreover, unlike previous editions, there is now at least one cartoon in every chapter reflecting the humorous sides of important themes in the text.

The outpouring of sociological studies and news stories over the last 3 years has been reviewed. As a result, this edition is strengthened with a number of new materials; the most significant ones are listed below.

Chapter 1   The Essence of Sociology
◆ A new chapter-opening vignette illustrates the influence of the global economy on U.S. workers.
◆ More information is given on the contributions of the first woman sociologist, Harriet Martineau.
◆ An introduction to the African American sociologist W.E.B. Du Bois as one of the early contributors to U.S. sociology has been added.
◆ A new discussion on ethnography has been added.
◆ A new section on research ethics discusses the conflict between privacy issues and the law.
◆ A new "Virtual World" box assesses the reliability of online surveys.

Chapter 2   Society and Culture
◆ A new chapter-opening vignette illustrates the impact of culture on social behavior.
◆ A new section discusses how democracy and capitalism influence U.S. pop culture.
◆ The sections on patriarchal and global influences of pop culture have been significantly revised.

◆ A new "Applied Sociology" box shows how we can enhance our sensitivity to others' cultures.

◆ A new "Virtual World" box discusses the increasing use of different languages on the Internet.

Chapter 3   Socialization

◆ The section on personality development has been revised to emphasize the processes of socialization—how children learn to think, feel, be normal, moral, and masculine or feminine.

◆ A new section on social diversity in socialization discusses how children of various ethnic groups are socialized in the United States.

◆ A new "Applied Sociology" box discusses how youngsters left at home alone by working parents can still be properly socialized.

◆ A new "Virtual World" box examines the emerging generation of young Internet users.

Chapter 4   Social Interaction in Everyday Life

◆ The introducton section has been revised to show more clearly how the three sociological perspectives illuminate the different facets of social interaction.

◆ The section on the sociology of humor has been revised to make clearer the subversive nature of humor.

◆ A new "Applied Sociology" box discusses how we can benefit from humor.

◆ A new "Virtual World" box shows how online chat is becoming increasingly popular.

Chapter 5   Groups and Organizations

◆ A new section on the social-psychological concept of idiosyncrasy credit explains why scandal-plagued President Clinton remains popular with the U.S. public.

◆ A new section underscores the value of social diversity in achieving the goals of a group or organization.

◆ A new "Applied Sociology" box illustrates how restaurants, banks, and other business establishments try to shorten the time customers spend standing in lines.

◆ A new "Virtual World" box discusses the tremendous speed at which the computer network transmits information to an enormous number of people everywhere.

Chapter 6   Deviance and Control

◆ A new chapter-opening vignette provides an example of school violence.

◆ Key portions of sections on drug use, criminal justice, and the war on drugs have been extensively revised and updated.

◆ New sections on binge drinking and pornography have been added to emphasize that deviance also includes noncriminal activities, as well as crimes.

◆ The discussion of Merton's strain theory has been revised to enhance understanding of the theory.

◆ A new section on social diversity focuses on how different races, different social classes, and both genders are involved in deviance.

◆ A new section analyzes the nature and impact of capital punishment.

◆ A new section discusses the increasing medicalization of deviance.

◆ A new "Applied Sociology" box presents an effective program for controlling violent youngsters.

◆ A new "Virtual World" box discusses the proliferation of pornography in cyberspace.

Chapter 7   U.S. and Global Stratification

◆ A new chapter-opener vignette presents a modern-day slavery system in a North African country.

◆ A new section presents a global view of the social stratification systems around the world.

◆ A new section offers the feminist perspective on social stratification.

◆ A new section on social diversity shows the role played by ethnicity and age in stratification.

◆ The section on reforming welfare has been extensively revised and updated, including discussion of the effects of recent changes in welfare laws.

◆ A new section on the conflict perspective on global stratification explains how rich nations exploit poor nations.

◆ A new section on feminist theory discusses how women's domestic work and gainful employment are related to global inequality.

◆ A new "Applied Sociology" box discusses how to become rich as suggested by a study of American millionaires.

◆ A new "Virtual World" box zeroes in on the emergence of social stratification in cyberspace.

Chapter 8   Race and Ethnicity

◆ A new chapter-opening vignette offers a glimpse into the growing racism in Western Europe.

◆ The section on affirmative action has been extensively revised and updated.

◆ The global analysis of race and ethnicity has been heavily revised and updated, to cover racial problems in various parts of the world, namely, the developing countries, Western and Eastern Europe, and the former Soviet Union.

♦ A new "Applied Sociology" box discusses how a unique program carries out affirmative action without any racial preference.

Chapter 9   Gender and Age

♦ A new section discusses how the women's movement battles gender inequality.

♦ A new section analyzes the nature and consequences of violence against women.

♦ A new section examines the relationship between social diversity and gender inequality.

♦ The last protion of the section about the functionalist perspective on gender inequality has been extensively revised.

♦ A new section on social diversity discusses the differences in again among men and women, as well as among vaious social classes and ethnic groups.

♦ A new section on the future of aging discusses the societal consequences of the growng population of older people.

♦ A new "Virtual World" box deals with the influences of gender inequality on computer games.

Chapter 10   Families

♦ A new chapter-opening vignette describes a two-career couple as an increasingly common example of modern American families.

♦ A new "Applied Sociology" box provides a new, effective way of solving marital problems.

♦ A new "Virtual World" box discusses how the Internet influences family relations.

Chapter 11   Education and Religion

♦ A new section on social diversity discusses the varied educational experiences of Native, African, Hispanic, and Asian American students.

♦ The section on school choice has been extensively revised and updated with recent data.

♦ A new section on social diversity presents the differences in religious experiences among Native, African, Hispanic, and Asian Americans.

♦ Two new sections discuss the proliferation of cults and the New Age movement in the United States.

♦ The section on American Islam has been significantly revised and updated.

♦ A new multipart section discusses the confrontation between religion and the secular world.

♦ A new "Applied Sociology" box shows how a unique private school produces academic excellence among Native American students while reinforcing their appreciation of their own culture.

Chapter 12   The Economy and Politics

♦ A new section on the feminist perspective provides insight into women's economic status.

♦ A new three-part section discusses various aspects of big corporations.

♦ A new section on social diversity focuses on the roles played by vaious ethnic minorities in the U.S. economy.

♦ A new multipart section analyzes the nature of political participation, anti-government militias, political parties, and interest groups.

♦ A new section on social diversity discusses the political experiences of Native, African, Hispanic, and Asian Americans.

♦ A new section examines the causes of war.

♦ A new "Virtual World" box shows how politicians woo voters via the Internet.

Chapter 13   Health and Population

♦ A new section discusses the government campaign against cigarette smoking, as well as who is likely to smoke and why.

♦ The discussion of the right to die has been expanded to include the issue of assisted suicide.

♦ The section on social diversity in seeking medical care includes a discussion of the Tuskegee experiments.

♦ The section on the U.S. population policy has been extensively revised and updated.

♦ A new "Virtual World" box discusses the increasing use of the Internet to seek medical services.

Chapter 14   Environment and Urbanization

♦ A new section on the feminist perspective explains how the exploitation of nature effectively reinforces the subjugation of women.

♦ A new theory of spatial pattern takes into account how a great number of cities have expanded into large metropolitan areas.

♦ A new critical analysis is presented of the three classical theories about city life.

♦ A new "Applied Sociology" box reveals how decaying cities can be revitalized.

Chapter 15   Collective Behavior, Social Movements, and Social Change

♦ A new chapter-opening vignette illustrates the dramatic social change involving the impact of the computer technology.

♦ A new section focuses on how U.S. society has changed significantly over the last two decades.

♦ A new "Virtual World" box discusses the emergence of e-mail etiquette.

LEARNING AIDS

The effective system of learning aids in this text motivates students and facilitates learning. Students are encouraged to think about the materials by themselves and to prepare for class discussion of important concepts and issues. It is frequently through such active involvement with what they read that students begin to sharpen their thinking skills. Then the understanding and absorption of ideas presented in this text and in the course will come easily.

Chapter-Opening Vignettes

Along with a chapter outline and a Myths and Realities box, each chapter opens with a thought-provoking story. This story will stimulate students' interest, as well as fix their attention on the main themes of the chapter.

Critical-Thinking Questions

A number of critical-thinking questions appear in the major sections of each chapter. These questions encourage students to think critically about society and the world around them, and to apply what they have learned from sociology to their own lives.

Stimulating Graphics

Many colorful figures, tables, maps, and photos are placed throughout the book. They are designed to spark student interest and, more important, to reinforce comprehension and retention of the points made in the text.

Questions for Discussion and Review

In every chapter there are questions at the end of each main section. Instructors can use them as a springboard for lively discussion in class. Students can use them to review the key ideas that have just been discussed before moving on to the next topic. Whether the questions are used in class or for review, or both, students will learn more as active thinkers than as recipients of ideas and facts.

Surfing the Net

In this edition, to capture and build on students' interest in the Internet, a list of Web sites, along with the two Internet exercises, is provided at the end of each chapter. Students who use these resources and exercises will gain additional knowledge about the subject matter of the chapter.

Chapter Summaries

Each chapter ends with a substantive summary in a question-and-answer format. The standard form of summary in an introductory text tends to turn students into passive consumers of knowledge. In contrast, the question-and-answer format encourages students to become actively involved by inviting them to join the author in thinking about important issues. Students who have actively thought about what they have read will more easily understand and remember the material later.

Key Terms

The most important words are boldfaced and defined when introduced. They are listed and defined again at the end of each chapter, with a page cross-reference to facilitate study. All key terms with their definitions are also presented in the Glossary at the end of the book.

Suggested Readings

To encourage further exploration of the chapter topic, suggestions for further reading are included at the end of each chapter. These suggestions include up-to-date books readily available in most school libraries.

Glossary

Absolute poverty The lack of minimum food and shelter necessary for maintaining life.

Achieved status A status that is attained through an individual's own actions.

Affirmative action A policy that requires employers and academic institutions to make special efforts to recruit qualified minorities for jobs, promotions, and educational opportunities.

Afrocentrism The view of the world from the standpoint of African culture.

Anti-Semitism Prejudice or discrimination against Jews.

Aptitude The capacity for developing physical or social skills.

Arranged marriage A marriage in which partners are selected by the couple's parents.

Ascribed status A status that one has no control over, such as status based on race, gender, or age.

Assimilation The process by which a minority adopts the dominant group's culture as the culture of the larger society.

Authority Legitimate power institutionalized in organizations.

Behavioral assimilation The social situation in which a minority adopts the dominant group's language, values, and behavioral patterns.

Belief An idea that is relatively subjective, unreliable, or unverifiable.

Bilateral descent The norm that recognizes both parents' families as the child's close relatives.

Biosphere A thin layer of air, water, and soil surrounding the earth.

Birth rate The number of babies born in a year for every 1,000 members of a given population.

Breakdown-frustration theory The theory that a social breakdown can cause a social movement by creating frustration among masses of people.

Bureaucracy A modern Western organization defined by Max Weber as being rational in achieving its goal efficiently.

Capitalism An economic system based on private ownership of property and competition in producing and selling goods and services.

Caste system A relatively rigid stratification system in which people's positions are ascribed and fixed.

Census A periodic head count of the entire population of a country.

Charisma An exceptional personal quality popularly attributed to certain individuals.

Church A relatively large, well-established religious organization that is integrated into the society and does not make strict demands on its members.

Collective behavior Relatively spontaneous, unorganized, and unpredictable social behavior.

Communism A classless society that operates on the principle of "from each according to his ability to each according to his needs."

Compensatory education A school program intended to improve the academic performance of socially and educationally disadvantaged children.

Competition An interaction in which two individuals follow mutually accepted rules, each trying to achieve the same goal before the other does.

Compositional theory The theory that city dwellers are as involved with small groups of friends, relatives, and neighbors as are noncity people.

Concentric-zone theory The model of land use in which the city spreads out from the center in a series of concentric zones, each used for a particular kind of activity.

Conflict An interaction in which two individuals disregard any rules, each trying to achieve his or her own goal by defeating the other.

Conflict perspective A theoretical perspective that portrays society as always changing and always marked by conflict.

Conglomerate A corporation that owns companies in various unrelated industries.

Content analysis Searching for specific words or ideas and then turning them into numbers.

Control group The subjects in an experiment who are not exposed to the independent variable.

Conventional morality Kohlberg's term for the practice of defining right and wrong according to the *motive* of the action being judged.

Convergence theory The theory that modernization will bring the West and non-West together by breaking down cultural barriers to produce a global society.

Cultural imperialism The practice of making minorities accept the dominant group's culture.

Cultural integration The joining of various values into a coherent whole.

Cultural pluralism The peaceful coexistence of various racial and ethnic groups, each retaining its own subculture.

Cultural relativism The belief that a culture must be understood on its own terms.

Cultural universals Practices found in all cultures as the means for meeting the same human needs.

Culture A design for living or a complex whole consisting of objects, values, and other characteristics that people acquire as members of society.

Cyclical theory The theory that societies move forward and backward, up and down, in an endless series of cycles.

Death rate The number of deaths in a year for every 1,000 members of a population.

De facto segregation Segregation resulting from tradition and custom.

De jure segregation Segregation sanctioned by law.

Demographic transition The theory that human populations tend to go through specific demographic stages and that these stages are tied to a society's economic development.

Demography The scientific study of population.

Dependency theory The theory that rich nations exploit poor ones for power and commercial gain, thereby perpetuating poverty, underdevelopment, or dependency on rich nations.

Detached observation A method of observation in which the researcher observes as an outsider, from a distance, without getting involved.

Developmental socialization The process by which people learn to be more competent in playing their currently assumed roles.

Deviance An act that is considered by public consensus, or by the powerful at a given place and time, to be a violation of some social rule.

Dramaturgy A method of analyzing social interaction as if the participants were performing on a stage.

Dual economy An economy that comprises a core of giant corporations dominating the market and a *periphery* of small firms competing for the remaining, smaller shares of business.

Ecology A study of the interactions among organisms and between organisms and their physical environment.

Economic globalization The interrelationship among the world's economies.

Economic institution A system for producing and distributing goods and services.

Ecosystem A self-sufficient community of organisms depending for survival on one another and on the environment.

Egalitarian family The family in which authority is equally distributed between husband and wife.

Ego Freud's term for the part of personality that is rational, dealing with the world logically and realistically.

Emergent-norm theory The theory that members of a crowd develop, through interaction, a new norm to deal with the unconventional situation facing them.

Empowerment zones The economically depressed urban areas that businesses, with the help of government grants, low-interest loans, and tax breaks, try to revive by creating jobs; also known as enterprise zones.

Endogamy Literally "marrying within," the act of marrying someone from one's own group.

Epidemiology The study of the origin and spread of disease within a population.

Equilibrium theory The theory that all the parts of society serve some function and are interdependent.

Ethicalism The type of religion that emphasizes moral principles as guides for living a righteous life.

Ethnic group A collection of people who share a distinctive cultural heritage.

Ethnocentrism The attitude that one's own culture is superior to that of others.

Ethnography An analysis of people's lives from their own perspective.

Experimental group The group that is exposed to the independent variable.

Expressive leaders Leaders who achieve group harmony by making others feel good.

Expressive role A role that requires taking care of personal relationships.

Extended family The family that consists of two parents, their unmarried children, and other relatives.

Fad A temporary enthusiasm for an innovation less respectable than a fashion.

Family of orientation The family in which one grows up, consisting of oneself and one's parents and siblings.

Family of procreation The family that one establishes through marriage, consisting of oneself and one's spouse and children.

Fashion A great though brief enthusiasm among a relatively large number of people for a particular innovation.

302   Glossary

Feminism The belief that women and men should be equal in various aspects of their lives.

Feminist theory A form of conflict theory that explains human life in terms of the experiences of women.

Feminization of poverty A huge number of women bearing the burden of poverty, mostly as single mothers or heads of families.

Functionalist perspective A theoretical perspective that focuses on social order.

Gender identity People's image of what they are socially expected to be and do on the basis of their sex.

Genderlects Linguistic styles that reflect the different worlds of women and men.

Gender role The pattern of attitudes and behaviors that a society expects of its members because of their being female or male.

Generalized others Mead's term for people who do not have close ties to a child but who do influence the child's internalization of society's values.

Genocide Wholesale killing of a racial or ethnic group.

Gentrification The movement of affluent people into poor urban neighborhoods.

Glass ceiling The prejudiced belief that keeps minority professionals from holding leadership positions in organizations.

Groupthink The tendency for members of a cohesive group to maintain a consensus to the extent of ignoring the truth.

References

AAMC (Association of American Medical Colleges). 1998. AAMC Web Site (hhttp://www.aamc.org/).

Abbott, Pamela, and Claire Wallace. 1990. *An Introduction to Sociology: Feminist Perspectives.* London: Routledge.

Abramson, Jeffrey. 1995. "Making the law colorblind." *New York Times,* October 16, p. A11.

Abramson, Jill. 1998. "The business of persuasion thrives in nation's capital." *New York Times,* September 29, pp. A1, A22.

Acton, H. B. 1967. *What Marx Really Said.* New York: Schocken.

AHA (American Heart Association). 1998. "Tobacco smoke biostatistical fact sheet." http://www.amhrt.org.

Alba, Richard D. 1990. *Ethnic Identity: The Transformation of White America.* New Haven, Conn.: Yale University Press.

Albert, Stew. 1996. "Militias and the broken heartland." *Tikkun,* 11, pp. 56–58.

Aldrich, Howard E. 1992. "Incommensurable paradigms? Vital signs from three perspectives." In Michael Reed and Michael Hughes (eds.), *Rethinking Organization: New Directions in Organization Theory and Analysis.* Newbury Park, Calif.: Sage.

Alexander, Karl L., and Martha A. Cook. 1982. "Curricula and coursework: A surprise ending to a familiar story." *American Sociological Review,* 47, pp. 626–640.

Allis, Sam. 1990. "Schooling kids at home." *Time,* October 22, pp. 84–86.

Alonso, William. 1964. "The historic and the structural theories of urban form: Their implications for urban renewal." *Journal of Land Economics,* 40, pp. 227–231.

Alter, Jonathan. 1998. "It's 4:00 p.m.: Do you know where your children are?" *Newsweek,* April 27, pp. 28–33.

Altman, Lawrence K. 1990. "Changes in medicine bring pain to healing profession." *New York Times,* February 18, pp. 1, 20–21.

Altman, Lawrence K. 1998. "Parts of Africa showing H.I.V. in 1 in 4 adults." *New York Times,* June 24, pp. A1, A8.

Ames, Katrine. 1990. "Our bodies, their selves." *Newsweek,* December 17, p. 60.

Andersen, Margaret L. 1993. *Thinking About Women,* 3rd ed. New York: Macmillan.

Anderson, C. Alan, and Deborah G. Whitehouse. 1995. *New Thought: A Practical American Spirituality.* New York: Crossroad.

Anderson, David C. 1994. "The crime funnel." *New York Times Magazine,* June 12, pp. 57–58.

Anderson, David C. 1998. *Sensible Justice: Alternatives to Prison.* New York: The New Press.

Anderson, Terry L. 1995. *Sovereign Nations or Reservations?: An Economic History of American Indians.* San Francisco: Pacific Research Institute for Public Policy.

Applebome, Peter. 1996. "Shootings at schools prompt new concerns about violence." *New York Times,* March 3, p. 8.

Archer, Dane, and Rosemary Gartner. 1984. *Violence and Crime in Cross-National Perspective.* New Haven, Conn.: Yale University Press.

Armstrong, Louise. 1993. *And They Call It Help: The Psychiatric Policing of America's Children.* Reading, Mass.: Addison-Wesley.

Arnette, June L., and Marjorie C. Walsleben. 1998. "Combating fear and restoring safety in schools." *Juvenile Justice Bulletin,* April, U.S. Department of Justice.

Arnold, Elizabeth A. 1996. "A new feminist agenda." *Wall Street Journal,* July 11, p. A16.

Asch, Solomon E. 1955. "Opinions and social pressure." *Scientific American,* 193, pp. 31–35.

Ashe, Arthur. 1977. "An open letter to black parents: Send your children to the libraries." *New York Times,* February 6, Section 5, p. 2.

Bader, Chris, Paul J. Becker, and Scott Desmond. 1996. "Reclaiming deviance as a unique course from criminology." *Teaching Sociology,* 24, pp. 316–320.

Baehr, Helen, and Ann Gray (eds.). 1996. *Turning It On: A Reader in Women and Media.* New York: St. Martin's.

304   References

Bailey, Kenneth D. 1994. *Methods of Social Research,* 4th ed. New York: Free Press.

Barnett, W. Steven. 1995. "Long-term effects of early childhood programs on cognitive and school outcomes." *The Future of Children,* 5, Winter, pp. 25–50.

Baron, James N. 1994. "Reflections on recent generations of mobility research." In David B. Grusky (ed.), *Social Stratification: Class, Race, and Gender in Sociological Perspective.* Boulder, Colo.: Westview.

Barringer, Felicity. 1989. "Doubt on 'trial marriage' raised by divorce rates." *New York Times,* June 9, pp. 1, 23.

Barringer, Felicity. 1991. "Population grows in state capitals." *New York Times,* January 26, pp. 1, 10.

Bart, Pauline B. 1991. "Feminist theories." In Henry Etzkowitz and Ronald M. Glassman (eds.), *The Renascence of Sociological Theory.* Itasca, Ill.: Peacock.

Basow, Susan A. 1986. *Sex-Role Stereotypes.* Monterey, Calif.: Brooks/Cole.

Basu, Kaushik. 1995. "The poor need child labor." *New York Times,* November 20, p. A17.

Baum, Dan. 1996. *Smoke and Mirrors: The War on Drugs.* Boston: Little, Brown.

Becerra, Rosina. 1988. "The Mexican American family." In Charles Mindel et al. (eds.), *Ethnic Families in America: Patterns and Variations,* 3rd ed. New York: Elsevier.

Beck, E. M., and Stewart E. Tolnay. 1990. "The killing fields of the Deep South: The market for cotton and the lynching of blacks, 1882–1930." *American Sociological Review,* 55, pp. 526–539.

Beck, Melinda. 1990a. "Trading places." *Newsweek,* July 16, pp. 48–54.

Beck, Melinda. 1990b. "The politics of cancer." *Newsweek,* December 10, pp. 62–65.

Becker, Howard S. 1963. *Outsiders.* New York: Free Press.

Becker, Howard S. 1982. "Culture: A sociological view." *The Yale Review,* 71, pp. 513–527.

Begley, Sharon. 1990. "The search for the fountain of youth." *Newsweek,* March 5, pp. 44–48.

Begley, Sharon. 1996. "The IQ puzzle." *Newsweek,* May 6, pp. 70–72.

Beirne, Piers, and James Messerschmidt. 1995. *Criminology,* 2nd ed. San Diego: Harcourt Brace Jovanovich.

Belkin, Lisa. 1990. "Many in medicine are calling rules a professional malaise." *New York Times,* February 19, pp. A1, A9.

Credits

Chapter 1

Page 2: © Hazel Hankin/Stock Boston; **5T**: © M. Steinbacher/Photo Edit; **5B**: © Jon Riley/Tony Stone Images; **6**: © Steven Starr/Stock Boston; **9**: © Corbis-Bettmann; **12**: © Archive Photos; **11T**: © Corbis-Bettmann; **11B**: © The University Library/University of Illinois at Chicago/Jane Addams Memorial Collection at Hull House; **14**: © Steve Helber/AP/Wide World Photos; **17**: © Bob Daemmrich/Stock Boston; **19**: © Monica Almeida/NYT Pictures; **24**: © R. Scott/The Image Works

Chapter 2

Page 32: © Jeremy Hartley/Panos Pictures; **35**: © Joe Marquette/AP/Wide World Photos; 38: © John Zich/AP/Wide World Photos; **40**: © DeVore/AnthroPhoto File; **41**: © Holland/Stock Boston; **43**: © Alan Levinson/Tony Stone Images; **46**: © Nicholas DeVore/Tony Stone Images; **48**: © To Wennstrom/AP/Wide World Photos; **50**: © Superstock; **51T**: © Peter Vandermark/Stock Boston; **51B**: © Amanda Merullo/Stock Boston; **53**: © Corbis-Bettmann; **57T**: © Joe Carini/The Image Works; **57M**: © Richard Dean/The Image Works; 57B: © Bob Daemmrich/The Image Works

Chapter 3

Page 66: © David Madison/Tony Stone Images; **69**: © Sam Abell; 72: © Susan Van Etten/Stock Boston; **73**: © Myrleen Ferguson/Photo Edit; **78**: © Brent Jones; **81**: © Eiler/Stock Boston; **83T**: © Penny Tweedie/Tony Stone Images; **84T**: © Leland Bobbe/Tony Stone Images; **84B**: © Will & Deni McIntyre/Photo Researchers; **86**: © Brenda Tharp/Photo Researchers; **90**: © Oddie/Photo Edit

Chapter 4

Page 94: © Superstock; **97**: © Jerry Irwin/Photo Researchers; **98**: © Gray Mortimore/Tony Stone Images; **103**: © Azzi/Woodfin Camp & Associates; **106T**: © Bruce Ayres/Tony Stone Images; **106B**: © Gary Conner/Photo Edit; **107**: © B. Daemmrich/The Image Works; **108**: © Mark Richards/Photo Edit; **111**: © Tom McCarthyUnicorn Stock Photos; **113**: © Tony Esparza/AP/Wide World Photos

Chapter 5

Page 118: © John Coletti/Stock Boston; **123**: © Will & Deni McIntyre/Photo Researchers; **124**: © Laima Druskis/Photo Researchers; **128**: © Ron Sherman/Stock Boston; **131T**: © Preuss/The Image Works; **131B**: © D. Wells/The Image Works; **132**: © Crandall/The Image Works; **134**: © Rick Browne/Stock Boston; **137**: © PBJ Pictures/Gamma Liaison; **140**: © Lawrence Migdale/Stock Boston; **143**: © Paola Koch/Photo Researchers

Chapter 6

Page 146: © A. Lichtenstein/The Image Works; **149**: © Leyla Umar/Gamma Liaison; **150T**: © Jim Pickerell/Tony Stone Images; **150B**: © Bill Truslow/Gamma Liaison; **154**: © Sipa Press; **157**: © David Young-Wolff/Photo Edit; **160**: © Fritz Hoffmann/The Image Works; **164**: © Martin R. Jones/Unicorn Stock Photos; **166**: © A. Ramey/Photo Edit

Chapter 7

Page 176: © Tony Savino/The Image Works; **179**: © Lewis Hine Photo/Library of Congress; **182**: © Zilloux/Gamma Liaison; **183**: © Superstock; **185**: © Frank Siteman/Tony Stone Images; **188T**: © Jeff Dunn/The Pictures Cube; **188B**: © Granitsas/The Image Works; **192**: © M. Siluk/The Image Works; **194T**: © Rob Crandall/Stock Boston; **194B**: © Archive Photos; **198**: © Bob Daemmrich/Stock Boston; **203**: © Mark Peters/Sipa Press

Chapter 8

Page 212: © John Eastcott/Momatiuk/The Image Works; **216**: © I. Berry/Magnum Photos; **219**: © Paul Conklin/Photo Edit; **221**: © Kathy Willens/AP/Wide World Photos; **225**: © M. Granitsas/The Image Works; **227T**: © Bachmann/The Image Works; **227B**: © Vicki Silbert/Photo Edit; **228**: © Lawrence Migdale/Tony Stone Images; **229**: © Robert Frerck/Odyssey/Chicago; **232**: © Lawrence Migdale/Photo Researchers; **236**: © Gerry Gropp/Sipa Press

305

Name Index

Subject Index

ACTIVITY 2

DIRECTIONS. Do an overview of one of the textbooks you are using in another course, and write a few paragraphs in which you discuss what you learned from your overview. If you do not have other textbooks at this time, ask your classmates who are using other books to share their paragraphs with you.

PREVIEWING TEXTBOOK CHAPTERS

Suppose you are invited to a party this Saturday night in an unfamiliar part of your state, and you are very excited about going because all your friends will be there. Unfortunately, you are working until 9 P.M. that night, which means that you have to travel alone and arrive late for the affair. When Saturday night comes around, you certainly would not get into your car and drive around aimlessly trying to find the party. Not only would you waste time and gas, but there is a real chance you would never arrive! Instead, you would have found out specifically where the party is, the best way to get there, and approximately how long the trip is going to take you. Furthermore, when getting directions, you would have asked for landmarks like traffic lights, service stations, and other structures to help guide your way. In short, you would have tried to become familiar with the route so that you could get to your destination as quickly and efficiently as possible.

We can apply the same principle to reading textbook chapters. Before starting an assignment, you should find out where you are going by familiarizing yourself with the material as much as possible. Not only will it ultimately save time and effort to do this, but it will result in much better comprehension because you know where you are going and what to look for along the way. The process by which you become acquainted with a textbook chapter is called **previewing.** Like overviewing, it involves skimming or quickly glancing over the material to determine what you will be reading about, how it is organized, and what aids to understanding are provided to help you with the task.

When previewing a textbook chapter, proceed through the following steps:

1. Take note of the title, which tells you the topic of the chapter. Once again, it is the answer to the question "What is this about?"

2. Check the length of the chapter so that you can gauge how long it will take you to read. While you are at it, try to get an idea how difficult the material is, because that also affects the time it will take you to get through it. The purpose here is for you to prepare yourself psychologically for the task and come up with a schedule for its completion, which could involve dividing up the assignment.

3. Check to see if there are objectives, goals, or outcomes at the beginning of the chapter. They tell you exactly what you are expected to know when you finish reading it, so they can serve as your personal study goals.

4. Skim the first several paragraphs, which are often an introduction to the main points to be covered and sometimes present the central message of the entire chapter.

5. Skim the last several paragraphs, which could serve as a summary of the most important information including, once again, the central message of the chapter. Keep in mind that writers sometimes provide a more formal summary or review in a separate section at the end of a chapter, which makes it easy to recognize.

6. Skim the major and minor chapter headings so that you become aware of the topics covered and how they are related to one another. As noted earlier, it is important to note connections between major and minor headings.

7. Look carefully at the **graphic aids,** which include charts, graphs, maps, pictures, and tables. They illustrate important information mentioned in the context of the textbook and often sum up major points made by the writer. Pay particular attention to the **captions** or **titles** and any explanations that appear over, under, or alongside the graphic aids, because you want to find out what they are about and be aware of the information that they stress. In short, no matter what graphic aid you encounter, you should always be able to answer the following two questions: "What is this graphic aid about?" and "What are the major points stressed?"

8. Check if there are questions within or at the end of the chapter. Because they also focus on the major points, you should keep any questions in mind and try to answer them as you read. At the very least, they can serve as guides to direct your reading to the most valuable information.

9. Take note of any other aids to understanding offered in the chapter, such as exercises, outlines, previews, vocabulary lists, or boldfaced and italicized vocabulary defined in context or in the margins. All of these aids can help make your reading more meaningful.

After you have completed your preview of a chapter, take a few moments to think carefully about what you have learned. As you read the chapter, remember what you have discovered from your preview so that you can focus on the most important information. Although it only takes a short time, previewing is an excellent way to get acquainted with textbook material. That familiarity will pay off later on by enabling you to read quicker and with much more understanding.

ACTIVITY 3

DIRECTIONS: Chapter 4 in this textbook contains very important information that will be used throughout the rest of the book. Familiarize yourself with that chapter by previewing it, and then answer the preview questions in your notebook.

Preview Questions

1. What is the chapter about?

2. How long will it take you to read it?

3. Are there objectives, goals, or outcomes at the beginning of the chapter that can serve as your personal study goals?

4. Is an introduction or a summary provided?

5. What is the central message of the entire chapter?

6. How many major and minor headings are there? Name them.

7. How many characteristics of critical thinking are there?

8. Are any graphic aids provided? If so, what are they about? What major points do they stress?

9. Are there questions within or at the end of the chapter?

10. What other aids to understanding are offered in the chapter that can help make your reading more meaningful?

Essay

Write a few paragraphs in which you discuss what you learned from your preview of the chapter and how it will help you read it more quickly and with greater understanding.

DIRECTIONS: Preview a chapter from one of the textbooks you are using in another course, and write a few paragraphs in which you discuss what you learned from your preview. If you are not using any other textbooks at this time, preview Chapter 5 in this textbook.

READING A TEXTBOOK CHAPTER CRITICALLY: QUESTIONS AND ANSWERS

In this textbook, you have several opportunities to play "the dashing detective." Enjoy them! When detectives investigate a real crime, they ask such questions as "When did the criminal activity occur?" "Are there any clues?" "Who was involved?" "Are there any witnesses?" "What were the possible motives?" Answers to these and questions like them enable detectives to piece together information so that they can solve the crime.

As a student, before you go into a test situation, you always ask your instructor questions to find out what the test will cover, what kind of test it will be, how many questions will be on it, and how many points each will be worth. The information gathered from the answers to those questions helps you to prepare more efficiently for the test and receive a higher grade for your efforts.

The importance of asking questions also applies to reading, as you saw in Chapter 2, when we discussed how to find the topic, main idea, details, and central message. Furthermore, in this chapter, questions were used to gather information for overviewing and previewing purposes. In the remaining chapters, you will be answering questions that help focus and improve your understanding and require that you evaluate or read critically material from various sources. Thus questioning has a very important role to play when it comes to dealing with textbooks and other kinds of reading as well.

How, then, do you actually apply **critical reading** to a textbook chapter? As you may have guessed, it involves the use of questions. When we discussed overviewing and previewing, we emphasized the importance of major and minor chapter headings because they make you aware of the topics covered and how the topics are related. Headings are generally highlighted in boldface or in colored type to stress their importance to the reader. *By simply turning those headings into questions, you are focusing your attention on the most important information in a textbook chapter and evaluating that information to answer your questions.* Sometimes writers actually provide headings that are already in question form, which makes your job even easier. Nevertheless, when you have to make headings into questions yourself, you can do so through the use of words often found in questions, such as *who, when, what, where, how,* and *why.* For example, look at the following headings and their corresponding questions.

Heading	*Question*
Booker T. Washington	Who was Booker T. Washington?
The Best Time to Study	When is the best time to study?
Physical Needs	What are physical needs?
The Cradle of Civilization	Where was the cradle of civilization?
Preventing Accidents	How do you prevent accidents?
The Need for Love	Why do we need love?

Sometimes it is very important to develop a question that relates a minor heading to a major one in order to understand how they are connected or related to each other. For instance, if the minor heading "Genetic Factors" is found under the major heading "The Development of Emotions" in a given chapter, then an appropriate question would read something like "What are genetic factors, and how do they contribute to the development of emotions?" By asking a question like this, you are focusing not only on the meaning of genetic factors but also on their relationship to the development of emotions. Certainly, that is what the textbook writer wants you to do.

When answering the questions that you have developed, you should always look for the central message of each chapter section and be aware of main ideas, patterns of organization, and context definitions. Although we have already discussed them at length in Chapters 1 and 2, it should be stressed again here that they are all extremely important because they provide the information with which to answer your questions. As discussed in Chapter 2, it is a very good idea to underline or highlight with a marker the information contained in main ideas, patterns of organization, and context definitions to separate it from the other material.

To review, underlining or highlighting is a useful technique that contributes to better comprehension because it requires that you evaluate carefully when deciding what information needs to be separated from the rest. That makes you into a more active, attentive reader, which is also an aid to concentration. Finally, this skill makes it easier to review the important information that you have separated in each section of a chapter without having to go back to reread everything. In short, underlining, highlighting, marking up, and even writing in your textbooks will help you master them by making you into a much more involved reader.

Carefully read the chapter section that follows. Make the heading into a question, and then answer your question by using the information provided in the passage. Pay particular attention to the sentences that have been underlined.

1   **Isolate and Locate the Source of the Problem** <u>This means finding the part of the environment that is most likely responsible for the issue. A source can be one of three things. First, the source of a problem might be other people in your life.</u> An organization I once consulted with was having trouble keeping its staff washrooms clean. They were used by staff and visitors. Management issued washroom keys to its staff and had visitors use a public washroom in the building. Unfortunately, the washrooms remained as messy as ever. The problem was incorrectly linked with visitors and not members of the organization. Once this was called to the staff's attention and washroom rules were discussed with people, the appearance of the washrooms improved.

2   <u>Second, the source of a problem might be some object in your environment.</u> A neighbor's car radio went out whenever he approached a local radio station. He complained to the station manager that its equipment was causing his radio to malfunction. As far as the radio station manager knew, my neighbor was the only person with this problem. Thus, it seemed unlikely that the radio station's equipment was in some way responsible. He had one of his technicians check my neighbor's radio. The technician found a loose wire that apparently turned the radio off when it was jarred by potholes in the street near the station. Those same potholes jarred the radio back into operation. Properly locating the problem led to a solution.

3   <u>The third source of a problem might be a relationship.</u> Whenever we have an interpersonal problem, a natural tendency is to blame the other person. "It couldn't be my fault," we might think to ourselves. Interpersonal problems are much easier to resolve when the relationship is viewed as the source.

4   A former neighbor and his wife, for example, used to argue over who would take the garbage out to their garbage cans, located in their backyard. One would think this would be a simple problem to solve. At the very least, the chore could be rotated. Unfortunately, whatever strategy they chose, one of them would inevitably break the deal. Each blamed the other for being absentminded, stubborn, and purposely irritating. They eventually entered counseling for other problems in their marriage and discovered that the techniques they employed to manipulate and control each other interfered with their relationship. Their therapist pointed out that the garbage became a symbol for "who is the garbage person in this relationship" and, by implication, the low-status person in the marriage. The source of the issue was not the garbage per se, but unresolved control and authority issues in their relationship.

Anthony F. Grasha, *Practical Applications of Psychology*, p. 91

If the question you developed from the heading reads something like "How or where do you isolate and locate the source of the problem?" you are correct. You never know for sure whether you have asked the right question until you have at least skimmed the material. However, just the process of thinking about possible appropriate questions forces you from the very beginning to consider the information in front of you carefully. For example, you might have been tempted to make up questions using the words *who, when,* or *why,* but a quick look at the section indicates that the information provides a better answer to a *how* or *where* question. Hence by trying to decide the best question to ask, you have already begun evaluating the section, which makes for much better comprehension in the long run.

You probably noticed that the first two sentences present the central message, and the major details—which are italicized—are organized into a simple listing-of-facts pattern. Together, they provide the answer to our question:

> Finding the part of the environment that is most likely responsible for the issue involves one of three things: other people in your life, some object in your environment, or a relationship.

Once again, we see the importance of recognizing central messages and patterns of organization, because they contain the most valuable information. You should always be on the lookout for them. The rest of the section consists of minor details that relate various examples designed to make the material clearer.

Reading a textbook chapter with a questioning mind helps focus your attention on the most important information. Furthermore, it makes you into a more active reader, who is thinking carefully about the chapter material in order to find answers. That in turn leads to greater concentration, improved comprehension, and a much better chance of remembering what you have read. In fact, all of the skills that we have discussed in this chapter and Chapters 1 and 2 are designed to help you deal more effectively with textbooks. As a result, the experience with your textbooks should be more meaningful and worthwhile. Take the time to use and improve on these skills as you continue with your education. Your efforts should enable you to increase your learning and achieve higher grades. That is a very good return for your hard work.

ACTIVITY 5

DIRECTIONS: The following passages are taken from various textbook chapters. For each of them, turn the heading into a question and answer it by using the central message and any main ideas, context definitions, and patterns of organization that may be present. Underline or highlight the most important information before writing out the answers in your notebook.

1
Marriage as an Exercise in Self-Interest

1   A number of couples, however, remain married for decades even when they know that their marriages are imperfect. To outsiders looking at such a married couple and observing one spouse silently suffering for years while the other spouse continually behaves in some socially unacceptable manner, the rationality of the marriage can be hard to fathom. To an economist, this makes the institution of marriage an especially interesting case study of human choice.

2   Throughout history, literally billions of people have chosen to be married and to put up with the faults of their matrimonial partners. Why do they do this? One reason that economists have offered is that spouses show consideration for their marriage partners in

the hope or expectation that the favor will be returned. This is self-interest at work. In addition, by entering into and staying faithful to a marriage, one spouse establishes a reputation with the other. By honoring their commitment to the marriage, they show more broadly that they are not afraid of commitments. This gives both a greater incentive to trust each other when they make joint financial decisions. By pooling their resources, both marriage partners can thereby make themselves better off than they would be alone. This is also an example of people responding in a self-interested way to incentives they face.

Roger LeRoy Miller, *Economics Today*, p. 14

2
Noise Pollution

1   Loud noise has become commonplace. We are often painfully aware of construction crews in our streets, jet airplanes roaring overhead, stereos blaring next door, and trucks rumbling down nearby freeways. Our bodies have definite physiological responses to noise, and noise can become a source of physical or mental distress.

2   Prolonged exposure to some noises results in hearing loss. Short-term exposure reduces productivity, concentration levels, and attention spans, and may affect mental and emotional health. Symptoms of noise-related distress include disturbed sleep patterns, headaches, and tension. Physically, our bodies respond to noises in a variety of ways. Blood pressure increases, blood vessels in the brain dilate, and vessels in other parts of the body constrict. The pupils of the eye dilate. Cholesterol levels in the blood rise, and some endocrine glands secrete additional stimulating hormones, such as adrenaline, into the bloodstream.

3   Sounds are measured in decibels. Hearing can be damaged by varying lengths of exposure to sound. If the duration of allowable daily exposure to different decibel levels is exceeded, hearing loss will result.

4   At this point, it is necessary to distinguish between sound and noise. Sound is anything that can be heard. Noise is sound that can damage the hearing or cause mental or emotional distress. When sounds become distracting or annoying, they become noise.

5   Unfortunately, despite gradually increasing awareness that noise pollution is more than just a nuisance, noise control programs at federal, state, and local levels have been given a low budgetary priority. In order to prevent hearing loss, it is important that you take it upon yourself to avoid voluntary and involuntary exposure to excessive noise. Playing stereos in your car and home at reasonable levels, wearing ear plugs when you use power equipment, and establishing barriers (closed windows, etc.) between you and noise will help keep your hearing intact.

Rebecca J. Donatelle, *Access to Health*, 7th ed., p. 574

3
Sports as Beneficial to Society

1   According to the functionalist perspective, sports contribute to the welfare of society by performing at least three major functions.

2   First, sports are conducive to success in other areas of life. Being competitive, sports inspire athletes to do their utmost to win, thereby helping them to develop such qualities as skill and ability, diligence and self-discipline, mental alertness, and physical fitness. These qualities can ensure success in the larger society. In the words of General Douglas MacArthur: "Upon the fields of friendly strife are sown the seeds that, upon other fields, on other days, will bear the fruits of victory." By watching athletes perform, spectators also learn the importance of hard work, playing by the rules, and working as a team player, characteristics that help ensure success in a career and other aspects of life.

3   Second, sports enhance health and happiness. Participants can enjoy a healthy and long life. The health benefit is more than physical. It is also psychological. Runners and joggers, for example, often find that their activity releases tension and anger as well as relieving anxiety and depression. Moreover, many people derive much pleasure from looking upon their participation as a form of beauty, an artistic expression, or a way of having a good time with friends. Similarly, sports improve the quality of life for the spectators. Fans can escape their humdrum daily routines, or find pleasure in filling their leisure time. They can savor the aesthetic pleasure of watching the excellence, beauty, and creativity in an athlete's performance. The fans can therefore attain greater happiness, life satisfaction, or psychological well-being (Smith, 1993).

4   Third, sports contribute to social order and stability. This is because sports serve as an integrating force for society as a whole. Sports are in effect a social mechanism for uniting potentially disunited members of society. Through their common interest in a famous athlete or team, people of diverse racial, social, and cultural backgrounds can feel a sense of homogeneity, community, or intimacy that they can acquire in no other way. Athletes, too, can identify with their fans, their community, and their country.

Alex Thio, *Sociology,* 5th ed., pp. 17–18

4
Why We Sleep

1   One likely function of sleep is to provide a "time out" period, so that the body can restore depleted reserves of energy, eliminate waste products from muscles, repair cells, strengthen the immune system, or recover physical abilities lost during the day. The idea that sleep is for physical rest and recuperation accords with the undeniable fact that at the end of the day we feel tired and crave sleep. Though most people can function fairly normally after a day or two of sleeplessness, sleep deprivation that lasts for four days or longer is quite uncomfortable. In animals, forced sleeplessness leads to infections and eventually death (Rechtschaffen et al., 1983), and the same may be true for people. There is a case on record of a man who, at the age of 52, abruptly began to lose sleep. After sinking deeper and deeper into an exhausted stupor, he developed a lung infection and died. An autopsy showed he had lost almost all of the large neurons in two areas of the thalamus that have been linked to sleep and hormonal circadian rhythms (Lugaresi et al., 1986).

2   Nonetheless, when people go many days without any sleep, they do not then require an equal period of time to catch up; one night's rest usually eliminates all symptoms of

fatigue (Dement, 1978). Moreover, the amount of time we sleep does not necessarily cor-
respond to how active we have been; even after a relaxing day on the beach, we usually
go to sleep at night as quickly as usual. For these reasons, simple rest or energy restoration cannot be the sole purpose of sleep.

3   Many researchers believe that sleep must have as much to do with brain function
as with bodily restoration. Even though most people still function pretty well after
losing a single night's sleep, mental flexibility, originality, and other aspects of creative thinking may suffer (Horne, 1988). Chronic sleepiness can impair performance
on tasks requiring vigilance or divided attention, and it can lead to automotive and
industrial accidents (Dement, 1992; Roehrs et al., 1990). Laboratory studies and observations of people participating in "wake-athons" have shown that after several days
of sleep loss, people become irritable and begin to have hallucinations and delusions
(Dement, 1978; Luce & Segal, 1966).

4   The brain, then, needs periodic rest. Researchers are trying to find out how sleep
may contribute to the regulation of brain metabolism, the maintenance of normal nerve-
cell activity, and the replenishment of neurotransmitters. It is clear, however, that during
sleep, the brain is not simply resting. On the contrary, most of the brain remains quite
active, as we are about to see.

Carol Tavris and Carole Wade, *Psychology in Perspective*, pp. 162–163

5
What Is Deviance?

1   Deviance is generally defined as any act that violates a social norm. But the phenomenon is more complex than that. How do we know whether an act violates a social
norm? Is homosexuality deviant—a violation of a social norm? Some people think so, but
others do not. There are at least three factors involved in determining what deviance is:
time, place, and public consensus or power.

2   First, what constitutes deviance varies from one historical period to another. Nearly
2,000 years ago, the Roman Empress Messalina won a bet with a friend by publicly having a prolonged session of sexual intercourse with twenty-five men. At the time, Romans
were not particularly scandalized, though they were quite impressed by her stamina (King,
1985). Today, if a person of similar social standing engaged in such behavior, we would
consider it extremely scandalous.

3   Second, the definition of deviance varies from one place to another. A polygamist
(a person with more than one spouse) is a criminal in the United States but not in Saudi
Arabia and other Muslim countries. Prostitution is illegal in the United States (except in
some counties in Nevada) but legal in Denmark, Germany, France, and many other countries. As a married man, President Clinton got into hot water for having an affair, but married leaders in China are fully expected to have girlfriends (Rosenthal, 1998).

4   Third, whether a given act is deviant depends on public consensus. Murder is unques-
tionably deviant because nearly all societies agree that it is. In contrast, drinking alcoholic beverages is generally not considered deviant. Public consensus, however, usually
reflects the vested interests of the rich and powerful. As Marx would have said, the ideas

of the ruling class tend to become the ruling ideas of society. Like the powerful, the general public tends, for example, to consider bank robbery a serious crime but not fraudulent advertising, which serves the interests of the powerful.

5   In view of these three determinants of deviant behavior, we may define **deviance** more precisely as an act considered by public consensus, or by the powerful at a given time and place, to be a violation of some social rule.

Alex Thio, *Sociology: A Brief Introduction,* 4th ed., pp. 148–149

ACTIVITY 6

DIRECTIONS: The three textbook selections that follow are longer than those in Activity 5. In addition, they contain both major and minor headings and two have graphic aids. Turn the headings into questions, taking into consideration the relationship or connection between the major and minor ones. Answer your questions by using the central message and any main ideas, context definitions, and patterns of organization that may be present. Underline or highlight the most important information before writing out the answers in your notebook. With regard to the graphic aids, answer the following two questions for each of them: "What is this graphic aid about?" and "What are the major points stressed?"

1
Smokeless Tobacco

1   Smokeless tobacco is used by approximately 5 million U.S. adults. Most users are teenage (20 percent of male high school students) and young adult males, who are often emulating a professional sports figure or a family member. There are two types of smokeless tobacco—chewing tobacco and snuff. Chewing tobacco comes in the form of loose leaf, plug, or twist. Chewing tobacco contains tobacco leaves treated with molasses and other flavorings. The user places a "quid" of tobacco in the mouth between the teeth and gums and then sucks or chews the quid to release the nicotine. Once the quid becomes ineffective, the user spits it out and inserts another. Dipping is another method of using chewing tobacco. The dipper takes a small amount of tobacco and places it between the lower lip and teeth to stimulate the flow of saliva and release the nicotine. Dipping rapidly releases the nicotine into the bloodstream.

2   Snuff can come in either a dry or moist powdered form or sachets (tea bag-like pouches) of tobacco. The most common placement of snuff is inside the cheek. In European countries, inhaling dry snuff is more common than in the United States.

Risks of Smokeless Tobacco

3   Smokeless tobacco is just as addictive as cigarettes due to its nicotine content. There is nicotine in all tobacco products, but smokeless tobacco contains more nicotine than do cigarettes. Holding an average-sized dip or chew in your mouth for 30 minutes gives

you as much nicotine as smoking four cigarettes. A two-can-a-week snuff dipper gets as much nicotine as a one-and-a-half-pack-a-day smoker.

4   One of the major risks of chewing tobacco is **leukoplakia,** a condition characterized by leathery white patches inside the mouth produced by contact with irritants in tobacco juice. Smokeless tobacco contains 10 times the amount of cancer-producing substances found in cigarettes and 100 times more than the Food and Drug Administration allows in foods and other substances used by the public. Between 3 and 17 percent of diagnosed leukoplakia cases develop into oral cancer. Users of smokeless tobacco are 50 times more likely to develop oral cancers than are nonusers. Warning signs of oral cancers include: lumps in the jaw or neck area; color changes or lumps inside the lips; white, smooth, or scaly patches in the mouth or on the neck, lips, or tongue; a red spot or sore on the lips or gums or inside the mouth that does not heal in two weeks; repeated bleeding in the mouth; difficulty or abnormality in speaking or swallowing.

5   The lag time between first use and contracting cancer is shorter for smokeless tobacco users than for smokers because absorption through the gums is the most efficient route of nicotine administration. A growing body of evidence suggests that long-term use of smokeless tobacco also increases the risk of cancer of the larynx, esophagus, nasal cavity, pancreas, kidney, and bladder. Moreover, many smokeless tobacco users eventually "graduate" to cigarettes.

6   Chewers and dippers do not face the specific hazards associated with heat and smoke, but they do run other tobacco-related risks. The stimulant effects of nicotine may create the same circulatory and respiratory problems for chewers as for smokers. Chronic smokeless tobacco use also results in delayed wound healing, peptic ulcer disease, and reproductive disturbances.

7   Smokeless tobacco also impairs the senses of taste and smell, causing the user to add salt and sugar to food, which may contribute to high blood pressure and obesity. Some smokeless tobacco products contain high levels of sodium (salt), which also contributes to high blood pressure. In addition, dental problems are common among users of smokeless tobacco. Contact with tobacco juice causes receding gums, tooth decay, bad breath, and discolored teeth. Damage to both the teeth and jawbone can contribute to early loss of teeth. Users of all tobacco products may not be able to use the vitamins and other nutrients in food effectively. In some cases, vitamin supplements may be recommended by a physician.

Rebecca J. Donatelle, *Health: The Basics*, 4th ed., p. 208

2
<u>Styles of Conflict</u>

1   There are four ways in which people can act when their needs aren't met. Each one has very different characteristics, as we can show by describing a common problem. At one time or another almost everyone has been bothered by a neighbor's barking dog. You know the story: every passing car, distant siren, pedestrian, and falling leaf seems to set off a fit of barking that leaves you unable to sleep, socialize, or study. By describing the pos-

sible ways of handling this kind of situation, the differences between nonassertive, directly aggressive, indirectly aggressive, and assertive behavior should become clear.

Nonassertive Behavior

2   There are two ways in which nonasserters manage a conflict. Sometimes they ignore their needs. Faced with the dog, for instance, a nonassertive person would try to forget the barking by closing the windows and trying to concentrate even harder. Another form of denial would be to claim that no problem exists—that a little barking never bothered anyone. To the degree that it's possible to make problems disappear by ignoring them, such an approach is probably advisable. In many cases, however, it simply isn't realistic to claim that nothing is wrong. For instance, if your health is being jeopardized by the cigarette smoke from someone nearby, you are clearly punishing yourself by remaining silent. If you need to learn more information from a supervisor before undertaking a project, you reduce the quality of your work by pretending that you understand it at all. If you claim that an unsatisfactory repair job is acceptable, you are paying good money for nothing. In all these and many more cases simply pretending that nothing is the matter when your needs continue to go unmet is clearly not the answer.

3   A second nonassertive course of action is to acknowledge your needs are not being met but simply to accept the situation, hoping that it might clear up without any action on your part. You could, for instance, wait for the neighbor who owns the barking dog to move. You could wait for the dog to be run over by a passing car or to die of old age. You could hope that your neighbor will realize how noisy the dog is and do something to keep it quiet. Each of these occurrences is a possibility, of course, but it would be unrealistic to count on one of them to solve your problem. And even if by chance you were lucky enough for the dog problem to be solved without taking action, you couldn't expect to be so fortunate in other parts of your life.

4   In addition, while waiting for one of these eventualities, you would undoubtedly grow more and more angry at your neighbor, making a friendly relationship between the two of you impossible. You would also lose a degree of self-respect, since you would see yourself as the kind of person who can't cope with even a common everyday irritation. Clearly, nonassertion is not a very satisfying course of action—either in this case or in other instances.

Direct Aggression

5   Where the nonasserter underreacts, a directly aggressive person overreacts. The usual consequences of aggressive behaviors are anger and defensiveness or hurt and humiliation. In either case aggressive communicators build themselves up at the expense of others.

6   You could handle the dog problem with direct aggression by abusively confronting your neighbors, calling them names and threatening to call the dogcatcher the next time you see their hound running loose. If the town in which you live has a leash law, you would be within your legal rights to do so, and thus you would gain your goal of bringing peace and quiet to the neighborhood. Unfortunately, your direct aggression would have other, less productive consequences. Your neighbors and you would probably cease to be on speaking terms, and you could expect a complaint from them the first time you violated even the most inconsequential of city ordinances. If you live in the neighborhood for any time at all, this state of hostilities isn't very appealing.

Indirect Aggression

7   In several of his works psychologist George Bach describes behavior that he terms "crazymaking." Crazymaking occurs when people have feelings of resentment, anger, or rage that they are unable or unwilling to express directly. Instead of keeping these feelings to themselves, the crazymakers send these aggressive messages in subtle, indirect ways, thus maintaining the front of kindness. This amiable façade eventually crumbles, however, leaving the crazymaker's victim confused and angry at having been fooled. The targets of the crazymaker can either react with aggressive behavior of their own or retreat to nurse their hurt feelings. In either case indirect aggression seldom has anything but harmful effects on a relationship.

8   You could respond to your neighbors and their dog in several crazymaking, indirectly aggressive ways. One strategy would be to complain anonymously to the city pound and then, after the dog has been hauled away, express your sympathy. Or you could complain to everyone else in the neighborhood, hoping that their hostility would force the offending neighbors to quiet the dog or face being a social outcast. A third possibility

Crazymakers: Indirect Aggression

1 What's your conflict style? To give you a better idea of some unproductive ways you may be handling your conflicts, we'll describe some typical conflict behaviors that can weaken relationships. In our survey we'll follow the fascinating work of George Bach, a leading authority on conflict and communication.

2 Bach explains that there are two types of aggression—clean fighting and dirty fighting. Either because they can't or won't express their feelings openly and constructively, dirty fighters sometimes resort to "crazymaking" techniques to vent their resentments. Instead of openly and caringly expressing their emotions, crazymakers (often unconsciously) use a variety of indirect tricks to get at their opponent. Because these "sneak attacks" don't usually get to the root of the problem, and because of their power to create a great deal of hurt, crazymakers can destroy communication. Let's take a look at some of them.

3 **The Avoider**   The avoider refuses to fight. When a conflict arises, he'll leave, fall asleep, pretend to be busy at work, or keep from facing the problem in some other way. This behavior makes it very difficult for the partner to express his feelings of anger, hurt, etc., because the avoider won't fight back. Arguing with an avoider is like trying to box with a person who won't even put up his gloves.

4 **The Pseudoaccommodator**   The pseudoaccommodator refuses to face up to a conflict either by giving in or by pretending that there's nothing at all wrong. This really drives the partner, who definitely feels there's a problem, crazy and causes him to feel both guilt and resentment toward the accommodator.

5 **The Guiltmaker**   Instead of saying straight out that she doesn't want or approve of something, the guiltmaker tries to change her partner's behavior by making him feel responsible for causing pain. The guiltmaker's favorite line is "It's O.K., don't worry about me..." accompanied by a big sigh.

6 **The Subject Changer**   Really a type of avoider, the subject changer escapes facing up to aggression by shifting the conversation whenever it approaches an area of conflict. Because of his tactics, the subject changer and his partner never have the chance to explore their problem and do something about it.

7 **The Distracter**   Rather than come out and express his feelings about the object of his dissatisfaction, the distracter attacks other parts of his partner's life. Thus he never has to share what's really on his mind and can avoid dealing with painful parts of his relationships.

8 **The Mind Reader**   Instead of allowing her partner to express his feelings honestly, the mind reader goes into character analysis, explaining what the other person really means or what's wrong with the other person. By behaving this way the mind reader refuses to handle her own feelings and leaves no room for her partner to express himself.

9 **The Trapper**   The trapper plays an especially dirty trick by setting up a desired behavior for her partner, and then when it's met, attacking the very thing she requested. An example of this technique is for the trapper to say, "Let's be totally honest with each other," and then when the partner shares his feelings, he finds himself attacked for having feelings that the trapper doesn't want to accept.

10 **The Crisis Tickler**   This person almost brings what's bothering him to the surface, but he never quite comes out and expresses himself. Instead of admitting his concern about the finances he innocently asks, "Gee, how much did that cost?" dropping a rather obvious hint but never really dealing with the crisis.

11 **The Gunnysacker**   This person doesn't respond immediately when she's angry.

Instead, she puts her resentment into her gunnysack, which after a while begins to bulge with large and small gripes. Then, when the sack is about to burst, the gunnysacker pours out all her pent-up aggressions on the overwhelmed and unsuspecting victim.

12 **The Trivial Tyrannizer**   Instead of honestly sharing his resentments, the trivial tyrannizer does things he knows will get his partner's goat—leaving dirty dishes in the sink, clipping his fingernails in bed, belching out loud, turning up the television too loud, and so on.

13 **The Joker**   Because she's afraid to face conflicts squarely, the joker kids around when her partner wants to be serious, thus blocking the expression of important feelings.

14 **The Beltliner**   Everyone has a psychological "beltline," and below it are subjects too sensitive to be approached without damaging the relationship. Beltlines may have to do with physical characteristics, intelligence, past behavior, or deeply ingrained personality traits a person is trying to overcome. In an attempt to "get even" or hurt his partner the beltliner will use his intimate knowledge to hit below the belt, where he knows it will hurt.

15 **The Blamer**   The blamer is more interested in finding fault than in solving a conflict. Needless to say, she usually doesn't blame herself. Blaming behavior almost never solves a conflict and is an almost surefire way to make the receiver defensive.

16 **The Contract Tyrannizer**   This person will not allow his relationship to change from the way it once was. Whatever the agreements the partners had as to roles and responsibilities at one time, they'll remain unchanged. "It's your job to...feed the baby, wash the dishes, discipline the kids,..."

17 **The Kitchen Sink Fighter**   This person is so named because in an argument he brings up things that are totally off the subject ("everything but the kitchen sink"): the way his partner behaved last New Year's eve, the unbalanced checkbook, bad breath—anything.

18 **The Withholder**   Instead of expressing her anger honestly and directly, the withholder punishes her partner by keeping back something—courtesy, affection, good cooking, humor, sex. As you can imagine, this is likely to build up even greater resentments in the relationship.

19 **The Benedict Arnold**   This character gets back at his partner by sabotage, by failing to defend him from attackers, and even by encouraging ridicule or disregard from outside the relationship.

would be to strike up a friendly conversation with one of the owners and casually remark about the terrible neighborhood you had just left, in which noisy dogs roamed the streets, uncontrolled by their thoughtless owners. (Or perhaps you could be more subtle and talk about noisy children instead!)

9   There are a number of shortcomings to such approaches as these, each of which illustrate the risks of indirect aggression. First, there is the chance that the crazymaking won't work: the neighbors might simply miss the point of your veiled attacks and continue to ignore the barking. On the other hand, they might get your message clearly, but either because of your lack of sincerity or out of sheer stubbornness they might simply refuse to do anything about the complaining. In either case it's likely that in this and other instances indirect aggression won't satisfy your unmet need.

10   Even when indirect aggression proves successful in the short run, a second shortcoming lies in its consequences over the longer range. You might manage to intimidate your neighbors into shutting up their mutt, for instance, but in winning that battle you could lose what would become a war. As a means of revenge, it's possible that they would wage their own campaign of crazymaking by such tactics as badmouthing things like your sloppy gardening to other neighbors or by phoning in false complaints about your allegedly loud parties. It's obvious that feuds such as this one are counter-productive and outweigh the apparent advantages of indirect aggression.

11   In addition to these unpleasant possibilities, a third shortcoming of indirect aggression is that it denies the people involved a chance of building any kind of honest relationship with each other. As long as you treat your neighbors as if they were an obstacle to be removed from your path, there's little likelihood that you'll get to know them as people. While this thought may not bother you, the principle that indirect aggression prevents intimacy holds true in other important areas of life. To the degree that you try to manipulate friends, they won't know the real you. The fewer of your needs you share directly with your coworkers, the less chance you have of becoming true friends and colleagues. The same principle holds for those people you hope to meet in the future. Indirect aggression denies closeness.

Styles of Conflict

	Nonassertive	Directly Aggressive	Indirectly Aggressive	Assertive
Approach to Others	I'm not O.K., You're O.K.	I'm O.K., You're not O.K.	I'm O.K., You're not O.K. (But I'll let you think you are.)	I'm O.K. You're O.K.
Decision Making	Let others choose	Choose for others. They know it.	Chooses for others They don't know it.	Chooses for self
Response of Others	Disrespect, guilt, anger, frustration	Hurt, defensiveness, humiliation	Confusion, frustration, feelings of manipulation	Mutual respect
Success Pattern	Succeeds by luck or charity of others	Beats out others	Wins by manipulation	Attempts "no lose" solutions

Adapted with permission from S. Phelps and N. Austin, *The Assertive Woman*. San Luis Obispo, CA: Impact, 1974 p. 11, and Gerald Piaget, American Orthopsychiatric Association, 1974.

Assertion

12   Assertive people handle conflicts skillfully by expressing their needs, thoughts, and feelings clearly and directly, but without judging others or dictating to them. They have the attitude that most of the time it is possible to resolve problems to everyone's satisfaction. Possessing this attitude and the skills to bring it about doesn't guarantee that assertive communicators will always get what they want, but it does give them the best chance of doing so. An additional benefit of such an approach is that whether or not it satisfies a particular need, it maintains the self-respect of both the asserters and those with whom they interact. As a result, people who manage their conflicts assertively may experience feelings of discomfort while they are working through the problem. They usually feel better about themselves and each other afterward—quite a change from the outcomes of no assertiveness and aggression.

13   An assertive course of action in the case of the barking dog would be to wait a few days to make sure that the noise is not just a fluke. If things continue in the present way, you could introduce yourself to your neighbors and explain your problem. You could tell them that although they might not notice it, the dog often plays in the street and keeps barking at passing cars. You could tell them why this behavior bothers you. It keeps you awake at night and makes it hard for you to do your work. You could point out that you don't want to be a grouch and call the pound. Rather than behaving in these ways, you could tell them that you've come to see what kind of solution you can find that will satisfy both of you. This approach may not work, and you might then have to decide whether it is more important to avoid bad feelings or to have peace and quiet. But the chances for a happy ending are best with this assertive approach. And no matter what happens, you can keep your self-respect by behaving directly and honestly.

Ronald B. Adler and Neil Towne, *Looking Out/Looking In*, pp. 198–204

3
Causes of Urban Problems

1   Almost every problem in U.S. society—drug abuse and crime, racism and poverty, poor education and environmental pollution—seems more severe in the cities, particularly in the older and more congested ones. Even as newer cities grow and age, their problems will probably become more severe. The difficulties that cities face and their ability to deal with them are shaped to a great extent by the intertwining effects of various social forces. We discuss some of them here.

Population Decline

2   In the last 10 years Detroit, Cleveland, Pittsburgh, St. Louis, and other big cities have lost more than 10 percent of their populations. In fact, most of the U.S. cities that have more than 200,000 people have suffered population declines (U.S. Census Bureau, 1998). On the face of it, this may look like good news for the cities' finances: fewer people should mean less demand for, and less spending on, police protection, fire protection, education, and other public services. In reality, however, population decreases have created serious problems.

3   As the years go by, a city must spend more to maintain its road, sewer, and water networks, even if it has fewer residents to pay for those services. Similarly, when families abandon the central city, the need for police and fire protection increases because abandoned homes can become magnets for vandalism and crime. They become fire hazards and finally must be torn down at the city's expense. Furthermore, behind the statistics of declining populations lies the fact that those who move out of the cities are largely middle-class whites, and with them go many businesses. Thus, the cities have fewer private-sector jobs and declining revenues. Those left behind in the city are typically less educated, poorer, and older—the people most in need of government spending for education, housing, health services, and welfare (Rybczynski, 1995; Gottdiener, 1994). In recent years, some efforts have been made to revitalize many cities by attracting tourists to spend money in the city, but more still needs to be done (see box).

Applied Sociology

How to Revitalize the City

According to a recent report by the U.S. Department of Housing and Urban Development, nineteen of the nation's thirty largest cities have suffered a population decline over the last two decades. The cities' poverty rate has also risen from 14 to 20 percent. The middle class continues to migrate to the suburbs, where significantly more jobs are created than in the cities. The urban poor are getting poorer and becoming more and more economically and physically isolated.

Confronted with these problems, a number of urban governments have recently expended a great deal of energy to revitalize their cities. Downtown Cleveland, once a dead zone of vacant lots, is now alive as a home to a new baseball stadium, a baseball arena, and the Rock-and-Roll Hall of Fame and Museum. The road to rebirth in New York City appears most clearly in the revitalization of Times Square and 42nd Street, and can be seen in 80 percent hotel occupancy rates throughout the city. Newark has built its splendid New Jersey Performing Arts Center as a symbol of urban resurgence, an example of what many consider necessary for a city to remake itself. In Detroit, many people are excited about the impending arrival of casinos, which are expected to bring in hordes of tourists and millions of dollars to the city.

As a result, many city centers do look better than they have in years. The influx of tourists, conventioneers, and suburbanites does help to enliven and enrich the cities to some degree. But these well-heeled people do not live in the cities and never will, while most inner-city neighbor-hoods, the heartbeat of any city, remain weak or depressed.

To accomplish more, cities should do more than simply transform themselves into entertainment satellites for people who do not reside there. Specifically, middle-class families should be encouraged to settle in cities. They will then have a strong, vested interest in urban schools and crime prevention because they will live in the city rather than just dabble in it. To lure the middle class into the city, however, the municipal government needs to reduce crime and improve schools as well as city services. The federal government should also provide economic incentives, such as income tax credits, low-interest loans, and other special mortgage programs to suburbanites who want to move back to the city.

Source: Bissinger, 1997.

Fiscal Squeeze

4   Urban problems stem largely from city governments' inability to generate sufficient income to provide various kinds of services to the public. Cities get most of their revenues from taxes on property, income, sales, and corporations. Some money comes from charging fees for services. But all these sources of revenue have shrunk over the last decade: the suburbs have drained off much of the cities' tax base by attracting industries and stores, as well as middle- and upper-class people.

5   There are other potential sources of revenue, but cities generally cannot tap them. In many states, cities are prohibited from raising as much in taxes as they wish. Cities are also deprived of other revenue-producing opportunities. When federal and state governments use city property, they are exempted from paying city taxes totaling billions of dollars. Suburbanites come into town, adding to traffic congestion, garbage, and wear and tear on roads and parks, while benefiting from police protection and other urban resources, but they pay no taxes to the city for these services.

6   Consequently, since the 1960s, cities have come to depend increasingly on the state and federal governments to help pay their bills. But since the late 1980s, the federal government has not been helpful after it was forced by stringent budget cuts to end the revenue-sharing program (Gottdiener, 1994; Schwab, 1992).

Political Dilemma

7   Part of the cities' fiscal problem originates with elected officials' unwillingness to raise taxes even if they have the power to do so and their citizens have the ability to pay. Given the unpopularity of tax increases, politicians tend to avoid risking taxpayers' anger even when taxes are low and necessary. But this political dilemma seems to have forced the cities to rely increasingly on private enterprise to tackle urban problems.

8   With their eyes on economic development, cities compete with one another to keep or attract businesses and industries. Low taxes and tax exemptions are used as lures. Although this may undermine the current tax base, the cities hope to build a larger tax base, through an increase in jobs, for the future.

9   Cities also set up **empowerment zones** (also known as *enterprise zones*), economically depressed urban areas that businesses, with the help of government grants, low-interest loans, and tax breaks, try to revive by creating jobs. In these special zones, thousands of jobs have been created for poor residents. A similar effort to solve public ills with private cures has appeared in another way. Grass-roots entrepreneurs known as *community development corporations (CDCs)* have rehabilitated abandoned homes, creating commercial enterprises and organizing social services in various large cities. Their objective is to succeed where governments have failed—by reclaiming city streets from crime and economic decline (Stout, 1996; Carlson, 1991; *New York Times,* 1991).

Housing Segregation

10   Every year billions of dollars are spent on housing in the United States. The government helps out by granting billions of dollars in tax deductions to landlords and homeowners. As a result, we are among the best-housed people in the world, with most of the nation's families owning their own homes. But it is difficult financially for minorities to own or rent a home. For one thing, minorities, especially African Americans, make up a high percentage of the population of the inner cities, where good housing at reasonable prices is scarce. While most African Americans living in metropolitan areas are concentrated in the inner cities, most of the metropolitan whites are spread out in the surrounding suburbs. In both the inner cities and the suburbs, African Americans are frequently segregated from whites and relegated to inferior housing.

11   Economics may be a factor in housing segregation. Because African Americans tend to have lower incomes, they often cannot afford to move into more expensive white neighborhoods. But racial discrimination is an even bigger factor. Real estate agents tend to steer potential African American buyers and renters away from white neighborhoods, perpetuating segregation, although this is an illegal practice. Banks are often more cautious in granting loans to African Americans than to whites, making it difficult for them to own or rehabilitate homes and thus encouraging the deterioration of African American neighborhoods. Many African Americans will not move into white neighborhoods because they want to avoid rejection by whites (Coulibaly, Green, and James, 1998).

Thinking Critically

What do you think would be the best ways to solve the problems of housing segregation?

Questions for Discussion and Review

1. What impact does population decline have on a city?
2. Why do many cities have serious financial problems?

3. How have cities dealt with the political dilemma of raising taxes?

4. What factors contribute to housing segregation?

Alex Thio, *Sociology: A Brief Introduction*, 4th ed., pp 427–430.

ACTIVITY 7

DIRECTIONS: For Activity 3, you previewed Chapter 4 from this textbook. Now turn all of the headings in that chapter into questions, and answer them in your notebook. Once again, use central messages, main ideas, context definitions, and patterns of organization to help you identify the most important information, and do not hesitate to underline or highlight it.

ACTIVITY 8

DIRECTIONS: Using the same chapter that you previewed for Activity 4, turn all of the headings into questions, and answer them in your notebook.

LOOKING BACK

Summarize and/or paraphrase the most important points you learned from this chapter and determine how they can be put to use in other classes. Be prepared to discuss with your classmates what you have written.

THINK AGAIN!

The following paragraphs are part of a graphic aid taken from a textbook chapter. Can you figure out the point or central message of all three stories taken together?

Picture These Scenes

1   A little league batter leaves the on-deck circle and enters the batter's box. The kid looks kind of scrawny, so you don't expect much, until you notice the gaze of determination and concentration in the batter's eyes and the coach's confident stance. The pitcher winds up, throws—and the kid swings, the bat cracks, and the ball sails sharply over the left-fielder's head. The kid rounds second to third, stares down the third baseman, and executes a perfect slide. Then the batter turns, takes off her cap and lets her long hair fall free, and flashes her winning smile at her third-base coach.

2   The nurse wipes the sweat from the surgeon's brow. The hip replacement surgery is going well, and the saw buzzes in the hand of the skillful surgeon as it is carefully moved through the pelvic bone. The work is demanding and physical. The nurse is adept at handing the surgeon each instrument at exactly the right moment; they have worked together

before and make a good team. Now it is time to close, and as the nurse prepares the sutures for the surgeon, a brief smile breaks out. "I am good at what I do," the nurse thinks to himself as he once again reaches over to wipe the surgeon's brow. The surgeon smiles in gratitude, grateful that she has such dedicated and able professionals working with her.

3   Robin undresses, feeling nervous and apprehensive, and then feels silly. After all, the photographer is a professional and has probably seen a thousand naked bodies, so what is one more? All that work in the weight room, the aerobics—why not show off, after all the work it took to get a such a tight body? "I should be proud," Robin thinks, slipping into the robe thoughtfully provided by the photographer. Once exposed to the lights of the studio, Robin gets another pang of doubt but dismisses it and drops the robe. The photographer suggests a seated pose, and Robin strikes it, but he drops his hands to cover his genitals. "Move your hands to your knees, please," the photographer says gently. After all, she is a professional and knows how to put her models at ease.

Janell L. Carroll and Paul Root Wolpe, Sexuality and Gender in Society, p. 162

The Dashing Detective

Remember to follow these steps:

- first, read the narrative and the question
- second, examine the picture carefully
- third, answer the question and come up with the solution

Have fun!

Wedding Day

After a night on the town with a few friends, young Lochinvar woke up in his bedroom on a gray, sunless morn and faced his wedding day as you see it. He was known to be compulsively late on practically all occasions, and the lovely Griselda, his bride-to-be, had said that if he was as much as one minute late for their 11:00 A.M. ceremony, the marriage would be off.

If you were young Lochinvar, what would you do?

Lawrence Treat, *Crime and Puzzlement*, p. 48

Name _____ Date _____

MASTERY TEST 3–1

DIRECTIONS: Fill in the blanks and answer the questions.

1. The method used to get acquainted with a new textbook is called _____.

2. The method used to familiarize yourself with a textbook chapter is called _____.

3. Questions, reference sources, and summaries are examples of _____ aids.

4. A textbook's organization can be seen in the
   a. index
   b. bibliography
   c. glossary
   d. all of the above
   e. none of the above

5. The preface is important because
   a. it gives the author's purpose
   b. lists features
   c. explains the aids to understanding
   d. all of the above
   e. none of the above

6. Page locations for very specific information can be found in the
   a. index
   b. preface
   c. table of contents
   d. appendix
   e. none of the above

7. A _____ provides definitions of words or combinations of words that fit the context of a given textbook.

8. Supplementary or additional information, such as maps and diagrams, can be found in the
   a. table of contents
   b. preface
   c. appendix
   d. index
   e. none of the above

9. For research purposes, it is useful to consult
   a. the bibliography
   b. a list of general reference sources

c. footnotes

d. a list of suggested readings

e. all of the above

10. A _____ contains sources used by the author to write the textbook.

11. The _____ states the topic of a given textbook chapter.

12. You can determine exactly what you are expected to know in a chapter and also set personal study goals by looking at the

a. objectives

b. goals

c. outcomes

d. all of the above

e. none of the above

13. _____ aids include charts, graphs, maps, pictures, and tables.

14. _____ or titles let you know what a graphic aid is about.

15. The _____ message of a chapter can sometimes be found in the first or last paragraph.

16. You can plan how to tackle a reading assignment by checking the length and difficulty of a chapter. True or false?

17. "Questions at the end of a chapter can help direct your reading to the most valuable information." Is this statement true or false?

18. Turning _____ into questions helps you focus your attention and evaluate the most important information in a chapter.

19. Underlining or highlighting textbook information is a useful technique that enables you to

a. comprehend better

b. review more quickly

c. concentrate better

d. all of the above

e. none of the above

20. The words _____, _____, _____,

_____, _____, and _____ should be used to make questions out of chapter headings.

Name _____   Date _____

MASTERY TEST 3-2

DIRECTIONS: For the two textbook selections that follow, turn the headings into questions, and write the questions in the space provided. Underline or highlight the most important information, and then write out the answers in your notebook. Also, indicate what two questions should be asked and answered concerning the graphic aids in the first selection.

1

Guidelines for Evaluating Sources

Determine relevance:
- Does the source devote some attention to your topic?
- Where in the source are you likely to find relevant information or ideas?
- Is the source appropriately specialized for your needs? Check the source's treatment of a topic you know something about, to ensure that it is neither too superficial nor too technical.
- How important is the source likely to be for your writing?

Judge reliability:
- How up to date is the source? If the publication date is not recent, be sure that other sources will give you more current views.
- Is the author an expert in the field? Look for an author biography, look up the author in a biographical reference, or try to trace the author over the Internet.
- What is the author's bias? Check biographical information or the author's own preface or introduction. Use book review indexes or citation indexes to learn what others have written about the author or the source.
- Whatever his or her bias, does the author reason soundly, provide adequate evidence, and consider opposing views?

Evaluating Electronic Sources

To a great extent, the same critical reading that serves you with print sources will help you evaluate online sources, too (see the box). But online sources can range from scholarly works to corporate promotions, from government-sponsored data to the self-published rantings of crackpots. To evaluate an online source, you'll first need to figure out what it is.

- *Checking the electronic address.* Look for an abbreviation that tells you where the source originates: edu (educational institution), gov (government body), org (nonprofit organization), mil (military), or com (commercial organization). With a source coming from compex.com, you should assume that the contents reflect the company's commercial purposes (although the information may still be helpful). With a source coming from harvard.edu, you can assume that the contents are more scholarly and objective (although you should still evaluate the information yourself).
- *Determining authorship or sponsorship.* Many sites list the person(s) or group(s) responsible for the site. A Web site may provide links to information about or other work

by an author or group. If not, you can refer to a biographical dictionary or conduct a keyword search of the Web. You should also look for mentions of the author or group in your other sources.

Often you will not be able to trace authors or sponsors or even identify them at all. For instance, someone passionate about the rights of adoptees might maintain a Web site devoted to the subject but not identify himself or herself as the author. In such a case, you'll need to evaluate the quality of the information and opinions by comparing them with sources you know to be reliable.

Guidelines for Evaluating Online Sources

- Check the electronic address for an idea of where the source originates.
- Determine who is responsible for the site.
- Gauge the purpose of the site: to build knowledge? to sell something? to create fear? to achieve another goal?
- Evaluate a Web site as a whole, considering its design, its readability, and the value of its links.

- Weigh contributions to discussion groups by putting them in the context of other contributions. Drop sources whose authors will not answer your direct questions.
- Check for references or links to reliable sources, watching especially for balance.
- Compare online sources with tested mainstream sources.

- *Gauging purpose.* Inferring the purpose of an online source can help you evaluate its reliability. Some sources may seem intent on selling ideas or products. Others may seem to be building knowledge—for instance, by acknowledging opposing views either directly or through links to other sites. Still others may seem determined to scare readers with shocking statistics or anecdotes.

- *Evaluating a Web site as a whole.* Consider both the design and the readability of a Web site and the nature of its links. Is the site thoughtfully designed, or is it cluttered with irrelevant material and graphics? Is it carefully written or difficult to understand? Do the links help clarify the purpose of the site—perhaps leading to scholarly sources or, in contrast, to frivolous or indecent sites?

- *Weighing the contributions to discussion groups.* You need to read individuals' contributions to discussion groups especially critically because they are unfiltered and unevaluated. Even on a discussion list, whose subscribers are likely to be professionals in the field, you may find wrong or misleading data and skewed opinions. With the more accessible Web forums and newsgroups, you should view postings with considerable skepticism.

  You can try to verify a contribution to a discussion group by looking at other contributions, which may help you confirm or refute the questionable posting, and by communicating directly with the author to ask about his or her background and publications. If you can't verify the information from a discussion group and the author doesn't respond to your direct approach, you should probably ignore the source.

- *Checking for references or links to reliable sources.* An online source may offer as support the titles of sources that you can trace and evaluate—articles in periodicals, other online sources, and so on. A Web site may include links to these other sources.

    Be aware, however, that online sources may refer you only to other sources that share the same bias. When evaluating both the original source and its references, look for a fair treatment of opposing views.
- *Comparing online and other sources.* Always consider online sources in the context of other sources so that you can distinguish singular, untested views from more mainstream views that have been subject to verification.

H. Ramsey Fowler and Jane E. Aaron, *The Little, Brown Handbook*, 8th ed., pp. 669–672.

QUESTIONS

_____

_____

_____

_____

_____

_____

_____

GRAPHIC AID QUESTIONS

_____

_____

_____

_____

_____

_____

_____

2
Homosexuality

1   Homosexuality may involve having the *feeling* of sexual desire for members of the same sex, the *experience* of having sex with persons of the same sex, or the *identification of oneself* as a gay or lesbian. Because of prejudice and discrimination against homo-

sexuality, most people with same-sex feelings or experiences do not identify themselves as gay. This is why a sex survey shows that only about 1.4 percent of U.S. women and 2.8 percent of men identify themselves as gay even though considerably more people (4 percent for women and 9 percent for men) have had a same-sex experience (*Society,* 1993).

THEORIES

2   Researchers in various disciplines have tried to explain the origin of homosexuality. Their explanations may be classified into three major types: biological, psychiatric, and sociological theories.

BIOLOGICAL THEORIES

3   Homosexuality has been linked to at least three kinds of biological factors: hormones, genes, and brain.

4   According to the *hormone theory,* gay men have lower levels of male sex hormones than nongay men, and lesbians have fewer female sex hormones than nonlesbians. But most studies have found no hormonal difference between gays or lesbians and straights (Burr, 1996; Porter, 1996).

5   According to the *genetic theory,* people are born rather than bred to be gay. Studies have suggested that the probability of two siblings becoming gay together is significantly higher among *identical* twins than among *fraternal* twins. This is taken to mean that homosexuality is largely determined by genes, because identical twins are more genetically alike than fraternal twins. But the findings do not necessarily mean that homosexuality can be traced to genes. Social environment may contribute to the development of homosexuality because, when compared with fraternal twins, identical twins are more likely to elicit similar responses from others—to be treated by parents, peers, strangers, and other members of society in the same way (Alessio, 1996; Burr, 1996; Porter, 1996).

6   A different kind of study claims to have found the "gay gene" somewhere on the X chromosome of gays. But the researchers studied only gay men, and it is quite possible that the so-called gay gene also appears in these gays' *heterosexual* brothers (Bishop, 1993; Burr, 1996; Porter, 1996).

7   The *brain theory* comes from a study in which Simon LeVay (1996) examined brain tissues from deceased gay and straight men. The researcher found, among other things, a difference in the size of the hypothalamus, the cluster of neurons, or nervous tissues, in the brain's lower area, which controls sex drive and body temperature. The gays' hypothalamuses were less than half the size of those in the straights. It was concluded that a relatively small brain could make a person gay. But it could be the other way around, namely, that homosexuality may affect the brain structure. There is evidence that the brain's neural networks can change in response to certain experiences. In people reading Braille after becoming blind, for example, the area of the brain controlling the reading finger usually grows larger (Ridley, 1996).

PSYCHIATRIC THEORIES

8   For many years most psychiatrists assumed that homosexuality was a form of mental illness. But in 1973 the American Psychiatric Association (APA) decided to define homosexuality as normal. Still today the APA continues to find some, though not most, gays and

lesbians to be suffering from what it calls *sexual orientation disturbance*. Most psychiatrists would help these troubled gays to accept their homosexuality and feel comfortable with themselves. But some psychiatrists would try to "cure" the "patients" of their homosexuality. Such psychiatrists continue to hold the belief that homosexuality is characterized by "hidden but incapacitating fears of the opposite sex" (Socarides et al., 1997; Berger, 1994; Bayer, 1987).

9   This pathological fear is often attributed to an abnormal parent-son relationship. A young boy is said to become gay later in life if he has a domineering, overprotective, or seductive mother and a weak, detached, or hostile father. Alienated from his father, the boy will not look on him as a model for learning the masculine role. Instead, being driven by his hostile father into the arms of his loving mother, the boy will learn to identify himself with her. As a consequence, the boy will likely grow up to become gay, according to this theory (Herman and Duberman, 1995; Bayer, 1987).

10   Many psychiatrists have found most of their gay patients to have had disturbed relationships with their parents, but these patients do not represent the majority of the gay population. Numerous studies on average, *non*patient gays have found them to be no different from heterosexuals in parent-child relationships (Ross and Arrindell, 1988).

SOCIOLOGICAL THEORIES

11   A basic problem with biological theories is their assumption that homosexuality is universally the same. Were this true, we should expect various societies to have about the same percentage of gays and lesbians. But the reality is that homosexuality varies greatly in form and frequency from one society to another.

12   Though relatively rare in many Western societies today, homosexual practices have been and are common in other societies such as ancient Greece, ancient Japan, the Azande of Africa, and New Guinea societies. In some of these societies, male teenagers have sex regularly with older men as a normal way of growing up, but later, in adulthood, marry women and have children (Herdt, 1990). This suggests that society has much to do with the development of homosexuality. To most sociologists, then, homosexuality is largely social behavior, no different from heterosexuality. Both are assumed to develop from past social experiences. Only the specific nature of their social experiences differs.

13   While they do not believe that certain hormones, genes, or brain size causes homosexuality, many sociologists nonetheless assume that gays and lesbians may be born with a biological *predisposition* that makes them more likely than other children to be attracted to members of the same sex. By itself, however, this biological predisposition does not automatically cause a person to become gay. As suggested by societal variations in the incidence of homosexuality, society can check—or encourage—it through a *socializing* process (Dickermann, 1995; Bullough, 1993).

14   The socializing process may involve children acquiring sexual orientation from physical contact with parents during the sensitive period between birth and age three. As research has suggested, if a mother kisses, touches, or caresses her little girl more than her little boy, as expected by the predominantly heterosexual society, then both the girl and the boy are likely to become heterosexual. But if, contrary to the expectation of heterosexual society, the mother has more physical contact with the boy than the girl, both children have a greater chance of growing up to be gay. Thus, parents can teach, though

often unintentionally, their children how to feel like members of the opposite sex by treating them as such (Fleishman, 1983).

15   This reflects an *essentialist* view of homosexuality, which regards sexual orientation as real and therefore seeks to explain how it has come about. But some sociologists are *social constructionists,* not interested in finding out what causes homosexuality. This is because they do not see homosexuality as real in and of itself, but as a social construct—society's definition of homosexuality as undesirable. To constructionists, then, how gays and lesbians live their lives has more to do with how society treats them than with their sexual orientation per se. Constructionists are therefore mostly interested in studying societal responses to homosexuality and how those responses affect the lives of gays and lesbians.

Alex Thio, *Sociology,* 5th ed., pp. 210–212

QUESTIONS

_____

_____

_____

_____

_____

_____

_____

_____

Name _____ Date _____

MASTERY TEST 3–3

DIRECTIONS: Pretend that you are in the following situation:

> You have been dating a person for the past year and have become very attached. Recently, another person has shown great interest in and started to pursue the person you have been dating, who apparently is very flattered by the extra attention.

Think about how would you handle this conflict situation. Now, based on the textbook passage "Styles of Conflict" which you focused on in Activity 6, identify *your* style of conflict.

_____

_____

_____

_____

_____

_____

_____

PLAYING SHERLOCK HOLMES AND DR. WATSON

Arthur Conan Doyle's fictional detective, Sherlock Holmes, is probably the greatest critical thinker of all time. This semester, you and a classmate will be given the opportunity to play Sherlock Holmes and his loyal companion, Dr. Watson. By putting your minds together, you will attempt to solve the case in "The Adventure of the Three Students."

At the end of each part of this textbook, the two of you will answer questions concerning the case, which ideally will lead you to the identity of the culprit. As a start, you and your partner should read the first part of the short story and then answer the questions that follow it. Write the answers in your notebooks. Have fun!

The Return of Sherlock Holmes
The Adventure of the Three Students: Part One

A. CONAN DOYLE

1   It was in the year '95 that a combination of events, into which I need not enter, caused Mr. Sherlock Holmes and myself to spend some weeks in one of our great University towns, and it was during this time that the small but instructive adventure which I am about to relate befell us. It will be obvious that any details which would help the reader to exactly identify the college or the criminal would be injudicious and offensive. So painful a scandal may well be allowed to die out. With due discretion the incident itself may, however, be described, since it serves to illustrate some of those qualities for which my friend was remarkable. I will endeavour in my statement to avoid such terms as would serve to limit the events to any particular place, or give a clue as to the people concerned.

2   We were residing at the time in furnished lodgings close to a library where Sherlock Holmes was pursuing some laborious researches in early English charters—researches which led to results so striking that they may be the subject of one of my future narratives. Here it was that one evening we received a visit from an acquaintance, Mr. Hilton Soames, tutor and lecturer at the College of St. Luke's. Mr. Soames was a tall, spare man, of a nervous and excitable temperament. I had always known him to be restless in his manner, but on this particular occasion he was in such a state of uncontrollable agitation that it was clear something very unusual had occurred.

3   "I trust, Mr. Holmes, that you can spare me a few hours of your valuable time. We have had a very painful incident at St. Luke's, and really, but for the happy chance of your being in the town, I should have been at a loss what to do."

4   "I am very busy just now, and I desire no distractions," my friend answered. "I should much prefer that you called in the aid of the police."

5   "No, no, my dear sir; such a course is utterly impossible. When once the law is evoked it cannot be stayed again, and this is just one of those cases where, for the credit of the college, it is most essential to avoid scandal. Your discretion is as well known as your powers, and you are the one man in the world who can help me. I beg you, Mr. Holmes, to do what you can."

6   My friend's temper had not improved since he had been deprived of the congenial surroundings of Baker Street. Without his scrap-books, his chemicals, and his homely

untidiness, he was an uncomfortable man. He shrugged his shoulders in ungracious acqui-escence, while our visitor in hurried words and with much excitable gesticulation poured forth his story.

7   "I must explain to you, Mr. Holmes, that to-morrow is the first day of the examina-tion for the Fortescue Scholarship. I am one of the examiners. My subject is Greek, and the first of the papers consists of a large passage of Greek translation which the candidate has not seen. This passage is printed on the examination paper, and it would naturally be an immense advantage if the candidate could prepare it in advance. For this reason great care is taken to keep the paper secret.

8   "To-day about three o'clock the proofs of this paper arrived from the printers. The exercise consists of half a chapter of Thucydides. I had to read it over carefully, as the text must be absolutely correct. At four-thirty my task was not yet completed. I had, how-ever, promised to take tea in a friend's rooms, so I left the proof upon my desk. I was absent rather more than an hour.

9   "You are aware, Mr. Holmes, that our college doors are double—a green baize one within and a heavy oak one without. As I approached my outer door I was amazed to see a key in it. For an instant I imagined that I had left my own there, but on feeling in my pocket I found that it was all right. The only duplicate which existed, so far as I knew, was that which belonged to my servant, Bannister, a man who has looked after my room for ten years, and whose honesty is absolutely above suspicion. I found that the key was indeed his, that he had entered my room to know if I wanted tea, and that he had very carelessly left the key in the door when he came out. His visit to my room must have been within a very few minutes of my leaving it. His forgetfulness about the key would have mattered little upon any other occasion, but on this one day it has produced the most deplorable consequences.

10   "The moment I looked at my table I was aware that someone had rummaged among my papers. The proof was in three long slips. I had left them all together. Now I found that one of them was lying on the floor, one was on the side table near the window, and the third was where I had left it."

11   Holmes stirred for the first time.

12   "The first page on the floor, the second in the window, the third where you left it," said he.

13   "Exactly, Mr. Holmes. You amaze me. How could you possibly know that?"

14   "Pray continue your very interesting statement."

15   "For an instant I imagined that Bannister had taken the unpardonable liberty of examin-ing my papers. He denied it, however, with the utmost earnestness, and I am convinced that he was speaking the truth. The alternative was that someone passing had observed the key in the door, had known that I was out, and had entered to look at the papers. A large sum of money is at stake, for the scholarship is a very valuable one, and an unscrupulous man might very well run a risk in order to gain an advantage over his fellows.

16   "Bannister was very much upset by the incident. He had nearly fainted when we found that the papers had undoubtedly been tampered with. I gave him a little brandy

and left him collapsed in a chair while I made a most careful examination of the room. I soon saw that the intruder had left other traces of his presence besides the rumpled papers. On the table in the window were several shreds from a pencil which had been sharpened. A broken tip of lead was lying there also. Evidently the rascal had copied the paper in a great hurry, had broken his pencil, and had been compelled to put a fresh point to it."

17   "Excellent!" said Holmes, who was recovering his good-humour as his attention became more engrossed by the case. "Fortune has been your friend."

18   "This was not all. I have a new writing-table with a fine surface of red leather. I am prepared to swear, and so is Bannister, that it was smooth and unstained. Now I found a clean cut in it about three inches long—not a mere scratch, but a positive cut. Not only this, but on the table I found a small ball of black dough, or clay, with specks of something which looks like sawdust in it. I am convinced that these marks were left by the man who rifled the papers. There were no footmarks and no other evidence as to his identity. I was at my wits' ends, when suddenly the happy thought occurred to me that you were in the town, and I came straight round to put the matter into your hands. Do help me, Mr. Holmes! You see my dilemma. Either I must find the man or else the examination must be postponed until fresh papers are prepared, and since this cannot be done without explanation there will ensue a hideous scandal, which will throw a cloud not only on the college, but on the University. Above all things I desire to settle the matter quietly and discreetly."

19   "I shall be happy to look into it and to give you such advice as I can," said Holmes, rising and putting on his overcoat. "The case is not entirely devoid of interest. Had any-one visited you in your room after the papers came to you?"

20   "Yes; young Daulat Ras, an Indian student who lives on the same stair, came in to ask me some particulars about the examination."

21   "For which he was entered?"

22   "Yes."

23   "And the papers were on your table?"

24   "To the best of my belief they were rolled up."

25   "But might be recognised as proofs?"

26   "Possibly."

27   "No one else in your room?"

28   "No."

29   "Did anyone know that these proofs would be there?"

30   "No one save the printer."

31   "Did this man Bannister know?"

32   "No, certainly not. No one knew."

33   "Where is Bannister now?"

34   "He was very ill, poor fellow. I left him collapsed in the chair. I was in such a hurry to come to you."

35   "You left your door open?"

36   "I locked up the papers first."

37   "Then it amounts to this, Mr. Soames, that unless the Indian student recognised the roll as being proofs, the man who tampered with them came upon them accidentally without knowing that they were there."

38   "So it seems to me."

39   Holmes gave an enigmatic smile.

40   "Well," said he, "let us go round. Not one of your cases, Watson—mental, not physical. All right; come if you want to. Now, Mr. Soames—at your disposal!"

41   The sitting-room of our client opened by a long, low, latticed window on to the ancient lichen-tinted court of the old college. A Gothic arched door led to a worn stone staircase. On the ground floor was the tutor's room. Above were three students, one on each story. It was already twilight when we reached the scene of our problem. Holmes halted and looked earnestly at the window. Then he approached it, and, standing on tiptoe with his neck craned, he looked into the room.

42   "He must have entered through the door. There is no opening except the one pane," said our learned guide.

43   "Dear me!" said Holmes, and he smiled in a singular way as he glanced at our companion. "Well, if there is nothing to be learned here we had best go inside."

44   The lecturer unlocked the outer door and ushered us into his room. We stood at the entrance while Holmes made an examination of the carpet.

45   "I am afraid there are no signs here," said he. "One could hardly hope for any upon so dry a day. Your servant seems to have quite recovered. You left him in a chair, you say; which chair?"

46   "By the window there."

47   "I see. Near this little table. You can come in now. I have finished with the carpet. Let us take the little table first. Of course, what has happened is very clear. The man entered and took the papers, sheet by sheet, from the central table. He carried them over to the window table, because from there he could see if you came across the courtyard, and so could effect an escape."

48   As a matter of fact he could not," said Soames, "for I entered by the side door."

49   "Ah, that's good! Well, anyhow, that was in his mind. Let me see the three strips. No finger impressions—no! Well, he carried over this one first and he copied it. How long would it take him to do that, using every possible contraction? A quarter of an hour, not less. Then he tossed it down and seized the next. He was in the midst of that when your return caused him to make a very hurried retreat—very hurried, since he had not time to replace the papers which would tell you that he had been there. You were not aware of any hurrying feet on the stair as you entered the outer door?"

50   "No, I can't say I was."

51   "Well, he wrote so furiously that he broke his pencil, and had, as you observe, to sharpen it again. This is of interest, Watson. The pencil was not an ordinary one. It was above the usual size, with a soft lead; the outer colour was dark blue, the maker's name was printed in silver lettering, and the piece remaining is only about an inch and a half long. Look for such a pencil, Mr. Soames, and you have got your man. When I add that he possesses a large and very blunt knife, you have an additional aid."

52   Mr. Soames was somewhat overwhelmed by this flood of information. "I can follow the other points," said he, "but really in this matter of the length—"

53   Holmes held out a small chip with the letters NN and a space of clear wood after them.

54   "You see?"

55   "No, I fear that even now—"

56   "Watson, I have always done you an injustice. There are others. What could this NN be? It is at the end of a word. You are aware that Johann Faber is the most common maker's name. Is it not clear that there is just as much of the pencil left as usually follows the Johann?" He held the small table sideways to the electric light. "I was hoping that if the paper on which he wrote was thin some trace of it might come through upon this polished surface. No, I see nothing. I don't think there is anything more to be learned here. Now for the central table. This small pellet is, I presume, the black, doughy mass you spoke of. Roughly pyramidal in shape and hollowed out, I perceive. As you say, there appear to be grains of sawdust in it. Dear me, this is very interesting. And the cut—a positive tear, I see. It began with a thin scratch and ended in a jagged hole. I am much indebted to you for directing my attention to this case, Mr. Soames. Where does that door lead to?"

57   "To my bedroom."

58   "Have you been in it since your adventure?"

59   "No; I came straight away for you."

60   "I should like to have a glance round. What a charming, old-fashioned room! Perhaps you will kindly wait a minute until I have examined the floor. No, I see nothing. What about this curtain? You hang your clothes behind it. If anyone were forced to conceal himself in this room he must do it there, since the bed is too low and the wardrobe too shallow. No one there, I suppose?"

61   As Holmes drew the curtain I was aware, from some little rigidity and alertness of his attitude, that he was prepared for an emergency. As a matter of fact the drawn curtain disclosed nothing but three or four suits of clothes hanging from a line of pegs. Holmes turned away and stooped suddenly to the floor.

62   "Halloa! What's this?" said he.

63   It was a small pyramid of black, putty-like stuff, exactly like the one upon the table of the study. Holmes held it out on his open palm in the glare of the electric light.

64   "Your visitor seems to have left traces in your bedroom as well as in your sitting-room, Mr. Soames."

65   "What could he have wanted there?"

66   "I think it is clear enough. You came back by an unexpected way, and so he had no warning until you were at the very door. What could he do? He caught up everything which would betray him and he rushed into your bedroom to conceal himself."

67   "Good gracious, Mr. Holmes, do you mean to tell me that all the time I was talking to Bannister in this room we had the man prisoner if we had only known it?"

68   "So I read it."

69   "Surely there is another alternative, Mr. Holmes. I don't know whether you observed my bedroom window?"

70   "Lattice-paned, lead framework, three separate windows, one swinging on hinge and large enough to admit a man."

71   "Exactly. And it looks out on an angle of the courtyard so as to be partly invisible. The man might have effected his entrance there, left traces as he passed through the bedroom, and, finally, finding the door open have escaped that way."

The Complete Original Illustrated Sherlock Holmes, pp. 566–570

QUESTIONS

1. What is the problem that confronts Holmes and Watson?
2. What are the clues?
3. At this point in the mystery, are there any suspects? If so, who are they, and why do you consider them suspects?

PART 2

DEALING WITH COMPLEXITY

CHAPTER 4
CRITICAL THINKING AND CONTEMPORARY ISSUES

CHAPTER OUTLINE

THINK ABOUT IT!

In a sentence or two, state the central message of each of the signs in the photographs—in other words, the overall point of each of them. Discuss your answers with your classmates.

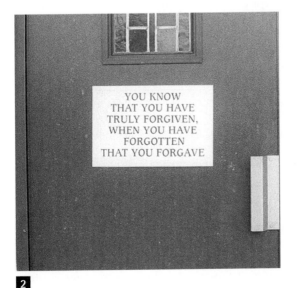

CHAPTER OUTCOMES

After completing Chapter 4, you should be able to:

■ Distinguish between critical thinking and random thinking

■ Discuss the benefits and uses of critical thinking

■ List, explain, and demonstrate the characteristics of critical thinking

■ Define a "contemporary issue"

■ Find topics and central messages in contemporary issue passages in order to determine what is at issue, distinguish among opposing viewpoints, and express personal viewpoints

CRITICAL THINKING VERSUS RANDOM THINKING

Take a few moments just to let some thoughts pass through your mind. What are you thinking about? Are you reflecting on what you did last night or what you intend to do this weekend? Are you worried about an assignment that is due or a test that is coming up? Maybe you are focusing on an important person in your life. Perhaps you are just thinking about how hungry or tired you are. The possibilities are endless.

What you just did was an example of **random thinking,** which is *thinking without a clear purpose or objective in mind.* We all do this kind of thinking countless times each day, often without even realizing it. Sometimes we are simply daydreaming, thinking about past experiences, or wondering or worrying about some future activity. Thoughts pop into mind and just as quickly out; they come and go without much effort on our part. Nothing is really accomplished as a result, except perhaps a rest or escape from whatever we may be doing at that particular time.

Random thinking is not critical thinking. How do they differ? Let's look at an example.

Suppose that you and a friend are considering whether to take a particular course next semester. The two of you approach another student who enrolled for that course last year, and she informs you that she dropped it after two weeks because it was so boring. On the basis of that conversation, your friend decides not to take the course. Although you are tempted to do the same thing, you decide instead to give the matter more thought because you do not think it wise to base your decision solely on the opinion of one student, who might have had a personal reason for not appreciating the course. For example, she could have had a problem at the time that interfered with her ability to fulfill the course requirements, or she could have been uncomfortable with the instructor's personality and teaching style. These may have been good reasons at the time for her not to stay in the course, but that does not mean that they should have an effect on your decision. Consequently, rather than automatically accepting one person's opinion, you decide to spend more time and effort getting additional information before coming to a final decision.

You organize your efforts by first getting a class schedule for next semester in order to find out the days and times that the course is offered and which faculty teach it. You want to determine if you can fit the course into your schedule and whether or not you have a choice of instructor. Second, you check the college catalog so that you can read the course description to see what it is about in a general sense and whether it can be used as part of your program of study. Third, you obtain a copy of a recent course syllabus from the department, a counselor, the instructor, or a student so that you can get additional information on assignments and grading. Fourth, you ask around so that you can find and talk to more students who have taken the course. Fifth, you discuss the course with a faculty member and your counselor or academic adviser.

After considering carefully all the information you gathered, you now feel confident about coming to a conclusion regarding whether or not to enroll in the course. You know that it fits into your program of study and your schedule, and you have a better understanding of its content. Furthermore, you are aware of who teaches the course and can determine if you are comfortable with his teaching style, grading policies, and personality. No matter what you ultimately decide to do, you have placed yourself in a much stronger position to make the right decision *for you.* However, you do continue to reconsider that decision right up until the time of registration, just in case you find out some additional information that changes your mind.

The process that you used in the example above involved **critical thinking,** which is best described as *a very careful and thoughtful way of dealing with events, issues, problems, decisions, or situations.* As you can see, it can be very helpful to you. Let's take a brief look at its many benefits and uses.

BENEFITS AND USES OF CRITICAL THINKING

Critical thinking is important because it makes you a much more careful decision maker who has the best chance of assessing situations accurately, making sense of issues and events, and coming up with solutions to problems. Because critical thinkers do not accept blindly everything they see, hear, or read, they place themselves in a better position to understand what is going on around them, to avoid costly mistakes, and to accomplish whatever they set out to do.

There are no limits to the uses of critical thinking. It can help you evaluate textbook material and other types of reading; uncover motivations and assess arguments; consider options, products, advertisements, and commercials; and judge policies and programs such as those offered by the various levels of government. The benefits of critical thinking for you are very real and substantial no matter what roles you play in life now and in the future, including those of student, professional, parent, and citizen. Make it a habit to think critically about everything!

CHARACTERISTICS OF CRITICAL THINKING

How do you know for sure when you are thinking critically? The answer to that question involves a discussion of its characteristics. Critical thinking requires:

- flexibility
- a clear purpose

- organization
- time and effort
- asking questions and finding answers
- research
- coming to logical conclusions

Let's consider each of these characteristics in more detail.

Flexibility

Critical thinking is **flexible thinking** because it involves a willingness to consider various possibilities before coming to a conclusion. Critical thinkers do not jump to conclusions or automatically accept what they first see, hear, or read. They are willing to gather and consider additional information, even if it does not support what they initially think or want to do. In the course selection example, it would have been easy for you simply to accept the first student's opinion and your friend's decision regarding the course. Even though you may have been tempted to take the quick and easy way out, you delayed your decision until you had a chance to gather more information. Realizing that your first reaction to the course was negative, you still managed to keep an open mind and were willing to consider carefully other viewpoints.

Critical thinkers, then, are aware of their initial feelings about decisions, issues, problems, or situations yet willing to look at other possibilities before taking action. *They are also willing to allow others the opportunity to voice their opinions, and they give careful consideration to those opinions before coming to their own conclusions.* In the end, critical thinkers may stick with their initial feelings, but only after much investigation and thought.

ACTIVITY 1

DIRECTIONS: Think about an example from your life in which you showed flexibility and an example from your life in which you did not. Be prepared to discuss your two examples.

ACTIVITY 2

DIRECTIONS: Read and think carefully about the following passage. Decide which side of the argument you disagree with and why, and show flexibility by writing a paragraph in support of that position. In other words, you are being asked to ignore your personal viewpoint and support the opposite one. You will be asked to provide the reasons why you disagree with the argument and also discuss the paragraph you wrote in support of it.

Pro & Con: Should Poor Immigrants Be Denied Free Medical Care?

The 1996 welfare reform law cuts off most health care benefits for new immigrants. It also permits states to end subsidized medical care for those already living in the United

States. Families that sponsor immigrants will now be required to pay their bills. If sponsors refuse, immigrants could go without care or turn to hospital emergency rooms, which cannot deny treatment in life-threatening situations.

Yes

1   Since this nation began, our policy has been to deport any noncitizen who becomes a public burden. The idea of immigration has always been to allow a limited number of people to come here for the opportunity to work, become self-sufficient, and contribute to the economy. To ensure self-reliance, all legal immigrants must have sponsors here who promise to support them if necessary. But those obligations have not been honored.

2   Instead, increasing numbers of legal immigrants are older people brought here by their children to go on Medicaid and supplemental security income. These elderly immigrants are our fastest growing welfare population. If the number of immigrants on Medicaid or ssi continues to increase at the present rate, the cost to taxpayers will be about $320 billion over the next ten years. This nation never intended to open its doors to people who would retire on welfare at the taxpayers' expense.

3   Denying nonemergency medical care to immigrants carries little health risk. We already screen immigrants for tuberculosis, and free vaccinations against contagious diseases are available to all at public health clinics. Some immigrants might turn to hospital emergency rooms for care, but in the long run most will stop coming to the United States once the free ride ends.

4   In a nation that spends 5 percent of its money on welfare benefits for the

No

1   Historically Congress has exempted sponsors' income when determining immigrants' eligibility for Medicaid. Our leaders recognized that medical care is too important—both to individuals in need and to public health—for anyone to go without. Subsidized treatment for the poor helps us control communicable diseases such as tuberculosis. And, just as important, it supports our system of hospitals, clinics, and doctors, which could otherwise be placed in financial jeopardy.

2   There is no evidence that immigrants bring their elderly parents here to get free medical care. They want to reunite with their mothers and fathers, and help care for them as they age. There's nothing wrong with that. That's family values.

3   The new policy is both inhumane and fiscally foolish. Arriving immigrants virtually always work and pay taxes, but they often don't earn enough to buy health insurance. The longer they go without basic care, the more likely they are to develop disabling conditions that could prevent them from paying taxes in the future. Further, all babies born here are U.S. citizens; they can't be deported. Providing prenatal care to immigrant mothers is much less expensive than caring for children born with severe and preventable health problems.

4   Besides, forcing immigrants to seek treatment in emergency rooms imperils the health of all Americans.

(continued)

Yes *(continued)*

poor, we need to encourage skilled immigrants who will contribute to our economic strength. Ending free health care is the first step.

Robert Rector is a senior policy analyst on welfare at the Heritage Foundation in Washington, D.C.

No *(continued)*

When the ERs are clogged with uninsured people, even the millionaire who gets in a car accident may not receive timely care.

Lucy Quacinella is an attorney at the Western Center on Law and Poverty in California.
Health, January/February 1997, p. 28

Clear Purpose

Critical thinking is deliberate thinking because it always involves a **clear purpose,** a specific goal. When you think critically, you are looking for reasons or explanations for events, considering various sides of an issue, attempting to solve a problem, coming to a decision, or making sense of a situation. For example, you may be trying to figure out how an event like an automobile accident occurred, distinguish among the arguments on both sides of an issue such as abortion, come up with a solution to a problem like a low grade in a course, decide where to go on vacation, or understand the reasons behind a political event such as a war or revolution. In the course example, the decision whether to register for the course was the purpose you, as a critical thinker, had in mind.

ACTIVITY 3

DIRECTIONS: Think about an experience from your past in which you demonstrated critical thinking by having a clear purpose—in other words, an example of an instance when you tried to reach a specific goal. It could involve your looking for reasons or explanations for events, considering various sides of an issue, attempting to solve a problem, coming to a decision, or making sense of a situation. Be prepared to discuss your example in class.

ACTIVITY 4

DIRECTIONS: Read the following article; then discuss it with a classmate. Together, try to come up with possible reasons or explanations for the actions of Joseph Chavis. Your purpose here is to try to make sense of the situation.

As a Lawyer, He's Exemplary; as a Robber, an Enigma

Christine Biederman

1   DALLAS, Jan. 19—Sitting beside his lawyer in Federal District Court today, a diminutive man in a conservative gray suit, starched, striped cotton shirt and conservative tie massaged his temples as if trying to banish a migraine.

2   When his case was called, he stepped before the bench and, in response to the judge's request to state his name and age, he cleared his throat and answered nearly inaudibly. Then, when the judge asked how much education he had, his wavering voice failed him; looking down at the podium, he began to cry.

3   Moments later, Joseph E. Chavis Jr., a 30-year-old lawyer known by colleagues and opponents alike as a quiet, studious and sincere man, would plead guilty to charges of bank robbery in a case that left many in disbelief.

4   A holder of a business degree from Texas A&M University and a law degree from Southern Methodist University, Mr. Chavis is recalled by his law professors as a model student and a caring mentor for other young black men and women making their way through the mostly white world of Dallas law firms.

5   After his arrest, just before Christmas, partners at Clark, West, Keller & Butler—the 100-year-old Dallas labor firm that has employed Mr. Chavis since he graduated from law school in 1990—stood by him and described him as a "terrific advocate and a first-rate lawyer." Friends say both Mr. Chavis and his wife, Debra Ann Lockhart, a fellow lawyer and law school classmate, devoted their spare time to Roman Catholic Church activities.

6   At first the charges against Mr. Chavis seemed a Kafkaesque nightmare of mistaken identity. After his arrest, members of his law firm, as well friends, relatives, former professors and even the dean of S.M.U.'s law school, said that the police had the wrong man, that the Joseph Chavis they knew could not have done this.

7   "So, on his way to work, he robs a bank," said Prof. William Bridge of the S.M.U. Law School. "It's just inconsistent with everything in his background and character, and therefore it's easier for me to believe that it's a mistake."

8   But the authorities continued to insist that there had been no mistake, and on Jan. 5, a Federal grand jury indicted Mr. Chavis.

9   In the course of robbing Bank United, a small bank in the exclusive University Park neighborhood, the authorities say, Mr. Chavis did everything but hold up a sign with his name and Social Security number.

10   The police and the Federal Bureau of Investigation say that about 9 A.M. on Dec. 18, Mr. Chavis left his condominium on the edge of the University Park area and drove two miles to the bank, which is within sight of S.M.U.'s law school in University Park. Once there, they say, Mr. Chavis walked in without a disguise and asked for two rolls of quarters in exchange for $20.

11   Mr. Chavis then left, only to return a few minutes later. This time, prosecutors say, he walked up to a teller and said: "Good morning. I have a gun in my pocket. Please give me your money." He received exactly $1,340 and fled on foot, the authorities said.

12   An F.B.I. spokeswoman, Marge Poche, said that the bank's camera had yielded "a great picture of the suspect" and that within minutes, the "police spotted someone they believed could fit the description of the bank robber in the vicinity of Renaissance Tower," the downtown high-rise where Mr. Chavis worked.

13   "They searched the area, and some units found some discarded money in a bathroom of the parking garage that had a lock," Ms. Poche said.

14   The Federal prosecutors said security cameras showed Mr. Chavis putting something in a trash can. A search of the trash can, they said, turned up white quarter wrappers as

well as the dark-brimmed baseball cap that the robber had been seen wearing. The baseball cap, which bore the logo of one of Mr. Chavis's clients, had been a gift for a legal job well done, his lawyer said.

15   About the same time, the police received a call saying banded bundles of money had been found under a water fountain in the hallway near a back entrance to the Clark, West law firm. An officer went to the firm and noticed that Mr. Chavis looked like the robber on the bank video; he was arrested that afternoon.

16   "All but about $10" of the bank's money was recovered, Ms. Poche said.

17   No one involved in the case has a satisfactory answer for the vexing questions it raises.

New York Times, January 20, 1996, p. 7

Organization

Students often complain that lack of time makes it difficult for them to accomplish everything that they have to do. There is no doubt that their lives are very busy, with classes to attend, assignments to be completed, studying to be done, and tests to be taken. As a typical college student, there are occasions when you must feel under a great deal of time pressure. For that reason, you probably schedule your daily activities very carefully so that you are able to get everything done. You have certain hours that you devote to going to and preparing for classes, and you work your other personal responsibilities around them. In other words, you use **organization** or careful planning, to make the most productive use of your limited time.

Critical thinkers also depend on organization to help them deal effectively with events, issues, problems, decisions, and situations. In the example, you certainly used an organized approach to help you to make a decision regarding whether you should take the course. You went through a series of specific steps in order to gather more information, which placed you in a much stronger position when deciding what to do. Critical thinking always involves that kind of organization.

Time and Effort

At this point, it is probably obvious to you that critical thinking requires much **time and effort.** Furthermore, critical thinkers are willing to take time away from other activities so that they can concentrate on a specific event, issue, problem, decision, or situation. The examples you have read about and the activities that you have been asked to complete all involve not only setting aside time but also putting in extra effort. In the example, the easy road would have been for you to follow your first reaction, which was not to register for the course. You opted instead to take some additional time to gather information, because you felt that it would help you make the right decision. In short, you were taking the time and making the effort that critical thinking requires.

ACTIVITY 5

DIRECTIONS: Pretend that you want to purchase or lease a new automobile. What steps would you follow to help organize your time and efforts? List them in your note-

The lease-or-buy game

Answer each question by
following the road marked
"yes" or "no." The route you
follow will show you whether
leasing is a good, indifferent,
or poor choice for you.

1 I typically get a new car
every three or four years.

2 I am unable to come up
with a down payment of at
least 20 percent, or I prefer
to put as little of my own money
into a car as possible.

3 I treat my vehicle gently
and maintain it faithfully.
It rarely gets dents and
scratches; small children and
pets are infrequent passengers.

4 I drive less than 15,000
miles per year; I foresee
no change in the next few
years that would significantly alter
the amount of driving I do.

CONSUMER REPORTS   DECEMBER 1997

Illustration by Jeffrey Polo

book. To help you decide whether to lease or buy, feel free to play the Lease-or-Buy
game presented above.

Asking Questions and Finding Answers

Critical thinkers are aware of what is going on around them. They observe their surroundings carefully and put substantial effort into looking for causes, explanations, or
reasons. In other words, critical thinkers **ask questions** continuously and are very
patient and persistent when trying to **find answers.** They often use words that are found
in questions, such as *who, when, what, where, how,* and *why.* For example, critical thinkers
would wonder: Who is responsible for determining the price of an automobile? Where
can I find information about a fair price for a particular automobile? Where can I find
information about a fair loan rate for an automobile? When is the best time to study for
a test? How do I decide what career to pursue? What are the requirements for the career
that I want to pursue? What provides the pressure that forces water through a faucet?
Where does electricity originate from? How is sewage carried through underground
pipes without clogging them? Why do leaves turn different colors in many areas of

the United States? Have you thought about answers to these questions and others like them? If you have, you have experience at being a critical thinker.

When considering whether to take the course in our example, you asked questions like "Will the course fit into my program of study?" "How will it affect my schedule?" "Do I have a choice of instructor?" "What is the course about?" and "How hard is it?" Furthermore, you were very persistent in trying to find answers *before* making a decision. In other words, you were being a critical thinker.

ACTIVITY 6

DIRECTIONS: During the next few days, take some time away from your usual routine to observe and think about your surroundings. Instead of rushing from one place to another, spend a few moments looking carefully at your neighborhood, school, or workplace, listening to what is going on, questioning what you see and hear, and finding answers by being patient and persistent. Then write an essay describing everything that you saw and heard, including possible answers to your questions. You will be asked to share your essay with your classmates.

ACTIVITY 7

DIRECTIONS: Look carefully at the scenes in the following photographs, and try to notice little things that seem interesting or unusual. Ask questions about what you see, and think about possible explanations. What is going on in photographs 1, 3, and 6? What is unusual in photographs 2, 4, and 5? What are the messages of the signs in photograph 5? Discuss your questions and possible explanations with your classmates.

1

2

3

4

5

6

ACTIVITY 8

DIRECTIONS: During the next few days, be patient and persistent when trying to find answers to the questions posed in the discussion in the text:

1. Who is responsible for determining the price of an automobile?

2. Where can I find information about a fair price for a particular automobile?

3. Where can I find information about a fair loan rate for an automobile?

4. When is the best time to study for a test?

5. How do I decide what career to pursue?

6. What are the requirements for the career that I want to pursue?

7. What provides the pressure that forces water through a faucet?

8. Where does electricity originate from?

9. How is sewage carried through underground pipes without clogging them?

10. Why do leaves turn different colors in many areas of the United States?

Be prepared to discuss your answers and how you found them.

ACTIVITY 9

DIRECTIONS: Read the following article, and develop questions that will perhaps help you make sense of the atrocious crime described in it and the reactions of the eyewitnesses. Think about possible answers to your questions, and discuss both your questions and answers with your classmates. Also, be prepared to discuss how you think you would have reacted had you been an eyewitness.

Witnesses Recall Beaten Woman's Fatal Leap

1   DETROIT, Sept. 1 (AP)—A city bus driver testified today that he and 40 to 50 other people watched as a woman, stripped of most of her clothing, was beaten for nearly half an hour last month before finally jumping off a bridge to her death to escape her attacker.

2   The witness, Harvey Mayberry, said the 19-year-old man charged with the attack, Martell Welch, had apparently been angry over a traffic accident involving his car and the woman's.

3   Mr. Mayberry said he saw Mr. Welch slam the woman's head five or six times against the hood of her car during the attack, which occurred on Aug. 19. The witness said Mr. Welch had then carried the woman toward the crowd, asking: "Does anybody want some of this bitch? Because she has to pay for my car."

4   Eventually, the woman, Deletha Word, 33, jumped off the side of the Belle Isle bridge, falling about 30 feet into the Detroit River. The authorities have said that two men who jumped

in to help her only caused her to swim to deeper waters, apparently in the fear that they, too, meant her harm. She drowned, and her body was recovered several hours later.

5   "I just felt bad," Mr. Mayberry said. "There was nothing I could do about it."

6   Mr. Mayberry was one of three witnesses who testified today at a preliminary hearing where Mr. Welch was ordered to stand trial on an open murder charge in Ms. Word's death. The charge means that the defendant could be convicted of either first- or second-degree murder. First-degree murder carries a mandatory sentence of life in prison; second-degree murder is punishable by up to life in prison.

7   Although the police initially said bystanders had cheered and egged on the attack, they later backed away from that account, and Mr. Mayberry testified that some people had yelled for Mr. Welch not to toss Ms. Word off the bridge.

8   Another witness, Tiffany Alexander, 23, said she and three companions came upon the attack when they drove onto the bridge and their way was blocked. Ms. Alexander testified that a cellular telephone was in their car but that no one used it to call the police. She did not say why.

9   Mr. Mayberry said he came upon the attack after it had begun. He testified that Mr. Welch had carried Ms. Word to a barrier separating the bridge's roadway from its sidewalk, had thrown her over it and had then gone after her with a car jack, saying he was going to "bust your brains out."

10   Ms. Word then climbed onto the railing at the very edge of the bridge, and Mr. Welch said, "You can't go out that way," Mr. Mayberry testified. As Mr. Welch got closer, the witness said, Ms. Word jumped.

11   Tyrone Gribble, 19, testified that Mr. Welch had yelled at Ms. Word not to jump but that after she did, he said, "Good for the bitch!"

New York Times, September 2, 1995

Research

Critical thinking is a way of dealing with events, issues, problems, decisions, or situations in a very thoughtful, careful manner. For that reason, it often requires **research,** *the process of looking for and gathering information to increase your knowledge and understanding of a given topic.* In the example that we have been using, you did research to place yourself in a stronger position in deciding whether to take the course. You studied the class schedule, the catalog, and a syllabus and talked with students, faculty, and your counselor to gather as much information as possible concerning the course. In other words, all of the research that you did provided you with more information to help you make a decision.

The kind of research that critical thinkers do and the sources of information that they use will vary with the matter at hand. In other words, research can involve using the Internet, going to libraries, reading official reports or documents, interviewing people, visiting various agencies and organizations, or some combination of these. For example, if a young man wants to find out more about the issue of gun control, he might go to the library or use the Internet to read about the topic in newspapers, magazines, books, or reports. In addition, he might talk with individuals who know something about the issue— perhaps police officials, gun owners, and members of various organizations that support and oppose gun control. By contrast, if he wants to investigate a traffic accident, he might study the police report, read newspaper accounts, talk with persons actually involved, and interview any witnesses who were present.

As these examples illustrate, critical thinkers are careful about using the sources that are most relevant, applicable, or appropriate and therefore most likely to provide useful, reliable information—information that is not only specific to the topic, but also accurate and trustworthy. Thus our young researcher would probably not seek information about gun control from a mechanic, a physician, or an accountant unless they were somehow involved with the issue, nor would he read general magazines or books to find out about a particular traffic accident. You certainly used appropriate sources when doing research for the course decision. Each of the individuals you talked with was in a good position to provide useful information, and the written sources were all relevant to the matter under consideration.

Critical thinkers are not only aware of their own feelings and opinions but also try to be aware of any **prejudice** or **bias** on the part of a given source. In other words, our researcher would determine if the source is providing information that supports a particular point of view instead of being impartial or evenhanded. For example, if he is discussing gun control with a representative of an organization that does not support it, like the National Rifle Association, he would keep in mind that the information he is getting is probably slanted in one direction. Similarly, if he is reading literature put out by that same organization, he realizes that it is likely to include only information supporting its viewpoint regarding the issue. This is not to say that he should necessarily ignore the information. However, at the very least, he would need to search for information from other sources that might offer opposing viewpoints. You were using critical thinking when you realized that the student who had dropped the course was only giving her personal point of view, which was not unbiased. That is precisely why you turned to additional sources of information before making a decision.

A Word of Caution When Using the Internet for Research   As you know, the Internet consists of an enormous number of desktop and much larger computers that are linked through a worldwide network. It is a very rapid means of sharing information, *some* of which is excellent and *some* of which is not very worthwhile. This results from the fact that unlike books and articles in periodicals and newspapers, there is no review by others before publication on the Internet. Thus anyone can publish personal views on a variety of topics without having the information evaluated first by editors, experts, or others who are knowledgeable about the subject matter. Therefore, in those instances, you as the researcher must be extra careful about determining not only the relevance and impartiality of the information presented but its reliability as well. How should you go about doing that?

First, as with all sources, use common sense to make sure that the information offered is useful or appropriate for your research needs. Ask yourself if a particular source focuses on the subject matter that is of interest to you and if it does so in a fair and thorough manner. For instance, if you are investigating the issue of capital punishment, a source that devotes several pages to a discussion of the opposing viewpoints would probably be more useful than one that devotes a few paragraphs to life on death row.

Second, try to use material published by educational institutions like Harvard (with Web addresses that end in *.edu*) or posted on governmental (*.gov*) and military (*.mil*) sites.

The information they provide is quite likely to be reliable. Sites maintained by professional organizations (*.org*), such as the American Medical Association, can usually be relied on for accurate information, but keep in mind that some organizations simply want to persuade you to accept their point of view. The National Rifle Association is a good example of such an organization. Commercial sources (sites that end in *.com*), like Philip Morris USA, are more questionable because they are often trying to sell you their products or influence your thinking so that they can continue to make profits. Thus if you were looking into the effects of cigarette advertising on young people, Philip Morris would probably not be a good source of information to use because of its obvious bias, whereas a report put out by the U.S. Office of the Surgeon General would be much more reliable.

Third, when possible, try to find the professional affiliation of the author in the credits or e-mail address so that you can determine his or her expertise on a given topic. For example, if you were investigating an issue involving medical ethics, a medical doctor who is also on the faculty of the University of Pennsylvania Medical School would probably be a more reliable source than an individual complaining about the high cost of medical treatment on a personal home page.

Fourth, see if the author lists a bibliography of the sources used so that you can gauge if they are reputable and scholarly. Publications like the *New York Times, Newsweek, New England Journal of Medicine*, and textbooks in general are usually recognized by most people as providers of accurate, well-researched, and well-documented information. Thus if sources like those are listed, you can feel a bit more secure about using the author's material.

Finally, there are online databases on the Internet, such as EBSCO, ProQuest, and LEXIS-NEXIS, that provide access to full-text articles from scholarly and popular periodicals like the *New England Journal of Medicine, Columbia Journalism Review, New York Times*, and *Newsweek*. Furthermore, there are online encyclopedias, like *World Book, Britannica*, and *Encarta*, that are good starting points for research. All of these sources can generally be relied upon for relevance, reliability, and impartiality. On the other hand, search engines, such as Yahoo and Google, use key words to find complete or condensed information from a variety of sources that should be evaluated carefully by the researcher.

As you recall, the first textbook passage in Mastery Test 3.2 provides some additional hints on evaluating sources, including electronic ones. If necessary, refer to it to refresh your memory. Remember that the Internet can be a very helpful source of information, but you must exercise great care when using it for research purposes.

ACTIVITY 10

DIRECTIONS: Assume you wanted to do research to answer the question "Does violence on television contribute to real violence in the United States?" How and where would you get information? Discuss this question with two of your classmates, and together come up with a list of possible sources that are appropriate to use. Be sure to include a variety of specific sources, and be ready to provide the reasons why you feel they are relevant to the issue. Also try to determine if you think they are likely to be reliable and impartial.

ACTIVITY 11

DIRECTIONS: With the same two classmates, look carefully at the following five sources taken from the Internet in order to determine if they are relevant, reliable, and impartial for the purpose of answering the question posed in Activity 10: "Does violence on television contribute to real violence in the United States?" In other words, for each source answer the following three questions:

1. Does the source focus on the subject matter and provide enough specific information to help me answer the question? (relevance)

2. Based upon my evaluation of the author and the source, is the information provided accurate and trustworthy? (reliability)

3. Is the information provided biased toward one particular point of view, or does it present opposing viewpoints? (impartiality)

1

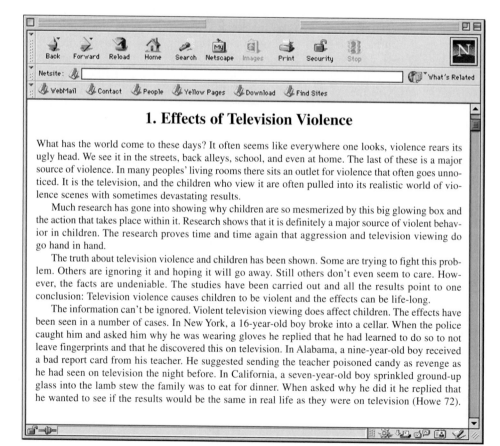

1. Effects of Television Violence

What has the world come to these days? It often seems like everywhere one looks, violence rears its ugly head. We see it in the streets, back alleys, school, and even at home. The last of these is a major source of violence. In many peoples' living rooms there sits an outlet for violence that often goes unnoticed. It is the television, and the children who view it are often pulled into its realistic world of violence scenes with sometimes devastating results.

Much research has gone into showing why children are so mesmerized by this big glowing box and the action that takes place within it. Research shows that it is definitely a major source of violent behavior in children. The research proves time and time again that aggression and television viewing do go hand in hand.

The truth about television violence and children has been shown. Some are trying to fight this problem. Others are ignoring it and hoping it will go away. Still others don't even seem to care. However, the facts are undeniable. The studies have been carried out and all the results point to one conclusion: Television violence causes children to be violent and the effects can be life-long.

The information can't be ignored. Violent television viewing does affect children. The effects have been seen in a number of cases. In New York, a 16-year-old boy broke into a cellar. When the police caught him and asked him why he was wearing gloves he replied that he had learned to do so to not leave fingerprints and that he discovered this on television. In Alabama, a nine-year-old boy received a bad report card from his teacher. He suggested sending the teacher poisoned candy as revenge as he had seen on television the night before. In California, a seven-year-old boy sprinkled ground-up glass into the lamb stew the family was to eat for dinner. When asked why he did it he replied that he wanted to see if the results would be the same in real life as they were on television (Howe 72).

(continued)

These are certainly startling examples of how television can affect the child. It must be pointed out that all of these situations were directly caused by children watching violent television.

Not only does television violence affect the child's youth, but it can also affect his or her adulthood. Some psychologists and psychiatrists feel that continued exposure to such violence might unnaturally speed up the impact of the adult world on the child. This can force the child into a kind of premature maturity. As the child matures into an adult, he can become bewildered, have a greater distrust towards others, a superficial approach to adult problems, and even an unwillingness to become an adult (Carter 14).

Television violence can destroy a young child's mind. The effects of this violence can be long-lasting, if not never-ending. For some, television at its worst, is an assault on a child's mind, an insidious influence tat upsets moral balance and makes a child prone to aggressive behavior as it warps his or her perception of the real world. Other see television as an unhealthy intrusion into a child's learning process, substituting easy pictures for the discipline of reading and concentrating and transforming the young viewer into a hypnotized nonthinker (Langone 48). As you can see, television violence can disrupt a child's learning and thinking ability which will cause life long problems. If a child cannot do well in school, his or her whole future is at stake.

Why do children like the violence that they see on television? ''Since media violence is much more vicious than that which children normally experience, real-life aggression appears bland by comparison'' (Dorr 227). The violence on television is able to be more exciting and enthralling than the violence that is normally viewed on the streets. Instead of just seeing a police officer handing a ticket to a speeding violator, he can beat the offender bloody on television. However, children don't always realize this is not the way thing are handled in real life. They come to expect it, and when they don't see it the world becomes bland and in need of violence. The children then can create the violence that their mind craves.

The television violence can cause actual violence in a number of ways. As explained above, after viewing television violence the world becomes bland in comparison. The child needs to create violence to keep himself satisfied (Dorr 127). Also the children find the violent characters on television fun to imitate. ''Children do imitate the behavior of models such as those portrayed in television, movies, etc. They do so because the ideas that are shown to them on television are more attractive to the viewer than those the viewer can think up himself'' (Brown 98). This has been widely seen lately with the advent of the Mighty Morphin' Power Rangers. Young children cannot seem to get enough of these fictional characters and will portray them often.

Another reason why television violence causes violence in children is apparent in the big cities. ''Aggressive behavior was more acceptable in the city, where a child's popularity rating with classmates was not hampered by his or her aggression'' (Huesmann 166). In the bigger cities, crime and violence is inevitable, expected and, therefore, is left unchecked and out of line.

Much research into the topic of children and television violence has been conducted. All of the results seem to point in the same direction. There are undeniable correlations between violent television and aggression. This result was obtained in a survey of London schoolchildren in 1975. Greensberg found in a significant relationship between violence viewing and aggression (Dorr 160).

In Israel 74 children from farms were tested as well as 112 schoolchildren from the city of Tel Aviv. The researchers found that the city children watched far more television then their farmland counterparts. However, both groups of children were just as likely to choose a violent program to watch then watching television. They city children had a greater tendency to regard violent television programs as accurate reflections of real life than the farm children. Likewise, the city boys identified most with characters from violent programs than did those living on the farms (Huesmann 166).

(continued)

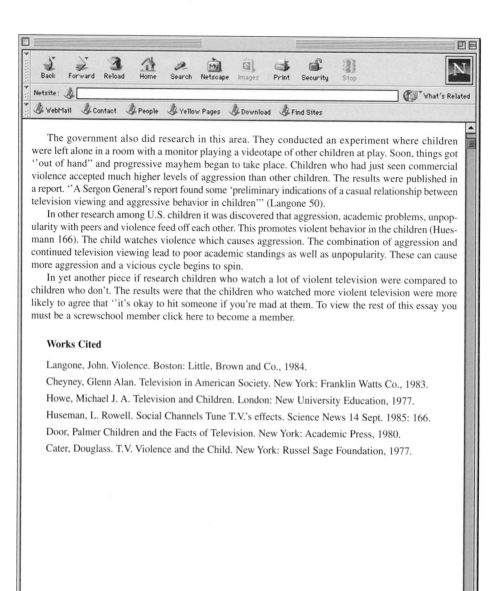

The government also did research in this area. They conducted an experiment where children were left alone in a room with a monitor playing a videotape of other children at play. Soon, things got ''out of hand'' and progressive mayhem began to take place. Children who had just seen commercial violence accepted much higher levels of aggression than other children. The results were published in a report. ''A Sergon General's report found some 'preliminary indications of a casual relationship between television viewing and aggressive behavior in children''' (Langone 50).

In other research among U.S. children it was discovered that aggression, academic problems, unpopularity with peers and violence feed off each other. This promotes violent behavior in the children (Huesmann 166). The child watches violence which causes aggression. The combination of aggression and continued television viewing lead to poor academic standings as well as unpopularity. These can cause more aggression and a vicious cycle begins to spin.

In yet another piece if research children who watch a lot of violent television were compared to children who don't. The results were that the children who watched more violent television were more likely to agree that ''it's okay to hit someone if you're mad at them. To view the rest of this essay you must be a screwschool member click here to become a member.

Works Cited

Langone, John. Violence. Boston: Little, Brown and Co., 1984.

Cheyney, Glenn Alan. Television in American Society. New York: Franklin Watts Co., 1983.

Howe, Michael J. A. Television and Children. London: New University Education, 1977.

Huseman, L. Rowell. Social Channels Tune T.V.'s effects. Science News 14 Sept. 1985: 166.

Door, Palmer Children and the Facts of Television. New York: Academic Press, 1980.

Cater, Douglass. T.V. Violence and the Child. New York: Russel Sage Foundation, 1977.

2

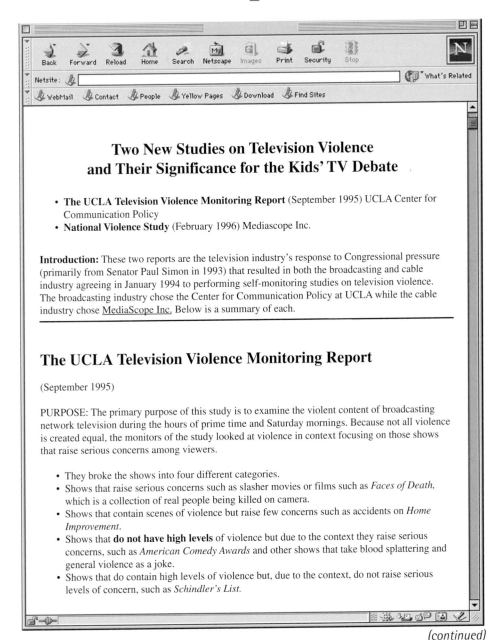

Two New Studies on Television Violence and Their Significance for the Kids' TV Debate

- **The UCLA Television Violence Monitoring Report** (September 1995) UCLA Center for Communication Policy
- **National Violence Study** (February 1996) Mediascope Inc.

Introduction: These two reports are the television industry's response to Congressional pressure (primarily from Senator Paul Simon in 1993) that resulted in both the broadcasting and cable industry agreeing in January 1994 to performing self-monitoring studies on television violence. The broadcasting industry chose the Center for Communication Policy at UCLA while the cable industry chose <u>MediaScope Inc.</u> Below is a summary of each.

The UCLA Television Violence Monitoring Report

(September 1995)

PURPOSE: The primary purpose of this study is to examine the violent content of broadcasting network television during the hours of prime time and Saturday mornings. Because not all violence is created equal, the monitors of the study looked at violence in context focusing on those shows that raise serious concerns among viewers.

- They broke the shows into four different categories.
- Shows that raise serious concerns such as slasher movies or films such as *Faces of Death*, which is a collection of real people being killed on camera.
- Shows that contain scenes of violence but raise few concerns such as accidents on *Home Improvement*.
- Shows that **do not have high levels** of violence but due to the context they raise serious concerns, such as *American Comedy Awards* and other shows that take blood splattering and general violence as a joke.
- Shows that do contain high levels of violence but, due to the context, do not raise serious levels of concern, such as *Schindler's List*.

(continued)

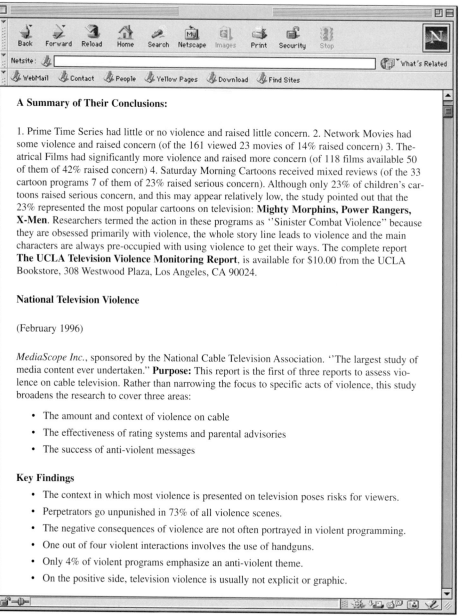

A Summary of Their Conclusions:

1. Prime Time Series had little or no violence and raised little concern. 2. Network Movies had some violence and raised concern (of the 161 viewed 23 movies of 14% raised concern) 3. Theatrical Films had significantly more violence and raised more concern (of 118 films available 50 of them of 42% raised concern) 4. Saturday Morning Cartoons received mixed reviews (of the 33 cartoon programs 7 of them of 23% raised serious concern). Although only 23% of children's cartoons raised serious concern, and this may appear relatively low, the study pointed out that the 23% represented the most popular cartoons on television: **Mighty Morphins, Power Rangers, X-Men**. Researchers termed the action in these programs as "Sinister Combat Violence" because they are obsessed primarily with violence, the whole story line leads to violence and the main characters are always pre-occupied with using violence to get their ways. The complete report **The UCLA Television Violence Monitoring Report**, is available for $10.00 from the UCLA Bookstore, 308 Westwood Plaza, Los Angeles, CA 90024.

National Television Violence

(February 1996)

MediaScope Inc., sponsored by the National Cable Television Association. "The largest study of media content ever undertaken." **Purpose:** This report is the first of three reports to assess violence on cable television. Rather than narrowing the focus to specific acts of violence, this study broadens the research to cover three areas:

- The amount and context of violence on cable
- The effectiveness of rating systems and parental advisories
- The success of anti-violent messages

Key Findings

- The context in which most violence is presented on television poses risks for viewers.
- Perpetrators go unpunished in 73% of all violence scenes.
- The negative consequences of violence are not often portrayed in violent programming.
- One out of four violent interactions involves the use of handguns.
- Only 4% of violent programs emphasize an anti-violent theme.
- On the positive side, television violence is usually not explicit or graphic.

(continued)

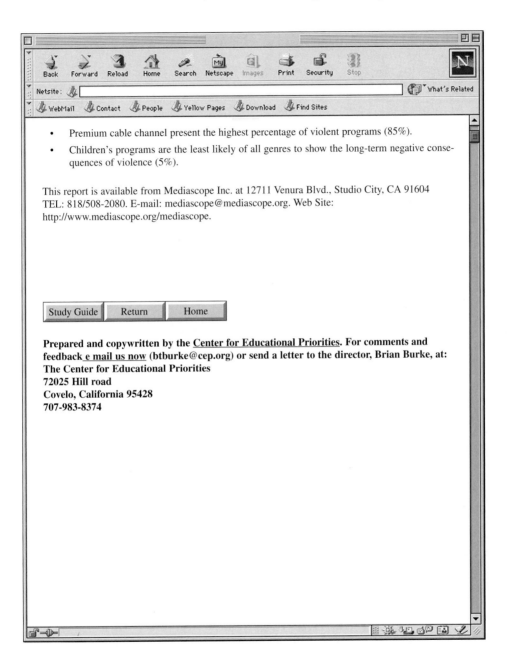

- Premium cable channel present the highest percentage of violent programs (85%).
- Children's programs are the least likely of all genres to show the long-term negative consequences of violence (5%).

This report is available from Mediascope Inc. at 12711 Venura Blvd., Studio City, CA 91604 TEL: 818/508-2080. E-mail: mediascope@mediascope.org. Web Site: http://www.mediascope.org/mediascope.

| Study Guide | Return | Home |

Prepared and copywritten by the <u>Center for Educational Priorities</u>. For comments and feedback <u>e mail us now</u> (btburke@cep.org) or send a letter to the director, Brian Burke, at: The Center for Educational Priorities
72025 Hill road
Covelo, California 95428
707-983-8374

3

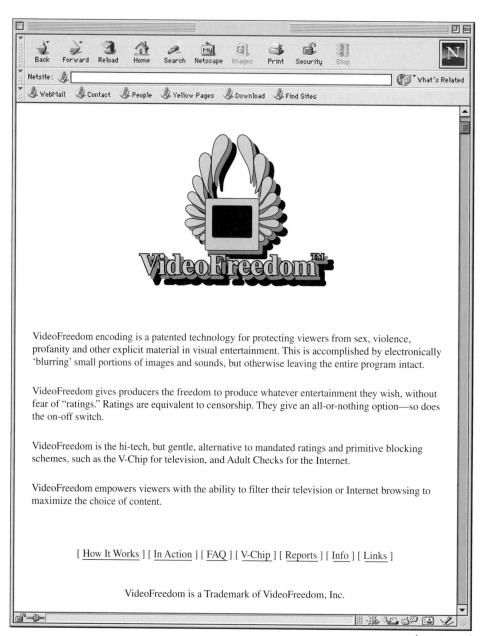

VideoFreedom encoding is a patented technology for protecting viewers from sex, violence, profanity and other explicit material in visual entertainment. This is accomplished by electronically 'blurring' small portions of images and sounds, but otherwise leaving the entire program intact.

VideoFreedom gives producers the freedom to produce whatever entertainment they wish, without fear of "ratings." Ratings are equivalent to censorship. They give an all-or-nothing option—so does the on-off switch.

VideoFreedom is the hi-tech, but gentle, alternative to mandated ratings and primitive blocking schemes, such as the V-Chip for television, and Adult Checks for the Internet.

VideoFreedom empowers viewers with the ability to filter their television or Internet browsing to maximize the choice of content.

[How It Works] [In Action] [FAQ] [V-Chip] [Reports] [Info] [Links]

VideoFreedom is a Trademark of VideoFreedom, Inc.

(continued)

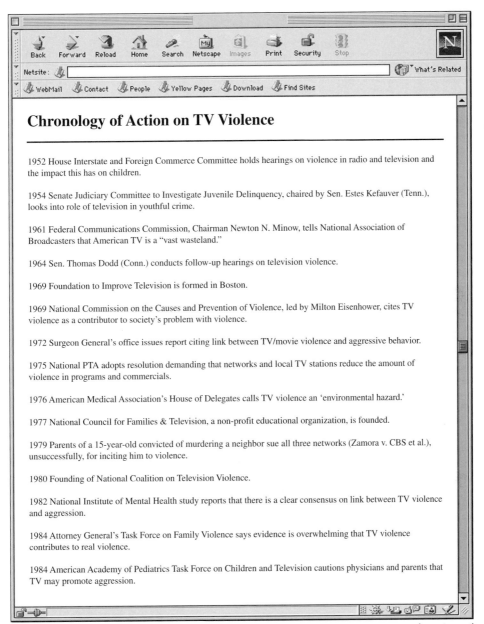

Chronology of Action on TV Violence

1952 House Interstate and Foreign Commerce Committee holds hearings on violence in radio and television and the impact this has on children.

1954 Senate Judiciary Committee to Investigate Juvenile Delinquency, chaired by Sen. Estes Kefauver (Tenn.), looks into role of television in youthful crime.

1961 Federal Communications Commission, Chairman Newton N. Minow, tells National Association of Broadcasters that American TV is a "vast wasteland."

1964 Sen. Thomas Dodd (Conn.) conducts follow-up hearings on television violence.

1969 Foundation to Improve Television is formed in Boston.

1969 National Commission on the Causes and Prevention of Violence, led by Milton Eisenhower, cites TV violence as a contributor to society's problem with violence.

1972 Surgeon General's office issues report citing link between TV/movie violence and aggressive behavior.

1975 National PTA adopts resolution demanding that networks and local TV stations reduce the amount of violence in programs and commercials.

1976 American Medical Association's House of Delegates calls TV violence an 'environmental hazard.'

1977 National Council for Families & Television, a non-profit educational organization, is founded.

1979 Parents of a 15-year-old convicted of murdering a neighbor sue all three networks (Zamora v. CBS et al.), unsuccessfully, for inciting him to violence.

1980 Founding of National Coalition on Television Violence.

1982 National Institute of Mental Health study reports that there is a clear consensus on link between TV violence and aggression.

1984 Attorney General's Task Force on Family Violence says evidence is overwhelming that TV violence contributes to real violence.

1984 American Academy of Pediatrics Task Force on Children and Television cautions physicians and parents that TV may promote aggression.

(continued)

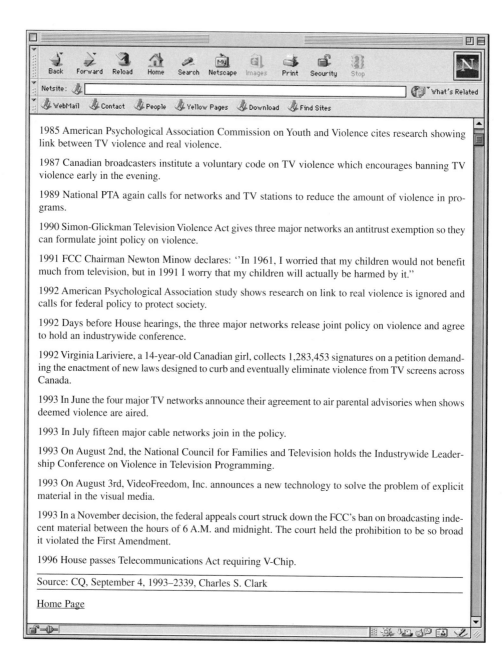

1985 American Psychological Association Commission on Youth and Violence cites research showing link between TV violence and real violence.

1987 Canadian broadcasters institute a voluntary code on TV violence which encourages banning TV violence early in the evening.

1989 National PTA again calls for networks and TV stations to reduce the amount of violence in programs.

1990 Simon-Glickman Television Violence Act gives three major networks an antitrust exemption so they can formulate joint policy on violence.

1991 FCC Chairman Newton Minow declares: ''In 1961, I worried that my children would not benefit much from television, but in 1991 I worry that my children will actually be harmed by it.''

1992 American Psychological Association study shows research on link to real violence is ignored and calls for federal policy to protect society.

1992 Days before House hearings, the three major networks release joint policy on violence and agree to hold an industrywide conference.

1992 Virginia Lariviere, a 14-year-old Canadian girl, collects 1,283,453 signatures on a petition demanding the enactment of new laws designed to curb and eventually eliminate violence from TV screens across Canada.

1993 In June the four major TV networks announce their agreement to air parental advisories when shows deemed violence are aired.

1993 In July fifteen major cable networks join in the policy.

1993 On August 2nd, the National Council for Families and Television holds the Industrywide Leadership Conference on Violence in Television Programming.

1993 On August 3rd, VideoFreedom, Inc. announces a new technology to solve the problem of explicit material in the visual media.

1993 In a November decision, the federal appeals court struck down the FCC's ban on broadcasting indecent material between the hours of 6 A.M. and midnight. The court held the prohibition to be so broad it violated the First Amendment.

1996 House passes Telecommunications Act requiring V-Chip.

Source: CQ, September 4, 1993–2339, Charles S. Clark

Home Page

4

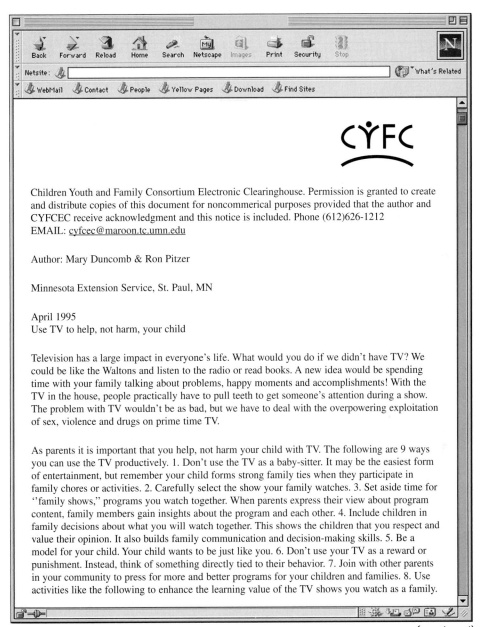

Children Youth and Family Consortium Electronic Clearinghouse. Permission is granted to create and distribute copies of this document for noncommerical purposes provided that the author and CYFCEC receive acknowledgment and this notice is included. Phone (612)626-1212
EMAIL: cyfcec@maroon.tc.umn.edu

Author: Mary Duncomb & Ron Pitzer

Minnesota Extension Service, St. Paul, MN

April 1995
Use TV to help, not harm, your child

Television has a large impact in everyone's life. What would you do if we didn't have TV? We could be like the Waltons and listen to the radio or read books. A new idea would be spending time with your family talking about problems, happy moments and accomplishments! With the TV in the house, people practically have to pull teeth to get someone's attention during a show. The problem with TV wouldn't be as bad, but we have to deal with the overpowering exploitation of sex, violence and drugs on prime time TV.

As parents it is important that you help, not harm your child with TV. The following are 9 ways you can use the TV productively. 1. Don't use the TV as a baby-sitter. It may be the easiest form of entertainment, but remember your child forms strong family ties when they participate in family chores or activities. 2. Carefully select the show your family watches. 3. Set aside time for ''family shows,'' programs you watch together. When parents express their view about program content, family members gain insights about the program and each other. 4. Include children in family decisions about what you will watch together. This shows the children that you respect and value their opinion. It also builds family communication and decision-making skills. 5. Be a model for your child. Your child wants to be just like you. 6. Don't use your TV as a reward or punishment. Instead, think of something directly tied to their behavior. 7. Join with other parents in your community to press for more and better programs for your children and families. 8. Use activities like the following to enhance the learning value of the TV shows you watch as a family.

(continued)

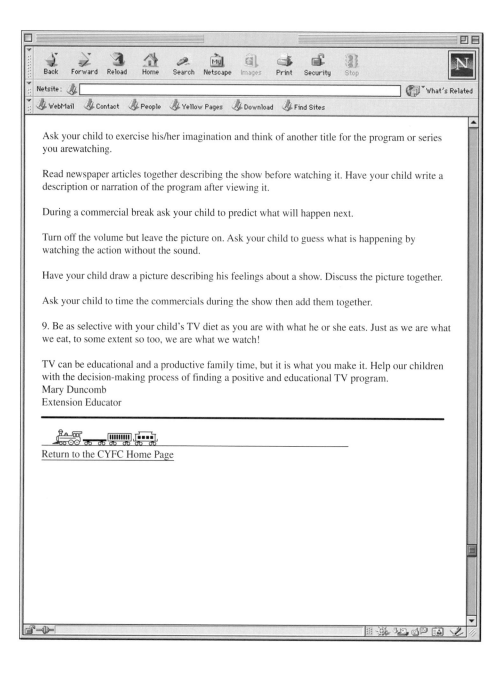

Ask your child to exercise his/her imagination and think of another title for the program or series you arewatching.

Read newspaper articles together describing the show before watching it. Have your child write a description or narration of the program after viewing it.

During a commercial break ask your child to predict what will happen next.

Turn off the volume but leave the picture on. Ask your child to guess what is happening by watching the action without the sound.

Have your child draw a picture describing his feelings about a show. Discuss the picture together.

Ask your child to time the commercials during the show then add them together.

9. Be as selective with your child's TV diet as you are with what he or she eats. Just as we are what we eat, to some extent so too, we are what we watch!

TV can be educational and a productive family time, but it is what you make it. Help our children with the decision-making process of finding a positive and educational TV program.
Mary Duncomb
Extension Educator

Return to the CYFC Home Page

5

Television Violence and Behavior: A Research Summary. ERIC Digest.

THIS DIGEST WAS CREATED BY ERIC, THE EDUCATIONAL RESOURCES INFORMATION CENTER. FOR MORE INFORMATION ABOUT ERIC, CONTACT ACCESS ERIC 1-800-LET-ERIC

Introduction
The National Association for the Education of Young Children (NAEYC) position statement on media violence and children (1990) reports that violence in the media has increased since 1980 and continues to increase, particularly since the Federal Communication Commission's decision to deregulate children's commercial television in 1982. The NAEYC statement cites the following examples: * Air time for war cartoons increased from 1.5 hours per week in 1982 to 43 hours per week in 1986. * In 1980, children's programs featured 18.6 violent acts per hour and now have about 26.4 violent acts each hour.

According to an American Psychological Association task force report on television and American society (Huston, et al., 1992), by the time the average child (i.e., one who watches two to four hours of television daily) leaves elementary school, he or she will have witnessed at least 8,000 murders and more than 100,000 other assorted acts of violence on television.

Indicating growing concern regarding the issue of television violence, recent commentaries in the Washington Post (Harwood, 1993; Will, 1993; "Televiolence," 1993) highlight: * a paper by Centerwall (1993) that examines several studies and argues that television violence increases violent and aggressive tendencies in young people and contributes to the growth of violent crime in the United States; * and a Times Mirror poll, reported in March 1993, that found that the majority of Americans feels that "entertainment television is too violent ... that this is harmful to society ... that we as a society have become desensitized to violence."

This digest describes the overall pattern of the results of research on television violence and behavior. Several variables in the relationship between television violence and aggression related to characteristics of the viewers and to the portrayal of violence are identified. Finally, concerns regarding the effects of television violence are summarized.

Research Findings
The overall pattern of research findings indicates a positive association between television violence and aggressive behavior. A Washington Post article (Oldenburg, 1992), states that "the preponderance of evidence from more than 3,000 research studies over two decades shows that the violence portrayed on television influences the attitudes and behavior of children who watch it." Signorielli (1991) finds that: "Most of the scientific evidence ... reveals a relationship between television and aggressive behavior. While few would say that there is absolute proof that watching television caused aggressive behavior, the overall cumulative weight of all the studies gives credence to the position that they are related. Essentially, television violence is one of the things that may lead to aggressive, antisocial, or criminal behavior; it does, however, usually work in conjunction with other factors. As aptly put by Dorr and Kovaric (1980), television violence may influence 'some of the people some of the time'" (pp. 94–95).

Characteristics of Viewers
The following characteristics of viewers, summarized by Clapp (1988), have been shown to affect the influence of television violence on behavior.

(continued)

- Age. "A relationship between television violence and aggression has been observed in children as young as 3 (Singer & Singer, 1981). Longitudinal data suggest that the relationship is much more consistent and substantial for children in middle childhood than at earlier ages (Eron and Hues-mann, 1986). Aggression in early adulthood is also related to the amount of violence watched in middle childhood, although it is not related to the amount watched in early adulthood (Eron, Huesmann, Lefkowitz, & Walder, 1972). It has been proposed that there is a sensitive period between ages 8 and 12 during which children are particularly susceptible to the influence of television violence (Eron & Huesmann, 1986)" (pp. 64–65).

- Amount of television watched. "Aggressive behavior is related to the total amount of television watched, not only to the amount of violent television watched. Aggressive behavior can be stimulated also by frenetic, hectic programming that creates a high level of arousal in children (Eron & Hues-mann, 1986; Wright & Huston, 1983)" (p. 65).

- Identification with television personalities. "Especially for boys, identification with a character substantially increases the likelihood that the character's aggressive behavior will be modeled (Huesmann & Eron, 1986; Huesmann, Lagerspetz, & Eron, 1984)" (p. 65).

- Belief that television violence is realistic. "Significant relationships have been found between children's belief that television violence is realistic, their aggressive behavior, and the amount of violence that they watch (Huesmann, 1986; Huesmann & Eron, 1986)" (p. 65).

- Intellectual achievement. "Children of lower intellectual achievement generally (1) watch more television, (2) watch more violent television, (3) believe violent television reflects real life, and (4) behave more aggressively (Huesmann, 1986)" (p. 65).

Comstock and Paik (1987, 1991) also identify the following factors that may increase the likelihood of television influence:

- Viewers who are in a state of anger or provocation before seeing a violent portrayal.

- Viewers who are in a state of frustration after viewing a violent portrayal, whether from an extraneous source or as a consequence of viewing the portrayal.

Portrayal of Violence
The following are factors related to how the violence is portrayed which may heighten the likelihood of television influence. Research on these factors is summarized by Comstock and Paik (1987, 1991):

- Reward or lack of punishment for the portrayed perpetrator of violence.

- Portrayal of the violence as justified.

- Cues in the portrayal of violence that resemble those likely to be encountered in real life. For example, a victim in the portrayal with the same name or characteristics as someone towards whom the viewer holds animosity.

- Portrayal of the perpetrator of violence as similar to the viewer.

- Violence portrayed so that its consequences do not stir distaste or arouse inhibitions.

- Violence portrayed as real events rather than events concocted for a fictional film.

- Portrayed violence that is not the subject of critical or disparaging commentary.

- Portrayals of violent acts that please the viewer.

- Portrayals in which violence is not interrupted by violence in a light or humorous vein.

(continued)

- Portrayed abuse that includes physical violence and aggression instead of or in addition to verbal abuse.
- Portrayals, violent or otherwise, that leave the viewer in a state of unresolved excitement.

Comstock and Paik (1991) argue that "these contingencies represent four dimensions: (a) efficacy (reward or lack or punishment); (b) normativeness (justified, consequenceless, intentionally hurtful, physical violence); (c) pertinence (commonality of cues, similarity to the viewer, absence of humorous violence); and (d) susceptibility (pleasure, anger, frustration, absence of criticism)" (pp. 255–256).

Concerns

Three major areas of concern regarding the effects of television violence are identified and discussed by the National Association for the Education of Young Children (1990):

- Children may become less sensitive to the pain and suffering of others.
- They may be more likely to behave in aggressive or harmful ways toward others.
- They may become more fearful of the world around them.

Of these, Signorielli (1991) considers the third scenario to be the most insidious: "Research ... has revealed that violence on television plays an important role in communicating the social order and in leading to perceptions of the world as a mean and dangerous place. Symbolic victimization on television and real world fear among women and minorities, even if contrary to the facts, are highly related (Morgan, 1983). Analysis also reveals that in most subgroups those who watch more television tend to express a heightened sense of living in a mean world of danger and mistrust as well as alienation and gloom" (p. 96).

Another concern addressed by the National Association for the Education of Young Children (1990) is the negative effect on children's play of viewing violent television: "In short, children who are frequent viewers of media violence learn that aggression is a successful and acceptable way to achieve goals and solve problems; they are less likely to benefit from creative, imaginative play as the natural means to express feelings, overcome anger, and gain self-control" (p. 19).

References

Centerwall, B.S. (1993). Television and violent crime. THE PUBLIC INTEREST, 111, pp. 56–77.

Clapp, G. (1988). CHILD STUDY RESEARCH: CURRENT PERSPECTIVES AND APPLICATIONS. Lexington, MA: Lexington.

Comstock, G. & Paik, H. (1987). TELEVISION AND CHILDREN: A REVIEW OF RECENT RESEARCH. Syracuse, NY: ERIC Clearinghouse on Information Resources. (ED 292 466).

Comstock, G. & Paik, H. (1991). TELEVISION AND THE AMERICAN CHILD. San Diego, CA: Academic.

Dorr, A., & Kovaric, P. (1980). Some of the people some of the time—But which people? In E. L. Palmer & A. Dorr (eds.), CHILDREN AND THE FACES OF TELEVISION: TEACHING, VIOLENCE, SELLING (pp. 183–199). New York: Academic.

Eron, L. D. & Huesmann, L. R, (1986). The role of television in the development of prosocial and antisocial behavior. In D. Olweus, J. Block, & M. Radke-Yarrow (eds.), THE DEVELOPMENT OF ANTISOCIAL AND PROSOCIAL BEHAVIOR: RESEARCH, THEORIES, AND ISSUES. New York: Academic.

(continued)

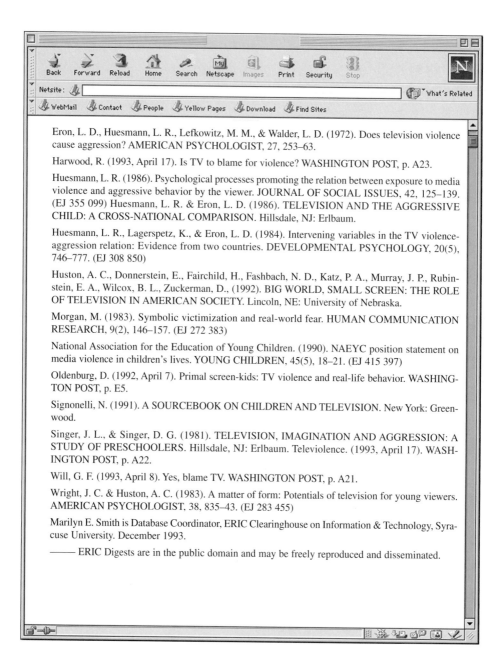

Eron, L. D., Huesmann, L. R., Lefkowitz, M. M., & Walder, L. D. (1972). Does television violence cause aggression? AMERICAN PSYCHOLOGIST, 27, 253–63.

Harwood, R. (1993, April 17). Is TV to blame for violence? WASHINGTON POST, p. A23.

Huesmann, L. R. (1986). Psychological processes promoting the relation between exposure to media violence and aggressive behavior by the viewer. JOURNAL OF SOCIAL ISSUES, 42, 125–139. (EJ 355 099) Huesmann, L. R. & Eron, L. D. (1986). TELEVISION AND THE AGGRESSIVE CHILD: A CROSS-NATIONAL COMPARISON. Hillsdale, NJ: Erlbaum.

Huesmann, L. R., Lagerspetz, K., & Eron, L. D. (1984). Intervening variables in the TV violence-aggression relation: Evidence from two countries. DEVELOPMENTAL PSYCHOLOGY, 20(5), 746–777. (EJ 308 850)

Huston, A. C., Donnerstein, E., Fairchild, H., Fashbach, N. D., Katz, P. A., Murray, J. P., Rubinstein, E. A., Wilcox, B. L., Zuckerman, D., (1992). BIG WORLD, SMALL SCREEN: THE ROLE OF TELEVISION IN AMERICAN SOCIETY. Lincoln, NE: University of Nebraska.

Morgan, M. (1983). Symbolic victimization and real-world fear. HUMAN COMMUNICATION RESEARCH, 9(2), 146–157. (EJ 272 383)

National Association for the Education of Young Children. (1990). NAEYC position statement on media violence in children's lives. YOUNG CHILDREN, 45(5), 18–21. (EJ 415 397)

Oldenburg, D. (1992, April 7). Primal screen-kids: TV violence and real-life behavior. WASHINGTON POST, p. E5.

Signonelli, N. (1991). A SOURCEBOOK ON CHILDREN AND TELEVISION. New York: Greenwood.

Singer, J. L., & Singer, D. G. (1981). TELEVISION, IMAGINATION AND AGGRESSION: A STUDY OF PRESCHOOLERS. Hillsdale, NJ: Erlbaum. Televiolence. (1993, April 17). WASHINGTON POST, p. A22.

Will, G. F. (1993, April 8). Yes, blame TV. WASHINGTON POST, p. A21.

Wright, J. C. & Huston, A. C. (1983). A matter of form: Potentials of television for young viewers. AMERICAN PSYCHOLOGIST, 38, 835–43. (EJ 283 455)

Marilyn E. Smith is Database Coordinator, ERIC Clearinghouse on Information & Technology, Syracuse University. December 1993.

—— ERIC Digests are in the public domain and may be freely reproduced and disseminated.

ACTIVITY 12

DIRECTIONS: Now that you and your two classmates have considered and evaluated various sources, write an essay in which you answer the question "Does violence on television contribute to real violence in the United States?" Your instructor will ask you to discuss your viewpoint in class.

ACTIVITY 13

DIRECTIONS: If a computer is available to you, use the Internet to find three relevant, reliable, and impartial sources in order to answer the question "Should there be organized, school-instituted prayer in our public schools?" Feel free to consult with the two classmates you worked with on Activities 10 and 11.

Coming to Logical Conclusions

After completing research, critical thinkers try to come to **logical conclusions** about the events, issues, problems, decisions, or situations they are considering. *Conclusions are logical or reasonable if they are based solidly on the information or evidence gathered.*

Let us look one last time at the example we have been using about whether you should enroll for a particular course. Suppose while doing the research you found that it fits both your schedule and program of study, that you are interested in at least some of its content, that you are comfortable with the instructor, assignments, and grading, and that most of the people you talk with like the course. Under those circumstances, it would be logical to conclude that it is good for you to take the course because most of the information supports that conclusion.

On the other hand, if you found that the course does not seem very interesting, that it is taught by only one instructor whom you are not too crazy about, and that only half the students you talked with liked it, a logical conclusion is that the course is not for you because most of the information points in that direction. Of course, the evidence could be approximately evenly divided, making it logical to conclude that it may or may not be the right course for you. In that instance, you would have to determine which factors— perhaps the content of the course, the instructor, or the requirements—are the most important to you and then decide accordingly. It is also important to emphasize that the information gathered could change in the future, thereby altering any one of those three possible conclusions. For instance, there could be a change of instructor, which could in turn affect course content, assignments, grading, and opinions regarding the course. That is why *critical thinkers always reconsider their conclusions to make sure that the evidence on which they are based has not changed or that no new information has been uncovered.*

To return to another example mentioned earlier, suppose that in your investigation of a traffic accident, the police report, newspaper accounts, and several witnesses all state that one person went through a red light. A logical conclusion would be that this driver was responsible for the accident—certainly, most of the information points in that direction. But if none of the evidence is clear as to who actually caused the collision, then the only reasonable conclusion is that no one person can be held responsible, at least at this particular time. However, that conclusion could change if additional evidence comes to light that points to one person as the culprit. Again, it is always necessary for critical thinkers to reconsider their conclusions from time to time.

ACTIVITY 14

DIRECTIONS: Pretend that there is an imaginary country with the following characteristics:

Rich and corrupt leaders

Crime on the increase

Extreme poverty among the masses

Many natural resources

What logical conclusions could you draw concerning the conditions in the country and what caused them, and what prediction can you make regarding its future? Discuss your conclusions with your classmates.

ACTIVITY 15

DIRECTIONS: With two of your classmates, look carefully at the six graphic aids that follow, paying particular attention to the captions and organization. For each, remember to answer the two questions we used in Chapter 3: "What is this graphic aid about?" and "What are the major points stressed?" Based on the information presented, draw as many logical conclusions as possible for each of the graphic aids.

Use of Tax Dollars.   The following pie chart shows how federal income tax dollars are spent.

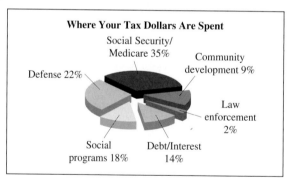

Where Your Tax Dollars Are Spent

Social Security/Medicare 35%

Community development 9%

Defense 22%

Law enforcement 2%

Social programs 18%

Debt/Interest 14%

1

Marvin L. Bittinger and David J. Ellenbogen, *Elementary Algebra,* 5th ed., p. 121

Health Among Industial Countries

The United States has virtually the lowest life expectancy and highest infant mortality in the industrial world. This is ironic because we spend more money on health care than does any other country.

Country	Life Expectancy*	Country	Infant Mortality Rate**
Japan	79.6	Japan	4.4
Australia	79.4	Sweden	4.5
Canada	79.1	Netherlands	4.9
France	78.4	Australia	5.5
Sweden	78.1	Germany	6.0
Italy	78.1	Canada	6.1
Netherlands	77.7	France	6.2
Britain	76.4	Britain	6.4
Germany	76.0	United States	6.7
United States	76.0	Italy	6.9

*Number of years infants at birth can expect to live.
**Number of infant deaths per 1,000 live births.
Source: U.S. Census Bureau, 1996

2

Alex Thio, *Sociology,* 5th ed., p. 474

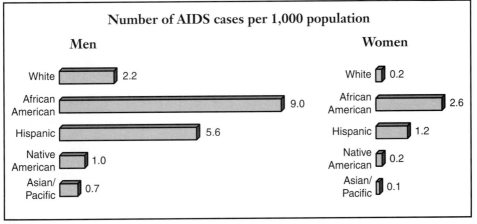

Number of AIDS cases per 1,000 population

Men

White — 2.2
African American — 9.0
Hispanic — 5.6
Native American — 1.0
Asian/Pacific — 0.7

Women

White — 0.2
African American — 2.6
Hispanic — 1.2
Native American — 0.2
Asian/Pacific — 0.1

3

Alex Thio, *Sociology: A Brief Introduction,* 4th ed., p. 381

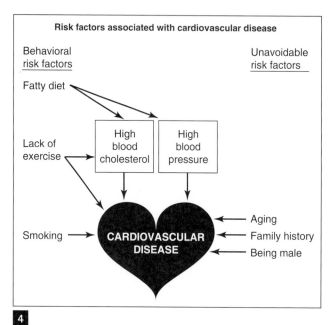

Neil A. Campbell et al., *Biology,* 3rd ed., p. 448

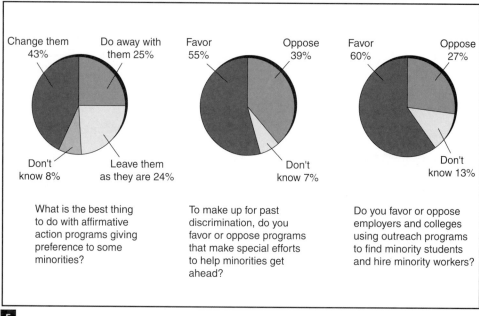

Who are the homeless?

No one knows precisely how many Americans are homeless. The National Coalition for the Homeless estimates that 750,000 Americans are homeless on any given night, and close to 2 million are homeless during the course of a year.

Federal officials recently issued a report on who these people are and where they come from, based on surveys of men and women served by shelters, soup kitchens, and other programs. Here are some of the report's key findings.

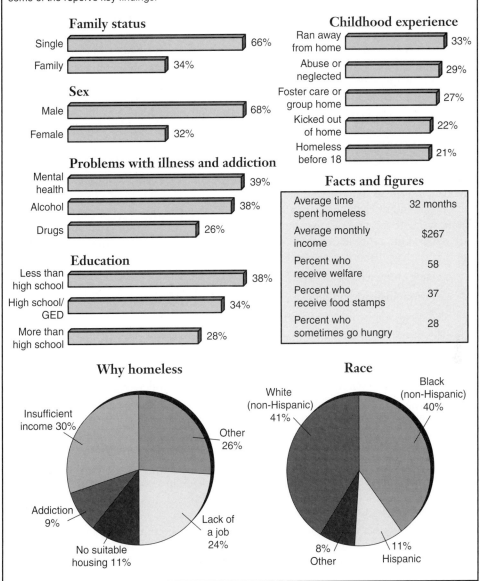

Family status
- Single 66%
- Family 34%

Sex
- Male 68%
- Female 32%

Problems with illness and addiction
- Mental health 39%
- Alcohol 38%
- Drugs 26%

Education
- Less than high school 38%
- High school/GED 34%
- More than high school 28%

Childhood experience
- Ran away from home 33%
- Abuse or neglected 29%
- Foster care or group home 27%
- Kicked out of home 22%
- Homeless before 18 21%

Facts and figures

Average time spent homeless	32 months
Average monthly income	$267
Percent who receive welfare	58
Percent who receive food stamps	37
Percent who sometimes go hungry	28

Why homeless
- Insufficient income 30%
- Addiction 9%
- No suitable housing 11%
- Lack of a job 24%
- Other 26%

Race
- White (non-Hispanic) 41%
- Black (non-Hispanic) 40%
- Hispanic 11%
- Other 8%

6

Urban Institute

WHAT IS A CONTEMPORARY ISSUE?

To review, *critical thinking is a careful, thoughtful way of dealing with events, issues, problems, decisions, or situations. It requires flexibility, a clear purpose, organization, time and effort, asking questions and finding answers, research, and coming to logical conclusions.* At this point, you have a good idea of what all of these characteristics mean and how they can be applied to the ordinary circumstances of everyday life. They can also be used in a broader sense as a way of dealing with and making better sense of topics of concern in the world around you, which are commonly called **contemporary issues.**

In this context, it is probably easiest to think of *contemporary* as a fancy word for "current." And an *issue* can be defined as a point, matter, or question to be disputed, decided, or debated—in other words, subject to very different and often conflicting interpretations, which we can call **opposing viewpoints.** A **contemporary issue,** then, is *a current point, matter, or question that is debatable and therefore subject to opposing viewpoints.*

Of course, we do not have to look very far to find a host of contemporary issues. Race relations, abortion, capital punishment, gay rights, violence in music, sexual harassment, teenage pregnancy, welfare, and gun control are obvious examples. It is precisely because they are debatable and often arouse our emotions when we read and talk about them that contemporary issues are appropriate topics for the careful, thoughtful treatment involved in critical thinking.

At the end of each chapter in this textbook, you will be asked to read about, think about, write about, and discuss some of the controversies surrounding many contemporary issues. Our approach to them will involve all of the characteristics of critical thinking that we have been discussing. In each case, you will:

1. Determine what is at issue
2. Distinguish among opposing viewpoints
3. Express a personal viewpoint

This three-step approach should enable you to understand the various viewpoints on the issues while at the same time giving you the opportunity to think carefully about your own point of view.

In many of the courses that you will be taking in your college career, you will be asked by instructors to read, write, or think about contemporary issues. For example, you may be required to read about racism for sociology, discuss the spread of AIDS in health, or write a paper on capital punishment for a criminal justice course. In addition, as an educated person, you will want to be able to speak knowledgeably with others about the major issues of the day, including the reasons behind the various points of view and your own personal viewpoints. For instance, you may find yourself in a position to discuss these matters with children and other family members or with colleagues on the job. As you can see, thinking critically about contemporary issues is useful to you not only as a college student but in the other roles that you play in life as well, both now and in the future. It is a skill that will serve you well throughout your life.

Before turning to a more detailed discussion of the three-step approach we will be using, read the following excerpt, which was taken from a typical college health textbook. Pay particular attention to the labels in the margins. Refer to this passage often as you read the explanation that follows it.

Topic (title)

Euthanasia

1   Medical science is now capable of prolonging the functioning of bodily systems long after the systems would normally have failed. It is not unusual to see patients in institutions living as near-vegetables for months and even years. Such individuals create a definite problem for family members and physicians: Would it not be better to put these patients out of their misery?

Context definition

2   On the question of this sort of "mercy killing," or *euthanasia*, Americans are divided into three groups. One group consists of the people who insist that all possible efforts be made to prolong the life of seriously ill patients. Those who take this stance maintain that any tampering with human life is a form of playing God and that the result is either murder or, if the patient concurs, murder combined with suicide.

Central message
First viewpoint

Rationale

Context definition

3   A majority of Americans, on the other hand, admit to a belief in *indirect euthanasia,* sometimes referred to as negative euthanasia. In forms of indirect euthanasia, death is not directly caused or induced; rather, it is allowed to take place through the withdrawal of specific treatments. Such indirect euthanasia is not uncommon in medical practice, though it is rarely acknowledged by doctors for fear of legal complications. This position has considerable authoritative backing, including that of the late Pope Pius XII, who declared that no extraordinary means need be taken to prolong human life.

Second viewpoint

Rationale

4   The third—and smallest—group consists of those who believe in *direct euthanasia.* The number of people who actually practice direct euthanasia is difficult to ascertain. Some physicians admit in private to having done so—either directly, by administering a lethal drug, or indirectly, by allowing the patient, the family, or the support staff to cause the death.

Third viewpoint

5   Such life-and-death decisions are far easier to make in the classroom than in the reality of a traumatic situation with a loved one. The primary difficulty does not involve logic so much as the poignancy of the environment in which decisions are made. Decision makers, plagued by long-standing illness, weary and bleary-eyed, emotionally drained, with daily life disrupted for many weeks or months (and perhaps feeling guilty, financially pressured, and involved with unfinished business), do not easily resort to the usual logic. Many a theoretically strong pro-life stance

Rationale

can use our knowledge of this issue to add here that miracles do occur, particularly with modern medicine, and therefore patients should be given every opportunity to survive.

The second viewpoint is favored by people who believe in indirect or negative euthanasia, in which "death is not directly caused or induced; rather, it is allowed to take place through the withdrawal of specific treatments." This point of view, according to the passage, has "considerable authoritative backing, including that of the late Pope Pius XII." Apparently, this "backing" is an important reason for the Americans who favor this particular position. If we have some background knowledge of this issue, we might add here that this viewpoint has the general support of the medical community and the courts, which is not the case with regard to direct euthanasia. This in turn could explain further why some people favor indirect over direct euthanasia.

The third viewpoint is supported by people who believe in direct euthanasia, which involves a doctor's "administering a lethal drug" or "allowing the patient, the family, or the support staff to cause the death." Although the passage gives no specific rationale for those who favor direct euthanasia, it does provide some additional reasons for people who favor both kinds of euthanasia: guilt, disruption of daily life, or the emotional, physical, and financial burden that go along with prolonged illness of a loved one. Thus we could guess that a possible rationale on the part of those favoring direct euthanasia would involve a quicker end to a terrible situation.

The details that support the central message of the passage have provided us with the opposing viewpoints and at least some of the rationale for each. We also have added some possible reasons of our own. As a critical thinker, you should always be prepared to do the same thing when dealing with contemporary issues.

Expressing a Personal Viewpoint

After determining what is at issue and distinguishing among opposing viewpoints, you can then express your personal viewpoint regarding the issue. Undoubtedly, you have your own opinions regarding many of the contemporary issues of the day, including those covered in this textbook. In fact, you will be asked to express your initial feelings toward each issue covered in this book *before* completing the three-step approach. Thus you can determine if your personal viewpoint changes after you have thoroughly considered the opposing viewpoints surrounding a given issue.

As already mentioned, it is important as a critical thinker that you be aware of your initial opinions and not permit them to interfere with a careful consideration of all viewpoints. For instance, you may have strong feelings of support or opposition regarding one or more of the viewpoints discussed in our textbook example dealing with euthanasia. That is fine, provided that you keep an open mind when distinguishing among the viewpoints, give careful thought to each of them, and at least consider the possibility that you might change your initial feelings after reading and thinking about the rationale for all points of view.

Having done that, you are in a better position to express your personal viewpoint even if it has not changed, because you have opened yourself up to other possibilities. When discussing your viewpoint, be sure to provide the reasons why you favor it over the others. For example, suppose that you support indirect euthanasia because you do not believe that extraordinary measures, such as a feeding tube or ventilator, should be taken to keep a person alive. Furthermore, in answer to those who do not favor any form of euthanasia, you believe that by using extraordinary measures, they are indeed playing God by preventing nature from taking its course. In addition, by doing so, they are perhaps prolonging a hopeless situation indefinitely, thereby placing loved ones under a tremendous physical, emotional, and financial burden. To those who support direct euthanasia, you respond that you do not favor that course of action because you believe it is playing God by deliberately bringing about certain death, to say nothing of the fact that it is both illegal and morally wrong.

Thus you have given your personal viewpoint regarding euthanasia and the reasons why you support it over the other two. Some of those reasons were mentioned in the passage you read, and others were not. It is always permissible to use your knowledge of an issue to supply additional rationale for your point of view.

Furthermore, you could have just as easily come out in favor of one of the other viewpoints or even some combination of them as long as you provide your reasons for doing so. For instance, in discussing this issue, one student supported indirect euthanasia only after three different doctors certify that the situation is hopeless; otherwise, she did not favor it at all. She wanted to be reasonably sure that there was little chance of improvement. Another student agreed with the use of a feeding tube to keep someone alive but was opposed to the attachment of a ventilator. Although he agreed with preventing a patient from starving, he did not support the use of a machine to do all of the patient's breathing. In other words, he considered only the second option to be extraordinary. Thus under one set of circumstances he was not in favor of indirect euthanasia, while under another set of circumstances he was.

Turning to the issue of capital punishment, there are people who oppose it under all circumstances no matter what the crime. On the other hand, some people support it for certain crimes, such as premeditated murder, but oppose it for others, like causing death in the course of a robbery. The possibilities for combinations of viewpoints are considerable when dealing with contemporary issues. As you focus on contemporary issues both in this textbook and in your daily life, do not stick automatically to just one point of view before considering others or some combination of them.

The diagram below illustrates the three-step approach to contemporary issues that we will be using:

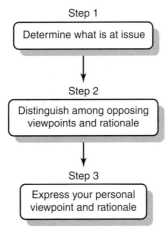

Step 1

Determine what is at issue

Step 2

Distinguish among opposing viewpoints and rationale

Step 3

Express your personal viewpoint and rationale

ACTIVITY 16

DIRECTIONS: Read the following five passages, and in your notebook answer the questions that follow each of them. You will use the three-step approach to contemporary issues. The *comprehension questions* will ask you to state the topic and central message of each passage before proceeding to determine what is at issue, distinguish among opposing viewpoints, and express a personal viewpoint. In addition, you will be asked to compare your personal viewpoint before and after you have thoroughly considered the opposing viewpoints brought out in the passages. Finally, to show flexibility, you will write a few paragraphs *in support of the viewpoint that you do* not *favor.* Keep in mind that some of the selections may deal with more than one issue.

The *thought and discussion questions* will often place you into *hypothetical* or imaginary situations involving the issues brought out in the passages. After thinking about them, feel free to discuss the questions with your classmates and together come up with possible answers. Finally, you will be asked to contribute any questions of your own that come to mind when reading the passages. You should be prepared to discuss possible answers to both your questions and those of your classmates.

EYE ON VOCABULARY

You are aware of the importance of vocabulary development, particularly in college. With that goal in mind, when reading each passage, take note of any unfamiliar words you come across. As suggested in Chapter 1, list them and their definitions in your notebook or on note cards. Use the context, word parts, or the dictionary to determine their meanings. After the completion of each passage, your instructor may ask to see your notebook or note cards and may discuss key words in class.

1

Down with Casual Fridays!
Can Laid-Back Clothes Set Working Women Back?
Don't Dress Down Until You Read This

John T. Molloy

1   Many working women today are happy that so many businesses have adopted dress-down days, or even casual dress all week long. But women shouldn't rejoice. The world's most clever male chauvinist could not have designed a more effective strategy to keep women out of power.

2   For more than 20 years, my company's research on wardrobe has shown that when women dress casually, their authority and competence are more likely to be challenged. In the 1970s, I found that women working in companies with strict dress codes earned

almost one third more than those who had the same levels of education and experience but worked in companies where they were allowed to dress casually. I redid the survey a dozen times, most recently in 1992. The gap between the salaries of women who dress formally and casually has narrowed—but only by 11 percent.

3   To figure out why, my firm used photographs of a man and a woman dressed professionally—the woman in a skirted suit and the man in a traditional men's suit. When we showed the pictures to businesspeople and asked which person was the vice president and which was the assistant, a slight but not overwhelming majority labeled the man the vice president. But when we showed respondents pictures of the same man and woman *without* their jackets, 80 to 90 percent of those questioned identified the man as more senior. When men dress casually, they lose some of their authority; when women do the same, they lose most of theirs.

4   The key to that authority—especially for women in male-dominated fields—is the jacket. In our latest survey, more than 90 percent of businesspeople assumed that women wearing jackets outranked those without. (Wearing a jacket especially helped young, petite women get taken seriously.)

5   So why ask women to dress for failure? The advocates of casual dress codes have wrapped their cause in virtue. A number of executives we talked to said they instituted casual days to build team spirit. True: If *everyone* wears jeans, including the company president, the change may have a positive effect on corporate culture. However, casual dress codes only break down hierarchies when they are first introduced. Within a year, most people in authority begin to dress more formally to identify their positions. If you go into these companies on a casual Friday, you can tell at a glance who is in charge.

6   A second claim in favor of dressing down is that employees have to spend less on clothing for work. This argument has a great deal of validity—for men. Take the experience of one of our clients. As far as Martha was concerned, she had to buy a second work wardrobe when her company instituted casual Fridays. Her husband and the other men at the company just started wearing their golf outfits to work, but Martha felt her weekend clothes would not do; many women's casual outfits are more revealing or sexier than men's, and Martha felt that as a manager, she had to maintain a professional image.

7   She's right. Many executives use casual days and social affairs as a way to appraise up-and-coming young people. The president of a Fortune 500 company openly admitted to me that when young employees, male and female, wore suits to work, they looked so cookie-cutter that he had a problem figuring out which of them would fit in best at corporate headquarters. He started using company outings—when employees were in more personal attire—to decide who was top-echelon material.

8   If your company institutes casual days, you can't ignore the new rules; you may look as if you're boycotting the program. But businesswomen are learning that to go to work in jeans and a T-shirt is a dangerous proposition. Many told us that when they dressed casually at work, they began to receive second-rate treatment; many started to dress as professionally as possible on casual days. They also adopted a wise strategy: keeping a jacket handy in case someone important shows up.

9   If the country's workplaces continue to go casual, jeans manufacturers will undoubtedly make money. But I doubt women will. When companies institute casual workdays, they are changing the rules of dress, but not the rules of nature. When executives tell

you that you can wear anything you want to work, they are telling you that you will not be officially censured for dressing as you wish. They are *not* telling you that you will be taken just as seriously as if you were dressed professionally.

10   It is up to women to make sure that casual days do not undermine their hard-won clout.

Glamour, October 1996, p. 196

COMPREHENSION QUESTIONS

1. What is the topic of the passage?

2. What is the central message of the passage?

3. Determine what is at issue. What is your initial personal viewpoint?

4. Distinguish among opposing viewpoints, and provide the rationale for each.

5. Think carefully about the viewpoints. Express a personal viewpoint, and give the reasons why you favor it. Does it differ from your initial personal viewpoint? Why or why not?

6. Write a few paragraphs *in support of the viewpoint that you do* not *favor.*

THOUGHT AND DISCUSSION QUESTIONS

1. Use the context to figure out what the author means when he states, "The world's most clever male chauvinist could not have designed a more effective strategy to keep women out of power."

2. As a businesswoman, how would you react if your company adopted casual dress all week long? Why? As a businessman, how would you react if your company adopted casual dress all week long? Why? If you answered these two questions differently, explain why.

3. List any questions that came to mind while you were reading this selection, and be prepared to discuss possible answers to them.

2
The Question of Reproductive Rights

Few issues have been as controversial over the past 20 years as whether women have the right to control their own reproduction, specifically, whether birth control and abortion should be available on demand. At the heart of this issue is a crucial question about individual rights: whether the mother has a right to individual self-determination or whether the rights of the unborn baby should be protected by the state. Two views follow, presenting both sides of this volatile question.

Self-Determination: A Basic Right

1   In 1973 the Supreme Court, in the landmark *Roe* v. *Wade* case, declared that abortion, like birth control, is included in the fundamental right to privacy that belongs to all individuals. The Court ruled that the decision to have an abortion during the first 3 months of pregnancy must be left to the pregnant woman and her doctor.

2   This ruling was based on the premise that our society values freedom and self-determination as a basic right. For this reason, the Court attempted to place the decision to bear a child—a decision inextricably related to the right of self-determination—beyond the reach of government. This ruling, along with earlier decisions allowing access to birth control, correctly leaves the choice to the individual most involved, the mother.

3   The mother is the person most closely concerned with the many issues concerning childbirth: Does she have the support a new mother needs? Will she be able to provide the child with a good home? How will an additional member affect the rest of her family? It is the mother who runs the emotional, social, spiritual, and physical risks of abortion or of not having the procedure.

4   Before *Roe* v. *Wade* millions of American women had dangerous and sometimes fatal illegal abortions, often driven to this extreme by poverty or fear. Since *Roe* v. *Wade* millions of women have taken advantage of their right to a safe, legal abortion. Considering the explosive growth in world population, this is a positive step contributing toward our stewardship of the planet.

5   There is no doubt that abortion is an emotionally charged and complex issue. However, the rights of the pregnant woman are paramount. She must have the right to choose and the fundamental right to control her own body and life.

Protecting the Rights of the Unborn Is the State's Duty

6   Beginning in the nineteenth century and extending through much of the twentieth, most states in the United States passed laws restricting or forbidding abortion. These laws were based on two general principles: the state's duty to protect those who cannot protect their own rights and the idea that life itself is an ultimate good.

7   Although various cases preceding *Roe* v. *Wade* established the right to birth control, there is a fundamental difference between birth control and abortion. The Supreme Court itself has declared that the decision to abort a fetus is inherently different from the decision to prevent a pregnancy, because a pregnant woman "cannot be isolated in her privacy." In other words, the pregnant woman is not just an individual but the source of a potential human life whose rights are equally important. Since the fetus cannot safeguard its own rights, it is the state's duty to intervene to ensure that they are protected.

8   Those who oppose abortion believe that the unborn child has a right to its own life and that this life begins at conception. No one has the right to take the life of an unborn child. To those who argue that a woman should not have to raise a child she does not want or cannot afford, they point to the thousands of childless couples who are desperate to adopt babies. The rights of the fetus, then, are of such importance that they must take precedence over the individual rights of the mother.

Marvin R. Levy, Mark Dignan, and Janet H. Shirreffs, *Life and Health*, p. 248

COMPREHENSION QUESTIONS

1. What is the topic of the passage?
2. What is the central message of the passage?
3. Determine what is at issue. What is your initial personal viewpoint?
4. Distinguish among opposing viewpoints, and provide the rationale for each.
5. Think carefully about the viewpoints. Express a personal viewpoint, and give the reasons why you favor it. Does it differ from your initial personal viewpoint? Why or why not?
6. Write a few paragraphs *in support of the viewpoint that you do* not *favor.*

THOUGHT AND DISCUSSION QUESTIONS

1. If your sixteen-year-old sister became pregnant and asked for your advice as to what she should do, what would you advise her? Why?
2. In the debate over abortion, some people oppose it in all circumstances while others oppose it except in cases of rape, incest, an abnormal fetus, or risk to the mother's health. Discuss these two viewpoints *objectively* by providing the rationale for each.
3. List any questions that came to mind while you were reading this selection, and be prepared to discuss possible answers to them.

3

Childless by Choice

Jeanne Safer

1   This year, the first wave of the baby boomers turns 50. For many of the 38 million women born during the baby boom, the biological clock so many watched anxiously is winding down forever.

2   But what about the 15 percent of those women—I am one—who intentionally never produced a baby boom of our own? Because our decision not to have children violates norms of feminine conduct, we face a different psychological task from our peers who became mothers or were infertile.

3   According to my own experience and the interviews I conducted with 50 women who are also childless by choice—the majority of them baby boomers—most of us have never been happier.

4   Contrary to popular assumptions, most women I've talked to who have made conscious decisions not to reproduce for personal or professional reasons are approaching their milestone birthdays with few regrets and with a lot of relief and excitement about the future.

5   At 35, Jane, a dancer, married a man who did not want children. At 40, she went to medical school. She has now established a child psychiatry practice and repaid her loans. "I make a difference in children's lives and still go out at night," she told me.

6   "My life is really beginning at 50," said Anna, an acupuncturist, as she and her new husband prepared for an around-the-world trip.

7   Reviewing a decade as a war correspondent in the Muslim world, one woman told me: "I've had such an eventful time I wouldn't mind dying now. Would I have been able to go into Afghanistan with the rebels if I'd had a child waiting at home?"

8   Robin, a secretary living in a Long Island suburb surrounded by other people's children, says: "There's no gene for motherhood. I'm happy with my life. I feel no need to undo what I didn't do—and I will leave lots of love behind me."

9   Lauren, a housewife and community activist, believes she has given up "a kind of self-knowledge you only get from having kids," but has gained "time to reflect that most people don't have."

10   It is only now as she approaches 50 that Leslie, a gallery owner, can volunteer that she chose not to be a mother. "I felt a stigma in my earlier years," she said. "I was afraid people would judge me or feel sorry for me, because I mistrusted my decision to be different. Now I know that I made that choice out of strength."

11   Many women attributed their satisfaction specifically to their decision to remain childless, a choice they believe has offered them rare opportunities for self-expression, service and creativity. Their need to be the center of their own attention is not based on selfishness or coldness, as is often assumed, but reflects a healthy wish to focus on their own lives.

12   All of them say they feel proud that they actively grappled with their motherhood dilemma. They say they do not regret the outcome, even though many had to mourn lost possibilities and accept being permanent outsiders to a principal preoccupation of their peers. Each told me she now enjoys her unconventional life, the intimacy of her marriage, her uncommon degree of freedom and privacy.

13   Conventional wisdom, the religious right and the psychologist Erik Erikson (who wrote, "A woman who does not fulfill her innate need to fill her uterus with embryonic tissue is likely to be frustrated or neurotic") are wrong. These "barren" women feel fully womanly as they reach menopause; many see themselves as models for the next generation, demonstrating that women can finally make informed choices about reproduction, see motherhood as a vocation that may or may not suit them, and be fulfilled whichever life they chose.

New York Times, January 17, 1996, p. A19

COMPREHENSION QUESTIONS

1. What is the topic of the passage?
2. What is the central message of the passage?
3. Determine what is at issue. What is your initial personal viewpoint?
4. Distinguish among opposing viewpoints, and provide the rationale for each.
5. Think carefully about the viewpoints. Express a personal viewpoint, and give the reasons why you favor it. Does it differ from your initial personal viewpoint? Why or why not?
6. Write a few paragraphs *in support of the viewpoint that you do not favor.*

THOUGHT AND DISCUSSION QUESTIONS

1. Is the writer of the passage being evenhanded or biased in her presentation of the material? Why?

2. Would you marry someone who did not want to have children? Why or why not? How would you handle the situation if you disagreed on that point?

3. List any questions that came to mind while you were reading this selection, and be prepared to discuss possible answers to them.

4

Shot in the Arm

Johnny Townsend

1   I cried yesterday upon leaving the doctor's office.

2   I know, it sounds melodramatic. Men in our society aren't supposed to cry. It's just that the news was so devastating.

3   My bill was $120.

4   I had received "two" injections of cortisone in my left shoulder for tendinitis. (Technically, it was one injection but included a dose of anaesthetic.) Each dose cost $6. That seemed reasonable to me.

5   But the office visit cost $45—a bit steep considering the doctor wasn't there for more than three minutes, and a minute of *that* consisted of his leaving the room to get the hypodermic and medicine. I understand there is a flat fee for office visits; shouldn't there then be a designated minimum amount of time that the doctor spends with each patient? This doctor ignored my questions, handed me the bill, and left while I was still putting on my shirt. Is it right to make me pay for his running behind schedule, when I've paid a fair fee?

6   As it was, I had waited an hour past my scheduled appointment to see him as it was. Even if I'm just a peon, my time is still worth a good $5.50 an hour. Can't I deduct that?

7   But the really painful part of the bill was the $63 for actually performing the injection, which lasted all of eight seconds. If I'm paying $63 for his skill, what was the $45 for—his ability to tell me to remove my shirt? (Don't tell me it was for his diagnosis, because he'd made that a month earlier when he gave me my first injection at a cost of $81.)

8   Basically, since the doctor was only in the room with me for two minutes, at $120 I paid him a dollar a second to see me. At those rates, maybe I should be glad he didn't stay longer.

9   My shoulder had been hurting for three months before I finally went to the doctor. I'd been hoping it would get better on its own, but when I tried to reach for something and realized I could no longer stretch my left arm as far as my right, I became frightened. I suppose this is the way most poor people let problems develop too far.

10   I have a couple of friends I take down to charity hospital every few weeks—one for arthritis and another for a shattered bone that won't heal. I took a third friend there when

he got the flu. Their waits of four, five, and six hours were demeaning and dehumanizing. Usually (except for the flu), they wouldn't even get to see a doctor but only set up an appointment to see one a month or two down the line. And when they showed up for *these* appointments, they had another four- to five-hour wait. Then they were diagnosed but often had to return in another few weeks to receive any treatment, with yet another four- to five-hour wait ahead of them.

11   I grew up in a middle-class home and just couldn't bear to go through all that myself. I am spoiled. I have three college degrees in English and work professionally as a college English instructor, where I earn $6,500 a year, with no benefits. I can't afford insurance. I don't know how I even saved enough for these two office visits, but they are the last.

12   After I had paid the $120, I walked in a daze to my car. I have finally become a complete nothing, I realized. People with money are everything, and people without it are nothing. It's certainly been said before, but I finally realized what it meant.

13   I don't expect anyone to feel sorry for me. As someone who frittered away his life on something so frivolous as English, I know exactly what society thinks of me. But as someone who grew up middle class, despite my miserable income of the past several years, I still managed to see myself as part of *us,* not *them.*

14   I, too, looked down on the poor somewhat, as ignorant or lazy or whatever. Oh, it's true that because of my liberal-arts background I was very nice and sensitive to *them,* but I hung on as long as I could to being part of *us,* believing I was only an honorary *them.* I was only clinging to respectability by my fingernails, but that doctor bill ripped my fingernails right off.

15   I was raised conservative but became much more liberal as an adult. Still, I am an odd mixture and maintain some strong views on both sides. I do think that entitlement programs and welfare too often promote dependence and lack of ambition, as well as punish those who try to escape poverty.

16   But honestly, how many people are going to say, "You know, the government is paying for my health care, so I think I'll go out and get appendicitis today"? Do people really say, "I hate rich people. I want them to pay more taxes for me. I was going to let that lump in my breast just sit there, but I think I'll go get it checked just to be spiteful"? Has anyone really been heard to remark, "Since I don't have to pay for it, I think I'll go develop some intestinal polyps. A colonoscopy sounds like a lot of fun. It'll liven up my boring, lazy week"?

17   The fact is that many people will never earn more than minimum wage and will be forever stuck in jobs with no benefits. And most people, even if they do work hard, will never be able to afford health care. If I'd had a torn rotator cuff, my doctor said it could cost a couple of thousand dollars to repair. We dregs of society may deserve to live in cruddy apartments and shop for clothes at thrift stores, but do we really deserve to wait half a year to be treated for something others are cured of in a week? Do only those who are smart enough or talented enough or lucky enough (or brutal enough or avaricious enough) to become wealthy deserve health care?

18   I've been back at school for a year now, taking my pre-med prerequisites with a grade-point average of 4.0. With or without health-care reform, I'm going to get the health care I deserve. It would be nice to think, though, that maybe the millions of other Americans

without health care might get some, too. No matter where we stand as individuals on the issue of reform, it is clear that the health-care system on some substantial level needs a shot in the arm.

The Humanist, November 1995, p. 4

COMPREHENSION QUESTIONS

1. What is the topic of the passage?
2. What is the central message of the passage?
3. Determine what is at issue. What is your initial personal viewpoint?
4. Distinguish among opposing viewpoints, and provide the rationale for each.
5. Think carefully about the viewpoints. Express a personal viewpoint, and give the reasons why you favor it. Does it differ from your initial personal viewpoint? Why or why not?
6. Write a few paragraphs *in support of the viewpoint that you do not favor.*

THOUGHT AND DISCUSSION QUESTIONS

1. If you were a doctor, how would you react to a patient who could not afford to pay your fees? Why? Would you agree to provide medical care to a homeless person? Why or why not?
2. If you were a doctor, what possible rationale would you give if you were accused of charging high fees?
3. List any questions that came to mind while you were reading this selection, and be prepared to discuss possible answers to them.

5

Should There Be Prayer in Our Public Schools?

Lynn Minton, Moderator

We spoke with a group of New York University students about the controversial issue of whether there should be prayer in our public schools. The students were taking part in an honors seminar on religion and the Constitution with John Sexton, dean of the NYU School of Law. They were Gregory A. Belinfanti, 19, of Elmont, N.Y.; Shaheen A. Khalfan, 20, of Searingtown, N.Y.; Victoria Kopolovich, 20, of Brooklyn, N.Y.; Molly Cowan, 20, of Fort Worth, Tex.; Brian J. Fitzpatrick, 20, of Brooklyn, N.Y.; Christopher Hughes, 20, of Secaucus, N.J.; Elie Fink, 21, of Bridgeport, Conn.; and Brooke E. Bell, 20, of San Jose, Calif.

1   **Greg:** Yes. Throughout our history, religion and the United States are intermingled— the first people who came here came to escape religious persecution. Every session of Congress begins with a prayer; on every coin is "In God we trust"; when we say the pledge

of allegiance, we say "under God." If you say, "No, you can't have prayer in the schools," you're negating the country's history.

2   **Shaheen:** I was born in Tanzania, and in Muslim countries religion is an inherent part of the school system. But I don't think that a public school education in America should have religion mixed in. You don't want to turn around one day and have the government tell you, "Now, you have to do *this* prayer." It's like you're brain-washing children. And I don't think the government should be saying, "I want you to believe in God." Or, "I want you to say this prayer before you start your school day." It may not even be your prayer. Who made up this prayer? Why should you have to say it if you don't believe in it?

3   **Greg:** At least 99% of the people, including the government, accept that there is this Being—and we'll call him God—who, as a nation, we live under. And all I'm saying is, at the beginning of the day, those of us who would like to say a nondenominational prayer should be given the opportunity. If you don't want to say the prayer, then don't say it.

4   **Victoria:** For you to say, "Well, you don't have to pray—you can leave the room"...well, we'll be looked upon as different. And it is our right to have an education in this country, and it is our right to stay in class. And I don't believe that there is such a thing as a general prayer that everyone could be part of.

5   **Molly:** That's the problem with school prayers—they try to combine all these religions, and so the prayer doesn't really represent any religion. A Christian prayer would say, "In Jesus' name I pray," but they're not going to say that in a public school. It's like the state is forming this pseudo-combo religion.

6   **Brian:** But even a nondenominational prayer to begin the school day is not constitutional—even a "moment of silence or voluntary prayer" is not allowed. It seems to me that in this country now there is a very strong anti-religious thread. There's this feeling that anyone who believes strongly in their religion is a fanatic, which of course isn't true. There is this feeling that if religion is allowed in schools, you're going to brainwash the children, which is ridiculous.

7   **Shaheen:** I don't mind a moment of silence, because a person can—if they want to—just sit and think about their plans for the day. But then the teacher should just announce a moment of silence. Not say, "We'll have a moment of silence or voluntary prayer." Just the fact that you're getting prayer involved with a public school education—it shouldn't be there.

8   **Molly:** Some people forget that you can pray anywhere. You don't need the school to "give" you time for prayer. You can sit in your class and pray. You can pray in the hall. Nobody's saying that they're going to hunt you down, listen to your thoughts and say, "No prayer!"

9   **Greg:** Perhaps you don't have the time. Perhaps you'd like to do it with your school-mates. But the Supreme Court said you can't have a moment of silence that is designed for meditation or voluntary prayer.

10   **Victoria:** I think it's just like, you give them a little bit, and then they'll want a lot. Then they'll start with spoken prayer. So the Supreme Court said, "No. We're stopping right here. We're drawing the line."

11   **Chris:** I'm definitely for a moment of silence. For meditation too. School is such a rat race, that's the last thing on your mind—to stop and collect your thoughts for a minute. So maybe it's like a reminder. And if you want to pray during that moment, then that's your choice.

12   **Lynn Minton:** What about people who don't pray silently? Or who kneel when they pray?

13   **Chris:** Those people can think about something else.

14   **Elie:** When you bring religion in any form into the public schools, it creates an opportunity to have the religion of the majority enforced. Children are very susceptible to peer pressure, and there's no way to regulate what goes on in every classroom.

15   **Brooke:** Once you bring religion into the schools, religious persecution will probably follow.

16   **Shaheen:** This country was founded to get away from religious persecution.

17   **Elie:** Even during a moment of silence, maybe some of the students are crossing themselves and others aren't—some kids could be ostracized.

18   **Greg:** Let's stop kickball too, because kids can be ostracized—a kid gets picked last, and he's got to stand against the fence.

19   **Brian:** We've heard religious persecution being thrown around. I don't think in this country, in this day and age....

20   **Brooke:** I don't mean the Holocaust happening in P.S. 20 or whatever, but I do think it can cause tension between kids and cause insults to be thrown around.

21   **Brian:** Those insults are around anyway. Let's say there's a Sikh, and he's wearing a turban. You don't think he's already going to have comments made to him, whether or not there are prayers in school?

22   **Greg:** Persecution doesn't stem from prayer. It stems from what's already in your head.

23   **Chris:** I don't think spoken prayer should be allowed.

24   **Brian:** I do.

25   **LM:** Who'd write the prayer?

26   **Brian:** Perhaps each district school board. Preferably with input from the students' parents—all working on a very local level.

27   **LM:** Would you be comfortable with their prayers?

28   **Brian:** It depends on what prayers they write. Let's just say the word "God" is used.

29   **LM:** Why is this important to you?

30   **Brian:** I feel religion in a group setting is very important.

31   **LM:** How about church?

32   **Greg:** You can't go to church on weekdays.

33   **Elie:** I go to synagogue every day.

34   **Greg:** And my grandmother goes to church every day. But I don't think it's realistic to expect high school kids to go to church every day.

35   **Molly:** Is it the responsibility of the government to bring the church to the school every day?

36   **Greg:** All they'd be doing is saying that we acknowledge that we are a religious people and that some people enjoy prayer before they start their day, and we will set aside this moment of time, and here is a prayer. If you don't want to say the prayer, you don't have to.

37   **Brian:** The idea of the First Amendment was not to deny people the right to say prayer. It was to prevent the government from meddling in and controlling people's lives.

38   **Victoria:** And prayer is not meddling?

39   **Greg:** The government is not supposed to tell people which religions to choose or to set up a national religion. By establishing prayer in the schools, the government is not doing those things.

40   **Molly:** You're saying you'd love to see prayer in school. There *is* prayer in school. I've done it. You could ask tons of students who have prayed in school.

41   **Brian:** But it's illegal.

42   **Molly:** It's not illegal! A private prayer, in class, in the hall ...

43   **Brian:** Why should people be afraid to freely announce their faith in God? Why should they have to go in the corner or in the hallway and secretly say it to themselves?

44   **Victoria:** They don't have to go into a corner. They don't have to pray silently—they can do what they want. But the government can't do it. The school can't do it.

45   **Greg:** It's sort of taboo to express your religious beliefs among your friends while you are at school, and I think it all stems from a misinterpretation of the First Amendment, which says "Congress shall make no law respecting an establishment of religion, or prohibiting the free exercise thereof." It does not say that the government can't say that we are *for* religion.

46   **LM:** Have you ever had a coach who held a pre-game prayer meeting in school?

47   **Chris:** Before every single game, our JV basketball coach would say, "All right, guys, hands in." And we'd say "The Lord's Prayer." And in the locker room, before every game, I would put my head down, say a prayer. A lot of kids would.

48   **Brooke:** I have a problem with the coach leading a prayer. Here the team is supposed to go out together and play, and yet right before, you divide up the group: If you want to pray, stay. If you don't ...

49   **Chris:** You have to realize, I went to a high school where almost everybody was Catholic.

50   **LM:** Is it okay where it's a public school, but everybody is the same religion?

51   **Molly:** I don't know. I mean, if none of the students have any problem with it, then it's okay.

52   **LM:** What if Elie moved into town and was on your team?

53   **Chris:** Actually, there were one or two Jewish kids on the JV team.

54   **Brian:** If no one objected, why would there be a problem?

55   **Elie:** The government has to worry about the guy who's sticking his hand in because he doesn't want to be different—but he really doesn't want to.

56   **Chris:** The coach knew that there were two Jewish kids on the team, but it wasn't an issue. If you do object, you could take that to him and say, "Listen, it really offends me that you say 'The Lord's Prayer.'"

57   **LM:** I'm thinking it takes a lot of courage to tell a coach, "I don't like the way you're doing that!"

58   **Greg:** We keep on saying that if you allow prayer in the school, some people will feel different. Well, the fact is that if you're not a Christian in the United States, then you're different. Because the majority, we're a Christian nation. If Elie went to a public school in my district, he'd be different. Regardless of whether there's prayer in the school.

59   **Brian:** It's a Judeo-Christian nation.

60   **Shaheen:** Are we all just putting aside that this country was established for religious freedom? Are the rest of us just going to have to go away?

61   **Greg:** You have religious freedom in a country that's a Judeo-Christian nation. We're not establishing a Judeo-Christian nation, we *are* one.

62   **Brooke:** What about the minority?

63   **Brian:** So what should we say—that it's Judeo-Christian-Islamic-Hindu...?

64   **Brooke:** No. You can just say it's a nation of different religions. What's wrong with that?

65   **Brian:** All you have to do is look at our motto, look at the prayer before Congress begins.

66   **Molly:** I'm uncomfortable just because I *am* part of the Christian majority. I know how I feel, but you have to consider how other people are going to feel. And there's something else: When you're in the majority and you don't take care of the minority's rights, then who is to say that, someday, somebody's not going to come along and take away *your* rights? And who will protect you?

Parade, November 27, 1994, pp. 4–5

COMPREHENSION QUESTIONS

1. What is the topic of the passage?

2. What is the central message of the passage?

3. Determine what is at issue. What is your initial personal viewpoint?

4. Distinguish among opposing viewpoints, and provide the rationale for each.

5. Think carefully about the viewpoints. Express a personal viewpoint, and give the reasons why you favor it. Does it differ from your initial personal viewpoint? Why or why not?

6. Write a few paragraphs *in support of the viewpoint that you do* not *favor.*

THOUGHT AND DISCUSSION QUESTIONS

1. How would you respond if your instructor asked the class to say a prayer today? Why?

2. Assume for a moment that you are a teacher who decides to start each school day with a prayer. How would you react to a student who refused to do so because he does not believe in God? Why?

3. Does God exist? Why or why not?

4. List any questions that came to mind while you were reading this selection, and be prepared to discuss possible answers to them.

ACTIVITY 17

DIRECTIONS: As a semester project, choose a contemporary issue that is of interest to you, and write an essay in which you discuss what is at issue, distinguish among the opposing viewpoints, and express a personal viewpoint. When you have completed your essay, you will be asked to make copies available for your classmates to read. After they have had an opportunity to consider what you have written, you will lead a classroom discussion of the issue during which you will present your conclusions and answer any questions that your fellow students may have.

ACTIVITY 18

DIRECTIONS: Your instructor is going to divide the class into groups, each of which will choose a contemporary issue to investigate. Each group will then be divided into two debate teams for the purpose of representing the major opposing viewpoints regarding the issue. Toward the end of the semester, the two teams will debate the issue in class, with your instructor serving as the moderator.

LOOKING BACK

Summarize and/or paraphrase the most important points you learned from this chapter and determine how they can be put to use in other classes. Be prepared to discuss with your classmates what you have written.

THINK AGAIN!

Suppose that you are alone in the forest with a friend, and you are both riding horses. An argument starts over whose horse is slower. After several minutes of bickering, you make a $100 bet and decide to have a race immediately. However, the race does not work because you each make your horse go as slowly as possible on purpose so that you can win the money. Assuming that you want to settle the matter right there on the spot, can you figure out a fair way to determine whose horse is slower?

The Dashing Detective

Remember to follow these steps:

- first, read the narrative and all the questions
- second, examine the picture carefully
- third, answer the questions in the order they appear and come up with the solution

Have fun!

An 8¢ Story

The day after Georgio Erysipelas lost fifteen dollars and eight cents to Hans Liverwurst in their weekly poker game, Georgio entered Hans's High Class Delicatessen. Both men were known to be short tempered and had previously come close to fighting over poker hands, but this time the fight was to the death, as Hans's body attests.

All that Detective Sharpeye could learn from witnesses who had heard the argument leading to the tragedy was that Georgio had shouted out in English, "That's all you'll get!" Hans had responded angrily in German, whereupon Georgio had switched into high gear, but in Greek.

Can you guess what they accused each other of?

Questions

1. Was Hans apparently eating when Georgio came into the store?   ☐ Yes   ☐ No

2. Whose footprints are shown?   ☐ Hans's   ☐ Georgio's

3. Did Hans stop at the pickle barrel?   ☐ Yes   ☐ No

4. Do you think Hans offered Georgio a pickle?   ☐ Yes   ☐ No

5. Do you think Hans and Georgio were on friendly terms when Georgio entered the store?
   ☐ Yes   ☐ No

6. Did Hans return to his table at any time after leaving it?   ☐ Yes   ☐ No

7. Do you think that Georgio came to pay his debt?   ☐ Yes   ☐ No

8. Do you think that Georgio came to the store with malice aforethought?
   ☐ Yes   ☐ No

9. Is there any evidence to show that Georgio may have acted in self-defense?
   ☐ Yes   ☐ No

10. Where did the murder weapon come from? _____

11. Do you think Hans objected to the fact that the five dollar bill was torn?
    ☐ Yes   ☐ No

12. What do you think the argument was about: ☐ The 8¢   ☐ The pickles
    ☐ The $10.00

Lawrence Treat, *Crime and Puzzlement*, pp. 46–47

Name _____ Date _____

MASTERY TEST 4–1

DIRECTIONS: Fill in the blanks and answer the questions.

1. _____ thinking has no clear purpose or objective.

2. Critical thinkers are in a better position to _____ what is

   going on around them, avoid costly _____, and

   _____ whatever they set out to do.

3. What is critical thinking? _____

   _____

   _____

4. What are the benefits and uses of critical thinking? _____

   _____

   _____

   _____

   _____

   _____

   _____

   _____

   _____

   _____

   _____

   _____

   _____

   _____

   _____

   _____

5. Name the characteristics of critical thinking, and describe each of them in a sentence

   or two. _____

_____

_____

_____

_____

_____

_____

_____

_____

_____

_____

_____

_____

_____

_____

_____

_____

_____

_____

6. When using the Internet for research, the critical thinker
    a. should first make sure that a particular source is both appropriate and relevant
    b. should try to use material from *.edu, .gov,* and *.mil* sites because they are most likely to be reliable
    c. should look for the professional affiliation and bibliography of the author
    d. should always be aware of possible bias
    e. all of the above
    f. none of the above

7. _____, _____, and _____ are online databases that provide access to full-text articles from scholarly and popular periodicals.

8. Name three online encyclopedias. _____

    _____

    _____

9. _____ and _____ are examples of search engines that use key words to find information.

10. What is a contemporary issue? _____

_____

_____

11. As a critical thinker it is important that you be aware of the _____, or

specific reasons, for a given viewpoint.

12. What is the central message of the following memo?

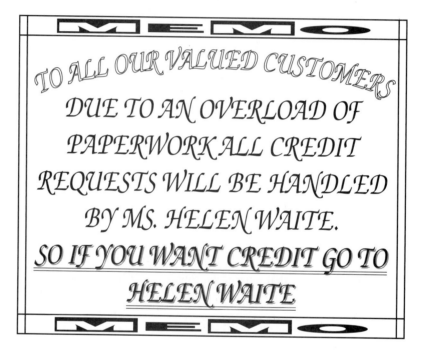

Central message: _____

_____

_____

Name _____ Date _____

MASTERY TEST 4-2

DIRECTIONS: For each of the following passages, determine what is at issue and distinguish among the opposing viewpoints, including the rationale for each.

1

PRO & CON: Putting Pig Parts into Human Bodies

Should researchers be permitted to experiment with the transplanting of pig cells or organs into humans?

[asks] *John O'Neil*

YES

1   The possibility of infection by retro-viruses is a hot topic, given Ebola and AIDS, but virologists say the risk is very small. Some people want to halt experiments—but halt them until when? It's almost impossible to identify a risk when you have no experience of something. It's true that if the benefits are not going to outweigh the risks, then any risk will be too great. But 60,000 people are waiting for organs in this country this year. About 12,000 are waiting for livers, but only 4,000 will get them. Even if everyone in the nation donated organs who could there wouldn't be enough. Where else do we have a life and death circumstance that's rationed? We can't create livers, hearts or kidneys. That's the reason to move forward, but cautiously.

2   Dr. Ronald Ferguson is chairman of the surgery department at Ohio State University Medical Center.

NO

1   I'm all for basic research in this field, but not human research. Before that, we have to consider who is going to be put at risk, and there's no argument that this risk exists. The danger, which nobody can quantify, is that a pig's infectious particle will infect a human recipient, mutate and infect the public in a way not unlike AIDS. The question then becomes an ethical one. If the general population is to be put at risk, shouldn't the population be informed about the risk and shouldn't there be a way of getting public input on whether clinical trials should go forward? We have suggested a moratorium on human trials until we find a way to involve the public. Lab experiments are fine, but don't impose risk on people to find out what the risk is.

2   Dr. Fritz H. Bach is an immunobiologist and the Lewis Thomas Professor at Harvard Medical School.

New York Times, October 27, 1998

Issue: _____

Opposing viewpoints and rationales: _____

_____

_____

_____

_____

_____

_____

_____

_____

_____

2

Do You Trust the Media?

1   These days, more and more news is *about* the news, thanks to a wave of media malfeasance that has Americans wondering whether they can trust anything they read, watch or hear. Among the biggest scandals: CNN and *Time*'s admission that their joint report about the United States' use of nerve gas in Vietnam had little basis in fact; the firing of a *Boston Globe* columnist and a *New Republic* writer for making up quotes and events; and prestigious news outlets caught spreading unfounded rumors during the early days of the Clinton-Lewinsky brouhaha.

2   These exposés arrive amid a growing credibility crisis. The percentage of Americans who think that news outlets usually get the facts straight has plummeted from 55 to 34 over the past 13 years, according to The Pew Research Center for The People & The Press.

3   Some say news quality is compromised by the intense, often minute-to-minute competition among a growing number of outlets, including cable shows, Internet sites and some dozen TV newsmagazines. As *Nightline*'s executive producer recently said, "Everybody is ratcheting up the speed and that's totally wrong....You can work too fast and make mistakes."

4   Others say the battle for ratings and advertising dollars also affects the news. "We're moving from journalism as a profession toward news as marketing," says Jim Naureckas of Fairness & Accuracy In Reporting, a watchdog group. Big-business media, he argues, would rather run "sensationalist stories that can be played for tears, fears or outrage" than cover serious political and economic issues.

5   Journalists' own biases are part of the problem too, adds Deborah Lambert of Accuracy in Media, a watchdog group that monitors the media for liberal bias. To "make a splash," she charges, some reporters give vent to personal passions instead of presenting information fairly. "To these journalists, truth has become a quaint relic."

6   Yet many believe news gathering is better than ever. "We never had a 'good old days' when no one made mistakes on deadline," says Dick Schwarzlose, a professor at Northwestern University's Medill School of Journalism. Nor are competition, sensationalism or bias anything new (the term *yellow journalism* was coined in the late nineteenth century); it's just that today, reporters as well as their audience are far more aware when the media

falls short. Says Schwarzlose, "The vast majority of people in the news business are doing their best to provide good information."

7   Robert Lichter, Ph.D., who heads the Center for Media and Public Affairs, questions whether bias-free news is ideal. The founding fathers' vision of a free press wasn't a few respected sources spooning out "objective" facts, he notes, but a welter of conflicting sources and viewpoints—precisely what today's consumer faces.

8   Journalism's defenders point out that most people know which sources are usually trustworthy and which play the news for thrills. The Pew survey, for example, found that 93 percent of Americans have little or no faith in the accuracy of supermarket tabloids. Meanwhile, believability of serious news outlets is becoming more of a concern—especially now that members of the media are watchdogging each other, says Bill Kovach, curator of Harvard's Nieman Foundation journalism fellowships. "When you make ratings your number-one priority and credibility number two, eventually you get slammed," he says. "I hope CNN and the others have learned that lesson by now."

9   Is the media less trustworthy than ever?

Glamour, October 1998, p. 240

Issue: _____

Opposing viewpoints and rationales: _____

_____

_____

_____

_____

_____

_____

_____

_____

_____

_____

_____

3

A Small Plea to Delete a Ubiquitous Expletive
Can't We Get Along Without the "F" Word?

Elizabeth Austin

1   Oh, f—.

2   The "F" word, as it's called in more polite circles (including magazines such as this one), is increasingly hard to escape. Those who rarely use it themselves nonetheless hear it frequently—on the street, on the job, at the health club, at the movies—anywhere

two or three disgruntled citizens might gather. Most people have uttered the word; everyone can define it. But even those who aren't particularly shocked by it don't want to hear it all the time. The toughest of tough guys cringes inwardly when somebody says it in front of his mother. Becoming a parent induces instant hypersensitivity to the word's ubiquitous presence in movies, on cable TV, in music, and in the loose talk of childless friends.

3   In its simplest and oldest usage, the "F" word refers to copulation. This usage has a long, frequently jolly, occasionally distinguished history. Shakespeare made glancing puns about it, and Scottish poet Robert Burns included it in his racier verses. More commonly today, though, the "F" word is used to express not desire but derision, not heat but hostility. Even when used as a kind of verbal space holder, a rougher, hipper equivalent of "you know" (as in "I f—ing love that f—ing movie," or in the Army patois that has been common for decades), it carries a rude message. It is both a gauge and an engine of our ever plummeting standards of civility. Yet enough people are fed up with it that it's possible to erase the "F" word from public parlance and civil discourse.

LAST WORD

4   A couple of generations back, calling for a public elimination of the "F" word would have been preposterous, since the word was never uttered in polite company (loosely defined as anywhere middle-class women were likely to hear it). In the late '60s, however, the loud, open use of the "F" word became a true shibboleth, dividing the student radicals from the Establishment "pigs" they delighted in tweaking. In Jerry Rubin's words, the "F" word was "the last word left in the English language. Amerika cannot destroy it because she dare not use it."

5   But America took that dare. From the early '70s on, the "F" word started turning up with increasing regularity in movies, literature, and real life, according to Jesse Sheidlower's exhaustive volume, *The F-Word*. Many linguists and social critics celebrated the "F" word's coming out as a healthy abandonment of prudishness; a few still do. But civic virtuecrats today make a stronger case that public use of the word is a prime example of the "broken window" theory of social decay. When we put private frustrations and the right to be foulmouthed ahead of public order and civility, we coarsen society and risk an avalanche of rage and violence. Despite its near universality, the "F" word remains a fighting word.

6   So let's get rid of it. Scholars of social norms say all that's necessary to remove offensive language from public speech is a critical mass of people willing to take up cudgels against it. University of Chicago law Prof. Randal Picker describes such sudden overthrows of social standards as "norms cascades." If society is ripe for change, he contends, a single, powerful catalyst can engineer swift, widespread transformation. Picker cites Jesse Jackson, whose call for a switch from "black" to "African-American" changed the nation's nomenclature almost overnight. A more subtle but equally effective norms cascade was engineered by a handful of feminist writers in the early 1970s. Author-activist Robin Morgan remembers furiously listing words then commonly used to describe women, both in conversation and in print. "Produce and animals is what we were," she recalls. "We were 'chicks' and 'lambs' and 'birds' and 'bitches,' and there was always the infamous 'cherry.'" When Morgan and other feminist leaders publicly insisted on being called women, they started a norms cascade that eventually erased not only chick and bitch but girl and lady as well.

7   The "F" word seems like a particularly ripe target for a new generation of linguistic activists from both sides of the ideological divide. Erasing the word from civil discourse is one goal that Phyllis Schlafly could share with Andrea Dworkin. Here are a few modest proposals to help make that happen:

- Police should start ticketing drivers who use the "F" word (or the correlating hand gesture), thereby boosting civility and calming road rage simultaneously. Although this could raise some First Amendment hackles, keep in mind that "fighting words" are not protected speech. One simple test of the fighting-words concept is whether a fight actually ensues. Slapping a $100 ticket on a driver whose uplifted finger sparked a collision should pass any constitutional test.
- The Motion Picture Association of America movie rating system should be overhauled to give an automatic NC–17 rating to any film that uses the "F" word even once. An NC–17 rating all but guarantees diminished viewership. Writers and directors who considered the word necessary to their artistic expression could still get their movies made; they'd just have to make the decision to trade lucrative ticket sales to teenagers for their artistic license.
- Authors who salt their books with gratuitous "F" words should get the same critical treatment as those who sprinkle their prose with casual racial epithets. Certainly, there are times when the "F" word expresses precisely what a writer means to convey. But we need literary critics who understand the distinction between necessary frankness and the adolescent desire to shock.
- Most important, we must delete the "F" word from our own lives. The most lasting shifts in social standards are those that begin at cocktail parties and around water coolers. We can wipe out the "F" word simply by refusing to use it ourselves and quietly but firmly objecting when others use it within earshot. The next time someone uses the "F" word in casual conversation, Judith Martin, better known as Miss Manners, suggests responding: "I'm not used to that sort of language." (If you can't say that line with a straight face, try: "We don't use that word anymore.")

8   Objecting to the "F" word isn't censorship. You can still use it as a punch line, if you like. You'll just risk the freezing silence and icy glares now reserved for white people who use the "N" word in public. Similarly, you're free to use it among your intimates, as a term of (in Sheidlower's words) "endearment, admiration, [or] derision." The rules of public civility have always included the naked-and-sweaty exemption. How you talk in the locker room or bedroom is up to you.

9   Ultimately, a social norm is nothing more, and nothing less, than the sum of individual decisions. In reconsidering the "F" word, you may prize your right to say it above your neighbor's right not to hear it. But personally, I'm swearing off.

U.S. News and World Report, April 6, 1998, pp. 58–59

Issue: _____

Opposing viewpoints and rationales: _____

_____

_____

_____

_____

_____

_____

_____

_____

_____

_____

_____

_____

_____

_____

4

Grappling with the Ethics of Stem Cell Research

Nicholas Wade

1   Can life be preserved at the expense of other life? The use of human embryonic stem cells presents a tight tangle of ethical questions.

2   The central issue is that biologists believe embryonic stem cells may help repair damaged tissues and organs, or grow new ones, laying the basis for a novel kind of therapy that some are calling regenerative medicine. But most embryonic stem cells are derived from early human embryos, the stage reached a week or so after the union of egg and sperm, and require the embryos' destruction.

3   Here are some of the principal arguments made by the two sides.

4   **Opponents:** The destruction of a human embryo is morally wrong, whatever the alleged benefits. A human life begins at the moment egg and sperm are united, and nothing should be done to an embryo that is not in its interest. The benefits to others, whatever they may be, cannot justify the destruction of a human life.

5   **Proponents:** Human embryos should be treated with respect, but the saving of lives through medical research is also a strong moral imperative.

6   The embryos at issue are created as part of a life-giving process—that of helping infertile couples conceive. A fertility clinic doctor mixes eggs and sperm in a dish, lets the

fertilized eggs develop a few days to the stage called a blastocyst and chooses the healthiest looking blastocyst to implant in the womb.

7   The others are frozen in case of future need, but most have no realistic prospect of coming to term and will eventually be destroyed, an inevitable consequence of the fertility treatment. If the parents have expressed a desire that their embryo be donated to research, rather than discarded unused, it is morally acceptable to use the embryo's cells for purposes that may bring great benefit to others.

8   Besides, it is not so clear that an individual life begins at fertilization. The beginnings of the nervous system do not appear until 14 days after fertilization. The early embryo can split, leading to the birth of twins, so that individuality, it could be argued, begins some days after fertilization. The full rights and protection due to an individual may not necessarily extend as far as the blastocyst.

9   **Opponents:** If embryonic stem cell research is permitted, the door may be opened to many further steps demeaning to human life. Scientists have a long research agenda, starting with the creation of embryos specifically for research purposes. If an absolute line is not drawn to protect the embryo, many grave abuses may follow.

10   **Proponents:** Each case should be considered on its merits. The frequent destruction of early embryos is already widely accepted in certain forms of contraception, such as the I.U.D., which prevents implantation, and in the fertility clinic treatment itself. Stem cell research requires very few embryos to be destroyed.

11   A special property of embryonic stem cells is that they grow and divide indefinitely. That means that in principle the cells from just a single blastocyst could satisfy all requirements. In practice, biologists would wish to establish a number of different lines, maybe 20 or 100, to make sure they had ones that were healthy and typical, and covered a spectrum of different immunological types. But the derivation of human cells would be a limited and occasional process, not an open-ended and continuing destruction.

12   **Opponents:** The federal guidelines on embryonic stem cell research are ethically flawed in allowing federally supported researchers to use the cells but not to derive them. This is like saying it is O.K. to use stolen property, provided you didn't steal it yourself.

13   **Proponents:** The guidelines may not be ethically immaculate but they reflect that same compromise that society has reached in the case of abortion, that abortion is legal but federal money may not be used to support it.

14   The guidelines would let the promise of embryonic stem cells be explored while respecting the view of those who believe the government should not lend its support to the destruction of embryos, as expressed in the Dickey amendment prohibiting federal money from being spent for such research.

15   **Opponents:** The medical benefits of embryonic stem cells are overstated but, in any event, could be obtained by using adult stem cells instead. The alleged benefits of embryonic stem cells are projections from experiments on mice and rats that have not yet been reproduced in people.

16   In any case, there is an alternative to embryonic stem cells. Many of the body's tissues possess a store of so-called adult stem cells with which to replenish themselves. In the body, adult stem cells seem to be tissue-specific. The blood stem cells make just new blood cells, the skin stem cells make new skin. But new research is showing that some adult stem

cells have a much wider repertoire and may be able to perform many of the tasks expected of embryonic stem cells.

17   Adult stem cells would be a better choice for treatment because patients could be repaired with their own adult stem cells instead of risking the immunological problems of embryonic stem cells from an unmatched donor.

18   **Proponents:** The promise of stem cell research is real, and both types of cells must be studied. True, scientists often get carried away with their enthusiasms. But there is solid ground beneath the high hopes held for embryonic stem cells.

19   The cells offer a powerful new way of treating intractable degenerative diseases like Parkinson's disease and diabetes. Adult stem cells are not nearly so prolific and versatile as embryonic stem cells and have not been proved to possess the same range of capabilities.

20   It is important to study both types of cells to discover which is best for each application. Embryonic stem cells do not seem very provocative to the immune system, and even if they are, there would be several ways to address the problem.

New York Times, July 24, 2001, p. F3

Issue: _____

Opposing viewpoints and rationales: _____

_____

_____

_____

_____

_____

_____

_____

_____

_____

_____

_____

_____

_____

Name _____   Date _____

MASTERY TEST 4–3

DIRECTIONS: As a critical thinker, read the following review of the movie *The Shining* which was taken from the Internet, and then answer the thought and discussion questions.

1   Terrifyingly, amazing achievement in filmmaking and the art of terror, this movie classic graces us with one of director Stanley Kubrick's sporadic directing gigs, only 5 years after his last acclaimed feature, *Barry Lyndon*, and 10 after his timely masterpiece *Clockwork Orange* (9/10). This movie is based on author Stephen King's best-selling novel of the same name, and stars the always-interesting Jack Nicholson.

PLOT:

2   A nice man, his wife and young boy, take on the task of overlooking a winter resort during its off season. The nice man is there for peace and quiet, as his profession as a writer requires just that. The boy has a special skill called "the shine" which allows him to hear and see things that others cannot. As their time in the grand hotel ticks away, the mansion begins to exude thoughts of the past and chills of the present. In time, the nice man transforms into a "not-so-nice" man, and begins to terrify his own flesh and blood.

CRITIQUE:

3   Chilling, majestic piece of cinematic fright, this film combines all the great elements of an intellectual thriller, with the grand vision of a director who has the instinctual capacity to pace a moody horror flick within the realm of his filmmaking genius that includes an eye for the original shot, an ice-cold soundtrack and an overall sense of dehumanization. This movie cuts through all the typical horror movies like a red-poker through a human eye, as it allows the viewer to not only feel the violence and psychosis of its protagonist, but appreciate the seed from which the derangement stems. One of the scariest things for people to face is the unknown and this film presents its plotting with just that thought in mind. The setting is perfect, in a desolate winter hideaway. The quietness of the moment is a character in itself, as the fermenting aggressor in Jack Torrance's mind wallows in this idle time, and breeds the devil's new playground. I always felt like the presence of evil was dormant in all of our minds, with only the circumstances of the moment, and the reasons given therein, needed to wake its violent ass and pounce over its unsuspecting victims. This film is a perfect example of this very thought.

4   And it is within this film's subtle touches of the canvas, the clackity-clacks of the young boy's big wheel riding along the empty hallways of the hotel, the labyrinthian garden representing the mind's fine line between sane and insane, Kubrick's purposely transfixed editing inconsistencies, continuity errors and set mis-arrangements, that we discover a world guided by the righteous and tangible, but coaxed away by the powerful and unknown. I have never read the book upon which the film is based, but without that as a comparison point, I am proud to say that this is one of the most terrifying films that I have ever seen. I thought that the runtime of the film could've been cut by a little bit, but then again, I am not one of the most acclaimed directors in the history of film, so maybe I should keep my two-cent criticisms over a superb film, to myself. All in all, this movie captures your

attention with its grand form and vision, ropes you in with some terror and eccentric direction, and ties you down and stabs you in the heart with its cold-eyed view of the man's mind gone overboard, creepy atmosphere and the loss of humanity.

www.joblo.com/shining.html

THOUGHT AND DISCUSSION QUESTIONS

1. Do you agree with the following statement:"Movies based on novels are not as good as the novels themselves."? Why or why not?
2. Pretend that you are a movie critic by watching the Stanley Kubrick version of *The Shining* and writing your review of it.
3. Which points made by the reviewer do you agree with? Which points do you disagree with? Why?
4. (Optional) During the course of the semester, read the novel and write a critical essay in which you compare the movie to it.

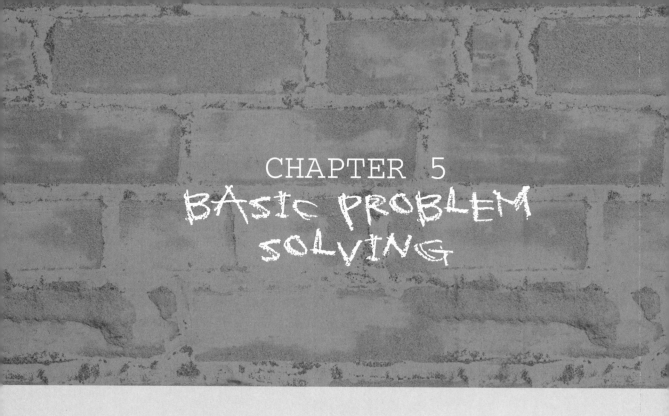

CHAPTER 5
BASIC PROBLEM SOLVING

CHAPTER OUTLINE

THINK ABOUT IT!

Look carefully at each of the signs in the photographs. What do you think is the specific problem being addressed in each? Discuss your answers with your classmates.

1

2

3

4

CHAPTER OUTCOMES

After completing Chapter 5, you should be able to:

- Define *problem* and *solution*
- List and describe the five steps involved in the basic method for personal problem solving
- Apply the method to a typical problem situation
- Continue to find topics and central messages in contemporary issue passages to determine what is at issue, distinguish among opposing viewpoints, and express personal viewpoints

Problem-Solving Exercise

For purposes of giving you the opportunity to practice both your thinking and problem-solving skills together, an exercise like this will be presented at the beginning of each of the remaining chapters in this textbook. The exercises will deal with a variety of hypothetical situations.

HYPOTHETICAL SITUATION

Suppose that you would really like to date a fellow student who is in one of your classes, but that person shows absolutely no interest in you. Every attempt that you make to start a conversation has failed. In fact, your glances and smiles are ignored with little or no eye contact in return. Nevertheless, you continue to be very attracted to your classmate and interested in starting a relationship because you think that this could be the "love of your life."

Think about this situation for a few moments, and then write a short essay in which you discuss how you would resolve it. Feel free to discuss your thoughts with your classmates.

WHAT IS A PROBLEM?

"I have a problem!" "We have a problem!" "You have a problem!" "She has a problem!" "There is a problem!" How often have you heard statements like these? Probably quite often. Problems are a big part of life. As one student aptly put it, "To have problems is to be alive." In that we cannot avoid them, what exactly do we mean when we talk about problems?

The dictionary defines a **problem** as "a question, matter, situation, or person that is perplexing or difficult" or "any question or matter involving doubt, uncertainty, or difficulty." These definitions are fine, but they really do not describe what it feels like to have a problem. We all have a wide variety of problems as we go through life yet really never think about an accurate definition of what it is we are experiencing.

To put it in simple terms, *there is a problem when we feel uncertain, dissatisfied, or upset with things, persons, or circumstances because they are either not doing what we think they should be doing or not going the way that we want or expected.* Thus we experience such problems as an automobile that will not start, a good friend that has been ignoring us lately, a boss that does not value our work, and an inability to stop smoking even though we want to quit. We can try to ignore problems like these and hope that they disappear, but usually they will not go away by themselves. Furthermore, they remain *our* problems and do not necessarily become anyone else's. Hence we are often forced to search on our own for possible solutions.

ACTIVITY 1

DIRECTIONS: Make a confidential list of personal problems that you have experienced recently.

WHAT IS A SOLUTION?

The dictionary defines a **solution** as "the act, method, or process of solving a problem" or "the act or process of explaining, settling, or disposing of a difficulty, problem, or doubt." In other words, *solutions are the means by which we rid ourselves of problems.* As a result, we no longer feel uncertain, dissatisfied, or upset with the things, persons, or circumstances that were either not doing what we thought they should be doing or not going the way that we wanted or expected.

The means that we choose to get us out of difficult situations will vary greatly. For instance, returning to the examples of the problems mentioned earlier:

The automobile that will not start can be fixed, junked, or traded in for another.

The good friend can be approached to talk about reasons for the change in behavior in order to come up with possible remedies, or the friendship can be ended if that is what is decided.

A discussion can be held with the boss to determine why our work is not appreciated, a higher-up can be consulted, or another job can be found.

Attempts can be made to stop smoking by wearing a nicotine patch, through the use of hypnosis, or by joining a support group.

There are always at least a few possible solutions to consider before deciding which one has the best chance of succeeding in eliminating a given problem.

ACTIVITY 2

DIRECTIONS: List the solutions that you came up with to solve the personal problems you noted in Activity 1.

HOW DO YOU SOLVE PROBLEMS?

In Activities 1 and 2, you listed problems that you experienced recently and their solutions. Is there a specific approach that you follow consistently when trying to solve problems? For example, do you run down all the possible solutions before choosing one, or do you go from one solution to the next by using trial and error? What approach did your classmates and you use to resolve the hypothetical situation presented in the problem-solving exercise at the start of the chapter?

Your approach to problem solving may not be clear to you and easy to describe. In fact, it is possible that you do not turn consistently to a definite method at all. Perhaps you use past experiences to help you sort things out. Maybe there are instances in which you do nothing, hoping that problems will go away by themselves. In short, there are different ways of dealing with problems, and we all have our individual preferences. However, we do agree on one thing: We want our problems to disappear quickly.

ACTIVITY 3

DIRECTIONS: Take a few moments to think carefully about the lists of problems and solutions that you drafted for Activities 1 and 2. See if there are any similarities in how you arrived at the solutions. Refer back to the discussion above and review the various approaches to problem solving that were mentioned. Did you use a specific approach, several different approaches, or no approach at all? Your instructor will ask for volunteers to discuss individual approaches to problem solving, without necessarily going into any details regarding the personal problems.

PROBLEM SOLVING AND CRITICAL THINKING

In Chapter 4, we noted that critical thinkers are careful and thoughtful in their approach to the world and that this enables them to make the most of limited time and helps them handle the complexities of life. That carefulness and thoughtfulness is particularly important when dealing with problems, because as a result of thinking critically, you place yourself in a stronger position to come up with the best solutions. In fact, all of the seven characteristics of critical thinking described in Chapter 4 are necessary ingredients for effective problem solving: *flexibility, a clear purpose, organization, time and effort, asking questions and finding answers, research, and coming to logical conclusions.*

A BASIC METHOD FOR PERSONAL PROBLEM SOLVING

The structured five-step approach to problem solving that follows may not eliminate all of your problems or guarantee perfect solutions, but it does provide a basic, simple, organized way of trying to deal with the things, persons, or circumstances that are disturbing you. As we proceed with the discussion, you may in fact discover that you are already using at least some of the steps as part of your approach to problems.

Step 1: Identifying the Problem

Before attempting to solve a problem, you have to make sure that you know what the problem is. This may seem obvious, but sometimes it is difficult to uncover what exactly is bothering you. For example, you may be angry at a friend who owes you money not because of the money itself but because she has ignored your constant reminders. Thus the real problem involves the fact that she is apparently not paying attention to you or not living up to her part of the bargain. In short, you may feel that you are being treated with a lack of respect or that a trust has been broken.

When defining a problem, you must be careful to go beneath the surface, to be very specific and not confuse means (ways of accomplishing goals) with the ends (the goals themselves). In the example just mentioned, the repayment of the money by your friend could simply be a means that really does not get at the overall problem of being ignored or treated with a lack of respect.

As part of this step, it is important to realize that the problem is yours and not necessarily anyone else's. *You* are the one who is uncertain, dissatisfied, or upset, and *you* have to take action to make things better. If other persons are involved, they may be perfectly happy to keep things exactly as they are. In fact, others may not even be aware that you are feeling unhappy about something. To take our example, your friend may not realize that you are angry about the money situation, or if she is aware of it, she may be quite willing to let things continue as they are indefinitely. With regard to the situation described in the problem-solving exercise at the beginning of the chapter, the problem of the fellow student not showing any interest in you may be very clear from your vantage point, but your classmate probably sees no problem at all and thus feels no need to take any kind of action.

Even if other people are not involved in what is bothering you, you must still come to terms with the fact that the solution to the problem requires action on your part. You may seek the advice of others, but ultimately you are the one who must do something to eliminate a given problem. Problems usually do not disappear by themselves, so you must take ownership of them.

Step 2: Gathering Information and Determining If the Problem Can Be Broken Down

After identifying the problem, defining it very specifically, and taking ownership of it, you need to gather as much information about it as possible. Depending on the nature of the problem, this could involve doing research and include discussions with various people who are knowledgeable about it, particularly those who have actually caused the problem or perhaps been involved in it in some other way. They can be very helpful in providing clarification.

As mentioned in Chapter 4, you must take into account whether the information gathered is relevant, reliable, and impartial. This may involve determining the motivations or purposes of the sources that you are using. Once you have evaluated and given careful thought to the information that you have gathered, you are in a much better position to proceed toward a solution.

As part of this step, you should determine if the problem can be broken down into smaller problems that can be worked on one at a time. Frequently, the solving of those smaller problems can lead to the solution of the overall one. For instance, you may be dissatisfied because you have a C average in your psychology course, and you really want to get a higher grade. Perhaps this problem can be broken down by subdividing it into smaller ones that are more specific and perhaps more manageable, such as ineffective note taking, poor test taking, lack of comprehension of the textbook, or not enough time spent on preparation for the class. By subdividing your problem, you can then focus on the problem areas that need improving and come up with strategies or solutions for them, thereby, ideally, resolving the overall problem. For example, you can take a note-taking or test-taking workshop to learn new techniques, improve on your reading skills by getting tutorial help and practicing, or simply spend more hours on course preparation. Over time, any of these could lead to a better grade in the course, thereby solving the major overriding problem of an average that is below what you want.

Looking back at the problem-solving exercise at the beginning of the chapter, after doing some research and gathering information from friends or other students, perhaps you find that your classmate is ignoring you because of involvement in another relationship or simply as a result of shyness. These facts help you break the problem down so that you can then decide whether to continue your pursuit and, if that is the case, arrive at a strategy such as getting involved in the same outside activities as your classmate. That might allow you to get acquainted in a more casual, less threatening atmosphere. As a result of breaking the problem down, you are in a better position to resolve it.

Step 3: Thinking About Possible Solutions and Weighing the Advantages and Disadvantages of Each

After you have identified the problem, defined it very specifically, taken ownership of it, gathered the facts, and determined if it can be broken down, you need to come up with a list of possible solutions. If the problem involves another person, as it often does, it is often advisable, if possible, to get that person involved at this stage even if he or she was already approached for information in Step 2. This is important for at least two reasons: First, the other party would likely supply additional information that is helpful when trying to devise a solution, and second, it is unrealistic to expect someone to cooperate with a given solution if the person had little or no part in the process through which it was decided on. In fact, as a result of not consulting with that other person, the proposed solution is likely to become no solution at all!

Obviously, to get another person involved, you have to communicate *your* specific definition of the problem—why *you* are uncertain, dissatisfied, or upset—and any of the information that you may have gathered concerning it. A *mutually* agreeable time has to be set up for that purpose. It is useless to try to discuss a problem if the other person is preoccupied with something else. In short, for this method to work, all concerned parties must be ready and willing to talk.

Whether you are working alone or with others, it is at this stage that a list of possible solutions is drawn up, indicating the advantages and disadvantages of each. It may help to *write these out* so that they can be properly analyzed and revised as you think them over. This is not something that can be rushed, so enough time should be set aside to review the options thoroughly. Remember, critical thinking is by definition a lengthy process, especially when trying to deal with problems.

Looking again at the problem-solving exercise at the beginning of this chapter, you might decide to take the direct approach and get your classmate involved at this stage by being totally honest about your interest in going out on a date. The big advantage of doing this is that it gets the matter out in the open and brings it to a head quickly. However, if the lack of interest has been a result of another relationship or shyness on the part of that student, then at this early stage, this possible solution could make matters even worse for you by scaring off your classmate. For that reason, it might be better in this particular situation for you to consider other possible solutions on your own.

Another possibility is to forget about the whole thing. This has the advantage of saving time and energy but the disadvantage of depriving yourself of the opportunity to date someone who is very appealing to you. Also, you may not want to accept defeat at this early stage without giving it your best shot.

One final possible solution was mentioned in Step 2, and it involves your finding out your classmate's interests so that you can participate in the same activities outside of class. The advantage of this possible solution is that you may get to know each other better, and your classmate may become friendlier after recognizing that you have similar interests. The major disadvantage involves your expenditure of much time and energy participating in activities that may not really excite you.

Step 4: Choosing a Possible Solution

After enumerating the advantages and disadvantages of as many potential solutions as you can think of, you select the one with the greatest chance of succeeding. This is likely to be the solution with advantages that outweigh the disadvantages. If the problem involves other people, the solution must of course be arrived at after discussion with them. Everyone concerned must agree that this is the very strongest possible solution at the time, the one that has the best chance of solving the problem. Once a decision has been made—whether you make it alone or with others—it is crucial that the solution chosen be supported completely and that the reasons for its selection be kept in mind always.

Turning once again to the problem-solving exercise, at this point you would choose the possible solution that you think has the best chance of resolving the problem to your satisfaction—in other words, the one that will result in a date with your classmate. Of the three possible solutions discussed in Step 3, the one that seems to be the strongest without having any important disadvantages involves your participation in some of the same outside activities as your classmate. As a result of this apparent interest in similar activities, the hope is that you would get to know each other, which in turn could lead ultimately to a date. The only real disadvantage is the time and energy you would use to participate in additional activities that you would not normally choose to do. Under the circumstances, that seems like a small price to pay, considering your strong desire to go out with your classmate.

Step 5: Checking Back on the Problem and the Possible Solution

You never know for sure if the possible solution chosen is going to work until you try it. For that reason, both the problem and the proposed solution must be reconsidered after enough time has gone by to allow the latter a chance to succeed. Once again, when others are using this approach with you, it is necessary to discuss together the extent of the progress made. If the proposed solution is not correcting the problem, either it has to be revised or another one has to be selected. This will necessitate that at least one or perhaps all of the previous steps be revisited.

Considering the problem-solving exercise one last time, if your involvement in those activities does seem to be changing your classmate's reaction to you, you will want to continue with your chosen solution, at least for a while longer. On the other hand, if there is no change after a reasonable period of time, you may want to turn to either of the remaining possible solutions that we discussed. For example, you could attempt the direct approach, thinking that at this point you have nothing to lose by being blunt, or decide instead to simply give up and go on with your life. Giving up the fight would not result in a date, but at least the problem has been eliminated to the extent that you can turn your attention perhaps in a more promising direction.

Although you will not be able to use Step 5 for the hypothetical problems used in this text, it is very important that you apply it to the real problems in your life. You want to be sure that you have arrived at the best possible solutions.

APPLYING THE METHOD TO A TYPICAL PROBLEM SITUATION

Let us look at one more example of how the basic five-step problem-solving approach was used in a personal situation. Richard and Susan have been married for 30 years and have experienced all the ups and downs that go along with a marriage of that duration. In recent years, Richard has been getting up at 4 A.M. to run 5 miles for health reasons. After finishing the run and taking a shower, he would take clean clothes from the dresser drawers in the bedroom. Unfortunately, Richard got into the bad habit of leaving the drawers half-open, which was starting to upset Susan. Although she mentioned it to him on several occasions, Richard did not attach much importance to the matter and continued to leave the drawers open.

Step 1: Identifying the Problem

Things went on like that for a while until Susan realized that this was her problem, because Richard was perfectly willing to continue what he was doing indefinitely. When she thought about it more thoroughly, it was not the half-open drawers per se that bothered her but the fact that Richard was apparently ignoring her. Furthermore, she saw no reason why she had to be the one to close them when Richard was perfectly capable of doing that for himself. After all, she was his wife, not his servant! The situation clearly required action on her part, or it would never be resolved to her satisfaction.

Step 2: Gathering Information and Determining If the Problem Can Be Broken Down

Because of the nature of this problem, Susan did not have to do research or consult other people about it, but she thought it appropriate to ask Richard why he was leaving his dresser drawers half-open. As it turned out, it was a good thing that she bothered to ask him, because he explained that the drawers stick, and he was afraid that by forcing them closed, he would make too much noise, thereby disturbing her sleep at that early hour. By making Susan aware of his thoughtful motivations, Richard clarified the situation for her. Although she appreciated his consideration, Susan continued to feel dissatisfied about the drawers' being left open and Richard's apparent assumption that it is her responsibility to close them. At this stage, she could not think of any way to break down the problem, so Susan proceeded to the next step.

Step 3: Thinking About Possible Solutions and Weighing the Advantages and Disadvantages of Each

Susan approached Richard on the matter, and they agreed to sit down and discuss it at length. She explained that even though she appreciated his consideration about not making too much noise in the morning, the fact that he continued to leave the dresser drawers half-open was upsetting to her. Susan was careful to emphasize that the real issues surrounding the problem involved his ignoring her constant complaints and his apparent belief that she was responsible for closing the drawers.

They agreed to consider the advantages and disadvantages of some possible solutions to the problem. One possible solution was for Richard not to run so early in the morning, but he explained that he could not fit a run in at any other time. Besides, he liked exercising at that early hour. For those two reasons, that proposed solution was unacceptable. Another possible solution was for Richard to force the drawers closed even if that made noise. Susan rejected that possibility because she was sure that it would disturb her sleep. A final possible solution involved Richard's taking out his clean clothing the night before so that he would not even have to go into the drawers in the early morning hours. Although this had the minor disadvantage of adding some clutter, it had the advantage of enabling Richard to adhere to his exercise schedule without disturbing Susan while at the same time eliminating her dissatisfaction with dresser drawers left half-open.

Step 4: Choosing a Possible Solution

After much discussion, they agreed that the third possible solution was the most acceptable because its advantages far outweighed its disadvantages. Apparently, it would solve the problem without creating any serious new problems for either Susan or Richard. They decided to give it a try.

Step 5: Checking Back on the Problem and the Possible Solution

Richard and Susan discussed both the problem and the agreed-on solution two weeks later after it became obvious that Richard was still leaving the drawers half-open at least some of the time. He explained that it was not intentional, but he was having a difficult time remembering to put his clothes out the night before. Because they had both thoroughly explored the other possible solutions and found them wanting, they decided to try to revise the one that they were currently using rather than going back through all the steps to find another solution. Susan certainly did not want to start nagging Richard about taking his clothes out the night before, so they came up with the idea that he would write a reminder to himself on the large message board in the kitchen until he got into the habit of gathering his clothes at night. With this slight adjustment, the problem was finally solved. Richard could run his heart out and have clean clothes while Susan slept in peace in a bedroom with closed dresser drawers.

Not all personal problems get resolved this easily, and of course there are much more serious ones that people face every day. Nevertheless, this example serves as a demonstration of how this basic method can be used to solve problems. The five-step approach is only one way of trying to deal with the complexities and difficulties of life that confront us all. When using it for the first several times, try to be very structured by following all of the steps in order. After a while, you will see that the steps can often be combined because the lines between them are not exact. In short, some flexibility is not only possible but desirable in most circumstances.

The diagram below illustrates the five-step approach to basic problem solving that you should apply to the problems encountered in your life.

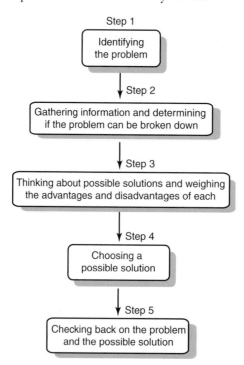

Step 1
Identifying the problem

Step 2
Gathering information and determining if the problem can be broken down

Step 3
Thinking about possible solutions and weighing the advantages and disadvantages of each

Step 4
Choosing a possible solution

Step 5
Checking back on the problem and the possible solution

ACTIVITY 4

DIRECTIONS: With two of your classmates, decide on a hypothetical problem, and apply the basic method for personal problem solving to it. Because it is a hypothetical problem, use only the first four steps of the approach.

ACTIVITY 5

DIRECTIONS: Using the first four steps of the approach, try to come up with possible solutions in the following problem situations. In each case, write an essay explaining step by step how you went about arriving at the solution. As you go through the steps with Problem 1, make sure that you identify specifically what you think the problem is after considering the various possibilities. Because the problem is not explicitly stated in this particular situation, you will have to come to a logical conclusion about what is wrong.

Problem 1

James is a good friend of yours, but lately he has been acting strange. His behavior is erratic, and his mood swings from silliness to depression to anger. He does not seem to care about college anymore, which has led to low grades and the strong possibility of his failing out. Furthermore, James has lost his part-time job because of continual tardiness and absenteeism. Consequently, he is often broke and seems desperate for money. He no longer talks with you much and is hanging around with a different group of friends. You are very concerned about his well-being.

Problem 2

In this situation, as in the first one, identify the problem by considering carefully the information presented and drawing a logical conclusion. Put yourself in Anita's place as you proceed through the first four steps of the approach. After you have completed your essay, your instructor will pair you off with a classmate *of the opposite sex* so that you can exchange essays and discuss your work.

1   Andy passed Anita's locker every morning on his way to first period class. He began by just staring at her when he walked by. Then she noticed that when he passed her in the hallways or stairwells, he kept on looking.

2   At first, the 14-year-old thought Andy was flirting, but as she paid more attention to his gaze, she realized something didn't feel right. Anita felt uncomfortable with Andy's looks. It felt dirty, as if Andy had some kind of X-ray vision and was trying to see through her clothes to what was underneath.

3   One morning. Anita was standing by her locker. Suddenly, from behind she felt a guy's body pressed full front up against her. As she turned to see who it was, she felt Andy Porter's hand grabbing tightly on her behind and squeezing it. Anita spun around with anger to look Andy in the eye. He glared at her with that ugly intensity she had experienced in the past. A sly smile emerged on Andy's lips, and Anita could feel her insides buckling.

4   Thoughts of Andy and his behavior distracted Anita in school for the next two weeks. She had difficulty concentrating. She found herself drifting off in class, thinking of ways

she could avoid Andy. Her Spanish teacher remarked about the decline in her class participation and the impact that would have on her "B" average. Mr. Marks, her history teacher, talked with Anita about her lateness to class and the negative consequences should she continue this behavior.

5   When Monday morning arrived, Anita once again experienced the gnawing knot of fear in her stomach as she approached the high school. Anita had shared her upset feelings with her close friends, but they just didn't understand. They thought she was lucky to have Andy Porter interested in her. He was one of the "hot" senior guys and having him "flirt" with her could only improve Anita's social status.

6   Anita could not relate to their opinion at all. She felt horrible. She lingered in the parking lot waiting for the first bell to ring. Although Anita realized she would be late again for Mr. Marks' class, she also knew that her tardiness would assure her of missing Andy in the hallway.

7   Anita finally entered the building and walked rapidly to her locker, head down, books held tightly against her chest. Suddenly overtaken by anger, she slammed her locker closed. Anita's eyes began to well up with tears, and the knot in her stomach began throbbing.

NJEA Review, March 1995, pp. 28–29

Problem 3

Last academic year, you took a science course in which a term paper was required. You spent much of the semester doing research and writing what turned out to be a 20-page paper. All of your effort and hard work paid off, because the instructor was very pleased with the result and gave you an A. During the summer, your best friend informed you that she will be taking the same course during the spring semester and expects to fulfill the term paper requirement by submitting your paper with her name on it. She believes strongly that favors like this one are what friends are for.

Problem 4

Your mother is suffering from malignant cancer and is in pain much of the time. Day after day, she remains in a near-comatose state but occasionally does awaken for short periods. During those times, she is fairly lucid when you have conversations with her. Although her doctors refuse to predict when she will die, they do not offer much hope for her survival. Because she is having difficulty breathing and is steadily losing weight from her inability to eat, the hospital has asked for your permission to attach a ventilator and feeding tube. These measures could keep her alive indefinitely, although they probably would not improve her deteriorating condition. You have no brothers or sisters, and your father, who has Alzheimer's disease, is in a nursing home. Furthermore, your mother does not have a living will, nor has she ever made her wishes known.

Problem 5

For the problem situation discussed in the following article, put yourself in the shoes of Anna and Camille as you go through the first four steps of the approach.

Love in the Time of AIDS

Camille McCausland

1   Devin sat on her great-uncle Richard's lap, playfully poking her fingers into his face. Richard took it in good humor, gurgling happily at his niece. That is, until her tiny fingers came away from his nose covered with blood. Then he gripped her arms while nine-month-old Devin struggled to get her fingers into her mouth.

2   "Hey, I need help," Richard yelled, his voice edging toward hysteria. Ignoring the blood running from his nose, he continued holding Devin's arms. "Get me a god-damned rag," he screamed.

3   "It only took a minute," my friend Anna said, when she told me this story. "I got a rag and disinfectant and cleaned her up. Still, it's scary." And scary it is, because Richard has AIDS.

4   Anna's voice faded into the background as I thought of my four-year-old daughter, Lauren, playing with Richard. Along with her dresses, she wore scraped knees, skinned elbows, and various other scratched parts common to toddlers. And I thought of AIDS. For a moment, I swear it was only a moment, I thought of not bringing Lauren around until Richard was gone.

5   Lauren's squeals, erupting as Richard chased her around the yard, interrupted my thoughts. I was reminded that Lauren's laugh always rings out when Richard is visiting. I remembered her tears that Richard dried when she fell off her bike. I remembered her joy when Richard hand-washed her muddied outfit so she could still wear it to school the next day. And I remembered Richard, old friend, almost family, loved one. Somehow, for that brief moment, I had forgotten Richard and what his life might be like without children in it.

6   Sanity returned as Richard came into focus: cropped hair, jeans, leather coat, T-shirt sleeves rolled just so. I thought of his annoyingly cheerful voice in the morning, his willingness to listen, and the advice bound to follow. And the laugh, never far away, making it impossible to stay mad at him for long.

7   Sanity returned, but it left behind a trace of fear so easily condemned in others.

8   I knew, standing in her yard, that Anna wouldn't be telling this story to any of her other friends. Most of Anna's friends were patiently awaiting Richard's departure to resume their visits. Just days before, I had told Anna what I thought of them. "The truth is," I had righteously claimed, "they prefer their ignorance to your company."

9   Now I am not so sure. Unlike Anna's other friends, I've known Richard for years. Diagnosed with ARC during a 1978 hepatitis B study and rediagnosed in the early '80s with HIV, Richard has lived with his disease for as long as I've known him. Years before my daughter was born, I was used to Richard's illness and had already lost other friends to AIDS. I've had plenty of time to adjust. And still I felt, that afternoon at Anna's, the fear that can erase a person simply by its presence. It was not born of ignorance.

10   The fact is that Anna's fear for her daughter was well founded. If Richard had been less careful of his disease than he was, Devin could have put blood carrying the HIV virus into her mouth. My own fear, while not as well founded, was certainly reasonable. For years I have equated that kind of fear with ignorance and bigotry. And then I felt it myself.

11   I wish I could say that my momentary lapse would not have been any longer even if I had not known Richard. But I am not so sure.

Problem 6

As you proceed through the four steps with the problem stated here, read the article that follows it as a way of gathering information for Step 2.

You are a single parent with a full-time job and an 8-year-old son. Thomas is a hyperactive child who is consistently disruptive in school. The teacher has called you several times about his behavior, and you have met with the principal regarding the matter. You have warned Thomas several times, but he just seems to be ignoring you. In fact, he has started to question your authority in other areas as well and constantly talks back to you. He refuses to follow your instructions, such as your request that he put his dirty clothes in the hamper. You have become angry and impatient with him, and you are starting to lose your temper. In fact, you have threatened to spank him on more than one occasion unless he changes his behavior.

Spanking Is Becoming the New Don't

Clare Collins

1   Have you ever spanked your child? Perhaps a better question is, would you admit to it?

2   "We spank as a last resort, when the children are either very rebellious or very rude," said Kellie Nienajadly, a Syracuse mother of a 2-year-old and a 3-year-old. "There's only so much reasoning you can do with children this young."

3   On the other hand, Rose Zagaja, who lives outside Hartford and has two children, ages 7 and 8, adamantly opposes spanking. "I think it's degrading and infuriating" to the child, she said.

4   Ms. Nienajadly's and Ms. Zagaja's differing views point to an emotional debate over a form of discipline that few of today's adults escaped as children. Is spanking merely a quick and decisive form of discipline, or is it to be shunned as ineffective, even cruel?

5   A recent Harris poll found that spanking is far from an uncommon parental act: 80 percent of the 1,250 adults surveyed said they had spanked their children. And 87 percent of those polled said that spanking is sometimes appropriate.

6   The telephone poll, conducted between Feb. 6 and 9, had a margin of error of plus or minus three percentage points. It did not ask respondents how frequently they spanked, nor did it define spanking.

7   The poll's findings run counter to the advice handed out by a growing number of child development experts who say spanking not only is ineffective but also breeds aggression.

8   "Spanking teaches kids that when someone is doing something you don't like and they won't stop doing it, you hit them," said Murray A. Straus, a professor of sociology at the

University of New Hampshire in Durham and the author of *Beating the Devil out of Them: Corporal Punishment in American Families* (Lexington Books, 1994), which argues against spanking.

9   Dr. Straus said that studies he had conducted found that children who are frequently spanked are more likely to act aggressively toward their peers and may then go on to be aggressive teenagers and depressed, abusive adults.

10   According to Dr. Straus's definition, spanking refers to any kind of swatting or slapping "intended to cause a child physical pain but not injury, for purposes of correction or control."

11   "Spanking is very subjective," Dr. Straus said. "Some people think you have to hit hard enough to leave a mark that doesn't last very long. Others would define that as abuse." He would like to see corporal punishment outlawed in this country. Spanking is illegal in many European countries.

12   "Parents spank young children because they don't know what else to do," said Alvin Rosenfeld, a child psychiatrist in Manhattan and co-author of *The Art of the Obvious* with the late Bruno Bettelheim. "Spanking does work. It puts a stop on certain behaviors. But the question is, does it achieve what you're trying to achieve?"

13   Even the strongest of statements against physical punishment usually stop short of condemning parents who have spanked. "We're all human," said Linda S. Budd, a St. Paul psychologist and the author of *Living with the Active Alert Child* (Parenting Press, 1993). "The fact that you lost it once and smacked your child doesn't mean you've ruined him for life. It does indicate a need to slow down and stop before you act."

14   Some experts condone spanking, usually on an extremely limited basis when the issue is safety or willful disobedience. One of the most widely quoted is James C. Dobson, the author of *The New Dare to Discipline* (Tyndale House Publishers, 1992).

15   Dr. Dobson, who writes that his theories are firmly rooted in Judeo-Christian beliefs, advocates spanking for children between the ages of 18 months and 10 years who directly challenge a parent's authority. He states in his book that spanking—which should be done in a calm, "I'm doing this for your own good" fashion—"is the shortest route to an attitude adjustment."

16   John Rosemond, a psychologist, supports spanking but suggests it be followed by consequences appropriate to the misbehavior. For instance, if a child leaves the house when told not to and is spanked, the parent should then take away television or other privileges. Mr. Rosemond says spanking can be far less detrimental than extreme verbal abuse or overly severe punishment.

17   More and more, though, spanking is emerging as the don't of the 1990's.

18   Dr. Budd said that she and most of her colleagues had given up on forms of therapy that change behaviors out of fear. She favors alternative methods of disciplining like time-outs and the taking away of privileges.

19   Although still a majority, the number of parents who spank is on the decline, said Dr. Straus, whose first study, in 1968, showed that "94 percent of the adult U.S. population believed it was sometimes necessary to give a child a spanking."

20   In a survey he conducted in 1994, Dr. Straus found that only 68 percent of the adult population—even fewer than in the Harris poll—believed in spanking. "In my line of work, that's actually an astronomical speed of social change," he said.

21   The Harris poll seems to support his contention that spanking is on the decline. It found that among the newest generation of parents—ages 18 to 24—31 percent said they had never spanked, compared with 19 percent among all parents. That trend is likely to continue, since the survey also found that most parents who were not spanked have not spanked their children.

22   Parents who do spank often feel they can't admit to it without risking harsh criticism. In a recent forum on Compuserve, the on-line service, only a handful of parents who responded to a query about spanking would speak for attribution. "It used to be parents who *didn't* spank were the ones who wouldn't be quoted," Dr. Straus said. "They were seen as the crackpots."

23   Spanking, Dr. Rosenfeld said, does nothing to further the long-term goal of successful parenting: raising happy, well-socialized adults. "Spanking deprives you of an opportunity to show your child that you have superior reasoning skills," he added.

24   "I came to the realization that spanking isn't all that effective," said Jebbie Crowe of Mystic, Conn., who is the mother of six children ages 14 to 28. She spanked her oldest children but changed her theory with her youngest. "My kids actually preferred it to other punishments because it was over quickly," she said. "It was an easy way out for both of us."

25   Dr. Budd says she believes that many parents spank because they have unrealistic expectations. "Often, parents just don't understand child development," she said. "They spank a child for being developmentally appropriate."

26   Dr. Budd said she had seen parents slap a toddler's hand because she kept pushing her plate off the highchair tray. "It would be better to just take the plate away," she said.

27   But what about matters of safety? "If a child is running in the street, it would be better to make her go inside for a while every time she does that, until she understands the limit," Dr. Budd said.

28   And rather than spanking a child who is rude or otherwise out of control, Dr. Rosenfeld recommended saying: "You must go to your room. I'm so disappointed in the way you're behaving. You are a good boy, a smart boy, but you are annoying me."

29   "In the long run," he added, "removing your approval works much better than spanking."

30   What if despite your best intentions, you do lose it? "Apologize," Dr. Budd said. "Own up to your mistake. That's parenting at its best."

New York Times, May 11, 1995

ACTIVITY 6

DIRECTIONS: Assume that your spouse and you are trying to decide whether or not to circumcise your infant son. After reading the following passage, use the first four steps of the problem solving approach in order to make a decision.

Circumcision: Take It or Leave It?

1   One decision facing parents of a newborn boy is whether to have him circumcised. Circumcision involves the surgical removal of the foreskin, a flap of skin covering the tip

of the penis. As a procedure, circumcision has been around for millennia, dating as far back as Egyptian times, more than 4,500 years ago, when priests performed circumcision on their newborn boys as a form of purification rite. To this day, it is an important religious ritual in Islamic and Jewish communities worldwide. It became popularized in the United States in the early 1900s in the belief that it promoted good hygiene and discouraged masturbation. During World War II, its benefits were extolled when it was discovered that, in the unsanitary conditions of the battlefield, circumcised male soldiers had far fewer infections than did their uncircumcised counterparts. Today, the American Academy of Pediatrics (AAP) estimates that nearly 1.2 million infant males, or about 70 percent of all newborn males, born in this country are circumcised each year. Outside of the United States, the practice is far less common.

2   For decades, the decision was relatively automatic for most parents in the United States, as the majority of circumcisions have been performed out of religious or cultural tradition or because of concerns over hygiene. In recent years, however, questions and issues over the procedure have surfaced. Some advocacy groups consider it to be cruel, barbaric, and unnecessary, citing studies that have questioned the potential harm of the loss of erogenous tissue and the possibility of long-lasting trauma to the child. Proponents of circumcision have pointed to studies that have suggested a slightly greater risk for penile cancer and some sexually transmitted infections among uncircumcised males. Who is right? Who is wrong? Probably nobody, as little conclusive evidence supports or refutes either side.

3   In an effort to draw closure to the issue, a special task force convened by the AAP recently concluded that although evidence indicates certain medical benefits of circumcision, they are not essential to the future health of the child. However, the AAP does not consider the findings compelling enough to recommend routine circumcision. What they do consider essential is that parents make an informed decision based on the known benefits and risks.

Possible Benefits of Circumcision:
- *Fewer urinary tract infections:* Boys who are not circumcised are at least four times more likely to develop a UTI in their first year of life. A history of chronic UTIs is speculated by some to lead to damaged kidneys in later life.
- *Reduced risk of penile cancer:* Although the rate of penile cancer is relatively low, uncircumcised males tend to be more susceptible.
- *Reduced risk of HIV and other STIs:* Uncircumcised men face a slightly greater risk of infection after exposure to HIV or other STIs. However, personal behavioral practices, notably attitudes toward safer sex and the use of a condom during all intercourse, still serve as the greatest risk indicator to all men.
- *Smaller risk of transmitting infectious pathogens to sex partners:* Uncircumcised males face a greater risk of bacterial and fungal growth development under the foreskin. However, men who clean this area fastidiously reduce the risk considerably, as well as the likelihood of transmitting any organisms to sex partners.

Potential Risks of Circumcision:
- *Pain:* Surprisingly, about 45 percent of circumcisions are performed without pain relief. Critics note the painful cries of infants and question whether such trauma

may leave permanent psychological damage. The AAP now recommends the use of an analgesic to reduce potential pain during the procedure.

- *Potential complications:* Although actual procedural risks of circumcisions are minor, complications can result, including mild bleeding and localized infection. Without a clear and essential benefit to a boy's well-being, either medically or emotionally, the risk is seen as unnecessary.
- *Loss of sensation at the tip of the penis:* Although some have reported this, it usually is only a very mild loss of sensation and may go away with time.

4   Ultimately, circumcision is more of a personal choice than a dramatic and inhumane event or a medical necessity. In summary, the trauma of thinking about circumcision may be worse than the actual event, both from the perspective of the infant and the man he will grow to be.

Rebecca J. Donatelle; *Health: The Basics,* 4th ed., p. 116

ACTIVITY 7

DIRECTIONS: During the course of the semester, try to solve two of your personal problems by using the five-step approach. Toward the end of the semester, your instructor will ask each student to discuss how well the approach worked. *You will not be asked to reveal the details of your personal problems.*

ACTIVITY 8

DIRECTIONS: For the following passages on contemporary issues, use the same procedure as in Chapter 4. First, answer the *comprehension questions,* which ask you to state the topic and central message of each passage before proceeding to determine what is at issue, distinguish among opposing viewpoints, and express a personal viewpoint. In addition, you will be asked to compare your personal viewpoint before and after you have thoroughly considered the opposing viewpoints brought out in the passages. Finally, to show flexibility, you will write a few paragraphs *in support of the viewpoint that you do* not *favor.* Keep in mind that some of the selections may deal with more than one issue.

You will then proceed to answer the *thought and discussion questions* before contributing any questions of your own that may come to mind while reading the passages. Feel free to discuss all of the questions with your classmates and together come up with possible answers.

EYE ON VOCABULARY

When reading each of the following passages in Activity 8, take note of any unfamiliar words you come across. List them and their definitions in your notebook or on note cards. Use the context, word parts, or the dictionary to determine their meanings. After the completion of each passage, your instructor will ask to see your notebook or note cards and may discuss key words in class.

1
Why the Poor Become Poorer

1   In recent years the poor have gotten *poorer,* particularly in big cities. Again, there are two contrasting explanations. One is sociological, attributing the increase in poverty to forces beyond the control of the individual. Over the last thirty years the middle class has largely left the cities for the suburbs, taking much of the tax base with it. Many well-paying, low-skilled jobs in manufacturing industries have also left the cities. As a result, the poor who are left behind, jobless, have become poorer (Wilson, 1996).

2   According to another explanation, a new version of the old "blame the victim" theory, poor people have gotten poorer because they do not want to work. There are still many jobs that match their skills, such as working in sweatshops, in fast-food restaurants, and as maids or servants. But poor people today consider these jobs demeaning and prefer to be on welfare instead, not seeing the first jobs as steppingstones from which to advance. Such an attitude is said to scorn the traditional view that almost any honest job, however unpleasant, confers independence and therefore dignity, is the first step on the ladder to better employment, and is better than taking something for nothing (Mead, 1992).

Alex Thio, *Sociology,* 5th ed., pp. 233–235

COMPREHENSION QUESTIONS

1. What is the topic of the passage?
2. What is the central message of the passage?
3. Determine what is at issue. What is your initial personal viewpoint?
4. Distinguish among opposing viewpoints, and provide the rationale for each.
5. Think carefully about the viewpoints. Express a personal viewpoint, and give the reasons why you favor it. Does it differ from your initial personal viewpoint? Why or why not?
6. Write a few paragraphs *in support of the viewpoint that you do not favor.*

THOUGHT AND DISCUSSION QUESTIONS

1. If you were the president of the United States, what policies would you recommend to help the poor? Why?
2. Can you think of any other instances in which the "blame the victim" theory has been used as an explanation?
3. List any questions that came to mind while you were reading this selection, and be prepared to discuss possible answers to them.

2
The Future of the Family

1   The death of the family has been predicted for decades. In 1949 Carle Zimmerman concluded from his study on the family that "We must look upon the present confusion of family values as the beginning of violent breaking up of a system." By the "confusion of family values," Zimmerman referred to the threat that individualism presented to the tradition of paternalistic authority and filial duty. He assumed that individualism would eventually do in the family. Today, many continue to predict the demise of the family, pointing out as evidence the increases in divorce, out-of-wedlock births, cohabitation, and singlehood.

2   However, the family is alive and well. The flaw in the gloomy forecast is that it confuses change with breakdown. Many of the traditional families—husbands as bread-winners and wives as homemakers—have merely changed into two-career families, which still hang together as nuclear families rather than disintegrate. Despite the increased number of people staying single, an overwhelming majority of those who now live alone will eventually marry. Although divorce rates have doubled over the last two decades, three out of four divorced people remarry, most doing so within three years of their marital breakup. Likewise, most of the young adults who live together before marriage will marry eventually. It is true that being part of a single-parent family, especially from an out-of-wedlock birth, is a problem for many mothers and their children. But the problem stems more from economic deprivation than from single parenthood as a new form of family.

3   Evidence from public opinion polls also points to the basic health of the U.S. family. Asked to describe their marriages in a recent national survey, 60 percent of married individuals said "very happy." 36 percent said "pretty happy," and only 3 percent said "not too happy" (NORC, 1994).

4   What will the U.S. family be like in the next 20 years? Most likely it will be much the same as it is today: manifesting *diversity* without destroying the basic family values. The continuing acceptance of these values comes through clearly in two studies. One shows that, compared with Europeans, people in the United States are more likely to marry, to do so at an earlier age, and to have slightly larger families, despite the higher incidences of divorce and single-parent families (Sorrentino, 1990). Another study, which tracked changes in family attitudes and values from the 1960s to the 1980s, shows that the vast majority of young people in the United States still value marriage, parenthood, and family life. They plan to marry, have children, and be successful in marriage (Thornton, 1989). Thus, Americans can be expected to continue supporting the family institution, even though their government is not as pro-family as those in Europe.

Alex Thio, *Sociology*, 5th ed., pp. 358–360.

COMPREHENSION QUESTIONS

1. What is the topic of the passage?

2. What is the central message of the passage?

3. Determine what is at issue. What is your initial personal viewpoint?

4. Distinguish among opposing viewpoints, and provide the rationale for each.

5. Think carefully about the viewpoints. Express a personal viewpoint, and give the reasons why you favor it. Does it differ from your initial personal viewpoint? Why or why not?

6. Write a few paragraphs *in support of the viewpoint that you do not favor.*

THOUGHT AND DISCUSSION QUESTIONS

1. In paragraph 2, the author writes: "It is true that being part of a single-parent family, especially from an out-of-wedlock birth, is a problem for many mothers and their children. But the problem stems more from economic deprivation than from single parenthood as a new form of family." Do you agree? Why or why not? Do you see any additional problems other than economic deprivation?

2. In your view, what will the family be like in the future?

3. List any questions that came to mind while you were reading this selection, and be prepared to discuss possible answers to them.

3

A True Crime Story

A Tragic Moment in New Mexico: Reflections on a Nation Gripped by Violence

Ken Englade and Tony Hillerman

1   Five Points, in a seedy South Valley section of Albuquerque, New Mexico, is a convergence of five streets, littered parking lots, and shopping centers half boarded up. A still, deserted place at 5:40 A.M. on a dark, 20-degree Sunday morning, January 9, 1994.

2   A man in his 60s enters one of the lots on his morning exercise walk, heading south. A Buick Riviera recently stolen by its two teen occupants cruises slowly along Five Points Road, also heading south. The car circles the lone figure.

3   On its fourth drive-by one of the youths jumps from the car, holding a police baton, demands money and clubs the man several times. The flat crack of a pistol shot pierces the air and Eddie Torres, 16, falls back and runs to the car, which screeches away. Dean Kern, 63, blood running down his cheek, gun in hand, staggers off looking for assistance.

4   Kern is hailed as a hero. Torres—after he has been arrested in the hospital and later sent to prison for aggravated battery—is dubbed a thug. But the phenomenon—civilians arming themselves and teens doing hard time—appears less a solution than a desperate, even dangerous, stopgap.

5   That a 63-year-old would resort to such drastic action is supported by a recent *USA Today*/CNN/Gallup poll: Americans have finally had it with youthful offenders. Sixty percent of respondents said a teen convicted of murder should get the death penalty, and more than 20 states (among them New Mexico) have or are planning tough new juvenile laws.

6   Meanwhile, because of crime's prevalence many older people are avoiding activities they felt safe taking part in a few years ago. That may be why those 65 and over are,

according to 1992 Bureau of Justice statistics, the least likely victims of violent crimes or theft. But at what cost to their quality of life?

7   To many, like Dean Kern, locking themselves indoors is not an option, yet continuing their activities as before is risky at best....Some believe their only recourse is to arm themselves when going out. Is this, truly, the final and only option?

8   Today Kern is cautious and fearful—he wouldn't allow his face to be photographed. Torres is bitter and vengeful—and could be released from prison as early as next year. Exactly what did happen between the two of them may unfortunately raise more questions than it can answer.

9   What *is* clear is that we generally perceive crime from one point of view, and from that perspective solutions may appear straightforward, even simple.

10   But if we examine this crime from all vantage points—and face its tempestuous issues of violence, an armed populace, and justice itself—it becomes evident that finding a viable solution is as complex as the moment of crime itself.

11   For 17 years Dean Kern has risen habitually at 4:30 and begun his day with a rigid physical regimen. In 1976 he suffered a severe heart attack. As part of his recovery program he took up jogging five miles a day around the perimeter of Kirtland Air Force Base where he used to work as manager of the telephone exchange.

12   After he retired in 1986, his knees could no longer take the hard pounding so he gave up jogging for swimming and walking. Three days a week he swam laps at a neighborhood pool; the other four days he walked a five-mile circle around his home, a tiny but comfortable bungalow he built in 1955 with a GI loan.

13   Shortly after 5:00 A.M. on Sunday, January 9, the tall, slim, sandy-haired man whose sartorial preferences run to jeans and Western-style snapfront shirts zipped up his padded down jacket, put on his hand-knit wool stocking cap (a gift from a neighbor grateful for a favor), and grabbed his .25 caliber Colt automatic from the top shelf of the hall closet.

14   Years earlier Kern had developed the habit of carrying the fist-sized pistol he originally bought for his wife but later appropriated for his own use because it was small and light—just the right size to fit in his jogging-suit pocket. He took it then to protect himself in case he encountered any of the stray or wild dogs that inhabited the desert around the Air Force base.

15   He continued to pack the weapon after he retired because part of the South Valley neighborhood where he walked in the mornings had become a campsite for the homeless, some of whom Kern feared might be strung out on drugs one day and come looking for a handy source of revenue.

16   About ten minutes into his route he came upon Five Points. "I was just walking, thinking, lining out my day." As he turned south on Sunset Road and was cutting through one of the parking lots, he suddenly became aware of a car.

17   "It came to the traffic signal but didn't want to wait for the light, so it cut across the lot I was in. Passed right in front of me, maybe 20 feet away." The windows were tinted and rolled up, but a street light showed two heads silhouetted in the front seat. The car exited the lot onto Sunset a block away. Then hesitated. Then turned around.

18   "When I saw it do that, I picked up my pace and crossed Sunset to get to the other side. It passed by again on the street."

19   The car backed up, turned around, and went by him a third time. "I knew then I was in big trouble." Kern was in front of a furniture store. Parked nearby was a truck with a for sale sign on it. "They made a U-turn and came back toward me again. I walked behind the truck to keep it between me and them."

20   When he came around the truck, a figure had already jumped out of the car and was slapping a sidehandled police baton in his hand.

21   Kern took off running. But workmen had been repaving the parking lot and planting trees there, and sand and gravel covered the pavement. Kern slipped and almost tumbled to the ground. Before he could regain his balance the attacker was all over him.

22   He felt one sharp blow bounce off his skull, two thud against his arm. He tried to outrun his assailant but couldn't. The baton cracked him two more times on the head. Despite Kern's thick cap and heavy jacket, the blows "took the hide off my arm and broke the skin on my head. I told myself, 'If I go down, I'm in bad shape.'"

23   Not able to get away, still being pummeled and honestly fearing for his life, Kern finally yanked the pistol from his pocket. "I put it against him and pulled the trigger."

24   The effect was instantaneous. The attacker cried out and threw up his arms, staggered backward, then ran back to the car. Tires screaming, the car spun around and sped away.

25   Kern stood there, dazed, and said a silent prayer. If it hadn't been for the wool cap's cushioning effect, he probably would have been knocked unconscious or his brains might have been leaking onto the sidewalk. Staggering to a pay phone, he dialed 911.

26   A lot of people think ironing is women's work, but it always gave Eddie Torres considerable pleasure. While his friends may have laughed if they had seen him hunched over the ironing board on the night of January 8 in the small trailer he shared with his mother, Torres wasn't worried about his macho image. Holding up his party shirt to inspect, he smiled in self-congratulation. A *cholo* (street-wise young Latino male) had to be respected. Looking sharp definitely earned him respect.

27   Torres was really pumped up for the party he was going to that night. Throwing it was an "older" woman (she was 25, he 16) he had met shortly after arriving in New Mexico two months before.

28   The party was everything he'd hoped for—good music, good booze, good dope. Then something happened that would change Eddie Torres's already grim life for the worse. "I was talking with the girl when somebody told me to chill out with her and swung me around," he said. Torres was more surprised than hurt. That would've never happened in the Los Angeles suburb where he'd grown up. Known by his fellow cholos there as "Crook," he had a reputation as someone to be reckoned with. His gang, East Side Paramount, was one of the largest and most violent in all of Los Angeles County, and its name was tattooed across the back of his neck and shoulders in inch-tall letters.

29   "I hit him, and they took him to the bathroom. A few minutes later the girl told me to leave." Drunk and upset, he stormed outside with two homeboys: one called "Gino," and Kevin Baca, 17, whom he'd met a month before.

30   Torres wandered into a nearby parking lot—and his eyes locked onto a solitary Buick Riviera. Quicker than most people can adjust the rear-view mirror, Torres broke in, hotwired it, and had the Riviera quietly rolling down the street.

31   Baca dropped Gino off at his home and Torres followed Baca's car to Baca's house. Then Baca jumped behind the wheel of the Buick and the pair went looking for some action, which meant a fight. "I was still hyper about what happened at the party. Then I see this *vato* (guy)."

32   There, in the middle of Five Points, a lone figure was crossing the parking lot. "The guy was acting crazy. He had his hand in his jacket like he had a gun, like he was tough or somethin'. I said, 'Go back towards him, I'll show him who's tough.'"

33   They drove back and passed real close, and the stranger stared at Torres. *"Me vió."* ("He looked at me.") Torres thought the man had challenged, or "mad-dogged," him. "I wanted to beat him up," Torres said.

34   They circled the man twice more ("I was scoping it out for cops") before Torres felt safe. Spotting a police baton under the seat of the Riviera, he grabbed it and lunged out of the Buick. "I don't know why I didn't just let him go," he said. "But I was drunk, I just wanted to get him." Blocking the man's path and smacking the polished wooden club, Torres barked, "Give me your money!"

35   "He tried to run away," Torres recalled later, "but I hit him [with the nightstick] on the head and shoulder."

36   All of a sudden the man straightened up and swung toward *him*. "I heard something real loud," Torres said. "There wasn't much pain, but I got dizzy. I felt something inside me."

37   He lurched back to the car and screamed at Baca to take him home. "I couldn't breathe. I said to myself, 'I'm going to die.'"

38   They picked up his mother at home and minutes later found a pay phone. As Torres waited, bleeding and shivering, his mother dialed 911.

39   The youngest of four gang-member brothers, Torres's indoctrination into their world started early on. He had his first serious brush with authorities—for breaking into a car—at eight. He went on to pile up arrests for burglary, auto theft, narcotics violations, and assault and battery ("I used to look for innocent-looking kids coming out of school and just beat 'em up. I knew it wasn't right, but it was what I liked to do").

40   There was a time, Torres says, when things might have turned out differently. For a while his father, Eddie Sr., a butcher, was able to keep his brothers clean and straight. "He was real strict, man, the way he grew my brothers up. He kept them in the right direction. Couldn't cuss, couldn't go out, nothin'."

41   And then, as in so many families, the arguments between their parents began, escalated, then eventually forced their mother, Dorie, to leave and take the boys. "After that, Mom would say the same things to us, but we wouldn't listen. That's when I started kicking back with my brothers and homeboys. I saw the things they were doing and thought it was all right."

42   Hoping to get her youngest son away from his brothers' and gang's influence and into a more stable environment, Dorie took Eddie Jr. to Albuquerque, where her sister lived.

43   Nine days after the shooting, while Torres was recuperating in the hospital, police arrested him on charges of aggravated battery with a deadly weapon, armed robbery, and conspiracy to commit armed robbery. Nancy Neary, the assistant district attorney, saw Torres as a classic sociopath. "Empathy is not a concept this kid has within himself," she said. "He was totally without remorse. He would kill Mr. Kern or anyone else the same way I'd swat a fly."

44   Feeling the county judges were lenient with juveniles and would never give him the maximum on all three counts, Neary made the boy an offer: Plead guilty to aggravated battery and she'd drop the other charges. Torres agreed. In New Mexico, victims have the right to be heard. So Kern drafted a letter that read, in part: "I feel I need to take this opportunity ... to plead with you to keep this man away from us for as long as the law permits....There is no way [law-enforcement officials] can prevent these types of crimes or protect us from these kinds of preditors [sic]. Only you can do that, Judge. Please put this young man away for as long as you can. Please keep him off us."

45   The Children's Court Judge Tommy E. Jewell has a reputation as a "liberal" jurist, always willing to give an offender a break if he believes the person can be rehabilitated. When Torres's case showed up on his calendar, however, the youth's record painted a grim picture. Jewell later stated that Torres was "a threat to society" and he was "pessimistic" that the young man would be changed by the experience.

46   The judge sentenced Torres to three years in prison. In a very few specified cases, courts can also add time to a sentence when there are "aggravating circumstances" for such things as the age of the victim. Because Kern was 63, Jewell tacked an extra year on to Torres's sentence. It was remarkably stiff considering the judge's reputation. When asked if such incarceration may only teach Torres to be a better criminal, Jewell replied, "A new and improved Eddie Torres in the crime-producing world is really a frightening thought." (As for Kevin Baca, he pleaded guilty to conspiracy to commit armed robbery and was eventually sentenced to two years' probation.)

47   According to Janet Velazquez, Torres's attorney, incarceration may actually be the young man's best—and last—chance to turn his life around. She noted that Torres tended to do well in structured environments, such as juvenile camps, where he got A's and B's. To date he's finished 10th grade, an anomaly in the gang world. "In school he's bright," she said. "But take him out of that structure ..."

48   The Southern New Mexico Correctional Facility is a medium-security prison built to house 480 men (and holding 570 at the time of this interview). It is surrounded not by walls but by two tall chain-link fences, one topped, the other covered, with razor wire. It sits low and half-hidden amid the pale desert scrub just off Interstate 10, a few miles west of Las Cruces.

49   On the day of his interview for this article, Eddie Torres strolls into the visitor's room in a lazy, liquid cholo gait. His eyes, sparkling in the bright overhead lights, reflect a detached, but shrewd, awareness. At 5-foot-8 and 140 pounds, he isn't physically threatening, but he certainly looks bigger and older than the average 16-year-old. He speaks quietly, with control—uncommonly mature for a youth his age—as he recalls the incident that had brought him there. "I was drunk," he says. "I knew I shouldn't have gone out there. I didn't want to rob him."

50   *Did you know at the time you were beating a 63-year-old?*

51   "I saw him, but I didn't know he was an older man. I regretted that *big time* afterwards. I knew how I'd feel if it had been my uncle or somebody."

52   *Are you bitter about being sent to prison?*

53   Torres slowly pulls his shirttail out and lifts it, exposing a long, ugly scar running from his navel to his sternum. "That *vato* didn't have to shoot me. He could've just pointed

the gun at me or fired it in the air—I would've run away. I only wanted to beat him up. I wasn't trying to kill him."

54   *Do you understand why he felt he had to shoot you?*

55   "He wasn't wrong to shoot me, but he didn't have to tell the police. I wouldn't have said nothing. I told 'em it was a drive-by."

56   *Mr. Kern has become a local hero for how he defended himself. Do you think he's a hero?*

57   "F— no, he's no hero! Shooting someone doesn't make anyone a hero. A lot of old people think if they go out and [shoot criminals], they're protecting society. *That pissed me off.* My brothers got real mad after they heard about that; they wanted to come out here and get the old guy."

58   *If you stay out of trouble when you get out, what do you want to do with the rest of your life?*

59   "Get a good job, a house, a lady and kids. Maybe my own business. Construction business. I'd like to build houses.

60   "But I'll probably be back [in prison] for something else."

61   *What would you do if you ran into Mr. Kern again?*

62   [*Softly*] "I'll probably kill him if I ever see him again."

63   Today, nearly a year after the crime, Dean Kern still worries about Torres's street philosophy of revenge, called *venganza* in the barrios. But what disturbs him more is the specter of the next "Torres" lurking in the early morning mist where he walks. "Suppose it happens again?" he asks. "Are people going to say, 'Ol' Dean must be out there trolling for these guys'?"

64   Kern poses the question but never answers it. Although carrying a concealed weapon in Albuquerque can be punishable by 90 days in jail and a fine, little was said about it during the proceedings. Defense attorney Velazquez, although asserting that carrying a concealed weapon "is a crime in my book," opted not to pursue the issue. "That was up to the prosecutor and D.A. By ignoring it, though, [they put] a stamp of approval on vigilante behavior. My concern is that *that* will be the message."

65   Prosecutor Neary shrugs off the violation. "Although Mr. Kern technically did something illegal, as far as I'm concerned he did nothing wrong. He didn't shoot immediately—he fired only after he'd been hit several times and couldn't get away. If it had been my mother-in-law, those blows would have destroyed her."

66   For his part, Kern admits he has changed his pre-dawn route—"I don't walk where cars go anymore"—but not his means of self-protection: He still carries his pistol.

67   To some experts and sociologists, youths like Eddie Torres seem destined to follow the criminal path on which—to whatever extent—family, culture or society has pushed them. They seem to have refused, or been unable, to resist their fate.

68   The fate of victims like Dean Kern, however, seems changed forever. After the incident he received more than 50 telephone calls and numerous letters applauding his action. "I didn't get one negative comment," he says.

69   One woman wrote saying that he was her hero. "But," he adds with a chuckle, "she also offered some advice: 'Practice, man, practice!'"

70   It's easy to be so sure, so brazen, from a comfortable distance. But ask Kern today how he feels about his entrance into the world of *venganza:* "I have no remorse;

I was defending myself. But I'm worried about his friends. He knows what I look like—and that's enough."

Modern Maturity, January/February 1995, pp. 22–31

COMPREHENSION QUESTIONS

1. What is the topic of the passage?
2. What is the central message of the passage?
3. Determine what is at issue. What is your initial personal viewpoint?
4. Distinguish among opposing viewpoints, and provide the rationale for each.
5. Think carefully about the viewpoints. Express a personal viewpoint, and give the reasons why you favor it. Does it differ from your initial personal viewpoint? Why or why not?
6. Write a few paragraphs *in support of the viewpoint that you do* not *favor.*

VOCABULARY QUESTION

Use the context to define the following words: *cholo, vato, me vió*, mad-dogged, *venganza.*

THOUGHT AND DISCUSSION QUESTIONS

1. In your view, why did Eddie Torres behave the way he did? Do you know anyone who behaves like him? How should you deal with a person like Eddie Torres? Why?
2. Is there any hope now for Eddie Torres? Why or why not?
3. How would you have reacted had the woman asked you to leave the party? Why?
4. If you were Dean Kern, what would you have done in a similar situation? Why? Should he be applauded for his action? Why or why not?
5. What can we do as a society to prevent conflicts like the one in this article from occurring?
6. List any questions that came to mind while you were reading this selection, and be prepared to discuss possible answers to them.

4

The Politics of Paternity Leave
Why Government Isn't Always the Problem

Tom McMakin

1   Valerie's asleep now, having snacked most of the morning, fussed and finally closed the brightest blue eyes I've ever seen. Quiet moments like these are rare when you are taking

care of a 4-month-old. When she sleeps, it's time for me to mix more formula, wipe the counter, call about life insurance and then, if time allows, break open the laptop and sit down to write for a few minutes. Welcome to paternity leave, a spicy stew of belches and smiles, DPT shots, heavy warm diapers and the odd moment of reflection.

2   The idea that fathers should take time off from work to be with their newborn children is a relatively new one, but it's an idea that is long overdue. Two years ago, time at home with Valerie would not have been possible. But thanks to the Family and Medical Leave Act of 1993, here I am changing my daughter's diapers and enjoying her first gurgles and giggles. Who would have thought it? A bunch of faraway lawmakers passed legislation, and it profoundly affected my life. Their law, PL103–3, requires that companies with more than 25 employees allow them to take up to 12 weeks of uncompensated time off to care for their children. Because of this legislation my life is richer.

3   Much richer. This bundle of sweet smells I call my daughter has given me the gift of new sight. A trip to the supermarket used to be a dreaded errand; now it is the highlight of my week. Valerie has taught me to look beyond our store's confusion of brands and hype and focus on the colors, shapes and happy chatter that make each visit a carnival of sight and sound. We squeal at the celery, spit heartily at the dairy rack and shrink in terror at the sight of the frozen turkeys. The moving counter by the cash register is a revelation.

4   A walk downtown has been similarly transformed. Everyone loves a baby. And we love them back for it. People I've never spoken with, but have passed on the street many times before, smile and ask how old she is. To be a baby, I've learned, is to live in a friendly, welcoming world. But it's not just her world; it's mine too. Because of my time home with Valerie, I'm also much more understanding of children and parents. I rush to help a mom with a stubborn car door or a dad whose youngest is on the verge of straying. I smile at mischievous kids, happy to see them speeding off in this direction or that, ruining their parents' best-laid plans.

5   I have paternity leave to thank for teaching me these and other lessons (never dump formula in cold water—it doesn't mix). I am grateful to my wife and to my employer for encouraging me in my decision to stay home and am grateful to a government that made taking this time possible.

6   Sadly, when Valerie and I walk downtown and stop at the local coffee shop, we hear people talking about government in two ways, neither of them very good. They say that government is either ineffective or misguided, with most agreeing that it is both. It is not hard to understand why the ranchers and business people clustered around the small Formica tables think this way. In our state of Montana, the public owns 39 percent of all land. That means there are legions of federal, state and local managers running around doing surveys, convening task forces, forming policy and interpreting regulations. With so much at stake and with so many bureaucrats in action, it is inevitable that these well-intentioned civil servants make mistakes. When they do, the mistakes are widely discussed and greatly criticized.

7   That's a shame. Somewhere in the rush to criticize, we have failed to see the forest for the trees. While Bozo the Clown may run a public agency or two, I cannot escape the fact that my sitting here today trading coos with my daughter is a salute to the possibility inherent in public action. On Feb. 5, 1993, our representatives in Washington decided it was important that families be allowed to spend time together when they most needed it and, more important, that wage earners should not lose their jobs while caring for a

dying mother or recuperating from a serious operation or spending time with a new-born. In my book, that bad boy of American culture, Congress, did something right when it passed this law.

8   The citizenry of this country has expanding and contracting tastes in what it wants its government to do, not unlike the members of the credit union to which I belong. One year we may ask the credit union's management to make sweeping changes, add more ser-vices and expand the types of loans it is willing to make. And then that energy runs its course and the membership elects a new board or hires a new manager to trim costs and services. When we ask the credit union to add services, we are not suggesting that credit unions ought to take over the world. By the same token, when we ask it to cut services, we are not saying credit unions are worthless. It's more like riding a horse up a hill: you might go to the left for a while and then to the right, but, even with the zigs and zags, you are still headed in one direction—toward the top.

9   In this current season of scaling back government—both Republicans and Democ-rats seem to agree that this is a good thing these days—my hope is we remember that gov-ernment is capable of doing things and doing them well. I work 40 hours a week because my great-grandfather voted for a reform Congress at the end of the last century. My savings at the credit union are insured because my grandmother voted for FDR. My dad put Eisenhower and a forward-looking Congress in place in the late '50s. As a result, it takes me one hour to travel to Butte and not two, on an interstate-highway system. Government isn't bad in and of itself. It isn't some malevolent Beltway-girdled ogre perched on the banks of the Potomac. It is, rather, an expression of our collective will.

10   But wait. Valerie is stirring. Little wet slimy hands await. I need to warm a bottle, find a fresh diaper, pad upstairs and quietly make sure she is serious about ending this nap, and finally peek over the side of the crib and drink in that bright, beautiful smile that never fails to remind me why I so like being a dad at home.

Newsweek, September 25, 1995, p. 26

COMPREHENSION QUESTIONS

1. What is the topic of the passage?

2. What is the central message of the passage?

3. Determine what is at issue. What is your initial personal viewpoint?

4. Distinguish among opposing viewpoints, and provide the rationale for each.

5. Think carefully about the viewpoints. Express a personal viewpoint, and give the reasons why you favor it. Does it differ from your initial personal viewpoint? Why or why not?

6. Write a few paragraphs *in support of the viewpoint that you do not favor.*

THOUGHT AND DISCUSSION QUESTIONS

1. Should fathers take time off from work to be with their newborn children? Why or why not? Are fathers as effective as mothers with newborn children? Why or why not?

2. Do you agree with the statement "To be a baby...is to live in a friendly, welcoming world"? Why or why not?

3. In your view, is the author expressing happiness, sadness, or both? Why?

4. List any questions that came to mind while you were reading this selection, and be prepared to discuss possible answers to them.

5
Why Women Make Better Cops

Tessa De Carlo

1   It's Friday night in Madison, Wisconsin, and officers from the police department's Blue Blanket team—a special drug, gang and gun squad—are cruising past an East Side low-income neighborhood, a site they've often had occasion to visit. Tonight the mood in the neighborhood, whose residents are mostly African American, is tense; a rumored party hasn't materialized and about 50 young people are now hanging around waiting for something to happen.

2   Just then an emergency call comes in, reporting that a young man has beaten up his girlfriend. As the officers, led by Sergeant Tony Peterson and Detective Marion Morgan, approach the crowd to see if they can find him, several kids cry out, "Marion! Marion!" She is the only black officer in the group, and the young people's voices are somewhere between affectionate and mocking.

3   The police approach a teenager who partly fits the reported batterer's description: young, black male; tall; denim jacket. But the man, who's apparently been drinking, isn't in any mood to cooperate. "I want to talk to my lawyer," he yells. "You're just doing this because I'm black!"

4   "We can do this the easy way, but now we're going to have to do it this way," says Peterson, as he and another officer deftly snap the man into handcuffs and lead him over to a police car to pat him down, check for outstanding warrants and ask a few questions. It turns out he isn't the man they're looking for, and after a few minutes he's released.

5   But in the meantime, one of his friends, another teenager in a black-and-red University of Wisconsin team jacket, has begun complaining loudly about the police, and a group of younger kids gathers around. Morgan puts her hand on the arm of the older boy, who towers over her. She's arrested him before on various charges, none of them very serious.

6   "You know we're here so everyone can live peacefully and safely," she tells him in a firm but not angry voice. "If *you* called in a complaint, you'd want us to come and deal with it. It doesn't help when someone like you, with standing in the neighborhood, cops an attitude and gets all these shorties going"—she nods toward the kids standing around. "I'm just telling you how it felt to me, and it felt like you were disrespecting me."

7   "I wouldn't disrespect you, you know that," the young man says, abashed.

8   She pats him on the arm, and he shrugs, looking a little embarrassed.

9   "We're not the enemy," she says.

10   "I know that," he answers.

A Better Kind of Cop?

11   According to many law enforcement officials, stories like this one show why women in police work aren't just as good as men—they're sometimes better.

12   "There's such an obvious need for more women in this business," says Nick Pastore, chief of police in New Haven, Connecticut. In his view, when it comes to the skills that really count, "women are much more effective."

13   America celebrates strong-arm police officers in movies and TV shows, but in real life, too much macho causes more problems than it solves. When police departments are permeated by "good old boy" attitudes and filled with what Pastore calls "young, male, suburban adventure-seekers eager to bash heads," they tend to confuse the war on crime with a war on minorities, women, gays and the rest of the community they're supposed to be serving.

14   Until two decades ago, a woman's only entrée into the hypermasculine world of policing was to become a clerk, or a "policewoman" restricted to working with juveniles. The passage of the Equal Employment Opportunity Act of 1972 prompted a flood of discrimination lawsuits and court orders that forced the stationhouse doors open—but not very far. Women still make up less than ten percent of the nation's police officers and about three percent of police supervisors.

15   That's a loss not only for women who want to be police officers but for everyone who wants safer communities and better policing. Because women—precisely because they don't conform to the locker-room mores of traditional law enforcement—often make better cops.

16   "Women officers are less authoritarian and use force less often than their male counterparts. They're better at defusing potentially violent confrontations, possess better communication skills and respond more effectively to incidents of violence against women," said Katherine Spillar, national coordinator for the Feminist Majority Foundation, in testimony before a commission investigating police brutality in Los Angeles.

17   Many police veterans agree. "Women officers are no less tough or strong or capable of dealing with the world of the streets," says Hubert Williams, president of the Police Foundation and former chief of police in Newark, New Jersey. "But on the whole they're better listeners, with a special knowledge of families and children, able to engage effectively and develop working relationships. That's why they're so valuable to law enforcement."

Women Fighting Crimes Against Women

18   The woman had called police in the Louisiana town several times before. Her marriage had fallen apart but her husband refused to leave. He hit her and threatened her and sabotaged her car so that she needed him to drive her to and from her job.

19   "This man beats me up, and the officers won't do anything," the woman sobbed when the police arrived yet again.

20   But this time the two officers who answered the call were women. "We told him, 'Look, whatever it was you did to her car, you get out there now and undo it,'" one of the officers recalls. "He was angry. If we'd been men, he would have fought. But I told him, 'I'm just a little-bitty person, so if you come at me, I'm not going to fight—I'll just shoot.'" The man decided to cooperate.

21   The officers wouldn't leave until he replaced the distributor cap on his wife's car. "Then we told him that if she ever called us again, we'd come back and kick his butt," the officer says.

22   The woman didn't call again, but a few months later one of the women officers ran into her on the street. Her husband had agreed to a divorce and moved out of state.

23   Why hadn't any of the other police who'd visited this woman helped her out? "This is an old-fashioned, good-old-boy place," says the Louisiana cop, who doesn't want her name used. "When the male officers go on a domestic, I hear them saying things like, 'The bitch don't keep the house clean—you *ought* to be whuppin' her ass.'"

24   Domestic violence is one of the most pressing issues in police work. A 1993 federal inquiry estimated that more than 21,000 domestic assaults, rapes and murders are reported to police each week. By some estimates, "family disturbances" account for more calls received by police each year than any other kind of crime.

25   But traditional male-dominated police departments take these calls less seriously than robberies and other crimes involving strangers. A study conducted by the Police Foundation cited police failure to make arrests in family violence cases as one of the most serious aspects of the nation's domestic violence problem.

26   One reason for poor police performance in this area may be that male officers are particularly prone to domestic violence themselves, and therefore resist treating it as a serious crime. "There's a lot of domestic violence being committed by officers," says a female cop from a large Southeastern city. "It's that macho image, saying, 'I'm the authority and I'm above the law.'"

27   Research bears her out. One 1991 study found that while violence—ranging from slapping to punching to stabbing—is an element in 16 percent of U.S. marriages, the rate among a sample of 425 police officers, 90 percent of them male, was as high as 41 percent.

28   A third study—concerning 72 male officers in the Midwest—bolstered a suspicion long held by observers of law enforcement: that the more violent an officer is at home, the more prejudiced he is against victims of domestic violence and the less likely he is to make arrests in such cases.

29   Arrest rates are influenced by many factors, including local laws and whether prosecutors are willing to bring cases to trial. But officers' attitudes do play a role. "Studies in the past 20 years show that women officers take domestic violence calls more seriously and treat it more seriously as a crime," says Katherine Spillar, who's now on the advisory board of the National Center for Women and Policing.

30   New Haven's Pastore noticed a difference in this area after he fast-tracked eight women into detective positions in his department. "These women have really concentrated on abuse against women and sexual assault," he says—crimes Pastore believes were given less focus when the system was all male. "Twice in the past year the same thing has happened: Friends of the accused have come to me and said, 'Since when do you have women doing these cases? They're so tenacious....Chief, can you take some heat off?' Their performance in this area alone is worth the presence of women on the force."

Are Women Cops Tough Enough?

31   The belief that women are less violent—and therefore less able to stand up to force or dish it out when necessary—used to be a prime argument for a male-only police force.

But once affirmative action opened policing to women, extensive research confirmed that although women are, in general, smaller and less powerful than men, especially in terms of upper-body strength, they are just as capable of policing as men.

32   For example, a 1987 study of 3,701 violent conflicts between police and citizens in New York City, including both assaults and gunplay, confirmed that female cops were just as brave as males. "Female officers, whether with a partner or alone, are more than willing to get involved in violent confrontations apparently without any fear of injury or death," the study concluded.

33   Take the case of San Francisco inspector Holly Pera, who before joining the force was a member of the San Francisco Ballet and then a teacher. A specialist in cases involving children, Pera teamed up with Inspector Kelly Carroll, a six-foot-one-inch male, to arrest a recently released ex-con who had reportedly robbed and sodomized several boys. High on crack cocaine, the man resisted arrest, attacking both officers. During the struggle, the suspect managed to get hold of Carroll's gun and was about to shoot him from a few feet away when Pera stepped between them. She and the ex-con both fired: His shots missed and hers hit him in the chest. He died of his wounds at the hospital. "I have never witnessed a single more courageous act," says Carroll. "There's no doubt she saved my life."

34   But the same research that showed women cops are as tough as their male colleagues discovered something equally important: Women officers *misuse* violence far less. In another study of New York City cops, for example, this one in 1989, researchers found that although female officers were involved in just as many violent confrontations as male officers, they received fewer civilian complaints, were involved in fewer shootings and used deadly force less often.

35   Women officers are frequently more effective in volatile situations because they focus on cooling everyone down, rather than asserting their own authority.

36   "I'm not going to get fired up because they call me a whore or a dyke," says a female trooper from Connecticut. "I just say, 'Forgive me, I have to be here. Now give me your side of the story.' Whereas a lot of male officers are going to say, 'What did you call me?' and—whoomp!—you've got another fight going."

37   "We tell officers that when you lose your temper, *you* are in danger," says Sheriff Jackie Barrett of Fulton County, Georgia. Staying cool and sidestepping unnecessary physical confrontations, she says, are "a function of maturity and of strength—*inner* strength."

38   Often courage can mean *not* using force and still getting results. In the Midwest two officers, a woman and a man, were called to a bar late at night by two frightened female bartenders. A nearby club had just let out, and although it was closing time at the bar, too, suddenly the bartenders were faced with a crowd of more than 200 people. With most of them drunk and refusing to leave, the scene was turning ugly.

39   The woman officer went into the bar and didn't notice until too late that the male officer had stayed outside. But there was no turning back. Using what she calls her mom voice ("You may not even like your mom, but you obey her"), she told the barful of rowdies, "It's time for you to go home now." Anyone who didn't leave would immediately be arrested, she told the crowd. "There are five police cars outside"—as far as she knew, there were only two, including hers—"and the doors will be locked and you'll all be processed right here."

40   "I got some lip," she recalls, "but everybody left. There were no fights and I didn't have to arrest a single person."

41   When she went outside she found four male officers standing around in the street. "They were waiting to see if I could handle the call," she says. "I'm considered not aggressive enough because I don't rush in and arrest the first person I see. But I don't get into fights, either, and I don't need 15 other officers for backup."

Los Angeles: Boys in Blue

42   Of course the absence of a Y chromosome doesn't automatically make someone a good cop, any more than it makes her a good mother or a bad driver. Some female officers are hot tempered and high-handed, and plenty of male cops are caring, compassionate people with excellent interpersonal skills.

43   However, traditional policing still tends to devalue those skills—in men as well as women—in favor of bullyboy aggressiveness and an "us against them" attitude toward not only crooks but the public at large. The result can be that police become part of the crime problem themselves.

44   This has been vividly demonstrated in Los Angeles, where cops were notorious for man-handling citizens long before the videotaped beating of Rodney King by four police officers in 1991. The gigantic cost of community ill will toward the L.A. Police Department was clear during the riots a year later, when police couldn't even enter riot-torn areas and citizens trying to defend their lives and property had to fend for themselves.

45   The independent commission formed to investigate the LAPD in the wake of the beating condemned the department's authoritarian, often confrontational policing style and found a direct connection between its proclivity for violence and its attitude toward women.

46   "Traditional views concerning the nature of police work in general—that is, that police work is a male-oriented profession with a major emphasis on physical strength—foster a climate in which female officers are discouraged," said the commission's final report. "A corollary of that culture is an emphasis on use of force to control a situation and a disdain for a more patient, less aggressive approach."

47   Transcripts of computerized transmissions between police cars show just how brutal the LAPD's internal culture had become. "I hope there is enough units to set up a powwow around the suspect so he can get a good spanking and nobody c it ..." was one typical computer transmission. Said another, "U wont believe this ... that female call again said susp returned ... I'll check it out then I'm going to stick my baton in her."

48   But one group of cops in L.A. did not succumb to run-amok machismo. The independent commission reported that female LAPD officers were much less likely to resort to use of excessive force. In 1991 women made up about 13 percent of the LAPD, but the commission found that of the 808 officers involved in frequent use of force, women accounted for only 30, or 3.7 percent. Among the 120 officers with the most use-of-force reports, not a single one was a woman.

49   As Katherine Spillar notes, one officer tried to stop the beating of Rodney King, "but the men told her to stay out of it."

50   The commission's findings aren't unique to Los Angeles. "In every department there's a small number of cops who get a huge number of civilian complaints," says Samuel Walker, a criminologist at the University of Nebraska at Omaha. "In all the cases where we've gotten information on who the bad boys are, female officers never show up on the list."

51   The Los Angeles City Council, which is currently paying out $28 million a year to settle civilian complaints against police, got the message. In 1992 it called on the LAPD to bring its percentage of female officers up to 43 percent—the percentage of women in the city's overall workforce, and far higher than that of any police department in the nation. Last year the council took the additional step, making 43 percent the LAPD's annual hiring goal.

Madison: Human Beings, Not Robocops

52   Right now, the city with one of the highest percentages of women cops is Madison, Wisconsin. Twenty-seven percent of its force is female; in addition, a third of its detectives and 25 percent of all those ranked above officer status are women.

53   Chief Richard Williams says women officers are essential to the department's community-oriented style of policing. "We want to reflect the community, and 50 percent of the people out there are women," he explains. "We want people to see us as human beings, rather than Robocops with dark glasses and no feelings." Williams says his department is doing that, not just by adding women to police ranks but by redefining what a police officer is.

54   Instead of recruiting eager young warriors with high-school educations and a couple of years in the military, Madison is voting for maturity and independent thinking by favoring candidates ages 25 to 29 with college degrees and well-developed communication skills.

55   Although women officers in Madison say the department isn't free of sexism, they describe many of the male officers as what Officer Carren Corcoran calls '90s guys: "They have good relationships with their wives, good communication with citizens, they don't try to take over our calls and they talk to suspects instead of just smashing the guy against the car."

56   The respect Madison officers feel for each other is paralleled by the force's relations with the community. In Los Angeles, officers often demand that suspects lie prone on the pavement. In Madison, officers address everyone as Sir or Ma'am and ask politely for identification and permission to pat a suspect down. Most of the time permission is given, and what is elsewhere a ritual of dominance and submission becomes a surprisingly good-natured interaction.

57   Madison officers say being respectful of citizens makes their job easier. "If you rip someone's self-respect and self-esteem away from them, that doesn't get you anywhere," says Sergeant Patricia Rickman.

58   Officers from Milwaukee and Chicago, whose departments are run on more traditional lines, "think we're all pansies here because we talk too much," she adds, laughing. "That's fine—we talk and we don't get hurt."

59   In other cities, social worker is the worst thing you can call a cop, but officers in the Madison Police Department see much of what they do in exactly those terms. Officer Sue Armagost has a master's degree in social work and worked with battered women for three years before becoming a cop. She says, "This is social work with a gun and a little more authority and a whole lot more job security."

60   Forget the gunfights and car chases in the movies and cop shows. Here are the crime-fighting highlights of one three-day weekend in Madison last fall:
- A six-year-old boy is accused of stealing a $1.99 toy gun from a supermarket.

- A man has beaten up his girlfriend. He leaves the house when she calls the police and has to be pursued for several blocks before he is arrested. The officers explain to the girlfriend her legal options for seeking protection from him in the future.
- A worried mother files a missing-person report on her pregnant 15-year-old, who has disappeared with a boyfriend. (She turns up six hours later.)
- A 17-year-old boy from a nearby farm town is hanging around a neighborhood at one o'clock in the morning with two small children in the back of his truck. He says they are from a nearby homeless shelter and that he gave their father a lift here, supposedly so he could cash a money order. The officers convince the boy to hand the children over to them and go home. They also call his parents.
- The children's parents are found a half hour later. The father has crack cocaine hidden in his mouth and is arrested. The mother and children are given some phone numbers for social services and taken back to the homeless shelter.
- A man reports he's been robbed, then admits he made up the story because he has spent his mother's bus money on drugs. He threatens suicide and must be taken to a crisis center.
- A confused 65-year-old woman turns up on a residential street several miles from where she lives. The officer finds her caregiver and returns the woman to her home.

61   This scenario is not unique to Madison. Even in the nation's largest, toughest cities, an officer on patrol spends 80 to 95 percent of work time answering service calls, talking to citizens and writing reports. Cops who don't like "social work" aren't well-suited to their jobs.

Toughing It Out

62   Despite their advantages, women police officers are still relatively rare. Although a 1990 Police Foundation survey of about 200 large municipal departments found that some 20 percent of police-academy applicants and graduates are now women, most major police department's female ranks remain stuck around the ten to 12 percent mark. *The Police Chief* magazine reports that women still make up only 8.6 percent of new hires nationally.

63   The biggest reason is that hostility to women officers is still rampant. A survey of 280 male officers in Washington, Oregon, Idaho and Montana, published in *The Police Chief* last year, found that 68 percent object to the idea of having a woman partner.

64   Often hostility takes the form of harassment. The LAPD is currently the target of a class-action lawsuit charging deliberate and systemic discrimination against women and minorities, ranging from rudeness and name-calling to sexual assault. Male resistance can sometimes take even harsher forms. In a story published last year about alleged harassment within the Maryland State Police, *The Baltimore Sun* reported one female trooper's charges about what happened when she refused a superior officer's requests for a date: He sent her into a riot situation with no backup. Baltimore attorney Kathleen Cahill, who is representing two female officers in sexual harassment suits against the agency, says one of her clients has received death threats that appear to have come from fellow officers. "If a woman speaks out in an office setting and her superiors retaliate, that's very serious," she says. "But women who blow the whistle on law enforcement are afraid they're going to die. When the police threaten your life, who do you call for help?"

65   Yet police departments are changing, whether the old guard likes it or not. And those changes will almost certainly mean an ever bigger role for women.

66   First, rising educational standards for police officers mean departments must recruit from the widest possible pool. "Agencies in major cities reject, on average, more than 90 percent of candidates," says the Police Foundation's Williams. "We would not be able to keep the police cars rolling without women."

67   Second, the future of policing is brain power, not muscle, which helps level the playing field for women. "In the future the really good cops are going to be preventing crime and disorder by understanding those things in an analytic way," predicts Karin Schmerler, a former researcher with the Police Executive Research Forum, a nonprofit law enforcement think tank. "Policing is becoming proactive rather than reactive, and therefore more of a thinking, creative kind of job."

68   One example of that is offered by Austin, Texas, chief of police Elizabeth Watson, one of only two women chiefs in major American cities. Old-style, control-oriented policing, she points out, has failed to stop drug dealing in residential neighborhoods. Unless police devote long hours to surveillance (unlikely in this budget-slashing era), they can't make arrests that hold up in court because they can't catch dealers in the act. As a result, says Watson, more and more police departments are helping local residents to organize and take action, for example, by slapping nuisance suits on crack-house landlords, agitating for better street lighting and creating citizen surveillance teams that can provide police with photos of drug deals, license-plate numbers and other evidence.

69   "We need to work in partnership with communities and other agencies, using problem-solving, communication and other interpersonal skills," says Watson. "Those are characteristics that were not considered as critical for officers in the past but that women are generally very good at."

70   Finally, women cops love their work with a fervor that can't help but attract more women to the ranks. Interviews with more than 30 women officers from around the country yielded many stories of harassment and discrimination, of on-the-job injuries and brushes with death. But not one of these women wishes she were doing anything else.

71   One lieutenant, the only woman supervisor in her Midwestern agency, has suffered intense harassment, including being stalked by a former fellow officer, but has never considered changing careers. "When you're on patrol you have a lot of autonomy; you're pretty much your own boss," she says. "You're taking care of people, helping them when they're hurt, protecting them. It's different each day. It's the best job in the world."

72   As a girl, Marianne Scholer noticed that women in TV crime shows were always the victims. "I didn't want to have to be helped—I wanted to do the helping," she says. "I knew that being feminine didn't have to mean being helpless." A lieutenant in the Orange County, Florida, sheriff's office, she recently won a medal of valor for rescuing three people, including a child, from a burning building. "This is what I want to do," she says. "Every day, every hour brings an opportunity for you to be there for somebody."

Glamour, September 1995, pp. 260–273

COMPREHENSION QUESTIONS

1. What is the topic of the passage?

2. What is the central message of the passage?

3. Determine what is at issue. What is your initial personal viewpoint?

4. Distinguish among opposing viewpoints, and provide the rationale for each.

5. Think carefully about the viewpoints. Express a personal viewpoint, and give the reasons why you favor it. Does it differ from your initial personal viewpoint? Why or why not?

6. Write a few paragraphs *in support of the viewpoint that you do* not *favor.*

THOUGHT AND DISCUSSION QUESTIONS

1. Should the police have put handcuffs on the teenager who partly fit the reported batterer's description? Why or why not? What would you have done if you had been one of the police officers present? Why?

2. In your view, are women cops tough enough? Why or why not?

3. Would you rather have a male or a female cop patrolling your neighborhood? Why?

4. In your view, does the author deal with the subject matter of the article in an unbiased way? Why or why not?

5. List any questions that came to mind while you were reading this selection, and be prepared to discuss possible answers to them.

LOOKING BACK

Summarize and/or paraphrase the most important points you learned from this chapter, and determine how they can be put to use in other classes. Be prepared to discuss with your classmates what you have written.

THINK AGAIN!

The following problem was given to me by one of my critical-thinking students:

Suppose you bought a house with two floors, plus a basement and an attic. There are three separate lights in the attic that are controlled by three separate switches in the basement.

One night you are all alone and decise to match each of the three switches in the basement with the specific light in the attic that it controls. Assume that you want to accomplish this task immediately and that you can only make one trip to the basement and one trip to the attic. Can you figure out how you would go about doing it?

The Dashing Detective

Remember to follow these steps:

- first, read the narrative
- second, examine the two pictures carefully
- third, identify as many dissimilarities between the pictures as you can find.

Have fun!

A ────── Back to the Classroom ──────

For a time Wilbur Unisex taught a class in investigative techniques at the police school in the local university. In order to test the ability of his students to observe accurately, he gave them the two pictures shown here and asked them to note as many dissimilarities between the two as they could find. Although Wilbur came up with a perfect score, very few of his students located all the discrepancies. (There are twelve.) Can you?

(Note: Some of Wilbur's students claimed that, since he had made the two sketches himself, he knew all the answers. He disdained comment.)

Lawrence Treat, *Crime and Puzzlement*, pp. 28–29

B

Name _____ Date _____

MASTERY TEST 5-1

DIRECTIONS: Answer the questions and fill in the blanks.

1. What is a problem?

   _____

   _____

   _____

2. What is a solution?

   _____

   _____

   _____

3. Name and describe briefly the steps involved in the basic method for personal problem solving.

   _____

   _____

   _____

   _____

   _____

   _____

   _____

   _____

   _____

   _____

4. When identifying a problem, it is important not to confuse _____ (ways of accomplishing goals) with the _____ (goals themselves).

5. If your problem concerns another person, is it necessary to get that person involved in all steps? Explain your answer.

6. Name two specific problems discussed in the following story.

Whose Job Is It?

This is a story about four people named Everybody, Somebody, Anybody, and Nobody. There was an important job to be done, and Everybody was asked to do it. Everybody was sure Somebody would do it. Anybody could have done it, but Nobody did it. Somebody got angry about that, because it was Everybody's job. Everybody thought Anybody could do it, but Nobody realized that Everybody wouldn't do it. It ended up that Everybody blamed Somebody when Nobody did what Anybody could have done.

Problems:_____

_____

_____

_____

Name _____   Date _____

MASTERY TEST 5–2

DIRECTIONS: Using the first four steps of the basic method for personal problem solving, try to come up with possible solutions in the following problem situations.

1

You have been dating the "love of your life" for the past year, and the two of you have decided to get married. One evening, while talking over wedding plans, you express your overwhelming desire to have children. During the course of the conversation, you are shocked to find out that your prospective spouse does not want kids. Even though the subject has never been discussed before, you always assumed that there would be no disagreement. You are madly in love but at a loss as to what to do because having children has been a lifelong dream.

_____

_____

_____

_____

_____

_____

_____

_____

_____

_____

Note: For the following situation, put yourself in the shoes of the Bodins.

2

The Eggs, Embryos and I
After Years of Infertility, IVF and Now Three Children, I'm Struggling with a Difficult Choice

Melissa Moore Bodin

1   I have six potential children on ice in a hospital in southern California, and I don't know what to do with them. For seven years my husband and I suffered with the '90s affliction—

infertility. Our problem started in 1986 when we threw out the diaphragm; the next month I was pregnant. Unfortunately, the embryo didn't make the whole journey. It started to develop in one of my tubes, and emergency surgery was necessary to remove it. "Don't worry, this happens, try again," the experts told us.

2   Eight months later, pregnant—again in the fallopian tube. More surgery. After an evaluation, we were told that my tubes weren't clear (what a surprise) but that an operation could help. By now I knew I was never wearing a bikini again, so what's another scar? After the procedure, we kept on trying, with no results. Then it was time for a little chemical help. I tried Clomid, a drug that increases the production of eggs from the normal one per month to four or more. The rationale is that the more eggs out there, the better the odds of hitting the jackpot. Finally, after a year and a half of monthly ovaries the size of softballs, another tubal pregnancy that needed surgery. You hit yourself in the head with a phone book enough times and something tells you to stop.

3   The last stop on the Infertility Highway is in vitro fertilization. IVF is expensive and not covered by insurance, but we scraped together every penny and went for it. To begin, I had to shut down my regular reproductive hormones by giving myself a shot in the thigh every morning for 10 days. It wasn't too bad, since I used a tiny diabetic needle. Then I moved on to the big guns, Metrodin and Pergonal, to chemically regulate my cycle. These drugs are suspended in sesame oil, so they have to be injected into the big gluteus muscles with a *large* needle. Now the husband comes into play, reluctantly. Although it was my body on the receiving end of the needle, David had a very hard time making the plunge. We had to do these injections twice a day for 10 days. One side effect: a lot of bruising and a huge lump at the site of each injection. Not a pretty picture, but since actual sex was not part of the process, looks weren't that important.

4   The big day came, and the infertility clinic harvested 15 eggs, an operation more unpleasant than it sounds. The eggs were then mixed with my husband's sperm in a petri dish. For 36 hours we waited to hear that we'd made 11 embryos. The doctor decided that six was the magic number for us and froze the other five. The only really happy part of the whole ordeal was that before the six embryos were placed in my womb, my husband was allowed to look through a microscope and see the tiny cells waiting to go home. Afterward I had to lie in an uncomfortable position: on my stomach, feet much higher than my head, for four hours in a dark room by myself. The nurse said to think positive thoughts—all I could think about was the enormous dent the end of the gurney was putting in the top of my head. The trip home was a sight to behold; suffice it to say I kept my feet higher than my head in the car, too. I stayed in bed for a week and watched afternoon talk shows about multiple births. Another week went by before the blood test.

5   Ever heard that you can't be "a little bit pregnant"? Wrong. The pregnancy test was positive, but the "numbers" weren't high enough. The test measures the level of a hormone in the mother's blood, and the doctors want to see a number around 100. Mine was 54. We spent a horrible week before the next blood test, half pregnant. In the end, the one tenacious embryo out of six slipped away. We had our frozen embryos left over, but only three survived the thaw, and that attempt was unsuccessful.

6   It took two years to recover from the failure, but after promising my husband that it would be the last attempt, we tried IVF again. The day of the pregnancy test I felt premenstrual and crampy, certain I wasn't pregnant. I made my husband call for results. "Does

positive mean positive?" he said into the phone. Nine months later Jesse was born. When Jesse had his first birthday, I began thinking about the 18 frozen embryos left over from this IVF cycle. I never thought I had a shot of succeeding (my odds were about 11 percent), but we went ahead and had six of the thawed embryos "put back." (Six others did not survive.) Two weeks later, when I had the pregnancy test, I'd already grown out of my bra, so I knew something was up. Not only was I pregnant, but the hormone level was 412. Our twins, Paul and Samuel, were born nine months later.

7   I am 42 and my husband is 50. We have three children in diapers—exactly three more than we ever thought we'd have. In Jesse's preschool class we're always 15 to 20 years older than the other parents. My silver-haired husband shows his buddies baby pictures and their response is "Are these your grandkids?" Parents in the play group are worried about buying their first house; I'm worried about menopause. Most parents are concerned about saving for college; we're concerned about being able to feed ourselves when the kids are college age. We've already spent their college money to get them. Our bank account is empty, and we're both going to have to work full time until we're in our 90s. Of course, we have three of the most wonderful, intelligent, beautiful children on earth, so none of this really matters.

8   But we still have six frozen embryos. We have only two choices—donate or destroy. As painful as the infertility was, we never considered adoption an alternative. Giving our embryos to another infertile couple would be like giving our children up for adoption. We know this is a very selfish attitude and have struggled mightily with the issue. After all we've gone through, the concept of destroying the embryos is hard to imagine.

9   So we pay our $50 a month storage fee, raise our boys and wonder what we are going to do.

Newsweek, July 28, 1997, pp. 14–15

_____

_____

_____

_____

_____

_____

_____

_____

_____

_____

_____

_____

_____

PLAYING SHERLOCK HOLMES AND DR. WATSON

DIRECTIONS: Along with your partner, read the second part of "The Adventure of the Three Students," and then answer the questions that follow it.

The Return of Sherlock Holmes
The Adventure of the Three Students: Part Two

A. Conan Doyle

1   Holmes shook his head impatiently.

2   "Let us be practical," said he. "I understand you to say that there are three students who use this stair and are in the habit of passing your door?"

3   "Yes, there are."

4   "And they are all in for this examination?"

5   "Yes."

6   "Have you any reason to suspect any one of them more than the others?"

7   Soames hesitated.

8   "It is a very delicate question," said he. "One hardly likes to throw suspicion where there are no proofs."

9   "Let us hear the suspicions. I will look after the proofs."

10   "I will tell you, then, in a few words the character of the three men who inhabit these rooms. The lower of the three is Gilchrist, a fine scholar and athlete; plays in the Rugby team and the cricket team for the college, and got his Blue for the hurdles and the long jump. He is a fine, manly fellow. His father was the notorious Sir Jabez Gilchrist, who ruined himself on the turf. My scholar has been left very poor, but he is hard-working and industrious. He will do well.

11   "The second floor is inhabited by Daulat Ras, the Indian. He is a quiet, inscrutable fellow, as most of those Indians are. He is well up in his work, though his Greek is his weak subject. He is steady and methodical.

12   "The top floor belongs to Miles McLaren. He is a brilliant fellow when he chooses to work—one of the brightest intellects of the University, but he is wayward, dissipated, and unprincipled. He was nearly expelled over a card scandal in his first year. He has been idling all this term, and he must look forward with dread to the examination."

13   "Then it is he whom you suspect?"

14   "I dare not go so far as that. But of the three he is perhaps the least unlikely."

15   "Exactly. Now, Mr. Soames, let us have a look at your servant, Bannister."

16   He was a little, white-faced, clean-shaven, grizzly-haired fellow of fifty. He was still suffering from this sudden disturbance of the quiet routine of his life. His plump face was twitching with his nervousness, and his fingers could not keep still.

17   "We are investigating this unhappy business, Bannister," said his master.

18   "Yes, sir."

19   "I understand," said Holmes, "that you left your key in the door?"

20   "Yes, sir."

21   "Was it not very extraordinary that you should do this on the very day when there were these papers inside?"

22   "It was most unfortunate, sir. But I have occasionally done the same thing at other times."

23   "When did you enter the room?"

24   "It was about half-past four. That is Mr. Soames's tea time."

25   "How long did you stay?"

26   "When I saw that he was absent I withdrew at once."

27   "Did you look at these papers on the table?"

28   "No, sir; certainly not."

29   "How came you to leave the key in the door?"

30   "I had the tea-tray in my hand. I thought I would come back for the key. Then I forgot."

31   "Has the outer door a spring lock?"

32   "No, sir."

33   "Then it was open all the time?"

34   "Yes, sir."

35   "Anyone in the room could get out?"

36   "Yes, sir."

37   "When Mr. Soames returned and called for you, you were very much disturbed?"

38   "Yes, sir. Such a thing has never happened during the many years that I have been here. I nearly fainted, sir."

39   "So I understand. Where were you when you began to feel bad?"

40   "Where was I, sir? Why, here, near the door."

41   "That is singular, because you sat down in that chair over yonder near the corner. Why did you pass these other chairs?"

42   "I don't know, sir. It didn't matter to me where I sat."

43   "I really don't think he knew much about it, Mr. Holmes. He was looking very bad— quite ghastly."

44   "You stayed here when your master left?"

45   "Only for a minute or so. Then I locked the door and went to my room."

46   "Whom do you suspect?"

47   "Oh, I would not venture to say, sir. I don't believe there is any gentleman in this University who is capable of profiting by such an action. No, sir, I'll not believe it."

48   "Thank you; that will do," said Holmes. "Oh, one more word. You have not mentioned to any of the three gentlemen whom you attend that anything is amiss?"

49   "No, sir; not a word."

50   "You haven't seen any of them?"

51   "No, sir."

52   "Very good. Now, Mr. Soames, we will take a walk in the quadrangle, if you please."

53   Three yellow squares of light shone above us in the gathering gloom.

54   "Your three birds are all in their nests," said Holmes, looking up. "Halloa! What's that? One of them seems restless enough."

55   It was the Indian, whose dark silhouette appeared suddenly upon his blind. He was pacing swiftly up and down his room.

56   "I should like to have a peep at each of them," said Holmes. "Is it possible?"

57   "No difficulty in the world," Soames answered. "This set of rooms is quite the oldest in the college, and it is not unusual for visitors to go over them. Come along, and I will personally conduct you."

58   "No names, please!" said Holmes, as we knocked at Gilchrist's door. A tall, flaxen-haired, slim young fellow opened it, and made us welcome when he understood our errand. There were some really curious pieces of mediæval domestic architecture within. Holmes was so charmed with one of them that he insisted on drawing it on his note book, broke his pencil, had to borrow one from our host, and finally borrowed a knife to sharpen his own. The same curious accident happened to him in the rooms of the Indian—a silent, little, hook-nosed fellow, who eyed us askance and was obviously glad when Holmes's architectural studies had come to an end. I could not see that in either case Holmes had come upon the clue for which he was searching. Only at the third did our visit prove abortive. The outer door would not open to our knock, and nothing more substantial than a torrent of bad language came from behind it. "I don't care who you are. You can go to blazes!" roared the angry voice. "To-morrow's the exam, and I won't be drawn by anyone."

59   "A rude fellow," said our guide, flushing with anger as we withdrew down the stair. "Of course, he did not realize that it was I who was knocking, but none the less his conduct was very uncourteous, and, indeed, under the circumstances rather suspicious."

60   Holmes's response was a curious one.

61   "Can you tell me his exact height?" he asked.

62   "Really, Mr. Holmes, I cannot undertake to say. He is taller than the Indian, not so tall as Gilchrist. I suppose five foot six would be about it."

63   "That is very important," said Holmes. "And now, Mr. Soames, I wish you good-night."

64   Our guide cried aloud in his astonishment and dismay. "Good gracious, Mr. Holmes, you are surely not going to leave me in this abrupt fashion! You don't seem to realize the position. To-morrow is the examination. I must take some definite action tonight. I cannot allow the examination to be held if one of the papers has been tampered with. The situation must be faced."

65   "You must leave it as it is. I shall drop round early to-morrow morning and chat the matter over. It is possible that I may be in a position then to indicate some course of action. Meanwhile you change nothing—nothing at all."

66   "Very good, Mr. Holmes."

67   "You can be perfectly easy in your mind. We shall certainly find some way out of your difficulties. I will take the black clay with me, also the pencil cuttings. Good-bye."

68   When we were out in the darkness of the quadrangle we again looked up at the windows. The Indian still paced his room. The others were invisible.

69   "Well, Watson, what do you think of it?" Holmes asked, as we came out into the main street. "Quite a little parlour game—sort of three-card trick, is it not? There are your three men. It must be one of them. You take your choice. Which is yours?"

70   "The foul-mouthed fellow at the top. He is the one with the worst record. And yet that Indian was a sly fellow also. Why should he be pacing his room all the time?"

71   "There is nothing in that. Many men do it when they are trying to learn anything by heart."

72   "He looked at us in a queer way."

73   "So would you if a flock of strangers came in on you when you were preparing for an examination next day, and every moment was of value. No, I see nothing in that. Pencils, too, and knives—all was satisfactory. But that fellow *does* puzzle me."

74   "Who?"

75   "Why, Bannister, the servant. What's his game in the matter?"

76   "He impressed me as being a perfectly honest man."

77   "So he did me. That's the puzzling part. Why should a perfectly honest man—well, well, here's a large stationer's. We shall begin our researches here."

78   There were only four stationers of any consequence in the town, and at each Holmes produced his pencil chips and bid high for a duplicate. All were agreed that one could be ordered, but that it was not a usual size of pencil and that it was seldom kept in stock. My friend did not appear to be depressed by his failure, but shrugged his shoulders in half-humorous resignation.

79   "No good, my dear Watson. This, the best and only final clue, has run to nothing. But, indeed, I have little doubt that we can build up a sufficient case without it. By Jove! my dear fellow, it is nearly nine, and the landlady babbled of green peas at seven-thirty. What with your eternal tobacco, Watson, and your irregularity at meals, I expect that you will get notice to quit and that I shall share your downfall—not, however, before we have solved the problem of the nervous tutor, the careless servant, and the three enterprising students."

80   Holmes made no further allusion to the matter that day, though he sat lost in thought for a long time after our belated dinner. At eight in the morning he came into my room just as I finished my toilet.

81   "Well, Watson," said he, "it is time we went down to St. Luke's. Can you do without breakfast?"

82   "Certainly."

83   "Soames will be in a dreadful fidget until we are able to tell him something positive."

84   "Have you anything positive to tell him?"

85   "I think so."

86   "You have formed a conclusion?"

87   "Yes, my dear Watson; I have solved the mystery."

88   "But what fresh evidence could you have got?"

88   "Aha! It is not for nothing that I have turned myself out of bed at the untimely hour of six. I have put in two hours' hard work and covered at least five miles, with something to show for it. Look at that!"

90   He held out his hand. On the palm were three little pyramids of black, doughy clay.

91   "Why, Holmes, you had only two yesterday!"

92   "And one more this morning. It is a fair argument that wherever No. 3 came from is also the source of Nos. 1 and 2. Eh, Watson? Well, come along and put friend Soames out of his pain."

93   The unfortunate tutor was certainly in a state of pitiable agitation when we found him in his chambers. In a few hours the examinations would commence, and he was still in the dilemma between making the facts public and allowing the culprit to compete

for the valuable scholarship. He could hardly stand still, so great was his mental agitation, and he ran towards Holmes with two eager hands outstretched.

94   "Thank Heaven that you have come! I feared that you had given it up in despair. What am I to do? Shall the examination proceed?"

95   "Yes; let it proceed by all means."

96   "But this rascal—?"

97   "He shall not compete."

98   "You know him?"

99   "I think so. If this matter is not to become public we must give ourselves certain powers, and resolve ourselves into a small private court-martial. You there, if you please, Soames! Watson, you here! I'll take the arm chair in the middle. I think that we are now sufficiently imposing to strike terror into a guilty breast. Kindly ring the bell!"

The Complete Original Illustrated Sherlock Holmes, pp. 570–574

QUESTIONS

1. Who are the suspects? Name and describe each of them.

2. At this point, do you suspect any one of them more than the others? Why or why not?

PART 3

CRITICAL READING: EVALUATING WHAT YOU READ

CHAPTER 6
USING INFERENCE

CHAPTER OUTLINE

THINK ABOUT IT!

Look at the message on the sign in photograph 1. Use your knowledge, experience, and the clues to make an "educated guess" regarding what the advertisement is really urging husbands to do. Discuss it with your classmates.

1

Assuming that you do not speak or understand Spanish, make an "educated guess" regarding what the message on the sign in photograph 2 is urging you to do. Discuss it with your classmates.

Make an "educated guess" why the author decided not to purchase a wall-to-wall carpet from the store in photograph 3. Discuss your guess with your classmates.

2

3

323

Make an "educated guess" why the cars in photograph 4 were parked on the lawn in front of a high school. Discuss your guess with your classmates.

4

CHAPTER OUTCOMES

After completing Chapter 6, you should be able to:

- Continue to apply the basic method for personal problem solving
- Define critical reading
- Define inference
- Use knowledge, experience, and clues to draw inferences in problem situations and when reading passages concerning contemporary issues
- Continue to find topics and central messages in contemporary issue passages to determine what is at issue, distinguish among opposing viewpoints, and express personal viewpoints

Problem-Solving Exercise

Using your notebook, apply the first four steps of the basic method for personal problem solving to the following hypothetical situation. Make sure to label each step clearly as you discuss what you would do.

HYPOTHETICAL SITUATION

You are very close friends with a married couple whom you have known for many years. While driving through town, you spot one of them entering a restaurant with a person of the opposite sex. The following afternoon, you see them once again going into the same restaurant together. They seem to be very comfortable with each other and in a rather jovial mood.

WHAT IS CRITICAL READING?

As a college student, you are expected to derive meaning from whatever information you encounter in textbooks and other sources. In Chapters 1, 2, and 3 we reviewed a number of reading skills:

- Using context, word parts, a glossary, and the dictionary to determine word meanings
- Distinguishing main ideas, major details, and minor details
- Recognizing patterns of organization
- Uncovering the central message of a selection
- Summarizing and paraphrasing
- Overviewing a textbook
- Previewing a textbook chapter
- Developing questions from chapter headings and answering them
- Underlining or highlighting

All of these skills help you comprehend reading material better, particularly material found in textbooks.

Critical reading can be defined as *very high-level comprehension of written material requiring interpretation and evaluation skills that enable the reader to separate important from unimportant information, distinguish between facts and opinions, and determine a writer's purpose and tone.* It also entails *using inference to go beyond what is stated explicitly, filling in informational gaps, and coming to logical conclusions.* These various skills require much thought, and that is why critical reading is dependent on critical thinking. Indeed, all of the characteristics of critical thinking discussed in Chapter 4 can be applied to critical reading. The diagram on the following page illustrates the relationship between critical thinking and critical reading skills.

You have already had some practice in separating important from unimportant information, particularly when answering questions developed from textbook chapter headings and when dealing with contemporary issues. In the remaining chapters, you will continue

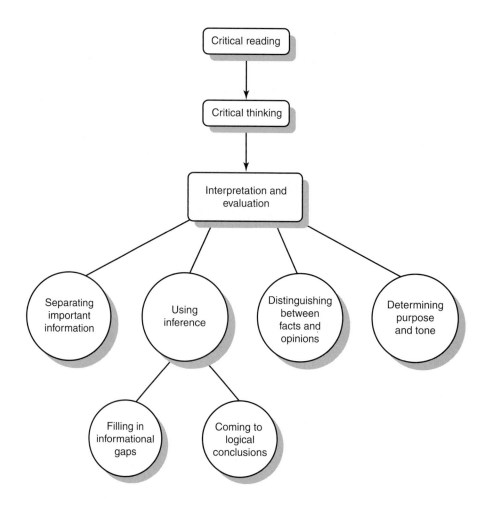

to practice that skill. The other critical reading skills—using inference, distinguishing between facts and opinions, and uncovering purpose and determining tone—are covered here in Part Three. Let's begin with a discussion of inference.

DRAWING INFERENCES

Pretend that you have had Professor Arlene Brown as a mathematics instructor for the past two semesters. She is a friendly person who always greets her classes in a warm manner. This past Tuesday, Professor Brown gave a difficult midterm examination in your algebra course. It covered rather complex material, and many of your classmates were concerned about their grades.

When the class met again on Thursday morning, Professor Brown arrived late, and when she came through the door she was not smiling at all. In fact, she walked briskly to the front of the room, slammed her briefcase on the desk, gruffly told the students to take out their notebooks, and began to cover new material immediately. Consequently, most of your classmates concluded that Professor Brown was upset about something.

They based that conclusion on three factors: first, their *knowledge* of the way people in general behave when they are upset; second, the *experience* they have had with Professor Brown in previous sessions; third, their using her behavior or actions as *clues*. That she was upset was a reasonable conclusion because it rested solidly on their knowledge and experience and flowed logically from the clues or facts at hand.

Some students went one step further by concluding that Professor Brown was upset because the class had done poorly on the midterm exam. Therefore, they became even more concerned about their test scores. However, you were skeptical and reluctant to go along with that line of reasoning. Although your classmates based their conclusion on knowledge and experience, you felt that it was not as solid as the previous one because there was a lack of specific clues pointing in that direction. They may ultimately end up being correct, but without additional information, their hunch was by no means certain. So it was probably wise for you to be cautious.

Now let's add some information to the story. Suppose Professor Brown, after slamming her briefcase on the desk, blurted out, "Men!" Could you then conclude reasonably that she had had an argument with her husband? Maybe, but you certainly might end up being wrong, because once again there are not enough clues. She could just as easily have had an argument that morning with some other male, such as a driver who cut her off on the way to school, her automobile mechanic, the dean, or another faculty member.

What if, instead, she had shouted, "Men! They are impossible to live with!" Would you then feel safe concluding that she had had an argument with her husband? Although that conclusion would be more likely in that it does rest on an additional clue, it might also turn out to be incorrect because she could be living with a boyfriend, son, brother, father, or roommate. It would become a much stronger conclusion if she had exclaimed, "Men! They are impossible to live with! Don't ever get married!" There would finally be enough clues to support the original conclusion that she had had a disagreement with her husband.

What we have been discussing here are **inferences**—"educated guesses" by which we go beyond what is explicit in order to fill in informational gaps, come to logical conclusions, and make sense of the world around us. They are "educated" because they are not wild guesses but are instead based on *knowledge, experience*, and the *clues or facts* of the situation. In short, the more knowledge, experience, and clues we have, the better our chances of coming up with sound inferences and hence logical and reasonable conclusions.

Using Knowledge to Infer

Knowledge of different subjects or topics varies from person to person: It comes down to what we have learned and experienced through the years. In that sense, knowledge really cannot be separated from experience because the latter adds to our knowledge base. On the other hand, our knowledge helps shape the way we interpret our experiences.

It follows, then, that the more we know and the more we have experienced, the easier it will be to draw inferences, depending of course on the circumstances. There will be occasions when we are in a much better position to make educated guesses and other occasions when we will not be able to do so with any degree of confidence. For example, look at the following photograph.

Certainly, most of us have enough knowledge to realize that this is a picture of a bus that is used for sightseeing purposes. However, what if I asked you to infer where the photograph was taken? There is one clue, and that is the name "Beantown." If you know the name of the city that is called "Beantown," you would feel very secure answering that the photograph was probably taken in the city of Boston. Thus your knowledge helped you use the clue to answer the question. People without that knowledge would be forced either to do some research or to take a wild guess. If they took a wild guess, the chances are fairly high that they would be wrong.

This is just one example of how knowledge can play a significant part when it comes to drawing inferences. We all need to accept the fact that we do not know everything, and no two people will possess the same degree of knowledge on every matter. In other words, we should not be embarrassed if we do not have enough knowledge in certain situations to draw inferences, and in those instances, it is probably better not to because there is a greater chance of being wrong. Keep in mind that there will be other situations in which we will find ourselves in a better position to come to logical conclusions. Furthermore, knowledge is not a constant but increases as we go through life.

Using Experience to Infer

We have already discussed the relationship between knowledge and experience. Our experiences add to our knowledge base and place us in a better position to come to logical conclusions about our surroundings. Once again, our experiences vary from person to person and therefore with regard to how much they help us draw inferences in different situations. For instance, look at the photograph below, and see if you can determine where it was taken.

If you have had the experience of visiting New York City around Christmastime, you probably came to the conclusion that the photograph is of the Christmas tree in Rockefeller Center. The Santa Claus, angels, size of the tree, and general layout of the buildings serve as clues. But if you have never had the experience of visiting Rockefeller Center in person at Christmastime, seen pictures of it in newspapers or magazines, or been introduced to it on television, it was much more difficult for you to make an accurate educated guess. Thus experiences—or lack of them—have an important effect on our ability to draw inferences.

Using Clues to Infer

As you have seen, in addition to knowledge and experience, we all depend on clues to help us draw inferences. The clues or facts present in a given situation interact with our knowledge and experiences, thus enabling us to make sense of our surroundings. For example, look at the following photograph, and list in your notebook at least three possible characteristics of the person who uses the study in the picture. When you are done, proceed to the explanation.

Although you do not know for sure, you can conclude reasonably that the person is a hockey fan because of the puck on the desk and the picture on the wall. In fact, judging by the uniform in the photograph, it would appear that the person is a New York Rangers fan. Furthermore, the other pictures on the wall suggest that he or she is a parent or that children are in some way an important part of his or her life. Also, the person obviously makes use of a portable computer, which is clearly visible on the desk. Finally, the can on the desk seems to indicate that the person drinks ale at least some of the time, and the golf club next to the desk would lead logically to the conclusion that he or she plays golf.

As you can see, by using the clues in the photograph in combination with your knowledge and experiences, you were able to infer some things about the person who uses the study. Much like a detective, you pieced together some important information that gave meaning to what you were observing. We all do this kind of exercise very often without even realizing it, and much of the time, our inferences are correct. Obviously, the more clues or facts available in a given situation, the better the chances of our inferences being accurate.

ACTIVITY 1

DIRECTIONS: For this activity, your instructor will divide the class into three groups. Each group will read only one of the three paragraphs that follow and use knowledge, experience, and clues to try to infer what person is being described. The paragraphs vary in terms of the clues that they provide, so be careful not to jump to a hasty conclusion unless your group is reasonably sure of that conclusion.

One Solitary Life

1   He was born in an obscure village, the child of a peasant woman. He grew up in another obscure village, where He worked in a carpenter shop until He was thirty. Then for three years He was an itinerant preacher. He never had a family or owned a home. He never set foot inside a big city. He never traveled two hundred miles from the place He was born. He never wrote a book, or held an office. He did none of the things that usually accompany greatness.

2   While He was still a young man, the tide of popular opinion turned against Him. His friends deserted Him. He was turned over to His enemies, and went through the mockery of a trial. He was nailed to a cross between two thieves. While He was dying, His executioners gambled for the only piece of property He had—His coat. When He was dead, He was taken down and laid in a borrowed grave.

3   Nineteen centuries have come and gone, and today He is the central figure for much of the human race. All the armies that ever marched and all the navies that ever sailed and all the parliaments that ever sat and all the kings that ever reigned, put together, have not affected the life of man upon this earth as powerfully as this "One Solitary Life."

ACTIVITY 2

DIRECTIONS: Read and think critically about the words to the Lee Ann Womack song "I Hope You Dance," which were found on the Internet (/http://lyrics.astraweb.com). In your notebook, use your inference skills to answer the questions that follow.

I Hope You Dance

Lee Ann Womack

I hope you never lose your sense of wonder,
You get your fill to eat but always keep that hunger,
May you never take one single breath for granted,
God forbid love ever leave you empty handed,
I hope you still feel small when you stand beside the ocean,
Whenever one door closes I hope one more opens,
Promise me that you'll give faith a fighting chance,
And when you get the choice to sit it out or dance

I hope you dance. I hope you dance.

I hope you never fear those mountains in the distance,
Never settle for the path of least resistance,
Livin' might mean takin' chances but they're worth takin',
Lovin' might be a mistake but it's worth makin',
Don't let some hell bent heart leave you bitter,
When you come close to sellin' out reconsider,
Give the heavens above more than just a passing glance,
And when you get the choice to sit it out or dance

I hope you dance. I hope you dance.
I hope you dance. I hope you dance.
(Time is a wheel in constant motion always rolling us along,
Tell me who wants to look back on their years and wonder where
those years have gone.)

I hope you still feel small when you stand beside the ocean,
Whenever one door closes I hope one more opens,
Promise me that you'll give faith a fighting chance,
And when you get the choice to sit it out or dance

Dance. I hope you dance.
I hope you dance. I hope you dance.
I hope you dance. I hope you dance.
(Time is a wheel in constant motion always rolling us along,
Tell me who wants to look back on their years and wonder where
those years have gone.)

http://lyrics.astraweb.com

QUESTIONS

1. In your view, to whom is the song being sung? Why?

2. Write your interpretation of the lines listed below:

   a. "I hope you never lose your sense of wonder"

   b. "You get your fill to eat but always keep that hunger"

   c. "I hope you still feel small when you stand beside the ocean"

   d. "Whenever one door closes I hope one more opens"

   e. "I hope you never fear those mountains in the distance"

   f. "Never settle for the path of least resistance"

   g. "When you come close to sellin' out reconsider"

   h. "Give the heavens above more than just a passing glance"

   i. "And when you get the choice to sit it out or dance. I hope you dance.
   I hope you dance"

LOOKING AT THE WORLD
WITH A QUESTIONING MIND

In Chapter 4, we noted that critical thinking involves asking questions, persistence in trying to find answers, and coming to logical conclusions that are based on sound reasoning and the information or evidence that has been gathered. In other words, to be a critical thinker, you must always be inquisitive about what is going on around you and constantly seeking answers. This in turn sometimes involves filling in the gaps by using your knowledge, experience, and the clues that are present to come to logical conclusions.

Now you see the connection between inferences and critical thinking, because in most instances in order to infer you must first question and then think carefully about what you see, hear, or read. Most of the time, no one is going to supply you with questions, so it is up to you to look at the world with a questioning mind. Then you must evaluate the information gathered to determine if you can answer your questions. It is at this point that you decide whether it is necessary to use inferences to help you.

USING INFERENCES WITH CONTEMPORARY ISSUES
AND PROBLEM SOLVING

When we read critically, it is often necessary to "read between the lines" by using inferences to fill in the gaps. We have already reviewed the importance of understanding a writer's stated and unstated messages in Chapter 2 when we talked about main ideas and central messages. As already mentioned, you will be introduced to facts/opinions, purpose and tone later on in this textbook.

In Chapter 4, when dealing with contemporary issues, you used inferences at times to help uncover unstated secondary issues, opposing viewpoints, and the rationale for those viewpoints. For example, for Selection 5, "Shot in the Arm," you not only had to infer the secondary issue involving how patients are treated by doctors but also had to supply reasons for one of the opposing viewpoints regarding why doctors often charge high fees.

Inferences can also be useful in basic problem solving. For instance, in Problem 1 in Activity 5 in Chapter 5, you were advised that because the problem was not stated explicitly, you would have to draw a logical conclusion about what was wrong. In other words, you were asked to use your knowledge, experience, and the facts that were given to infer what was bothering James. After thinking about the situation and discussing it in class, it was decided that one of the most likely possibilities was that James had some kind of substance abuse problem. Problem 2 in the same activity also required that you come to a logical conclusion by inferring from the information given that sexual harassment was the problem that Anita was experiencing.

Finally, in the hypothetical situation for the problem-solving exercise at the beginning of this chapter, you had to be very careful to gather additional information as part of Step 2, *before* trying to infer the nature of your friend's relationship. You could not possibly address the situation with any degree of certainty until completing that important step. Thus you saw the importance of questioning what you observe and the necessity for caution when using inferences.

As you make your way through college, remember to read and think with a questioning mind. This is a very important part of being both a critical reader and a critical thinker! Go beneath the surface, and do not accept information at face value. Use your knowledge, experience, and the clues or facts available to help you draw inferences so that you can fill in some of the gaps and come to logical conclusions. However, remember not to go too far beyond the information presented, because your conclusions may not have a solid foundation, and therefore they could be wrong.

ACTIVITY 3

DIRECTIONS: Your instructor is going to divide the class into small groups in order to apply the basic method for personal problem solving to the following situation. This was a real-life problem I encountered that required the use of inference skills in order to come to a logical conclusion regarding the doctor's motivations. When discussing the situation in your group, try to figure out what logical conclusion the author came to and what solution he decided on. Because this problem actually occurred, your instructor will let you know what I found in Step 5 when I "checked back on the problem and the possible solution." In other words, your instructor will tell you how the entire episode turned out.

You are in the surgeon's office with your daughter three weeks after he operated successfully on her for a thyroid tumor, and you ask him to recommend an internist because you have a lump on the side of your neck. Dr. Rosin informs you that the neck area is one of his specialties and starts immediately to examine you. After about two minutes, he advises you that one of your salivary glands is swollen. He proceeds to prescribe two antibiotics, schedules an X-ray for you at the hospital to determine if there is a stone in the gland, and sets up another appointment with him in three weeks.

On your return visit, you tell Dr. Rosin that you think the lump changes in size and is smaller at least some of the time. After reexamining you for about three minutes, he declares that the X-ray showed no evidence of a stone, the antibiotics have been ineffectual, and in his opinion the lump has gotten bigger. You ask him if the X-ray showed anything else, and he advises you that he was only testing for a stone. Furthermore, Dr. Rosin warns that either the gland is inflamed or it has a tumor that has a 50–50 chance of being malignant. Even if it is just inflamed, he continues, you will probably wake up one morning in excruciating pain with the lump three times bigger. He adds that he would not wish that kind of pain on his worst enemy.

Dr. Rosin explains further that he could do a needle biopsy in his office to determine if the lump is malignant, but he does not advise doing that because in his opinion those kinds of biopsies usually do not give accurate readings. He urges you to have surgery and explains how the operation will be performed, adding cautiously that he will not know for three days after surgery whether or not the lump is malignant. Finally, Dr. Rosin explains that the chances are high that during surgery, a nerve in your neck will get severed, affecting your lower lip when you smile. However, he assures you that the functioning of your mouth will not be affected. After listening, you tell him that you will have to think about what to do, and he agrees with that course of action. As you are leaving, he concludes by saying that if you decide on the operation, you should schedule it through his office. Otherwise, he would like to see you in about a month.

ACTIVITY 4

DIRECTIONS: First, read and think critically about the following short story written by Kate Chopin. Then, without looking back at it, summarize and/or paraphrase the story in your notebook. Finally, use your inference skills to determine why the author titled the story "The Storm." Be prepared to discuss your summary and conclusions with your classmates.

The Storm
A Sequel to "The 'Cadian Ball"

Kate Chopin

I

1   The leaves were so still that even Bibi thought it was going to rain. Bobinôt, who was accustomed to converse on terms of perfect equality with his little son, called the child's attention to certain sombre clouds that were rolling with sinister intention from the west, accompanied by a sullen, threatening roar. They were at Friedheimer's store and decided to remain there till the storm had passed. They sat within the door on two empty kegs. Bibi was four years old and looked very wise.

2   "Mama'll be 'fraid, yes," he suggested with blinking eyes.

3   "She'll shut the house. Maybe she got Sylvie helpin' her this evenin'," Bobinôt responded reassuringly.

4   "No, she ent got Sylvie. Sylvie was helpin' her yistiday," piped Bibi.

5   Bobinôt arose and going across to the counter purchased a can of shrimps, of which Calixta was very fond. Then he returned to his perch on the keg and sat stolidly holding the can of shrimps while the storm burst. It shook the wooden store and seemed to be ripping great furrows in the distant field. Bibi laid his little hand on his father's knee and was not afraid.

II

6   Calixta, at home, felt no uneasiness for their safety. She sat at a side window sewing furiously on a sewing machine. She was greatly occupied and did not notice the approaching storm. But she felt very warm and often stopped to mop her face on which the perspiration gathered in beads. She unfastened her white sacque at the throat. It began to grow dark, and suddenly realizing the situation she got up hurriedly and went about closing windows and doors.

7   Out on the small front gallery she had hung Bobinôt's Sunday clothes to air and she hastened out to gather them before the rain fell. As she stepped outside, Alcée Laballière rode

in at the gate. She had not seen him very often since her marriage, and never alone. She stood there with Bobinôt's coat in her hands, and the big rain drops began to fall. Alcée rode his horse under the shelter of a side projection where the chickens had huddled and there were plows and a harrow piled up in the corner.

8   "May I come and wait on your gallery till the storm is over, Calixta?" he asked.

9   "Come 'long in, M'sieur Alcée."

10   His voice and her own startled her as if from a trance, and she seized Bobinôt's vest. Alcée, mounting to the porch, grabbed the trousers and snatched Bibi's braided jacket that was about to be carried away by a sudden gust of wind. He expressed an intention to remain outside, but it was soon apparent that he might as well have been out in the open; the water beat in upon the boards in driving sheets, and he went inside, closing the door after him. It was even necessary to put something beneath the door to keep the water out.

11   "My! what a rain! It's good two years sence it rain' like that," exclaimed Calixta as she rolled up a piece of bagging and Alcée helped her to thrust it beneath the crack.

12   She was a little fuller of figure than five years before when she married; but she had lost nothing of her vivacity. Her blue eyes still retained their melting quality; and her yellow hair, dishevelled by the wind and rain, kinked more stubbornly than ever about her ears and temples.

13   The rain bear upon the low, shingled roof with a force and clatter that threatened to break an entrance and deluge them there. They were in the dining room—the sitting room—the general utility room. Adjoining was her bed room, with Bibi's couch alongside her own. The door stood open, and the room with its white, monumental bed, its closed shutters, looked dim and mysterious.

14   Alcée flung himself into a rocker and Calixta nervously began to gather up from the floor the lengths of a cotton sheet which she had been sewing.

15   "If this keeps up, *Dieu sait* if the levees goin' to stan' it!" she exclaimed.

16   "What have you got to do with the levees?"

17   "I got enough to do! An' there's Bobinôt with Bibi out in that storm—if he only didn't left Friedheimer's!"

18   "Let us hope, Calixta, that Bobinôt's got sense enough to come in out of a cyclone."

19   She went and stood at the window with a greatly disturbed look on her face. She wiped the frame that was clouded with moisture. It was stiflingly hot. Alcée got up and joined her at the window, looking over her shoulder. The rain was coming down in sheets obscuring the view of far-off cabins and enveloping the distant wood in a gray mist. The playing of the light-ning was incessant. A bolt struck a tall chinaberry tree at the edge of the field. It filled all vis-ible space with a blinding glare and the crash seemed to invade the very boards they stood upon.

20   Calixta put her hands to her eyes, and with a cry, staggered backward. Alcée's arm encircled her, and for an instant he drew her close and spasmodically to him.

21   "*Bonté!*" she cried, releasing herself from his encircling arm and retreating from the window, "the house'll go next! If I only knew w'ere Bibi was!" She would not compose her-self; she would not be seated. Alcée clasped her shoulders and looked into her face. The contact of her warm, palpitating body when he had unthinkingly drawn her into his arms, had aroused all the old-time infatuation and desire for her flesh.

22   "Calixta," he said, "don't be frightened. Nothing can happen. The house is too low to be stuck, with so many tall trees standing about. There! aren't you going to be quiet?

say, aren't you?" He pushed her hair back from her face that was warm and steaming. Her lips were as red and moist as pomegranate seed. Her white neck and a glimpse of her full, firm bosom disturbed him powerfully. As she glanced up at him the fear in her liquid blue eyes had given place to a drowsy gleam that unconsciously betrayed a sensuous desire. He looked down into her eyes and there was nothing for him to do but to gather her lips in a kiss. It reminded him of Assumption.

23   "Do you remember—in Assumption. Calixta?" he asked in a low voice broken by passion. Oh! she remembered; for in Assumption he had kissed her and kissed and kissed her; until his senses would well nigh fail, and to save her he would resort to a desperate flight. If she was not an immaculate dove in those days, she was still inviolate; a passionate creature whose very defenselessness had made her defense, against which his honor forbade him to prevail. Now—well, now—her lips seemed in a manner free to be tasted, as well as her round, white throat and her whiter breasts.

24   They did not heed the crashing torrents, and the roar of the elements made her laugh as she lay in his arms. She was a revelation in that dim, mysterious chamber; as white as the couch she lay upon. Her firm, elastic flesh that was knowing for the first time its birthright, was like a creamy lily that the sun invites to contribute its breath and perfume to the undying life of the world.

25   The generous abundance of her passion, without guile or trickery, was like a white flame which penetrated and found response in depths of his own sensuous nature that had never yet been reached.

26   When he touched her breasts they gave themselves up in quivering ecstasy, inviting his lips. Her mouth was a fountain of delight. And when he possessed her, they seemed to swoon together at the very borderland of life's mystery.

27   He stayed cushioned upon her, breathless, dazed, enervated, with his heart beating like a hammer upon her. With one hand she clasped his head, her lips lightly touching his forehead. The other hand stroked with a soothing rhythm his muscular shoulders.

28   The growl of the thunder was distant and passing away. The rain beat softly upon the shingles, inviting them to drowsiness and sleep. But they dared not yield.

29   The rain was over; and the sun was turning the glistening green world into a palace of gems. Calixta, on the gallery, watched Alcée ride away. He turned and smiled at her with a beaming face; and she lifted her pretty chin in the air and laughed aloud.

III

30   Bobinôt and Bibi, trudging home, stopped without at the cistern to make themselves presentable.

31   "My! Bibi, w'at will yo' mama say! You ought to be ashame'. You oughtn' put on those good pants. Look at 'em! An' that mud on yo' collar! How you got that mud on yo' collar, Bibi? I never saw such a boy!" Bibi was the picture of pathetic resignation. Bobinôt was the embodiment of serious solicitude as he strove to remove from his own person and his son's the signs of their tramp over heavy roads and through wet fields. He scraped the mud off Bibi's bare legs and feet with a stick and carefully removed all traces from his heavy brogans. Then, prepared for the worst—the meeting with an over-scrupulous housewife, they entered cautiously at the back door.

32   Calixta was preparing supper. She had set the table and was dripping coffee at the hearth. She sprang up as they came in.

33   "Oh, Bobinôt! You back! My! but I was uneasy. W'ere you been during the rain? An' Bibi? he ain't wet? he ain't hurt?" She had clasped Bibi and was kissing him effusively. Bobinôt's explanations and apologies which he had been composing all along the way, died on his lips as Calixta felt him to see if he were dry, and seemed to express nothing but satisfaction at their safe return.

34   "I brought you some shrimps, Calixta," offered Bobinôt, hauling the can from his ample side pocket and laying it on the table.

35   "Shrimps! Oh, Bobinôt! you too good fo' anything!" and she gave him a smacking kiss on the check that resounded. "*J'vous réponds,* we'll have a feas' tonight! umph-umph!"

36   Bobinôt and Bibi began to relax and enjoy themselves, and when the three seated themselves at table they laughed much and so loud that anyone might have heard them as far away as Laballière's.

IV

37   Alcée Laballière wrote to his wife, Clarisse, that night. It was a loving letter, full of tender solicitude. He told her not to hurry back, but if she and the babies liked it at Biloxi, to stay a month longer. He was getting on nicely; and though he missed them, he was willing to bear the separation a while longer—realizing that their health and pleasure were the first things to be considered.

V

38   As for Clarisse, she was charmed upon receiving her husband's letter. She and the babies were doing well. The society was agreeable; many of her old friends and acquaintances were at the bay. And the first free breath since her marriage seemed to restore the pleasant liberty of her maiden days. Devoted as she was to her husband, their intimate conjugal life was something which she was more than willing to forego for a while.

39   So the storm passed and everyone was happy.

ACTIVITY 5

DIRECTIONS: Read the following passages, and answer the questions that follow. Continue to use inferences, when needed, to draw logical conclusions.

EYE ON VOCABULARY

When reading each of the following passages, take note of any unfamiliar words you come across. List them and their definitions in your notebook or on note cards. Use the context, word parts, or the dictionary to determine their meanings. After the completion of each passage, your instructor will ask to see your notebook or note cards and may discuss key words in class.

1

Killing Animals
Raising of Fenced-In Quarry for "Hunters" Spawns a Debate

Alfred Lubrano

1   Beer was waiting. Now was the killing time.

2   "I wanna peg one of these babies and get to my Silver Bullet," Rex Perysian shouted, fitting an arrow into his crossbow.

3   The beefy redhead and his four buddies arranged themselves in a semicircle around an animal feeder in a clearing at the Renegade Ranch Hunting Preserve.

4   In the frigid nowhere of northern Michigan, the 300-acre ranch is a fenced patch of snow and jack pines stocked with buffalo, exotic deer and other trophy animals that can be killed for a price. Today, the men—dressed in camouflage and sporting walkie-talkies—were shooting for Russian boars, normally $450 per head, marked down to $350.

5   To help the hunt, the ranch owner's son chased a snorting black line of boars along an animal trail toward the boars' breakfast bin, and the poised arrows.

6   Hiding behind a tree, Perysian fired first, hitting the first boar in line in its hindquarters. The 250-pound animal writhed and squealed as the whizzing arrow pierced skin and muscle with a muffled whack. The boar hobbled up a ridge toward an 8-foot fence, staining the snow with its blood.

7   Unable to escape, the animal cried, startling three rams out of a stand of trees. Perysian delivered a second arrow, then a third, both from closer than 10 feet. The boar shuddered and twitched, then lay still, four minutes after the first arrow hit.

8   "I was pumpin', man," Perysian, 31, a commercial-sign installer from Michigan, said into the camcorder his buddy pointed at him. "The first arrow was high. The second hit liver. The third took lung. I like it."

9   Perysian stood astride the boar and, after cleaning blood off its nose, lifted its head by the ears for the camera. "I'll grab it like I grab my women," he told his pals.

10   Then Perysian dropped the animal's head and bellowed into the woods, boasting that the kill had sexually aroused him. His voice echoed in the woods and frightened the rams, who ran off. In the next 30 minutes, three more boars would go down at Renegade.

11   They're known pejoratively as "canned hunts," a different kind of killing experience.

12   People without the time, ability or inclination to spend days in the woods tracking trophy-quality animals visit fenced-in places like Renegade to bag their prey.

13   "It's like taking a gun to the zoo," said Michael Carlton, a former hunting writer who visited the fenced-in Stony Fork Hunts in Wellsboro, Pa., 25 years ago, then vowed never to hunt again.

14   The hunts are fomenting national debate. Animal-rights activists are appalled. Members of pro-hunting groups that advocate "ethical," non-fenced hunting label the hunts "despicable." Meanwhile, breeders of animals used in the hunts defend their $100 million-a-year industry, saying it's their right to raise animals for whatever purposes they desire. Similarly, canned-hunt owners say no one can tell them what to do on their property. Even

Congress has weighed in, with a proposed bill that would criminalize the use of animals for such hunts.

15   What riles most opponents of canned hunts is how the deck seems stacked against the animals. Many such hunts guarantee a kill. Customers rarely need hunting licenses and may hunt any time of the year.

16   As at Renegade, many ranch owners set up hunting blinds where shooters can sit and await their prizes near the troughs where the animals eat. It's so easy to kill an animal that a few places, like the J.W. Hunting Preserve in Henryetta, Okla., specialize in wheelchair hunts. At Hunters Quest Game Ranch in southern Michigan, a disabled hunter who can't use his arms fires his rifle by pulling with his teeth on a leather strap attached to the trigger.

17   At canned hunts, many animals are accustomed to seeing and being fed by people daily, which means they may not flee hunters as truly wild animals would. If they do run, they can't get far: The ranches are surrounded by high fencing.

18   Sometimes, Pennsylvania Game Commission officials report, ranch owners drug animals to make them easier to handle. "At one hunt, they stood up a drugged sheep like a silhouette, and guys shot arrows at it and it didn't even flinch," said Jim Beard, assistant director of the commission's Bureau of Law Enforcement.

19   Some animals aren't given the chance to wander preserves—they are shot by hunters in—or just outside—their cages, Beard and others said.

20   Most of the animals in the camps are known as exotics—species of deer and antelope, sheep, goat, boars, gazelles, yaks and other creatures not native to the United States.

21   Many are grown on ranches and sold to hunting camps by people like Bill Dyroff, an Austin, Pa., math teacher who found that raising fallow deer for hunts is more profitable than raising cattle. "Only people who don't put pork chops on their plates can criticize," he asserted.

22   Other animals are believed to come from circuses and—less frequently—from zoos.

23   Canned hunts are legal in 39 states, including Pennsylvania, which is believed by the Humane Society to be among four states that have the most hunting preserves. The Humane Society estimates that Texas has more than half of the nation's 1,000 hunting preserves, although no one knows the exact number. The hunts are outlawed in 11 states, including New Jersey.

24   Lately, there's been movement to make the hunting of captive exotics illegal everywhere. Two bills being considered by the U.S. House of Representatives and the Senate would prohibit the transport and possession of exotics held in captivity on a ranch with fewer than 1,000 acres for "purposes of allowing the killing ... of that animal for entertainment or the collection of a trophy."

25   Canned hunts are so controversial, many "legitimate" hunters rail against them.

26   "It's cheating," said Lark Ritchie, a Cree Indian who guides hunts in northern Ontario. "The men involved do it to show off [their manhood], for status. There's a lot of 'hunters' I call killers."

27   Some believe canned hunts violate the widely held hunting ethic of "fair chase," which demands that a hunter pursue and take wild game in a manner that doesn't afford him improper or unfair advantage.

28   The Boone and Crockett Club, a hunting and conservation organization founded by Teddy Roosevelt that keeps track of wild-game hunting records (biggest antlers, widest

head) won't allow the entry of any animal taken in a hunting preserve into its books. Fences, club members say, render the chase unfair.

29   The National Rifle Association's federal lobbyist, Heather Wingate, said, "We are not in favor of canned hunts." Still, the NRA is opposing the proposed captive-exotics legislation, for fear it could lead to restrictions on all forms of hunting.

30   While Perysian went after the first boar at Renegade, 25-year-old Eric Heiss aimed for the second.

31   "I never shot an animal before," said Heiss, who works for a Michigan chemical company. His eyes were wide, he spoke rapidly. "But I shot an artery with the first arrow. You can see the blood. The second shot slashed heart and lung. I was more scared than anything. But it was a rush."

32   Beaming for the camcorder, Heiss said to his buddies: "I used to raise hogs for the state fair. I once won a blue ribbon." He paused, allowing the irony to float away. "Oh, well. How's my hair?"

33   A ranch hand came by to gut the animal, pulling its internal organs into a pile. The hunters told Heiss to sit astride his boar and lift up its head for the camera, as Perysian had.

34   "Poor thing, abusing it like this," Heiss suddenly said.

35   Jim Kurdziel, the videographer, was puzzled by the remark: "You shoot him, then you feel bad?"

36   As the men spoke, vapor from the boar's newly hollowed body cavity wafted into the freezing air, like the smoke from a barbecue.

37   Some hunters feel that hunting on game ranches is a perversion of a noble American sport.

38   "I feel most alive when I'm hunting," said the Rev. Theodore Vitali, chairman of the philosophy department at St. Louis University, an avid hunter, and a member of the Boone and Crockett Club. But Father Vitali finds "canned hunts despicable."

39   "I'm celebrating life. There is no life without death. When I kill an animal, my immediate response is gratitude to the animal and nature ... for giving me his life. It's the dialectic of life and death. There's no other game in town."

40   Asked whether killing animals is at odds with being a priest, Vitali, who mounts the heads of the animals he's killed on his walls to "honor them," said: "It's not against Christianity to kill, unless we take illicit pleasure in it."

41   His friend Dan Pletscher, a biologist at the University of Montana, said hunting was natural for a predator like man. Still, he added, "Predation is hard to understand because it is not pretty. But if you eat meat, you're part of the food chain. I always feel better because when I hunt, I know where it comes from."

Newark (N.J.) Star-Ledger, February 11, 1996, pp. 39–40

COMPREHENSION QUESTIONS

1. What is the topic of the passage?

2. What is the central message of the passage?

3. Determine what is at issue. What is your initial personal viewpoint?

4. Distinguish among opposing viewpoints, and provide the rationale for each.

5. Think carefully about the viewpoints. Express a personal viewpoint, and give the reasons why you favor it. Does it differ from your initial personal viewpoint? Why or why not?

6. Write a few paragraphs *in support of the viewpoint that you do* not *favor.*

THOUGHT AND DISCUSSION QUESTIONS

1. Would you ever participate in a "canned hunt"? Why or why not?

2. What can you infer from the article regarding Rex Perysian's view of women? Why? Can you infer that those who participate in "canned hunts" have a similar view of women? Why or why not?

3. How do you interpret the statement "Only people who don't put pork chops on their plates can criticize" (paragraph 21)?

4. List any questions that came to mind while you were reading this selection, and be prepared to discuss possible answers to them.

2

An "Amos 'n' Andy" Christmas

Henry Louis Gates Jr.

1   The Christmas season—that perilous time between Thanksgiving indigestion and midnight Mass on Christmas Eve—is an emotional gauntlet for me. It's a month of almost irresistible appeal for "essential" items that I can't afford and could easily have done without—followed by the sticker shock of credit card statements after New Year's. Besides, I find relentless holiday cheer inexpressibly depressing.

2   It wasn't always so.

3   Last year, determined to recapture the warm glow of childhood memories, I decided to spend Christmas back home in Piedmont, the West Virginia village in the Allegheny Mountains where I spent my first 18 Christmases.

4   It was a hard sell with my two daughters, who are 12 and 14 years old. No manual for parenting ever prepares you for the battle of wills when you try to persuade adolescents to spend a vacation away from their friends. Reason soon fails, leaving only the recourse of the desperate: "Because I say so, that's why." (One of the cruelest features of parenthood is the gradual discovery that your children have lives—their own lives.) "Going back to Piedmont is like traveling in a time machine," Liza, the younger child, remarked tartly. "A time machine to nowhere." The cruelty of youth!

5   Walking with my wife, Sharon Adams, and daughters down the main drag, Ashfield Street, which resembles those frontier sets you see in bad Westerns, I sorted through my abundant reserves of nostalgia to find my happiest Christmas memory.

6   As we passed what used to be the five-and-ten-cent store—it's now a warehouse—I remembered Christmas 1956, when I was 6 years old. That year, my father invited me to "ring the bell" for the Salvation Army sidewalk appeal, installed between the two double doors of the five-and-dime. Although it meant standing in the snow, half-frozen, I enjoyed myself—more because my father kept me supplied with hot cocoa than because shoppers were tossing money into the red kettle.

7   I was gulping my umpteenth cup of cocoa when an old black man walked by. His name was Mr. Smoke Clagett. "Evenin', Mr. Smoke," my father said. "How's it going today?"

8   "White man still in the lead," Mr. Smoke mumbled as he tossed a quarter into the kettle, then shuffled off through the snow.

9   "What's that mean, Daddy?" I blurted. My father laughed.

10   "He always says that," he replied. "I'll explain later." I don't know that he ever did; he must have realized I was bound to figure it out on my own one day. We had other things on our mind just then.

11   Back home, while I was still shivering and about drowned in all that hot chocolate, my parents consoled me by letting me and my older brother open one present early. We picked a big box, ripped open the wrapping paper to find a record player and a package of 45's that came with it. While my brother sang "The Great Pretender" along with the Platters, his arms spread wide and his eyes closed, I tried to puzzle out what kind of thrill Fats Domino had found up on Blueberry Hill.

12   But the big event of Christmas Eve was always the "Amos 'n' Andy" Christmas television episode, "Andy Plays Santa Claus." We watched it on a 12-inch set, which seemed mammoth in those days.

13   The episode opens with the miserly Kingfish visiting his friends' homes, pulling out a Christmas card, reading it out loud, then leaving. "I just bought one," he explains, proud of his thrift, "and I goin' around readin' it."

14   But what really captivated me was that in the all-black world of Amos 'n' Andy's Harlem, there was an all-black department store, owned and operated by black attendants for a black clientele, whose children could sit on the lap of a black Santa Claus—even if that Santa was a red-robed and white-bearded Andy (that's Andrew H. Brown to you). Andy had taken the job late on Christmas Eve just so he could buy a present for Amos's daughter, Arbadella: an expensive talking doll, which Amos "just couldn't afford this year."

15   And then I saw it. As the camera panned across an easel and paint set (marked $5.95) and a $14.95 perambulator set, there in the heart of Santa Claus Land, perched high on the display shelf, was Arbadella's talking doll. She was wearing a starched, white fluffy dress, made all the brighter by contrast with the doll baby's gleaming black skin. A black doll! The first I'd ever seen.

16   How fortunate those people in Harlem are, I thought. Not only do they have their own department stores; those department stores sell black dolls! My cousins had about a zillion dolls, but none of them black, brown or even yellow. You could bet your bottom dollar that Piedmont's five-and-ten would stock no such item. That Arbadella was one lucky little girl. And Andy Brown was not as dumb as he looked.

17   Last Christmas, in Piedmont, I found myself struggling against the gravitational force of family and time, feeling drawn into the same old family roles, helplessly watching the re-emergence of "little Skippy" Gates as we assembled for dinner with so many aunts, uncles and cousins that our children needed a scorecard to tell the players.

18   Somehow childhood anxieties were easier to tap than childhood merriment. "Have you washed your hands?" Uncle Harry asked me as we sat down, as if I were still 6. I realized that to him I would always be stuck in a time zone of ancient Christmases. Then I remembered our collection of "Amos 'n' Andy" videotapes and decided to show it to the girls.

19   While the dishes drip-dried in the kitchen, I set up the VCR and told Liza and Maggie to take off their CD headphones and discover that marvelous world of warmth and solidarity that makes the "Amos 'n' Andy" Christmas show such a rare and poignant memory. I found myself laughing so hard at Kingfish's malapropisms and Andy's gullibility that it took me a while to realize that I was laughing alone.

20   They'll get it—eventually—I thought. Just wait until they see Arbadella's doll and the scene when Amos tucks his daughter in bed and teaches her the Lord's Prayer while the kindhearted Andy sneaks the doll under the Christmas tree.

21   So how did these two post-modernists, reared on "A Very Brady Christmas," Kwanzaa festivals, multicultural Barbies and a basement full of black dolls with names like Kenya and Kianja, respond to my desperate effort to drag them down my memory lane?

22   "It was garbage," Liza pronounced, to my disbelief. Maggie volunteered, "Fake, pathetic and stupid." Liza added: "No 8-year-old's gonna lay there while their father recites them the Lord's Prayer. Yeah, Amos, cut the prayer stuff."

23   Then Maggie demanded, "Why can't we watch *Ernest Saves Christmas?*"—a 1988 movie for children about a goofy white Florida cabdriver who helps to find Santa's successor.

24   My father, who had entered the room near the end of the program, listened quietly to this aftermath. "Looks like the white man's still in the lead," he said.

New York Times, December 23, 1994

COMPREHENSION QUESTIONS

1. What is the topic of the passage?

2. What is the central message of the passage?

3. Determine what is at issue. What is your initial personal viewpoint?

4. Distinguish among opposing viewpoints, and provide the rationale for each.

5. Think carefully about the viewpoints. Express a personal viewpoint, and give the reasons why you favor it. Does it differ from your initial personal viewpoint? Why or why not?

6. Write a few paragraphs *in support of the viewpoint that you do not favor.*

THOUGHT AND DISCUSSION QUESTIONS

1. How do you interpret the statement "White man still in the lead" (paragraphs 8 and 24)?

2. Why did the author believe that Piedmont's five-and-ten would not stock black dolls?

3. Relate the following statement to the article: "The more things change, the more they stay the same." What things changed? What things stayed the same?

4. Was the author wrong to make his children go back with him to Piedmont for Christmas? Why or why not? What would you have done? Why?

5. List any questions that came to mind while you were reading this selection, and be prepared to discuss possible answers to them.

3
Can We Become Caught in the Web?

Maia Szalavitz

1   I've lived and worked on the Internet for nine years now. At first, the online world threatened to engulf me. But now it has made possible a life I love and couldn't sustain any other way.

2   I have an intense relationship with the Net. Because my boyfriend lives in England, it is our primary means of communicating. And since I work as a freelance journalist, I spend much of my time doing research on the Web and communicating with editors by e-mail. I'm online at least half my day.

3   When I began my wired life, the Web hadn't been invented. A friend founded a "bulletin board" in New York City in 1990 called Echo, and invited me to help start the conversation. I was immediately hooked by a world where what you write—not how you look or sound—is who you are. It had definite appeal to someone who has always found socializing difficult. And as a writer, I even had an advantage. My style online is conveyed by my sentences and syntax, not my fashion sense or physical appearance.

4   But there are some serious problems with an online existence. If you aren't careful to limit yourself, you can start to find human contact frightening—even phone calls become scary. Computers do what you want for the most part, but life outside is noisy, unpredictable and crowded. Seeing friends comes to seem a chore; getting groceries an unwanted adventure.

5   The repetitive nature of online tasks—checking e-mail, searching for data, sending replies—has a soothing, ritualistic quality, somewhat like preparing and using drugs. The Net also offers druglike distractions: engaging in flame-fest arguments with people you will never meet, discussing topics you love but rarely get a chance to share in real life. You write, but don't feel isolated as your words generate near-instant responses. The sense of connection—whether true or false—is compellingly attractive.

6   Still, I wouldn't call my Internet use an addiction. As a former heroin and cocaine addict, I know that experience all too well. Addiction inherently moves you away from love and work. My relationship to the Internet is far more complex.

7   While heroin and cocaine failed to deliver what I thought they'd promised, the Internet lived up to its billing. For one, I don't know how people sustain long-distance relationships without it. My boyfriend and I use a chat program that allows us to see what the other is writing as we type. We usually spend at least an hour a day communicating this way. Many couples who live together don't spend that much time "listening" to each other.

8   In today's mobile world, the Net also provides community that geography sometimes can't. While many pundits claimed that the Web helped push the Columbine High School shooters to the edge, I figure that it may have prevented many other such situations. After all, outcast teens can now find friends online—without fear of ridicule or attack. I wish I'd had the Net when I felt there was no one in the world who understood me.

9   My sister's life has also been bettered by the Net. When Kira conceived her first child in 1995, she joined an online group of mothers around the world who were due to give birth in the same month. Over the years, they've shared the ups and downs of parenting. They've met in person only rarely.

10   When Kira posted about her profound postpartum depression the other mothers became concerned. Since Kira lives in Florida and most of her family is in New York, the list members offered to fly me down for support. Kira was so moved that she cried when she was told I was coming and how it had been arranged.

11   Her depression had made her feel that no one cared. Her husband's frequent relocation had given her little chance to set local roots. But online, she found companionship. And it wasn't limited to words on a screen: it was real, practical and vital.

12   Like anything else that is pleasurable, the Net can be misused. My boyfriend's first few years on the Net included a lot of 18-hour days online.

13   Such compulsive use can be harmful—but it is probably less so than many other distractions. People can and do use everything from methamphetamine to mountaineering to avoid doing what they should. If you can't face the world, you'll always find somewhere to hide. And even my boyfriend's Net overdose wasn't entirely negative: he now knows UNIX, Linux and other programs I can't even name and has started a Net-related business.

14   I think psychologists looking to treat "Internet addiction" and fear-mongering pundits hype the bad side of the Net for their own purposes: profits and ratings. What you find in the vast chaos of the Web is mainly what you choose to look for. If you don't look for trouble, chances are, you won't find it.

Newsweek, December 6, 1999, p. 11

COMPREHENSION QUESTIONS

1. What is the topic of the passage?
2. What is the central message of the passage?
3. Determine what is at issue. What is your initial personal viewpoint?
4. Distinguish among opposing viewpoints, and provide the rationale for each.
5. Think carefully about the viewpoints. Express a personal viewpoint, and give the reasons why you favor it. Does it differ from your initial personal viewpoint? Why or why not?
6. Write a few paragraphs *in support of the viewpoint that you do* not *favor.*

THOUGHT AND DISCUSSION QUESTIONS

1. In your view, is the Internet addictive? Why or why not?
2. Can one find companionship online? Why or why not?
3. Do you agree with the author when she states, "If you can't face the world, you'll always find somewhere to hide"? Why or why not?
4. Is it safe to infer that the author believes that couples living together do not communicate enough? Why or why not?

5. Is the author on safe ground when she concludes, "I think psychologists looking to treat 'Internet addiction' and fear-mongering pundits hype the bad side of the Net for their own purposes: profits and ratings." Why or why not?

6. List any questions that came to mind while you were reading this selection, and be prepared to discuss possible answers to them.

4

Body Piercing and Tattooing: Risks to Health

1   One look around college campuses and other enclaves for young people reveals a trend that, while not necessarily new, has been growing in recent years. We're talking, of course, about body piercing and tattooing, also referred to as forms of "body art." For decades, tattoos appeared to be the sole propriety of bikers, military guys, and general rough-necks; and in many people's eyes, they represented the rougher, seedier part of society. Body piercing, on the other hand, was virtually nonexistent in our culture except for pierced ears, which didn't really appear until the latter part of the twentieth century. Even then, pierced ears were limited, for the most part, to women. Various forms of body embell-ishment, or body art, however, can be traced throughout human history when people "dressed themselves up" to attract attention or be viewed as acceptable by their peers. Examinations of cultures throughout the world, both historic and contemporary, provide evidence of the use of body art as a medium of self- and cultural expression. Ancient cultures often used body piercing as a mark of royalty or elitism. Egyptian pharaohs under-went rites of passage by piercing their navels. Roman soldiers demonstrated manhood by piercing their nipples.

2   But why the surge in popularity in current society, particularly among young peo-ple? Today, young and old alike are getting their ears and bodies pierced in record num-bers, in such places as the eyebrows, tongues, lips, noses, navels, nipples, genitals, and just about any place possible. Many people view the trend as a fulfillment of a desire for self-expression, as this University of Wisconsin-Madison student points out:

> "... The nipple [ring] was one of those things that I did as a kind of empow-erment, claiming my body as my own and refuting the stereotypes that people have about me.... The tattoo was kind of a lark and came along the same lines and I like it too.... [T]hey both give me a secret smile."

3   Whatever the reason, tattoo artists are doing a booming business in both their tra-ditional artistry of tattooing as well as in the "art" of body piercing. Amidst the "oohing" and "aahing" over the latest artistic additions, however, the concerns over health risks from these procedures have been largely ignored. Despite the warnings from local health offi-cials and federal agencies, the popularity of piercings and tattoos has grown.

4   The most common health-related problems associated with tattoos and body pierc-ing include skin reactions, infections, and scarring. The average healing times for piercings depend on the size of the insert, location, and the person's overall health. Facial and tongue piercings tend to heal more quickly than piercings of areas not commonly exposed to open

air or light and which are often teeming with bacteria, such as the genitals. Because the hands are great germ transmitters, "fingering" of pierced areas poses a significant risk for infection.

5   Of greater concern, however, is the potential transmission of dangerous pathogens that any puncture of the human body exacerbates. The use of unsterile needles—which can cause serious infections and can transmit HIV, hepatitis B and C, tetanus, and a host of other diseases—poses a very real risk. Body piercing and tattooing are performed by body artists, unlicensed "professionals" who generally have learned their trade from other body artists. Laws and policies regulating body piercing and tattooing vary greatly by state. While some states don't allow tattoo and body-piercing parlors, others may regulate them carefully, and still others provide few regulations and standards by which parlors have to abide. Standards for safety usually include minimum age of use, standards of sanitation, use of aseptic techniques, sterilization of equipment, informed risks, instructions for skin care, record keeping, and recommendations for dealing with adverse reactions. Because of the varying degree of standards regulating this business and the potential for transmission of dangerous pathoges, anyone who receives a tattoo, body piercing, or permanent make-up tattoo cannot donate blood for one year.

6   Anyone who does opt for tattooing or body piercing should remember the following:

- Look for clean, well-lit work areas, and ask about sterilization procedures.
- Before having the work done, watch the artist at work. Tattoo removal is expensive and often undoable. Make sure the tattoo is one you can live with.
- Right before piercing or tattooing, the body area should be carefully sterilized and the artist should wear new latex gloves and touch nothing else while working.
- Packaged, sterilized needles should be used only once and then discarded. A piercing gun should not be used because it cannot be sterilized properly.
- Only jewelry made of noncorrosive metal, such as surgical stainless steel, niobium, or solid 14-karat gold, is safe for new piercing.
- Leftover tattoo ink should be discarded after each procedure.
- If any signs of pus, swelling, redness, or discoloration persist, remove the piercing object and contact a physician.

Rebecca J. Donatelle, *Health: The Basics,* 4th ed., pp. 322–323

COMPREHENSION QUESTIONS

1. What is the topic of the passage?
2. What is the central message of the passage?
3. Determine what is at issue. What is your initial personal viewpoint?
4. Distinguish among opposing viewpoints, and provide the rationale for each.
5. Think carefully about the viewpoints. Express a personal viewpoint, and give the reasons why you favor it. Does it differ from your initial personal viewpoint? Why or why not?
6. Write a few paragraphs *in support of the viewpoint that you do* not *favor.*

THOUGHT AND DISCUSSION QUESTIONS

1. What does the author mean by "'oohing' and 'aahing' over the latest artistic additions"?

2. In your view, why have tattoos and body piercings become popular among young people? Do you agree with those who assert that it is done only for purposes of showing off? Why or why not?

3. If you had a thirteen-year-old son, would you permit him to be pierced or tattooed? Why or why not? If you had a thirteen-year-old daughter, would you permit her to be pierced or tattooed? Why or why not? If your answers to the two questions above are different, explain why.

4. Is it safe to conclude that the author is opposed to tattoos and body piercing? Why or why not?

5. List any questions that came to mind while you were reading this selection, and be prepared to discuss possible answers to them.

5

Macbeth as Hero

Michael Spinter
Professor Nelson
English 211
May 6, 2000

1   When we think of a tragic hero, we probably think of a fundamentally sympathetic person who is entangled in terrifying circumstances and who ultimately dies, leaving us with a sense that the world has suffered a loss. For instance, Hamlet must avenge his father's murder, and in doing so he performs certain actions that verge on the wrongful, such as behaving cruelly to his beloved Ophelia and his mother and killing Rosencrantz and Guildenstern; but we believe that Hamlet is fundamentally a decent man and that Denmark is the poorer for his death.

2   Macbeth, however, is different. He kills King Duncan and Duncan's grooms, kills Banquo, attempts to kill Banquo's son, and finally kills Lady Macduff and her children and her servants. True, the only people whom he kills with his own hands are Duncan and the grooms—the other victims are destroyed by hired murderers—but clearly Macbeth is responsible for all of the deaths. He could seem an utterly unscrupulous, sneaking crook rather than a tragic hero for whom a reader can feel sympathy.

3   Certainly most of the other characters in the play feel no sympathy for Macbeth. Macduff calls him a "hell-kite," or a hellish bird of prey (4.3.217), a "tyrant" (5.7.14), a "hell-hound" (5.8.3), and a "coward" (5.8.23). To Malcolm he is a "tyrant" (4.3.12), "devilish Macbeth" (4.3.117), and a "butcher" (5.8.69). Readers and spectators can hardly deny the truth of these characterizations. And yet Macbeth does not seem merely villainous. It would be going too far to say that we always sympathize with him, but we are deeply interested in him

and do not dismiss him in disgust as an out-and-out monster. How can we account for his hold on our feelings? At least five factors play their parts.

4   First, Macbeth is an impressive military figure. In the first extended description of Macbeth, the Captain speaks of "brave Macbeth—well he deserves that name" (1.2.16). The Captain tells how Macbeth valiantly fought on behalf of his king, and King Duncan exclaims, "O valiant cousin! Worthy gentleman!" (1.2.2). True, Macbeth sometimes cringes, such as when he denies responsibility for Banquo's death: "Thou canst not say I did it" (3.4.51). But throughout most of the play, we see him as a bold and courageous soldier.

5   Of course, Macbeth's ability as a soldier is not enough by itself to explain his hold on us. A second reason is that he is in some degree a victim—a victim of his wife's ambition and a victim of the witches. Yes, he ought to see through his wife's schemes, and he ought to resist the witches, just as Banquo resists them, but surely Macbeth is partly tricked into crime. He is responsible, but we can imagine ourselves falling as he does, and his status as a victim arouses our sympathy.

6   A third source of his hold on us is that although Macbeth engages in terrible deeds, he almost always retains his conscience. For instance, after he murders Duncan he cannot sleep at night. When he tells Lady Macbeth that he has heard a voice saying, "Macbeth does murder sleep" (2.2.35), she ridicules him, but the voice is prophetic: he is doomed to sleepless nights. We in the audience are glad that Macbeth is tormented by his deed, since it shows that he knows he has done wrong and that he still has some decent human feelings.

7   A fourth reason why we retain some sympathy for Macbeth is that he eventually loses all of his allies, even his wife, and he stands before us a lonely, guilt-haunted figure. On this point, scene 2 of act 3 is especially significant. When Lady Macbeth asks Macbeth why he keeps to himself (line 8), he confides something of the mental stress that he is undergoing. But when she asks, "What's to be done?" (44), he cannot bring himself to tell her that he is plotting the deaths of Banquo and Fleance. Instead of further involving his wife, the only person with whom he might still have a human connection, Macbeth says, "Be innocent of the knowledge, dearest chuck [...]" (45). The word <u>chuck</u>, an affectionate form of <u>chick</u>, shows warmth and intimacy that are touching, but his refusal or his inability to confide in his wife and former partner in crime shows how fully isolated he is from all human contact. We cannot help feeling some sympathy for him.

8   Finally, Macbeth holds our interest, instead of disgusting us, because he speaks so wonderfully. The greatness of his language compels us to listen to him with rapt attention. Some speeches are very familiar, such as "My way of life / Is fall'n into the sear, the yellow leaf [...]" (5.3.23–24) and "Tomorrow and tomorrow and tomorrow / Creeps in this petty pace from day to day [...]" (5.5.19–20). But almost every speech Macbeth utters is equally memorable, from his first, "So foul and fair a day I have not seen" (1.3.38), to his last:

> Before my body
> I throw my warlike shield. Lay on, Macduff:
> And damned be him that first cries, "Hold, enough!"
>
> (5.8.32–34)

9   If we stand back and judge Macbeth only by what he does, we of course say that he is a foul murderer. But if we read the play attentively, or witness a performance, and give due weight to Macbeth's bravery, his role as a victim, his tormented conscience, his

isolation, and especially his moving language, we do not simply judge him. Rather, we see that, villain though he is, he is not merely awful but also awesome.

Work Cited

Shakespeare, William. <u>The Tragedy of Macbeth</u>. Ed. Sylvan Barnet. Rev. ed. New York: NAL, 1987.

H. Ramsey Fowler et al., *The Little Brown Handbook*, 8th ed., pp. 814–816

COMPREHENSION QUESTIONS

1. What is the topic of the passage?

2. What is the central message of the passage?

3. Determine what is at issue. What is your initial personal viewpoint?

4. Distinguish among opposing viewpoints, and provide the rationale for each.

5. Think carefully about the viewpoints. Express a personal viewpoint, and give the reasons why you favor it. Does it differ from your initial personal viewpoint? Why or why not?

6. Write a few paragraphs *in support of the viewpoint that you do not favor.*

THOUGHT AND DISCUSSION QUESTIONS

1. Is it safe to conclude that the passage above was written by a student? Why or why not?

2. In your view, does the author believe that Macbeth is a "tragic hero?" Why or why not?

3. Name two or three people *you* believe to be "tragic heroes," and explain why you consider them as such.

4. Is it safe to infer that the author believes that Macbeth, like Hamlet, "is fundamentally a decent man?" Why or why not?

5. List any questions that came to mind while you were reading this selection, and be prepared to discuss possible answers to them.

LOOKING BACK

Summarize and/or paraphrase the most important points you learned from this chapter, and determine how they can be put to use in other classes. Be prepared to discuss with your classmates what you have written.

THINK AGAIN!

The following passage came from a psychology textbook. After reading it carefully, use your inference skills to figure out what suggestion the colleague made to remedy the backward curtain problem without having to replace the motor.

The Case of the Backward Curtain

A colleague of mine was in the hospital suffering from a bad back. He was confined to his bed and was dependent upon others to do many things for him. One of the few tasks he could do for himself was to open and close the curtains in his room by pressing buttons on a console beside his bed. But when he pressed the button labeled "Open," the curtains closed; pressing "Close" opened the curtains. A hospital maintenance man was called to fix the mechanism. He defined the problem as a defective motor that controlled the curtain and began to disconnect the motor when my colleague suggested, "Couldn't we look at this problem differently?"

Anthony F. Grasha, *Practical Applications of Psychology,* p. 93

The Dashing Detective

Remember to follow these steps:

- first, read the narrative and all the questions
- second, examine the picture carefully
- third, answer the questions in the order they appear, and come up with the solution

Have fun!

Footsteps in the Dark

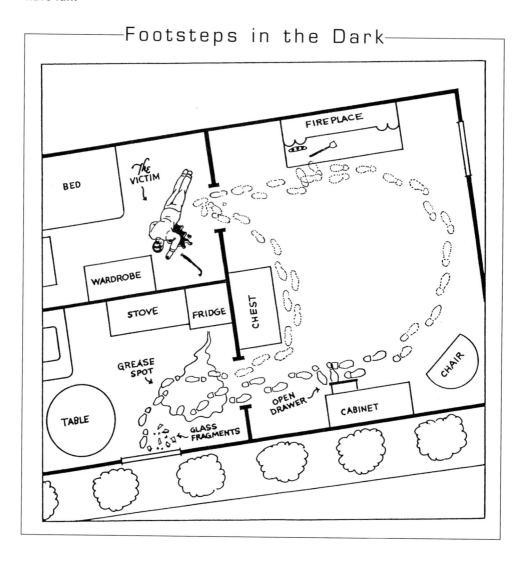

Detective Mercymee's sketch of C. T. Jenny's bungalow is here reproduced. Jenny, a coin collector, had a valuable collection, which is now missing. He was killed by a savage blow from a poker. The footsteps, made by traversing the grease spot, matched the shoes of a cat burglar known as Meeow. Meeow admitted having been in Jenny's house, but when interrogated he denied killing Jenny and made the statements copied down here. By examining the sketch, can you decide whether Meeow told the truth and was innocent of the Jenny homicide?

Questions

Do you think that the following statements are true, false, or that there is insufficient evidence to support any conclusions?

1. "I busted the kitchen window to get in."   ☐ True   ☐ False   ☐ Insufficient evidence

2. "I stop at the kitchen door to give the joint the once-over, but I don't see nothing."
   ☐ True   ☐ False   ☐ Insufficient evidence

3. "I walk over to the cabinet and yank open a drawer."   ☐ True   ☐ False
   ☐ Insufficient evidence

4. "I circle the room to kind of see what's what."   ☐ True   ☐ False   ☐ Insufficient evidence

5. "In front of the fireplace I stop cold."   ☐ True   ☐ False   ☐ Insufficient evidence

6. "Because I see a dead body lying there in the next room."   ☐ True   ☐ False
   ☐ Insufficient evidence

7. "I want nothing to do with what I see, so I beat it straight out."   ☐ True   ☐ False
   ☐ Insufficient evidence

8. Do you think that Meeow killed Jenny?   ☐ Yes   ☐ No

Lawrence Treat, *Crime and Puzzlement*, pp. 26—27

Name _____   Date _____

MASTERY TEST 6–1

DIRECTIONS: Answer the questions and fill in the blanks. Use your inference skills to answer questions 4 through 8.

1. A very high level comprehension of written material requiring interpretation and evaluation skills is called

   a. critical thinking
   b. inference
   c. literal comprehension
   d. critical reading
   e. none of the above

2. Inferences are _____ guesses by which we go beyond what is

   _____ in order to fill in informational _____, come to

   _____ conclusions, and make sense of the _____ around us.

3. Inferences should be based on _____, _____, and

   _____.

4. What gifts are being referred to on the sign in the photograph? How do you interpret the rest of the message?

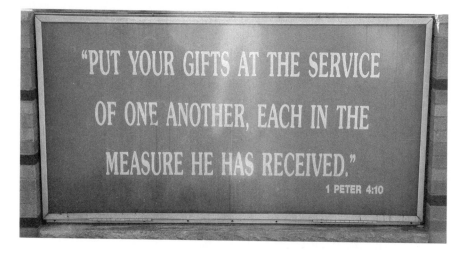

"PUT YOUR GIFTS AT THE SERVICE OF ONE ANOTHER, EACH IN THE MEASURE HE HAS RECEIVED."

1 PETER 4:10

_____

_____

_____

5. Can you figure out what is being carried by the truck in the photograph?

_____

_____

_____

_____

_____

6. What war is being discussed in the following passage?

1   The war affected black Americans in many ways. Several factors operated to improve their lot. One was their own growing tendency to demand fair treatment. Another was the reaction of Americans to Hitler's barbaric treatment of millions of Jews, which compelled millions of white citizens to reexamine their views about race. If the nation expected blacks to risk their lives for the common good, how could it continue to treat them as second-class citizens? Black leaders pointed out the inconsistency between fighting for democracy abroad and ignoring it at home. "We want democracy in Alabama," the NAACP announced, and this argument too had some effect on white thinking.

2   Blacks in the armed forces were treated more fairly than they had been in World War I. They were enlisted for the first time in the air force and the marines, and they were given more responsible positions in the army and navy. The army commissioned its first black general. Some 600 black pilots won their wings. Altogether about a million served, about half of them overseas.

John A. Garraty, *A Short History of the American Nation*, p. 473

7. Read the passage; then answer the questions following it.

As a group, they are a very special breed apart from the rest of us. They have one goal on their minds from the moment they wake up in the morning until the moment they go to sleep at night. Although promises make up a big part of their speeches, those promises are seldom kept. Their remarks are often couched in glowing terms that are difficult to understand but always focused on the things they think we want to hear. We can't trust them! It has been that way for centuries, and it is not going to change any time soon.

a. What group is the writer discussing?
b. What goal is the writer referring to?
c. Is the writer optimistic or pessimistic about the future?
d. Is the passage mostly fact or mostly opinion?

8. Read the passage; then answer the questions following it.

I have been here for so many years that I can barely remember what it is like on the outside. The fight has been long and hard, but it all comes to an end at midnight. Although there is one last chance, that chance now seems slim at best. How I wish I could turn back the clock to that warm day in July when everything went up in smoke. If only I had ignored what he did, it might have turned out differently. Will God forgive me?

a. What is going to happen to the person in the passage?
b. What is her "one last chance"?
c. How did she get into this situation?
d. To whom is she speaking?

Name _____   Date _____

MASTERY TEST 6-2

DIRECTIONS: What is the central message of *all* the people quoted here?

1   **Diane:** I had a sinus infection, so I called one of the doctors on my HMO's list. When I checked in with the receptionist, she couldn't find my name on the computer, and she told me I'd have to pay. Since I had run out of the house with only $20 in my pocket, I argued with her a little. She summoned the doctor in charge of the entire clinic, the doctor I was supposed to see. He proceeded to tell me, in front of everyone, how he hated managed care and how my HMO owed him hundreds of thousands of dollars. Meanwhile I'm standing there with my head pounding, my sinuses clogged. I wanted to walk out and say, "Screw you and your clinic," but I knew I needed antibiotics. It made me feel so small and powerless.

2   **Cathleen:** I was pregnant and I started spotting, something that hadn't happened in my first pregnancy. It made me nervous, so I called my doctor's office, even though it wasn't during office hours. When she called me back she was clearly irritated that I had bothered her. She said. "Oh well, a lot of people miscarry at this stage, you had to have known that." She was very matter-of-fact. When I asked her what I could do, she told me if the bleeding got really heavy to call back and we could confirm the miscarriage with a sonogram. She was exasperated with my emotions.

3   **Cynthia:** I was going through infertility treatment. I didn't like the doctor very much, but he was highly recommended and there are continuous hormonal cycles involved, so it's hard to break away. One day he was inseminating me with my husband's sperm, and he said, "Now that's what I call a quickie." It was so disdainful I never went back. I gave up trying to have a baby for a year. It was just so offensive.

4   **Jerry:** My father was dying, supposedly of complications from diabetes, and I moved home to take care of him. I learned how to change IV's, I was dealing with a lot of body fluids. It was only later that I found out he had AIDS. His doctors knew he hadn't told me, knew I was doing all this stuff, but they never warned me about the risk of infection. I think under the circumstances that they should have told me *something.*

5   **Rebecca:** My mother had been pushing me to get a nose job. I didn't really think I needed one, but I went for the consultation anyway. She sent me to a family friend, a plastic surgeon. When I walked into his office, the first thing he said was, "What took you so long?" I felt that he disapproved of my imperfection, that any imperfection was an offense to his eye. He had a little God complex going. I blame myself because I didn't have the courage or self-esteem to say, "I'm out of here." I felt I was at his mercy. He knew how to prey on everything I was worried about with regard to my appearance.

6   **Joanne:** I was at the gynecologist's for the first time, being fitted for a diaphragm. I was uncomfortable, and I must have squirmed. The doctor was irritated. He said, "Would you sit still so I can examine you?" Then he told me I'd better go on the Pill because if I

couldn't sit still for an exam, I'd never be able to use a diaphragm. I was humiliated. He made me feel like a baby.

Elizabeth De Vita, "The Decline of the Doctor-Patient Relationship,"
American Health, June 1995, pp. 63–67, 105

_____

_____

_____

_____

Name _____   Date _____

MASTERY TEST 6-3

DIRECTIONS: First, read and think critically about the words to the following poem. Then, use your inference skills to identify the central message of the poem and interpret the meaning of each stanza.

Come With Me

Mark Hillringhouse

1   Don't go off shopping at the mall.
     You'll only curse yourself for getting stuck in so much traffic.
     You'll walk a mile just to find your car.
     No one will be around to help you.
     And you'll have to hold your stomach in
     just to fit into those new pants.
     When you get home all your purchases will look tawdry,
     and you'll only have to drive back to return everything.
     Come with me and instead we will spread a blanket
     over the long grass and lie on our backs
     and watch the orange leaves tumble under a blue sky.

2   Don't go running for high office.
     Politics are a poor nourishment for the tired soul.
     Come election you'll realize you'll be stumping every night
     shaking hands for a few meager votes.
     After losing, no one will remember your name.
     Let the city run itself, let others fight for a seat on the council.
     Come with me and together we will find a bar
     in a crowded city and spend the evenings there
     drinking and talking to strangers.

3   Don't go off and become a teacher,
     you'll only make yourself miserable.
     Come June you'll realize you'll be out working all summer
     just to make ends meet.
     When it's time for bed, you'll be up grading papers.
     The IRS will hit you over and over for new taxes
     and you'll never be able to save more than a week's pay.
     Come with me and together
     we will launch a boat and watch the ripples
     our oars make in the water as we row
     far, very far, away from shore.

4   Don't go off and become a poet,
    you'll only learn to regret it.
    Poetry is too solitary a craft for a lonely traveler.
    After years of trying you'll never attain greatness.
    Everything you write will pass into obscurity.
    Even your own family will suffer from your own lack of meaning.
    Let others climb over each other for a place at the podium,
    each one thinking his work better than the next.
    Up there the light is pale and the air is thin.
    Throw away your notebooks and pen
    and forget about the immortals.
    Come with me and together
    we will tilt our heads into the night air
    and laugh at the thousand brilliant stars.

Directions: First, read and think critically about the following short story. Then, without looking back at it, summarize and/or paraphrase the story in your notebook. Finally, use your inference skills first to identify the central message and then to determine the reasons why the boy said, "Thank you, m'am."

Thank You, Ma'm

Langston Hughes

1   She was a large woman with a large purse that had everything in it but hammer and nails. It had a long strap and she carried it slung across her shoulder. It was about eleven o'clock at night, and she was walking alone, when a boy ran up behind her and tried to snatch her purse. The strap broke with the single tug the boy gave it from behind. But the boy's weight, and the weight of the purse combined caused him to lose his balance so, instead of taking off full blast as he had hoped, the boy fell on his back on the sidewalk, and his legs flew up. The large woman simply turned around and kicked him right square in his blue jeaned sitter. Then she reached down, picked the boy up by his shirt front, and shook him until his teeth rattled.

2   After that the woman said, "Pick up my pocketbook, boy, and give it here."

3   She still held him. But she bent down enough to permit him to stoop and pick up her purse. Then she said, "Now ain't you ashamed of yourself?"

4   Firmly gripped by his shirt front, the boy said, "Yes'm."

5   The woman said, "What did you want to do it for?"

6   The boy said, "I didn't aim to."

7   She said, "You a lie!"

8   By that time two or three people passed, stopped, turned to look, and some stood watching.

9   "If I turn you loose, will you run?" asked the woman.

10   "Yes'm," said the boy.

11   "Then I won't turn you loose," said the woman. She did not release him.

12   "I'm very sorry, lady, I'm sorry," whispered the boy.

13   "Um-hum! And your face is dirty. I got a great mind to wash your face for you. Ain't you got nobody home to tell you to wash your face?"

14   "No'm," said the boy.

15   "Then it will get washed this evening," said the large woman starting up the street, dragging the frightened boy behind her.

16   He looked as if he were fourteen or fifteen, frail and willow-wild, in tennis shoes and blue jeans.

17   The woman said, "You ought to be my son. I would teach you right from wrong. Least I can do right now is to wash your face. Are you hungry?"

18   "No'm," said the being-dragged boy. "I just want you to turn me loose."

19   "Was I bothering *you* when I turned that corner?" asked the woman.

20   "No'm."

21   "But you put yourself in contact with *me*," said the woman. "If you think that that contact is not going to last awhile, you got another thought coming. When I get through with you, sir, you are going to remember Mrs. Luella Bates Washington Jones."

22   Sweat popped out on the boy's face and he began to struggle. Mrs. Jones stopped, jerked him around in front of her, put a half nelson about his neck, and continued to drag him up the street. When she got to her door, she dragged the boy inside, down a hall, and into a large kitchenette-furnished room at the rear of the house. She switched on the light and left the door open. The boy could hear other roomers laughing and talking in the large house. Some of their doors were open, too, so he knew he and the woman were not alone. The woman still had him by the neck in the middle of her room.

23   She said, "What is your name?"

24   "Roger," answered the boy.

25   "Then, Roger, you go to that sink and wash your face," said the woman, whereupon she turned him loose—at last. Roger looked at the door—looked at the woman—looked at the door—*and went to the sink.*

26   "Let the water run until it gets warm," she said. "Here's a clean towel."

27   "You gonna take me to jail?" asked the boy, bending over the sink.

28   "Not with that face, I would not take you nowhere," said the woman. "Here I am trying to get home to cook me a bite to eat and you snatch my pocketbook! Maybe you ain't been to your supper either, late as it be. Have you?"

29   "There's nobody home at my house," said the boy.

30   "Then we'll eat," said the woman. "I believe you're hungry—or been hungry—to try to snatch my pocketbook."

31   "I wanted a pair of blue suede shoes," said the boy.

32   "Well, you didn't have to snatch *my* pocketbook to get some suede shoes," said Mrs. Luella Bates Washington Jones. "You could of asked me."

33   "M'am?"

34   The water dripping from his face, the boy looked at her. There was a long pause. A very long pause. After he had dried his face and not knowing what else to do dried it again, the boy turned around, wondering what next. The door was open. He could make a dash for it down the hall. He could run, run, run, run, *run!*

35   The woman was sitting on the day-bed. After awhile she said, "I were young once and I wanted things I could not get."

36   There was another long pause. The boy's mouth opened. Then he frowned, but not knowing he frowned.

37   The woman said, "Uh-hum!" You thought I was going to say *but,* didn't you? You thought I was going to say, *but I didn't snatch people's pocketbooks.* Well, I wasn't going to say that." Pause. Silence. "I have done things, too, which I would not tell you, son—neither tell God, if he didn't already know. So you set down while I fix us something to eat. You might run that comb through your hair so you will look presentable."

38   In another corner of the room behind a screen was a gas plate and an icebox. Mrs. Jones got up and went behind the screen. The woman did not watch the boy to see if he was going to run now, nor did she watch her purse which she left behind her on the day-bed. But the boy took care to sit on the far side of the room where he thought she could easily see him out of the corner of her eye, if she wanted to. He did not trust the woman *not* to trust him. And he did not want to be mistrusted now.

39   "Do you need somebody to go to the store," asked the boy, "maybe to get some milk or something?"

40   "Don't believe I do," said the woman, "unless you just want sweet milk yourself. I was going to make cocoa out of this canned milk I got here."

41   "That will be fine," said the boy.

42   She heated some lima beans and ham she had in the icebox, made the cocoa, and set the table. The woman did not ask the boy anything about where he lived, or his folks, or anything else that would embarrass him. Instead, as they ate, she told him about her job in a hotel beauty-shop that stayed open late, what the work was like, and how all kinds of women came in and out, blondes, red-heads, and Spanish. Then she cut him a half of her ten-cent cake.

43   "Eat some more, son," she said.

44   When they were finished eating she got up and said, "Now, here, take this ten dollars and buy yourself some blue suede shoes. And next time, do not make the mistake of latching onto *my* pocketbook *nor nobody else's*—because shoes come by devilish like that will burn your feet. I got to get my rest now. But I wish you would behave yourself, son, from here on in."

45   She led him down the hall to the front door and opened it. "Good-night! Behave yourself, boy!" she said, looking out into the street.

46   The boy wanted to say something else other than, "Thank you, m'am," to Mrs. Luella Bates Washington Jones, but he couldn't do so as he turned at the barren stoop and looked back at the large woman in the door. He barely managed to say, "Thank you," before she shut the door. And he never saw her again.

CHAPTER 7
DISTINGUISHING BETWEEN FACTS AND OPINIONS

CHAPTER OUTLINE

THINK ABOUT IT!

Look carefully at photographs 1, 2, 3, and 5. Then for each, write a paragraph in your notebook in which you describe what you see in detail. What caption or title would you give each of the photographs?

After you have written your paragraphs and captions, read them carefully, and try to distinguish between the facts and your opinions. Discuss your conclusions with your classmates.

Is the central message of the sign in photograph 4 a fact or an opinion? Discuss your answer with your classmates.

1

2

3

4

5

CHAPTER OUTCOMES

After completing Chapter 7, you should be able to:

- Continue to apply the basic method for personal problem solving
- Define *fact* and *opinion*
- Define *unbiased*
- Distinguish between facts and opinions and understand why it is important to do so, particularly when dealing with problems and contemporary issues
- Continue to find topics and central messages in contemporary issue passages to determine what is at issue, distinguish among opposing viewpoints, and express personal viewpoints

Problem-Solving Exercise

Using your notebook, apply the first four steps of the basic method for personal problem-solving to the following hypothetical situation. Make sure to label clearly each step as you discuss what you would do. This situation is similar to a real-life one experienced by one of my students.

HYPOTHETICAL SITUATION

You are a single parent living alone with a 2-year-old child. This past September, you enrolled as a full-time college student with the hope of pursuing a career in social work so that you can make a better life for you and your son. So far, college has been a challenging but rewarding experience.

Because you have no immediate family living in this part of the country, you have to bring your son to a day care center while you attend classes. Although financial aid covers your books and tuition, you are forced to work at home as a typist for an agency to support the two of you. However, there never seems to be enough money to make ends meet.

Furthermore, it is very difficult to get either typing or schoolwork done with your son running around the apartment. Thus you are living under a great deal of stress, which is affecting your performance at school and your relationship with your child. You lose your temper often and yell at him constantly. Things have to change quickly.

WHY DISTINGUISH BETWEEN FACTS AND OPINIONS?

Read the list of ten statements below, and place an *O* next to the ones that you think are opinions, an *F* next to those that you think are facts.

1. Washington, D.C., which is the capital of the United States, is a beautiful city.
2. World War II was the last major war to be fought in the twentieth century.
3. The winters in Canada are really horrible because they are usually very cold.
4. Ronald Reagan, who was the fortieth president of the United States, was a wonderful leader.
5. The Berlin Wall, which separated East from West Berlin, has been taken down.
6. There are 50 states in the United States, and it is a widely accepted fact that Puerto Rico will become the fifty-first.
7. Experts tell us that the Mercedes-Benz is the best automobile on the market today.
8. Carbon monoxide is a poisonous gas that can be extremely deadly.
9. The United States is the most powerful country in the world.
10. Heart disease, which strikes people of all ages, can be caused by high blood pressure, smoking, and lack of exercise.

Now let's examine the responses.

Statement 1 combines both *fact* and *opinion* because Washington *is* the capital of the United States, but whether or not it is a beautiful city is a matter of opinion. Certainly, some people would agree that it is beautiful while others may not. It could depend on both the definition of the word *beautiful* and the other cities to which Washington is being compared.

Statement 2 is an *opinion* because it could be argued convincingly that there have been other major wars fought since World War II, including the one in Vietnam, which caused the loss of many American and Vietnamese lives. Furthermore, it really depends on one's definition of the word *major*. For example, does it mean many casualties, number of countries involved, or something else?

Statement 3 is a combination of *fact* and *opinion* because although it is true that the winters in Canada are usually very cold, some people would argue that cold does not necessarily make them horrible. For instance, many Canadians like cold weather because it enables them to earn a living or do things that they enjoy doing, such as skiing, skating, and playing hockey.

It is a fact that Ronald Reagan was the fortieth President of the United States, but not everyone is of the opinion that he was a wonderful leader. Thus statement 4 is also a combination of *fact* and *opinion*.

Statements 5, 8, and 10 are all *facts* that can be supported by checking various sources. They can be proved and are generally accepted by everyone.

Statement 6 is a combination of *fact* and *opinion*. Whereas the first part of the statement is obviously a fact, the second part is an opinion because it is a prediction and a matter of conjecture that Puerto Rico will become the fifty-first state. Also, the use of the word *fact* in the sentence does not necessarily prove that the information is indeed factual.

Statement 7 is an *opinion* for two reasons: First, the "experts" are not identified, so we do not know if they are reliable, and second, no data are presented that would indicate how the word *best* is being used in the sentence. For example, does it refer to economical gas mileage, reliability, extensive safety equipment, exceptional good looks, or all of those pluses taken together?

Finally, statement 9 is also an *opinion* because the meaning of the word *powerful* as used in the sentence is not clear. If it refers to military power, a strong case can be made for the accuracy of the statement, although some people would argue that as long as other countries possess nuclear weapons, no single country, including the United States, is all-powerful. By contrast, if it refers to economic power, more people might argue that the United States is indeed *not* the most powerful country in the world.

As you can see, it is sometimes not simple to distinguish between opinions and facts, yet if you expect to think and read critically, you must be able to separate fact from opinion as part of evaluating what you see, hear, and read. In other words, you should not automatically accept information without first considering its accuracy, its source, and the motivations of whoever is presenting it. Otherwise, you are in danger of accepting opinions as facts, and that could have a negative effect on the decisions you make in life. For example, you could end up taking the wrong course, choosing the wrong solution to a problem, accepting the wrong version of a story, buying the wrong product, dating the wrong person, or voting for the wrong candidate. Thus the cost of confusing facts and opinions can be quite substantial. Let's take a closer look at how to distinguish between them.

WHAT IS A FACT?

A **fact** is *something that can be or has been proved, verified, or confirmed in an unbiased manner*. As you know, *unbiased* means "evenhanded," "objective," "impartial," or "without prejudice." You can prove, verify, or confirm a fact by personal observation, by using the observations of others, or by checking with reliable sources, such as studies that have been conducted, reputable books that have been written, or noted experts in a given field.

Personal observation simply involves checking something for ourselves, such as going to a person's home to verify that the person lives there. However, for practical reasons, we sometimes have to rely on the observations of others who serve as witnesses when we are unable to be present ourselves. For information about an event that occurred in the past or one that is happening in a far-off place that we cannot get to—such as the taking down of the Berlin Wall in Germany—we must rely on the eyewitness accounts of others. Finally, sometimes we must rely on written materials or other people who have more expertise than we do in a particular subject to determine if something is indeed factual. For instance, most people would rely on what they have read in the medical literature, including the results of studies conducted by prominent physicians, to conclude that statement 10, dealing with heart disease, is factually accurate.

One of the keys to uncovering facts, then, is our determination that they have been or can be proved in an unbiased way. In other words, we have to be reasonably certain that the observations, experts, and any additional sources that we use or that are presented to us by others are as evenhanded as possible and not clouded by personal opinion.

Also, keep in mind that facts can change over time as conditions change, resulting in the elimination of some facts and the addition of others. For example, it was once a fact that there were 48 states in the United States, but that was no longer a fact after the addition of the states of Alaska and Hawaii in 1959, thereby bringing the total to 50. Thus one fact was replaced by another. In short, determining whether or not something is a fact is an ongoing process that involves careful evaluation and continuous reevaluation, both of which are important characteristics of critical thinking.

ACTIVITY 1

DIRECTIONS: In your notebook, list ten facts, and be prepared to discuss them in class.

WHAT IS AN OPINION?

An **opinion** is *someone's personal judgment about something that has not been proved, verified, or confirmed in an unbiased manner.* In the more obvious cases, words like *good, bad, right,* or *wrong* are often used with opinions. However, sometimes people are more subtle when offering their opinions, which makes them more difficult to recognize. For example, the statements "Bill Clinton was a bad president" and "Bill Clinton, as president, left something to be desired" both express negative opinions, but the first is stronger and more obvious than the second.

Also, be on the lookout for opinions that are couched in factual terms, such as "The fact of the matter is that abortion is wrong!" Just because the word *fact* is used does not make the statement a fact. You saw another example of an opinion couched in factual terms in statement 6, which asserted that "it is a widely accepted fact that Puerto Rico will become the fifty-first [state]."

Finally, opinions can sometimes turn into facts after they have been proved, veri-fied, or confirmed in an unbiased manner. For instance, a week before your birthday, you can claim that it is going to rain on that day, which is your opinion. However, if it does rain on that day, your original claim has become a fact, which can now be proved. Thus opinions, like facts, can change over time and should therefore be reevaluated.

When dealing with opinions in general, you should not automatically disregard them. First of all, you need to take into consideration who is offering a given opinion. *An expert or some other person who has extensive education, training, or experience in a given area is in a strong position to offer an opinion in that area.* That kind of opinion, sometimes called an **informed opinion,** should be taken seriously. For example, the foreign policy views of the chair of the U.S. Senate Foreign Relations Committee are worth careful considera-tion, as are those of a cancer researcher if the subject involves the causes of that disease. Opinions in general are also worth looking at because they can give you new ideas and viewpoints that you may not have thought about before. In short, always make it a prac-tice to evaluate the opinions you encounter and give special consideration to their sources.

ACTIVITY 2

DIRECTIONS: In your notebook, list ten opinions, and be prepared to discuss them in class.

FACTS AND OPINIONS IN COMBINATION

As you saw at the beginning of this chapter, often facts and opinions are used in combi-nation, which makes it more difficult to distinguish between them. Sometimes this is done inadvertently when we are trying to express ourselves orally or in writing, but it can also be an intentional device to influence or persuade others. Commercials that influence our decisions as to what to purchase or whom to vote for and propaganda that attempts to persuade people to think in a certain way or support a certain course of action come to mind immediately as examples of how this technique can be used effectively.

For instance, a political commercial that states "Inflation is rising dramatically. But don't worry—our candidate has the answer! Remember that when you vote next Tues-day!" is probably a combination of fact and opinion. A rising inflation rate can be proved by published statistics, but whether or not the candidate has the answer to the problem is not so simple to prove, at least not at this time. Of course, the whole purpose of the commercial is to get you to vote for that candidate. If indeed the official does eventu-ally solve the inflation problem after the election, the latter part of the original commercial has become a fact. Once again, you must carefully evaluate and continuously reevaluate what you see, hear, and read.

ACTIVITY 3

DIRECTIONS: In your notebook, list ten statements that combine facts and opinions, and be prepared to discuss them in class.

RELATING FACTS AND OPINIONS TO PROBLEM SOLVING AND CONTEMPORARY ISSUES

When engaged in problem solving, you are already aware of the importance of gathering information as part of Step 2 of the approach that we have been using. No matter where the information comes from, it is crucial that it be as factual as possible. Otherwise, you could base your possible solutions on opinions or biased information, in which case they may not turn out to be solutions at all.

For example, if you are trying to solve the problem of a car engine that is smoking and you accept the opinion of a person who knows little about car engines, you are likely to waste your time, effort, and money. But if you consult a reliable car repair manual or take the advice of a reputable mechanic, you will probably end up with a solution to the problem. In short, the more you base possible solutions on facts, the better your chances of resolving problems.

As you already know, the ability to distinguish between facts and opinions is an important part of critical reading in general, no matter what kind of material you have in front of you. When you read, you should know whether or not you are dealing with information that is reliable and factual. Textbook material, for the most part, fits into that category due to its educational focus and because it is usually reviewed and approved by publishers and scholars prior to publication. When doing other kinds of reading, you need to be more vigilant, because facts and opinions are often interspersed.

That is certainly the case with contemporary issues, which tend to arouse emotions and bring out an array of opinions and opposing viewpoints. Furthermore, the ratio of facts to opinions will vary widely from passage to passage. Some will consist mostly of facts, some will consist mostly of opinions, and some will fall somewhere in between.

In addition, writers will not always make their purpose, tone or mood, obvious or mention the sources from which they have gotten their information. In those instances, you will either have to do research yourself or make a decision on the spot regarding the credentials of the writer and the reliability of the publication in which the information appeared. As you know, you can spend a great deal of time doing research, and sometimes that will be necessary if your purpose, for example, is to write a term paper for one of your courses. However, on other occasions, when you may be reading for pleasure, you can use your inference skills to come to a logical conclusion as to the writer's purpose and the reliability of the publication so that you can ultimately determine if the information is unbiased.

We will deal more thoroughly with purpose and tone in Chapter 8, but keep in mind at this point that recognizing purpose is an important part of determining what proportion of the material before you is factual and how much is opinion. As you can see, uncovering bias is not an exact science. It does require time and effort on your part, but that is what critical reading and critical thinking are all about.

 **ACTIVITY 4**

DIRECTIONS: Refer to the information you gathered for Step 2 in the problem-solving exercise at the beginning of this chapter. Was it mostly fact, mostly opinion, or a combination of both? Why?

ACTIVITY 5

DIRECTIONS: Write a three-paragraph essay on a contemporary issue of your choice. Make the first paragraph mostly fact, the second paragraph mostly opinion, and the third paragraph a combination of both. Be prepared to read your essay aloud in class.

ACTIVITY 6

DIRECTIONS: The following problem was taken from a psychology textbook. After reading and thinking about it carefully, get together with one of your classmates to discuss how to gather facts to solve it.

> Suppose that you live in a town that has one famous company, Boopsie's Biscuits and Buns. Everyone in the town is grateful for the 3B company and goes to work there with high hopes. Soon, however, an odd thing starts happening to many employees. They complain of fatigue and irritability. They are taking lots of sick leave. Productivity declines. What's going on at Boopsie's? Is everybody suffering from sheer laziness?
>
> Carol Tavris and Carole Wade, *Psychology in Perspective,* p. 437

ACTIVITY 7

DIRECTIONS: Read the following passages and answer the questions that follow. When reading each passage, try to make a determination as to what is fact and what is opinion. As part of that process, it will be helpful for you to take note of the writer's credentials if they are included, any sources mentioned, and the publication from which the passage was taken. Also, remember to use inference skills when appropriate.

EYE ON VOCABULARY

When reading each passage, take note of any unfamiliar words you come across. List them and their definitions in your notebook or on note cards. Use the context, word parts, or the dictionary to determine their meanings. After the completion of each passage, your instructor will ask to see your notebook or note cards and may discuss key words in class.

1
It's More Influential Than TV Advertising. So Why Do They Call It "Junk Mail"?

1   Any advertising medium that can influence consumers better than television deserves more respect.

2   And, in fact, most people like direct mail advertising. More than half the population read it promptly and completely, and say they find it useful. Some even say they'd like more. Over half the people in America order goods and services through catalogs or other advertising that comes by mail.

3   All of which is probably why direct mail is the U.S. Postal Service's fastest-growing business. Marketers large and small like it because it's inexpensive, goes straight to specific customers, invites response and gets results. And direct mail pays for i tself, which is reassuring to customers who think first-class postage rates subsidize third-class mail.

4   Direct mail is an essential component of the American retail economy. It benefits marketers and consumers alike. In 1995, it generated almost $385 billion in sales revenues for marketers. And it brought happiness to a lot of people who like browsing through catalogs, discovering unique products, or finding out about neighborhood bargains without leaving the comforts of home.

5   And now direct mail is going international. In 1995, the U.S. Postal Service sent to Japan the one millionth package for a major catalog retailer who is building a customer base there. And that helps the balance of payments.

6   So, call it Direct Marketing, call it Ad Mail—but please, don't call it junk mail.

United States Postal Service. We Deliver For You.

COMPREHENSION QUESTIONS

1. What is the topic of the passage?
2. What is the central message of the passage?
3. Determine what is at issue. What is your initial personal viewpoint?
4. Distinguish among opposing viewpoints, and provide the rationale for each.
5. Think carefully about the viewpoints. Express a personal viewpoint, and give the reasons why you favor it. Does it differ from your initial personal viewpoint? Why or why not?
6. Write a few paragraphs *in support of the viewpoint that you do not favor.*

THOUGHT AND DISCUSSION QUESTIONS

1. Would you prefer to call this mail "junk mail," "direct marketing," or "ad mail"? Why?
2. If you had the option of never receiving this kind of mail again, would you take that option? Why or why not?
3. Do you think the information presented is mostly fact, mostly opinion, or a combination of both? Why? Provide specific examples.
4. Do you think the article is unbiased? Why or why not?
5. List any questions that came to mind while you were reading this selection, and be prepared to discuss possible answers to them.

2
_____

Making the Grade

*Many Students Wheedle for a Degree
as If It Were a Freebie T-Shirt*
_____

Kurt Wiesenfeld

1   It was a rookie error. After 10 years I should have known better, but I went to my office the day after final grades were posted. There was a tentative knock on the door. "Professor Wiesenfeld? I took your Physics 2121 class? I flunked it? I wonder if there's anything I can do to improve my grade?" I thought: "Why are you asking me? Isn't it too late to worry about it? Do you dislike making declarative statements?"

2   After the student gave his tale of woe and left, the phone rang. "I got a D in your class. Is there any way you can change it to 'Incomplete'?" Then the e-mail assault began: "I'm shy about coming in to talk to you, but I'm not shy about asking for a better grade. Anyway, it's worth a try." The next day I had three phone messages from students asking *me* to call *them*. I didn't.

3   Time was, when you received a grade, that was it. You might groan and moan, but you accepted it as the outcome of your efforts or lack thereof (and, yes, sometimes a tough grader). In the last few years, however, some students have developed a disgruntled-consumer approach. If they don't like their grade, they go to the "return" counter to trade it in for something better.

4   What alarms me is their indifference toward grades as an indication of personal effort and performance. Many, when pressed about why they think they deserve a better grade, admit they don't deserve one but would like one anyway. Having been raised on gold stars for effort and smiley faces for self-esteem, they've learned that they can get by without hard work and real talent if they can talk the professor into giving them a break. This attitude is beyond cynicism. There's a weird innocence to the assumption that one expects (even deserves) a better grade simply by begging for it. With that outlook, I guess I shouldn't be as flabbergasted as I was that 12 students asked me to change their grades *after* final grades were posted.

5   That's 10 percent of my class who let three months of midterms, quizzes and lab reports slide until long past remedy. My graduate student calls it hyperrational thinking: if effort and intelligence don't matter, why should deadlines? What matters is getting a better grade through an unearned bonus, the academic equivalent of a freebie T shirt or toaster giveaway. Rewards are disconnected from the quality of one's work. An act and its consequences are unrelated, random events.

6   Their arguments for wheedling better grades often ignore academic performance. Perhaps they feel it's not relevant. "If my grade isn't raised to a D I'll lose my scholarship." "If you don't give me a C, I'll flunk out." One sincerely overwrought student pleaded, "If I don't pass, my life is over." This is tough stuff to deal with. Apparently, I'm responsible for someone's losing a scholarship, flunking out or deciding whether life has meaning. Perhaps these students see me as a commodities broker with something they want—a grade. Though intrinsically worthless, grades, if properly manipulated, can be traded for what has value: a degree, which means a job, which means money. The one thing college actually

offers—a chance to learn—is considered irrelevant, even less than worthless, because of the long hours and hard work required.

7   In a society saturated with surface values, love of knowledge for its own sake does sound eccentric. The benefits of fame and wealth are more obvious. So is it right to blame students for reflecting the superficial values saturating our society?

8   Yes, of course it's right. These guys had better take themselves seriously now, because our country will be forced to take them seriously later, when the stakes are much higher. They must recognize that their attitude is not only self-destructive, but socially destructive. The erosion of quality control—giving appropriate grades for actual accomplishments—is a major concern in my department. One colleague noted that a physics major could obtain a degree without ever answering a written exam question completely. How? By pulling in enough partial credit and extra credit. And by getting breaks on grades.

9   But what happens once she or he graduates and gets a job? That's when the misfortunes of eroding academic standards multiply. We lament that schoolchildren get "kicked upstairs" until they graduate from high school despite being illiterate and mathematically inept, but we seem unconcerned with college graduates whose less blatant deficiencies are far more harmful if their accreditation exceeds their qualifications.

10   Most of my students are science and engineering majors. If they're good at getting partial credit but not at getting the answer right, then the new bridge breaks or the new drug doesn't work. One finds examples here in Atlanta. Last year a light tower in the Olympic Stadium collapsed, killing a worker. It collapsed because an engineer miscalculated how much weight it could hold. A new 12-story dormitory could develop dangerous cracks due to a foundation that's uneven by more than six inches. The error resulted from incorrect data being fed into a computer. I drive past that dorm daily on my way to work, wondering if a foundation crushed under kilotons of weight is repairable or if this structure will have to be demolished. Two 10,000-pound steel beams at the new natatorium collapsed in March, crashing into the student athletic complex. (Should we give partial credit since no one was hurt?) Those are real-world consequences of errors and lack of expertise.

11   But the lesson is lost on the grade-grousing 10 percent. Say that you won't (not can't, but won't) change the grade they deserve to what they want, and they're frequently bewildered or angry. They don't think it's fair that they're judged according to their performance, not their desires or "potential." They don't think it's fair that they should jeopardize their scholarships or be in danger of flunking out simply because they could not or did not do their work. But it's more than fair; it's necessary to help preserve a minimum standard of quality that our society needs to maintain safety and integrity. I don't know if the 13th-hour students will learn that lesson, but I've learned mine. From now on, after final grades are posted, I'll lie low until the next quarter starts.

Newsweek, June 17, 1996, p. 16

COMPREHENSION QUESTIONS

1. What is the topic of the passage?

2. What is the central message of the passage?

3. Determine what is at issue. What is your initial personal viewpoint?

4. Distinguish among opposing viewpoints, and provide the rationale for each.

5. Think carefully about the viewpoints. Express a personal viewpoint, and give the reasons why you favor it. Does it differ from your initial personal viewpoint? Why or why not?

6. Write a few paragraphs *in support of the viewpoint that you do* not *favor.*

THOUGHT AND DISCUSSION QUESTIONS

1. In your opinion, is "hyperrational thinking" ever acceptable? Why or why not? Have you ever engaged in it? When and why?

2. Do you agree with the author that the erosion of quality control with regard to academic standards can be socially destructive? Why or why not?

3. If you were a college instructor, would you permit students to raise their grades by doing extra credit work? Why or why not?

4. Do you think the information presented is mostly fact, mostly opinion, or a combination of both? Why? Provide specific examples.

5. Do you think the article is unbiased? Why or why not?

6. List any questions that came to mind while you were reading this selection, and be prepared to discuss possible answers to them.

3

Fertility for Sale

As reproductive technology has advanced, the law of supply and demand has inevitably clicked in. Some clinics have had trouble finding women to donate their eggs for implantation in infertile women. That has led to a medical and ethical debate over whether donors should charge for their eggs and, if so, how much. The St. Barnabas Medical Center in Livingston, N.J., recently accelerated that debate by offering $5,000 for donors, double the rate of many clinics. A variety of experts were asked whether women should be permitted to sell their eggs on the open market:

Robert Wright is the author *of The Moral Animal: Evolutionary Psychology and Everyday Life.*

1   Is a woman who gets several thousand dollars for a few eggs being exploited? The claim is not on its face ridiculous; a donor undergoes an unpleasant and risky procedure that is invasive both physically and in a less tangible sense. What *is* ridiculous is the idea that the woman is more exploited if she gets $5,000 than if she gets $2,000. Yet that is the implicit logic of some who argue for limiting fees lest we degrade women by turning their eggs into commodities.

2   Critics of high fees say it's all right to compensate donors, just not to entice them. But that distinction faded years ago, when infertile women began paying more than a few hundred dollars for eggs. They found that if they didn't pay real money, they'd get no eggs. This is the market at work: a willing buyer, a willing seller. Is there any reason to get between them?

3   Sometimes society plausibly says yes, as with drug sales and prostitution. Personally, I don't see a comparably strong argument in this case. If there is one, maybe we should take eggs off the market. But what's the point of pretending they aren't already there?

Cynthia Gorney is the author of *Articles of Faith: A Frontline History of the Abortion Wars.*

4   A precedent for limiting compensation for egg donation was set 15 years ago, when the most heated argument in infertility circles was about surrogate mothers—women who volunteered to undergo artificial insemination and carry a baby to term for infertile couples. The ethical consensus then was that if a woman offers to lend out her own reproductive system because she wants to help someone else, we suppose we can't stop her, but she shouldn't be tempted to do it because she wants or needs money: a surrogate should be paid for medical expenses and lost time at work, and perhaps offered some modest extra cash to offset the physical discomfort of pregnancy. But the money should not be generous enough to make surrogacy an attractive line of work.

5   And as a rule, surrogate mothers still don't collect much money, nor should they. To be sure, this is partly because they deliver up fully developed human beings, which by law and venerable tradition may not be bought and sold. But it is also because surrogate mothers deliver up their own bodily organs—their eggs and the use of their wombs—and we have equally venerable tradition forbidding people to sell their body parts for profit.

6   Galloping technology and the escalating hopes of infertile couples are working together to push us much too far, too fast. There has got to be a point at which society declares to the infertile couple: We are sorry for your situation, but you cannot buy everything you want. We will not let you offer that young woman $10,000 for some of her eggs, just as we will not let you offer her brother $10,000 for one of his kidneys. The potential cost to both of them—and to all the rest of us—is too high.

Lee M. Silver, a biology professor at Princeton, is the author of *Remaking Eden: Cloning and Beyond in a Brave New World.*

7   Why are physicians and bioethicists—who are mostly male—trying to limit monetary compensation to women who donate their eggs? In no other part of the economy do we limit the amount of money that can be paid to people who participate in risky or demeaning activities. Indeed, college students have long been enticed by high fees into participating in risky medical experiments.

8   But society expects women to be altruistic, not venal. And it insists that women be protected from themselves, on the assumption that they are unable to make rational decisions about their own bodies. And perhaps men feel threatened by the idea that women now also have a way to spread their seed upon the earth.

Robert Coles, a physician, is a professor of social ethics at Harvard and the author, most recently, of *The Youngest Parents: Teen-Age Pregnancy as It Shapes Lives.*

9   We really don't know the long-term medical consequences for women who donate their eggs. There have been a few reports of serious side effects, like renal failure. But have researchers studied carefully enough what exposure to these fertility drugs does to women? If poor women become repeat donors because the process keeps getting more lucrative, will they increase their risk down the line for ovarian cancer? These are unanswered questions.

10   Most important, the widening divide between the rich and the poor poses an ethical dilemma: can we condone the "harvesting" of eggs from poor women, who may be
putting their health at risk, for the benefit of the affluent?

Elizabeth Bartholet, a professor at Harvard Law School, is the author of *Family Bonds:
Adoption and the Politics of Parenting.*

11   The selling of human eggs puts at risk the donors' health and sacrifices their human
dignity. It also encourages women to bear children who are not genetically related to
them, so that their mates can have genetic offspring. This practice produces children
who have lost one genetic parent—in a world that already has an abundance of orphans
who need homes.

12   We need to call a halt to further commercialization of reproduction to give policy
makers a chance to consider the ethical issues involved in reproductive technology like
egg selling, cloning and sex selection. We should follow the lead of other countries
and establish a national commission to resolve these issues rather than leave them to
the market.

Lori Arnold is a doctor at the Fertility and I.V.F. Center of Miami.

13   Most women who donate their eggs at our clinic do so because they want to help provide the gift of life. Many have children of their own; they want to help others experience the joys of motherhood.

14   The motive is altruistic, but that should not blind anyone to the practical difficulties. Donors are required to undergo treatment with fertility drugs, counseling, screen-
ing, ultrasound monitoring, blood work and numerous office visits. It takes weeks. And
retrieving the eggs from their ovaries is a surgical procedure.

15   Also worth factoring in is that the donors are giving a couple the chance to have a
family, with a child who has the father's genetic makeup. The donor also gives the recipient a chance to experience pregnancy, delivery and breast-feeding, thereby facilitating
mother-baby bonding.

16   Thus compensation given to an egg donor is well deserved. Of course, there comes
a point when a fee becomes self-defeating, since the cost is paid by the recipient—few
couples can afford to pay an unlimited amount. But donors deserve something more
than a token. Ours receive $1,500 to $2,000; no one should begrudge them that.

New York Times, March 4, 1998

COMPREHENSION QUESTIONS

1. What is the topic of the passage?

2. What is the central message of the passage?

3. Determine what is at issue. What is your initial personal viewpoint?

4. Distinguish among opposing viewpoints, and provide the rationale for each.

5. Think carefully about the viewpoints. Express a personal viewpoint, and give the
   reasons why you favor it. Does it differ from your initial personal viewpoint?
   Why or why not?

6. Write a few paragraphs *in support of the viewpoint that you do not favor.*

THOUGHT AND DISCUSSION QUESTIONS

1. If your spouse and you were infertile, would you agree to having a surrogate mother carry a baby to term for you? Why or why not?

2. If your spouse and you were infertile, would you agree to having donor eggs implanted? Why or why not?

3. If you are a woman, would you agree to be a surrogate mother or an egg donor if the price were right? Why or why not? If you are a man, would you support your wife's decision to be a surrogate mother or an egg donor if the price were right? Why or why not?

4. Do you think the information presented is mostly fact, mostly opinion, or a combination of both? Why? Provide specific examples.

5. Do you think the article is unbiased? Why or why not?

6. List any questions that came to mind while you were reading this selection, and be prepared to discuss possible answers to them.

4

Do Competitive Sports Teach Valuable Life Lessons to Youth?

YES

1   Several factors, such as one's attitude toward competition, the manner in which competition is organized, and the behavior of important adults—such as parents and coaches—can contribute to making competition either worthwhile or hurtful. The current crisis in youth sports will be resolved only if we dedicate ourselves to ensuring that youth sports programs are indeed worthwhile, and by working together to eliminate destructive attitudes and behaviors.

2   There are four important reasons that I believe we should tackle the problems in youth sports by encouraging—not prohibiting—competitive sports for children. First, if children are taught emotional skills and psychological skills to help them be effective competitors, these skills will be helpful throughout life.

3   Examples of some of these coping skills include: knowing how to relax and calm down in pressure situations or when being evaluated, using one's imagination in support of reaching one's goals, being able to receive and utilize criticism and learning how to focus attention.

4   Second, competitive sports expose children to losing. Learning how to deal with loss is a valuable experience for children. Third, competitive sports show children that there are standards of excellence in each sport. Such experience is an important part of developing a mastery approach.

5   Competition provides performers in any given area with a way to measure their progress. Those who would argue that competition should be abolished must propose an alternative means of measuring improvement. I think that simply looking at our own performance over time is not adequate....Expertise develops when the urge to improve, to become as good as other skilled performers, or even better, occurs. This urge is the

ego side of the competitive instinct. But without competition, it is nearly impossible to imagine how excellence could develop.

6   Finally, competitive youth sports programs provide children with the opportunity to learn new skills and work on existing skills, to set goals and try to achieve them and to work with others in team situations. These experiences can be fundamental in providing children with a sense of self-esteem. Good physical self-esteem can help children develop fitness and health habits, which build a strong foundation for an active and healthy life.

Shane Murphy, *The Cheers and the Tears: A Healthy Alternative to the Dark Side of Youth Sports Today*
(Jossey-Bass, 1999)

NO

7   Competing drags us down, devastates us psychologically, poisons our relationships, interferes with our performance. But acknowledging these things would be painful and might force us to make radical changes in our lives, so instead we create and accept rationalizations for competition: It's part of "human nature." It builds character.

8   The last of these beliefs is the most remarkable. The contention that competition is psychologically beneficial contradicts the intuitive knowledge that I believe most of us possess. Despite direct awareness of what competition does to people...some individuals persist in claiming that its effects are constructive. This is a powerful example of how it is possible to adjust our beliefs so as to escape the threatening realization that we have been subjecting ourselves to something terrible, that we have internalized a corrosive personality attribute.

9   Also, this may be why the traditional assumption that "competitive sport builds character" is still with us today in spite of overwhelming contrary evidence. Apart from the absence of data to support it, the adage itself is exceedingly slippery. One sports sociologist reports that of all the writers he has encountered who repeat this assertion, not one actually defined the word character, let alone provided evidence for the claim. Character was typically assumed to be understood as desirable and wholesome, or it was defined implicitly by association with such adjectives as "clean-cut," "red-blooded," "upstanding," "desirable" and so forth. For the late Gen. Douglas MacArthur, competition was a "vital character builder" in the sense that it "make[s] sons into men." This definition, besides being irrelevant to half the human race, tells us nothing about which features of being a man are considered desirable.

10   In what may be the only explicit research of this claim, [authors] Ogilvie and Tutko could find "no empirical support for the tradition that sport builds character. Indeed, there is evidence that athletic competition limits growth in some areas." Among the problematic results they discovered were depression, extreme stress, and relatively shallow relationships. [They] also found, as mentioned before, that many players "with immense character strengths" avoid competitive sports. Finally, they discovered that those who do participate are not improved by competition; whatever strengths they have were theirs to begin with.

Alfie Kohn, *No Contest: The Case Against Competition* (Houghton Mifflin, 1992)

COMPREHENSION QUESTIONS

1. What is the topic of the passage?

2. What is the central message of the passage?

3. Determine what is at issue. What is your initial personal viewpoint?

4. Distinguish among opposing viewpoints, and provide the rationale for each.

5. Think carefully about the viewpoints. Express a personal viewpoint, and give the reasons why you favor it. Does it differ from your initial personal viewpoint? Why or why not?

6. Write a few paragraphs *in support of the viewpoint that you do* not *favor.*

THOUGHT AND DISCUSSION QUESTIONS

1. Do you agree with Shane Murphy when he states, "Learning how to deal with loss is a valuable experience for children"? Why or why not?

2. How do you define "character"? Do you believe that "competitive sport builds character"? Why or why not?

3. Use your inference skills to determine what Alfie Kohn means when he states that General Douglas MacArthur's definition is "irrelevant to half the human race."

4. Do you think the information presented is mostly fact, mostly opinion, or a combination of both? Why? Provide specific examples.

5. Do you think the statements are unbiased? Why or why not?

6. List any questions that came to mind while you were reading this selection, and be prepared to discuss possible answers to them.

LOOKING BACK

Summarize and/or paraphrase the most important points you learned from this chapter, and determine how they can be put to use in other classes. Be prepared to discuss with your classmates what you have written.

THINK AGAIN!

Assume that *you* are the person making the statement "Brothers and sisters, I have none. But that man's father is my father's son." What is the relationship of *that man* to you? Get together with a classmate, and discuss the possibilities.

The Dashing Detective

Remember to follow these steps:

- first, read the narrative and all the questions
- second, examine the picture carefully
- third, answer the questions in the order they appear and come up with the solution

Have fun!

Burglars broke a window and entered the home of Samuel F. Whippersnapper, a coin collector, and rifled his collection. He grappled with them and was shot and fatally wounded in the course of the struggle. He had time, however, to call the police, who stopped a car with these four suspects in it and brought them to the station house, together with the coat, which had some of the stolen coins in a pocket.

Whippersnapper died clutching the button which is shown. The police were satisfied that the other objects sketched, which were found at Whippersnapper's, belonged to the burglars. From the above facts and an examination of the evidence and the four suspects, can you decide who shot Whippersnapper?

Questions

1. Who do you think broke the window?   ☐ Dan Jurous   ☐ "Bull" Dozer
   ☐ Helen Wheels   ☐ "Brains" B. Heind

2. At what time did the struggle occur?

3. Do you think that more than one person was involved in the burglary?   ☐ Yes   ☐ No

4. Does the button come from the coat found in the car?   ☐ Yes   ☐ No

5. Do you think that "Bull" Dozer was involved in the struggle?   ☐ Yes   ☐ No

6. Do you think that the wearer of the coat killed Whippersnapper?   ☐ Yes   ☐ No

7. Who do you think shot Whippersnapper?   ☐ Dan Jurous   ☐ "Bull" Dozer
   ☐ Helen Wheels   ☐ "Brains" B. Heind

Lawrence Treat, *Crime and Puzzlement*, pp. 44–45

Name _____ Date _____

MASTERY TEST 7–1

DIRECTIONS: Answer the questions and fill in the blanks. For statements 7 through 10, indicate whether it is a fact, an opinion, or a combination of both.

1. What is a fact? _____

_____

_____

2. What is an opinion? _____

_____

_____

3. A statement is unbiased when it is
   a. evenhanded
   b. objective
   c. impartial
   d. without prejudice
   e. all of the above

4. You can prove or verify a fact by personal _____, by using the observations of _____, or by checking with reliable _____.

5. "As a critical thinker, you must disregard all opinions." Is this statement true or false?

6. An _____ opinion is one given by a person with extensive education, training, or experience in the particular area being discussed.

7. It is a fact that capital punishment serves as a deterrent to murder._____

8. Although the Supreme Court has made a landmark decision regarding abortion, the issue is far from settled._____

9. The Clinton-Lewinsky matter was given extensive coverage by the media.

   _____

10. The Soviet Union no longer exists, but there still is much instability in Europe.

   _____

Name _____   Date _____

MASTERY TEST 7-2

DIRECTIONS: Does the paragraph below consist of fact or opinion?.

1

When Nixon became president in 1969, the major economic problem facing him was inflation. It was caused primarily by the heavy military expenditures and "easy money" policies of the Johnson administration. Nixon cut federal spending and balanced the 1969 budget, while the Federal Reserve Board forced up interest rates in order to slow the expansion of the money supply. When prices continued to rise, there was mounting uneasiness. Labor unions demanded large wage increases. In 1970 Congress passed a law giving the president power to regulate prices and wages.

John A. Garraty, *A Short History of the American Nation*, p. 52

_____

_____

DIRECTIONS: The two passages that follow deal with the same issue. What is that issue? Alongside each passage, indicate whether it consists of mostly fact, mostly opinion, or a combination of both.

2

Perhaps the most unfortunate victims of drug prohibition laws have been the residents of America's ghettos. These laws have proved largely futile in deterring ghetto-dwellers from becoming drug abusers, but they do account for much of what ghetto residents identify as the drug problem. Aggressive, gun-toting drug dealers often upset law-abiding residents far more than do addicts nodding out in doorways. Meanwhile other residents perceive the drug dealers as heroes and successful role models. They're symbols of success to children who see no other options. At the same time the increasingly harsh criminal penalties imposed on adult drug dealers have led drug traffickers to recruit juveniles. Where once children started dealing drugs only after they had been using them for a few years, today the sequence is often reversed. Many children start using drugs only after working for older drug dealers for a while....Legalization of drugs, like legalization of alcohol in the early 1930s, would drive the drug-dealing business off the streets and out of apartment buildings and into government-regulated, tax-paying stores. It also would force many of the gun-toting dealers out of the business and convert others into legitimate businessmen.

Ethan A. Nadelmann, "Shooting Up," *New Republic*, June 1988

_____

_____

3

All studies show that those most likely to try drugs, get hooked, and die—as opposed to those who suffer from cirrhosis and lung cancer—are young people, who are susceptible to the lure of quick thrills and are terribly adaptable to messages provided by adult society. Under pressure of the current prohibition, the number of kids who use illegal drugs at least once a month has fallen from 39 percent in the late 1970s to 25 percent in 1987, according to the annual survey of high school seniors conducted by the University of Michigan. The same survey shows that attitudes toward drug use have turned sharply negative. But use of legal drugs is still strong. Thirty-eight percent of high school seniors reported getting drunk within the past two weeks, and 27 percent said they smoke cigarettes every day. Drug prohibition is working with kids; legalization would do them harm.

Morton M. Kondracke, "Don't Legalize Drugs," *New Republic,* June 27, 1988

Name _____   Date _____

MASTERY TEST 7-3

DIRECTIONS: For each of the longer selections that follow, indicate whether the information presented is mostly fact, mostly opinion, or a combination of both. Also, indicate which of the passages, if any, present information that is *informed opinion.*

1
America's Favorite Food: The Hamburger

1   It's not only the President who enjoys a good hamburger.

2   Americans consume some 38 billion hamburgers a year. And, according to a fast food expert, they account for nearly 60 percent of all sandwiches sold over the counter, replacing the hot dog as the nation's most popular food item.

3   "Hamburgers are popular because they are great tasting and basic, yet can be adapted to suit various tastes," suggested Linda Vaughan, vice president of new products for Jack in the Box restaurants, which sold 200 million hamburgers last year.

4   Americans consume about 25 percent of their meals away from home, and about half of that in fast food restaurants, she said. So it's no wonder that nearly five billion hamburgers and cheeseburgers were served in commercial restaurants in 1993, according to the National Restaurant Association.

5   No one can claim the exact date the first hamburger was made, but America's favorite sandwich got its name in the 18th century from German immigrants from the city of Hamburg who brought their popular broiled chopped steak to the United States. The rest is hamburger history.

6   What makes today's hamburger perfect is a matter of debate, but no matter. Variety in hamburgers has become the norm, Vaughan said. Though some restaurants specialize in basic burgers, others pride themselves on making every condiment count.

7   But whether it's a secret sauce or bacon and onion rings that draws people to hamburgers, Americans have many ways of creating a sandwich unique to them. "They can be made to suit individual tastes from the basic to the exotic," said Vaughan.

8   "In our research, we discovered many people literally crave the taste of a hamburger, some claiming that they can eat a good burger every day of the week." In fact, she said, Jack in the Box, a fast food chain targeted primarily to more adult tastes, is refocusing its efforts on the hamburger in its many varieties as a business strategy. "It's a taste people don't get tired of, even as food trends come and go."

Smart Publications, September 16, 1995, p. 13

_____

_____

2

Should Humans Be Cloned?

New methods can create a baby who is your genetic twin.

YES

1   The cloning of human beings is now possible. Scientists can take an egg cell, remove its DNA, insert DNA from a cell of any person, and create an embryo who is that person's younger but identical twin. This technology offers a miracle option for families who cannot have children of their own by any other method. After 25 years as a fertility specialist, trying to help couples have babies, I have joined with scientists in Europe and elsewhere to develop that option. By doing so, I believe, we will be helping humanity.

2   It is true that the cloning of animals—such as Dolly the sheep, created in Scotland in 1997—has so far had a high failure rate and is fraught with risks. But those risks have been exaggerated, and many of them have resulted from improper cloning. Meanwhile, I can show you e-mails from thousands of families eager to accept those risks. They say in their messages that if they are able to have a child through cloning, they will love that son or daughter just as much as they would any other.

3   Believe it or not, the genie is out of the bottle. Human cloning will be done whether we like it or not. I think we should accept it, make it legal, regulate it, and make sure it is done in a responsible, scientifically correct way—not left to unscrupulous black-market exploiters.

Panos Zavos, Ph.D., Director, Andrology Institute of America Lexington, Ky.

NO

4   Don't think about human cloning from the point of view of the person being cloned. Think about it as if you were the younger, duplicated copy. If you do, you'll see at once why cloning a human being is deeply unethical.

5   First, the known grave risks of abnormality and deformity seen in animal cloning make attempts at human cloning an immoral experiment on the resulting child-to-be. Second, even if you were a healthy clone, would you want to be constantly compared with the adult original in whose image you have been made? Wouldn't you want to have your own unique identity and an open-ended future, fully a surprise to yourself and the world?

6   If you were the clone of your "mother," would it help your adolescence to turn into the spitting image of the woman Daddy fell in love with? If you were the clone of your "father" but your parents later divorced, would you like to look just like the man your mother now detests?

7   Third, don't you think it is a form of child abuse for parents to try to determine in advance just exactly what kind of a child you are supposed to be? Do you want to live under the tyranny of their biologically determined expectations?

8   Finally, would you like to turn human procreation into manufacture, producing children as artifacts? Cloning is tyrannical and dehumanizing. We should have none of it.

Leon R. Kass, M.D., Professor, Committee on Social Thought, University of Chicago, New York Times Upfront,
April 30, 2001, p. 26

CHAPTER 8
RECOGNIZING PURPOSE AND TONE

CHAPTER OUTLINE

The Importance of Recognizing Purpose

To Inform

To Persuade

To Entertain

Combination of Purposes

The Importance of Recognizing Tone

Matter-of-Fact Tone

Humorous Tone

Angry Tone

Sad Tone

Ironic Tone

THINK ABOUT IT!

Use your inference skills to determine the *purpose* of the message on each of the signs in the following photographs. In other words, what are readers being urged to do or not do? Discuss the purposes with your classmates.

1

2

3

4

5

CHAPTER OUTCOMES

After completing Chapter 8, you should be able to:

- Continue to apply the basic method for personal problem solving
- Define *purpose* and *tone*
- Recognize the various kinds of purpose
- Recognize the various kinds of tone
- Continue to find topics and central messages in contemporary issue passages to determine what is at issue, distinguish among opposing viewpoints, and express personal viewpoints

Problem-Solving Exercise

Using your notebook, apply the first four steps of the basic method for personal problem solving to the following hypothetical situation. Be sure to label each step clearly as you discuss what you would do. This situation is similar to a real-life one experienced by several of my students.

HYPOTHETICAL SITUATION

For several weeks, you have been enrolled in an introductory business course that is required in your program of study. From the beginning of the semester, you have not been comfortable with the instructor. His lectures are difficult to follow, and he is gruff and impatient when you ask questions, both in and out of class. Furthermore, you feel that he grades your test papers unfairly by taking off too many points for answers that are basically correct. In short, you get the impression that he simply does not like you.

Although you have a C average, you need a much higher grade in your major courses in order to continue your education and eventually secure a better job. In fact, you have not received a grade lower than B in all the other courses that you have taken to this point. You fear that this predicament is not going to get any better, and you are at a loss as to what to do about it.

THE IMPORTANCE OF RECOGNIZING PURPOSE

Throughout this textbook, we have emphasized the importance of evaluating what you see, hear, and read as a necessary part of critical thinking. You have been cautioned not to rush to judgment by accepting everything at face value but instead to take the time to consider what you have before you, regardless of your personal viewpoint. When reading, part of the evaluation process involves recognizing the writer's **purpose,** or *reasons for writing*. That, in turn, can help you distinguish between facts and opinions, uncover bias, and assess the overall reliability of information.

Although writers always have a purpose for writing, they usually do not come right out and say what it is. Consequently, it is up to the reader to make an inference or an educated guess regarding their motivations, based on:

- Author's background or affiliation
- Publication in which the writing appears
- The information itself
- How the information is presented

For example, a physician who is a member of the American Medical Association may write a piece in a popular magazine dealing with the high cost of malpractice insurance in order to persuade readers to be sympathetic to rising medical fees. In doing so, she may not state that purpose explicitly but instead present convincing information that supports that point of view without providing any contradictory information. Thus the reader could infer her purpose by taking into consideration the fact that she is a physician who is affiliated with the major medical association representing doctors, by keeping in mind that the article appears in a magazine that is read widely by the general public, and by recognizing that the information provided appears to be one-sided.

Generally speaking, a writer's purpose for writing is usually to *inform*, to *persuade*, to *entertain*, or some combination of the three. The ease with which you will be able to recognize these purposes will often depend on how obvious a particular writer chooses to be in the presentation of the material. As noted, it will sometimes be necessary for you to use your inference skills. Let us look more closely at each of the three purposes.

To Inform

When the purpose is to inform, *a writer simply provides facts, data, or information about a given subject so that you can learn more about it.* Textbook writers generally have this as their overall purpose. For example, read the following passage from a biology textbook.

Biology Is Connected to Our Lives in Many Ways

1   Global warming, air and water pollution, endangered species, genetic engineering, test-tube babies, nutrition, aerobic exercise and weight control, medical advances, AIDS and the immune system—is there ever a day that we don't see several of these issues featured in the news? These topics and many more have biological underpinnings. Biology, the science of life, has an enormous impact on our everyday life, and it is impossible to take an informed stand on many important issues without a basic understanding of life science.

2   Much of biology's impact on modern society stems from its contributions to technology and medicine. Technology is the application of scientific knowledge. Many discoveries in biology have practical applications. The technology of modern birth control, for instance, grew out of an understanding of the structure and function of the human reproductive system.

3   Perhaps the most important application of biology to our lives today is in helping us understand and respond to the environmental problems we currently face. One of our biggest environmental challenges is the possibility of global changes in weather and climate. Rain forests, which we have featured in this chapter, have a major effect on climate. In this capacity, tropical rain forests are vital to life as far away as Siberia and Antarctica.... Every year, as human demands for wood, food, and minerals increase, vast areas of tropical rain forest are destroyed. (At least 85% of North America's rain forests have been heavily logged.) Destroying rain forests kills off untold numbers of species. It also produces large amounts of carbon dioxide (CO_2) gas. The CO_2 traps heat from sunlight and can warm the atmosphere. Many scientists contend that the destruction of rain forests at the current rate, coupled with CO_2 (and other gases) increases from sources such as industrial pollution, is raising global temperatures. Higher temperatures might melt glacial and polar ice, cause worldwide flooding, and alter the world's climates even more drastically.

4   Evaluating news reports on problems of this magnitude requires critical thinking and familiarity with many aspects of biology. For instance, in considering the possible effects of rain forest destruction, it is useful to know something about whole plants, cells, and molecules, as these subjects relate to photosynthesis and other kinds of energy transformation. It is also useful to know about carbon and water cycling in ecosystems, the growth patterns of the human population, and the effect of climate and soil conditions on the distribution of life on Earth.

5   Biology—from the molecular level to the ecosystem level—is directly connected to our everyday lives. It may also help us find solutions to the many environmental problems that confront us. Biology offers us a deeper understanding of ourselves and our planet, and a chance to more fully appreciate life in all its diversity.

Neil A. Campbell et al., *Biology*, 3rd ed., p. 12

The writer's purpose here is to inform the reader about the many important connections that the subject of biology has to our everyday lives, including its contributions to technology and medicine and its help in finding solutions to environmental problems. Several examples are provided for support and clarification.

Keep in mind that sometimes a writer wants to inform us in order to suggest, in a subtle or clever way, that we do something. For instance, as you read the following passage, think about its purpose.

Getting Help When Anger Turns Inward

Thomas H. Matthews

1   When Jerome W. was 13 years old, he tried to kill himself. He thought that pressures in his life had grown so large that ending his life was the only solution.

2   He had thought for weeks about how he would do it. Then one day, with family gathered around him, he simply walked to the window of his fifth-floor apartment in Brooklyn and began to crawl to the ledge. As he poised for the jump, his mother realized what Jerome was doing and pulled him back into the house.

3   "I was very serious," Jerome said. "I wanted to die. I began to ask myself, 'Why am I here?'"

4   Jerome said his problems stemmed from his relationship with his mother. After he was 9, there was no father in his house, so he was responsible for his brother and sister. He helped care for them, making their breakfast every day and taking them to and from school. He felt a great deal of pressure trying to go to school himself and care for his siblings.

5   He also began to feel that his mother was turning against him.

6   "There was a fight every day," he said. "I couldn't figure out why she was doing this to me."

7   After the suicide attempt, his mother chided him, saying that if he tried it again, she would let him. And that response, coupled with the ongoing arguments, he said, caused Jerome to shut down and say, "No more."

8   "I couldn't believe she said those things to me," he recalled. "From that day on, I blocked my mother out. I no longer showed any emotion. I didn't expect it to go as far as it did."

9   It went on for more than 10 years.

10   A psychotherapist for Jerome was recommended by the UJA-Federation of New York, one of seven agencies supported by The New York Times Neediest Cases Fund, now in its 84th year. The Times pays the fund's administrative costs, so donations go directly to the charities.

11   The therapist, Kiki Vouyiouklis, quickly realized that Jerome had successfully isolated himself from the world. "He had lost touch with everyone," she said.

12   While seeing Ms. Vouyiouklis over a 10-month period, Jerome was able to let out what he had held back for years. "I was forced to hate, but I was able to release all of that," he said. "It was a big-time relief."

13   "I've come such a long way," said Jerome, 25, who now works as a freelance production assistant in the television and movie industry. "I'm proud of what I have been able to do. I feel like a whole person now."

New York Times, February 16, 1996, p. B2

The passage above is intended for the most part to inform the reader about how Jerome W. overcame much adversity and developed into a successful person. However, the reader is also told that he was able to accomplish this through the help of one of seven agencies supported by the New York Times Neediest Cases Fund, which depends in part on donations. Hence, in a subtle way, the writer is suggesting that others like Jerome could be helped similarly if readers of the passage would donate money. It is not unusual for writers to present facts with the intention of encouraging us to do something.

ACTIVITY 1

DIRECTIONS: Write a short informational essay in your notebook dealing with a contemporary issue in which you present only facts. Then, using the same essay, add some material that encourages the reader to do something.

ACTIVITY 2

DIRECTIONS: Bring to class an example of a passage that was written to inform readers.

To Persuade

When a writer's purpose is to persuade, *the writer is trying to get the reader to think in a certain way or take a particular action.* Although some facts may be presented, the writer's real intention is to get others to agree with the opinion being expressed or to engage in some activity in support of that point of view. For instance, as you read the following passage, think about the author's purpose.

The Littlest Killers
Lord of the Flies, Chicago Style

Brent Staples

1   Imagine the terror of a 5-year-old child, dangling 14 stories above the pavement, as his brother tries fruitlessly to save him from two other boys, ages 10 and 11, who are determined to see him drop.

2   The image of Eric Morse, hurled to his death in Chicago in 1994, has been a recurrent one in both local and national politics. Newt Gingrich cited it in speeches. Henry Cisneros, the Secretary of Housing and Urban Development, called it a clinching fact in the Government's decision to take over the Chicago Housing Authority, deemed by Federal authorities the most dangerous and ill managed in the country. The Illinois Legislature easily passed a bill permitting 10-year-old children to be charged with murder and—as "super predators"—sent to maximum-security jails. The rush to jail young children is catching on elsewhere as well. Nationwide last year, 700 pieces of legislation were introduced aimed at prosecuting minors as adults.

3   The judge who last week sent Eric Morse's killers to jails for juveniles came near to rending her robes as she described Eric's plunge and asked how the boys who caused his death had become so indifferent to human life. No one who has spent time in, or even near, Chicago public housing projects should need to ask such a question. Eric's fall—and the world he lived in—bears a disturbing resemblance to *Lord of the Flies,* William Golding's novel about a band of British schoolboys marooned on a jungle island. Without adults to keep them in check, the boys turn to blood lust and murder. A boy who tries to reason gets his skull split open when he is thrown from a cliff.

4   Eric was killed for refusing to steal candy for his tormentors. The public housing complex where he died qualifies as an "island" in Golding's sense—an island of poverty and pathology, cut off from the city proper. Of the 15 poorest census tracts in America, 11 are Chicago public housing communities. The city designed and treated them as pariah states, even while they were bright, shining steppingstones for the black middle class. Public housing was far too densely built, walled off with freeways and railroad lines used as ghetto walls. As the poverty deepened, there was simply no way to dilute it.

5   Chicago's Ida B. Wells housing development has few adult men. The women are disproportionately teenagers. At the time of Eric's death, a third of the complex's 2,800 apartments were abandoned, used primarily by drug dealers who hawked heroin from the windows. In a survey at a nearby high school, half the students said they had been shot at; 45 percent said they had seen someone killed. The boys who dropped Eric from the window did not originate the act. The gangs, which both boys knew well, occasionally used such punishment on members who tried to quit. Bear in mind that this environment is sustained with Federal dollars.

6   The conduct of the two young killers was all the more understandable given that they have I.Q.'s of 60 and 76, with perhaps less emotional maturity than 5-year-old Eric. The judge in the case has ordered psychiatric treatment and follow-up care. But in light of what experts describe as Illinois's poor record with treatment—and its high failure rate with juveniles—the prospects for treatment seem poor. In Massachusetts or Missouri, the two

would have been sent to facilities with fewer than two dozen beds and extensive psy-chiatric help. In Illinois, the boys could go to lockdowns with hundreds of others—many of them gangsters who will re-create the projects behind bars.

7   Few things are more horrifying than the murder of a child. But in view of the antecedents, Eric Morse's death was almost a naturally occurring event. The projects have become factories for crime and killers, with homicide taking younger and younger vic-tims each year. The judge who sentenced Eric's killers called it "essential to find out how these two young boys turned out to be killers, to have no respect for human life and no empathy for their victim." We know quite well what made them killers. What we need is the political will to do something about it.

New York Times, February 6, 1996, p. A22

The passage above does present facts regarding the murder of Eric Morse by two other boys and the very poor conditions in the Chicago public housing projects that have led to crimes like that. However, the writer concludes by stating: "We know quite well what made them killers. What we need is the political will to do something about it" (paragraph 7). We can infer from those statements that the writer is urging readers to support measures that will help correct the conditions in the housing projects or politicians who favor such mea-sures. In short, he is trying to get us to agree with his point of view regarding the causes of crimes like the murder of Eric Morse and asking us to take action to eliminate them.

ACTIVITY 3

DIRECTIONS: Write a short essay in your notebook dealing with a contemporary issue in which you try to persuade the reader to think in a certain way or take a particular action.

ACTIVITY 4

DIRECTIONS: Bring to class an example of a passage that was written to persuade readers.

To Entertain

A writer whose purpose is to entertain must try to *bring enjoyment to readers by treating a topic in a light, cheerful, funny, or laughable manner.* For example, as you read the passage that follows, think about its purpose.

The Dark Menace

Richard Pirozzi

1   I will never forget my first encounter with a bat; it is an experience that will live in my memory forever. It all started at 3:00 A.M. on a muggy summer morning in late July when I got out of my bed to use the bathroom. As I left the bedroom, in what can best

be described as a near comatose state, something went whizzing by my head. With half-closed eyes, I looked up and saw what I thought was a large moth flying around in circles. It made several more sweeps around the periphery of the room before I realized that this was no moth.

2   Never at a loss as to what to do in a potentially dangerous situation, I did what any intelligent, if not courageous, person would do: I ran back into the bedroom, quickly slamming the door behind me. At that point, my wife woke to ask why I was exercising so early in the morning. I explained what was happening and suggested that she investigate immediately. My offer was rejected promptly with a look of utter disappointment at my obvious lack of courage.

3   My last hope was our big, bad 115-pound golden retriever, who was fast asleep on his back on our bedroom floor. After much prodding he managed to get up, although he had a look about him of total annoyance. Ignoring his reaction, I pushed him out of the bedroom into the living room and quickly slammed the door shut behind him. Now, I gloated, the bat was finished!

4   I listened intently by the door for the sound of what surely would be a fierce struggle, but there was total silence. After a few more impatient moments, I opened the door a crack and peered into the living room. To my shock, our great protector was waiting anxiously to return to the bedroom, which he did with great speed nearly knocking me down in the process. It was only a matter of minutes before he was—like my wife—again fast asleep. What a disappointment!

5   With no clear remedy to the situation, I became increasingly upset and disillusioned. Through the years I had heard several unpleasant "bat stories," which only contributed to my apprehension: bats fly into people's hair; bats attack; bats drink people's blood; bats can have rabies. After much thought and soul-searching, it became clear to me that I was going to have to be the saviour of the household. Armed with nothing, but dressed like a soldier ready for combat, I made my way into the living room to confront the dark menace.

6   The bat was not at all impressed with my presence as she whisked by my head several times while circling the room. Although her body was relatively small, her wing span was wide, much the way an airplane is proportioned. I marveled at her exceptional grace as she flew within the confines of the darkened room never once hitting a wall or anything else. She made no sound as she glided through the air. It was only later that I learned that bats do emit high-frequency sounds as they fly, which after striking various objects, bounce back as echoes. Using these echoes that cannot be heard by the human ear, bats navigate in total darkness without running into anything. This explains why bats function so well as nocturnal beings and can sleep away virtually all of their days. Although they are able to see, they do not have to depend on their eyes to fly. In short, they are extraordinary flying machines.

7   Eventually I put my admiration for the bat aside and returned to the immediate problem of ridding the premises of her company. I theorized that if I could entice her to fly into the front hall, the inside door could be closed quickly trapping her in that small area. If I then ran out the back door and came around to the front of the house, I could open that door and send her on her merry way. In case you are wondering why the front door would be open at 3:00 A.M., the answer is simple. I always leave my keys in it, which is

very convenient for me as well as for any uninvited guests who decide to visit. Needless to say, the rest of the family is not particularly impressed with my hospitality.

8   By the way, the plan worked perfectly for both the bat and me. In the years since this episode, I have learned much about bats through extensive reading. Although bats can be rabid, they are basically peaceful creatures who generally do not attack humans unless provoked. They are not particularly interested in human hair, which in my case is irrelevant because I have so little. Finally, some bats, who live mainly in South and Central America, are indeed called vampire bats, but they *usually* enjoy the blood of animals of the nonhuman variety and do not spend much time biting people's necks. When they do take blood, they drink very little, and the unsuspecting victim is in fairly good shape when they leave.

9   With my expanding knowledge, I have come to appreciate these strange creatures of the night with their magnificent flying abilities. They may not be beautiful, but they sure are fascinating to watch. Unlike many people, I am not nearly as terrified of them as was once the case. Nevertheless, I would just as soon meet my next bat in the zoo!

The passage above deals with the author's encounter with a bat that found its way into his home. Much of the material is presented in a humorous manner designed to bring enjoyment to readers. Phrases like "near comotose state" (paragraph 1) and "dressed like a soldier ready for combat" (paragraph 5), and sentences like "They are not particularly interested in human hair, which in my case is irrelevant because I have so little" (paragraph 8) are obvious examples that attempt to be funny. They are meant to entertain readers by making them laugh.

ACTIVITY 5

DIRECTIONS: Write a short essay in your notebook dealing with a contemporary issue that has entertainment as its purpose.

ACTIVITY 6

DIRECTIONS: Bring to class an example of a passage that was written to entertain readers.

Combination of Purposes

Sometimes a writer has more than one purpose, as illustrated in the passage dealing with Eric Morse. As you recall, the writer provided factual information but also tried to persuade readers to accept his viewpoint and take action. The passage above about bats was designed not only to entertain but to inform as well by providing useful information. These examples are not at all unusual, especially when you are reading material that deals with controversial contemporary topics.

When there is a combination of purposes, try to uncover and concentrate on the writer's *overall* or *main purpose* by focusing on the most important messages and the information that lends direct support to them. Remember that recognizing the purpose (or purposes) helps you evaluate the reliability and objectivity of reading material. This is very important when dealing with issues that involve conflicting, debatable, and sometimes emotional viewpoints.

ACTIVITY 7

DIRECTIONS: Write a short essay in your notebook dealing with a contemporary issue that demonstrates a combination of purposes.

ACTIVITY 8

DIRECTIONS: Bring to class an example of a passage that has a combination of purposes.

ACTIVITY 9

DIRECTIONS: Read the following passages and answer the questions. When reading each passage, keep in mind the writer's background or affiliation, the publication in which the writing appears, and how the most important information is presented, all of which should help you recognize the writer's overall or main purpose. Remember to use inference skills when appropriate.

EYE ON VOCABULARY

When reading each passage, take note of any unfamiliar words you come across. List them and their definitions in your notebook or on note cards. Use the context, word parts, or the dictionary to determine their meanings. After the completion of each passage, your instructor will ask to see your notebook or note cards and may discuss key words in class.

1
Pornography

1   It is against the law to distribute pornography, "obscene" or sexually explicit materials in the media. The general public also opposes the distribution as well as the use of pornography. Yet pornography has become an enormous industry today. A major reason is that the demand for sexually explicit materials has soared over the last decade. The number of hard-core video rentals, for example, skyrocketed from only 75 million in 1985 to 665 million in 1996. Today, the United States has become by far the world's leading producer of hard-core videos, churning them out at the astonishing rate of about 150 new titles a week (Schlosser, 1997; Weber, 1997). Pornography has also gone online; whatever X-rated, hard-core material is available in adult bookstores or video stores can be accessed via the Internet (see box). But is pornography harmful?

2   According to some conservatives, pornography is harmful to society. The studies most often cited to support this view, conducted in laboratories, suggest that exposure to pornography increases aggression. In these studies, male subjects were first made to feel

irritated, angry, or ready to behave aggressively. Then they were exposed to pornographic materials. In general, their level of aggression increased significantly (Soble, 1996; Linz and Malamuth, 1993). But the artificial laboratory setting is quite different from the real world. At home, pornography users may not become more aggressive because they can do something—such as masturbating or copulating—to satisfy their sexual arousal.

3   According to some liberals, pornography is harmless. To support this view, studies that fail to show a connection between pornography and rape are often cited. Cities with high circulation of sexually oriented magazines, for example, have largely the same rates of rape as cities with low circulation. But the pornography in such studies is mostly *nonviolent,* depicting merely nudity and consensual sex (Strossen, 1996; Linz and Malamuth, 1993).

4   Other studies suggest that *violent* pornography is harmful, as some feminists assert. For example, research often finds that men who see slasher movies, in which a female rape victim is cut up, show less sympathy for rape victims in general. Studies of rapists suggest that men who lack sympathy for rape victims are more likely to assault women (Kipnis, 1996; Cole, 1995; Linz and Malamuth, 1993). We may therefore conclude that nonviolent pornography may be harmless but that violent pornography is harmful.

Virtual World: The Proliferation of Cyberporn

5   Pornography in cyberspace is not new. Soon after the Internet came on the technological scene, people started to exchange dirty pictures on the Net. But amateur swapping has now given way to commercial ventures. By mid-1997, according to an online guide to cyberporn, there were already about 900 sex sites on the Web. Only 1 year later, this number had soared to somewhere between 20,000 and 30,000. These commercial sites vary in size from small outfits with just a few hundred paying members to major networks with thousands of subscribers.

6   Cyberporn has become big business, raking in some $700 million a year. Sex sites are comparable in popularity to sports or weather sites and have only slightly fewer visitors than business and travel sites. A onetime stripper's site brings in so much revenue that she has given up stripping for good. In her former profession, she made only $1,500 a month, but immediately after going on the Web, her monthly earnings jumped to $10,000 to $15,000. A 23-year-old man formed a company called Internet Entertainment in 1997 and now makes $20 million annually by offering a wide range of online shows. One type, called "live video," features exotic nude dancers in full color on the computer screens of customers, who can chat on the phone with the gyrating performers. Customers can also click their way to different virtual rooms: in the "bedroom" the visitor can see a naked dancer rolling around on a giant mattress, and in the "health club" the performer works out on a step exerciser with no clothes on.

7   Cyberporn has become so popular primarily because customers can view racy material in the privacy of their homes. They no longer have to sneak into a sleazy adult bookstore or the back room of a video shop.

Alex Thio, *Sociology: A Brief Introduction,* 4th ed., pp. 154–155

COMPREHENSION QUESTIONS

1. What is the topic of the passage?

2. What is the central message of the passage?

3. Determine what is at issue. What is your initial personal viewpoint?

4. Distinguish among opposing viewpoints, and provide the rationale for each.

5. Think carefully about the viewpoints. Express a personal viewpoint, and give the reasons why you favor it. Does it differ from your initial personal viewpoint? Why or why not?

6. Write a few paragraphs *in support of the viewpoint that you do* not *favor*.

THOUGHT AND DISCUSSION QUESTIONS

1. In your view, should pornography be permitted in cyberspace? Why or why not?

2. Can you safely infer from the passage that the author is opposed to the use of pornography? Why or why not?

3. Have you ever used pornography? Why or why not?

4. In your view, did the studies that first made male subjects angry or ready to behave aggressively and then exposed them to pornographic materials prove that exposure to pornography increases aggression? Why or why not?

5. What is the author's *overall* or *main purpose?* Give specific reasons for your answer.

6. List any questions that came to mind while you were reading this selection, and be prepared to discuss possible answers to them.

2
A New Sales Incentive

Isadore Barmash

1   A creative brainstorm recently came to me during a period of personal discomfort. Waiting endlessly for my wife to finish her shopping in a cavernous department store, it occurred to me that the patient men and women who accompany their spouses when they shop are really the forgotten consumers of today. The partners who give moral support to shoppers, cheerfully hold bags, stare into space, concentrate on where they parked and keep their eyes on the time so that dinner doesn't slip by unnoticed, desperately need some support of their own. America's 1 million-plus stores—which constitute the nation's biggest industry—are just over their exhausting, frustrating, agonizing Christmas season. Now they are balefully looking ahead to the new year, hoping that it may bring an improvement. Anything positive they do will surely help to stem the downsizings, closings and mergers that have dogged American retailing in the last few years. Any new wrinkle that retailers can offer to create more good will and turn a discomfited grouser into a gratified shopper's companion makes good sense.

2   Let's examine why, in addition to business reasons, it's important morally and socially to please those who accompany their partners when they buy that merchandise. We are

forbearing. We provide moral support just in case our companion wants some advice (even if it is usually ignored). We are security symbols when the two of us go into the parking lot. If need be, we stand as a credit confirmation. If the salesclerk has some doubts, they vanish as she or he sees us standing stolidly beside the shopper. And we are a sort of sober authority figure, flashing indignant, even threatening expressions to a clerk giving our companion a hard time. We're a great backup.

3   So what should the merchants do for us? They should provide some physical comforts. Some chairs or benches, preferably inside the store and preferably in the most popular departments, would be useful, so that our backs and feet do not protest so badly that our patience just oozes away, leading to a potential argument with our spouses when they come up for air. It wouldn't take much room, but it would be so welcomed. The bigger the stores, the more flexibility they offer for such amenities. Actually, one reason that they range to as much as two or three football fields is that it allows them the capability of easily moving things around, like a giant stage. Aisles, nooks and crannies, corners, and dead ends flourish in the big stores.

4   Going a bit further, it would be very pleasant to find a large store setting aside a small area as a lounge for men (and women) as in airports. A TV, the latest newspapers, perhaps some magazines could be placed there, along with a few upholstered chairs and perhaps a couple of vending machines. One per floor—OK, one per store—would be appreciated. Is it really too much to ask? I'm not asking for a Dow-Jones stock ticker or a Bloomberg news wire. But if the store wants to provide them, who would say no?

5   As a couple, my wife and I have traveled a bit and seen chairs and benches made available to shoppers at the Mitsukoshi stores in the Ginza in Tokyo and at Stockmann's, the big department store in Helsinki. If they can do it, why can't we?

6   To be fair, when my wife and I were recently in a Macy's, I began wandering around while waiting and experienced a pleasant shock. The store actually has two upholstered chairs and two wooden chairs on the main selling floor. Sitting there were four men with soulful looks as if savoring a celestial pleasure. Would that one would have given a seat to a well-dressed soul nearby whom I observed leaning up against a post, his face pressed against it as if in terminal despair. Anecdote's moral: great, but give us more chairs!

7   Not so long ago, in another department store, I was waiting as usual when a woman wandered by. She glanced at me and announced, "I've lost my husband." I answered, innocuously enough, "And I am waiting for my wife." But she didn't hear me because she was wandering around, shouting, "Maurice, Maurice!" What an argument they are going to have when they finally meet, I thought.

8   Why is it, I wondered, that the sexes have such a hard time with each other in the nation's stores? Women buy about three times as much merchandise as men, but it is not a problem of socio-demographics. What it is, I concluded, is just a matter of (1) comfort and (2) communications. Marital relations would certainly blossom if the man were happily ensconced in a leisure area while his wife shopped. At least she would know where he was.

9   But better yet, what the retailers might well consider are walkie-talkies so that shopping companions can keep in touch with each other. It's manageable—show credit cards, get a pair of walkie-talkies, return them when leaving. Ridiculous? Maybe, but think how many arguments it would avoid. After all, when you have these multi-football-field-size sites, communications are vital, aren't they?

10   Stores lately seem to love initials in their display signs. In the women's department, they have LIZ, DKNY and I.N.C., and others in the men's wear department. So how about SCSC, for Shoppers' Companion Support Center? It may not directly beef up a store's business, but can it hurt? What it will do is improve good will, something that retailers pay a lot for when they swallow up one another, as they have been doing a lot lately. Yet it is something that can't be truly measured in dollars but in the intangibles that really count. What is certain is that it would relieve those tired, aimless souls who just wait around but would like nothing better than to fade into the woodwork.

11   And consider how it would motivate shoppers knowing their companions were relaxing in comfort, not brooding or nursing anger. They might even buy more.

Newsweek, January 29, 1996, p. 12

COMPREHENSION QUESTIONS

1. What is the topic of the passage?

2. What is the central message of the passage?

3. Determine what is at issue. What is your initial personal viewpoint?

4. Distinguish among opposing viewpoints, and provide the rationale for each.

5. Think carefully about the viewpoints. Express a personal viewpoint, and give the reasons why you favor it. Does it differ from your initial personal viewpoint? Why or why not?

6. Write a few paragraphs *in support of the viewpoint that you do* not *favor.*

THOUGHT AND DISCUSSION QUESTIONS

1. In your view, do men and women shop differently? Why or why not?

2. Do you agree with the author that spouses might buy more if they knew that their partners were waiting comfortably for them? Why or why not?

3. In your view, is this article sexist? Why or why not?

4. What is the author's *overall* or *main purpose*? Give specific reasons for your answer.

5. List any questions that came to mind while you were reading this selection, and be prepared to discuss possible answers to them.

3

Thinking About Racism and Our Children

Richard Pirozzi

1   Two African American women—a mother and her daughter—are shopping for clothing at a major department store. As they browse through the aisles trying to decide what to buy, they are followed and watched closely by the salespeople. Meanwhile, there are two Caucasian girls one aisle over who are going unnoticed as they put various articles

of clothing into a shopping bag without paying for them. The mother and her daughter purchase some items and proceed to leave the store. As they reach the door, they are joined by the two white girls, who quickly go through the exit at the same time. When the alarm goes off, the salespeople rush to the door and ask the mother and daughter to return to the counter in order to check the contents of their bags. In the meantime, the two girls walk toward their car, having stolen hundreds of dollars' worth of merchandise.

2   A young professional African American man waits for a cab in the middle of New York City at midnight. As he waves, several taxis pass right by him, the drivers fearful of picking him up at that hour and possibly having to drive through an unsafe part of town. On the other hand, they do not hesitate to stop for white passengers just a few blocks away. Growing increasingly impatient after standing in the same spot for half an hour, the man decides to use public transportation.

3   Two black college students are driving back to school along an interstate highway in the middle of the afternoon. They and the drivers of three other automobiles are traveling about five miles over the speed limit. A state trooper pulls the college students over for speeding and proceeds to question them suspiciously about drugs, while the other drivers continue down the highway on their merry way. The trooper and the drivers of the three other cars happen to be white.

4   Do these three stories sound familiar to you? If you are black, your answer is probably yes. If you are white, chances are your answer is no. Yet situations like these confront black people every day, and they cut at the very soul of the country. The result is outrage and resentment on the part of African Americans toward the white establishment, while most Caucasians display an unbelievable inability to recognize the problem, no less try to correct it.

5   This was brought home clearly by the reaction to the verdict in the O. J. Simpson trial. While many whites had a look of anger or disbelief on their faces because they felt that a guilty man had been set free, most blacks responded with spontaneous joy and much satisfaction. For many of them it was not even a question of guilt or innocence but rather a case where, at last, one of their own had won out against a tainted criminal justice system that has consistently proven itself to be prejudiced and unfair. To understand their reaction one does not have to look any further than the Rodney King episode where the four white cops who beat him on camera were exonerated by a jury devoid of any black people. Although that is one of the most blatant and well-publicized cases, it does epitomize what happens all too frequently. Consequently, for many African Americans it was a refreshing change of pace to see Simpson walk. On the other hand, the white people who thought that he was guilty felt the bitterness, frustration and disillusionment that blacks have had to deal with for a very long time. It is doubtful, however, that whites were able to make that connection and appreciate what African Americans have been coping with through the years.

6   There are those who will argue that much progress has been made in race relations in this century. Certainly, from a legislative point of view, there are laws now on the books that provide protection for minorities by eliminating the more blatant forms of racism, and they have helped to bring about at least some behavioral change over the last forty or so years. I can never forget the experience I had in the early 1950s as a six-year-old, when my mother sat me down at a table in a small restaurant located in Paterson, New Jersey. She had some more shopping to do so she asked the owner if he would

keep an eye on me for fifteen minutes. While my mother was gone, a very dignified older black woman sat down across from me at my table. The owner, in an abrupt manner, immediately asked her to sit someplace else. The look of hurt on her face will stay with me forever. Then there were all those experiences in the mid-1960s when I was attending a small Southern junior college where local black people were treated by some of the students as if they were something other than human.

7   Perhaps these instances of outright racist behavior no longer occur as frequently, but how much have attitudes really changed? It seems that the most obvious examples of racism—the Rodney King episode notwithstanding—have for the most part disappeared, only to be replaced by a more subtle strain. In this day and age, I am always amazed at the frequent use of racial epithets and stereotyping by professional and nonprofessional white people. And it certainly does not help matters when black people use those same epithets and stereotypes to refer to themselves and each other. Blacks are also guilty of stereotyping whites and perceiving them as all the same. In fact, years of mistreatment and degradation have led to such suspicion that on many of our college campuses African Americans generally prefer to stick together rather than mix with white students.

8   Can it be that deep down inside, we are all racists? What hope then is there for racial harmony in this country? There are some things that need to be done quickly. First of all, a real effort has to be made by both races to reach out, communicate and empathize with each other. Whites have to come to appreciate what has been the black experience for most of the history of this nation, and they must speak out strongly against all forms of racism whether blatant or subtle. On the other hand, blacks should never forget their history as victims of discrimination, but they must also attempt to rise above it and not assume that all whites are cut from the same mold. African Americans should also take great pride in their accomplishments against what must have seemed like insurmountable odds to their forefathers. They must keep in mind that change is often gradual and sometimes very painful for all those involved, and for that reason, animosity is frequently its by-product.

9   Most important, parents of both races must teach their children that racist behavior of any kind is totally unacceptable. Kids should know about the history of race relations in this country and be advised of the role they can play—now and as adults—to make the situation more harmonious. At the very least, this should include a familiarity with the diverse groups that make up American society. In short, parents need to go out of their way to introduce their children at an early age to people of different races so that they are better equipped to interact with them today and in the future. Progress cannot be made unless we start to really get to know each other. In the end, improvement in race relations does not rest exclusively with our generation but will depend ultimately on generations still to come.

The Humanist, July–August 1996, pp. 40–41

COMPREHENSION QUESTIONS

1. What is the topic of the passage?

2. What is the central message of the passage?

3. Determine what is at issue. What is your initial personal viewpoint?

4. Distinguish among opposing viewpoints, and provide the rationale for each.

5. Think carefully about the viewpoints. Express a personal viewpoint, and give the reasons why you favor it. Does it differ from your initial personal viewpoint? Why or why not?

6. Write a few paragraphs *in support of the viewpoint that you do* not *favor.*

THOUGHT AND DISCUSSION QUESTIONS

1. Do you agree with the author that racism today is more subtle than in the past? Why or why not?

2. Can you safely infer from the passage that the author believes we are all racists? Why or why not? Do you believe that "deep down inside, we are all racists"? Why or why not?

3. In your view, what will race relations be like in the United States 50 years from now? Why?

4. Do you think the information presented is mostly fact, mostly opinion, or a combination of both? Why? Cite specific examples.

5. What is the author's *overall* or *main purpose*? Give specific reasons for your answer.

6. List any questions that came to mind while you were reading this selection, and be prepared to discuss possible answers to them.

THE IMPORTANCE OF RECOGNIZING TONE

A writer's **tone** or **mood** is *a reflection of the writer's attitude or feelings toward a given topic or issue.* It is expressed by the words and phrases used in the information presented. As with purpose, it is important for you to recognize the tone, because it helps you determine a writer's motivations or reasons for writing, which can in turn make it easier to recognize bias and distinguish between facts and opinions. Furthermore, it is part of the whole evaluation process that you should use when considering not only what you read but also what you see and hear.

Thus tone is an important consideration when you deal with contemporary issues and also when you gather information from people and written sources for problem-solving purposes. When interacting face to face, a person's *tone of voice* and *body language* will sometimes reveal the person's feelings on a given matter, so you may find yourself in a better position to assess the quality of the information the person is giving you. This, in turn, may help you solve a problem more efficiently. The same benefit applies when dealing with written sources for problem solving, when you want to weigh their objectivity.

As with purpose, writers don't always come right out and say what they are feeling about a particular topic or issue. In those instances, it becomes necessary to "read between the lines" and use inference skills to help determine tone. Thus the words and phrases a writer uses will serve as the clues to the writer's attitude. As you will recall, it is often necessary to use those same clues to infer a writer's purpose when it is not explicit. In fact, tone and purpose are related, and therefore each can be used sometimes to help figure out the other. For example, if a writer's tone is humorous, it would probably indicate that the writer's purpose is to entertain and vice versa. On the other hand, if the tone is matter-of-fact, the purpose is likely to be informational.

When trying to recognize the tone, there are several possibilities to be considered. This is certainly the case when dealing with contemporary issues, where writers sometimes have more than one purpose. In addition, they may also express more than one attitude toward the subject matter. On those occasions, follow the same procedure that you used when dealing with a combination of purposes: Concentrate on the most important messages and the information that lends direct support to them. This should help you uncover the *overall tone*.

We will focus on five common tones or moods that are often expressed by writers: matter-of-fact, humorous, angry, sad, and ironic. Each one represents an overall feeling or attitude by a given writer toward a particular subject. Let us look at each of these.

Matter-of-Fact Tone

When adopting a matter-of-fact tone, which is common in textbooks, *the writer sticks to the facts and presents them in a straightforward, unemotional manner*. In other words, there is a concerted attempt to be evenhanded and objective. The purpose is informational. For example, read this paragraph:

> Although progress has been made with regard to women's rights in the United States, it appears that there is room for improvement. There are still jobs not open to them, and they are sometimes paid less than men occupying the same or similar positions. Furthermore, some women have been the victims of out-and-out sexual harassment on the job. In short, it will take a while longer before we can safely say that there is equality between the sexes.

The paragraph expresses little emotion as the author attempts to present the information in a straightforward and unbiased way. For the most part, the words used are not extreme or slanted.

ACTIVITY 10

DIRECTIONS: In your notebook, write a paragraph with a matter-of-fact tone on any topic that interests you.

ACTIVITY 11

DIRECTIONS: Bring to class an example of a passage with a matter-of-fact tone.

Humorous Tone

A humorous tone is one in which *a writer presents information in a lighthearted manner designed to entertain or make the reader laugh*. For instance, read the following paragraph, which deals with the same subject matter as the previous one:

> If you believe that there has been much progress with regard to women's rights in the United States, you probably also believe in the Tooth Fairy. Wake up and smell the

aftershave lotion! Women are still excluded from some jobs as if they were suffering from some weird contagious disease. And just compare their pay scales to those of men in certain positions—you could die laughing. Not to mention that some males turn into cavemen when they are around women on the job. Equality between the sexes? Give me a break!

Although the paragraph makes basically the same points as the previous matter-of-fact one, it does so in a much more lighthearted way. The use of expressions like "Tooth Fairy," "weird contagious disease," "you could die laughing," "turn into cavemen" and the various exclamations are an attempt to be funny and make the reader laugh.

ACTIVITY 12

DIRECTIONS: In your notebook, write a paragraph with a humorous tone on the same topic that you used for Activity 10.

ACTIVITY 13

DIRECTIONS: Bring to class an example of a passage with a humorous tone.

Angry Tone

An angry tone lets you know that *the writer is annoyed, irritated, or bothered in some way about the subject matter being presented.* For example, read the following paragraph, which deals with the same topic as the previous ones:

I am sick and tired of hearing how much "progress" has been made with regard to women's rights in the United States. Women are prevented from filling some jobs and are paid ridiculously low wages in certain positions, compared to men. Furthermore, some men behave obnoxiously when they are around women on the job. It is absurd to say that we have achieved equality between the sexes.

Although the paragraph is similar to the other two in terms of the points being made, it presents them in a much more emotional manner. The use of the expressions "sick and tired," "ridiculously low," "behave obnoxiously," and "absurd" clearly express the writer's anger.

ACTIVITY 14

DIRECTIONS: In your notebook, write a paragraph with an angry tone on the same topic that you have been using.

ACTIVITY 15

DIRECTIONS: Bring to class an example of a passage with an angry tone.

Sad Tone

A sad tone *presents information in a gloomy, melancholy, or sorrowful way*. For instance, read the following paragraph on the same topic as the previous ones:

> Although some slight progress has been made with regard to women's rights in the United States, there is, regrettably, ample room for improvement. It is discouraging to realize that some jobs are still not open to women and that women are too often paid less than men occupying the same or similar positions. Furthermore, some women are still the unfortunate victims of sexual harassment on the job. In short, equality between the sexes at this point remains far beyond our grasp. What a sad state of affairs!

Once again, the points that are made in the paragraph are similar to those found in the others, but this time they are presented in a downcast manner. The use of "regrettably," "discouraging," "unfortunate," and "sad state of affairs" and the generally negative approach to the material indicate that the writer is pessimistic about the situation.

ACTIVITY 16

DIRECTIONS: In your notebook, write a paragraph with a sad tone on the same topic that you have been using.

ACTIVITY 17

DIRECTIONS: Bring to class an example of a passage with a sad tone.

Ironic Tone

The dictionary defines **irony** as "a method of humorous or sarcastic expression in which the intended meaning of the words used is the direct opposite of their usual sense" or "a combination of circumstances or a result that is the opposite of what might be expected or considered appropriate." Thus an ironic message *conveys its meaning by using words to mean the opposite of what they usually mean*, and an ironic event is an occurrence that is *the opposite or reverse of what is normally expected*. We might describe a bad day in a sarcastic manner by saying "What a wonderful day I've had!" or we might observe the irony in the fact that the first ship specifically designed to be unsinkable, the *Titanic*, sank on its very first voyage. A writer generally uses irony to present messages in a catchy, unusual way so that readers will take notice and remember them. For instance, read the following paragraph, which deals once again with women's rights:

> Now that women are in business suits, why don't we just assume that no further progress needs to be made with regard to women's rights in the United States? We can simply ignore the fact that some jobs are still not open to them and that they are sometimes paid less than men occupying the same or similar positions. It really doesn't even matter that some women are still being subjected to sexual harassment on the job. Let's just proclaim equality between the sexes a *fait accompli* and get the whole issue behind us.

Notice how the writer takes what is essentially the same information but this time uses expressions that mean the *opposite* of the points he really wants to convey. By using this somewhat unusual technique, he hopes that the reader will be jolted into taking note of and remembering the *intended* messages.

Let us look at another example of irony, an occurrence that is the opposite of what is normally expected:

1   Earnest, lean Regilio Tuur, looking like a strip of copper wire with muscles, was no-nonsense as he shadowboxed outside the bloodstained ring at Gleason's Gym near the Brooklyn waterfront. But he permitted himself an ironic laugh when his workout was over and he talked about how his craft had changed.

2   He remembers when his big concern was how to keep from being cut badly. These days, he worries more when an opponent starts gushing blood. You never know any-more, said this young man.... Who can say where the other fellow has been?

3   "I've fought four times in the last year and had four H.I.V. tests, and my manager made sure that my opponents were tested, too," said Mr. Tuur, a Suriname-born Dutchman now living on Long Island. "This is a blood sport. You can't be careful enough. People talk about testing and the right to privacy, but that's a crock. We're talking about lives here. Going into the ring with some who's tested positive, that's an act of suicide, isn't it?"

Clyde Haberman, "H.I.V. Testing for Boxers: Is Rule Fair? Is Anything?"
New York Times, February 16, 1996, p. 132

Here the irony involves how one circumstance has changed completely in the sport of boxing. In the past, the boxer discussed in the passage was concerned about sustain-ing a bad cut, whereas now, with the AIDS problem, he is more worried about an oppo-nent's getting cut. Thus what is happening is the opposite of what normally has been expected. Notice that the writer explicitly lets the reader know that there is irony in this situation by calling the boxer's laugh "ironic."

ACTIVITY 18

DIRECTIONS: In your notebook, write two paragraphs in an ironic tone on any topics that are of interest to you. In one of them, convey a message by using words to mean the oppo-site of what they usually mean, and in the other, discuss an occurrence that is the oppo-site or reverse of what is normally expected. Use the two examples in the text to guide you, and feel free to discuss your paragraphs with your classmates.

ACTIVITY 19

DIRECTIONS: Bring to class an example of a passage with an ironic tone.

ACTIVITY 20

DIRECTIONS: Read the following passages and answer the questions. When reading each passage, concentrate on the most important messages and the information that lends direct support to them to help you uncover the overall tone. Remember to use inference skills when appropriate.

EYE ON VOCABULARY

When reading each passage, take note of any unfamiliar words you come across. List them and their definitions in your notebook or on note cards. Use the context, word parts, or the dictionary to determine their meanings. After the completion of each passage, your instructor will ask to see your notebook or note cards and may discuss key words in class.

1
Double Exploitation

Bob Herbert

1   With the show's rat-a-tat theme music blaring in the background, the television announcer, already planning future shows, says to the national viewing audience: "Is your teen daughter *obsessed* with sex? If so, call us at 800-93-SALLY and tell us about her."

2   For those who find enjoyment, excitement and lots of laughs in the sexual exploitation of children, I offer you the Sally Jessy Raphael experience. I had the misfortune to see last Monday's show, which was titled "My Teen Can't Go Without Sex." It was like spending an hour in an unclean bathroom.

3   The show opened with several comments like the following:

4   "Sally, my little girl is only 12 years old, but she's already had sex with 25 guys!"

5   Loud prurient cheers erupted from the studio audience and the music intensified as Ms. Raphael kicked off a show that was unrelentingly vile and degrading, and brutally abusive to its young guests. The girls (no boys) were encouraged, cajoled and all but coerced into revealing excruciating details of their promiscuity. They were then roundly denounced, cursed, reviled, laughed at and otherwise humiliated by the rowdy audience. They were even chastised by Ms. Raphael, an empty-headed and maddeningly self-righteous host.

6   A 15-year-old, who was booed because she had slept with 17 guys, wept and blurted out that she had been sexually abused by her mother's boyfriend.

7   "How far did he get?" Ms. Raphael asked. "Tell us, *Steffi*. How far?"

8   However far the abuser got, it was no reason—as far as the host was concerned—to give the girl a break. Ms. Raphael told her, "If you take all the women in the world who have been abused, they don't go and do what you've been doing."

9   Microphones were handed to members of the audience who wanted to denounce the girls. "You make me sick!" a woman shrieked at the 15-year-old. She told the girl that if she ever got pregnant, the child (apparently predestined to be female) would be a "slut" just like her mother. "There's going to be one slut in the other one," the woman said.

10   That was one of the milder comments. You got the impression that if rocks had been distributed to the nitwits in the audience, they would have eagerly thrown them at the wretched offenders.

11   That was the tenor of the entire show. The star was the 12-year-old, which was not surprising. She was the youngest and the whole point of the program was to titillate the audience by eroticizing children. The girls were heavily made up and repeated references were made to their relationships with older men, their reluctance to use condoms, and so on. It was a form of ritualized, legalized child abuse.

12   The host and the audience, equally reprehensible, attempted to immunize themselves and safeguard their enjoyment by portraying the children as demons and seductresses, rather than as the victims of the men and boys who preyed upon them, the parents who were unwilling or unable to protect them, and a society capable of viewing programs like Ms. Raphael's as entertainment, rather than as a menace.

13   A 12-year-old who has slept with dozens of boys needs professional counseling in a safe and compassionate environment, not the hoots and derisive shouts of a mob masquerading as an audience. If Ms. Raphael had even the slightest sensitivity to the needs of a child who had been sexually molested, she could never think that outing that child on national television was a good idea.

14   The children on Ms. Raphael's show last Monday were betrayed. By definition, they were excessively needy. That is the case with all sexually exploited children. But instead of getting help from a powerful authority figure like the host of a nationally syndicated television show, these children were brutally victimized again.

15   The abuse was not limited to the young. The mother of the 12-year-old seemed to be mentally impaired, perhaps retarded. When she made a tearful comment that was uttered with difficulty and was grammatically incorrect, the audience and Ms. Raphael broke into uncontrollable laughter. The daughter, distressed, looked on helplessly.

16   What fun. Maybe they can do an entire show on mental illness. It ought to be at least as entertaining as child sex abuse.

New York Times, February 26, 1996, p. A13

COMPREHENSION QUESTIONS

1. What is the topic of the passage?

2. What is the central message of the passage?

3. Determine what is at issue. What is your initial personal viewpoint?

4. Distinguish among opposing viewpoints, and provide the rationale for each.

5. Think carefully about the viewpoints. Express a personal viewpoint, and give the reasons why you favor it. Does it differ from your initial personal viewpoint? Why or why not?

6. Write a few paragraphs *in support of the viewpoint that you do not favor.*

THOUGHT AND DISCUSSION QUESTIONS

1. Why did the author title the passage "Double Exploitation"?

2. Should shows like the one mentioned in the passage be permitted on the air? Why or why not? Do you watch shows like the one mentioned in the passage? Why or why not?

3. Do you think the information presented is mostly fact, mostly opinion, or a combination of both? Why? Cite specific examples.

4. Which one of the five tones discussed is expressed by the author when he states: "What fun. Maybe they can do an entire show on mental illness. It ought to be at least as entertaining as child sex abuse" (paragraph 16)? Give reasons for your answer.

5. What is the *overall tone* of the passage? Give specific reasons for your answer.

6. List any questions that came to mind while you were reading this selection, and be prepared to discuss possible answers to them.

2
You're in My Spot

Sharon White Taylor

1   While my husband, Cliff, and I were sitting in our car outside a restaurant recently, a man pulled into a space clearly reserved for the handicapped. When he bounded out of his car and sprinted into the restaurant, all my senses stood at attention.

2   Since becoming disabled by a stroke three years ago, I've waged a campaign against the able-bodied who are too lazy to walk extra steps. In this case, the man had a choice of nearby parking spots, but he opted for the reserved space in front of the door.

3   This wasn't the first time I have challenged a parking cheat. Often, from my car, I've spotted a nonqualified person parked illegally and have called out: "Excuse me, you are parked in a handicapped zone." I have clumped after people with my walker and chased them down with my wheelchair to point out the errors of their ways.

4   While family members agree with my reasons for pursuing my mission, they worry about my methods. One winter's day my sister, Nancy, questioned my sanity when I forced her to push my wheelchair through an icy parking lot to confront a woman without a limp (or a parking sticker) walking away from a handicapped space. Later, Nancy was glad she had given me the chance to challenge the offender. The woman confessed: "I should know better. I'm a nurse." She moved her car. Not long ago, when I reminded another woman that she was parked in a handicapped zone, she retorted in a huff, "I know all about you people. I work in a convalescent home."

5   Most people don't apologize. Many are rude. Some offer nonsensical excuses. I confronted one man as he briskly headed into a grocery store. "My mother is handicapped," he snapped.

6   Before I joined the ranks of the disabled, I often eyed those coveted spots on rainy days or when I stopped for milk or bread after a long work day. I passed them by. After suffering a broken leg some years ago, I understood their importance. In my state permits are not issued for temporary handicaps. When my husband pulled into a typical narrow parking space, he had great difficulty trying to maneuver the wheelchair out of the car without hitting a neighboring vehicle. Pushing a wheelchair in the snow and rain or across a rutted parking lot can be hazardous.

7   The switch from temporary to permanent disability hasn't been easy. Following a brief bout with depression, I decided to accept what can't be changed. I have even learned to appreciate the perks. It is comforting to find a spot close to the store while other shoppers trek through snow or heat.

8   My adult children joke about taking me and my parking permit to concerts so they can have privileged parking. Of course, they quip, you have to wait in the car.

9   All kidding aside, others envy my parking status. One blistering hot summer day, a woman saw me getting out of my car at a crowded mall. She was obviously wilted after walking the length of the large lot. "You are so lucky," she said. "I'll trade places with you." I smiled. "Gladly," I answered. "I would love to walk."

10   Though I rarely feel sorry for myself these days, it would be nice to leave my house without wondering if my destination has stairs I can't negotiate or whether privileged parking will be available. In many places there are only one or two designated spots and they may be occupied. There have been times when being unable to find a space has meant we've had to forgo plans to attend an event. The frustration of finding the marked places filled by nondisabled drivers has spurred me to continue my battle against abusers.

11   Until recently, if I found a car illegally parked with no driver in sight, I would leave a hastily scribbled note on the windshield. Now I am armed with professionally printed, bright orange notices given to me by another family waging the same war. In large black letters the placards read: "This is not a ticket but a reminder. You are parked in a space that is reserved for the handicapped. These facilities are provided for individuals whose physical disabilities make their use a necessity."

12   Having left more than 50 handwritten notes and about a dozen printed notices, I was curious about their effect on the offenders. The very-abled man who had parked illegally in front of the restaurant would be a perfect gauge to test whether the placards made a difference.

13   I suggested to Cliff that we eat our sandwiches in the car and wait to see how the transgressor reacted. Cliff agreed, but he made me promise not to confront the man directly. Cliff is always conscious of my safety and blanches when I face off with scofflaws.

14   I'm sure he won't forget the day I spotted a burly oaf pulling a huge truck with monster tires into a reserved spot. Cliff refused to take my wheelchair out of the car and the guy was too far away to hear me shouting. I think of him as the big one that got away. I wasn't about to let that happen again.

15   So we munched our sandwiches, sipped coffee and discussed what the latest offender's reaction might be. Even though I'm an optimist, I didn't expect him to flagellate himself and cry *mea culpa*. Perhaps he would look sheepish and glance around to see if anyone had noticed the big orange flier under his windshield wiper. Maybe in the future he would be more considerate. My husband is a pessimist. His prediction proved more accurate.

16   After about 20 minutes, the man returned to his car. He saw the notice, pulled it off the windshield and quickly read it. Looking as if he had smelled something vile, he threw it down next to a trash container, spat on the ground and drove away.

17   We had our answer. People who illegally park in spaces for the handicapped also litter and spit.

18   Oh, dear, am I being politically incorrect? Have I stereotyped people who usurp hand-icapped parking? If you feel maligned, defend your position. Point out that you may self-ishly inconvenience the disabled, but you never litter or spit in public.

Newsweek, February 19, 1996, p. 20

COMPREHENSION QUESTIONS

1. What is the topic of the passage?

2. What is the central message of the passage?

3. Determine what is at issue. What is your initial personal viewpoint?

4. Distinguish among opposing viewpoints, and provide the rationale for each.

5. Think carefully about the viewpoints. Express a personal viewpoint, and give the reasons why you favor it. Does it differ from your initial personal viewpoint? Why or why not?

6. Write a few paragraphs *in support of the viewpoint that you do not favor.*

THOUGHT AND DISCUSSION QUESTIONS

1. In your view, are handicapped parking spaces justified? Why or why not?

2. Do you ever park in handicapped parking spaces? Why or why not?

3. Is the writer on solid ground when she infers that "people who illegally park in spaces for the handicapped also litter and spit" (paragraph 17)? Why or why not?

4. What is the *overall tone* of the passage? Give specific reasons for your answer.

5. List any questions that came to mind while you were reading this selection, and be prepared to discuss possible answers to them.

3
The F-Word ... or, Isn't a Mink Bred to Be a Coat?

Evelyn Renold

1   Not long ago, my eightysomething aunt asked me if I wanted her luxurious mink coat. She planned on leaving it to me in her will, she said, but why didn't I just take it now? I remember feeling a rush of excitement, immediately followed by an avalanche of anxiety: Given the fervor of the animal-rights movement, would I ever have the courage to wear it? And how did I really feel about carving up little creatures to make a fashion statement?

2   It's not as if I'd spent my whole life lusting after fur. I grew up in Southern California, and though I can recall a few L.A. country-club types preening in their mink stoles, fur was pretty exotic out there. Even after migrating east, I never seriously considered such an extravagance. Fur coats, I remember thinking, were the province of older women with more lavish lifestyles than mine.

3   Still, like every warm-blooded American girl, I fantasized. Suppose I were to acquire a posher lifestyle. What kind of fur would I choose? And how would it look on me as I

swept into charity balls and Monday nights at the opera? (Unspoken answers: *fox* and *very good indeed.*) Now and again, I would furtively try on a fur coat belonging to a friend, if only to keep this harmless little fantasy alive.

4   Then one day, the fantasy stopped being harmless. Almost overnight, fur coats went the way of red meat and unprotected sex—bygone relics of a more licentious, less politically correct era. I'd missed my chance, and I felt a little cheated. If I wanted to be considered a caring, compassionate person, fur was definitely out—though I have to confess that its appeal was somewhat enhanced for me by its newly forbidden status.

5   Not that I'm indifferent to furry creatures. Having cohabited with cats, I get more than a little squeamish when I read about scientific experiments conducted on living felines. (Yes, animal research is necessary; I just wish they'd draft rats rather than kittens.) And I was outraged by last year's news story about the Colombian drug dealers who smuggled cocaine into this country in a sheepdog's belly. So I understand the argument—at least I think I do—that even though minks are less charismatic than canines and cats, we ought to care about them too. Nonetheless, I've always been suspicious of people who worry more about animals than humans (the English are notorious for this). "Get a life—a human life," I feel like telling them.

6   Pets, of course, are garnering some very good press these days, as psychologists recognize the support and companionship they provide their human masters. But the truth is, animals—even our favorite domesticated ones—are still animals, and they have their limitations. You can't take them dancing or to the movies. And while many are sympathetic listeners, they're totally useless when it comes to offering advice. More damning yet, not a single one has run for public office or contributed to the cultural life of the country (unless you count Mickey Mouse, Kermit the Frog, or the Lion King). Animals are different, and it's foolish to pretend otherwise.

7   Which doesn't mean we should kill them heedlessly, or inflict needless pain on them. But I do find myself increasingly concerned about our priorities. Recently, a British magazine declared animal rights to be the number one "hip" cause on the planet. And a reporter for an American magazine, interviewing some female members of PETA (People for the Ethical Treatment of Animals), suggested that in another era, these smart, committed young women would have been marching for civil rights or the Equal Rights Amendment—causes that, I don't think it's denigrating animals to say, seem infinitely more important.

8   Maybe we're looking to help our four-footed friends because we feel so hopeless about our two-footed ones. After all, spray-painting women in fur (a favorite PETA tactic) is a whole lot easier—and clearly more fun—than trying to figure out how to end racial strife, cure AIDS, or fix welfare. What's more, it seems to be effective. The number of mink farms in this country has declined precipitously in recent years, and fur sales are nowhere near what they were a decade ago (though they've improved some in the last couple of years). Celebrities are increasingly wary of lending themselves to the Blackglama What Becomes a Legend Most? advertising campaign. And many fashion designers have bailed out of the fur trade, partly because a large number of their steady customers now find fur offensive—and partly because of pressure from PETA.

9   What happens, exactly, to those minks (or foxes or chinchillas) on their way from the wild to the showroom that has the people at PETA so exercised? PETA claims that trappers kill most of the fur-bearing creatures that end up as coats, employing sadistic means

10 to subdue their prey. Fur spokespeople, however, counter that the animals used for fashion come from farms that follow strict humane standards, further arguing that if the animals were mistreated, they wouldn't produce good pelts.

10 It's hard to know whom to believe. But given PETA's eccentric views, I'm not sure I would pick them. Not only do they want us to forswear fur; these fashion fundamentalists insist we lay down all clothing made of leather, suede, shearling, down, wool, and silk. Today your fur coat, tomorrow your cashmere sweater. They also want us to dispense with all food that comes from animals—including milk and eggs. Finally, and most alarming, the group opposes all forms of medical research that involve animal experimentation—even for AIDS and cancer.

11 Still, PETA has managed to make the antifur movement as trendy as push-up bras—trendier, really. Everyone has seen those bare-bottomed supermodels in the PETA ads posing under the slogan *I'd rather go naked than wear fur.* (Tell *that* to the Eskimos: I can see them now in their synthetic furs, polyester pants, and plastic shoes.) It's as though you have to be old, fat, and morally depraved to challenge the antifur dogma.

12 In truth, we live in a man-eat-chicken world—the point being that there's a food chain and we're at the top. That's nature. Speaking of which: Consider for a moment what happens to those furry creatures that are not pressed into service as high-fashion coats. It's a mistake to believe they live out their days sipping piña coladas at some animal version of Club Med. Many are killed, brutally and unapologetically, by predators in their own habitat, while others die of equally grisly so-called natural causes.

13 And yet the antifur folks are hard to dismiss. Sometimes they get to me—like when they argue that years from now we'll have come to realize mistreating animals was no different from mistreating any other defenseless, disenfranchised minority group. As for my aunt's mink, it's still hanging in her closet. Wistfully, I think of it from time to time. And I can only make a guess as to why I haven't claimed it: caution perhaps, cowardice no doubt, and maybe a tiny twinge of conscience.

Cosmopolitan, February 1996, p. 30

COMPREHENSION QUESTIONS

1. What is the topic of the passage?

2. What is the central message of the passage?

3. Determine what is at issue. What is your initial personal viewpoint?

4. Distinguish among opposing viewpoints, and provide the rationale for each.

5. Think carefully about the viewpoints. Express a personal viewpoint, and give the reasons why you favor it. Does it differ from your initial personal viewpoint? Why or why not?

6. Write a few paragraphs *in support of the viewpoint that you do* not *favor.*

THOUGHT AND DISCUSSION QUESTIONS

1. Do you agree with those who are antifur when they claim that "years from now we'll have come to realize mistreating animals was no different from mistreating any other defenseless, disenfranchised minority group"? Why or why not?

2. Do you agree with the author that civil rights or the Equal Rights Amendment are more important causes than animal rights? Why or why not?

3. Would you wear a fur coat or some other item of clothing that was trimmed with fur? Why or why not?

4. What can you infer regarding whether or not the writer will ever wear her aunt's mink coat? Why?

5. What is the *overall tone* of the passage? Give specific reasons for your answer.

6. List any questions that came to mind while you were reading this selection, and be prepared to discuss possible answers to them.

LOOKING BACK

Summarize and/or paraphrase the most important points you learned from this chapter, and determine how they can be put to use in other classes. Be prepared to discuss with your classmates what you have written.

THINK AGAIN!

The following message, along with a picture of the local museum of art, appeared on the side of a bus in Atlanta, Georgia:

The real barrier between people and great art is not money. It is parking!

What is the purpose of the message? What is its tone?

The Dashing Detective

Remember to follow these steps:

- first, read the narrative and all the questions
- second, examine the picture carefully
- third, answer the questions in the order they appear and come up with the solution

Have fun!

Dropout

As the clock struck five, ninety-year-old Mrs. Mirabel Fallwell dropped out of the window of her spacious twelfth-floor apartment. On the fourth stroke she struck.

Detective Amos Shrewd investigated shortly afterwards and found the room as you see it. Jerry Jarvis, Mrs. Fallwell's nephew and heir, said that the portrait on the wall of his beloved aunt was one that he himself had painted. Under questioning, he claimed that he had been at the far end of the apartment at the time of the tragedy and that he knew nothing about it until informed by the police.

If you were Shrewd, would you charge Jarvis with homicide?

Questions

1. Is there a reason why Mirabel interrupted her phone call and went to the window?
   ☐ Yes   ☐ No

2. Did Mirabel rush to the window?   ☐ Yes   ☐ No

3. Is it likely that she brought a footstool to the window?   ☐ Yes   ☐ No

4. Is it reasonable to suppose that Mirabel had a dizzy spell while at the window?
   ☐ Yes   ☐ No

5. Did she try to keep herself from falling out of the window?   ☐ Yes   ☐ No

6. Do you think she committed suicide?   ☐ Yes   ☐ No

7. What do you think was the cause of death?   ☐ Accident   ☐ Murder

Lawrence Treat, *Crime and Puzzlement,* pp. 30–31

Name _____ Date _____

MASTERY TEST 8–1

DIRECTIONS: Answer the questions.

1. What is a writer's purpose?

   _____

2. What is a writer's tone?

   _____

3. When a writer simply provides facts, data, or information about a subject so that we can learn more about it, the purpose is
   a. to persuade
   b. to inform
   c. to entertain
   d. all of the above
   e. none of the above

4. When a writer is trying to get us to think in a certain way or take a particular action, the purpose is
   a. to inform
   b. to entertain
   c. to persuade
   d. all of the above
   e. none of the above

5. When a writer is trying to amuse or bring enjoyment to us, the purpose is
   a. to entertain
   b. to persuade
   c. to inform
   d. all of the above
   e. none of the above

6. It is important for the critical reader to recognize a writer's purpose and tone to
   a. distinguish between facts and opinions
   b. uncover bias
   c. assess the overall reliability of information
   d. all of the above
   e. none of the above

7. When a writer sticks to the facts and presents them in a straightforward, unemotional manner, the tone is
   a. matter-of-fact
   b. humorous
   c. angry
   d. sad
   e. ironic

8. When a writer is mad, annoyed, irritated, or bothered by the subject matter presented, the tone is:
   a. sad
   b. angry
   c. humorous
   d. matter-of-fact
   e. ironic

9. When a writer presents information in a lighthearted, funny manner, the tone is
   a. ironic
   b. matter-of-fact
   c. humorous
   d. angry
   e. sad

10. When a writer presents information in a gloomy, melancholy, or sorrowful way, the tone is
    a. angry
    b. ironic
    c. sad
    d. matter-of-fact
    e. humorous

11. When a writer uses words to mean the opposite of what those words usually mean, the tone is
    a. ironic
    b. angry
    c. sad
    d. matter-of-fact
    e. humorous

12. What is the purpose and tone of the message on the sign in this photograph taken in Chicago?

Purpose: _____

Tone: _____

Name _____   Date _____

MASTERY TEST 8-2

DIRECTIONS: Determine the purpose and tone for each of the passages.

1

Happy National Apathy Day

Will Durst

1   Don't vote. You don't have to. No one's going to make you. This isn't the Soviet Union in the 50's. You won't be forced from your bed and dragged to the polls against your will. Relax. None of your friends are voting. And things are pretty good the way they are, right? If it ain't broke, don't fix it. What do you care if some barren deserted beach does or doesn't get blanketed by a thick film of 30-weight because of offshore drilling? Find another beach. What's the big deal?

2   Don't vote; you know you don't want to. Parking is a pain, the print is so tiny, and it's always on a Tuesday—what's that all about, anyway? Besides, haven't the pollsters already told us who's going to win? Why beat your head against a wall? It's a done deal. Out of your hands. Don't even need to wash them. It'd be totally different if it actually mattered. But it's not as it we have any real choice. If voting were effective they would have made it illegal by now.

3   Don't vote. Everyone knows the big corporations have the politicians so deep in their pockets they've got to brush the lint out of their hair before photo ops. It's common knowledge. Conventional wisdom. You'll only end up encouraging them.

4   You must have better things to do. Jog on over to the library before it gets closed down and read up on other people who never voted. Or you could work on that extra room for Grandma when Medicare fails and she has to move in. Or take a farewell trip on your local mass transit and wave bye-bye to the neighborhood rec center. That would be fun.

5   Besides, what difference does it make? One lousy little vote. A spit in the ocean. Don't worry. Be happy. Stay home. This is still a free country, last time I looked. Who cares? Not you.

New York Times, November 2, 1998, p. A27

Purpose: _____

Tone: _____

2

My Father's Keeper

Richard Pirozzi

1   We buried my mother on my twenty-fourth wedding anniversary, after her short battle with pancreatic cancer. She succumbed to the disease a few days after surgery in the early morning hours during her stay at a hospital in southern New Jersey. Although I was prepared as much as one possibly can be for the departure of a mother, I cannot make the same claim regarding the care of my 85-year-old father. That very year he had survived open-heart surgery only to lose his wife of over 50 years. His feelings for her are best expressed by the words he uttered tearfully the day she died: "I have lost everything."

2   In fact, my mother was the centerpiece of the entire family. At a very early age, I discovered that, if you wanted to get anything done in our house, you simply had to know just one word: *Jo.* That was what everyone called my mother instead of Josephine, which was her formal name. She did everything for my father—from serving as his personal secretary to satisfying his every need. It became so extreme that, as he watched television, he would occasionally use a bell to beckon her when he needed something, which was often. I grew up wondering if my mother was a wife or a slave left over from pre–Civil War days. Not only would she be an impossible act to follow, no one even wanted to try.

3   There was little time for me to grieve her loss because we were all too busy trying, unsuccessfully, to ease my father's pain. My brother, who is my only sibling, lives with his family in Georgia, so it became painfully obvious almost immediately who would be given the responsibility of looking after my father. It was both a necessary and logical arrangement because at the time he was still living in southern New Jersey, while my home was an hour away in the northern part of the state.

4   Caring for my father for the next three years would be an experience that had moments of hilarity, moments of frustration, and moments of great sadness. Most of the lighter times were a result of his pursuit of romance, which came as a complete shock to the rest of the family. It seems he came to the conclusion that he was irresistible to women of all ages. This phase really began right after he moved to my neighborhood in order to be closer to me. I enrolled him in the senior citizens day-care center, where he met a woman whom *he* thought was to be his next true love. It did not make a bit of difference to him that she was 40 years old and already had a boyfriend. Much to everyone's chagrin, he tried unsuccessfully to talk her out of the relationship by extolling his own unlimited virtues. It was not a coincidence that she happened to be a nurse who could provide him with the necessary medical services. His affection for her explains, in no small part, why he would often claim not to be feeling well while at the center, so that he could be sent to the nurse's office. Believe me, I received telephone calls about it.

5   Next on his list was a 24-year-old whom he politely told one day that her impending marriage would be over in a year because her prospective husband was not in the same league as he. (She took a chance and went through with the wedding anyway.) Virtually all of the housekeepers I hired to clean his apartment were, according to my father, desperately trying to corral him. He called them all "bimbos" and pretended to express no real interest, although he did enjoy their supposed attention. I guess he did not want to mix

business with pleasure. Then he went through a series of waitresses, ranging in age from 16 to 30, before finally settling for a 70-year-old woman whom he had met at the senior citizen residence where he lived for a few months. In fact, we went on a double date with them—the highlight of which was his attempt to kiss her goodbye. The problem was that she did not realize what he was attempting to do!

6   As startling as these escapades were, at least they involved real people. There was the time my father, in trying to find a bathroom in a restaurant, began to have a conversation with his reflection in a full-length mirror. Because of very poor eyesight, he mistook his reflection for a lovely woman (which must explain why he had the most radiant smile on his face). I waited a moment to help him, not out of indifference or cruelty but because I had not seen him so happy in years. Love does that to people.

7   There were, of course, the bad times as well that go along with aging and the loss of a lifelong partner. The obvious emptiness that he experienced at major family events, the endless appointments with doctors, the various tests that needed to be taken, and the general deterioration of my father's body and mind made his final years anything but "golden." On top of all this, I came to the sad realization that, when you are old and failing, no one seems to want to be with you anymore. I will never forget how one of my father's business associates turned around and walked in the other direction when he saw him coming; how members of his family disappeared, forgetting all the things that he had done for them through the years; and how even his sons sometimes thought of our own needs over his. There was the time, for example, when he showed up at my house on New Year's Eve with his blanket because he did not want to sleep at the senior citizen residence. I had plans, so I angrily talked him into going back there to be with the other residents. Later, I found out that he had had an argument with the head nun earlier in the day. I can never forgive myself for not letting him sleep over that night. Unfortunately, there would be no chance to redeem myself, for it would be my father's last New Year's Eve.

8   My father was not happy at the residence because he did not like the head nun. In fact, he called her Sister Baccala to her face. (For those who do not know, *baccala* is the Italian word for dried cod fish, which has the most abominable smell.) But my father's dislike for her did not extend to the other nuns who worked there, to one of whom he proposed marriage. Apparently, he thought it was time to liberalize the rules of the Catholic church.

9   The end came almost three years to the day after my mother's death. Those intervening years saw a rapid decline in energy and spirit. A benign brain tumor called a meningioma took from May to September to kill my father. By that time, he was emaciated from weight loss: a mere shadow of the man I had affectionately called Charlie. But even in the final days, he managed to humor us twice more by coming out of a near-comatose state to yell, "Get rid of her!" when he heard me mention one of the housekeeper's names, and by defiantly holding his mouth tightly closed so the nurse could not suction it out. He could still make us laugh even when he wasn't trying to be facetious.

10   Those years as my father's keeper were difficult ones which have had a lasting effect on me. Although several people were very helpful, I was primarily responsible for his well-being, serving as his part-time moving agent, financial adviser and manager, nurse, transportation planner, chauffeur, and a host of other roles. Because of his feeble condition, I was forced to do things for him that I never dreamed I would have to do, including helping him to dress and cleaning him up after the inevitable accidents in the bathroom.

11 The obvious role reversal bothered me a great deal then, and it still does now whenever I think about it. My patience was tried to the limit, and my emotions were on a nonstop roller-coaster. There were times when I was angry, times when I was depressed, and many times when I felt guilty for not doing more. And yet, through it all, there were still humorous moments that will stay in my memory forever. In the end, perhaps they should serve as my father's legacy.

The Humanist, March/April 1996, pp. 47–48

Purpose: _____

Tone: _____

3
I Was a Teen Mom

Kimberly Evanovich

1 Not long ago I was having lunch with the CEO of a software company that was considering me as a consultant for a lucrative overseas project. All had gone well, and we were waiting for the check when a very young, very pregnant woman passed by pushing a stroller and checking a bus schedule.

2 My companion snorted with disgust. "That makes me sick," he said, shaking his head. "You'd think she would stop creating new mouths for the government to feed."

3 Like most of my business associates, this man was not aware that I, at age 28, even *had* children—let alone kids old enough to be in the fourth and fifth grades. He saw my suit and my Gold Card and assumed I shared his view that teen mothers deserve no compassion. Nothing could be further from the truth.

4 When I accidentally became pregnant at 17, I was terrified. I cried when I got my first positive pregnancy test and promptly got three more. My friends encouraged me to have an abortion, but as logical as their arguments seemed (I barely knew the baby's father; I had my future to think about), I just couldn't do it. Yet the shock of becoming a parent was paralyzing. I remember looking in the mirror after my daughter was born, trying to connect my face to my new identity. Another human being was going to see me and think, "mother," but all I could think was that I wanted my *own* mother.

5 Although I was married to my daughter's father for a while—and had another child with him—I found myself completely on my own before my twentieth birthday, with no earning power and two babies in diapers. My parents were unable to offer me support, but I decided not to go on welfare; I just didn't think of that option at first, and by the time I did, I had found other ways to squeak by, working two jobs while I earned my college degree.

6 Over the years I came to accept, and love, my life as a parent. What I couldn't accept was the way I was treated.

7 While it is not unusual for two toddlers to break into noisy tears upon being denied an ice cream, when it happened with *my* children, strangers made snide comments—as if someone who couldn't control her own fertility certainly couldn't control a child. Once, an older woman who had stopped to admire my daughter's huge blue eyes—and who then

noticed my young face and pregnant figure—remarked, "You poor thing. I bet you wish you were more careful with birth control." Another woman, with pro-life stickers on her van, muttered "welfare mother" after I parked my dilapidated car next to hers. What was she saying—Keep your baby alive, but keep it away from me?

8   Professionally, I soon realized that as long as I was just an ambitious student, employers were friendly and doors opened. But once I let on that I was also a mother of two, smiles faded. Some people said, "I don't understand ... *you* have kids?" They were genuinely confused. Once they understood, I was often ushered out. They had no image of the life I was trying to live, and the stereotype they usually came up with was that of the irresponsible tramp.

9   Even pediatricians often acted as if I were to blame for my children's infrequent illnesses. Once, my four-year-old daughter woke screaming in pain and I rushed her to the emergency room. When it turned out to be a bladder infection, the doctor wanted to know if "a lot of men" used my toilet.

10   Indignant, I responded that the only males who used my toilet were my fiancé (an engineering graduate student who is now my husband) and my three-year-old son.

11   "Well then," he continued, "Is this 'boyfriend' of yours a *clean* person?"

12   His attitude was not unusual. In fact, if anyone made me doubt my future, it was the people employed to *help* young mothers and their children.

13   When my son was diagnosed with diabetes, a California children's services worker insisted that I would need her group's help in paying his medical bills for the rest of my life. When I protested that no, I had nearly finished college and had bright prospects, she laughed. "Do you realize," she said, "that only high-paying executive positions offer the medical coverage you will need? I think we can safely say that your chances of providing for your son on your own are extremely slim."

14   Two weeks before graduation, I was hired by a Big Six accounting firm. My insurance, I learned, was of the high-paying executive sort, and it was with great pleasure that I called the children's services worker to let her know that I would not, after all, be needing her for the rest of my life.

15   I now own my own marketing consulting company and am blissfully remarried; my children are happy and healthy. My daughter claims that nothing is better than having a mom who's young because you "like the same CDs and can share earrings."

16   As I near 30, remarks about teen moms simply annoy me; when I was 18, they stung. The difference between success and failure was, for me, the belief that I *could* make it— yet I often got the message that the game was already over. Why struggle to win when the world is convinced you have lost?

17   Many people think that to offer kind words to young mothers is to endorse their deviant behavior. I know otherwise. Treating teen moms as worthwhile and responsible can only help them live up to the challenge of their lives.

Glamour, April 1996, p. 156

Purpose: _____

Tone: _____

Name _____ Date _____

DIRECTIONS: Read the following short story, and discuss its ironies.

The Story of an Hour

Kate Chopin

1   Knowing that Mrs. Mallard was afflicted with a heart trouble, great care was taken to break to her as gently as possible the news of her husband's death.

2   It was her sister Josephine who told her, in broken sentences, veiled hints that revealed in half concealing. Her husband's friend Richards was there, too, near her. It was he who had been in the newspaper office when intelligence of the railroad disaster was received, with Brently Mallard's name leading the list of "killed." He had only taken the time to assure himself of its truth by a second telegram, and had hastened to forestall any less careful, less tender friend in bearing the sad message.

3   She did not hear the story as many women have heard the same, with a paralyzed inability to accept its significance. She wept at once with sudden, wild abandonment, in her sister's arms. When the storm of grief had spent itself she went away to her room alone. She would have no one follow her.

4   There stood, facing the open window, a comfortable, roomy armchair. Into this she sank, pressed down by a physical exhaustion that haunted her body and seemed to reach into her soul.

5   She could see in the open square before her house the tops of trees that were all aquiver with the new spring life. The delicious breath of rain was in the air. In the street below a peddler was crying his wares. The notes of a distant song which some one was singing reached her faintly, and countless sparrows were twittering in the eaves.

6   There were patches of blue sky showing here and there through the clouds that had met and piled one above the other in the west facing her window.

7   She sat with her head thrown back upon the cushion of the chair quite motionless, except when a sob came up into her throat and shook her, as a child who has cried itself to sleep continues to sob in its dreams.

8   She was young, with a fair, calm face, whose lines bespoke repression and even a certain strength. But now there was a dull stare in her eyes, whose gaze was fixed away off yonder on one of those patches of blue sky. It was not a glance of reflection, but rather indicated a suspension of intelligent thought.

9   There was something coming to her and she was waiting for it, fearfully. What was it? She did not know; it was too subtle and elusive to name. But she felt it creeping out of the sky, reaching toward her through the sounds, the scents, the color that filled the air.

10   Now her bosom rose and fell tumultuously. She was beginning to recognize this thing that was approaching to possess her, and she was striving to beat it back with her will—as powerless as her two white slender hands would have been.

11   When she abandoned herself a little whispered word escaped her slightly parted lips. She said it over and over under her breath: "Free, free, free!" The vacant stare and the look of terror that had followed it went from her eyes. They stayed keen and bright. Her pulses beat fast, and the coursing blood warmed and relaxed every inch of her body.

12   She did not stop to ask if it were not a monstrous joy that held her. A clear and exalted perception enabled her to dismiss the suggestion as trivial.

13   She knew that she would weep again when she saw the kind, tender hands folded in death; the face that had never looked save with love upon her, fixed and gray and dead. But she saw beyond that bitter moment a long procession of years to come that would belong to her absolutely. And she opened and spread her arms out to them in welcome.

14   There would be no one to live for her during those coming years; she would live for herself. There would be no powerful will bending her in the blind persistence with which men and women believe they have a right to impose a private will upon a fellow creature. A kind intention or a cruel intention made the act seem no less a crime as she looked upon it in that brief moment of illumination.

15   And yet she had loved him—sometimes. Often she had not. What did it matter! What could love, the unsolved mystery, count for in face of this possession of self-assertion which she suddenly recognized as the strongest impulse of her being.

16   "Free! Body and soul free!" she kept whispering.

17   Josephine was kneeling before the closed door with her lips to the keyhole, imploring for admission. "Louise, open the door! I beg; open the door—you will make yourself ill. What are you doing, Louise? For heaven's sake open the door."

18   "Go away. I am not making myself ill." No; she was drinking in the very elixir of life through that open window.

19   Her fancy was running riot along those days ahead of her. Spring days, and summer days, and all sorts of days that would be her own. She breathed a quick prayer that life might be long. It was only yesterday she had thought with a shudder that life might be long.

20   She arose at length and opened the door to her sister's importunities. There was a feverish triumph in her eyes, and she carried herself unwittingly like a goddess of Victory. She clasped her sister's waist and together they descended the stairs. Richards stood waiting for them at the bottom.

21   Some one was opening the front door with a latchkey. It was Brently Mallard who entered, a little travel-stained, composedly carrying his grip-sack and umbrella. He had been far from the scene of accident, and did not even know there had been one. He stood amazed at Josephine's piercing cry; at Richards' quick motion to screen him from the view of his wife.

22   But Richards was too late.

23   When the doctors came they said she had died of heart disease—of joy that kills.

Literature for Composition, 5th ed., ed. Sylvan Barnet et al., pp. 12–13

Ironies:_____

_____

_____

CHAPTER 9
LOOKING AT ADVERTISEMENTS WITH A CRITICAL EYE

CHAPTER OUTLINE

THINK ABOUT IT!

What is advertisement 1 trying to get readers to do? What is the tone? Discuss your answers with your classmates.

To whom is advertisement 2 appealing? What is it trying to get readers to do? What is its tone? Discuss your answers with your classmates.

1

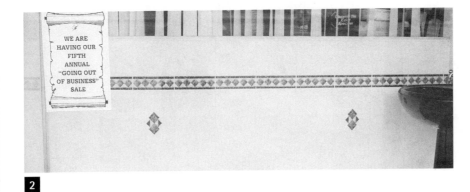

2

To whom is advertisement 3 appealing? What is it trying to get readers not to do? What is its tone is? Discuss your answers with your classmates.

3

Assuming that you do not speak or understand Spanish, use your inference skills to determine whom advertisement 4 is appealing to, what it is trying to get readers to do, and what is its tone. Discuss your answers with your classmates.

4

CHAPTER OUTCOMES

- ■ After completing Chapter 9, you should be able to:
- ■ Continue to apply the basic method for personal problem solving
- ■ Evaluate an advertisement by determining how it tries to catch the interest of readers; to whom it is designed to appeal; what it is trying to persuade readers to buy, do, or think; the benefit to readers that it is stressing; and how convincing it is
- ■ Continue to find topics and central messages in contemporary issue passages to determine what is at issue, distinguish among opposing viewpoints, and express personal viewpoints

Problem-Solving Exercise

Apply the first four steps of the basic method for personal problem solving to the following hypothetical situation. Your instructor will divide the class into four groups for purposes of dealing with the problem from the different perspectives of José, Maria, Carlotta, and Pedro. In other words, Group 1 will tackle the problem from José's point of view, Group 2 from Maria's point of view, Group 3 from Carlotta's point of view, and Group 4 from Pedro's point of view. After all four groups have completed their work, a person from each one will speak on behalf of the other members as the entire class attempts to come up with a possible solution acceptable to all groups.

HYPOTHETICAL SITUATION

José and Maria have been married for many years and had three children two years apart. Their oldest son is now residing in another state, while their 23-year-old daughter, Carlotta, and their 21-year-old son, Pedro, still live at home.

Pedro, as the youngest child, has been somewhat spoiled through the years to the extent that his siblings feel a certain amount of resentment toward him. To them, Pedro has always seemed to demand and receive more attention, time, and money.

In recent years, the situation has gotten very tense at home, particularly between José and Pedro. It seems that they clash about everything and are constantly shouting at each other, which is causing much stress for the entire family. José, who gets very angry, feels that Pedro is selfish and much too demanding. As head of the family, he has decided to draw the line. Otherwise, he fears that he will lose control of the household to Pedro. In fact, on several occasions, they have almost come to blows.

Maria believes that her husband is being much too firm with Pedro, and she really does not like the way José talks to him. She has told José many times that he is using insulting, degrading language in his arguments with their son. Pedro also gets very mad at his father and always tends to go to his mother as an ally who is more receptive to his wishes. José interprets her actions as a lack of support for him, and as a result, he is losing his self-respect and has become very resentful.

Consequently, José and Maria have had some very heated arguments, which have affected the stability of their marriage. Carlotta, feeling the tension, has withdrawn from the situation and tends to stay in her room much of the time. She has become totally disgusted with the entire household!

ADVERTISEMENTS AND CRITICAL THINKING

Pretend that you are a skier and read the following advertisement in the newspaper:

> Every item in every Princeton Ski Shop has been reduced to the lowest price ever. Guaranteed.

Would you rush right out to the nearest Princeton Ski Shop and buy everything in sight? One hopes not! At the very least, you would first want to know if the advertisement is referring to the lowest prices ever at the Princeton Ski Shop or at all stores that sell those items. Furthermore, you would wonder how Princeton Ski Shop can prove to customers that the prices are indeed the lowest ever or, for that matter, how *you* would be able to find out that information for yourself. Finally, you would be interested in what the guarantee involves. For example, if you could prove to Princeton that it once sold a particular item at a cheaper price than it is now or that you can find it for less at a competing ski shop, what is the store prepared to do under the terms of its guarantee?

As a critical thinker and reader, you are very aware of the importance of evaluating what you see, hear, and read so that you are in a better position to make the best possible decisions. This is particularly important when dealing with advertisements, which are designed specifically to influence your thinking, which of course in turn has an effect on your purchasing, political, and philosophical decisions. In fact, in today's world, you are overwhelmed with advertisements which attempt to persuade you to *buy* something, *do* something, or *think* something. You are urged to buy certain products, including foods, drinks, automobiles and clothing; to take advantage of particular services, such as tax return preparation, cleaning, or pest control; to attend social affairs, workshops, or classes; to vote or not to vote for certain candidates or political issues; and to support or oppose particular viewpoints regarding such issues as abortion, health care, and school prayer. There is no end to the stream of claims and counterclaims, all designed to sell you something.

If you do not pick and choose among the products, services, and ideas pushed by advertisers, you could soon go broke, become confused about who and what to vote for, or perhaps not even know what to think. You can avoid those unattractive possibilities by taking the time to think critically about advertisements so that you can evaluate them *before* acting. In short, critical thinking can help you sift through all the information thrown your way. How, then, should you think critically about advertisements? By answering a series of questions designed to uncover their purposes and strategies.

EVALUATING AN ADVERTISEMENT

One way to evaluate an advertisement is to ask and answer the following questions:

- How does it try to catch the interest of readers?
- To whom is it designed to appeal?
- What is it trying to persuade readers to buy, do, or think?
- What benefit to readers is it stressing?
- How convincing is it?

As you know, looking at the world with a questioning mind to find answers to questions like these is an important aspect of critical thinking. This certainly applies when dealing with advertisements, which are often very clever in their attempts to sway our minds.

Although we will be concerned only with advertisements in print, the same questions are relevant to all forms of advertising. They should enable you to evaluate advertising claims more effectively so that you can make informed decisions regarding what to buy, what to do, and what to think. Let's look at each of the questions in turn.

How Does It Try to Catch the Interest of Readers?

One of the keys to successful advertising is to catch the interest of readers. In your busy life, there is little time to read every page in front of you, so you have to be very selective. Being aware of this, advertisers go to great lengths to arouse your curiosity in what they have to say. You should know when advertisers are trying to catch your interest so that you keep in mind that they are attempting to influence you. Look at advertisement 5.

As you can see, it is picture of a burglar breaking into a home and, in large, dark print, the statement: "When you go away, the burglars will stay." Both the picture and the statement that rhymes are designed to catch the interest of readers. Also, "Summer Sale!" in large print may attract attention.

To Whom Is It Designed to Appeal?

Advertisers always have an intended audience targeted for their messages—men, women, or children of specific ages, from various ethnic groups, and with certain interests. It is important that you know to whom an advertisement is designed to appeal so that you can decide whether or not you should spend your time giving serious consideration to what it has to say. Because of the picture and statement, for example, the SND Security System ad was obviously meant to appeal to homeowners. Look at advertisement 6 and determine its intended audience.

If you answered that the ad is designed to appeal to students, you are correct. More specifically, it is intended for high school students who want to attend college and college students who are interested in going to graduate school. Notice how it catches their attention with the happy student who just opened an acceptance letter and the statement in large, dark print that she will need a bigger mailbox because she will be receiving so many more acceptance letters.

What Is It Trying to Persuade Readers to Buy, Do, or Think?

Obviously, the whole point of a given advertisement is to get you to purchase a product, take a certain action, or think a certain way. In the examples so far, the advertisers were trying to get readers to buy an SND Security System and take the Princeton Review course. It is important that you recognize the point of an advertisement so that you can determine if it has relevance to your life and is therefore worthy of your time. Read advertisement 7 and determine what it is trying to persuade readers to buy, do, or think.

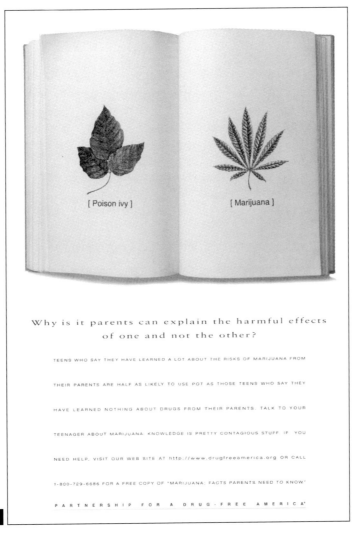

[Poison ivy]   [Marijuana]

Why is it parents can explain the harmful effects of one and not the other?

TEENS WHO SAY THEY HAVE LEARNED A LOT ABOUT THE RISKS OF MARIJUANA FROM

THEIR PARENTS ARE HALF AS LIKELY TO USE POT AS THOSE TEENS WHO SAY THEY

HAVE LEARNED NOTHING ABOUT DRUGS FROM THEIR PARENTS. TALK TO YOUR

TEENAGER ABOUT MARIJUANA. KNOWLEDGE IS PRETTY CONTAGIOUS STUFF. IF YOU

NEED HELP, VISIT OUR WEB SITE AT http://www.drugfreeamerica.org OR CALL

1-800-729-6686 FOR A FREE COPY OF "MARIJUANA: FACTS PARENTS NEED TO KNOW."

PARTNERSHIP FOR A DRUG-FREE AMERICA®

7

The ad, which attempts to catch the interest of readers through pictures of poison ivy and marijuana leaves, is appealing to parents to talk to their teenagers about the harmful effects of marijuana. Thus the target group—parents of teenagers—are being urged to do something.

What Benefit to Readers Is It Stressing?

An effective advertisement is very specific about the benefit to readers as a result of their buying, doing, or thinking whatever is being urged by the ad: Buying an SND Security System will prevent burglars from breaking into homes, and save buyers money because of the summer sale. Taking the Princeton Review course will help students get higher test scores to gain easier admission to colleges and graduate schools; teenagers whose parents talk to them about the harmful effects of marijuana are much less likely to use it. It is extremely important that you recognize the benefit stressed by an advertisement so that you can make a sound decision as to whether or not to follow its advice. Look at advertisement 8 and determine what benefit it is stressing.

As you can see, the advertisement catches the interest of readers by pretending to be an ad for ski wax when in fact it is really making an appeal to drivers to buy a Blazer truck because it will go through all kinds of snow conditions.

How Convincing Is It?

From your perspective as a critical thinker, the most important consideration concerning the evaluation of a given advertisement involves how convincing it is in terms of the benefit stressed. In short, your decision as to whether or not to buy, do, or think what an ad is suggesting is based almost solely on the degree to which you become convinced that the benefit to you is both relevant and valid.

The examples that we have been using do not do a very good job in that respect, which could lead you to the conclusion that those advertisers believe most readers are not critical thinkers.

> In the SND Security System ad, homeowners are not told how or why an SND system will prevent a burglar from breaking into their homes, nor are they informed how much money they will save because of the summer sale. However, the statistic provided apparently comes from a reliable source (1993 FBI Uniform Crime Report).

> Students are not informed how their enrollment in the Princeton Review course, with its "proven test-taking strategies," is going to result in higher test scores, nor are they given any statistics regarding success rates of other students who have completed the course.

> Parents are given one statistic in the ad dealing with the harmful effects of marijuana that supports the claim that teens who have been warned by parents are half as likely to use pot as those who have learned nothing about drugs from their parents. However, they are never told how that statistic was arrived at or where it comes from. Nevertheless, at least there is an offer of additional free information from Partnership for a Drug-Free America, which *seems* like a reputable organization that favors what *apparently* is a very good cause. Hence readers have the option of investigating the matter further.

> Finally, the advertisement for the Blazer gives drivers no indication how that vehicle will enable them to go through all kinds of snow conditions.

Let's take a look at advertisement 9 to determine how convincing it is. This advertisement, which was posted on a college classroom door, is designed to appeal to students who are suffering from "math anxiety," and it tries to catch their interest through the use of large boldface lettering and a somewhat humorous cartoon figure. In addition, it does deal with a topic that is of obvious concern to many students. As you can see, the ad is trying to persuade readers to attend a math anxiety workshop, but it only *implies* that attendance will help students with the problem. Furthermore, there is absolutely no indication of exactly how this workshop is going to assist students who suffer from math anxiety. For instance, are certain techniques or specific methods that will help going to be suggested, or is the workshop simply a review session dealing with mathematical principles? Although some students may attend anyway because this is a rather common problem, the advertisement really does not do a very effective job of convincing readers of the benefit resulting from their attendance.

MATH ANXIETY WORKSHOP!!!
TUESDAY, APRIL 21ST
2:00 PM IN ROOM H107

DOES MATH MAKE YOU SHAKE???

DO YOU FREEZE DURING MATH TESTS?

DO YOU FORGET ANSWERS TO QUESTIONS YOU KNOW?

DOES YOUR SLEEP OR APPETITE SUFFER BEFORE A TEST?

COME TO A MATH ANXIETY WORKSHOP:

TUESDAY, APRIL 21ST AT 2:00 PM ROOM H107

9

In the end, if an advertisement does not convince you of the benefit of buying, doing, or thinking what it is urging, you have no good reason to follow its advice. If you did, you might end up making a decision that you will regret, such as buying the wrong (for you) product or service, voting for the wrong candidate, accepting the wrong idea, or supporting the wrong viewpoint. Thus you must remember always to evaluate the advertisements you come in contact with by answering the five questions that we have been using. The time spent should make you a more informed, careful consumer who thinks before acting.

ACTIVITY 1

DIRECTIONS: Complete the following exercise, which appeared in a psychology textbook.

What's Wrong Here?

All of the statements below were taken from claims and assertions found in the popular media. Indicate in the space provided why you should be suspicious.

"No other smoking-cessation program works better than Quitters Anonymous."

_____

_____

"Ache-Be-Gone contains twice as much pain relief medication as its competitors, and that's why it's the most effective product on the market today."

_____

_____

Portions of an article in the newspaper read, "*The Last Body Count* was a very successful feature film and later video store release. Unfortunately, it was ranked last in its time slot when shown on network television. A news magazine show and three situation comedies competing with it were ranked higher in the ratings. Viewers are obviously losing their taste for violence on television."

_____

_____

"According to industry records, last year, Trans-Caribbean Airlines had the best 'on-time' record of any other airline in the industry. Fly with us, and be sure of getting to your destination on time today!"

_____

_____

"Students who use a word processor get higher grades."

_____

_____

"This SAT refresher course is guaranteed to raise your combined SAT scores an average of 100 points higher than your PSAT or last SAT scores."

_____

_____

Anthony F. Grasha, Practical Applications of Psychology, p. 78

ACTIVITY 2

DIRECTIONS: For this activity, your instructor will divide the class into groups of three. Evaluate each of the following advertisements within your group by asking and answering these five questions:

- How does it try to catch the interest of readers?
- To whom is it designed to appeal?
- What is it trying to persuade readers to buy, do, or think?
- What benefit to readers is it stressing?
- How convincing is it?

Be prepared to discuss your answers with the rest of the class.

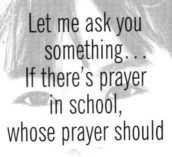

Let me ask you
something…
If there's prayer
in school,
whose prayer should

it be?

Official prayer sessions in public school seem
like a good idea to many Americans,
provided they get to choose the prayer.
But in such a diverse society, how can one prayer
satisfy every religious belief?
How would you feel if your child were required to
say a Catholic prayer in school every day?
Or a Baptist prayer or Muslim prayer?
What about a Jewish prayer or a Buddhist prayer?
There are over 1,500 religious denominations
in America. How many of us would want our
children to recite someone else's prayer?
Maybe prayer is just too personal to let
the government or any one particular religious
group decide what prayers our children should
be saying in school.
Think about it.

Ira Glasser
Executive Director of the American Civil Liberties Union
125 Broad Street
New York, New York 10004
www.aclu.org

1

TV is Good.

For years the pundits, moralists and self-righteous, self-appointed preservers of our culture have told us that television is bad. They've stood high on their soapbox and looked condescendingly on our innocuous pleasure. They've sought to wean us from our harmless habit by derisively referring to television as the Boob Tube or the Idiot Box.

Well, television is not the evil destroyer of all that is right in this world. In fact, and we say this with all the disdain we can muster for the elitists who purport otherwise – TV is good.

TV binds us together. It makes us laugh. Makes us cry. Why, in the span of ten years, TV brought us the downfall of an American president, one giant step for mankind and the introduction of Farrah Fawcett as one of "Charlie's Angels." Can any other medium match TV for its immediacy, its impact, its capacity to entertain? Who among us hasn't spent an entire weekend on the couch, bathed in the cool glow of a Sony Trinitron‚ only to return to work recuperated and completely refreshed? And who would dispute that the greatest advancement in aviation over the last ten years was the decision to air sitcoms during the in-flight service?

Why then should we cower behind our remote controls? Let us rejoice in our fully adjustable, leather-upholstered recliners. Let us celebrate our cerebral-free non-activity. Let us climb the highest figurative mountaintop and proclaim, with all the vigor and shrillness that made Roseanne a household name, that TV is good.

2   Sony and Trinitron are trademarks of Sony.

TomPaine.common sense
A Journal of Opinion

Eating in the Dark

FDA Will Not Require Labeling of Genetically Engineered Foods

Americans have a right to know what's in our food.

So how come the Food and Drug Administration wants us eating in the dark?

The FDA has proposed new rules that would not require genetically engineered food to be labeled as such. The rules would also continue to allow these foods to be sold without any required safety testing.

Very little independent research has been published on the safety of genetically engineered (GE) foods. The FDA's own scientists have warned that there's not enough evidence to declare them safe. Yet, in what amounts to an uncontrolled human experiment, the FDA has already allowed GE foods to become part of our diet.

We don't know what these foods might do to people with allergies or weak immune systems, or if they have any long-term effect on children. Biotechnology companies might know, but in the name of protecting trade secrets they have kept most of their test results private and away from peer review.

We do know this: Credible polling shows consumers overwhelmingly support GE food labeling. Yet the FDA has ignored the public's desire, proposing rules that give the biotech industry just what it wants. And no wonder. Generous contributions to both political parties give the industry special access to FDA's overseers in Congress and the White House.

The new FDA rules are not yet final. **Consumers have one more week – until May 3 – to let the agency know what they think.** They can do so through the website **www.TrueFoodNow.org.**

The 15-nation European Union, Japan, Australia, New Zealand, South Korea and Russia all mandate the labeling of genetically engineered food.

But if the FDA's new rules go through as drafted, Americans will be left eating in the dark.

This Week at TomPaine.com –
Eating in the Dark
Featuring a detailed critique of the FDA's proposed rules... "The A-B-C's of GE Food" by Rachel Massey... and "Common Sense on Biotech" by Michael F. Jacobson.

■ *TomPaine.com. Money and Politics. Environment. Media Criticism. History.*
© 2001 The Florence Fund, PO Box 53033, Washington, DC 20009.

3

This is my brother Omar.

He had a hole in his tummy.

A bullet hit him.

I saw red grass.

A gun was in the garage.

I didn't mean to shoot daddy's gun.

I didn't mean to shoot daddy's gun.

An unlocked gun could be the death of your family.
Please lock up your gun.

www.unloadandlock.com

NATIONAL CRIME PREVENTION COUNCIL

4

Old Age

PERCEPTIONS

REALITIES

Percent of Americans **18-34** who expect these things to happen when they get old.		Percent of Americans **65 and Over** who have experienced these things.
77	More Travel	46
76	More Hobbies	56
69	Less Active	41
64	New Skills	28
62	More Respect	53
58	Less Stress	50
48	Serious Illness	25
46	Get Social Security	90
47	Can't Drive	15
44	Get Medicare	80
43	Fewer Responsibilities	50
41	Trouble Walking	30
38	Lose Bladder Control	14
32	Less Sex Life	37
29	Become Senile	2
29	Dependent on Kids	5
26	Be Lonely	24
13	Be Poor	18

There are surprises ahead for today's young people. Old age is different than what they anticipate. This is one finding of a nationwide survey we conducted to help frame a national discussion about the future of Social Security in an aging society.

Our premise: the more we all understand about how we and our fellow citizens view old age, the easier it will be to figure out what role Social Security should play in it.

If you'd like more information, give us a call at (888) 735-ADSS (2377) or visit us on the Web at www.americansdiscuss.org. *Americans Discuss Social Security* is a non-partisan initiative to help secure the future of Social Security by publishing information, hosting discussions and helping to deliver Americans' views to America's policy makers.

SOCIAL SECURITY
Americans
Discuss
Social
Security

A PROJECT FUNDED BY THE PEW CHARITABLE TRUSTS

2001 Pennsylvania Avenue, Suite 825
Washington, DC 20006

5

Less than 2% of condoms actually fail.

Every percent counts.
bankrate.com

bankrate.com is an independent, objective listing of all the best rates on mortgages, car loans, credit cards, CDs and more. No commitment required.

6

YOU CAN'T STOP
YOUR PET FROM...

BUT YOU CAN STOP YOUR
PET FROM SHEDDING!

Mrs. Allen's SHED-STOP®

The Veterinarian-Recommended Natural Miracle
Available at Caldor, FEDCO, Pet Supplies Plus, PETsMART,
STOP&SHOP, other fine retailers & veterinary offices.
Or call 1-800-327-0098 www.shed-stop.com

7

To Put
This Problem Into
Perspective,
Imagine Someone
Breaking Your Arm
Because You
Missed A Putt.

This December, the Lexus Challenge Hosted by Raymond Floyd will provide more than dramatic competition.
It will provide solace for abused and neglected children by raising funds for Childhelp USA, a national
non-profit organization dedicated to the prevention of child abuse. Please join us in watching this prestigious
tournament on NBC December 21st and 22nd. For the love of the game, and for the sake of the children.

Childhelp USA

LEXUS CHALLENGE
HOSTED BY RAYMOND FLOYD

8

9

Source: Reprinted with permission of the publisher.
© 2002 by Merriam-Webster, Incorporated.

TV, Movie & Music Company Heads...

PARENTS & GRANDPARENTS:
THIS IS FOR OUR CHILDREN

How Can You Sleep At Night?
We Find You Guilty Of A Monstrous Evil

We're a group of parents and grandparents who are DISGUSTED with all the sex, violence, killings, vulgar humor, profanity, perversion, filth and sleaze you allow your companies to spew forth on our children.

We're OUTRAGED that the OVERWHELMING EVIDENCE OF THE TRAGIC CONSEQUENCES is not being publicized so you are able to get away with denying the horrendous harm you are causing. For example:

You're Teaching Children That Violence Is Acceptable

The National Institute of Mental Health has over 1000 studies showing TV violence increases violence among children. When one rural town began receiving TV signals, violent behavior among children jumped 160 percent within the next 2 years. The American Medical Association, the American Academy of Pediatrics, the American Psychological Association and the American Academy of Child and Adolescent Psychiatry all agree: violence in entertainment is increasing violence among children, making them less sensitive to real-life violence and more likely to consider violence an answer to conflict.

You're Encouraging Kids To Use Drugs

A University of Michigan study has found that the music industry has been "an important determinant" of increased use of drugs by teenagers. 67 percent of adults surveyed say TV, movies, magazines and music encourage the illegal use of drugs. 76 percent of 12-to 17-year olds report that the entertainment industry encourages drug use.

You're Leading Children To Early Sex

One poll of children between the ages of 10 and 16 found that 62 percent said sex on television and in movies influences children to have sex. 77 percent said there is too much sex before marriage on TV. A U.S. Senator says, "Steamy sex scenes, crude innuendo and outright obscenities – material we never even imagined being on commercial television – are now the nightly norm." He said sex is being sold to children "not only as desirable, but good, regular and normal."

You're Causing A Teenage Venereal Disease Epidemic

The Institute of Medicine has issued a major report titled "The Hidden Epidemic," which says our mass media encourage the conduct responsible for a Sexually Transmitted Disease Epidemic. The Federal Centers for Disease Control and Prevention estimates approximately three million teenagers contract a venereal disease EACH YEAR!

Your Role In School Shootings

A 1999 survey found that two-thirds of America's teens think violence in television and music is "partially responsible for crimes like the Littleton shootings." An Associated Press poll found that Americans' top choice for effectively stopping school violence is reducing violence in popular entertainment. "Meet The Press" reported that the Littleton killers idolized the music of shock-rocker Marilyn Manson, who's songs brazenly encourage shooting.

Your Role In Teen Suicides

As long ago as 1985 the National Education Association warned that many of the 5000 teenage suicides each year are linked to depression fueled by fatalistic music and lyrics.

We're Not Going To Let You Deny The Truth Any Longer!

We now know there is a massive number of studies, reports and polls like those above that make crystal clear the horrendous consequences caused by entertainment companies. We're outraged that Hollywood spokesman Jack Valenti is being paid over $1 million a year to DENY the consequences and DIVERT CRITICISM from film and TV companies ... and that the record industry's spokesperson DENIES the tragic consequences caused by music lyrics. No consequences?

A 19-year old boy shot and killed a state trooper. His lawyer said he'd been under the spell of a music album's cop-killer lyrics.

Two teenagers are convicted of murder. They say they were inspired to kill by a movie.

A boy who killed himself left a suicide note telling his family to watch a TV show to understand what prompted his decision to end his life.

A 15-year old boy accused of sexually abusing his 8-year old half-sister says he got the idea from watching a TV show.

Three teenage boys murder and then rape a 15-year old girl. One of the boys said they were inspired by the music of a heavy-metal band.

No consequences? We say SHAME on the heads of companies who look the other way and allow entertainment like this.

Parents and Grandparents: It's Up To US!

We Must Get Them To Stop

If what you've read above angers you as much as it does us, now you can do something to stop it. Actually and literally. And here's how.

Accuracy In Media (AIM), America's oldest news watchdog organization, angered because the news media are not telling the public the shocking facts revealed on this page, is paying for ads like this so YOU, armed with the TRUTH, can bring your influence to bear on your local TV and radio stations and their

advertisers demanding they stop airing material destructive of the morals, health and lives of America's children.

Outraged Parents of America will provide you with the OVERWHELMING EVIDENCE plus the advice and support that will help you bring about change. It costs nothing to join. You can join by writing us, or calling the toll free number below, requesting information on how you can become a volunteer in this vital program.

Outraged Parents of America, Dept. 4
4455 Connecticut Avenue, N.W., Suite 330
Washington, DC 20008

1-800-644-4453

10

ACTIVITY 3

DIRECTIONS: Read the following passages, and answer the questions. Remember to use inference skills when appropriate.

EYE ON VOCABULARY

When reading each passage, take note of any unfamiliar words you come across. List them and their definitions in your notebook or on note cards. Use the context, word parts, or the dictionary to determine their meanings. After the completion of each passage, your instructor will ask to see your notebook or note cards and may discuss key words in class.

1
Obedience to Authority

Harmful Consequences

1   In September of 1987, a protest against the shipment of military equipment to Nicaragua occurred outside of the Naval Weapons Station in Concord, California. Three of the protestors stretched their bodies across the railroad tracks leading out of the Naval Weapons Station to prevent a train from passing. *The civilian crew of the train had been given orders not to stop. In spite of being able to see the protestors 600 feet ahead, they never even slowed the train.* Two of the men managed to get out of the way; a third was not fast enough and had two legs severed below the knee. Naval medical corpsmen at the scene refused to treat him or allow him to be taken to the hospital in their ambulance. Onlookers tried to stop the flow of blood for 45 minutes until a private ambulance arrived. (Kelman and Hamilton, 1989).

Embarrassing Moments

2   A colleague sent a graduate student to be the "substitute teacher" in an introductory psychology class. The undergraduate students had never seen her before. The substitute began the class by saying, "I'm in charge today, and I want to get this session started by asking each of you to stand. Fine, now I want you to clap your hands three times and pat the person standing next to you on the shoulder five times. Now jump up and down for ten seconds. OK, sit down and put your pencils and notebooks on the floor." *Each of the 240 students in the class followed the commands of the teacher without questioning them.* My colleague then entered the room and began a well-listened-to presentation on obedience to authority.

Doing What I'm Told Versus What's Right for Me

3   I was once hired by a company to be part of a workshop on making effective personal decisions. The company maintained and repaired electronic equipment used to mon-

itor radiation levels in nuclear facilities. Some technicians balked at entering an abandoned facility, fearing that it was dangerous to do so.

4   The company decided it only wanted to use technicians who had made an informed choice to maintain and repair the equipment. Experts in the area of radiation as well as those familiar with the site presented information and showed that the site was safe. I was asked to provide some principles of personal decision making that would help the employees decide whether or not they wanted to volunteer for the work.

5   Afterwards, I rode in an elevator with five of the technicians. One of them broke the silence by saying, *"You know, every one of us would have agreed to enter the facility if our boss had simply ordered us to do it. Having all of you experts brought in to talk to us only made us suspicious that the site was, in fact, dangerous."*

Anthony F. Grasha, *Practical Applications of Psychology*, p. 357

COMPREHENSION QUESTIONS

1. What is the topic of the passage?

2. What is the central message of the passage?

3. Determine what is at issue. What is your initial personal viewpoint?

4. Distinguish among opposing viewpoints, and provide the rationale for each.

5. Think carefully about the viewpoints. Express a personal viewpoint, and give the reasons why you favor it. Does it differ from your initial personal viewpoint? Why or why not?

6. Write a few paragraphs *in support of the viewpoint that you do not favor.*

THOUGHT AND DISCUSSION QUESTIONS

1. What would you have done if you had been a member of the civilian crew of the train? Why? What would you have done if you had been one of the undergraduate students? Why?

2. Do you agree with what the naval medical corpsmen did? Why or why not?

3. Under the circumstances, would you have felt confident that the nuclear site was safe? Why or why not?

4. Is there any connection between "obedience to authority" and advertising? Why or why not?

5. List any questions that came to mind while you were reading this selection, and be prepared to discuss possible answers to them.

2

A Nation of Hookers

Jesse Bier

1   Prostitution is the selling of one's person for money. I think we can all agree on that; it seems a safe enough definition. Matters turn inconvenient only when we start considering

that a person can offer himself or herself as an entire self or personality for sale. The prostitution of the whole person is, after all, a far more thorough spectacle of corruption than the merely sexual. As a matter of fact, the literal streetwalker often tries to disengage himself or herself from the sex act itself in order to salvage vestiges of self-respect.

2   I emphasize these comparisons and call attention to the pertinent metaphor going the rounds in the world of advertising and entertainment, especially television. Celebrities who resist the sale of themselves for commercials are called "virgins."

3   All kinds of celebrities and people are included. I am not talking only of entertainers—although many come to mind who recruit spouse and children as well in a comprehensive family abasement for any and all products. Athletes qualify just as well, and astronauts and—well, anybody. However, it is not absolutely essential that we focus on public personalities. One of our superlatively American democratic perversions is that *anyone* can qualify as a moral prostitute, even or especially "ordinary" people—or actors posing as such—in their testimony about a dish detergent or a car or an antacid tablet. Average men confess and advertise love for their wives and sweethearts under the influence of a gerontological patent medicine; normal but aging executives press ancient "formula" into their hair in order to stay young-looking, quite literally prostituting at least part of their body for business and social purposes. And so on.

4   Still, the spectacle of celebrities in brazen cynical self-devaluation has had a certain undeniable force over the years. A lovable comedian, trading on warmth, kept saying, "Believe me ..." about anything from coffee crystals to sweepstake lotteries. And a certain famous and rotund actor and former movie director with a deep compelling voice solemnly linked Beethoven and California wine. One of my all-time favorites, however, comes from the world of sports. A fresh-faced champion skier changed her last name, in an ad featuring her, to "Chapstick," obliging the company by wiping herself out utterly—not quite on the ski slopes, only in life.

5   As to our general population itself, "Miss America" winners are programmed to laugh or cry at exact moments, especially at victory—a necessary forfeiture of the emotional self for the spectacle. And game-show contestants must pass virtual rehearsals demonstrating their capacity to emote in wide-mouthed commodity joy. And there are programs like *The Newlywed Game*, where our scrubbed young brides and grooms recall—or should we say, expose—private and often intimate moments for public exhibition, for a price or a prize.

6   Let's not forget a species of child prostitution, to round things out. Separately, countless children advertise breakfast cereals, toys, puppy food, and the like. Or they are all put together, as by a prominent entertainer who used to mimic kids around the block but has graduated to the simpler and easier use of them in cute dessert ads. My favorite combinative ad, however, features a one-time kid now grown up to a kind of professional celebrityhood himself, as the look-alike son of one of America's most beloved twentieth-century comedians; in an endearing flashback, he recalls his father's supposed advice about natural foods—and then advertises the whole-grain cereal himself. It is brilliant reversalism: grown kids trading on their deceased parents, neatly closing the familial circle by the selling of private and precious affections.

7   There are other subtle variations of the nostalgia effect. An aging movie actor, who long ago made his name as a Frank Capra–styled honest American character, has touted

the tires of the one company accused of criminal negligence in steel radials. And another all-American movie actor, dressed in his Naval Reserve uniform, has advertised for a commercial "Veterans Insurance Company," in a soft-spoken sincere exploitation of his own patriotism. As we veer toward politics, let's not overlook the former mayors, former governors, former House Speakers, and even former presidents who have sold their authority in one commercial forum or another.

8   Nothing is sacred—least of all religion. There is a whole network dedicated to smiling, glamorized personalities in slick witness to the Lord. Sooner or later I expect the ultimate ad, which will begin with a medium shot of Jesus on the crucifix. Suddenly he awakens, tears himself off the cross, and descends to us. In closeup, he plucks out a nail and says, "Only at —'s can you find old-fashioned, truly tempered precision nails. Buy some—today!"

9   Few will even object. Because by that time we shall have become so used to the vulgar sale of self, so ready to barter our most precious values, models, and icons, that any prostitution will seem only natural—the logical end of a long series.

10   We can do one thing, though. We can still look down on the call girl and out-and-out hooker. When we're slipping so far ourselves, we need any sense of superiority we can get.

The Humanist, November-December 1995, p. 41

COMPREHENSION QUESTIONS

1. What is the topic of the passage?

2. What is the central message of the passage?

3. Determine what is at issue. What is your initial personal viewpoint?

4. Distinguish among opposing viewpoints, and provide the rationale for each.

5. Think carefully about the viewpoints. Express a personal viewpoint, and give the reasons why you favor it. Does it differ from your initial personal viewpoint? Why or why not?

6. Write a few paragraphs *in support of the viewpoint that you do* not *favor.*

THOUGHT AND DISCUSSION QUESTIONS

1. In your view, what are the similarities and differences between a "moral prostitute" and an "out-and-out hooker"?

2. If you were a celebrity, would you be a prostitute or a virgin? Why?

3. Would you agree to do a commercial for a product that you did not like as much as a competing one or a product that you never really used at all? Why or why not?

4. What is the tone of the writer's comments on Jesus? What point is he trying to make?

5. List any questions that came to mind while you were reading this selection, and be prepared to discuss possible answers to them.

3
Does Alcohol Advertising Get a "Free Ride?"

1   Unless we've been cut off from virtually every contact with American civilization, each of us is well aware that cigarette smoking is not a healthful pursuit. Indeed, we're aware that it can be extremely harmful in any number of ways, many of which we can tick off with some confidence—e.g., increased risk of various cancers, emphysema, high blood pressure, and possible birth defects, not to mention stained teeth, smelly clothing, and on and on. We know these things because we've been told them in schools, by various health agencies, by news programs, by magazine articles, and, not unimportantly, by the cigarette producers themselves, who are required to include health warnings in every advertisement.

2   Now, do you know as well that:

- Alcohol is a great national killer?
- About 20,000 people a year die in alcohol-related automobile accidents?
- Half of all those imprisoned for murder were under the influence of alcohol when arrested?
- Alcohol is involved in about 37 percent of rapes and in the majority of aggravated assaults?
- Spousal abuse is twice as likely to occur if one of the partners has been drinking?
- Very great proportions of violent acts of all kinds have alcohol present and indeed have intoxicated actors?
- Alcohol is far more deadly than tobacco to *innocent bystanders?*
- Alcohol is the drug of choice for young people and certainly the one most likely to be abused?
- A typical 18-year old, still 3 years below the legal drinking age in most states, has seen an estimated 100,000 beer commercials?

3   Unlike cigarettes, beer advertising (and, to some extent, ads for spirits) can, and does, appear in the broadcast media, often in highly popular sports programming. Joe Camel has left the scene, but the Budweiser frogs and lizards are still memorable, complete with *"Frank & Louie's Greatest Hits,"* a CD featuring 11 pop rock party classics, as well as commercials.

4   Is there an ethical issue here?

5   First, there is predictable disagreement about facts. A letter from the President of the Beer Institute stated bluntly, "Study after study has concluded that beer advertising does not cause alcohol abuse or underage drinking." Yet, columnist Charles Krauthammer refers to a study that found that 56 percent of students in grades 5 through 12 say alcohol advertising encourages them to drink, and researchers Grube and Wallach's study of 468 children whose average age was approximately 12 was interpreted as concluding that, "kids who were more aware of beer advertising displayed more knowledge about ads and slogans, held more favorable views on drinking and stated that they intended to drink more often as adults than children who were less knowledgeable."

6   Next, there is the clear disagreement about what is intended by beer advertising. The beer advertisers, like their tobacco counterparts, maintain that their advertising is

not meant to recruit, but rather to retain product loyalty among existing drinkers and, if possible, encourage brand switching. They point to voluntary efforts to discourage under-age drinking and/or promote responsible drinking of those of a legal age such as Bud-weiser's "know when to say when" and "friends don't let friends drive drunk," campaigns in addition to contributions to the Century Council, an industry organization dedicated to reducing drunk driving and underage drinking, as well as such acts of self-restraint as voluntarily pulling such popular icons as Budweiser's Spuds McKenzie and Stroh's Swedish bikini team. As for not targeting underage audiences, the President of the Beer Institute asserts, "Ads are to be placed in media where most of the audience is reasonably expected to be above the minimum drinking age," (for example, Budweiser pulled off MTV in favor of VH1 and its predominantly adult viewing audience.)

7   As you might imagine, critics see the picture somewhat differently. Not appealing to potential underage drinkers? "TV sports in particular, a staple of adolescents, is one long hymn to the glories of beer," asserts Krauthammer. And what of *Frank & Louie's Great-est Hits,* distributed through mass retailers such as Kmart and Wal-Mart? (The record com-pany observed, "When you take a brand like Budweiser it has a certain power." "You see evidence in the selling of [Budweiser] T-shirts and hats. Why not music? This is a good hook for the consumer.") *Advertising Age* called it the "Wrong gig for Bud ads," and stated force-fully, "Anheuser-Busch should know better." "Know when to say when?" One survey of 300 high school and college students revealed that 40 percent interpreted the message to mean it was acceptable for older teenagers to get drunk occasionally. And what of the ads them-selves? One [mid–1990s] study of alcohol advertising in televised sports found that 15 per-cent of the ads used celebrity endorsers (often athletes or entertainers) while another 37 percent involved either water sports or driving.

8   Certainly there can be no debate that there *is* use and abuse of alcoholic beverages among those under the legal age, and that purposefully or not young people *are* exposed to a great deal of alcohol advertising, particularly of beer. What, if anything, should be done, ethically?

9   The brewers might argue that they are already being socially responsible through self-regulation and brewer and industry public service ads. Yet critics might contend that, unlike the ads on behalf of the Partnership for a Drug-Free America, these efforts are not well coordinated or focused. Commentator William Beaver, for example, contends that in addi-tion to what public service and anti-drinking advertising that now exists, "the public must be made aware of the link between alcohol, youth, and crime in much the same way it has come to know the problems associated with drunk driving." Is the public fully aware of the connections between alcohol and the varied social dysfunctions centered on crime mentioned earlier? Probably not nearly as well as the connection between drinking and dangerous driving. Would it be useful if they knew more, and, if so, who should tell them? The brewers? Special interest groups? The government?

10   The brewers seem to endorse the idea that public service advertising is something the business should do, either as individual brewers or through the Century Council. Would they then be willing to focus their social responsibility on the more extensive menu of problems associated with alcohol abuse, thus perhaps raising the level of awareness of alcohol as a major societal problem beyond drinking and driving? Or, is it in their utili-tarian interests to keep the problems associated with alcohol relatively well focused, thus

11   avoiding the intervention of special interest or government who might have a more extensive agenda.

     Returning to the thesis that, compared to cigarettes, alcohol is getting a relatively free ride in terms of regulation, Krauthammer offers us the ultimate test. "Ask yourself this," he writes, "if you knew your child was going to become addicted to either alcohol or tobacco, which would you choose?"

Clifford G. Christians et al., Media Ethics, 6th ed., pp. 155–157

COMPREHENSION QUESTIONS

1. What is the topic of the passage?
2. What is the central message of the passage?
3. Determine what is at issue. What is your initial personal viewpoint?
4. Distinguish among opposing viewpoints, and provide the rationale for each.
5. Think carefully about the viewpoints. Express a personal viewpoint, and give the reasons why you favor it. Does it differ from your initial personal viewpoint? Why or why not?
6. Write a few paragraphs *in support of the viewpoint that you do* not *favor.*

THOUGHT AND DISCUSSION QUESTIONS

1. Do you agree with the authors when they state, "alcohol is far more deadly than tobacco to *innocent bystanders*"? Why or why not?
2. Do you agree with beer advertisers that "their advertising is not meant to recruit, but rather to retain product loyalty among existing drinkers and, if possible, encourage brand switching"? Why or why not? Does beer advertising encourage you to drink beer or drink a certain brand of beer? Why or why not?
3. In your view, who is responsible for making the public aware of the link between alcohol, youth, and crime: the brewers, special interest groups, the government, or all of the them? Why?
4. How would you answer the question posed at the end of the passage: "if you knew your child was going to become addicted to either alcohol or tobacco, which would you choose? Why?
5. List any questions that came to mind while you were reading this selection, and be prepared to discuss possible answers to them.

4

All Shook Up

Jeannie Ralston

1   Eileen Plazek has a drinking habit: Every morning without fail, she whips up a frothy concoction—a cup of water, two scoops of 40-30-30 Balance drink mix, and some ice

cubes—in her blender. Plazek, a sales representative who lives in Sacramento, California, says that the protein in the drink gives her the energy to survive until noon. "I knew I needed protein," she says, reporting that her chiropractor prescribed the 40-30-30 ratio of carbohydrates, protein, and fat, respectively. "If I made a regular breakfast, I would have to cook, and that takes time. I'm not a morning person, so I like ready-made food. There's no greasy frying pan to clean up. I can't do without shakes now."

2   People used to be too busy to cook meals; now they're too busy to eat them. As a result, they're turning to the slew of nutrient-packed shakes that have flooded the market. There are weight-loss shakes, energy shakes, and bodybuilding shakes. They come in a can or in a powder form that requires a spin through the blender with water, milk, or juice. And there are now chains of stores that make shakes for their customers (at these places the drinks are usually called smoothies, perhaps to avoid association with those fattening shakes sold at Dairy Queen). As more people seek sustenance through a straw, sales have boomed. Last year grocery stores moved $226 million worth of shakes, a fourfold increase over 1993.

3   There are nutritional differences among the canned shakes. Bodybuilding shakes have a little more protein, weight-loss shakes are a tad lower in fat, and energy shakes have a few more carbohydrates. The counter-bought smoothies, which contain fresh fruit, yogurt, and supplements, are usually more substantial than the others. All are touted as self-contained nourishment that requires no thought and no time—Nutrition for Dummies, essentially. But though these concoctions provide a significant percentage of the recommended daily allowances for dozens of nutrients, experts aren't sold on the benefits of the adult population's regressing to infant formula.

4   The general consensus is that downing these liquid meals is better than resorting to a Coke and fries but worse than eating a salad. "Drinking a canned supplement is better than eating junk food or fat-saturated fast food," says George Blackburn, an associate professor at Harvard Medical School and director of the Center for the Study of Nutrition and Medicine at Boston's Beth Israel Deaconess Medical Center. "But in the long run, a can a day won't keep the doctor away."

5   The chief criticism of these shakes is that people miss out on a complex collection of nutrients in real food that liquids can't duplicate. Mainly, they lack adequate fiber and phytochemicals such as isoflavones, carotenoids, and other plant-derived compounds that maintain health and prevent disease. "These drinks don't contain everything you need to stay healthy," says Bonnie Liebman, director of nutrition for the Center for Science in the Public Interest in Washington, D.C. "We don't know exactly what it is in fruits and vegetables that leads to lower rates of heart disease and cancer, but whatever it is, it's probably not in a can." Even smoothies, which provide some fiber and phytochemicals, don't make the grade. "Smoothies are fine as a snack or as part of a meal but not as a complete meal," says Larry Lindner, executive editor of the *Tufts University Health & Nutrition Letter.*

6   No argument there, says Pete Paradossi, a spokesman for Boost. "We don't think people should drink every meal. We think people should eat more fruits and vegetables. We're not telling people to give up their apples and bagels, but we recognize that there's a big difference between what's ideal as far as healthy eating and what humans actually do."

7   The current crop of canned and powdered shakes grew out of the success of a drink called Ensure, which was developed in the early '70s for the older set by Ross Products Division of Abbott Laboratories, a manufacturer of infant formula. Its major competitor is Sustacal, produced by fellow baby-food maker Mead Johnson. Products such as Designer Protein and Met-Rx are distributed through health-food shops and drugstores. The smoothie craze went nationwide with a company called Jamba Juice, which in seven years has grown to 80 outlets.

Into the Drink

Shake	Cal. per serving	Protein grams	Fat grams	Calcium %DV*	Iron %DV*	Vitamin C %DV*
Boost	240	10	4	30	20	100
Sustacal High Protein	240	15	6	20	20	20
ReSource	180	9	0	15	15	60
Ensure	250	9	6	30	25	50
Nestlé Sweet Success	200	10	2.5	35	25	25
Ultra Slim-Fast	220	10	3	40	15	35
40-30-30 Balance**	180	14	6	25	30	30
Met-Rx**	250	37	2	100	45	60
Designer Protein**	85	18.5	1	9.5	1	0
Jamba Powerboost	347	9.4	1.7	112	128	879

*Percentage of daily values, according to recommended dietary allowance
**Mixed with water

8   Nutritionists complain that some of the ingredients in smoothies and other shakes may not be as effective as their manufacturers claim. For example, some producers imply that the protein in their shakes is superior to the protein found anywhere else. Some of these drinks are made from whey peptide protein. It's an adequate protein but no better than what's in a piece of meat or an egg. While the high protein levels in these shakes help mitigate swings in insulin levels and subsequent hunger pangs, scientists say that extra protein does not build muscle more efficiently, as some producers suggest. "What builds bodies is training, not food," says Lindner. "Extra protein does not add bulk. If it did, we'd all look like Arnold Schwarzenegger." New Image Power Shakes and something called the Venice Burner at Robeks chain of juice bars contain chromium picolinate, which supposedly burns fat. It's true that chromium picolinate is key in the transfer of sugar from blood to muscles, which allows the sugar to fuel the muscles' activities. However, Lindner warns, "Interpreting that to mean that taking chromium can build muscle and decrease fat is taking a giant leap of faith. It's not proven."

9   In addition to being attractive to people who lack time, shakes also appeal to dieters who lack willpower. Someone who has trouble curbing portions may prefer to reduce temptation by avoiding food when possible. It is a universally acknowledged truth in the industry that dieters who rely on these shakes usually regain the weight lost once they resume

normal eating, but the maker of Slim-Fast insists that its product can work long-term. Not surprisingly, the company touts an ongoing study indicating that by staying on Slim-Fast, 73 percent of men and 62 percent of women lost weight—and kept off more than half of it—for some three years. Smoothies, however, can be a dieter's enemy; even if they are low-fat or fat-free, honey or sweeteners are often added (a typical Jamba Juice drink has 320 to 500 calories).

10   At least the smoothies taste good—which is more than can be said about canned shakes. Not many people drink the canned varieties because they find them delicious. Elizabeth Stewart, a New York fashion stylist, downs Ensure for breakfast every morning because she has trouble keeping weight on. "I get full so fast—one cookie will do it," says Stewart, who is five feet seven and weighs 118 pounds. She packs cans of Ensure when she travels to Paris to cover the fashion shows. It's almost sacrilegious to be drinking milk in the home of croissants and foie gras, but Stewart says she's too busy to eat. "It's just laziness," she says. "I wouldn't say that they are yummy. I'd definitely rather have a real milk shake, but real milk shakes are more of a project."

11   There are certainly more appealing and satisfying ways to spend 250 calories. When Anne Dubner, a Houston dietitian, broke her jaw and had to drink liquid food for three weeks, she says she began craving real food, a phenomenon that could explain why people often gain back weight quickly after a liquid diet. "I missed chewing," she says. "I craved something crunchy. I knew I couldn't have it, which is why I wanted it."

12   When people turn to liquid lunches, they deprive themselves of the pleasures of food, with all its varied textures and smells, say nutritionists. "Why do Americans have to spurn healthy meals for something that doesn't taste very good and costs a lot?" laments Lindner. "Why do people feel food has to be punishing to be good for them?" Good question.

Allure, June 1998, pp. 100, 102, 109

COMPREHENSION QUESTIONS

1. What is the topic of the passage?
2. What is the central message of the passage?
3. Determine what is at issue. What is your initial personal viewpoint?
4. Distinguish among opposing viewpoints, and provide the rationale for each.
5. Think carefully about the viewpoints. Express a personal viewpoint, and give the reasons why you favor it. Does it differ from your initial personal viewpoint? Why or why not?
6. Write a few paragraphs *in support of the viewpoint that you do not favor.*

THOUGHT AND DISCUSSION QUESTIONS

1. In your view, what role, if any, does advertising play in the popularity of nutritional shakes? Why?
2. What does the popularity of nutritional shakes say about current attitudes and lifestyles?

3. If you were interested in losing weight, bodybuilding, or increasing your energy, which shakes from the list provided would you choose to drink for each of those purposes? Why?

4. Nutritionally speaking, would it be better for a person to have spaghetti and meatballs or a nutritional shake? Why?

5. List any questions that came to mind while you were reading this selection, and be prepared to discuss possible answers to them.

5
African Ritual Pain: Genital Cutting

Celia W. Dugger

1   MAN, Ivory Coast—Marthe Bleu is 12 years old, a shy, pretty girl with a heart-shaped face, dressed in flip-flops and a lacy, white pinafore trimmed in pink satin. But already her body is taking on the soft, rounded shape of womanhood. And these days she wants more than anything to do what she believes stands between her and being grown up. She wants to have her genitals cut off.

2   In the lament of pubescent girls everywhere, she says that all her friends are getting ahead of her. Their parents have sent them into the woods where village women "cut what is down there," she said, gesturing to her lap.

3   After the rite, the girls are showered with gifts of money, jewelry and cloth. Their families honor them with celebrations where hundreds of relatives and friends feast on goat, cow and chicken.

4   "It is the custom, and I want to respect it," she said.

5   The tradition of female genital cutting is woven into the everyday life of the Yacouba people here, just as it is for hundreds of ethnic groups in a wide band of 28 countries across Africa. In Man, it is part of a girl's dreams of womanhood, a father's desire to show off with a big party and a family's way of proving its conformity to social convention.

6   The rising chorus of international condemnation of this age-old practice, voiced in recent years from the podiums of United Nations assemblies in Vienna, Cairo and Beijing, echoes only faintly in places like Man, a tourist town deep in the interior, surrounded by the craggy, cloud-shrouded Toura mountains.

7   On the coast, in the cosmopolitan hubbub of Abidjan, and in other parts of Africa, the debate about female genital cutting is slowly moving into the public arena. Only in the last few years have African nations even begun measuring the prevalence of genital cutting as part of national health surveys or in other research.

8   In the Ivory Coast and the Central African Republic, two out of five women have been cut. In Togo, it is one in eight. In the Sudan—the only country that already had reliable national estimates—it is 9 out of 10. In Mali, it is 93 percent.

9   "It looks like women in most countries are nearly as likely to undergo these procedures as their mothers and grandmothers," said Dara Carr, a researcher at Macro International

Inc., the Maryland-based company that is assisting the countries in conducting the health surveys. "But there are some seeds of change."

10   In the Sudan, the prevalence of the practice has dropped from 96 percent to 89 percent over the course of a decade. And there has been a shift toward a less severe form of genital cutting. In Togo, a survey found that half of the mothers who had been cut wanted to spare their daughters. And while three-quarters of the women in Mali favor continuing the practice, a majority in the Central African Republic want to end it.

11   But what women want and what they have the power to accomplish are very different things. In most of the countries where tens of millions of girls and women have been cut, organizations have sprung up to combat the practice.

12   Like mosquitoes attacking an elephant, the small, ill-financed groups are struggling within societies where men rule women's lives, and old people, including old women, rule the young.

13   There are, for example, Ivoirian laws against physical violence that could be used to stop the cutting, said Idrissa Fofana, a high-ranking official in the Justice Ministry.

14   But the Government has no interest in imposing them on unwilling families, antagonizing village chiefs and family elders who are pillars of society and guardians of tradition.

15   "If there was a complaint from parents that their child had been excised against their wishes, the Justice Ministry could pursue the case," Mr. Fofana said. "But if there is no complaint, we cannot disturb the peace of the family and the village."

16   Like most Yacouba girls in Man, Marthe Bleu is an eager initiate. But even if she resisted, her father, Jean-Baptiste Bleu, a trim, genial, neatly dressed waiter at a local hotel, would insist on her cutting.

17   "If your daughter has not been excised, the father is not allowed to speak at village meetings," he said. "No man in the village will marry her. It is an obligation. We have done it, we do it and we will continue to do it."

18   "She has no choice. I decide. Her viewpoint is not important."

19   The Bleus have not yet chosen who will cut Marthe, but not far from their home, through a maze of dirt pathways, lives Madeleine Douan, 47, one of the local excisers.

20   The tall, sinewy woman refused to show the ceremonial knife she uses, but brought out other accouterment of her calling: a long strand of metal bells and cloth sacks filled with bottle caps. While she cuts a group of 10 to 15 girls on the ground of the forest, other women shake the noisemakers, covering the cries of pain. Mrs. Douan herself sings traditional songs.

21   She introduced several of the girls she had recently cut. Natalie Sahi, 15, sat on the side of her thigh outside Mrs. Douan's windowless mud hut to avoid putting direct pressure on the wound. "I wanted it to happen," she said. "It's natural."

22   Patricia Vehgolou, 13, her hair neatly braided in corn rows, buried her face in her hands and would only giggle when asked if the cutting hurt. Mrs. Douan explained that the girls must swear before leaving the forest that they will not share the secrets of the rite with the uninitiated.

23   The purpose of the cutting, Mrs. Douan said, is to help insure a woman's fidelity to her husband and her family. "It's a tradition from antiquity," she said. A woman's role in life

is to care for her children, keep house and cook. If she has not been cut, Mrs. Douan said, a woman might think instead about her own sexual pleasure.

The Origins: Pride, Tradition and Ignored Risks

24   It is not known when, where or why the practice of female genital cutting originated. Scholars believe that it started in Egypt or the Horn of Africa more than 2,000 years ago, before the advent of Christianity or Islam. It then spread west across the continent, all the way to the Atlantic Ocean, with the migration of dominant tribes and civilizations.

25   The practice knows no class or religious boundaries. Most prevalent among Muslims, it is also performed by Christians and followers of traditional African religions. The practice is more widespread among the illiterate, but it is also common among the educated.

26   The nature of the cutting, the reasons for it and the age at which it is done vary greatly by region and ethnic group.

27   The practice involves amputating some or all of the external genitalia—the clitoris, the small genital lips and the large ones—diminishing a woman's ability to experience sexual pleasure. It can also cause serious health problems, including hemorrhaging and infection.

28   Typically, the cutting is done by traditional village women without anything to dull the pain. But sometimes, when midwives or nurses are brought in to do the job, they apply a local anesthetic.

29   Many believe that cutting helps insure a girl's virginity before marriage and fidelity afterward by reducing sex to a marital obligation. Often, people follow the custom simply because it has always been done.

30   "Children are born and the parents do it," said Awa Kone, a Malian washerwoman in Abidjan, who plans to take her baby daughter, Kadia, to an exciser in the near future.

31   In the Horn of Africa—Djibouti, Somalia, the Sudan and parts of Ethiopia—the most severe and harmful form of cutting, infibulation, is practiced.

32   In this procedure, the clitoris and some or all of the small genital lips are cut away. Then an incision is made in the large lips so the raw surfaces can be stitched together, covering the urethra and most of the vagina. Only a small opening, as tiny as a matchstick or as large as a small fingertip, is left to pass urine and menstrual blood, said Nahid Toubia, a Sudanese surgeon who is an associate professor at Columbia University.

33   Infibulation comes with its own set of rationales. Some men say the artificial tightness heightens their sexual enjoyment. The smoothness of the scar is found esthetically beautiful. And the stitching itself forms a chastity belt of flesh.

34   There is a common thread to all forms of cutting. Economic realities underlie the practice. Women typically have no way to survive without a husband. Parents insist on the rite so their daughters are marriageable.

35   "People do know the health risks," said Ellen Gruenbaum, a medical anthropologist at California State University, San Bernardino. "They have seen people get sick. On rare occasions, a girl might die. But you will not change people's minds by preaching to them or telling them they're primitive. They undertake the risks for reasons important to them."

36   After the cutting, more pain lies ahead. Women who have endured the more extreme forms of the practice have particularly agonizing and complicated deliveries. The scarring narrows the vaginal opening and makes the flesh inelastic, doctors and midwives say. The pressure of a baby's emerging head often causes grave tearing of the vagina.

CASE STUDIES

Census of an Ancient Rite

The World Health Organization, advocacy groups and news accounts often cite the estimate that 85 million to 115 million girls and women have undergone genital cutting. But these numbers are considered uncertain because there have been few scientific surveys. The rite is known to be practiced in 28 African countries, shaded in map.

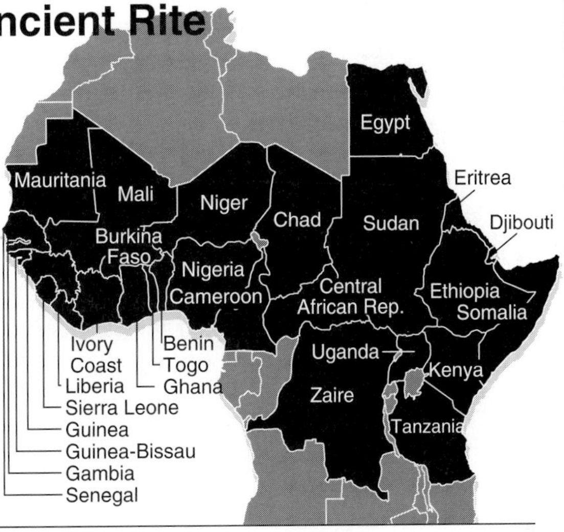

Map labels: Mauritania, Mali, Niger, Chad, Sudan, Egypt, Eritrea, Djibouti, Burkina Faso, Nigeria, Cameroon, Central African Rep., Ethiopia, Somalia, Ivory Coast, Benin, Togo, Ghana, Uganda, Kenya, Liberia, Zaire, Sierra Leone, Tanzania, Guinea, Guinea-Bissau, Gambia, Senegal

Large-scale surveys have been released from five countries, providing the first solid data.

Percentage of different groups that has undergone genital cutting.

LEVEL OF EDUCATION	RELIGION
None	Christian
Primary	Muslim
Secondary or more	Traditional

Prevalence of practice

Country	Prevalence	None	Primary	Secondary or more	Christian	Muslim	Traditional
Central African Republic	43%	48%	45	23	not available		
Ivory Coast	43%	55	25	22	32%	80	37
Mali	93%	94	94	90	85	94	88
Sudan	89%	not available			47	90	
Togo	12%	16	6	4	3	64	10

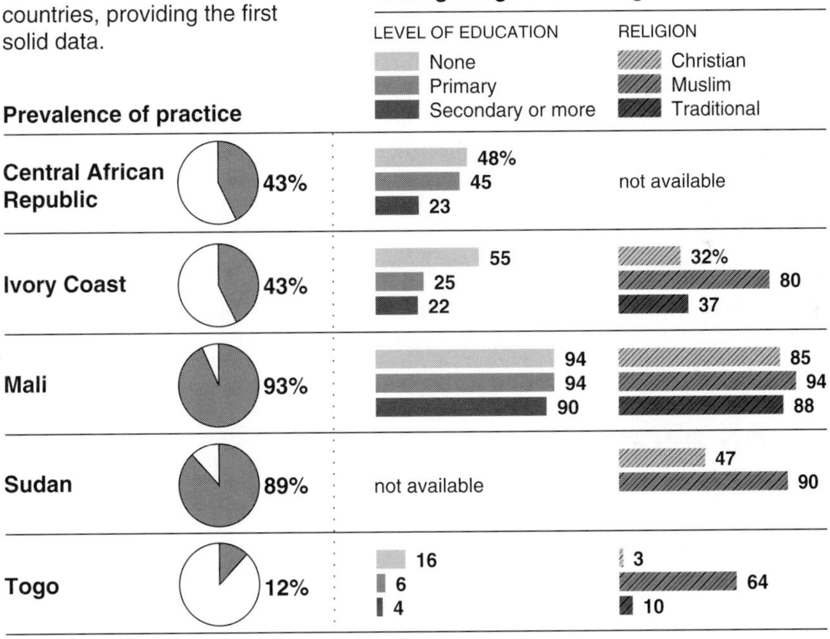

Sources: Demographic and Health Surveys, Marco Intl. Inc., Calverton, Md. Years of reports: Sudan, 1989-90; Ivory Coast, 1994; Central African Republic, 1994-95; Mali, preliminary report, 1995-96. Togo source: Demographic Research Unit, University of Benin, Lomé, Togo, June 1996.

New York Times

37   Women who bear a child in their villages without a doctor to widen the vagina surgically sometimes arrive torn and bleeding at the Maternal Health Center in Man. On occasion, the tearing goes up into the urethra and bladder, down into the anus, as well as side to side. The women must then be sent to a hospital in Abidjan for surgery.

38   Clautilde Yenon, a midwife at the health center, tried to think of a way to convey the excruciating damage. Finally, she had an idea. She picked up a sheet of paper and ripped it into jagged pieces.

New York Times, October 5, 1996, pp. 1, 6

COMPREHENSION QUESTIONS

1. What is the topic of the passage?
2. What is the central message of the passage?
3. Determine what is at issue. What is your initial personal viewpoint?
4. Distinguish among opposing viewpoints, and provide the rationale for each.
5. Think carefully about the viewpoints. Express a personal viewpoint, and give the reasons why you favor it. Does it differ from your initial personal viewpoint? Why or why not?
6. Write a few paragraphs *in support of the viewpoint that you do* not *favor.*

THOUGHT AND DISCUSSION QUESTIONS

1. Genital cutting is sometimes referred to as the "rite of anguish." How do you interpret that phrase?
2. What effect, if any, does level of education and religion have on the practice?
3. In your view, are the statistics presented in the passage relevant, reliable, and impartial? Why or why not?
4. Will genital cutting be as prevalent in Africa 50 years from now? Why or why not?
5. List any questions that came to mind while you were reading this selection, and be prepared to discuss possible answers to them.

LOOKING BACK

Summarize and/or paraphrase the most important points you learned from this chapter, and determine how they can be put to use in other classes. Be prepared to discuss with your classmates what you have written.

THINK AGAIN!

Evaluate your survival skills by taking the following "self-discovery test." Be prepared to discuss your responses in class.

Rate Your Survival Skills

Laura Billings

Most of us have mastered everyday safety basics: Always wear a seat belt. Don't let strangers into your home. Look both ways before you cross the street. But what if you were faced with a more immediate threat to your health and your life? Say a thug demands your car keys. Or a riptide carries you out to sea. Or the earth suddenly shakes beneath you. Would you know what to do—and what not to do? We've picked several high-pressure, panic-inducing situations and asked how you'd react in each case. See how many times you select the best strategy, or the worst.

1. The rain is coming down in sheets on the curvy country road ahead. You lose control of your car and steer yourself right off the pavement and into a river. How do you get out alive?
   a. Get out of the car any way you can.
   b. Stay in the car until help arrives—river currents are too dangerous for the average swimmer.
   c. Wait until the car sinks to the bottom and water pressure equalizes before you open the door to swim out.

2. On a hike, you stumble upon a mother bear and her cubs. She doesn't seem happy. What now?
   a. Run and climb up the nearest tree.
   b. Stand your ground and don't move.
   c. Charge at the bear and wave your arms to scare her and the cubs away.

3. It's been a record snowfall, and you're trapped on the side of the road. The radio says that even the tow trucks are spinning their wheels in the snow and ice, so you:
   a. hike off to find a service station.
   b. put the car in neutral and push until your tires find some traction.
   c. huddle up for warmth inside the car, turn on your dome light and check occasionally to make sure that your tailpipe isn't clogged.

4. You and your surfboard are not alone—a shark is in the neighborhood. Any way to reduce the chance that you'll end up as its afternoon snack?
   a. Leave the board and swim to shore.
   b. Pull your arms and legs on top of the board and remain still.
   c. Float face up in the water, with your limbs at your side—a shark won't attack if you look dead.

5. You hiked solo up a mountainside and are feeling very Maria Von Trapp. But now it's getting dark, and you don't remember how to get back down. You:
   a. find your way out by following flowing water downhill.
   b. build a fire and wait for rescue.
   c. spend the night retracing your tracks—you might have a hard time finding them the next day.

6. On your way out of a fast-food drive-through, a young thug asks you for your money and your car. He and his gun seem very insistent, so you:
   a. hand over your car keys and your wallet and step away from the car.
   b. lock the doors, floor the accelerator and peel out of there.
   c. scream "Help!" to attract the attention of passersby.

7. You wake up in the middle of the night to the sound of a fire alarm and the smell of smoke. Best plan:
   a. Hang a sheet from your window and jump out if the fire comes too close.
   b. Gather up important belongings and race for the door as fast as you can.
   c. Crawl to the door, check the conditions on the other side and proceed if it's safe. If not, retreat and wait for rescue.

8. You're in a Los Angeles parking lot when the Big One finally hits. You:
   a. run to your car and hop in.
   b. stop where you are, crouch into a squat and cover your head.
   c. rush to the doorway of a building, where it's structurally sound; you don't want to be in a wide-open space.

9. It's a Saturday night and you're all by yourself, tossing grapes in the air and catching them in your mouth when, suddenly, one goes down the wrong way. It's getting hard to breathe. How do you save yourself?
   a. Try sticking your fingers in your throat to pull out the offending fruit.
   b. Give yourself the Heimlich maneuver with your fists wrapped together in a ball.
   c. Throw yourself over the top of a high-backed chair with enough force to expel the grape.

10. You and three coworkers are in the office elevator when it gets stuck between floors. The lights dim, the alarm goes off and everyone is starting to panic. How to deal?
    a. Help each other climb out of the ceiling vent and up the cable to the nearest elevator landing.
    b. Take shallow breaths until help arrives—air flow may be limited.
    c. Hit the emergency button, use the elevator phone to call building security or 911, and wait for rescue.

11. You wake at night and hear a prowler. The safest strategy:
    a. Get out of the house and call 911 from a pay phone or neighbor's place.
    b. Grab your baseball bat and stand behind the door, ready to surprise him when he enters.
    c. Call the police, barricade your bedroom door and hide.

12. A rattlesnake clamped its fangs into your leg, then slithered away. Now what?
    a. Use a sharp knife or rock to cut into the site of the bite and suck the venom out, making sure not to swallow it.
    b. Wrap a tourniquet above the bite.
    c. Immobilize the leg and get medical attention immediately.

13. You planned on a dip, but a riptide has carried you far from shore. How do you stay afloat?
    a. Turn straight toward the beach and paddle as hard as you can.
    b. Swim parallel to shore, or at a 45-degree angle to it, until the wave action starts carrying you back to land.
    c. Wave while you're riding the rip out to the calmer waters behind the waves and hope a lifeguard sees you.

Mademoiselle, March 1998, pp. 126–127

The Dashing Detective

Remember to follow these steps:

- first, read the narrative and all the questions
- second, examine the letter carefully
- third, answer the questions in the order they appear and come up with the solution

Have fun!

Extortion

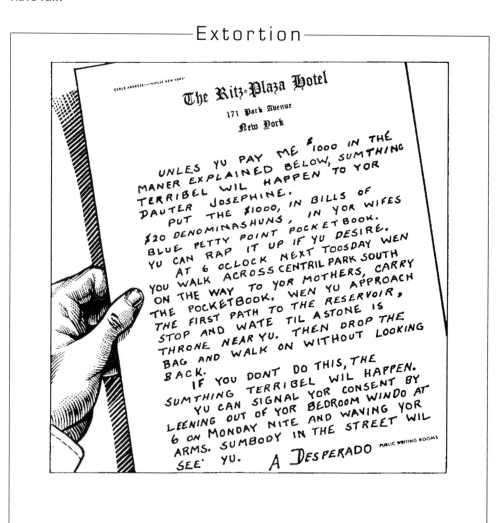

Pictured here is a kidnapping threat which was mailed to Iver Nutmeg, wealthy gumshoe manufacturer.

From this information and an examination of the paper, can you discover who sent the extortion letter?

Questions

1. Did the writer know Nutmeg's address?   ☐ Yes   ☐ No

2. Did the writer misspell because he was unfamiliar with English?   ☐ Yes   ☐ No

3. Do you think the writer misspelled intentionally?   ☐ Yes   ☐ No

4. Do you think the writer used print as a disguise to his handwriting?   ☐ Yes   ☐ No

5. Would you say the writer was probably a shabbily dressed person?   ☐ Yes   ☐ No

6. Do you think the writer was a professional gangster?   ☐ Yes   ☐ No

7. Did the writer know Nutmeg by sight?   ☐ Yes   ☐ No

8. Was the writer familiar with Nutmeg's habits?   ☐ Yes   ☐ No

9. Was the writer familiar with Nutmeg's apartment?   ☐ Yes   ☐ No

10. Do you think the writer was a man?   ☐ Yes   ☐ No

11. Who wrote the extortion letter?   ☐ A gangster   ☐ An elevator boy   ☐ A discharged English governess   ☐ A discharged office clerk   ☐ A waitress from the restaurant where Nutmeg eats lunch   ☐ A discharged Irish chambermaid   ☐ A discharged chauffeur   ☐ A delivery boy

Lawrence Treat, *Crime and Puzzlement*, pp. 22–23

Name _____   Date _____

MASTERY TEST 9-1

DIRECTIONS: Choose one of the options below to complete the statement:

Advertisements require critical reading and critical thinking because they:

     a. affect our purchasing decisions
     b. affect our political decisions
     c. affect our philosophical decisions
     d. influence our thinking
     e. all of the above

DIRECTIONS: Read and think critically about the following advertisements. Then answer these questions for each one:

1. How does it try to catch the interest of readers?

2. To whom is it designed to appeal?

3. What is it trying to persuade readers to buy, do, or think?

4. What benefit to readers is it stressing?

5. How convincing is it?

_____

_____

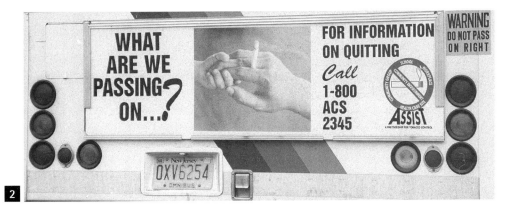

2

CHARLTON HESTON DIDN'T WRITE THE SECOND AMENDMENT.

—

HE JUST ACTS THAT WAY.

The NRA, not our Constitution,
is preventing sane gun laws.

It's a sad and shameful fact that thousands of kids are killed by firearms every year in this country. What's even more shameful is the National Rifle Association's misrepresentation of the Second Amendment. The NRA's rhetoric undermines efforts to pass reasonable gun laws, such as those mandating child-safety features. Neither the U.S. Supreme Court nor any federal appellate court has ever struck down a gun regulation on Second Amendment grounds. Yet the NRA continues to spend millions of dollars each year convincing the public and media that effective gun laws are unconstitutional. Former U.S. Supreme Court Chief Justice Warren Burger called the NRA's interpretation "one of the greatest pieces of fraud, I repeat the word *fraud*, on the American public by special interest groups that I have ever seen in my lifetime."

Today NRA president Charlton Heston received a letter, signed by many of our nation's most prominent historians and legal scholars, urging the NRA to end its misrepresentation of the Second Amendment.

We're Legal Community Against Violence. We provide legal assistance to communities seeking effective solutions to the national epidemic of gun-related violence. To find out what you can do to save lives in your community, visit our website at www.lcav.org.

The Second Amendment to the U.S. Constitution: "A well regulated Militia, being necessary to the security of a free State, the right of the people to keep and bear Arms, shall not be infringed."

Legal Community Against Violence
(www.firearmslawcenter.org).

3

Source: Courtesy of Legal Community Against Violence

4

_____
_____
_____
_____
_____
_____

_____
_____
_____
_____
_____
_____

5

6

7

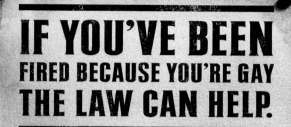

8

Name _____   Date _____

MASTERY TEST 9-2

DIRECTIONS: In the space below, create a convincing advertisement that catches the interest of readers, appeals to a certain audience and, by stressing the benefits to readers, tries to persuade them to buy, do, or think something.

_____

_____

_____

_____

_____

_____

_____

_____

_____

_____

_____

_____

_____

_____

_____

_____

_____

_____

_____

_____

_____

_____

_____

_____

_____

Name _____ Date _____

MASTERY TEST 9-3

DIRECTIONS: Read and think about the passages below, and answer the questions that follow.

1
Dead Body Photo

1   John Harte was the only photographer working on Sunday, July 28, at the Bakersfield *Californian.* After some routine assignments, he heard on the police scanner about a drowning at a lake twenty-five miles northeast of Bakersfield. When he arrived on the scene, divers were still searching for the body of five-year-old Edward Romero, who had drowned while swimming with his brothers.

2   The divers finally brought up the dead boy, and the sheriff kept onlookers at bay while the family and officials gathered around the open body bag. The television crew did not film that moment, but Harte ducked under the sheriff's arms and shot eight quick frames with his motor-driven camera.

3   The *Californian* had a policy of not running pictures of dead bodies. So managing editor Robert Bentley was called into the office on Sunday evening for a decision. Concluding that the picture would remind readers to be careful when kids are swimming, Bentley gave his approval. On Monday, Harte transmitted the picture over the Associated Press wire "after a 20-minute argument with an editor who was furious we ran the picture ... and accused [Harte] of seeking glory and an AP award."

4   Readers bombarded the 80,000 circulation daily with 400 phone calls, 500 letters, and 80 cancellations. The *Californian* even received a bomb threat, forcing evacuation of the building for ninety minutes.

5   Distraught by the intensity of the reaction, Bentley sent around a newsroom memo admitting that "a serious error of editorial judgment was made.... We make mistakes—and this clearly was a big one." He concluded that their most important lesson was "the stark validation of what readers—and former readers—are saying not just locally but across the country: that the news media are seriously out of touch with their audiences."

6   For photographer John Harte, Bentley's contrition was "disappointing to me and many of my co-workers." And editorial page editor Ed Clendaniel of the *Walla Walla* (Washington) *Union Bulletin* was not apologetic either about running it in his paper, even though it was out of context. "First, the foremost duty of any paper is to report the news," he argued. "One of the hard facts of life is that the world is filled with tragic moments as well as happy moments.... Second, we believe the photograph does more to promote water safety than 10,000 words could ever hope to accomplish."

7   Later Bentley entered Harte's photo in the Pulitzer Prize competition. "I really don't see any contradiction," he explained. "I think the photograph should never have been published.... But the Pulitzer Prize is given for journalistic and technical excellence. It is not given for reader approval."

8   Michael J. Ogden, executive director of the *Providence Journal-Bulletin,* condemns photographs that capitalize on human grief:

I can understand the printing of an auto accident picture as an object lesson. What I can't understand is the printing of sobbing wives, mothers, children.... What is the value of showing a mother who has just lost her child in a fire? Is this supposed to have a restraining effect on arsonists? I am sure that those who don't hesitate to print such pictures will use the pious pretense of quoting Charles A. Dana's famous *dictum* that "whatever the Divine Providence permitted to occur I was not too proud to print." Which is as peachy a shibboleth to permit pandering as I can image.

9   But Ogden is a rare editor. Every day in newspapers and on television, photographs and film footage emphasize grief and tragedy. Though Harte's photo did not win the Pulitzer, in fact, professional awards are regularly given to grisly pictures regardless of whether they pander to morbid tastes.

10   Defending photos of this type usually centers on newsworthiness. The broken-hearted father whose child was just run over, a shocked eight-year-old boy watching his teenage brother gunned down by police, the would-be suicide on a bridge—all pitiful scenes that communicate something of human tragedy and are therefore to be considered news. Photojournalists sum up a news event in a manner the mind can hold, capturing that portrayal "rich in meaning because it is a trigger image of all the emotions aroused by the subject." Harte in this case acted as an undaunted professional, fulfilling his role as reporter on everyday affairs—including the unpleasantries. From the photographer's perspective, to capture the newsworthy moment is an important self-discipline. Photographers are trained not to panic but to bring forth the truth as events dictate. They are schooled to be visual historians and not freelance medics or family counselors.

11   On what grounds, however, can the photographer's behavior be condoned in the Bakersfield drowning? The principals at the scene tried to prevent him from intruding, though, it should be granted, the authorities' judgment is not always correct. The warning bell thesis was generally used by the picture's proponents, asserting that the photo could make other parents more safety conscious. However, this utilitarian appeal to possible consequences has no factual basis. Perhaps in the name of reporting news, the photojournalist in this case was actually caught in those opportunistic professional values that build circulation by playing on the human penchant for morbidity.

12   No overarching purpose emerges that can ameliorate the direct invasion of privacy and insensitivity for these innocent victims of tragedy. In all jurisdictions, the reporting of events of public concern involves no legal issue of privacy invasion. But it is here that the photographer should consider the moral guideline: that suffering individuals are entitled to dignity and respect, despite the fact that events may have made them part of the news.

13   Photojournalism is an extremely significant window on our humanity and inhumanity. In pursuing its mission, the ethical conflict typically revolves around the need for honest visual information and for respecting a person's privacy. Bob Greene of the *Chicago Tribune* is exaggerating only slightly in calling the Harte picture "pornography." "Because of journalistic factors they could not control," he wrote, "at the most terrible moment of their lives" the Romeros were exposed to the entire country. The older brother's hysteria for not watching his little brother closely enough is presented without compassion before an audience who

had no right to become a participant in this traumatizing event for a suffering family. And even those who find the photo acceptable are upset by the context: The *Californian* printing the photo right next to a headline about teen killings by a satanic cult.

Clifford G. Christians et al., Media Ethics, 6th ed., pp. 123–126.

COMPREHENSION QUESTIONS

1. What is the topic of the passage?
2. What is the central message of the passage?
3. Determine what is at issue. What is your initial personal viewpoint?
4. Distinguish among opposing viewpoints, and provide the rationale for each.
5. Think carefully about the viewpoints. Express a personal viewpoint, and give the reasons you favor it. Does it differ from your initial personal viewpoint? Why or why not?
6. Write a few paragraphs *in support of the viewpoint that you do* not *favor.*

THOUGHT AND DISCUSSION QUESTIONS

1. If you were John Harte, would you have taken the photograph? Why or why not?
2. Do you agree with Robert Bentley, "that the news media are seriously out of touch with their audiences?" Why or why not?
3. Do you support "the warning bells thesis?" Why or why not?
4. "Every day in newspapers and on television, photographs and film footage emphasize grief and tragedy." Do you agree with this statement? Why or why not?
5. Do you think the information presented in the passage is mostly fact, mostly opinion, or a combination of both? Why? Provide specific examples.
6. Do you think the passage is unbiased? Why or why not?

2

Arguments For and Against Capital Punishment

1   Those who support the death penalty usually base their argument on one of four grounds: (1) The death penalty is a necessary punishment as retribution for the life unlawfully taken; (2) the death penalty will deter others from committing murder; (3) the death penalty is less expensive to administer than life imprisonment; and (4) errors in executing innocent persons are rare. Let us examine the evidence that exists to support these claims.

CAPITAL PUNISHMENT AS RETRIBUTION

2   The retributionist argument is perhaps the oldest of all justifications for punishment. It can be traced at least as far back as the Old Testament. The books of Exodus (21:12–25), Leviticus (24:17–21), Numbers (35:30–31), and Deuteronomy (19:11–12), all warn that

> in case a man strikes any soul of mankind fatally, he should be put to death without fail.... And in case a man should cause a defect in his associate, then just as he

has done, so it should be done to him. Fracture for fracture, eye for eye, tooth for tooth; the same sort of defect he may cause in the man that is what should be caused in him. And the fatal striker of a heart should make compensation for it, but the fatal striker of a man should be put to death.

Although modern Israel, established in 1948, quickly abandoned the Mosaic law of "life for life" (except in cases of wartime treason or Nazi collaboration), many people continue to apply this notion of retribution in support of the death penalty. In fact, Christians sometimes use this justification for capital punishment despite Christ's teachings to the contrary. For example, the Gospel according to Matthew (5:38–39) recounts Jesus' stating, "You heard that it was said, 'Eye for eye and tooth for tooth.' However, I say to you: Do not resist him that is wicked; but whoever slaps you on the right cheek, turn the other also to him." Such teachings prompted the disciples of early Christianity to oppose capital punishment. Adherence to this principle wavered, however, when non-Christians came to be seen as heretics and deserving of death. This change of heart relied heavily on Paul's declaration to the Romans (13:1–2):

Let every soul be in subjection to the superior authorities, for there is no authority except by God; the existing authorities stand placed in their relative positions by God. Therefore he who opposes the authority has taken a stand against the arrangement of God.

Some believed that Paul's statements meant that if the state permitted capital punishment, capital punishment must be God's will, because government exists only by God's will. This line of reasoning continues to be employed today by those who defend the death penalty on the basis of Biblical interpretation.

3   Regardless of the basis of the argument, there is little evidence that capital punishment has been effective as a form of retribution. Examinations of willful homicides in the United States have shown that fewer than half are murders involving premeditation or homicides committed during the course of a felony. Further, fewer than 25 percent of homicides are prosecuted as capital cases. In these capital cases males and blacks have been executed much more often than have females and whites convicted of the same crimes. Even when a person is prosecuted for murder, the defendant's odds of actually receiving retribution is extremely small. For example, in Massachusetts between 1931 and 1950, a murder defendant faced a 29 percent chance of being convicted and a 4 percent chance of being put to death. In California between 1950 and 1975, only 29 percent of homicide convictions were capital cases; 6 percent of defendants were sentenced to death, and fewer than 2 percent were executed. In fact, the death penalty has been imposed on only a small minority of offenders convicted of homicide. During its greatest usage in the 1930s, death sentences were handed down in only 1 of 50 homicide convictions. And as criminologist Thorsten Sellin has pointed out, these examples actually *overestimate* the use of the death penalty as retribution:

Considering that these adjudicated murderers were only a part of a group that included the never-discovered offenders and those arrested but not prosecuted or convicted for lack of sufficient evidence, it is obvious that if retribution by death could be measured in relation to the number of actual murders, its failure would be even more evident.

Although in recent years supporters of retribution have succeeded in passing death penalty laws, it can be seen that only a small proportion of criminal homicides are actually subject to the death penalty. Moreover, the penalty is rarely imposed even in cases in which it is applicable. When it is applied, males and blacks receive a disproportionate share of the death sentences imposed.

4   It appears, therefore, that the goal of the retributionists has yet to be achieved. Even if the number of executions were to rise dramatically, it is unlikely that more than 2 percent of all homicide offenders sentenced would ever be executed. After all, the rate was 2 percent during the 1930s, when executions numbered more than 200 per year. Limits on appellate review of sentences in death penalty cases have resulted in more executions in recent years, but the numbers are quite small compared to those in the 1930s. Trends in the number of people executed in the United States from 1930 to 1998 are illustrated in the figure below. It is clear that the increase in executions during the 1990s is dwarfed by the number of executions that took place each year from 1930 to 1950.

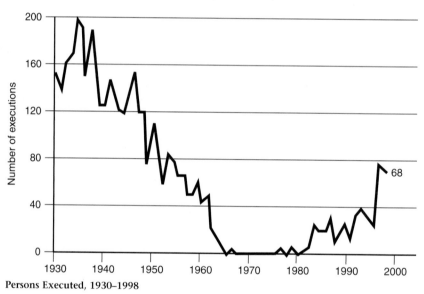

Persons Executed, 1930–1998

Source: Tracy L. Snell, Capital Punishment (Washington, DC: U.S. Bureau of Justice Statistics, 1999).

THE DEATH PENALTY AS DETERRENCE

5   The belief that the death penalty will prevent crime by deterring future murders is another common argument in support of capital punishment. One aspect of this argument suggests that police officers in states without the death penalty are more likely to be killed than officers in states that provide for capital punishment for murder (or at least for murder of police officers). Studies consistently have found, however, that the numbers of police officers killed do not differ in death penalty and non-death penalty states.

6   The deterrence argument also holds that capital punishment prevents the offender from committing another murder if released on parole. In the four-year period from

1969 to 1973, when no death sentences were carried out, 6,835 male offenders serving sentences for murder were released on parole from state prisons. Fewer than 5 percent of those released were returned to prison for additional crimes. Fewer than one-half of 1 percent committed willful homicides. From 1930 to 1962, when executions were more frequent, only 63 offenders convicted of first-degree murder in New York State were released on parole; of these, one person was returned to prison for committing an additional crime (a burglary). Other follow-up studies have had similar results. It is clear that murderers are very rarely released on parole and that when they are, it is extremely uncommon for them to be involved in another homicide.

7   Another way to assess the deterrent effect of capital punishment is to determine whether homicide rates increase when states abolish capital punishment, or to examine the homicide rates in neighboring states, one of which has a death penalty while the other does not. Obviously, if capital punishment prevents murders, states without a death penalty law should have higher homicide rates than neighboring states that employ the death penalty. A comparison of homicide rates and use of the death penalty in Maryland, Delaware, and New Jersey from 1920 through 1974 found no difference in homicide rates, even though each of these states retained, abolished, and sometimes reinstituted capital punishment during this fifty-five-year period. The number of executions in these states varied from none to a high of twenty-six per year, but in no case was a higher number of executions accompanied by a lower homicide rate. Comparable findings were uncovered in tristate comparisons of Arizona, California, and New Mexico and of Indiana, Ohio, and Michigan, as well as of other states. As Brian Forst concluded, "it is erroneous to view capital punishment as a means of reducing the homicide rate." Likewise, Scott Decker and Carol Kohlfeld found that "several different methods of examining the deterrent effect of executions resulted in the same finding; there is no evidence of a deterrent effect of executions in the state of Texas." These findings mirror the conclusions of other criminologists.

8   Studies that appear to show a deterrent effect have been repudiated on methodological grounds. In fact, there is evidence from two studies that there may be a slight *increase* in the number of homicides following a legal execution. These studies found a few more homicides after executions than one would normally expect to occur. It has been suggested that a legal execution may "provoke" homicides by conveying the message that vengeance by means of killing is justified.

9   There are several important reasons that the death penalty is not a deterrent to criminal homicide. Most significant is that the offender must consider the consequences of his or her actions if deterrence is to take place. If a person does not consider the possibility of being penalized for his or her actions, no penalty, however severe, will act as a deterrent. The crime of murder is rarely carried out in such a rational fashion. First, those who commit murder rarely set out to do it. Most homicides occur as an unplanned act during the commission of a robbery or other felony. Thus, the death penalty is not considered as a possible outcome because murder was not an anticipated part of the crime. Second, offenders rarely believe that they will be caught. Because police solve only a small percentage of all serious crimes, the likelihood of punishment is very low. Certainty of punishment is extremely important if deterrence is to work. The lower the chances of being

caught, the lower the deterrent effect of any penalty. Third, when criminal homicides occur, they usually are committed during a moment of intense anger or emotion in which reason is distorted. Police estimate that about half of all homicides occur during arguments between an offender and a victim who know each other. Also, it is not unusual for the offender to be under the influence of alcohol or a drug, which certainly affects rational thinking. All these circumstances work against the exercise of rational behavior, which is pivotal to the notion of deterrence.

ECONOMICS AND CAPITAL PUNISHMENT

10   Some claim that the death penalty is more economical than housing an offender in prison for life. A study conducted in New York State during the 1980s found that it would cost a total $648,560 to incarcerate a thirty-year-old murderer if he lived to age seventy. On the other hand, at that time the costs of the trials and multiple appeals involved in capital cases amounted to more than $1.8 million. Currently, it costs $20,100 per year to imprison the average inmate, but the cost is usually higher on death row because of segregation practices for those awaiting execution. The average inmate on death row is now twenty-eight years old, suggesting that living thirty or more years in prison is quite possible. A 1998 study found that the cost of defending a federal death penalty case through trial was $269,139, plus the cost of subsequent appeals. In Florida, each execution costs the state $3.2 million—six times the cost of life imprisonment. The high cost of capital punishment cases arises from the fact that virtually all death penalty states provide for automatic appellate review of death sentences. To guard against the possibility of a mistake, states usually conduct this review regardless of the offender's wishes. Because of this time-consuming process, the average time between sentencing and execution of offenders executed since 1977 has been more than eight years. Limitations on the right to appeal, enacted in 1996, will reduce the time between sentencing and execution; but it remains to be seen whether the difference will be significant.

11   The economic argument for the use of the death penalty thus does not hold up under scrutiny. It also overlooks the fact that the proportion of offenders who ever face the death penalty is extremely small. As the New York State report concluded, "a criminal justice system with the death penalty is inordinately more expensive than a criminal justice system without the death penalty."

ERRORS IN APPLYING THE DEATH PENALTY

12   A major criticism of capital punishment is its finality. Proponents of the death penalty argue that errors are rare; but in a criminal justice system based on inexact legal standards such as "probable cause" and "proof beyond a reasonable doubt," there is always room for error. There have been cases in which offenders who were executed have later been found to be innocent. In Illinois, for example, at least 13 offenders who were convicted of murder and sentenced to death later were found to be innocent. A systematic nationwide study found 400 erroneous convictions in death penalty cases. In 1999 and 2000, both Nebraska and Illinois put a hold on executions because of errors, and possible prosecution misconduct, that put innocent suspects on death row. The 1996 Antiterrorism and Effective Death Penalty Act places restrictions on the appeals available to offenders

sentenced to death. Some fear that these new limits will result in additional erroneous convictions in murder cases.

13   Advances in testing for deoxyribonucleic acid (DNA) have been instrumental both in convicting and in exonerating suspects linked to serious crimes. Reliable DNA testing emerged during the late 1980s, and although testing procedures are still improving, DNA tests now are generally accepted as evidence in court. DNA evidence has revealed that eyewitness testimony is sometimes mistaken, that jailhouse informants can be unreliable, and that those with criminal records often become suspects in criminal cases without strong evidence of their involvement in the crime. In one case a rape victim identified her assailant, but DNA evidence later showed she was mistaken. In another case a man was wrongly convicted in the rape of an eleven-year-old girl, even though eleven witnesses had testified he was 300 miles away at the time of the rape. Errors like these are troubling, because they reveal that weak evidence sometimes results in erroneous criminal convictions. DNA samples taken from hair or body fluids from the victim or crime scene has revealed these errors to the shock of many, resulting in attempts to halt executions in eleven states in order to study the reasons for these errors.

14   From 1977, the year after the U.S. Supreme Court reinstated the death penalty in *Gregg v. Georgia,* through 1998, a total of 5,709 offenders were sentenced to death. Of these, 500 were executed, but 2,137 were removed from death row by appellate court review, sentence reductions, or death. The large number of prisoners whose sentences are reduced or overturned, often because errors are discovered, has caused many to question the use of so final a penalty as capital punishment in so uncertain a process as the American criminal justice system.

Jay S. Albanese, *Criminal Justice,* pp. 334–339

COMPREHENSION QUESTIONS

1. What is the topic of the passage?
2. What is the central message of the passage?
3. Determine what is at issue. What is your initial personal viewpoint?
4. Distinguish among opposing viewpoints, and provide the rationale for each.
5. Think carefully about the viewpoints. Express a personal viewpoint, and give the reasons why you favor it. Does it differ from your initial personal viewpoint? Why or why not?
6. Write a few paragraphs *in support of the viewpoint that you do* not *favor.*

THOUGHT AND DISCUSSION QUESTIONS

1. In your view, is capital punishment God's will? Why or why not?
2. In your view, are eyewitness testimonies reliable? Why or why not?
3. In your view, are jailhouse informants reliable? Why or why not?
4. In your view, should those with criminal records automatically become suspects in criminal cases? Why or why not?

5. Is it safe to conclude that the author believes it is okay to place murderers on parole because they are unlikely to murder again? Why or why not?

6. Is it reasonable to infer that the author believes the American criminal justice system should not be used to make capital punishment decisions? Why or why not?

7. Do you think the information presented is mostly fact, mostly opinion, or a combination of both? Why? Provide specific examples.

8. Do you think the passage is unbiased? Why or why not?

9. What is the author's overall purpose and tone? Give specific reasons for your answer.

10. Would you recommend the death penalty in a case where a husband kills his wife in the heat of an argument? Why or why not? How about if their roles were reversed? Why or why not?

Name _____   Date _____

MASTERY TEST 9–4

DIRECTIONS: Apply the first four steps of the basic method for personal problem solving to the two *real-life problems* that follow. Be sure to label each step.

For this problem, place yourself in the position of Michael Alvear's sister as you proceed through the steps.

1

A Family Dilemma: To Scout or Not to Scout?
*America's most wholesome group makes my sister
feel she has to choose between her gay brother and her son.*

Michael Alvear

1   My sister constantly tells me how much her 6-year-old son Ricky (not his real name) adores me. So when he came home with a flier about joining a fun and exciting group for kids his age, she had a tough decision to make. Should she let him join a group that doesn't like his beloved uncle Michael?

2   When the Supreme Court ruled that the Boy Scouts have the constitutional right to fire Scout leaders for being gay, my sister was caught in an agonizing moral dilemma: allowing her son to become a member of America's most family-friendly group meant dishonoring part of her family.

3   The political backlash since the ruling against the Boy Scouts is clear to anyone who reads the local papers. Many cities, believing the Scouts are engaging in discrimination, have told local Scout troops that they can't use parks, schools and other municipal sites. Companies and charities have withdrawn hundreds of thousands of dollars in support. But what isn't so easy to see is the division the Supreme Court ruling created in millions of families like mine.

4   When my sister first called to tell me she was thinking of putting Ricky in the Cub Scouts (a program run by the Boy Scouts of America), I could hear the torment in her voice. Ricky is a bright, athletic boy who suffers from a shyness so paralyzing he doesn't have any friends. The other day my sister asked who he had played with during recess. "Nobody," he mumbled, looking at the floor. "I just scratched the mosquito bites on my leg till it was time to go back to class."

5   It breaks my sister's heart to see what Ricky's shyness is doing to him. Karate, softball and soccer leagues helped, but not nearly enough. In another age, my sister wouldn't have thought twice about letting him join the Scouts. But now the decision has taken on an unsettling ethical dimension.

6   "I don't understand why they're making me take sides in my own family," she said about the Boy Scout policy. "In order to help my son I have to abandon my brother."

7   My sister was up against some disturbing questions. Should she violate her sense of family loyalty for the social needs of her son? Or keep her values intact and deny her

son the possibility of overcoming his shyness? By saying that troops have the right to fire gay leaders, the Boy Scouts created the unimaginable: a moral quandary about joining the most wholesome group in America.

8   My sister was afraid she'd be doing the same thing many parents did a generation ago when they joined country clubs that didn't allow blacks and Jews. They, too, must have rationalized their membership by saying the clubs' wholesome activities would be good for their kids.

9   There was one thing my sister and her husband were not conflicted about: me. "No way are we putting Ricky in the Scouts if this is an issue for you," she said. "Blood is thicker than camping." Still, she wanted to know how I'd feel if my nephew became a Scout.

10   I felt completely torn, but I answered with as much certainty as I could muster. "I am not getting in the way of what's best for a 6-year-old," I told her. Ironically, I found myself trying to persuade her to let Ricky join the Scouts. It's families that teach morality, I argued, not after-school groups. Besides, I added, it's not like the issue will come up during any of the Scouting activities.

11   Or will it? Is it really inconceivable that kids who know why the president of the United States was impeached would ask their Scout leader why gay people aren't allowed in the organization? And what would the scoutmaster's response be? I was shaken by the possibility of my nephew hearing a trusted grown-up trying to convince him that his uncle Michael is someone to be scared of.

12   One night I had a terrible dream of a Boy Scout official pointing me out to Ricky and saying, "See that guy? The one you love more than any other man except your father? He's not allowed in here."

13   I woke up feeling a kind of enraged helplessness. How could I mean so much to my family and so little to so many outside it? Ultimately, I knew I could live with the indignity of my nephew belonging to a group that discriminates against his uncle; what I couldn't live with was the guilt of denying Ricky a chance to improve his life.

14   How can Ricky's parents know what the right thing to do is in this situation? For starters, they plan to get more information before they make a decision. And so my sister, a mom torn between her devotion to her brother and concern for her son, will go to next month's Scout meeting with her husband.

15   Will they put Ricky in the Scouts? I don't know. But as the date of the meeting approaches, I can't help thinking how unfair it is that my sister will have to pass under that imaginary sign that hangs over every Scout gathering: YOUR SON IS WELCOME, BUT YOUR BROTHER IS NOT.

Newsweek, November 6, 2000, pp. 12–13

_____

_____

_____

_____

_____

2

DIRECTIONS: This problem confronted one of my critical thinking students. Place yourself in her position as you proceed through the steps.

You are the mother of three young children who live with you and your boyfriend, who is not their father. Your two daughters are four- and two-years-old respectively, and your son has just turned five. Although the children's biological father lives in the vicinity, he does not see them much nor does he provide any financial assistance. For those reasons, your relationship with him has been so strained that you barely talk to each other.

Your boyfriend and you plan on getting married in about two years. You are a full-time college student, while he attends only part-time because he holds two jobs. As a result, he is usually extremely tired. In addition, both money and living space in your two-bedroom apartment are very limited. Furthermore, your children demand much attention, which you are not always able to give. Although you feel guilty, you are simply too exhausted and overextended. In short, the situation has become very stressful.

To make matters even worse, two weeks ago you found out that you are pregnant with your boyfriend's child, and you are beside yourself as to what to do. As it stands now, there's not enough money or space in your apartment for the five of you, no less for a new baby. Your parents have lost patience with you and are not very sympathetic to your predicament.

_____

_____

_____

_____

_____

_____

_____

_____

_____

_____

_____

_____

The Dashing Detective

Remember to follow these steps:

- first, read the narrative and all the questions
- second, examine the two pictures carefully
- third, answer the questions in the order they appear and come up with the solution

Have fun!

The Three Graces

Few of those who were invited to the Nineties' benefit affair, held on the estate of the Baroness Calvados-Slivovitz, had ever heard of either akrokanthera or of Hector Moneylove, so let me explain.

Both are poison. Akrokanthera is an African arrow poison that acts almost instantly, and Hector Moneylove is a more subtle form and comes from Chicago. Hector is (or was) a large, handsome man who kicked dogs, slapped children, and robbed their piggy banks whenever he had the chance. That, however, was a mere hobby, and his true vocation was gypping widows and orphans of their inheritances. Several of his victims had been reduced to committing suicide.

Among those who had survived, however, were the Three Graces—the graces respectively of youth, maturity, and old age. It was certainly no coincidence that they met with Hector at the baroness's party, flirted outrageously, plied him with the special Slivovitz distilled from the baroness's own sloes, and then left him stretched out on what became his deathbed.

Sketch A is the replica of a photograph taken by one of the guests at the party. Sketch B shows the Three Graces a few minutes later when they were among those questioned concerning Hector's death. Shortly afterwards, all were released for lack of evidence, but when the autopsy showed that death had resulted from a needlelike puncture in which akrokanthera had been injected, the trio was questioned again. Each of the three said she could have obtained a vial of the poison, but hadn't.

On the basis of the facts above, who do you think killed Hector?

Questions

1. Did each of the Three Graces have a motive for killing Hector?

2. Do you think they deliberately set out to get Hector drunk?

3. Do you think that they planned the murder in advance?

4. Who had the physical opportunity of injecting or applying the akrokanthera?

5. Who do you think killed Hector?

Lawrence Treat, *My Cousin Phoebe*, pp. 32–33

PLAYING SHERLOCK HOLMES AND DR. WATSON

DIRECTIONS: With your partner, answer the questions that follow. *After you have discussed your answers and conclusions with the rest of the class,* your instructor will distribute the last part of the short story so that you can determine if you are ready to compete with the "real" Sherlock Holmes and Dr. Watson:

1. Why did Holmes look through the window into the tutor's room?

2. Why did Holmes draw in his notebook, break his pencil, and borrow a pencil and knife from two of the students?

3. Why did Holmes want to know Miles McLaren's exact height?

4. After thinking critically about this case, who do you believe is the culprit? Why did you and your partner come to that conclusion?

5. Once you and your partner have read the last part of the short story and know the identity of the guilty party, write a different ending to the mystery using the same clues.

HOLMES AND WATSON TO THE RESCUE ONE LAST TIME

DIRECTIONS: Read and think very carefully about the following passage. Now that the two of you are successful critical thinkers and accomplished detectives, what would you advise the poor merchant's daughter to do? Be prepared to discuss your solution to her predicament with your classmates.

Many years ago when a person who owed money could be thrown into jail, a merchant in London had the misfortune to owe a huge sum to a money-lender. The money-lender, who was old and ugly, fancied the merchant's beautiful teenage daughter. He proposed a bargain. He said he would cancel the merchant's debt if he could have the girl instead.

Both the merchant and his daughter were horrified at the proposal. So the cunning money-lender proposed that they let Providence decide the matter. He told them that he would put a black pebble and a white pebble into an empty money-bag and then the girl would have to pick out one of the pebbles. If she chose the black pebble she would become his wife and her father's debt would be cancelled. If she chose the white pebble she would stay with her father and the debt would still be cancelled. But if she refused to pick out a pebble her father would be thrown into jail and she would starve.

Reluctantly the merchant agreed. They were standing on a pebble-strewn path in the merchant's garden as they talked and the money-lender stooped down to pick up the two pebbles. As he picked up the pebbles the girl, sharp-eyed with fright, noticed that he picked up two black pebbles and put them into the money-bag. He then asked the girl to pick out the pebble that was to decide her fate and that of her father.

Edward de Bono, *Newthink,* p. 11

GLOSSARY

aids to understanding elements that make a book easier to use

antonyms words that have opposite meanings

appendix section of a book containing supplementary information

asking questions and finding answers engaging in *critical thinking*

bias lack of impartiality or objectivity

bibliography list of works consulted while researching a book or an article

caption explanation of a *graphic aid*

cause and effect *pattern of organization* based on explaining why something happened

central message the *main idea* of a piece of writing longer than one paragraph

clear purpose a specific objective of *critical thinking*, such as an explanation, solution, or decision

comparison and contrast *pattern of organization* for presenting *details* by pointing out similarities and differences

contemporary issues current topics of interest and debate

context the surrounding words in a sentence that make the specific meaning of a word clear

credits list of sources of material appearing in a book but not original to it

critical reading high-level comprehension of written material

requiring interpretation and evaluation skills that enable the reader to separate important information, use inference to come to logical conclusions, distinguish between facts and opinions, and determine a writer's purpose and tone

critical thinking a very careful and thoughtful way of dealing with events, issues, problems, decisions, or situations.

details bits of information that flesh out the *main idea* of a paragraph

fact a piece of knowledge that can be confirmed as accurate in a reliable and unbiased manner

finding answers part of engaging in *critical thinking*

flexible thinking considering various possibilities before coming to a conclusion

glossary list of relevant terms and their definitions, arranged alphabetically

graphic aids illustrative *aids to understanding* such as charts, graphs, maps, pictures, and tables

highlighting using a marker to stress and focus on the most important information in a passage

index list of cross-references, arranged alphabetically by topic

inference an "educated guess" based on knowledge, experience, and circumstantial evidence or clues

495

informed opinion   the *opinion* of an expert who is well versed in the relevant *facts*

irony   the use of words to mean their opposite for humorous or sarcastic effect

learning aids   see *aids to understanding*

logical conclusions   determinations based on rational consideration of all the *facts*

main idea   a sentence (stated or not) that summarizes the sense of an entire paragraph

major details   bits of information that explain the *main idea* of a paragraph

minor details   bits of information that make *major details* more specific

mood   see *tone*

notes   additional information or source identification, usually collected at the end of a chapter or book

opinion   a personal judgment

opposing viewpoints   conflicting *opinions* regarding the same issue

organization   making the most productive use of limited time

overviewing   *skimming* a text to get acquainted with it

paraphrasing   shortening or condensing information or the main points of a passage by rewording or substituting your own words for those of the author

patterns of organization   arrangements of *facts* to clarify *details* and *main ideas*

preface   introductory chapter in a book

prefix   a word part added before a root or word to change its meaning or create a new word

prejudice   viewpoint adopted without consideration of all the *facts* or other possible viewpoints

previewing   *skimming* to familiarize oneself with the material

problem   any question or matter involving doubt, uncertainty, or difficulty

purpose   reasons for writing

random thinking   thinking with no clear purpose in mind

rationale   specific reason or reasons supporting a viewpoint

reference sources   works recommended for further reading on a given subject

research   process of gathering information to increase knowledge of a topic

root   the basic part or stem from which words are derived

simple listing of facts   lists of *details* used as a *pattern of organization*

skimming   glancing over a text quickly

solution   means by which we rid ourselves of problems

suffix   a word part added after a root or word to create a new word or affect the way a word is used

suggested readings   see *reference sources*

summarizing   shortening or condensing information or the main points of a passage by using many of the writer's own words

synonyms   words that have the same meaning

table of contents   list of the parts, chapters, and subheadings of a book

time and effort   essential requirements of *critical thinking*

time sequence *pattern of organization* in which events are recounted chronologically

title formal name given to a book, article, chapter, *graphic aid*, or other book element

title page page indicating title, author, publisher, and edition of a book

tone a writer's attitude or feeling toward the *topic* being written about

topic the subject of a paragraph

topic sentence a sentence in a paragraph stating the *main idea* of that paragraph

transition words words used to introduce *patterns of organization*

unstated main idea a statement not appearing in a paragraph that summarizes the *main idea* of that paragraph

word part a root, prefix, or suffix

CREDITS

TEXT CREDITS

Chapter 1

From Jay Albanese, *Criminal Justice*, Second Edition. Copyright © 2002 by Allyn & Bacon. Reprinted/adapted by permission.

Excerpt from *The American Heritage Dictionary of English Language*, Fourth Edition. Reprinted by permission of Houghton Mifflin Co. All rights reserved.

Neil A. Campbell, Lawrence G. Mitchell, and Jane Reece, *Biology*, Third Edition. Copyright © 2000 by Longman Publishers. Reprinted by permission of Pearson Education, Inc.

From F. Kurt Cylke, *The Environment*. Copyright © 1993 by Allyn & Bacon. Reprinted/adapted by permission.

Rebecca J. Donatelle, *Access to Health*, Seventh Edition. Copyright © 2002 by Addison-Wesley Publishers. Reprinted by permission of Pearson Education, Inc.

Rebecca J. Donatelle, *Health: The Basics*, Fourth Edition. Copyright © 2001 by Addison-Wesley Publishers. Reprinted by permission of Pearson Education, Inc.

From H. Ramsey Fowler and Jane E. Aaron, *The Little, Brown Handbook*, Eighth Edition. Copyright © 2001 by Longman Publishers. Reprinted by permission of Pearson Education, Inc.

From Roger LeRoy Miller, *Economics Today*, Ninth Edition. Copyright © 1997. Reprinted by permission of Pearson Education, Inc.

From Roger LeRoy Miller, *Economics Today*, 1999–2000 Edition. Copyright © 1999, pp. 1–4 (Glossary). Reprinted by permission of Pearson Education, Inc.

From Richard Sweeney, *Out of Place: Homelessness in America*. Copyright © 1993 by Allyn & Bacon. Reprinted/adapted by permission.

From Carol Tavris and Carole Wade, *Psychology in Perspective*, Second Edition. Copyright © 1997 by Allyn & Bacon. Reprinted/adapted by permission.

From Alex Thio, *Sociology: A Brief Introduction*, Fourth Edition. Copyright © 2000 by Allyn & Bacon. Reprinted/adapted by permission.

From Lawrence Treat, *Crime and Puzzlement*. Illustrations by Leslie Cabarga. Reprinted by permission of David R. Godine, Publisher, Inc. Copyright © 1981 by Lawrence Treat, Illustrations by Leslie Cabarga.

From George D. Zgourides, *Human Sexuality: Contemporary Perspectives*. Copyright © 1996 by Allyn & Bacon. Reprinted/adapted by permission.

Chapter 2

Excerpts from Ronald B. Adler and Neil Towne, *Looking Out/Looking In: Interpersonal Communication*, Third Edition, Copyright © 1981 Thomson Learning Publishers.

Mel Allen, "Letter to Olivia." From *Bowdoin Magazine*, Winter 2000. Copyright 2000, Bowdoin College. Reprinted by permission.

"Are Car Phones Too Dangerous?" from *Glamour*, September 1997. Reprinted by permission.

Eric Asimov, "Close Your Eyes. Hold Your Nose. It's Dinner Time." Copyright © 1997 by The New York Times Co. Reprinted by permission.

Chapter 3

From Alex Thio, *Sociology*, Fifth Edition. Copyright © 1998 by Allyn & Bacon. Reprinted/adapted by permission.

From Alex Thio, *Sociology: A Brief Introduction*, Fourth Edition. Copyright © 2000 by Allyn & Bacon. Reprinted/adapted by permission.

From Lawrence Treat, *Crime and Puzzlement*. Illustrations by Leslie Cabarga. Reprinted by permission of David R. Godine, Publisher, Inc. Copyright © 1981 by Lawrence Treat, Illustrations by Leslie Cabarga.

Chapter 4

Elizabeth Austin, "A Small Plea to Delete a Ubiquitous Expletive." Copyright © 1998, *U.S. News & World Report, L.P.* Reprinted with permission.

Christine Biederman, "As a Lawyer, He's Exemplary; as a Robber, an Enigma." Copyright © 1996 by The New York Times Co. Reprinted by permission.

Marvin L. Bittinger and David J. Ellenbogen, *Elementary Algebra: Concepts and Applications*, Fifth Edition, p. 2, figure p. 121, © 1998. Reprinted by permission of Pearson Education, Inc.

Neil A. Campbell, Lawrence G. Mitchell, and Jane Reece, *Biology*, Third Edition. Copyright © 2000 by Longman Publishers. Reprinted by permission of Pearson Education, Inc.

Tessa DeCarlo, "Do You Trust the Media," from *Glamour*, (October 1998). Reprinted by permission.

Mary Duncomb and Ron Pitzer, from the transcript of "Use TV to Help, Not Harm, Your Child," Reprinted by permission of the author and Children Youth and Family Consortium Electronic Clearinghouse.

"Effects of Television Violence." Term paper found on school@screwschool.com.

From JoBlo's Movie Emporium (www.joblo.com). Copyright © 2001. Berge Garabedian.

From Marvin R. Levy, Mark Dignan, and Janet H. Shirreffs, *Life and Health*, Copyright © 1992 by McGraw-Hill, Inc. Reprinted with permission of The McGraw-Hill Companies.

Lynn Minton, "Should There Be Prayer in our Public Schools?" Reprinted with permission from *Parade*, copyright © 1994.

John T. Molloy, "Down with Casual Fridays." Copyright © by Warner Books Inc. Originally published in *Glamour*.

John O'Neil, "Putting Pig Parts into Human Bodies." Copyright © 1998 by The New York Times Co. Reprinted by permission.

Jeffrey Pelo, "The Lease-Or-Buy Game." Copyright © 1997 by Consumers Union of U.S., Inc. Yonkers, NY 10703-1057, a nonprofit organization. Reprinted with permission from the December, 1997 issue of CONSUMER REPORTS for educational purposes only. No commercial use or photocopying permitted. To learn more about Consumers Union, log onto www.ConsumerReports.org.

Robert Rector & Lucy Quacinella, "PRO/CON: Should Poor Immigrants Be Denied Free Medical Care?" Copyright © 1997 *Health Magazine*. For subscriptions, please call 1-800-274-2522.

Jeanne Safer, "Childless by Choice." Copyright © 1996 by the New York Times Co. Reprinted by permission.

From Alex Thio, *Sociology*, Fifth Edition. Copyright © 1998 by Allyn & Bacon. Reprinted/adapted by permission.

From Alex Thio, *Sociology: A Brief Introduction*, Fourth Edition. Copyright © 2000 by Allyn & Bacon. Reprinted/adapted by permission.

Johnny Townsend, "Shot in the Arm." From *The Humanist*, November 1995, p. 4. Reprinted with permission of the author.

From Lawrence Treat, *Crime and Puzzlement*. Illustrations by Leslie Cabarga. Reprinted by permission of David R. Godine, Publisher, Inc. Copyright © 1981 by Lawrence Treat, Illustrations by Leslie Cabarga.

"Two New Studies on Television Violence and Their Significance for the Kids' TV Debate." Copyright © Center for Educational Priorities. Reprinted by permission.

From the Urban Institute, "Who Are the Homeless?" The Urban Institute Press, January 31, 2000.

From "VideoFreedom Chronology of Action on TV Violence." Copyright © VideoFreedom Inc. Reprinted by permission.

Nicholas Wade, "Grappling with the Ethics of Stem Cell Research." Copyright © 2001 by The New York Times Co. Reprinted by permission

"Witnesses Recall Beaten Woman's Fatal Leap." Copyright © 1995. Reprinted with permission of The Associated Press.

Chapter 5

Melissa Moore Bodin, "The Eggs, Embryos and I." From *Newsweek*, July 28, 1997. All rights reserved. Reprinted by permission.

Clare Collins, "Spanking Is Becoming the New Don't." Copyright © 1995 by The New York Times Co. Reprinted by permission.

Tessa DeCarlo, "Why Women Make Better Cops." From *Glamour*, September 1995, pp. 260–263, 272–273. Reprinted with permission.

Rebecca J. Donatelle, *Health: The Basics*, Fourth Edition. Copyright © 2001 by Addison-Wesley Publishers. Reprinted by permission of Pearson Education, Inc.

Ken Englade and Tony Hillerman, "A True Crime Story." From *Modern Maturity*, January/February 1995, pp. 22–26, 28–31. Reprinted by permission of the author.

"Fighting Harrassment." Reprinted with permission from the NJEA REVIEW, official journal of the New Jersey Education Association, Vol.. 68, No. 7, March 1995, pp. 28–31.

Camille McCausland, "Love in the Time of AIDS." From *New Age Journal*, October 1995, p.176. Reprinted with permission of the author.

Tom McMakin, "The Politics of Paternity Leave." From *Newsweek*, September 25, 1995. All rights reserved. Reprinted by permission.

From Alex Thio, *Sociology*, Fifth Edition. Copyright © 1998 by Allyn & Bacon. Reprinted/adapted by permission.

From Lawrence Treat, *Crime and Puzzlement*. Illustrations by Leslie Cabarga. Reprinted by permission of David R. Godine, Publisher, Inc. Copyright © 1981 by Lawrence Treat, Illustrations by Leslie Cabarga.

Chapter 6

Elizabeth DeVita, "The Decline of the Doctor-Patient Relationship." From *American Health*, June 1995, pp. 63, 64, 66, 67, 105.

From Rebecca J. Donatelle, *Health: The Basics*, Fourth Edition. Copyright © 2001 by Addison-Wesley Publishers. Reprinted by permission of Pearson Education, Inc.

From H. Ramsey Fowler and Jane E. Aaron, *The Little, Brown Handbook*, Eighth Edition. Copyright © 2001 by Longman Publishers. Reprinted by permission of Pearson Education, Inc.

Henry Louis Gates Jr. "An Amos n' Andy Christmas." Copyright © 1994 by The New York Times Co. Reprinted by permission.

From Anthony F. Grasha, *Practical Applications of Psychology*, Fourth Edition. Copyright © 1995 by Allyn & Bacon. Reprinted/adapted by permission.

Mark Hillringhouse "Come With Me." Reprinted by permission.

From Langston Hughes, *The Collected Poems of Langston Hughes*. Copyright © 1994 by The Estate of Langston Hughes. Used by permission of Alfred A. Knopf, a division of Random House, Inc.

From Alfred Lubrano "Killing Animals." Reprinted with permission of Knight-Ridder/Tribune Media Services.

Mark Sanders and Tia Sellers "I Hope You Dance." Universal-MCA Music Publishers o-b-o itself and Soda Creek Song and Hal Leonard.

Maia Szalavitz, "Can We Become Caught in the Web?" From *Newsweek*, December 6, 1999. All rights reserved. Reprinted by permission.

From Lawrence Treat, *Crime and Puzzlement*. Illustrations by Leslie Cabarga. Reprinted by permission of David R. Godine, Publisher, Inc. Copyright © 1981 by Lawrence Treat, Illustrations by Leslie Cabarga.

Chapter 7

"America's Favorite Food—The Hamburger" from *Smart Publications*, September 16, 1995, p. 13. Reprinted by permission.

The Cheers and the Tears: A Healthy Alternative to the Dark Side of Youth Sports Today, Jossey-Bass. Copyright © 1999 as published in *The Congressional Quarterly*, March 23, 2001. This material is used by permission of John Wiley & Sons, Inc.

"Fertility for Sale." Copyright © 1998 by The New York Times Co. Reprinted by permission.

Excerpt from Alfie Kohn, *No Contest: The Case Against Competition*. Copyright © 1986, 1992 by Alfie Kohn. Reproduced by permission of Houghton Mifflin Company. All rights reserved.

Morton M. Kondracke "Don't Legalize Drugs." Excerpted by permission of The New Republic, Copyright © 1988, The New Republic, Inc.

Ethan A. Nadelmann, "Shooting Up." Excerpted by permission of The New Republic, Copyright © 1988, The New Republic, Inc.

From *The New York Times Upfront Magazine*. Copyright © 2000, 2001 by Scholastic Inc. Reprinted by permission of Scholastic Inc.

From Carol Tavris and Carole Wade, *Psychology in Perspective*, Second Edition. Copyright © 1997 by Allyn & Bacon. Reprinted/adapted by permission.

From Lawrence Treat, *Crime and Puzzlement*. Illustrations by Leslie Cabarga. Reprinted by permission of David R. Godine, Publisher, Inc. Copyright © 1981 by Lawrence Treat, Illustrations by Leslie Cabarga.

Kurt Wiesenfeld, "Making the Grade." From *Newsweek*, June 17, 1996. All rights reserved. Reprinted by permission.

Chapter 8

Isadore Barmash, "A New Sales Incentive." From *Newsweek*, January 29, 1996. All rights reserved. Reprinted by permission.

From Neil A. Campbell, Lawrence G. Mitchell, and Jane Reece. *Biology*, Third Edition. Copyright © 2000 by Longman Publishers. Reprinted by permission of Pearson Education, Inc.

Will Durst, "Happy National Apathy Day." Copyright © 1998 by The New York Times Co. Reprinted by permission.

Kimberly Evanovich, "I Was a Teen Mom." From *Glamour*, April 1996. Reprinted with permission.

Clyde Haberman, "HIV Testing for Boxers: Is Rule Fair? Is Anything?" Copyright © 1996 by The New York Times Co. Reprinted by permission.

Bob Herbert, "Double Exploitation." Copyright © 1996 by The New York Times Co. Reprinted by permission.

Thomas Matthews, "Getting Help When Anger Turns Inward." Reprinted by permission.

Evelyn Renold, "The F-Word...or, Isn't a Mink Bred to be a Coat?" From *Cosmopolitan*, February 1996, p. 30. Reprinted by permission of the author.

Brent Staples, "The Littlest Killers." Copyright © 1996 by the New York Times Co. Reprinted by permission.

From Alex Thio, *Sociology: A Brief Introduction*, Fourth Edition. Copyright © 2000 by Allyn & Bacon. Reprinted/adapted by permission.

From Lawrence Treat, *Crime and Puzzlement*. Illustrations by Leslie Cabarga. Reprinted by permission of David R. Godine, Publisher, Inc. Copyright © 1981 by Lawrence Treat, Illustrations by Leslie Cabarga.

Sharon White Taylor, "You're in My Spot." From *Newsweek*, February 19, 1996. All rights reserved. Reprinted by permission.

Chapter 9

From Jay Albanese, *Criminal Justice*, Second Edition. Copyright © 2002 by Allyn & Bacon. Reprinted/adapted by permission.

Michael Alvear, "A Family Dilemma: To Scout or Not to Scout?" From *Newsweek*, November 6, 2000. All rights reserved. Reprinted by permission.

Jesse Bier, "The Popular Condition, A Nation of Hookers." *From The Humanist*, November/December 1995, p. 41. Reprinted with permission of the author.

Excerpts from Clifford G. Christians et al., *Media Ethics*, Sixth Edition. Copyright © 2001 by Longman Publishers. Reprinted by permission of Pearson Education, Inc.

From Edward de Bono, *New Think: The Use of Lateral Thinking in the Generation of New Ideas*. Copyright © 1967 by Edward de Bono. Reprinted by permission of Basic Books, a member of Perseus Books, L.L.C.

Celia W. Dugger, "African Ritual Pain: Genital Cutting." Copyright © 1996 by The New York Times Co. Reprinted by permission.

From Anthony F. Grasha, *Practical Applications of Psychology*, Fourth Edition. Copyright © 1995 by Allyn & Bacon. Reprinted/adapted by permission.

Manning Marable, "An Idea Whose Time Has Come" and Shelby Steele, "Or a Childish Illusion of Justice." From *Newsweek*, August 27, 2001. All rights reserved. Reprinted by permission.

Jeannie Ralston, "All Shook Up." From *Allure*, June 1998. Reprinted with permission.

"Rate Your Survival Skills," from *Mademoiselle*, March 1998. Reprinted by permission.

From Lawrence Treat, *Crime and Puzzlement*. Illustrations by Leslie Cabarga. Reprinted by permission of David R. Godine, Publisher, Inc. Copyright © 1981 by Lawrence Treat, Illustrations by Leslie Cabarga.

PHOTO CREDITS

INDEX